International Organizational Behavior

International Organizational Behavior is a study of individual, group, and team behavior in organizations as they interact to achieve both personal and organizational goals. Topics include individual differences, interpersonal communication, leadership, decision-making, reward systems, and conflict management. It also includes a study of general cross-cultural differences and the development of cross-cultural frameworks in decision-making, negotiation, conflict management, communication, and general business relations. The primary emphasis of the book is on understanding how and why cultures differ.

Dean McFarlin is a Professor and Chairperson in the Department of Management & Marketing and NCR Professor of Global Leadership Development at the University of Dayton, USA.

Paul Sweeney is a Professor at the University of Dayton, USA.

International Organizational Behavior

Transcending Borders and Cultures

Dean McFarlin and Paul Sweeney

Routledge
Taylor & Francis Group

NEW YORK AND LONDON

Please visit the Companion Website at www.routledge.com/cw/mcfarlin

First published 2013
by Routledge
711 Third Avenue, New York, NY 10017

Simultaneously published in the UK
by Routledge
2 Park Square, Milton Park, Abingdon, Oxon OX14 4RN

Routledge is an imprint of the Taylor & Francis Group, an informa business

Library of Congress Cataloging in Publication Data

McFarlin, Dean B.
   International organizational behavior: transcending borders and cultures /
Dean McFarlin & Paul Sweeney.—1st ed.
      p. cm.
   Includes bibliographical references and index.

1. Organizational behavior.   2. International business enterprises—
Management.   I. Title.
HD58.7.M394   2012
658'.049—dc23   2012002660

ISBN: 978-0-415-89255-1 (hbk)
ISBN: 978-0-415-89256-8 (pbk)
ISBN: 978-0-203-10782-9 (ebk)

Typeset in Berling Roman and Futura
by Apex CoVantage

Certified Sourcing
www.sfiprogram.org
SFI-00453

Printed and bound in the United States of America by Edwards Brothers Malloy.

To Laurie, Andrew, Elizabeth, and Nathaniel
—Dean B. McFarlin

To Mary, Emma, and Farrell
—Paul D. Sweeney

Contents

Preface

This is the first edition of our book and, needless to say, we are excited to present it to you! This is especially the case because the study of international organizational behavior (IOB) has been growing and evolving rapidly in recent years—encompassing everything from how cultural differences shape employee attitudes, to why conflicts arise in internationally diverse work groups, to the tricky task of managing alliances between firms from different countries. IOB is also an inherently complex area, where actions in corporate contexts are often hard to fathom, thanks to cultural differences in perspectives as well as the simple fact that the motivations behind those actions are not directly observable. Consequently, the management challenges associated with understanding, much less responding to, IOB issues are significant.

TRANSCENDING BORDERS AND CULTURES

The theme of our book is reflected in its subtitle —*Transcending Borders and Cultures*. Managers and employees alike need to be able to transcend the challenges that inevitably arise when borders—and cultural boundaries—are crossed. Indeed, in today's increasingly diverse, multicultural business world, managers and employees alike need to move across borders (literally or figuratively) and grasp a wide variety of cultural nuances on a routine basis. Doing this well requires both a sophisticated understanding of cultural differences and a repertoire of skills and management tactics that can be brought to bear to build and maintain a competitive global workforce.

Our book provides both the conceptual framework needed for a transcendent understanding of culture and plenty of practical advice for managing international challenges with organizational behavior. In doing so, we emphasize that firms need to develop corporate leaders with cross-cultural management skills. This first edition is designed to help both employees and managers better understand and effectively respond to IOB issues. Clearly, employees and managers must build their international skills in ways that provide the adaptability and flexibility they need to be effective in an increasingly globalized business environment that remains rife with cultural differences. Those differences will inevitably be reflected in people's values, perspectives, and behaviors at work.

Because IOB is a fairly new and rapidly changing area, there is no specific set of topics that must be covered in a text. This provides plenty of alternatives in both our choice of topics and how we treat them. Hopefully, you will conclude that our choices in this regard are good ones. You will see that we do not shy away from making recommendations: each chapter presents state-of-the-art practices used by companies dealing with IOB issues, as well as expert advice that is supported by the latest research. In doing so, we take a fresh, lively, and engaging approach to presenting material. Throughout the book, our guidance for international managers will emphasize flexibility and adaptability, which are attributes that we feel are essential for thriving in today's complex and volatile international business environment.

In essence, both employees and managers need to understand the IOB challenges they face to be able to respond quickly and appropriately. Put simply, many international business opportunities are missed because companies fail to anticipate people-related complexities and complications. These both subtle and overt cultural challenges probably trip up international firms as much, if not more, than misguided business strategies do. Consequently, cross-cultural skills are important for everyone who works in an internationally oriented company.

OUR INTENDED AUDIENCE

Our book is designed to appeal to professors seeking a primary text in cross-cultural organizational behavior, cross-cultural management, or international management courses. It also will work well as a management-oriented supplement in broader, more traditional international business and organizational behavior courses. The book is designed to appeal to a wide variety of students. Students with limited exposure to IOB issues will appreciate the basic foundations laid out in each chapter, while students with some international coursework or work experience will be attracted by the applied focus and depth on key topics. Indeed, our focus on applications, combined with a variety of applications-oriented features in each chapter, is designed for both students and instructors who desire a hands-on approach to IOB.

BOOK STRUCTURE AND CHAPTER PREVIEW

The book is made up of 12 chapters, within three parts, which provide balanced coverage and flow while complementing and improving on other texts on the market. Specifically, each part of the book includes four interrelated chapters. First is **Part 1—The Role of Culture in Organizational Behavior.** In this first section, we lay the groundwork for the rest of the text—providing the essential foundation for understanding and managing organizational behavior across cultural boundaries. **Chapter 1** starts this process by briefly reviewing trends impacting the management of organizational behavior across borders and how companies develop their overseas business strategies. We also introduce the concept of culture and how cultural differences may impact everything companies do and how employees behave. Along the way we focus on the cultural challenges associated with managing organizational behavior across borders. From there, **Chapter 2** lays out several conceptual frameworks for understanding and managing cultural differences—material that is referenced throughout the rest of the book. **Chapter 3** and **Chapter 4** tackle basic management tasks that cut across industries (e.g., communication and negotiation, respectively) and where an understanding of cultural differences is critical—both in terms of accurately interpreting behavior and crafting solutions that work.

Part 2—**Leading People and Teams across Cultural Boundaries**—builds on Part 1 and begins with two chapters on individual employee behavior management. **Chapter 5** addresses theories of motivation and their applicability across cultures while **Chapter 6** presents frameworks for understanding and adapting leadership styles to better fit different cultural contexts. The final two chapters in this section address behavior management from group- and organization-level perspectives. **Chapter 7** examines decision making in a multicultural environment, with particular focus on the challenges of managing internationally diverse groups. **Chapter 8** takes things a step further, addressing the thorny behavioral challenges associated with managing everything from international work teams to joint ventures to other types of international alliances.

We conclude the book with **Part 3—Building and Managing a Global Workforce**. This final section examines how culture shapes the "nuts and bolts" of managing a workforce. **Chapter 9** covers the selection of international personnel as well as how best to evaluate and provide feedback to those employees. **Chapter 10** then addresses how culture can shape compensation and reward strategies—and how international managers can handle the associated challenges. **Chapter 11** examines various options for staffing international positions, with an extensive focus on traditional expatriates (this includes both emerging alternatives as well as recent trends in expatriation). Finally, **Chapter 12** considers how international firms can effectively manage relations with their workforces on a broad scale, something that is often essential for building employee commitment on a global basis. In doing so, this chapter focuses on labor relations, especially on how unions are structured and function in various places in the world—something that may vary significantly from country to country.

FEATURES THAT SET US APART

Up-to-Date and Quality Sources. Our book relies on the most recent and most prestigious publications available from both a practitioner (e.g., *The Economist, Harvard Business Review*) and academic perspective (e.g., *Journal of International*

Business Studies). Consequently, we capture cutting-edge thinking and practices seen around the world as international managers grapple with organizational behavior issues. We believe students must also become good consumers of new knowledge and have an appreciation for research about IOB. After all, research provides the building blocks for most successful applications in international management.

Concise, Engaging, and Action-Oriented Writing. The course, dealing with IOB is ultimately about *application* and figuring out what works. Consequently, each chapter is full of examples from firms around the world. We also include concrete action recommendations in each chapter. In doing so, we use an engaging writing style that gets right to the point.

Chapter-Ending Case. Each chapter concludes with a case under the banner **Making the Case for International Understanding.** These two- to three-page cases present real-life organizational behavior challenges that managers face in international contexts. Cases cover content areas relevant to each chapter and include cultural dimensions. Also included are assignment questions for students to address (e.g., diagnosing situations, making recommendations). These questions can be used to guide class discussion and/or a written case analysis prepared by students.

Culture Clash. Each chapter contains this innovative feature, which provides concrete examples of how international firms or managers have made cultural mistakes that caused significant problems or that raise important issues related to organizational behavior. Designed to bring some of the relevant conceptual material from each chapter to life, these boxes will also examine how companies or managers responded to these cultural errors or challenges.

Global Innovations. Another feature found within each chapter, this reports on cutting-edge and creative approaches taken by various companies and managers in response to international organizational behavior issues described in the accompanying text. The focus is on innovative solutions to behavioral challenges that are indigenous to a particular country or region.

Developing Your International Career. This feature appears at the end of every chapter. It presents students with a developmental exercise or self-assessment designed to build self-insight or develop skills to help them prepare for international careers while dealing with the behavioral challenges presented in the chapter.

Coverage Reflecting the Shifting Balance of Power. Throughout the text we provide examples from a wide variety of cultures (e.g., from Africa, the Americas, Asia, Europe, and the Middle East). Also provided are many comparisons against the United States as the world's largest economy and single largest source of research on international organizational behavior issues. That said, our coverage and examples also emphasize the rapidly growing countries and regions that have gained impressive traction in global business. Specifically, the book reflects this shifting balance of power in international business, focusing more on what are now referred to as the BRIC nations (i.e., Brazil, Russia, India, and China). Indeed, we pay special attention to China and India.

Coverage of Emerging Issues in IOB. The text covers how culture impacts employee behaviors associated with important emerging issues. For example, we cover the challenges of managing international labor relations as well as those related to interacting with employees or contractors in outsourced or off-shored roles. Likewise, we examine management challenges associated with various types of alliances as well as international employee performance appraisal and compensation.

Other Features and Support for Professors. Each chapter concludes with **Chapter Summary** and **Discussion Questions** sections, designed to help students review the important points of the text and to facilitate conversations about chapter material. The extensive use of exhibits throughout the book makes it easier to digest important information as well as to increase readability and visual appeal. For professors, our book includes a support package consisting of an **Instructor's Manual, PowerPoint** presentations, and a **Test Bank.** Such a comprehensive support package is rarely found with concise texts.

Acknowledgments

Behind every successful book are professionals who provide the support, guidance, and advice needed to make everything click. We are most grateful for the reviewers who kindly contributed their time, energy, and academic expertise toward the development of this first edition:

Ramudu Bhanugopan, Charles Sturt University
Arthur DeGeorge, University of Central Florida
Gordon E. Dehler, College of Charleston
Dail Fields, Regent University
Lauryn Migenes, University of Central Florida
Maria L. Nathan, Lynchburg College
Luciara Nardon, Carleton University
Richard A. Posthuma, University of Texas at El Paso
Yunxia Zhu, University of Queensland

Likewise, we owe a huge debt of gratitude to John Szilagyi and his entire team at Routledge. We admire John greatly—he is a consummate professional and knows the ins and outs of business books better than anyone. Indeed, we have learned a tremendous amount and gained many new insights about the publishing business from John in the 15 years that we have known him. We also wish to thank a very patient—and very persistent—Lauren Athmer and her editorial colleagues at LEAP Publishing Services for helping to keep us on track and get things done. We are grateful for their help.

Part 1

The Role of Culture in Organizational Behavior

Chapter 1

International Organizational Behavior
Challenges for Management

MANAGING PEOPLE IN A DYNAMIC GLOBAL CONTEXT

> People need to come first in the mix. As companies seek to build local operations in countries such as Brazil, Russia, India and China, identifying and tapping local talent pools becomes increasingly important. Striking the right balance between standardization and localization is always a work-in-progress, but the vast cultural and language gaps from country to country demand it. The days of overseas operations run exclusively by expats are over.
>
> —Miles White, CEO
> of medical/pharmaceutical firm Abbott[1]

White's comments succinctly capture some of the common management and talent challenges facing multinational companies today. They also underscore where multinationals see the biggest growth opportunities—in rapidly developing countries such as India. Indeed, successfully expanding overseas requires a variety of critical management skills and abilities, including being adaptable and innovative. It also means being able to recruit, develop, motivate, and coordinate a far-flung global workforce, one that might be operating in dozens of countries worldwide. In doing so, international managers must somehow grasp and then bridge myriad cultural differences while scouring the planet for the best talent. At the same time, they must also fight off nimble competitors that can pop up overnight with new products and services driven by the latest technological innovations. In short, successfully managing organizational behavior in today's dynamic international environment is a tall order.[2]

Advances in technology have made it possible to operate businesses around the world 24/7—simultaneously lowering barriers between nations while enabling firms to manage their global supply chains with maximum flexibility. And since employees anywhere can interact at any time, recruiting people from all corners of the world, as well as sending jobs offshore, is easier than ever. Indeed, the process of globalization (the increasing interconnectedness of national economies around the world) is fueled, in part, by technological advances. Over the long haul, globalization should continue to spur international business growth and reduce trade barriers.[3]

That said, optimistic scenarios can be derailed quickly. The interdependence that globalization brings also means that problems in one part of the world can have ripple effects elsewhere. Moreover, rapidly growing nations such as China and India are producing homegrown companies in recent years that are giving multinationals from established markets such as Japan, Europe, and the United States competitive fits. This growth is challenging established multinationals' ability to keep up in everything from innovation to hiring the best talent. Several developing countries now have a total gross domestic product (GDP) over $1 trillion, with China surpassing Japan in 2010 to become the world's second-largest economy behind the United States. Indeed, experts predict that China will overtake the United States for the top spot in less than two decades. Small wonder, then, that in a recent survey, increased international competition and the loss of key talent were listed among the top five business threats executives said they were most concerned about.[4]

Goals for the Chapter

Of course, international business encompasses a wide variety of opportunities and threats. Our view is that the challenges associated with managing organizational behavior across national and cultural boundaries are among the most vexing that an international firm must deal with. Consequently, a key goal for this first chapter is to set the stage for the rest of the book and provide a context for discussion. In particular, we will sketch out the important shifts that have taken place in recent years with respect to developing nations—some of which we have already alluded to. Next, we will examine key trends facing companies today as they manage people across cultures and borders. After that, we will present important conceptual foundations that will be used throughout the book. These will include the concept of culture as well as a brief review of how firms evolve internationally and the strategies they use to compete abroad.

International Business Growth: Globalization and the Rise of Emerging Markets

The strongest growth in international business has been in developing countries rather than in traditional economic heavyweights such as the European Union (EU), Japan, and the United States. Consider that over the last three decades or so, China's economy grew some 1,000%. This trend is also on display when we look at how foreign direct investment (FDI) has been flowing into countries recently. While developed nations such as Germany continue to attract considerable investment, developing countries have been climbing the list of the top 20 recipients of FDI. And that includes Brazil, Russia, India, and China—now commonly referred to as the BRIC countries. This acronym underscores the increasing economic clout of these and other developing countries. Indeed, in 2008 developing nations received 43% of the world's total FDI compared to just 30% in 2005.[5]

Likewise, gross domestic product (GDP) is also growing at a much faster clip in developing nations. By 2020 or so, developing nations may account for more than half of the GDP growth in the world and be home to 700 million new members of the middle class. In short, this means that developing countries will have a citizenry that is more affluent and has more disposable income to spend than ever. No wonder established multinationals view developing nations as huge potential sources of new customers. For instance, McDonald's is hoping to build several hundred new drive-through restaurants in China over the next few years as that nation's love affair with the automobile deepens (thanks, at least in part, to 30,000 miles of new freeways constructed in the past 10 years).[6]

But while BRIC nations garner a lot of attention, multinational firms are increasingly looking to countries such as Indonesia, Turkey, and Vietnam for new opportunities in the developing world. Africa is one of the last great untapped frontiers for international business. There are huge unmet market needs, young populations with growing incomes, impressive natural resources, and aggressive local firms to work with. This explains why companies as diverse as General Electric (GE), French food giant Danone SA, restaurant holding company Yum Brands, and retailing powerhouse Wal-Mart have all made significant moves into African markets in recent years. Yum Brand's KFC restaurant unit wants to double sales in Africa to $2 billion by 2014. To put this in perspective, Yum Brand's CEO noted that "Africa wasn't even on our radar screen 10 years ago, but now we see it exploding with opportunity."[7]

Indeed, many large international firms see developing countries as more than just sources of cheap labor. They offer increasingly affluent populations eager for better products and services. They also offer talented "frugal innovators"—people who can create on the cheap because of their extensive experience with local constraints (e.g., lack of access to capital). Not surprisingly, these are individuals both local and international companies are eager to employ. Especially attractive in developing countries are innovative homegrown products that are priced to match the lower incomes of local citizens. For instance, in recent years Indian firms such as Tata Motors have been designing and selling $2,000 cars as well as $100 stoves and refrigerators. And established companies from developed nations have started paying attention, creating locally designed products for emerging markets (e.g., GE's ultra-cheap ultrasound equipment).[8]

More than ever, developing countries are also producing world-class companies that are challenging their competitors in more developed countries. For instance, how many Europeans and Americans would have recognized names such as Infosys (the information technology giant of India) or Haier (the home appliance maker in China) a decade ago? Today, these firms, and others like them, are giving more established companies such as U.S.-based IBM and Whirlpool a run for their money. In 2010, 139 of the 500 biggest firms in the world were U.S. companies compared to 185 firms in 2002. Conversely, developing countries had just a single representative among the 500 biggest companies back in 1997. But in 2010, there were 67 firms among the world's largest 500 firms—just from BRIC countries alone.[9]

International Challenges in Doing Business and Managing Talent

On top of facing a dynamic competitive environment when they venture abroad, companies also must cope with management challenges that are unique to international business. This section will touch on these challenges, including specific issues related to managing talent. On a broader level, however, international managers must be able to grasp foreign cultures and adapt their own behavior accordingly to be effective.[10]

Emerging Market Complexity: The Case of China

Of course, this is easier said than done. Consider China, a complex place where business is driven more by relationships based on mutual reciprocity and dispensing of favors (known as *guanxi*, pronounced "gwan-shee") than on policies or laws. Establishing those relationships can be frustrating for impatient foreigners who would rather "get down to business" than spend time building relationships and trust with prospective Chinese partners.[11]

And that is just for starters. Foreign firms in China face major regional differences in culture and languages as well as a host of competitors. And while the nation is modernizing at an amazing rate, incomes in much of rural China are insufficient to buy expensive electronics, cars, and homes. As a result, foreign companies may struggle in China, especially when selling directly to consumers. At the same time, the pace of competition in China is frenetic. Over 660,000 foreign companies were operating there in 2009, nearly double the number in 2000, plus millions of local firms. For instance, foreign consumer products companies may face thousands of small local competitors in a major city like Shanghai. Overall, economic power has been shifting China's way. For more on this point, read the accompanying *Culture Clash* box.[12]

CULTURE CLASH

Tilting East: China as the New Economic Center

Interactions between the United States and China on economic issues have been prickly in recent years, with plenty of sniping back and forth about the value of China's currency, trade imbalances, and so on. Especially interesting is how harshly Chinese officials sometimes react to economic comments made by their U.S. counterparts (for example, certain U.S. suggestions have been called "uncontrolled" and "irresponsible").

The increased testiness and harsher tone of Chinese officials may reflect China's rising power and its pent-up resentment about the last 500 years of Western predominance. Flash back to Beijing half a millennium ago and you would be in the capital of a Ming dynasty that exerted influence across Asia. Foreign trade was expanding and times were good in the newly built Forbidden City. That description is just as apt now to China in the twenty-first century. While per capita income in China was still only 19% of that in the United States in 2010, it is still a sharp improvement over the 3% figure back in 1980. Clearly, China is headed where countries such as South Korea and Singapore have gone before, becoming richer in the process.

Yet China's rise has been fastest of all. How did this happen? One view is that the Chinese government decided to "download" the economic "killer apps" used by Western powers for years. In China this is referred to as the pursuit of the Four Mores: more consumption, more importing, more investing abroad, and more innovation. In terms of consumption, China recently passed the United States as the world's largest auto market. By 2035, China will consume one-fifth of all energy used worldwide, a 75% increase since the late 2000s. By consuming more, China will reduce trade imbalances with other countries and make friends along the way, especially in other developing nations. Consuming more also means that China imports more. For example, China imports more goods from Australia than any other country and is also a significant importer of Brazilian, Indian, Japanese, and German products. Indeed, because it now accounts for one-fifth of global growth, China is increasingly a market for other countries' goods, allowing it to wield more influence in the process.

Regarding China's drive for more innovation, the country recently overtook Germany and is closing on others in total patent applications. In 2008, the total number of patents from China, India, Japan, and South Korea exceeded those from Western nations. And in certain industries, China is already a world leader. Good examples include wind turbine and photovoltaic panel technologies—areas strategically important given China's massive energy needs. All of this helps explain why China may feel entitled to a new global swagger. Having just passed Japan in total GDP, China is positioned to overtake the United States relatively soon. Still, it is not completely clear whether the United States is coming to the end of hundreds of years of Western economic prominence. But a major power shift is occurring, and the focus is on China as the world tilts east.[13]

Another Management Headache: Currency Volatility

A major set of challenges facing international managers is rapid change in currency values that produce havoc and have serious ripple effects across countries. For instance, the euro rose 50% higher against the U.S. dollar between 2001 and early 2004. During the euro's rise, Volkswagen's European-made cars became much more expensive to export to the United States, hurting profits. At the same time, the weaker dollar helped U.S. farm equipment maker Deere & Company sell in Europe—making its products cheaper and boosting profits.[14]

Currency swings can be a response to rapidly changing business dynamics or merely the whims of investors and traders. Trillions of dollars are traded daily in currency markets, with billions moving in and out of nations electronically in minutes. Consequently, international managers need to pay attention to currency swings if they want to avoid sudden losses. Some managers use currency hedging to protect against big currency swings. In essence, they are buying what amounts to an insurance policy that effectively freezes currency rates for a fixed period. Currency hedging is expensive, though, and hardly foolproof. For instance, a South Korean company may buy a hedge to protect its earnings in Europe against a falling euro, only to see the euro rise instead. Another option for reducing the impact of currency volatility is to make products where they are sold, relying on local suppliers in the process. This natural hedging is used by many big firms to insulate themselves from currency problems. For example, Honda makes most of the cars it sells to Americans in U.S. factories, meaning that it can protect U.S. revenues from a rising yen.[15]

Of course, using natural hedging means that companies must manage more facilities in a wider variety of countries. That can produce new challenges, especially those related to managing talent effectively across borders. Firms operating internationally need to build a workforce with productive and innovative employees to compete successfully. Today, many firms look worldwide for the best possible employees at the best possible price. We tackle some of these talent-related issues next.[16]

Offshoring and Onshoring: Recent Trends

Offshoring involves sending jobs abroad, often to places where labor is cheap. Both large and small firms have been engaging in offshoring for decades. Traditionally, companies based in developed nations with expensive labor have sent jobs to cheaper countries to cut personnel costs (up to 75% in some cases). For example, employees at foreign affiliates or subsidiaries of U.S. firms rose by over 700,000 from 2006 to 2008 to nearly 12 million—due, at least in part, to offshoring. In 2010 alone, major firms that were offshoring jobs from the United States included Hewlett-Packard, Hilton, and JPMorgan Chase. Among popular offshoring destinations are China, Mexico, and, increasingly, the Philippines.[17]

India is another common offshoring recipient. In many ways, India is an ideal offshoring destination, with a deep reservoir of inexpensive, highly educated, technical talent with good English-speaking skills. Not surprisingly, many firms, including General Electric, Microsoft, and Intel, have research and development operations in India. On top of that, some 200 of the largest international companies in the world offshore their information technology (IT) work to leading Indian firms such as Infosys and Wipro. These Indian IT powerhouses are not content to simply be offshoring recipients. They also compete against foreign multinationals such as IBM for IT consulting and IT systems integration contracts.[18]

Offshoring comes with management challenges. Difficult logistics, poor work quality, lousy customer service, high shipping costs, long delivery times, intellectual property theft, cultural differences, and communication problems are common offshoring issues. As a result, some firms have shifted once-offshored jobs back home. This trend, labeled onshoring, occurs when firms conclude that the costs outweigh the benefits of offshoring (in a recent survey of manufacturers, 55% were dissatisfied with offshoring). Indeed, this led General Electric to shift water heater production from a plant in China back to the United States in 2011. Similarly, Dell Computer returned some call center operations to the United States from India because of rising customer complaints. Some firms are trying to capitalize on this trend by offering themselves as alternatives to offshoring. For more on this, see the accompanying *Global Innovations* box. Of course, offshoring can work if management bridges cultural and communication differences, provides sufficient support, and sets clear expectations. Firms need to think carefully about what work should be offshored and then search diligently to hire the best foreign employees.[19]

GLOBAL INNOVATIONS

Out of India? An Onshoring Alternative to Bangalore

With its large, well-trained, and inexpensive English-speaking workforce, Indian companies have raked in roughly $50 billion in revenue in the IT and customer service industries, just to name a few, while serving foreign multinationals. Moreover, Indian companies will likely grow their share of this lucrative business in the years ahead.

Yet in the background, some U.S. firms are onshoring IT service work back to the United States. More surprising is that onshoring activity is being promoted in small, rural communities around the United States. Among other places, Pendleton, Oregon; Duluth, Minnesota; and Joplin, Missouri, seem to be on the leading edge of what may become an innovative new trend in onshoring. Consider Pendleton-based IT firm Cayuse Technologies. Cayuse is 100% owned by the Confederated Tribe of the Umatilla Indian Reservation (CTUIR). The CTUIR partnered with Accenture to develop Cayuse Technologies; the goals were to help diversify the local economy and create living-wage jobs for tribe members and the community. It is working; sales soared 700% from 2007 to 2009, hitting nearly $8 million, with plans for additional expansion in the works.

Cayuse is one of a growing number of small to medium-sized U.S. IT companies that deliberately locate in rural America and offer themselves as an alternative to offshoring. It is not that rural onshorers like Cayuse are cheaper than popular offshore locations—on paper they cost 10% to 150% more for their services. But that does not tell the whole story. For example, offshored work carries plenty of hidden expenses because of the significant management oversight needed (e.g., to bridge culture gaps). In the end, the total cost difference between offshoring work to India and onshoring work to firms such as Cayuse can be negligible. Indeed, this is the sweet spot for Cayuse and other small onshoring firms located in rural U.S. settings. These small companies can undercut bigger U.S. competitors on prices because, among other things, places such as Pendleton, Duluth, and Joplin are cheaper places to do business in than Los Angeles, New York, and Boston. Add these cost savings to the hefty challenges of managing offshored work, and firms such as Cayuse have a compelling value proposition.

And the Cayuse phenomenon is gaining steam, with dozens of similar companies now also in this niche. Examples include Saturn Systems, RuralSourcing, and Onshore Technology Services—all U.S. firms with around 150 employees that have enjoyed nearly triple-digit growth in the past few years. American customers find them easy to work with because there are no culture barriers and few worries about data security. And when total costs are factored in, customers find rural onshorers attractive. For example, Ascensus, a firm that creates retirement planning software, decided to onshore some of its work to Duluth-based Saturn Systems. Saturn was more expensive up front than Indian competitors, but what tipped the balance in Saturn's favor were the considerable added hassles and costs of managing work done on the other side of the world.

While rural onshorers are still dwarfed by offshoring activity, they are growing at a faster rate. Moreover, they could benefit over time from rising labor costs in places such as India and China. That said, rural outsourcers face challenges, too, not the least of which is the availability of skilled employees in places like Bedford, Indiana. On the other hand, some 60 million Americans live in rural settings—many of who are hungry for work. And nimble rural onshorers are capitalizing on this large pool of labor by retraining unemployed workers from other industry sectors using boot-camp style programs. Look out Bangalore, here comes Duluth.[20]

The reality is that the practice of offshoring is not going away anytime soon. Many executives view offshoring as part of the global competition for jobs and talent. Millions of customer service–related jobs are expected to be offshored from developed nations to places like Russia, the Philippines, India, and China over the next few years. For example, Spain's Telefonica has thousands of employees based in Morocco who take service calls from European customers.[21]

And while many offshored jobs involve basic service support, firms are increasingly offshoring sophisticated work, including new product development and innovation. Moreover, the motivation, particularly when complex work is involved, has less to do with cutting labor costs than being able to hire the best employees in the world, developing the firm into a global power, achieving faster revenue growth, and entering foreign markets more quickly. The bottom line is that skilled knowledge workers—especially given globalization, technology advances, and intense competition—are at a premium. That helps explain why IBM performs considerable software development work in India, something that leverages the large pool of skilled local programmers there. Indeed, many of the more than 17,000 employees who work for General Electric in India are professionals and scientists. Put simply, skilled professional jobs in a variety of scientific areas are increasingly found in centers of excellence around the world.[22]

Competitiveness: The Best Talent Wins

Underscoring many of the trends discussed so far is that developing countries such as India are increasingly sources of highly skilled technical talent. The most competitive and talented workforce usually wins—and winning means keeping the lion's share of the best jobs. But what constitutes a world-class competitive workforce? There is no simple answer, but training, educational quality, motivation, and having cutting-edge skills are part of the equation. The quality of a nation's workforce relates to how competitive that country is, both in job creation and in its ability to produce outstanding companies that can excel globally. Table 1.1 lists the top 25 most competitive nations for 2010. One common characteristic that is shared by top nations is the quality of their workforces. Keep in mind, however,

Table 1.1
The 25 Most Competitive Nations in 2010

2010 Rank	Nation
1	Singapore
2	Hong Kong
3	United States
4	Switzerland
5	Australia
6	Sweden
7	Canada
8	Taiwan
9	Norway
10	Malaysia
11	Luxembourg
12	Netherlands
13	Denmark
14	Austria
15	Qatar
16	Germany
17	Israel
18	Mainland China
19	Finland
20	New Zealand
21	Ireland

22	United Kingdom
23	Korea
24	France
25	Belgium

Source: Adapted from The International Institute for Management Development's *2010 World Competitiveness Scoreboard* (see www.imd.org/research/publications/wcy/).

that sophisticated work can be done *anywhere* with a good supporting infrastructure (such as high-speed Internet connections) and employees who are properly trained and educated (witness the success of India and Mexico in attracting jobs from abroad, though neither is in the top 25).[23]

On the Rise: Workforce Diversity

One consequence of the global hunt for talent is that workforces are an increasingly complicated mix of cultures, backgrounds, and ethnic groups. Moreover, demographic changes within countries are also contributing to greater workforce diversity. For example, Hispanics will make up nearly 25% of the U.S. population in a few decades (compared to just 10% in 1995). While diversity brings challenges, it also offers opportunities to leverage differences for the benefit of the firm. Moreover, a diverse workforce makes it easier for companies to reach important customer populations. In the United States, for instance, Hispanics' disposable income exceeds $650 billion—customers that Procter & Gamble (P&G) has been able to sell to more effectively after establishing a bilingual team of employees to reach them.[24]

But managing workforce diversity is not easy. Managers often battle outdated attitudes and perceptions that can derail their best efforts. For instance, since many important decisions are made in cross-functional teams of employees with diverse backgrounds, effective interaction is critical. Moreover, building cultural diversity into decision-making teams is often essential for making the best decisions in the long run, raising the stakes for management to make the process work. Sadly, relatively few companies take diversity management seriously.[25]

Effectively Managing International Organizational Behavior: A Skills Profile

How *should* international managers approach issues related to workforce diversity, the global talent hunt, and employee motivation, just to name a few? How can they adapt in the face of cultural values, languages, and business practices that can change across (and sometimes within) countries, a backdrop that impacts all aspects of management? Imagine the difficulty of managing people in far-flung corporate operations that literally circle the globe. For example, in 2011 consumer products giant P&G had over $82 billion in revenue, nearly 130,000 employees, and operations in 180 countries. Managing people in such a behemoth is no easy chore.[26]

When companies such as P&G have an extensive global footprint, everything they do has international implications. Building an international workforce staffed by open-minded, flexible people who can comfortably operate across multiple cultures and languages may take years. Consequently, it is dangerous to rely on

Table 1.2
Measuring Up: Desired Skills and Attributes for Managing International Organizational Behavior

Area	Description of Desired Skills and Attributes
Business practices	Understands differences in business practices across countries
Change agent	Record of successfully initiating and implementing change
Cultural adaptability	Adapts quickly to foreign cultures, diverse cross-cultural experience
Cultural sensitivity	Effective leading people from many cultures, nationalities, and religions
Decision making	Successful strategic planner across different international situations
Delegation	Delegates effectively in cross-cultural contexts
Line management	Record of success in overseas projects and assignments
Mental maturity	Possesses the endurance required for the rigors of foreign postings
Multidimensional perspective	Extensive multifunctional, multicountry, and multienvironment experience
Negotiation	Record of successful business negotiations in multicultural contexts
Resourcefulness	Record of acceptance by host country's government and business elite
Team building	Record of creating culturally diverse work groups that meet firm goals
Vision	Quickly spots and responds to threats and opportunities in the host country

Source: Adapted from Briscoe, D. R., Schuler, R. S., & Claus, L. (2009). *International Human Resource Management* (3rd ed.). New York: Routledge.

only a few managers with significant international skills. Instead, understanding how culture, business practices, and laws change from place to place is something that, ideally, all managers should grasp. Table 1.2 presents the specific skills and attributes needed to effectively manage organizational behavior across countries.[27]

To be effective across borders, executives need to have deep multicultural experience and embrace diversity. They must be comfortable sharing information and teaming with local employees to succeed in local markets. They also need to offer high-performing employees everywhere fair pay, excellent development opportunities, and plenty of recognition. International managers will struggle if they remain wedded to a command-and-control mentality—something that does not fully leverage local employee know-how nor allow for rapid reaction to change. Put simply, international companies need mature, sophisticated, and experienced managers who are comfortable with ambiguity and change.[28]

CONCEPTUAL BUILDING BLOCKS

Underpinning many of the issues discussed so far are a variety of management concepts, including those related to how firms develop and grow internationally. This final section presents many of these concepts. Some will be covered in more detail later, while others will provide a frame of reference that will help you understand material in subsequent chapters.

The Pervasive Impact of Culture

We have already alluded to the fact that culture can impact just about everything associated with managing employees. Of course, many definitions of culture exist. But we like international management expert Geert Hofstede's definition of culture as "the collective programming of the mind which distinguishes one group or category of people from another." This "programming" is something that we can only infer from observing how people behave, and culture's usefulness as a concept depends on how well it can predict people's actions. Complicating matters is that managers may not fully recognize the impact of culture on their own views and behaviors, much less their subordinates'.[29]

But that is just the tip of the iceberg. For instance, large cultural differences may exist within countries. Recent research suggests that it might be better to view cultural differences as embedded in a mosaic of dimensions that should shape and inform strategies for managing employees across borders. These could include how economic, financial, legal, and political systems vary across countries as well as national differences in demographic characteristics and knowledge production.[30]

Regardless, culture can shape everything from how employees expect to be treated to how expatriates adapt, to the international strategies adopted by executives and even to the dividends that firms pay. Likewise, human resource practices, organization structures, negotiation tactics, and leadership styles are impacted by culture and can vary widely across countries. Cultural differences in beliefs about the importance of work may shape employee motivation in ways that are reflected in national economic growth rates. The reasons that entrepreneurs start companies may reflect cultural influences. In certain Asian countries (such as Indonesia), interest in entrepreneurship tends to be more tightly linked to concerns about social status (for example, gaining a good reputation from being successful) than in the United States. Finally, the impact of cultural differences depends, in part, on how managers respond. For instance, failing to understand how best to motivate foreign employees can result in bad outcomes, while successfully adapting management styles to match local values may lead to outstanding performance. Even foreign subsidiaries perform better when they manage employees in ways that are aligned with local culture.[31]

That said, many international executives tend to underestimate the difficulty and time needed to effectively manage cultural differences. Culture is complex, rooted in language, history, geography, religion, and economic developments, just to name a few. Moreover, culture is always evolving and changing, and individuals may not espouse the values of their cultural group. For instance, it is not difficult to find Americans who have a collectivistic outlook (versus being self-absorbed individualists) or Japanese who are obsessed with individual achievement (versus being group-oriented conformists).[32]

International managers must also resist oversimplifying culture. Many believe that people everywhere are increasingly thinking and acting alike. This belief in cultural convergence (that it will soon be possible to manage everyone the same way everywhere) is unlikely to be achieved in the near future. To the contrary, globalization and other forces have intensified the desire of some to adhere to their cultural traditions. Consequently, it is not likely that cultural differences have faded to a great extent.[33]

Perhaps an even more common oversimplification is when managers treat cultural differences as broad-brush labels that can be slapped on people with little or no analysis. While such labels are easy to use and give managers a rough impression of different cultures, relying on them is problematic to say the least. Part of the problem is that in developing helpful advice for managers, many experts reduce cultural complexities to more generic categories that are easier to grasp. But managers would be well served to remember that categories and labels, however helpful, do not fully describe the nuances and complexities associated with specific cultures.[34]

Multinational Enterprises: History, Development, and Strategic Options

This last section takes a step back and discusses the history and evolution of international corporations before we conclude with some of the basic strategic choices firms make in tackling global markets. A general understanding of how companies approach international markets should prove helpful as you read subsequent chapters.

The term *multinational* refers to a large, well-developed international firm that operates in many foreign locations—European consumer products giant Unilever is a good example. Multinationals spend significant resources abroad (e.g., building or buying production facilities), and their worldwide impact is staggering. Today there are over 63,000 multinationals plus more than 800,000 foreign subsidiaries. Half of the largest 100 economies in the world are multinationals. Collectively, multinationals employ over 90 million people globally, paying them $1.5 trillion in annual wages.[35]

But multinationals are hardly identical. Some compete in industries where they can basically sell the same products everywhere, while others must tailor their products extensively to meet local needs. Multinationals may also operate differently within industries. Some embrace standardization, using similar structures, technologies, and management practices everywhere. In essence, "home" is the country where the headquarters resides and where key decisions are made. Other multinationals give local subsidiaries more freedom to make decisions and better serve local needs. In this case, headquarters offers guidance, but local managers make operational decisions and are relied on much more than expatriates from the home country.[36]

Regardless, multinationals have evolved considerably over the past century. From 1900 to 1960, multinationals typically did their innovating in the home country. Eventually, many realized that good ideas could come from anywhere. So, in the 1970s and 1980s, firms started setting up research units overseas to capture ideas in key markets. Yet these outposts had trouble attracting headquarters' attention. Since the 1990s, multinationals have continued to pursue new ideas in a more democratic fashion, especially from parts of the firm directly connected to customers. Today, many multinationals feel their most innovative ideas will come from the periphery of the company rather than its center. Still, how best to leverage such ideas remains an important challenge for management.[37]

Stages in International Corporate Development

Many companies evolve through distinct stages as they expand international activities. As firms gain experience overseas, their level of involvement in international markets grows, allowing them to master more complicated foreign operations. Small companies often step into international markets by exporting, an option not requiring expensive foreign facilities. Eventually, some companies transition from exporting to building facilities overseas. Firms also may jump over developmental stages or not follow a clear series of development steps (e.g., by making overseas acquisitions). Indeed, some multinationals from emerging economies have taken a more rapid developmental path than their counterparts in developed countries. Nevertheless, many firms develop through distinct stages as they become more sophisticated internationally. Table 1.3 examines the six specific stages of corporate internationalization.[38]

Table 1.3
Typical Developmental Stages in Corporate
Internationalization

Stage 1:   Exporting

Stage 2:   Sales subsidiaries

Stage 3:   International division

Stage 4:   Multinational

Stage 5:   Global or transnational

Stage 6:   Alliances and partnerships

Source: Adapted from Briscoe, D. R. (1995). *International Human Resource Management*.
Englewood Cliffs, NJ: Prentice Hall.

Stage 1: Exporting. Domestic firms often begin their international experiences by exporting. Firms usually rely on small internal staffs to handle exporting activities or use consulting firms with expertise in foreign contracts, currency hassles, and letters of credit. For instance, clothing retailer L. L. Bean initially served only the U.S. market but later began exporting to foreign customers, and now the company exports to more than 160 countries.[39]

Stage 2: Sales Subsidiaries. Once overseas sales are growing significantly, companies may establish overseas distributors or representatives to market their products and provide customer service. Thanks to strong export growth in overseas markets, U.S. motorcycle maker Harley-Davidson began setting up overseas offices and retail outlets for better marketing and sales support.[40]

Stage 3: International Division. Harley-Davidson has continued to expand its foreign operations. The firm opened its first Chinese dealership in 2006 and plans to have 28 in place there by 2016. At the time of this book's publication, the company's goal is to boost its foreign sales to 40% of total revenues by 2014. In short, Harley-Davidson has evolved to Stage 3 and now assembles motorcycles overseas. Its first foreign assembly operation was in Brazil, where it shipped motorcycle kits for final assembly. While most Harley-Davidson motorcycles are still made in the United States, the firm's Brazilian assembly operation is a common next step up from foreign sales subsidiaries. Having an international division requires a more sophisticated structure to manage foreign business activity—one that typically requires staff who are experienced in international business.[41]

Stage 4: Multinational. Multinational firms understand that while headquarters may make key strategic decisions, foreign operations often perform best when they are run by local employees steeped in local market know-how. Indeed, foreign subsidiaries in Stage 4 firms typically focus on supporting the national or regional market where they are located. Sometimes the best way to do that is to tap a foreign subsidiary's local ties. To enter the Brazilian market, U.S. retailer JCPenney purchased local store chain Lojas Renner. Along with Lojas Renner's Brazilian managers, JCPenney also kept the Lojas Renner name on its new stores to capitalize on local expertise and reputation. In the next two years, Lojas Renner grew over 100%. Likewise, Dutch retailer Ahold operates under different store names overseas, emphasizing local brands in the countries where it does business. Yet successful multinationals can stumble if they are not prepared, as French retailer Carrefour did in pulling out of Russia to cut its losses.[42]

Stage 5: Global or Transnational. Some firms never reach this stage because they do not need operational integration worldwide in their industries. But companies that have developed to this point will manufacture or source materials anywhere if it helps minimize costs and maximize returns. For example, Logitech International bases its senior manufacturing executive in Taiwan, where key Asian computer component suppliers are located. This allows for faster decisions about what suppliers it can source product from. Managing dispersed operations well requires flexibility, expertise in bridging cultures, and a global perspective. Yet a transnational orientation still allows for market-specific tailoring of products—we'll say more about this later.[43]

Stage 6: Alliances and Partnerships. In this stage, multinationals connect with other firms to leverage combined resources (e.g., people, technology, facilities, or other capabilities). Joint ventures, which are separate entities created and resourced by both partnering firms, are a popular type of partnership because they give multinationals access to resources that are too expensive to secure alone. For instance, auto companies have repeatedly joined forces to develop new engines, joining their collective know-how while reducing huge development costs. Service companies also engage in joint ventures, such as Wal-Mart's recent partnership with Indian retailer Bharti Enterprises Ltd., which allowed Wal-Mart to open its first store in India. One challenge that exists with international alliances and partnerships is building trust between firms, particularly when cultural differences exist. If trust issues can be overcome, alliances and partnerships will likely flourish.[44]

Different Drummers: Emerging Market Multinationals

Not every company, however, evolves through the stages sketched out above. This is especially true for multinationals that have grown in developing countries where plenty of disadvantages exist, such as political instability, lousy infrastructures, and weak legal systems. Yet such adversity may make multinationals from developing countries stronger and nimbler competitors. Indeed, home market difficulties can better prepare these multinationals than traditional multinationals based in rich nations. Multinationals based in developing countries are often very quick to expand overseas, aggressively building their capabilities in many cases by acquiring or forming partnerships with more established multinationals from developed nations. This is exactly what Chinese energy firms, including Chinalco, China National Petroleum Corp., Cnooc, and Sinopec, have done in recent years. All four companies have been offering billions of dollars to buy energy firms based in places as diverse as Argentina, Britain, Norway, and Switzerland. While not all of these deals have gone through, the Chinese firms behind them clearly aspire to be global competitors.[45]

Strategic Choices for International Business

Due to global competition, multinationals typically follow a corporate strategy to guide their business across countries. Indeed, some multinationals use several strategies depending on the needs of particular business units. For instance, General Electric has international business units in appliances, jet engines, lighting, and medical diagnostic systems, among others. The extent to which GE tailors its products to local customer preferences varies across these units based on industry and competitive demands.[46]

Global Integration and Local Responsiveness

In short, multinationals face different levels of pressure for local responsiveness. In certain industries, tailoring to meet market-specific customer preferences is critical. For instance, food preferences vary widely and reflect cultural differences. While pizza is found in many countries, squid is a topping found mainly in Asian nations. In other cases, what drives local customization are nation-specific regulations governing certain products (e.g., pharmaceuticals). But customization is unnecessary when identical products can be sold anywhere—such as computer chips. Industries also vary regarding the pressure for global integration. In some industries, multinationals face powerful competitors. To increase profitability, multinationals in this situation often seek efficiency and economies of scale (such as concentrating production in low-wage locations) to help cut costs and respond faster to competitive threats. But if multinationals have superior products and face weak competition, there is relatively little pressure for integration, at least not until stronger competitors emerge. In any case, the five corporate strategies typically used by multinationals are a direct response to industry pressures for global integration and local responsiveness. Figure 1.1 presents these strategies graphically.[47]

The International Strategy

Multinationals that face little pressure to tailor products across markets or to become highly efficient to combat competitors often pursue an international strategy

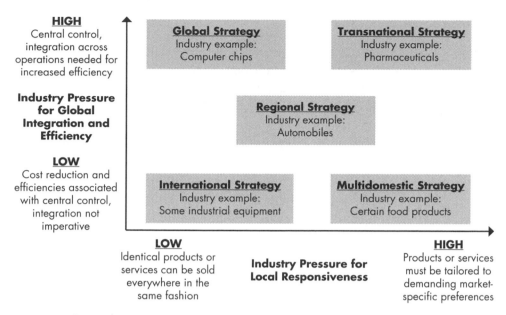

FIGURE 1.1 Choosing an International Strategy: Horses for Courses

Sources: Adapted from Beamish, P. W., Morrison, A. J., Rosenzweig, P. M., & Inken, A. C. (2000). *International Management: Text and Cases* (4th ed.). Burr Ridge, IL: Irwin McGraw-Hill, 143; Daniels, J. D., & Radebaugh, L. H. (2001). *International Business: Environments and Operations* (9th ed.). Upper Saddle River, NJ: Prentice Hall, 529; Hill, C. W. L. (2008). *Global Business Today* (5th ed.). New York: McGraw-Hill/Irwin.

of selling similar products everywhere. In doing so, they usually perform product development in their home market while maintaining outposts in foreign markets (e.g., distribution facilities) with headquarters making key decisions. This strategy is a good match when multinationals face few competitors for their unique products. For instance, Harley-Davidson, known for its iconic motorcycles, earns most of its revenues in the United States. But it has also done well distributing its American-made machines overseas. In 2009, the firm started selling expensive models in India, where no competition exists for luxury motorcycles. Likewise, in the past, all of P&G's products were developed in the United States and then sold overseas. Today, the competition P&G faces is much tougher, and it no longer uses the international strategy.

In specialized product niches, firms can dominate with the international strategy. For example, some German firms have combined engineering prowess with sophisticated information technology while employing world-class manufacturing specialists. This combination has allowed these companies to make some of the finest industrial equipment anywhere while not worrying too much about costs. Customers flock to these German specialists for their specific industrial needs. One such example is Kuka, a German robotics firm that serves the worldwide auto industry.[48]

The Multidomestic Strategy

In some industries, multinationals face huge pressure to tailor products and services to meet local preferences even while pressure for integration and efficiency is relatively low. If so, the best bet may be a multidomestic strategy, aligning products and services to customer needs in specific foreign markets. This works particularly well if multinationals can charge more for their customized products. With the multidomestic strategy, local country managers typically have the freedom to respond to local preferences as they see fit—leading to many product variations across countries. But the trade-off for local independence can be inefficiency, costly duplication (with each country operation run like a mini version of the firm), and poor information sharing across markets. For instance, at one point country managers at beauty giant Avon could develop unique products in their local markets. The result was soaring costs and product proliferation (e.g., 13,000 products for the Mexican market alone). This became intolerable as business in key markets slowed. Eventually, Avon dropped its multidomestic approach, centralizing marketing and manufacturing globally to save money. Once strong competitors or business problems emerge, pressures for efficiency and cost saving make the multidomestic strategy less attractive.[49]

Still, the need to respond to different local preferences may offset any advantages from centralized or integrated operations. For instance, centralized manufacturing makes little sense for Nestlé and Unilever when it comes to food products. Shipping costs would wipe out savings from economies of scale, while centralization would make it much harder to tailor products (e.g., by taste, packaging, etc.) to begin with.[50]

The Global Strategy

Global integration can be critical for profitability in certain industries, especially when the same products or services can be sold everywhere. In this case, the global strategy is a good option. Boeing basically sells the same airliners worldwide with few differences. Customers can typically select just a few limited variations (such as cabin seating layouts).[51]

With the global strategy, corporate headquarters keeps control over worldwide operations to gain efficiencies and economies of scale while improving quality. For instance, chip giant Intel has plants in a few countries (among them China, the United States, and Ireland) to concentrate efficiencies, but its products are used worldwide. Intel must support its most important customers while keeping costs low and margins high.[52]

Boeing also centralizes its design and manufacturing process. The firm's center in Moscow designs plane parts and coordinates the activities of foreign suppliers such as Mitsubishi. All Boeing planes are assembled in the United States (with many parts coming from foreign suppliers and partners) and then exported to airlines globally.[53]

The global strategy does, however, present challenges, including the difficulty of effectively coordinating dispersed international operations. Boeing has had bitter experience in this area with its newest plane, the 787 Dreamliner. Because the Dreamliner was costly to develop, Boeing asked a large number of companies, many of them foreign, to not only provide 787 components, but to design them and to take on the financial risks in doing so. This complex quilt of suppliers and their responsibilities created huge management headaches for Boeing that led to missed deadlines and quality problems. Boeing had to take back production of some parts and improve its coordination of subcontractors.[54]

The Transnational Strategy

In some industries, multinationals are pressured to tailor products to local preferences *and* improve efficiencies by integrating operations worldwide. They may move key activities to wherever they can be done cheapest and most efficiently while maintaining quality and responsiveness to local preferences. This transnational strategy is a best-of-both-worlds blend of global and multidomestic approaches. It comes, however, with the potential for conflict given the competing demands of local responsiveness (which undercuts standardization) and global efficiency (which undercuts the ability to tailor products for local markets).[55]

Indeed, firms pursuing a transnational strategy often tilt toward the global side to minimize product variation wherever possible to cut costs. P&G did just that when it simplified its personal care products worldwide. For instance, some P&G hair care products now use a single fragrance worldwide that is tweaked for local tastes. Less fragrance is used in markets where subtlety is preferred (such as in Japan), and more fragrance is used where a strong scent is preferred (including many European countries). But juggling efficiency against local preference is tough. While standardizing products more is cheaper and more efficient, it risks alienating customers with strong preferences in specific markets.[56]

One way to deal with this is to produce the underlying components used in a variety of products in a few locations to capture efficiencies. Final assembly can then occur at facilities in key markets, where features important to local customers are added. For example, Caterpillar sells earthmoving equipment in 180 countries. The firm makes most components in the United States but assembles final products in 60 facilities in 23 countries. Naturally, balancing local preferences with efficiency requires excellent management.[57]

The Regional Strategy

Sometimes customer preferences vary regionally instead of nationally. In that case, multinationals may opt for the regional strategy, which allows managers in a regional area (Europe, for example) to make decisions, set goals, and tweak products.

It also means pursuing efficiencies and economies by leveraging any location advantages within a region (e.g., locate plants in low-wage countries within a region).[58]

For example, France's Thomson used a regional strategy for TVs. Its European plants made televisions for the European market, while Thomson's North American operations produced TVs for that market, largely using regional suppliers. While the regional approach precludes worldwide integration, it allows for more local product customization than a global strategy. The regional strategy also offers more coordination than a multidomestic strategy, where foreign subsidiaries are largely independent.[59]

The regional strategy is a good bet for many industries. For instance, in the auto industry, while national tastes vary, broad regional preferences also exist. Compared to Americans, Europeans prefer smaller, more fuel-efficient cars because Europe has much higher gas prices. To deal with this, Toyota relies on a small number of vehicle platforms that are adaptable for regional customization. Key Toyota factories then produce a limited number of unique models to be sold across their respective regions.[60]

Creating Buy-In When Developing International Strategy

Regardless of the strategies that multinationals use, they will not work if local managers drag their feet. So multinationals should ensure that the ways they

FIGURE 1.2 Developing International Strategy: Recommendations for a Fair Process

Source: Adapted from Kim, W. C., & Mauborgne, R. A. (2005). *Blue Ocean Strategy: How to Create Uncontested Market Space and Make the Competition Irrelevant.* Boston: Harvard Business School Press.

develop international strategies are seen as fair by the people who are asked to carry them out—particularly when that strategy is a departure from the status quo. But what constitutes fairness in strategy development? Top executives should thoroughly familiarize themselves with foreign operations. They should treat foreign subsidiaries consistently and promote two-way communication. They should also encourage local employees to challenge the perspectives of senior executives and explain to them the strategic decisions ultimately made. Figure 1.2 summarizes how these recommendations can help strategy execution abroad. By engaging foreign employees, explaining strategic options, and clarifying expectations, multinationals can improve trust and commitment. Committed employees are more likely to take steps to ensure that the firm's strategy is implemented successfully.[61]

CHAPTER SUMMARY

This chapter examined the challenges associated with managing organizational behavior in a dynamic international business context. While developed nations such as the United States, France, and Germany continue to attract considerable outside investment, developing nations, which include BRIC countries (Brazil, Russia, India, and China), have been climbing the list of foreign direct investment recipients. International managers face a number of difficulties, and there are countless complexities associated with developing countries like China, such as currency volatility and global job movement (e.g., offshoring). The second half of the chapter provided conceptual building blocks for the rest of the book. The role of *culture* is an important one in international management.

Next, *multinationals* were discussed, as well as six common stages in their development. Also discussed were five international business strategies used by multinationals given industry pressures for local responsiveness and global integration. The international strategy may be best when relatively low pressures for global integration and local responsiveness exist. The multidomestic strategy may be best when product preferences vary across nations and integration pressures are low. The global strategy works best when the same products can be sold everywhere and integration pressures are high. The transnational strategy may be best when integration and efficiency are key but customer preferences still vary across nations. Finally, the regional strategy blends elements of both global and multidomestic approaches. Discussion concluded with analysis of international strategies, where we urged firms to develop their strategies in a fair manner if they want managers worldwide to embrace them. To create a fair process, managers should familiarize themselves with local operations and ensure two-way communication with local employees when developing international strategy.

DISCUSSION QUESTIONS

1. What are the implications of globalization and the rise of developing countries (such as China and India) for managing organizational behavior effectively?

2. What do you make of the debate around the issues of offshoring and onshoring? What are the pros and cons of each? What decision factors should be considered?

3. What is culture? Why is it important for managing people around the world?

4. What are the key differences between international, global, transnational, multidomestic, and regional strategies?

Developing Your International Career

DO YOU HAVE A GLOBAL MIND-SET?

One of the themes in this book is that success in an international context requires a deep understanding of cultures, organizational behavior, and yourself. Having self-insight sufficient enough to grasp your strengths and weaknesses is the key to effectively managing organizational behavior, especially on an overseas assignment. But how can you build self-insight? Moreover, what specific strengths or attributes are critical for successful overseas leadership, broadly defined—and how can you actually assess them?

Individuals who possess the three elements of a global mind-set—social, psychological, and intellectual capital—are most likely to do well abroad. **Social capital** has to do with how well you build trusting relationships, especially with individuals unlike yourself. This includes being comfortable communicating and networking with people from other cultures, particularly when they have perspectives different than yours. **Psychological capital** has to do with your openness to new experiences—being energized by foreign contexts, having a sense of adventure, and being passionate about engaging with other parts of the world. Finally, **intellectual capital** reflects your grasp of your firm's global business operations. This includes understanding how competitors and customers act abroad as well as your ability to cognitively juggle all the complexities associated with international business. It also includes whether you have a genuine interest in the histories, cultures, and political systems in different parts of the world.

Fortunately, an instrument has been created to measure the elements of a global mind-set. It has over 70 items and has been tested on nearly 1,000 executives. Indeed, executives who had higher scores also tended to receive better performance evaluations in international leadership roles (see www.globalmindset.com for more information). Presented in this feature is this instrument, with questions from all three elements. Please rate yourself on these items and reflect on what they might mean for your own mind-set, your suitability for international assignments, and your possible areas of weakness. A variety of steps can be taken, either individually or by your company, to help improve any areas of weakness. Intellectual capital tends to be the easiest to improve (e.g., by greater preparation), while psychological capital tends to be the hardest.

GLOBAL MIND-SET SAMPLER

Please answer the following questions with the scale below.

1	2	3	4	5
Not at all	Small extent	Moderate extent	Large extent	Very large extent

Element 1—Social Capital Questions: Do You...

_____ 1.... understand the nonverbal expressions made by people in several different cultures?

_____ 2.... have the skills to work to achieve a goal with people from different cultures?

_____ 3.... easily coordinate your work efforts with other people?

_____ 4.... work well with people who are very different from you?

_____ **Total Social Capital Score**

Element 2—Psychological Capital Questions: Do You...

_____ 1.... feel comfortable even when you aren't in control of a situation?

_____ 2.... seek to challenge yourself in new ways?

_____ 3.... seek to learn more about other cultures and their customs?

_____ 4.... enjoy exploring different parts of the world?

_____ **Total Psychological Capital Score.**

Element 3—Intellectual Capital Questions: Do You...

_____ 1.... discuss ramifications of world events with friends and colleagues?

_____ 2.... know about major religions in the world and their impact on society?

_____ 3.... know about key business and cultural leaders, as well as the history and geography, of several countries?

_____ 4.... know about business strategies for expanding globally?

_____ **Total Intellectual Capital Score**

INTERPRETING YOUR SCORES

The questions above will give you a snapshot about how likely you are to perform at a high level in an international position. We suggest you add up your scores and see how well you did in each of the three elements associated with a global mind-set.

Element score above 16: This is a strong area for you and bodes well for performance
Element score between 12 and 16: Good showing, but could use some improvement
Element score below 12: A potential area of weakness, may need major improvement

Adapted from: Javidan, M., Teagarden, M., & Bowen, D. (2010). Making it overseas. _Harvard Business Review_, April, 109–113.

Making the Case for International Understanding

THE NEW BRIC GIANTS: FOLLOWING THE PATH OF JAPAN INC.?

Back in the 1980s and 1990s, every other magazine cover seemed to feature a new management technique that was helping Japanese firms succeed internationally. We heard all about the Toyota Way, the Honda Way, and the Mitsubishi Way—and with good reason, since Japan led the world at the time.

But since the late 1990s, the news has not been nearly as good for Japan. In fact, by 2000 Japan had only 68 firms on the Global 500 list (down from 141 in 1995), a figure that has not changed much since then (71 Japanese firms were on the 2010 list). So which countries have gained at Japan's expense? Companies from Brazil, Russia, India, and China have grown tremendously during Japan's slide—these BRIC countries saw their combined share of Global 500 revenues rise from 0.9% to nearly 11%. But do firms that rise meteorically fall rapidly as well? If so, what does this mean for the recent success of companies from BRIC countries and other developing nations? Will they lose steam like Japan did, or will they find ways to adjust and protect their gains, a trajectory followed by some U.S. and European firms?

Several factors will determine whether BRIC countries can stay globally competitive over time. The inability of some of Japan's most successful firms to maintain their competitive positions offers some valuable lessons. Specifically, the features that were responsible for Japan's early success were also impediments to continued success. Japanese firms were unable to adapt their management approaches and cultures—features responsible for the growth of their export economy—into something sustainable. Japanese firms gave too much credit to their cultures, as defined by corporate policies and ways of viewing problems (devotion to the "Way").

Indeed, Japanese firms enjoyed their early successes while continuing to drive down costs via economies of scale and developing (or borrowing) methods that ensured quality production. Many Japanese firms recognized the appeal of exporting, and so began the Japanese miracle. By 1986, over 95% of all Japanese products sold globally were made in Japan. In building super-efficient and competitive systems, the Japanese used a set of unique corporate approaches, policies, values, and employment practices to shore up their gains. Because of their success, soon everyone wanted to know more about the Toyota Way or the Toshiba Way. Years of success reified the "Ways," amplified by an obsessive media. During a five-year period in the late 1980s, the *Harvard Business Review* alone published 36 articles featuring Japanese management prowess.

But while their methods helped Japanese firms grow exports, they hindered success in setting up foreign operations. The automatic application of the Way was a mistake reflecting the assumption that what worked at home would also work in foreign operations. In exporting their methods abroad, Japanese firms sent many more expats overseas than did their U.S. and European counterparts—on average, twice as many. Once abroad, Japanese expatriates searched for loyal adherents. As one Japanese manager said,

"I don't want to hire someone who is too American or German. They will not fit our company and way of doing things." Subsequently, Japanese firms began to stumble. In the mobile phone industry, Japanese firms such as Sharp, Panasonic, Fujitsu, NEC, Toshiba, and Sony all tried to replicate abroad what had worked in Japan using home-market thinking. The results were phones not tailored to specific foreign markets. All of these firms, with the exception of Sony (thanks to its partnership with Ericsson), lost their shirts.

Then there was the nature of the Japanese home market. During their growth periods, Japanese firms faced few foreign rivals at home. From the 1970s to the 1990s, foreign investment in Japan was just 0.30% of GDP, with only about 1,000 foreign firms operating in the country. Onerous regulations, a complex legal system, and tight interconnections among Japanese firms made it difficult for foreign firms to grab a foothold in Japan. While advantageous as Japan's exports grew, the isolation of their home market from foreign competition meant that Japanese firms had little experience dealing with foreign competitors head-to-head. For instance, Japanese investment giant Nomura struggled to compete against Goldman Sachs, UBS, and others in foreign financial capitals like London and New York. Nomura simply did not have the market sophistication and knowledge needed to compete and floundered for years.

Another factor to consider is the nature of the labor force. Simply put, the Japanese labor force has been homogeneous, docile, and compliant for decades—just what you need when quality, precision, and efficiency are the coins of the realm. The Japanese population is very uniform with few ethnic subgroups, and immigration is low. In 1960, only 1% of the population was non-Japanese, and that figure is not much higher today (1.6% in 2010). Compare this to the substantial rise in immigrants as a percentage of the population in both the United States (from 5% to 13%) and Germany (from 1% to 13%) over the same time period.

But a homogeneous, cooperative workforce at home didn't help prepare Japanese firms for their ventures abroad. Indeed, many Japanese firms encountered human resource management setbacks overseas. Take the masculine culture that characterizes many Japanese firms, for example. These views, and the behaviors that accompany them, might be overlooked, if not appreciated, in Tokyo. But in the United States, such attitudes can prove costly and damage reputations. At a Mitsubishi plant in Illinois, sexist attitudes in employment ads led to lawsuits about systematic harassment of women and resulted in a $35 million fine. Other Japanese firms have experienced similar problems.

Finally, a close look at top management teams in Japanese firms reveals a similar pattern—a strength when exporting from home but a potential handicap when operating in foreign countries. For the most part, Japanese firms are led by Japanese. Of the Japanese firms still on the Global 500, about 98% of corporate officers are Japanese. Consider Matsushita Electric (now Panasonic), an outstanding exporter during the 1980s and 1990s. Senior managers were all Japanese. Moreover, nearly all of these managers had graduated from one of the four top Japanese universities and had spent their whole careers at the company. This contrasts with U.S. firms such as IBM, where 30% of top managers are foreign nationals. Likewise, European firms such as French grocery giant Carrefour contrast sharply with Japanese firms in this regard. Carrefour has successfully expanded in dozens of countries by hiring local nationals to run foreign outposts, rotating them across countries before promoting them into senior management.

So the question remains—are BRIC countries and the companies that call them home well positioned for the future, or do they have big challenges to face down the line? Japan Inc. rose to international prominence in a short period of time, only to fall back. Perhaps the BRIC countries can learn from this cautionary tale—and your analysis.

ASSIGNMENT QUESTIONS

1. Identify one firm on the current Global 500 list from each of the four BRIC countries. Do these firms rely on and promote a set of "Ways" for operating? If so, what are those ways? Do they parallel what we saw in Japanese firms?

2. What is the nature of the domestic markets in BRIC countries? How are foreign companies treated? Do you see any parallels with Japan's experience?

3. What is the nature of the domestic labor force in BRIC countries? How homogeneous and cooperative is the workforce compared to Japan's? What are the implications of this in your view?

4. For the four BRIC-based firms identified in Question 1, what is the makeup of their top management? How much foreign experience is represented?

5. Taking everything into consideration, how likely is it that BRIC countries, and the firms based there, will eventually experience what happened in Japan?

Adapted from: Black, J. S., & Morrison, A. J. (2010). A cautionary tale for emerging market giants. *Harvard Business Review,* September, 99–103; http://money.cnn.com/magazines/fortune/global500/2010/countries/Japan.html.

NOTES

1. White, M. D. (2010). The four Ps of global business expansion. *Wall Street Journal,* November 12, A19.

2. White, M. D. (2009). The long climb. *The Economist,* October 3, 3–5; Guillen, M. F., & Garcia-Canal, E. (2009). The American model of the multinational firm and the "new" multinationals from emerging economies. *Academy of Management Perspectives,* 23(2), 23–35; McFarlin, D. B., & Sweeney, P. D. (2011). *International Management: Strategic Opportunities and Cultural Challenges* (4th ed.). New York: Routledge.

3. Anderson, J., Kupp, M., & Moaligou, R. (2009). Lessons from the developing world. *Wall Street Journal,* August 17, R6; Baker, S. (2004). Jobs go overseas—under water. *Business Week,* April 5, 13; Engardio, P. (2000). The barons of outsourcing. *Business Week,* August 28, 177–178; Friedman, T. (2004). The incredible shrinking world. *Dayton Daily News,* March 6, A8; McFarlin, D. B., & Sweeney, P. D. (2011). *International Management: Strategic Opportunities and Cultural Challenges* (4th ed.). New York: Routledge.

4. The BRICS: The trillion-dollar club. *The Economist,* April 17, 2010, 64–66; Champion, M. (2004). CEOs' worst nightmares. *Wall Street Journal,* January 21, A13; Carpenter, M. A., &

Fredrickson, J. W. (2001). Top management teams, global strategic posture, and the moderating role of uncertainty. *Academy of Management Journal*, 44, 533–545; McDonald, J. (2010). China surges past Japan as No. 2 economy; U.S. next? *Dayton Daily News*, August 17, A7.

5. The cutting edge. *The Economist*, February 24, 2001, 80; World trade. *The Economist*, December 6, 2003, 94; Trade in the Americas: All in the familia. *The Economist*, April 21, 2001, 19–22; Deans, B. (2001). Popular resistance barrier to trade pact. *Dayton Daily News*, April 22, 16A; Engardio, P. (2001). America's future: Smart globalization. *Business Week*, August 27, 132–137; Sachs, J. D. (2003). Welcome to the Asian century. *Fortune*, December 29, 53–54; Seager, A. (2009). China becomes world's third largest economy. *The Guardian*, January 14. Available at www.guardian.co.uk; Wonacott, P., & King, N. (2003). Chinese wield quiet clout at trade talks. *Wall Street Journal*, September 15, A18; www.economywatch.com/economies-in-top/; www.investopedia.com/terms/b/bric.asp; www.unctad.org.

6. Burkitt, L. (2010). China's car economy revs up. *Wall Street Journal*, October 7, B1, B11; Wooldridge, A. (2010). The emerging emerging markets. In *The World in 2011* (131–132). London: The Economist.

7. Business is transforming Africa for the better. *The Economist*, June 12, 2010, 76; Farzad, R. (2010). Drop Russia add Indonesia: The debate is on. *Bloomberg Businessweek*, November 22–28, 26–27; Jargon, J. (2010). KFC savors potential in Africa *Wall Street Journal*, December 8, B1, B2; Passariello, C. (2010). Danone expands its pantry to woo the world's poor. *Wall Street Journal*, June 29, A1, A16; Stewart, R. M. (2010). Wal-Mart sets African offer. *Wall Street Journal*, November 30, B2; Wooldridge, A. (2010). The emerging emerging markets. In *The World in 2011* (131–132). London: The Economist.

8. The power to disrupt (A special report on innovation in emerging markets). *The Economist*, April 17, 2010, 16–18; Bellman, E. (2009). Indian firms shift focus to the poor. *Wall Street Journal*, October 20, A1, A18; Cooper, J. C., & Madigan, K. (2004). The economy is showing real muscle. *Business Week*, May 3, 33–34; Engardio, P. (2001). America's future: Smart globalization. *Business Week*, August 27, 132–137; www.economywatch.com/world_economy/world-economic-indicators/world-gdp.html; www.nationmaster.com.

9. The power to disrupt (A special report on innovation in emerging markets). *The Economist*, April 17, 2010, 16–18; Mero, J. (2008). Power shift. *Fortune*, July 21, 161–182; http://money.cnn.com/magazines/fortune/global500/2010/full_list/.

10. McFarlin, D. B., & Sweeney, P. D. (2011). *International Management: Strategic Opportunities and Cultural Challenges* (4th ed.). New York: Routledge.

11. Time to change the act. *The Economist*, February 21, 2009, 69–71; Gimpel, L. (2008). Global hot spots. *Entrepreneur*, June, 62–70; Roberts, D., & Engardio, P. (2009). The China hype. *Business Week*, November 2, 36–42.

12. China's economic power: Enter the dragon. *The Economist*, March 10, 2001, 23–25; Bremner, B., Balfour, F., Shari, M., Ihlwan, M., & Engardio, P. (2001). Asia: The big chill. *Business Week*, April 2, 48–50; Higgins, A. (2004). As China surges, it also proves a buttress to American strength. *Wall Street Journal*, January 30, A1, A8; Powell, B. (2009). China's hard landing. *Fortune*, March 16, 114–120; Schlevogt, K. A. (2000). The business environment in China: Getting to know the next century's superpower. *Thunderbird International Business Review*, 42 (January–February), 85–111.

13. Ferguson, N. (2010). In China's orbit: The world is tilting back to the East. *Wall Street Journal*, November 20–21, C1, C2.

14. Competitive sport in Boca Raton. *The Economist*, February 7, 2004, 65–68; Tested by the mighty euro. *The Economist*, March 20, 2004, 61–62; Glasgall, W. (1995). Hot money. *Business Week*, March 20, 46–50; Hitt, M. A., Keats, B. W., & DeMarie, S. M. (1998). Navigating in the new competitive landscape: Building strategic flexibility and competitive advantage in the 21st century. *Academy of Management Executive*, 12, 22–42; Miller, R., Arndt, M., Capell, K., & Fairlamb, D. (2003). The incredible falling dollar. *Business Week*, December 22, 36–38.

15. Currency hedging: Holding back the flood. *The Economist*, February 21, 2004, 72; Tested by the mighty euro. *The Economist*, March 20, 2004, 61–62; Bianco, A., & Moore, P. L. (2001). Downfall: The inside story of the management fiasco at Xerox. *Business Week*, March 5, 82, 90; Glasgall, W. (1995). Hot money. *Business Week*, March 20, 46–50; Phillips, M. M. (2001). Financial contagion knows no borders. *Wall Street Journal*, July 13, A2; Sparks, D. (2000). Business won't hedge the euro away. *Business Week*, December 4, 157; Zaun, T. (2001). As the yen weakens, Japan's car makers smile. *Wall Street Journal*, April 10, A15, A19.

16. A survey of the new economy: Knowledge is power. *The Economist*, September 23, 2000, 27; Siekman, P. (2000). The big myth about U.S. manufacturing. *Fortune*, October 2, 244C–244E.

17. Ante, S. E., & Hof, R. D. (2004). Look who's going offshore. *Business Week*, May 17, 64–65; Lee, D. (2010). Outsourcing trend could hamper economy. *Dayton Daily News*, October 17, C2.

18. The world is rocky. *The Economist*, December 13, 2008, 9; Einhorn, B., Kripalani, M., & Engardio, P. (2001). India 3.0. *Business Week*, February 26, 44–46; Kripalani, M., & Clifford, M. L. (2000). India wired. *Business Week*, March 6, 82–91; Sharma, A., & Worthe, B. (2009). Indian tech outsourcers aim to widen contracts. *Wall Street Journal*, October 5, B1, B7.

19. Ante, S. E. (2004). Shifting work offshore? Outsourcer beware. *Business Week*, January 12, 36–37; Barrett, R. (2010). Outsourcing isn't worth it, some companies finding. *Dayton Daily News*, November 21, C5; Maher, K., & Tita, B. (2010). Caterpillar joins "onshoring" trend. *Wall Street Journal*, March 12, B1, B7; Thurm, S. (2004). Lesson in India: Some jobs don't translate overseas. *Wall Street Journal*, March 3, A1, A10.

20. Leiber, N. (2010). "Rural outsourcers" vs. Bangalore. *Bloomberg Businessweek*, September 27–October 3, 51–52.

21. The great hollowing out myth. *The Economist*, February 21, 2004, 27–29; Bridis, T. (2004). Firms want freedom to move jobs overseas. *Dayton Daily News*, January 8, D1; Haberman, S. (2004). Software: Will outsourcing hurt America's supremacy? *Business Week*, March 1, 84–94; Kripalani, M., & Engardio, P. (2003). The rise of India. *Business Week*, December 8, 66–78; Nussbaum, B. (2004). Where are the jobs? *Business Week*, March 22, 36–52; Schlender, B. (2004). Peter Drucker sets us straight. *Fortune*, January 12, 115–118; Schroeder, M. (2004). Outsourcing may create U.S. jobs. *Wall Street Journal*, March 30, A2; Teves, O. (2003). Philippines latest to feel jobs surge. *Dayton Daily News*, December 6, D1, D4.

22. Outsourcing to India: Back office to the world. *The Economist*, May 5, 2001, 59–62; Clifford, M., & Kripalani, M. (2000). Different countries, adjoining cubicles. *Business Week*, August 28, 182–184; Koretz, G. (2000). Solving a global growth enigma. *Business Week*, November 20, 32; Lavin, D. (2002). Globalization goes upscale. *Wall Street Journal*, February 1, A18; Lewin, A. Y., Massini, S., & Peeters, C. (2010). Why are companies offshoring innovation? The emerging global race for talent. *Journal of International Business Studies*, 40, 901–925.

23. Borrus, A. (2000). Give me your tired, your poor—and all your techies. *Business Week*, November 13, 48; Clifford, M., & Kripalani, M. (2000). Different countries, adjoining cubicles. *Business Week*, August 28, 182–184; Kripalani, M., Hamm, S., & Ante, S. (2004).

Scrambling to stem India's onslaught. *Business Week*, January 26, 81–81; Koretz, G. (2000). The economy's Achilles' heel? *Business Week*, November 13, 42; Montgomery, C. (2002). Chief: No delivery from labor pains. *Dayton Daily News*, March 2, 1E, 8E.

24. Adler, N. J., & Gundersen, A. (2008). *International Dimensions of Organizational Behavior* (5th ed.). Mason, OH: Thompson South-Western; Coy, P. (2000). The creative economy. *Business Week*, August 28, 76–82; Grow, B. (2004). Hispanic nation. *Business Week*, March 15, 59–67; Malpass, A. (1998). Ready for that job on the street? *Business Week*, March 16, 118; Valbrun, M. (2000). Immigrants find economic boom brings more than higher pay. *Wall Street Journal*, August 16, B1, B4.

25. Adler, N. J., & Gundersen, A. (2008). *International Dimensions of Organizational Behavior* (5th ed.). Mason, OH: Thompson South-Western; Gentile, M. C. (1996). *Managerial Excellence through Diversity*. Chicago: Irwin; Joplin, J. R. W., & Daus, C. S. (1997). Challenges of leading a diverse workforce. *Academy of Management Executive*, 11, 32–47; Robinson, G., & Dechant, K. (1997). Building a business case for diversity. *Academy of Management Executive*, 11, 21–31.

26. Murray, M. (2001). As huge companies keep growing, CEOs struggle to keep pace. *Wall Street Journal*, February 8, A1, A6; Roberts, K., Kossek, E. E., & Ozeki, C. (1998). Managing the global workforce: Challenges and strategies. *Academy of Management Executive*, 12, 93–106; Stanek, M. B. (2000). The need for global managers: A business necessity. *Management Decision*, 38, 232–242; http://www.hoovers.com; http.//www.pg.com.

27. Briscoe, D. R., Schuler, R. S., & Claus, L. (2009). *International Human Resource Management* (3rd ed.). New York: Routledge.

28. Birkinshaw, J., & Hood, N. (2001). Unleash innovation in foreign subsidiaries. *Harvard Business Review*, March, 79, 131–138; Dwyer, P., Engardio, P., Schiller, Z., & Reed, S. (1994). Tearing up today's organization chart. *Business Week*, November 18, 80–90; Stanek, M. B. (2000). The need for global managers: A business necessity. *Management Decision*, 38, 232–242; McFarlin, D. B., & Sweeney, P. D. (2011). *International Management: Strategic Opportunities and Cultural Challenges* (4th ed.). New York: Routledge; Shrader, R. C. (2001). Collaboration and performance in foreign markets: The case of young high-technology manufacturing firms. *Academy of Management Journal*, 44, 45–60.

29. Hofstede, G. (1993). Cultural constraints in management theories. *Academy of Management Executive*, 7, 81–94; Triandis, H. C. (1996). The psychological measurement of cultural syndromes. *American Psychologist*, 51, 407–415.

30. Berry, H., Guillen, M. F., & Zhou, N. (2010). An institutional approach to cross-national distance. *Journal of International Business Studies*, 41, 1480–1560; McFarlin, D. B., & Sweeney, P. D. (2011). *International Management: Strategic Opportunities and Cultural Challenges* (4th ed.). New York: Routledge.

31. Adler, N. J., & Gundersen, A. (2008). *International Dimensions of Organizational Behavior* (5th ed.). Mason, OH: Thompson South-Western; Begley, T. M., & Tan, W. L. (2001). The socio-cultural environment for entrepreneurship: A comparison between East Asian and Anglo-Saxon countries. *Journal of International Business Studies*, 32, 537–553; Earley, P. C., & Singh, H. (2000). New approaches to international and cross-cultural management research. In P. C. Earley & H. Singh (eds.), *Innovations in International and Cross-cultural Management* (1–14). Thousand Oaks, CA: Sage; Granato, J., Inglehart, R., & Leblang, D. (1996). The effect of cultural values on economic development: Theory, hypotheses, and some empirical tests.

American Journal of Political Science, 40, 607–631; Gupta, V., & Fernandez, C. (2009). Cross-cultural similarities and differences in characteristics attributed to entrepreneurs: A three nation study. *Journal of Leadership and Organizational Studies*, 15, 304–318; Thomas, D. C., Au, K., & Ravlin, E. C. (2003). Cultural variation and the psychological contract. *Journal of Organizational Behavior*, 24, 451–472; Shenkar, O. (2001). Cultural distance revisited: Towards a more rigorous conceptualization and measurement of cultural differences. *Journal of International Business Studies*, 32, 519–535.

32. Morris, M. W., Podolny, J. M., & Ariel, S. (2000). Missing relations: Incorporating relational constructs into models of culture. In P. C. Earley & H. Singh (eds.), *Innovations in International and Cross-cultural Management* (52–90). Thousand Oaks, CA: Sage; Sampson, E. E. (2000). Reinterpreting individualism and collectivism. *American Psychologist*, 55, 1425–1432.

33. Schneider, S. C., & Barsoux, J. L. (2003). *Managing across Cultures* (2nd ed.). Harlow, England: Pearson Education.

34. Osland, J. S., & Bird, A. (2000). Beyond sophisticated stereotyping. Cultural sensemaking in context. *Academy of Management Executive*, 14, 65–79.

35. Melloan, G. (2004). Feeling the muscles of the multinationals. *Wall Street Journal*, January 6, A19; http://yaleglobal.yale.edu/about/globalinc.jsp.

36. McFarlin, D. B., & Sweeney, P. D. (2011). *International Management: Strategic Opportunities and Cultural Challenges* (4th ed.). New York: Routledge.

37. Birkinshaw, J., & Hood, N. (2001). Unleash innovation in foreign subsidiaries. *Harvard Business Review*, March, 131–138.

38. Cavusgil, S. T., Knight, G., & Riesenberger, J. R. (2008). *International Business: Strategy, Management, and the New Realities*. Upper Saddle River, NJ: Prentice Hall; Negandhi, A. (1987). *International Management*. Boston: Allyn & Bacon; Welch, L. S., & Luostarinen, R. (1988). Internationalization: Evolution of a concept. *Journal of General Management*, 14, 55–71.

39. Black, J. S., Gregersen, H. B., & Mendenhall, M. E. (1992). *Global Assignments: Successfully Expatriating and Repatriating International Managers*. San Francisco: Jossey-Bass; Milliman, J., Von Glinow, M. A., & Nathan, M. (1991). Organizational life cycles and strategic international human resource management in multinational companies: Implications for congruence theory. *Academy of Management Journal*, 16, 318–339; www.llbean.com.

40. Aeppel, T. (2009). Harley-Davidson profit plunges. *Wall Street Journal*, October 16, B5; www.harley-davidson.com.

41. Aeppel, T. (2009). Harley-Davidson profit plunges. *Wall Street Journal*, October 16, B5; Lin, L., Clothier, M., & Ying, T. (2011). Why Harley can't rev up in China. *Bloomberg Businessweek*, October 24–30, 24–25; See www.harley-davidson.com.

42. Wal around the world. *The Economist*, December 8, 2001, 55–57; Bellman, E. (2009). Wal-Mart exports big box concept to India. *Wall Street Journal*, May 28, B1; Bianco, A., & Zellner, W. (2003). Is Wal-Mart too powerful? *Business Week*, October 6, 100–110; Ellison, S. (2001). Carrefour and Ahold find shoppers like to think local. *Wall Street Journal*, August 31, A5; Landers, P. (2001). Penney blends two business cultures. *Wall Street Journal*, April 5, A15, A17; Smith, G. (2002). War of the superstores. *Business Week*, September 23, 60; Spencer, M. (2009). Carrefour, in shift, to exit Russia as it reports 2.9% drop in sales. *Wall Street Journal*, October 16, B5; Zellner, W., Schmidt, K. A., Ihlwan, M., & Dawley, H. (2001). How well does Wal-Mart travel? *Business Week*, September 3, 82–84; Zimmerman, A., & Fackler, M. (2003). Wal-Mart's foray into Japan spurs a retail upheaval. *Wall Street Journal*, September 19, A1, A6.

43. Hamm, S. (2003). Borders are so 20th century. *Business Week*, September 22, 68–72; Rohwer, J. (2000). GE digs into Asia. *Fortune*, October 2, 165–178.

44. Ball, J., Zaun, T., & Shirouzu, N. (2002). Daimler explores idea of "world engine." *Wall Street Journal*, January 8, A3; Bellman, E. (2009). Wal-Mart exports big box concept to India. *Wall Street Journal*, May 28, B1; Briscoe, D. R. (1995). *International Human Resource Management*. Englewood Cliffs, NJ: Prentice Hall; Dyer, J. H. (2000). Examining interfirm trust and relationships in a cross-national setting. In P. C. Earley & H. Singh (eds.), *Innovations in International and Cross-cultural Management* (215–244). Thousand Oaks, CA: Sage; Tse, D. K., Pan, Y., & Au, K. Y. (1997). How MNCs choose entry modes and form alliances: The China experience. *Journal of International Business Studies*, 28, 779–803.

45. Guillen, M. F., & Garcia-Canal, E. (2009). The American model of the multinational firm and the "new" multinationals from emerging economies. *Academy of Management Perspectives*, 23(2), 23–35; Poon, A. (2009). Chinese oil firms bid $17 billion to expand. *Wall Street Journal*, August 11, B1, B2.

46. Ghoshal, S., & Bartlett, C. A. (1990). The multinational organization as an interorganizational network. *Academy of Management Review*, 15, 603–625; Malnight, T. W. (1996). The transition from decentralized to network-based MNC structures: An evolutionary perspective. *Journal of International Business Studies*, 27, 43–65.

47. Cavusgil, S. T., Knight, G., & Riesenberger, J. R. (2008). *International Business. Strategy, Management, and the New Realities*. Upper Saddle River, NJ: Prentice Hall.

48. Bellman, F. (2009). Harley to ride India growth. *Wall Street Journal*, August 28, B1, B2; Cavusgil, S. T., Knight, G., & Riesenberger, J. R. (2008). *International Business: Strategy, Management, and the New Realities*. Upper Saddle River, NJ: Prentice Hall; Ewing, J. (2009). Amazing machines may lead Europe out of recession. *Business Week*, August 24 & 31, 60–61; Hill, C. W. L. (2008). *Global Business Today* (5th ed.). New York: McGraw-Hill/Irwin; see also: http://www.harley-davidson.com/wcm/Content/Pages/Company/company.jsp?locale = en_US.

49. Byrnes, N. (2007). Avon: More than cosmetic changes. *Business Week*, March 12, 62–63; Cavusgil, S. T., Knight, G., & Riesenberger, J. R. (2008). *International Business: Strategy, Management, and the New Realities*. Upper Saddle River, NJ: Prentice Hall; Ewing, J. (2009). Amazing machines may lead Europe out of recession. *Business Week*, August 24 & 31, 60–61; Hill, C. W. L. (2008). *Global Business Today* (5th ed.). New York: McGraw-Hill/Irwin.

50. Bartlett, C. A., & Ghoshal, S. (1989). *Managing across Borders: The Transnational Solution*. Boston: Harvard Business School Press; Hout, T., Porter, M. E., & Rudden, E. (1982). How global companies win out. *Harvard Business Review*, September–October, 99–108; Lovelock, C. H., & Yip, G. S. (1996). Developing global strategies for service businesses. *California Management Review*, 38, 64–85; Luo, Y. (2001). Determinants of local responsiveness: Perspectives from foreign subsidiaries in an emerging market. *Journal of Management*, 27, 451–477; Prahalad, C. K., & Doz, Y. L. (1987). *The Multinational Mission: Balancing Local Demands and Global Vision*. New York: Free Press; Tomlinson, R. (2000). Can Nestle be the very best? *Fortune*, November 13, 353–360.

51. Lunsford, J. L. (2003). Boeing may risk building new jet despite a lack of U.S. customers. *Wall Street Journal*, October 15, A1, A13.

52. Cavusgil, S. T., Knight, G., & Riesenberger, J. R. (2008). *International Business: Strategy, Management, and the New Realities*. Upper Saddle River, NJ: Prentice Hall; Hitt, M. A., Ireland, R. D., & Hoskisson, R. E. (2009). *Strategic Management: Competitiveness and*

Globalization (8th ed.). Mason, OH: South-Western Cengage Learning; MacMillian, I. C., van Putten., A. B., & McGrath, R. G. (2003). Global gamesmanship. *Harvard Business Review,* May, 62–73; Ramstad, E., & Juying, Q. (2006). Intel pushes chip production deep into China's hinterlands. *Wall Street Journal,* May 23, B1, B3; Wheelen, T. L., & Hunger, J. D. (1995). *Strategic Management and Business Policy* (5th ed.). Reading, MA: Addison-Wesley.

53. Holmes, S. (2003). A plane, a plan, a problem. *Business Week,* December 1, 40–42; Boeing's high-speed flight. *Business Week,* August 12, 2002, 74–75.

54. Cavusgil, S. T., Knight, G., & Riesenberger, J. R. (2008). *International Business: Strategy, Management, and the New Realities.* Upper Saddle River, NJ: Prentice Hall; Michaels, D., & Sanders, P. (2009). Dreamliner production gets closer monitoring. *Wall Street Journal,* October 7, B1, B2.

55. Cavusgil, S. T., Knight, G., & Riesenberger, J. R. (2008). *International Business: Strategy, Management, and the New Realities.* Upper Saddle River, NJ: Prentice Hall; Hitt, M. A., Ireland, R. D., & Hoskisson, R. E. (2009). *Strategic Management: Competitiveness and Globalization* (8th ed.). Mason, OH: South-Western Cengage Learning; Morrison, A. J., Ricks, D. A., & Roth, K. (1991). Globalization versus regionalization: Which way for the multinational? *Organizational Dynamics,* 19, 17–29; Prahalad, C. K., & Doz, Y. L. (1987). *The Multinational Mission: Balancing Local Demands and Global Vision.* New York: Free Press; Wheelen, T. L., & Hunger, J. D. (1995). *Strategic Management and Business Policy* (5th ed.). Reading, MA: Addison-Wesley.

56. Schiller, Z., Burns, G., & Miller, K. L. (1996). Make it simple: That's P&G's new marketing mantra—and it's spreading. *Business Week,* September 9, 96–104.

57. Cavusgil, S. T., Knight, G., & Riesenberger, J. R. (2008). *International Business: Strategy, Management, and the New Realities.* Upper Saddle River, NJ: Prentice Hall; Luo, Y. (2003). Market-seeking MNEs in an emerging market: How parent-subsidiary links shape overseas success. *Journal of International Business Studies,* 34, 290–309; Bartlett, C. A., & Ghoshal, S. (1989). *Managing across Borders: The Transnational Solution.* Boston: Harvard Business School Press; See also: http://www.cat.com/corporate-overview/offices-and-facilities.

58. Birkinshaw, J., Morrison, A., & Hulland, J. (1995). Structural and competitive determinants of a global integration strategy. *Strategic Management Journal,* 16, 637–655.

59. Hitt, M. A., Ireland, R. D., & Hoskisson, R. E. (2009). *Strategic Management: Competitiveness and Globalization* (8th ed.). Mason, OH: South-Western Cengage Learning; Morrison, A. J., Ricks, D. A., & Roth, K. (1991). Globalization versus regionalization: Which way for the multinational? *Organizational Dynamics,* 19, 17–29.

60. Ghemawat, P. (2005). Regional strategies for global leadership. *Harvard Business Review,* December. Available at www.hbrreprints.org.

61. Kim, W. C., & Mauborgne, R. A. (2005). *Blue Ocean Strategy: How to Create Uncontested Market Space and Make the Competition Irrelevant.* Boston: Harvard Business School Press. Kim, W. C., & Mauborgne, R. A. (1991). Implementing global strategies: The role of procedural justice. *Strategic Management Journal,* 12, 125–143; Making global strategies work. *Sloan Management Review,* Spring 1993, 11–25.

Chapter 2

Cultural Frameworks

Understanding Differences in Employee Attitudes and Behavior

I tried to integrate the strengths of both Western and Eastern management approaches, but without losing the essential qualities of each culture.

—Stan Shih, cofounder and chairman emeritus of
Taiwan's Acer Group, on Acer's management system[1]

Entrepreneur Stan Shih grew Taiwan's Acer Group from nothing to the second largest provider of PCs on the planet. In doing so, he always envisioned Acer as a global brand and as a global corporate citizen. Moreover, his sophisticated understanding of cultural differences is impressive and is captured in his blended management approach, which helped form a new type of Asian management. Visualizing, much less implementing, a style that straddles cultural boundaries effectively is a huge challenge to say the least.[2]

THE DEVELOPMENT OF AND NEED FOR CULTURE FRAMEWORKS

If anything, Shih's challenge to integrate Western and Eastern strengths without losing the most valued qualities of each culture underscores the warning discussed in chapter 1 regarding the dangers of oversimplifying something as complex as culture, particularly when the focus is on managing organizational behavior. International managers sometimes feel in desperate need of tools that can help sort out culture, even at the risk of oversimplifying matters. This partly explains why so many cultural frameworks have popped up over the past few decades. A cultural framework attempts to summarize and classify a set of norms, behaviors, customs, and traditions that are common to a given society. Yet cultural frameworks are seductive in that they can encourage management tendencies to rely on time-saving analytical shortcuts. In turn, this can inhibit managers' ability to be effective as they oversimplify culture and paint employees around the world with a set of broad-brush generalizations.

Nevertheless, if used judiciously, cultural frameworks can prove helpful. That is especially the case if managers treat them not as one-size-fits-all labeling devices but as guidance and starting points for helping to make sense of different business cultures and the people who are a part of them. Managers also need to remember that all cultural frameworks have limitations. For instance, three key influential frameworks reviewed in this chapter attempt to capture cultural differences through sets of bipolar dimensions (e.g., individualism–collectivism). Nations can then be categorized based on where they tend to fall on each cultural dimension. But this reductionism cannot fully capture the complexities and apparent paradoxes in specific cultures. For instance, if Americans are so individualistic, then why are they so generous with charities and so willing to help when natural disasters strike (hurricanes, floods, etc.)? And if Central American countries are so well known for showing warmth in interpersonal interactions, then why do service workers in those countries often seem indifferent to customers? Indeed, in one survey, bank customers in Costa Rica preferred to interact with "polite" machines (ATMs) instead of human tellers.[3]

With these limitations in mind, we will present three cultural frameworks that have attracted the most attention among international managers. Then we will turn our attention to some common manifestations of cultural differences in the global workplace, such as how culture may shape work attitudes (such as job satisfaction and leadership) and perceptions (such as about time, people, space, etc.). We will wrap up the chapter by suggesting ways that managers and multinationals alike can combat cultural stereotypes and bridge cultural differences—as Stan Shih did at Acer.

Hofstede's Seminal Effort: Clustering Countries by Cultural Values

Geert Hofstede's cultural framework is arguably the most well known in the world. Originally published in 1980, its influence and impact is hard to overestimate, especially because it is the largest effort (before or since) to cluster countries by cultural values. Today, Hofstede's framework is widely used by academics, international managers, and cultural training consultants. It has also spawned a variety of efforts by other scholars to create alternative frameworks. The next two frameworks we will consider are, in effect, the offspring of Hofstede's earlier work.[4]

Hofstede developed his framework using questionnaires collected from more than 116,000 employees across more than 70 countries. This monumental set of data yielded four bipolar cultural dimensions: individualism–collectivism, masculinity–femininity, power distance, and uncertainty avoidance. Hofstede devised scores for each dimension that ranged from 1 to 100 and could be applied to specific countries for comparison purposes. He also developed a series of cultural maps that allowed nations to be positioned in relative terms along two of the four culture dimensions. And because nations tended to cluster together, it was also possible to make relative comparisons across sets of countries. Hofstede's framework involving four (original) cultural dimensions offers guidance for managers who interact with employees from around the world.[5] Table 2.1 lists the country abbreviations used in Hofstede's culture maps.

Table 2.1
Countries and Regions in Hofstede's Culture Maps

ARA	Arab countries (Egypt, Lebanon, Libya, Kuwait, Iraq, Saudi Arabia, United Arab Emirates)	JPN	Japan
		KOR	South Korea
ARG	Argentina	MAL	Malaysia
AUL	Australia	MEX	Mexico
AUT	Austria	NET	Netherlands
BEL	Belgium	NOR	Norway
BRA	Brazil	NZL	New Zealand
CAN	Canada	PAK	Pakistan
CHL	Chile	PAN	Panama
COL	Colombia	PER	Peru
COS	Costa Rica	PHI	Philippines
DEN	Denmark	POR	Portugal
EAF	East Africa (Kenya, Ethiopia, Zambia)	SAF	South Africa
EQA	Ecuador	SAL	El Salvador
FIN	Finland	SIN	Singapore
FRA	France	SPA	Spain
GBR	Great Britain	SWE	Sweden
GER	Germany	SWI	Switzerland
GRE	Greece	TAI	Taiwan
GUA	Guatemala	THA	Thailand
HOK	Hong Kong	TUR	Turkey
IDO	Indonesia	URU	Uruguay
IND	India	USA	United States
IRA	Iran	VEN	Venezuela
IRE	Ireland	WAF	West Africa (Nigeria, Ghana, Sierra Leone)
ISR	Israel		
ITA	Italy	YUG	Former Yugoslavia
JAM	Jamaica		

Source: Adapted from Hofstede, G. (1991). *Cultures and Organizations: Software of the Mind*. London: McGraw-Hill, 55.

Individualism–Collectivism

This dimension addresses the question of whether people in a culture tend to see themselves as individuals or as part of a group. In cultures where individualistic values hold sway, a common belief is that people should take responsibility for themselves. Consequently, autonomy, personal achievement, and privacy are highly valued. On the other hand, in cultures where collectivism tends to dominate, group membership is highly valued, with people seeing themselves as belonging to groups that protect and care for them. As a result, people tend to be loyal and devoted to the groups they belong to, whether a family, a clan or tribe, or a firm. Although this dimension has been studied extensively, it is arguably the most complicated. In short, individualism–collectivism appears to cover several multifaceted values with a variety of components.[6]

For example, individualism seems to include economic (e.g., "I achieve things by being competitive") as well as expressive (e.g., "I would like to be viewed as a unique individual") components. Collectivism appears to also include both economic (e.g., "group members should share their resources") and expressive (e.g., "group members should be emotionally attached to each other") elements. These components, however, may be viewed quite differently across cultures. For instance, while cultures rooted in Latin American and Confucian traditions both tilt toward collectivism, they tend to interpret expressiveness toward group members differently. Specifically, warm displays of emotion are common in many Latin American countries—something that is much less likely to be seen in Japan. Similarly, being competitive in the individualistic United States can easily extend to friends, but not as commonly in Australia where a "mate" takes on special significance. Put simply, how collectivism or individualism are interpreted can differ across cultures.[7]

Masculinity–Femininity

This aspect describes whether people are more likely to value the assertive acquisition of material success (such as money, power, etc.) or quality of life and good relationships with coworkers. The masculine side of this dimension comes from Hofstede's observation that, in most cultures, men were more likely to value the assertive (masculine) side of things. Consequently, cultures in which people tend to be strongly motivated by achievement, have a positive view of ambitious career pursuits, and feel that men are best able to handle powerful positions are considered masculine. Institutions, such as schools and companies, tend to focus on cultivating high performers and promoting the idea that a successful career is an important, worthy goal. Not surprisingly, workplaces in masculine cultures are often competitive and stressful. In contrast, people in feminine cultures are more likely to value a harmonious workplace, emphasize gender equality, and feel that it is important to care for the less fortunate. As a result, work environments tend to be less stressful with less careerism. Job security tends to be higher and relations between labor and management less conflict prone.[8]

Power Distance

This dimension captures whether or not people accept wide differences in power between individuals. The question is whether the culture is accepting of having power unequally distributed (large distance) or not (small distance). In cultures where power distance is large, people tend to be accepting of their roles in life as well as the dictates or directions coming from those in positions of authority. Put simply, people tend to accept the premise that some are destined, or are otherwise deserving, to be in positions of power while others are not. Consequently, when a firm's structure involves large gaps in authority where power is dispersed unequally, it can be regarded as normal. After all, those in charge are viewed as different kinds of people than those who are not in positions of leadership. Generally speaking, executive authority and discretion is more centralized in cultures where power distance is large.

In cultures where power distance is small, people tend to be more skeptical and wary of concentrated power. As a result, companies tend to be more flat, with fewer management layers and authority pushed down to lower levels in a decentralized manner. Managers in small power distance cultures tend to be more open and trusting with subordinates, developing closer relationships in the process. They wield their authority cautiously; conspicuous displays of power are viewed negatively, and the misuse of power is constrained by procedures, policies, and laws that can create serious problems for managers if violated.[9]

Uncertainty Avoidance

People tend to react differently to ambiguous or uncertain events. Hofstede's framework contends that culture, in the form of uncertainty avoidance, partly determines those reactions. In cultures where uncertainty avoidance is small, people are more likely to believe that life has an inherent amount of unpredictability or uncertainty. Consequently, people tend to be less enamored with, or concerned about, complying with procedures, following rules, or respecting organizational hierarchies. If anything, taking risks, particularly when seeking personal achievement, is encouraged. In essence, life in organizations means that a certain level of competition, conflict, and ambiguity are inevitable.

In cultures where uncertainty avoidance is large, people are more likely to feel threatened by risk and ambiguity. As a result, people tend to desire predictable, stable workplaces and will do whatever they can to create them. This is one reason that procedures and policies aimed at reducing ambiguity about how employees should be treated proliferate. Moreover, when uncertainty avoidance is high, people are more likely to embrace absolute truths and be less tolerant of ideas or behaviors that are different. Not surprisingly, there tends to be less willingness to take risks when making decisions—either on the company's behalf or for one's personal career.

Mapping Hofstede's Cultural Framework

By crossing pairs of cultural dimensions and plotting scores by country, Hofstede developed some useful culture maps. These maps identify countries whose scores cluster together in one of four quadrants that reflect different combinations of the cultural dimensions. Countries that tend to cluster together may have specific combinations of cultural values that managers should consider carefully.

Let's begin with the positions of nations mapped on the individualism–collectivism and power distance dimensions. As Figure 2.1 illustrates, Costa Rica is the only

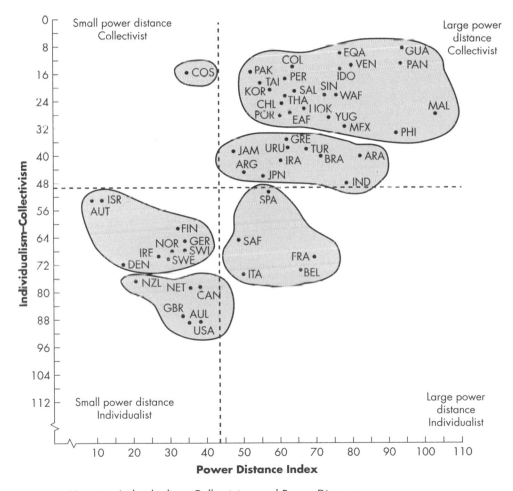

FIGURE 2.1 Mapping Individualism–Collectivism and Power Distance

Source: Hofstede, G. (1991). *Cultures and Organizations: Software of the Mind*. London: McGraw-Hill, 54. Used with permission.

country combining collectivism and small power distance. Much more common is collectivism and large power distance—many of the nations in this quadrant are either Asian or Latin American. Likewise, individualism and small power distance are common combinations among Anglo and Northern European countries (e.g., Great Britain, Sweden).

Figure 2.2 maps uncertainty avoidance and masculinity–femininity. Starting in the upper right quadrant, countries combining weak uncertainty avoidance and masculine values tend to be *achievement oriented* according to Hofstede. Most nations in this group are Anglo countries or former colonies (e.g., India, the Philippines). The lower right quadrant combines masculinity and strong uncertainty avoidance, producing what Hofstede called *security motivation* (i.e., where both

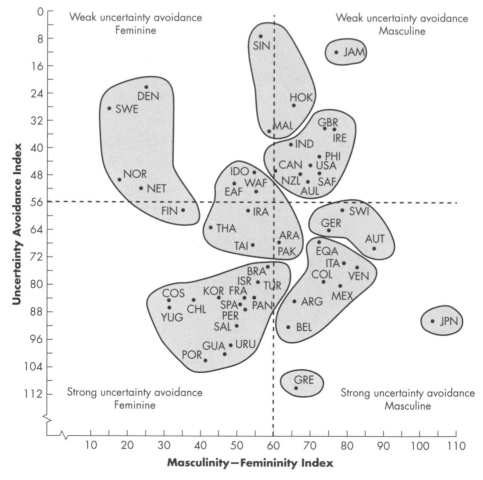

FIGURE 2.2 Mapping Uncertainty Avoidance and Masculinity–Femininity

Source: Hofstede, G. (1991). *Cultures and Organizations: Software of the Mind.* London: McGraw-Hill, 123. Used with permission.

performance and job security are valued). Conversely, the map quadrant combining feminine values with strong uncertainty avoidance results in *social motivation*. In these countries, job security, positive relationships, and a high quality of life are valued. In the last quadrant, Scandinavian countries are well represented. Here feminine values and weak uncertainty avoidance dominate—meaning that, while taking risks and performing well are acceptable, a high quality of work life and social relationships are prized more.

Figure 2.3 displays the final map, crossing uncertainty avoidance and power distance. Most nations in the *family quadrant* (large power distance combined with weak uncertainty avoidance) are Asian—where loyalty to strong, paternal leaders has traditionally been more important than policies and procedures.

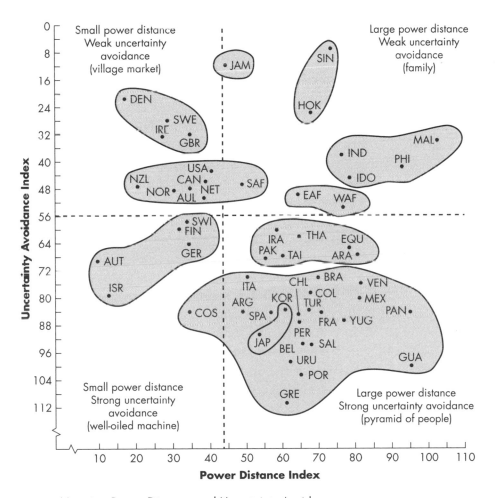

FIGURE 2.3 Mapping Power Distance and Uncertainty Avoidance

Source: Hofstede, G. (1991). *Cultures and Organizations: Software of the Mind*. London: McGraw-Hill, 141. Used with permission.

Conversely, countries in the *pyramid of people quadrant* (large power distance plus strong uncertainty avoidance) tend to have cultures that embrace powerful leaders but in a more hierarchical and rule-oriented work context (e.g., with clear chains of command, etc.). This clarity helps make organizations more predictable.

The *well-oiled machine quadrant* (small power distance combined with strong uncertainty avoidance) is populated by Germanic countries. Here, leaders tend to be less important than are clear policies and procedures that drive efficiency. And finally, Anglo and Scandinavian nations dominate the *village market quadrant* (small power distance combined with weak uncertainty avoidance). Countries in this quadrant are known for having cultures that embrace risk taking and people who generally prefer leaders with limited power. Good conflict management and negotiation skills may be important for accomplishing things here given that hierarchies tend to be relatively flat with fewer formal controls over employees.[10]

Long-Term versus Short-Term Orientation

After developing his original framework, Hofstede later added a fifth cultural dimension: long-term versus short-term orientation. Evolving out of his work on Asian societies, this dimension distinguishes cultures with a forward-looking view on life (long-term) from those more concerned with the past and present (short-term). People in long-term oriented cultures tend to feel that future-focused values such as hard work, persistence, and adaptability are most important. Long-term orientation characterizes a number of Asian societies—which may have provided part of the foundation for the economic success achieved by countries such as China and South Korea in recent decades. In contrast, people in short-term oriented cultures tend to feel that values emphasizing the past and present, such as respect for tradition, stability, and fulfilling social obligations, are most important (e.g., Pakistan, the Philippines). While Asian nations tend to have the strongest long-term orientation, this value can also be found in a variety of Eastern and Western countries. See Figure 2.4 for a visual representation. The connection between long-term versus short-term orientation and Hofstede's original cultural dimensions is complex. Some evidence suggests that richer nations that tend to have a long-term orientation also tend to be low on individualism and have large power distance (e.g., South Korea).[11]

Limitations of Hofstede's Framework

Despite all of its obvious pluses, Hofstede's framework does have some drawbacks. An obvious limitation is that Hofstede's framework is missing a variety of countries,

More long-term oriented

China
Hong Kong
Taiwan
Japan
South Korea
Brazil
India
Thailand
Singapore
Netherlands
Bangladesh
Sweden
Poland
Germany
Australia
New Zealand
United States
Great Britain
Zimbabwe
Canada
Philippines
Nigeria
Pakistan

More short-term oriented

FIGURE 2.4 Long-Term or Short-Term Orientation for Selected Nations

Source: Adapted from Hofstede, G. (2001). *Culture's Consequences* (2nd ed.). Thousand Oaks, CA: Sage, 356.

CULTURE CLASH

Japanese Management Practices Rub Chinese Employees the Wrong Way

Japanese firms were first in line when China began opening its doors to foreign multi-nationals over three decades ago. But China is not the same place it was then—today, the country is much better off and has shifted from being an export platform for manufactured goods to a more consumer-driven market. Workers are becoming more demanding about pay and working conditions. Workplace unrest, including strikes, has buffeted a variety of multinationals in China, including Japanese firms such as Honda, Mitsumi Electric, and Toyota. This increased employee activism is working, as annual wages have been rising for Chinese workers at a double-digit clip in recent years.

Managing Chinese employees can be thorny for foreign multinationals. Compound-ing the problem for Japanese multinationals are management practices that are not well aligned to the Chinese context—a particularly vexing issue since Japanese firms commonly expect their expatriates to adhere to homeland management practices when sent abroad. For instance, Japanese management values are rooted in a collective society and include patience, harmony, efficiency, and hierarchy. Many Japanese managers expect employees to be compliant company loyalists, willing to make personal sacrifices for the good of the firm. Indeed, the vaunted production efficiency of the Japanese is based on both just-in-time systems and employees willing to do whatever it takes to make things work, often for relatively little in the way of extra pay or perks.

While this has worked well in Japan, China is another story. When problems pop up in China, getting them resolved quickly before they blow up into something serious enough to slow or shut down operations is a huge challenge. That is because Japanese expatriates managing in China typically have little power and authority. Given Japanese respect for hierarchy, expatriate managers usually must solicit orders from headquarters back in Japan. This might be fine if they receive speedy answers, but they often do not thanks to the slow process of consensual decision making for which Japanese firms are famous. Indeed, many of the problems that Japanese firms have in China are due to slow response time from Japanese executives back home.

But Japanese firms are learning and making adjustments, which bodes well for the future. Besides giving their Chinese employees better pay and benefits (e.g., Honda hiked pay nearly 25% for its Chinese workers in 2010), some Japanese firms are also looking to relocate work to friendlier cultural contexts. Yet relocating may not be the best solution for Japanese companies that want to sell higher-end products in China. Instead, adjustments to these management practices, some very innovative, have been made by Japanese firms in China. For example, heavy equipment maker Komatsu decided that the best way to adapt to China's cultural and workplace environment was to stop relying on Japanese expatriates to manage there. By the end of 2012, Komatsu planned to have all 16 of its Chinese subsidiaries run by local Chinese managers more familiar with the local culture. Clearly, the stakes for doing a better job of managing Chinese employees has never been higher given that China is now Japan's top partner when it comes to trade. Consequently, look for Japanese firms to continue to up the ante when it comes to making an effort to adapt to Chinese values, culture, and workplace preferences.[15]

including ones from Eastern European nations, and some emerging Asian markets such as Vietnam. Naturally this reflects, at least in part, the fact that the world has changed since Hofstede collected his original data more than 30 years ago. Fortunately, Hofstede's latest work does include cultural value estimates for new emerging market powerhouses such as China and Russia. Hofstede characterizes China as a long-term-oriented nation that scores relatively low on individualism while moderate on uncertainty avoidance and masculinity. In contrast, he views Russia as a short-term-oriented nation with large power distance, strong uncertainty avoidance, moderate individualism, and low masculinity. Still, some areas of the world remain underrepresented even in Hofstede's latest work.[12]

Hofstede's framework also ignores differences that exist between countries within a specific cluster or quadrant. For instance, despite having similar scores, important cultural differences may separate Americans and Australians. One study found that Americans were more interested in intrinsic rewards like responsibility and recognition, while Australians were more interested in having job security and a good income. Similarly, Hofstede's framework does not account for differences that may exist within nations. For example, studies have found that strong regional subcultures in Brazil differ in important values linked to motivation, which, in turn, can significantly impact business performance. Hofstede's framework has a hard time explaining both cases.[13]

Limitations aside, Hofstede's framework remains enormously influential in international management as a guide for understanding the impact of culture. Recent studies have underscored the value and applicability of the cultural dimensions. For example, business leaders tend to establish strategic priorities in ways that reflect their national cultures. And failing to understand how your own cultural values may impact effectiveness outside your home environment can prove costly. Take a look at the following *Culture Clash* box to see what we mean.[14]

Trompenaars's Cultural Dimensions

Following in Hofstede's footsteps, Fons Trompenaars's more recent framework makes some similar distinctions (e.g., on individualism). On other cultural dimensions, however, Trompenaars presents an alternative perspective, due in part to his newer data and use of different methods. His ambitious effort included collecting data from over 15,000 managers in 28 nations across a decade-long period. After sifting through these data, Trompenaars identified several bipolar cultural dimensions that constitute the heart of his framework—many of which focus on relationships, as you will see.[16]

Outer- versus Inner-Directed Views of the Environment

People who are outer-directed tend to believe that what happens in life is not something that they can directly control. Consequently, they tend to accommodate themselves to their station in life. They also seek stability and harmonious relationships in the workplace. On the other hand, people who are inner-directed tend to feel that they are in control of their own fate and, as a result, are more willing to embrace change and to pursue personal goals. Trompenaars's results suggested, for instance, that Americans are more likely to be inner-directed, while Chinese are more likely to be outer-directed. Likewise, one study comparing American and

Arab managers showed that Americans tended to endorse inner-directed values while their Arab counterparts were more likely to endorse outer-directed values. The dominance of outer-directed values in many Arab countries typically means that business practices place more emphasis on relationships than they do in Western countries. Arab business culture emphasizes high-contact experiences with business partners; they often seek to know their potential partner well before engaging in negotiation. Inner-directed cultures may view this great emphasis on personalizing business contacts, such as negotiation, as a digressive.[17]

Universalism versus Particularism

This dimension relates to rules and whether relationships or situations should impact their application. People who embrace universalism tend to feel that everyone should follow the same set of rules and practices, while people who subscribe to particularism believe that rules should be adapted or adjusted depending on the situation or person. For instance, in many countries, rules and procedures are bent to maintain, if not strengthen, good relationships with family and friends (particularism). Managers who embrace particularism are more likely to consider workers' job demands and family issues when appraising performance and doling out raises than are managers who embrace universalism. Examples of countries with cultures that tend toward particularism include China, Indonesia, and Venezuela. In the United States, however, the universalism perspective tends to be stronger, with relationships and contexts subordinate to procedures governing things like performance evaluations. Simply put, in U.S. firms, you would be more likely to see the same procedures, standards, and forms applied regardless of the situation or who is being evaluated.

Neutral versus Emotional

Stoicism and suppression of emotional displays are the tendencies on the neutral side of this dimension. For instance, Japanese are known for the value they tend to place on emotional composure and reserve. A famous Japanese saying is, "The first person to raise [his or her] voice loses the argument." On the other end of the spectrum are cultures that value emotional expression—Mexico is an example of a country where expressing feelings is common and accepted. Needless to say, mixing employees with these divergent perspectives can produce some management challenges. A safe rule of thumb if you find yourself in such a situation is to adjust to the local context by either being more reserved when the local culture is neutral or being more animated when the local culture is emotional.

Specific versus Diffuse

Compartmentalization is typically the order of the day in the United States and other specific cultures. In other words, work and family roles tend to be treated separately. For example, how formally people carry themselves, the titles they use, and the behavior they display will depend on the role they are in at the time (i.e., boss versus family member or friend). Moreover, in specific cultures, relationships are often constrained to particular roles—which limits their impact. The classic workplace example here would be the all-too-common situation in the United States, where employees are quite friendly with each other at work but never see each other or socialize outside the workplace. Contrast that scenario with the environment in a diffuse culture like China, where distinctions between roles are ambiguous and boundaries fuzzy. Your job title may significantly impact how you are perceived and treated across a variety of life contexts. This may help explain why it takes so much time to build trust and relationships in China—people in diffuse cultures may be cautious at first when interacting with new people since giving others access to one sphere of life can mean access to all.

Achievement versus Ascription. The United States is a good example of an achievement culture, where an individual's status is a function of how he or she has performed (e.g., securing a big promotion) or what goals have been reached (e.g., getting an MBA from a top school). Put simply, tremendous clout is earned by being excellent in your chosen endeavors. On the other side of the ledger are ascription cultures, in which an individual's status has less to do with performance and more to do with things such as social class, connections, age, or gender. Family connections, for example, tend to play a much bigger role in ascription cultures (e.g., Indonesia, China) than they do in achievement cultures.

Individualism versus Communitarianism. This dimension seems identical to Hofstede's view of individualism (you see yourself as an individual first) and collectivism (communitarianism means that you see yourself as part of a group first). But there are real differences between the two frameworks. For example, Argentina and Mexico are relatively collectivistic according to Hofstede, while Trompenaars classifies them as individualistic. As we alluded to earlier, such contrasts may reflect methodological differences in the way Hofstede and Trompenaars conducted their original research (e.g., how each defined terms, measured survey items, etc.). Plus, since Trompenaars's data are newer, his results may have uncovered cultural values that have been shifting in recent years. Indeed, cultures are always changing and evolving, sometimes slowly and sometimes at a faster clip. Trompenaars's work may underscore that argument—as does the cultural framework that evolved from the even more recent GLOBE study.[18]

The GLOBE Cultural Framework

The most comprehensive and far-reaching efforts to identify cultural dimensions and use them to classify countries is the Global Leadership and Organizational Behavior Effectiveness (GLOBE) project. GLOBE's reach is impressive, starting with its team of 200-plus researchers hailing from more than 60 countries. Thanks to their cooperative efforts, this team collected survey data from 20,000 middle managers working in almost 1,000 firms that were operating in a variety of industries. Countries from every region of the world were included. Designed, in part, to replicate, if not extend, Hofstede's earlier work, GLOBE also assessed cross-cultural perspectives on leadership (examined later in Chapter 6). For instance, compared to Hofstede, GLOBE cast a wider geographic net and included many companies and industries (versus Hofstede's exclusive focus on IBM).[19]

The main tool used by GLOBE was a survey designed to assess nine different cultural dimensions. These dimensions were developed from the GLOBE team's assessment of existing frameworks, particularly Hofstede's, as well as from interviews and focus groups conducted in a variety of countries. Table 2.2 describes the nine GLOBE cultural dimensions and presents examples of nations that rank high and low on these dimensions. Six of the nine GLOBE dimensions appear to overlap with dimensions in Hofstede's framework.

The GLOBE team has argued that its study is a major step forward and that some of its dimensions that parallel Hofstede's are actually improvements, given more refined definitions and improved measurements. Moreover, the team also contends that its new dimensions represent a significant advance. The first three dimensions listed in Table 2.2 parallel those that we have discussed while presenting Hofstede's framework. The fourth dimension in Table 2.2, however, focuses on a specific type of collectivism that emphasizes loyalty and closeness to in-groups such as family or coworkers as opposed to societal collectivism (GLOBE dimension number 3). Indeed, in-group ties are common and fundamental for understanding how business operates and deals get done in a variety of nations (e.g., the Philippines). South Korea is particularly well known for its *chaebol*, huge and powerful multinational conglomerates that are partially controlled by extended family dynasties (Samsung and Hyundai among them).[20]

The next two dimensions listed in Table 2.2 (gender egalitarianism and future orientation) also have roots in Hofstede's work. But the final three dimensions in Table 2.2 are new GLOBE additions that can be helpful to international managers. For instance, performance orientation may be especially helpful for grasping motivation issues across cultures. This dimension reflects the extent to which good performance and striving for improvement are valued in a culture (somewhat paralleling Trompenaars' achievement-versus-ascription dimension and partially overlapping with Hofstede's masculinity–femininity dimension). Interestingly, of the 62 countries assessed by GLOBE, Hong Kong, Singapore, and Switzerland scored the highest on performance orientation; the United States fell in the middle of the pack; and Greece, Russia, and Venezuela scored the lowest. Of course, this does not mean that low-scoring nations such as Russia cannot improve economically or even become outstanding successes in the global marketplace. Rather, it simply means that these countries are characterized by cultures in which a person's background, connections, and family ties may be seen as more important than performance-related factors.

Table 2.2
GLOBE Cultural Dimensions

Dimension and Definition	Countries Ranked High	Countries Ranked Low
1. Uncertainty avoidance (Hofstede)	Switzerland, Sweden, Singapore	Guatemala, Hungary, Russia
2. Power distance (Hofstede)	Morocco, Nigeria, El Salvador	Denmark, Netherlands, Israel
3. Collectivism I, societal (Hofstede)	Sweden, South Korea, Japan	Argentina, Germany, Hungary
4. Collectivism II, in-group—the degree to which people are loyal and close to families or organizations	Philippines, Iran, India	New Zealand, Sweden, Denmark
5. Gender egalitarianism—does society minimize gender role difference and promote gender equality? (Hofstede's masculinity—femininity dimension)	Russia, Poland, Denmark	Egypt, Kuwait, South Korea
6. Future orientation (Hofstede's long-term orientation)	Singapore, Switzerland, Netherlands	Poland, Argentina, Russia
7. Assertiveness—are people generally assertive in their relations with others?	Albania, Germany, Hong Kong	Switzerland, New Zealand, Sweden
8. Performance orientation—degree to which society encourages and provides rewards for performance and excellence	Switzerland, Singapore, Hong Kong	Russia, Venezuela, Greece
9. Humane orientation—does society encourage and reward for being fair, altruistic, generous, caring, and kind to others?	Philippines, Ireland, Thailand	Germany, Singapore, Greece

Source: Adapted from House, R. J., et al. (2004). *Culture, Leadership, and Organizations: The GLOBE Study of 62 Societies*. Thousand Oaks, CA: Sage.

Note: U.S. ranking: 1 (middle), 2 (low), 3 (middle), 4 (low), 5 (middle), 6 (high), 7 (middle), 8 (high), 9 (middle).

The last dimension in Table 2.2, humane orientation, reflects the extent to which a culture encourages and rewards people who are kind, fair, and considerate to others. Ireland, the Philippines, and Thailand are all examples of countries that score very high on humane orientation. In such nations, people tend to focus more on the powerless and underprivileged. Consequently, it is important to be friendly toward, and tolerant of, others who are less fortunate, including in the workplace. In contrast, people in low-scoring nations, such as Germany and Singapore, are more likely to be concerned about improving themselves and the pursuit of power, influence, and material possessions.[21]

Looking Ahead: The Future of the GLOBE–Hofstede Debate

While the GLOBE effort is clearly comprehensive and impressive in many ways, it has not escaped criticism. One concern is that, while GLOBE was designed to replicate, if not extend, Hofstede's earlier work, it nonetheless defined and measured key concepts quite differently. Consequently, some have suggested that GLOBE's findings cannot be directly compared with Hofstede's or that it is not completely clear what GLOBE was actually measuring (e.g., did it really measure cultural values or merely differences in circumstances between groups of people in various countries?). On the other hand, GLOBE participants have argued that their changes were designed to respond to, and improve on, shortcomings in Hofstede's work. In essence, they claim that their results offer a more nuanced and sophisticated perspective on the complexities of culture.[22]

Another line of criticism has to do with Hofstede's 30-year track record of successful applications (e.g., in cross-cultural training programs) and external validation for key concepts. Critics have pointed out that GLOBE has enjoyed much less success in the marketplace for its ideas and does not offer a meaningful advance over what we have already learned from Hofstede. Of course, GLOBE cannot match Hofstede in the sense that it simply has not been around as long. Nevertheless, it is important to assess the impact of the GLOBE effort over time, particularly

---

GLOBAL INNOVATIONS

More than Face Value: Facebook Takes the Plunge in Russia and Indonesia

With over 500 million members, Facebook is a social networking giant. But it's not really a global brand—at least not yet. Indeed, despite the popularity of the Internet in China and Brazil, Facebook has a low profile in both countries. Still, underestimating Facebook would be a mistake. The company has made some impressive strides in two nations—Russia and Indonesia—that might not strike people as great markets to leap into. Yet Facebook has done exactly that, armed with an understanding of the culture of both countries and how that culture impacts a customer's willingness to use the firm's services.

In Russia, local networking sites are quite popular—an important signal to Facebook. Indeed, Facebook launched its Russian site in 2010 and saw its user base jump nearly 400% in the first eight months. One of the factors that attracted Facebook to Russia is the fact that Russians average almost 10 hours monthly on social networking sites, more than twice the global average. Many parts of Russia are isolated and frigid for much of the year, making online interaction an attractive option.

But a bigger reason for the pull of social networking is the Russian cultural tradition of using informal networks as sources of information. Given Russia's long history of closed institutions and opaque systems that cannot be trusted or relied upon, informal networks can be a powerful substitute for information source. Plus, with historically limited press and civil freedoms, Russians often feel isolated. And unlike in China, Russian authorities allow pretty much anything to happen online. Moreover, Facebook gives its Russian customers a measure of control, allowing them to create and then vote on Russian names for various website features. Finally, Russia is a very relationship-oriented society, one where connections are key for everything from securing good jobs to addressing problems with local officials. This also bolsters the attractiveness of social networking online.

Turning to Indonesia, many citizens of the world's largest Muslim country love to chat and share—and increasingly, they want to do it online. Thanks to skyrocketing growth, Indonesia has already become Facebook's number-two market in the world, despite the fact that less than 20% of Indonesians have access to the Internet. Interestingly, Facebook recognized that certain elements of Indonesia's culture make people there especially open to using social networking. First, friendships are very important in Indonesian society. Combined with a tendency to embrace trends, a desire for publicity, and relatively little concern about privacy, Indonesians are ideal customers for Facebook.

That said, Indonesia does have some peculiarities as a market for social networking. Few Indonesians have bank accounts or credit cards, so the advertising model that Facebook uses to make money in the United States (i.e., where people routinely buy something after being enticed to click on ads displayed on the screen) does not apply to nearly the same degree. Instead, Facebook is trying to construct partnerships with other firms in ways that will allow Indonesian customers to barter for goods or use online "currency"—while still making money somehow on these transactions. In any case, another unusual aspect of Indonesians' social networking behavior is their tendency to use avatars, often with completely different physical characteristics, instead of their own photos to represent themselves on Facebook. Indonesians who interact online about their real lives while using idealized avatars as self-images underscore why Facebook cannot take foreign markets at face value. Instead, Facebook and other companies need to better understand how culture impacts social networking complexities in different markets.[25]

as the differences between GLOBE and Hofstede are sorted out by researchers. This process is critical since, as one expert put it, "heavy emphasis is often placed on the managerial implications flowing from cross-cultural research generally."[23]

The sense is that, while it may never match Hofstede's impact, GLOBE will continue to play a role in shaping how international managers view culture for the foreseeable future. And that is what matters for our purposes here. All approaches to culture we have described can be used by managers to triangulate on the often thorny cultural issues they face. Efforts to classify countries by cultural values offer an important starting point and enhance managers' sensitivity about how their behavior may need to change if they want to be effective across cultural boundaries.

MANIFESTATIONS OF CULTURE IN THE WORKPLACE

To this point, we have said relatively little about specific ways in which cultural differences can impact international managers, much less how they should respond. Granted, we have already noted that culture plays a role in virtually everything associated with business, often in surprising ways. For instance, in addition to influencing corporate strategies and human resources practices, culture can impact entrepreneurship rates across countries as well as whether knowledge transfer is inhibited or enhanced in international acquisitions. We will examine some of these issues in subsequent chapters, including how a keen understanding of culture can help some of the world's leading companies decide which foreign markets to enter in the first place. For a snapshot of how one company is doing just that, please see the *Global Innovations* box, which addresses how cultural factors helped Facebook decide to take the plunge in Russia and Indonesia. In the meantime, the rest of this section will stay focused on individual employees, exploring how culture can shape work-related perceptions as well as important work attitudes.[24]

How Culture Shapes Work-Related Perceptions and Attitudes

Culture can shape how we perceive the world and those around us in a variety of ways. We will consider three sets of examples of the impact of culture on perception—about people, about events, and about time. All three can have important implications for managers and employees in the workplace.

People

In one study, Chinese and Australians were asked to read detailed descriptions of fictitious people that included attributes related to conscientiousness, sensitivity, and so on. Next, respondents were asked about how they expected these people to behave. The idea was to uncover whether the Chinese and Australians in the study would focus on different bits of information in forming their perceptions.[26]

The two groups of respondents were selected because of their cultural differences. Australians are more individualistic, and the Chinese more collectivistic. As predicted, the Chinese focused more on characteristics involving consideration of others, while the Australians emphasized outgoingness (a person-centered attribute) when developing their perceptions of others. Both groups used information selectively when forming perceptions, focusing on attributes most consistent with their cultural tendencies. Of course, this has implications in the workplace since our perceptions also shape how we communicate, negotiate, and do business with others.[27]

Other studies have found similar results. For instance, one study examined the impact of power distance on perceptions, comparing Americans, who tend to be less deferential to people with power and status, to Chinese, who tend to value power and status more highly. Participants read a story describing a meeting in which a manager insulted an employee in front of others. In one version of the story, the manager had low status, and in the other version, the manager had high status. When asked about their perception, Americans tended to view the manager in negative terms regardless of whether they had read the high- or low-status version of the story. In contrast, the Chinese reading the high-status version of the story tended to be less critical of the manager than if they had read the low-status version. Once again, these results suggest that the cultural importance of power distance can shape perceptions, this time of managers. In turn, this has implications for how leadership styles may need to be adapted depending on the cultural context.[28]

Events

Culture also shapes perceptions of events. For instance, in another study comparing more individualistic Australians with their more collectivistic Chinese counterparts, both groups were asked to rate a list of common events (such as eating lunch and socializing with friends) on a variety of dimensions (e.g., from boring to interesting). As expected, the Chinese participants tended to pay more attention to events involving other people and felt that they were more important than events not involving others. Interestingly, the Australians tended to see events involving others as more interesting than their Chinese counterparts. While group events may have simply been seen as more fun by the Australians, for the Chinese, they may have produced a greater sense of social obligation.[29]

Perceptions of People and Events: More Implications

It is important to mention that culture operates like an automatic filtering and organizing process when shaping people's perceptions. We tend to use cultural filters to quickly form perceptions of our coworkers and business partners without really understanding how those filters work. As a result, most of us have a hard time stepping back to understand and appreciate the cultural filters that other people are using. Needless to say, this can create problems.

For instance, Westerners tend to use abstract, universal principles when forming perceptions, while many East Asians tend to rely on more nuanced principles that are specific to the context of the meeting. Imagine how this might play out in a performance appraisal situation, where managers have to both perceive the situation accurately and decide what to do. In one study, managers were asked about how they would treat a subordinate who had been an above-average performer for more than a decade, but whose performance had slipped considerably to below average in the past year. Nearly 80% of the American and Canadian participants in the study said they would terminate the employee, compared to just 20% of the participants from Singapore and Korea. In short, contextual circumstances were more likely to be taken into account by East Asians when judging subordinate performance. In contrast, the Westerners were more analytical, emphasizing formal procedures that were detached from the broader circumstances. That said, these tendencies are hardly immutable. Like anything else, over time the impact of culture can become more salient as well as morph and shift depending on a person's experiences. For example, studies show that Asians who live in the West and Westerners who spend extended time in Asia often learn to recognize how local values shape perceptions—leading to enhanced understanding and a greater capability to adapt.[30]

Time

To underscore the pervasive influence of culture on perceptions, consider something as seemingly objective as time. Most of us carry timepieces of one sort or another, and we have to set schedules, arrange for meeting times, and so on, all using the same seconds-minutes-hours system of measurement. Nevertheless, there are significant differences across cultures in how time is perceived. For instance, time is seen as a commodity (e.g., "time is money") in many Western cultures. But in Eastern cultures, time is often perceived as something more fluid and flexible. This distinction has sometimes been referred to as "event time" versus "clock time." Event time is more characteristic of many Asian and Middle Eastern cultures, where scheduling revolves around people and events rather than specific times. For example, instead of scheduling meals to take place at a particular hour, they can occur whenever the food is ready. Likewise, appointments may be set loosely, around events rather than specific dates and times.[31] In contrast, clock time tends to be emphasized in Western cultures. Events are scheduled closely and strictly by the clock.

Researcher Robert Levine has systematically studied the connection between culture and time, and his results are shown in Table 2.3. Levine's interest was piqued when he taught in Brazil. He noticed that the times displayed on clocks and watches around his campus in Brazil seemed to vary considerably. And many of his students didn't show up on time for his classes, with many arriving 30 minutes late—or more—without showing any signs of fuss or distress. This was in direct contrast to Levine's experience teaching in the United States, where students are expected to be on time (at the same time) for the start of class. Moreover, when class was over, many of Levine's Brazilian students stayed to interact and ask questions (often for more than 30 minutes)—very unlike their American counterparts, who tended to bolt the minute class ended and became fidgety if class did not end on time.[32] In a subsequent study, Levine found that Americans carefully monitored time and defined "late" in more strict ways than did Brazilians. About 20 minutes was considered late on average by Americans, but for Brazilians it was over 30 minutes. Interestingly, perceptions also varied as to what was an acceptable reason for being late. Compared to Americans, Brazilians were more forgiving and more likely to attribute blame to unexpected circumstances rather the late person's insensitivity. Moreover, to many Brazilians, chronic tardiness was a sign of success—late people are late because they have more business partners and more friends to chat with. Americans, however, tended to feel that punctuality was important.

In a more elaborate study, Levine relied on several objective measures of time to assess the impact of culture across several countries. He measured bank clock accuracy across banks in different countries by comparing their displayed times against true local times. Banks were selected because they tend to be formal institutions that closely monitor time and that are connected to a variety of business activities, including across countries (e.g., currency exchange, letters of credit, etc.). Consequently, if national differences can be found in this important and tightly controlled area, many other perceptual differences about time are likely to exist in other areas. Japanese and U.S. bank clocks were tops in accuracy, while Indonesian banks were the farthest off, more than three minutes slow on average.[33]

Table 2.3 also displays Levine's results for walking and post office speed. In a variety of large cities in each country, Levine measured how long it took people walking alone to cover a 100-foot distance on a downtown street. The Japanese were the quickest, taking just about 20 seconds to walk 100 feet, with Americans and British close behind at about 22 seconds or so. At the other end of the spectrum, Indonesians were the slowest, taking roughly 30% longer to cover the same 100 feet (approximately 27 seconds on average) than the Japanese. Postal clerk speed was also assessed in each country by making a uniform request (giving clerks a note in their native language that asked for a stamp for a regular letter and paying with the equivalent of a five-dollar bill). Once more, service speed varied considerably, ranging from Japan's speedy 25-second average to Italy's 45 seconds.

Collectively, these results using objective time measures reveal the influence of culture on something as fundamental and indisputable as time. So it should come as no surprise that other seemingly objective issues (e.g., measuring profitability

Table 2.3
Eye of the Beholder: Time across Countries

Country	Bank Clock Accuracy	Walking Speed	Post Office Speed
Japan	1	1	1
United States	2	3	2
United Kingdom	4	2	3
Italy	5	4	6
Taiwan	3	5	4
Indonesia	6	6	5

Source: Adapted from Levine, R. V., & Bartlett, K. (1984). Pace of life, punctuality, and coronary heart disease in six countries. *Journal of Cross-Cultural Psychology, 15,* 233-255.

Note: Numbers refer to the ranking of each country on a time measure (1 = top ranking).

and setting business strategies) are also influenced by culture in subtle ways. And therein lies the potential for conflict, management trouble, and lost opportunities. Fortunately, at least when it comes to time, we can mitigate some of this and promote understanding by classifying countries by their orientation toward time.[34]

Classifying Countries by Time Orientation

Researchers have distinguished between *monochronic* and *polychromic* orientations toward time. These orientations center on whether people in a culture tend to focus on doing one thing at a time or tend to juggle a variety of tasks at once. While there is plenty of room for variation on time orientation within countries, we will focus here on differences across countries.[35]

In cultures with a monochronic orientation, schedules tend to be exact and time is seen as a commodity to be measured precisely—with plenty of economic terminology used in the process (e.g., time must be "saved," "spent," or "not wasted"). The monochronic perspective characterizes the United States and some European nations. That said, if you have traveled across Europe by train, you know that major differences exist about how precise train schedules are across countries. Arrive a minute or two late for a German train and it is likely to have already left the station. In Spain or Italy, you might still be able to catch your train several minutes past its scheduled departure.

Cultures that are polychronic, however, embrace a more fluid perspective on time that can be very hard to grasp for Americans, Canadians, and others coming from a monochronic perspective. For instance, in many South American countries (often polychronic), people are inclined to finish conversations when they run into friends or colleagues rather than abruptly cut off the interaction just to be on time for an appointment. Put simply, the polychronic orientation does not rely on an economic perspective on time.

Indeed, what would be considered interruptions (i.e., the unscheduled derailing of some activity) in a monochronic culture tend to be taken more in stride in a polychronic environment, where time is seen as ebbing and flowing in response to events or the juggling of multiple activities. Put another way, people with a polychronic perspective view unscheduled and irregular events or changes as more consistent with how life actually happens. But mix the two orientations in a business context and problems can erupt.

For instance, a monochronic Canadian manager with an appointment at a Brazilian bank may start seething if, 10 to 15 minutes past the scheduled start time, she continues to sit while the polychronic banker she is waiting on finishes conversations with several other people. After all, when time is a commodity, to keep people waiting is perceived as rude and should prompt an apology. But the Brazilian banker may hardly want to apologize—if anything, he may think the miffed Canadian is demanding and self-absorbed. The bottom line, of course, is that these two managers are not likely to start off well in their relationship, with obvious negative implications for their business dealings, all because neither understands the other's orientation toward time. Table 2.4 lists common tendencies of people with monochronic and polychronic orientations toward time, many of which have been connected to national cultures.[36]

Table 2.4
Differences between Monochronic and Polychronic Time Orientations

Monochronic Time	Polychronic Time
Does one thing at a time	Does many things at once
Task oriented	People oriented
Comfortable with short-term relations	Needs longer-term relations
Sticks to plans	Often changes plans
More internally focused	More externally focused

Culture and Key Work Attitudes

While work is clearly an enormously important activity for people worldwide, culture shapes how they feel about and react to their jobs. In this section we turn our attention to how culture can impact key work attitudes such as job satisfaction and organizational commitment.

Job Satisfaction

Despite occasional press reports to the contrary, large-scale studies show that Americans tend to be quite satisfied with their jobs compared to people in other countries. One such study found that Japanese employees were much less satisfied with their jobs than their American counterparts—even after controlling for the American tendency to be overly positive and the Japanese tendency to be less expressive or more modest. Perhaps most striking was that about 70% of the Americans in the study indicated that they would take their current job again compared to less than 25% of the Japanese.[37]

Other research comparing Americans and Japanese finds similar results, using a variety of different methodologies. One study comparing managers from several countries found that the Japanese were the least satisfied with their jobs. Yet in looking at Japanese reactions to specific aspects of their jobs (e.g., working conditions, pay), their responses varied—on some aspects, they were among the most satisfied. This seems to suggest that any purported Japanese tendency to be modest does not systematically reduce all evaluations of their jobs. Indeed, another study found considerable variation among Japanese workers, with older and more senior employees expressing greater job satisfaction, among other factors. Older Japanese employees are the people most likely to display traditional modesty, yet they are among the most satisfied with their jobs.[38]

While many studies have focused on differences between Japanese and Americans in terms of job satisfaction, researchers have expanded their methodological and cultural reach in recent years. A recent study examined some 130,000 employees working in 39 nations for a large multinational and found that job level (blue collar versus white collar) was positively connected to job satisfaction in individualistic cultures like the United States but not in collective cultures. This was especially true when jobs gave employees a real opportunity to use their skills. Likewise, some studies have recently focused on assessing employee engagement across cultures. Related to job satisfaction, employee engagement includes confidence in company leaders and their concern for employees as well as the extent to which jobs are found challenging and offer growth opportunities. One study found that workers in India and Brazil had the highest levels of employee engagement anywhere in the world, with the United States placing third. China, by way of comparison, placed twelfth in the study, and Japanese workers scored quite low in the rankings. Only about one in three of the Japanese who participated in the survey were engaged to any degree—possibly a reflection of the difficult economic environment that has plagued Japan for some time.[39]

In general, culture seems to impact job satisfaction and related work attitudes in a variety of ways. Overall, employees in Western cultures tend to have higher job satisfaction than employees in Eastern cultures. While extrinsic factors such as pay predict job satisfaction across cultures, intrinsic factors such as responsibility and growth opportunities tend to be more important in richer countries characterized by high individualism and low power distance.[40]

Organizational Commitment

Another key work attitude is organizational commitment. Less well studied than job satisfaction, we still know quite a bit about this work attitude, including how it plays out across cultures. For instance, in one study, workers from the United States, Japan, and Korea were asked to complete a scale measuring organizational commitment (e.g., "I am willing to work harder than I have to help this company," and "I would turn down another job for more pay in order to stay with this company"). On balance, American workers displayed higher organizational commitment than either Japanese or Korean employees. This seems to contradict the commonly held view that Asian employees, particularly from Japan, are more committed to their firms than supposedly self-interested Americans.[41]

Part of this apparent contradiction may involve the difference between organizational commitment and work commitment—something that researchers are careful to distinguish. Work commitment is not about loyalty to the firm or a willingness to help the company succeed. Instead, it reflects how important work itself is in people's lives. So in terms of organizational commitment, American workers tend to be as committed as, if not more so than, their Korean or Japanese counterparts. But when it comes to work commitment, the Japanese come out on top.[42]

That said, we also want to point out that factors other than culture can, and do, influence work commitment. Some research suggests, for instance, that occupation level plays a bigger role in shaping work commitment than national culture. Indeed, across 20 countries, work commitment was very similar when broken down by occupation level. So, as workers rise through the ranks in companies—regardless of their country and culture—work commitment also seems to rise. Another complicating factor in all research on commitment (and job satisfaction for that matter), is that measurement methods vary. And measures may be perceived differently across cultures, making it challenging to know whether culture or measurement differences are driving the results.[43]

Culture and Perspectives on Leadership

How leaders are viewed is shaped by cultural factors, which include shared experiences and history. In the United States, leadership is commonly seen in terms of motivating others to achieve firm goals; it is the process of successfully influencing people. Executive leaders are typically seen as important for achieving great things in companies and for changing things when circumstances require it. But in Germany, engineers, not executives, tend to be held in high regard. Given their shared traditions of craftsmanship and apprenticeships, which date back to the Middle Ages, many Germans view management's purpose as solving technical challenges and distributing work rather than motivating people.

Studies reinforce the notion that culture influences how leadership is viewed. For instance, in one investigation, less than 20% of the U.S., Dutch, and Swedish managers surveyed felt that it was critical to have precise answers ready when subordinates asked them questions. Instead, managers in these nations believed that their role was to help employees solve their own problems and to find their own answers. In stark contrast, having precise answers at the ready was important to many German (46%), French (53%), and Italian (66%) managers. This orientation of having answers for subordinates was even more strongly endorsed by Indonesian (73%) and Japanese (78%) managers. In many cultures, an important part of the leader's role is to project authority and expertise, something that gives subordinates a feeling of comfort and stability.

The source of leaders also varies across nations thanks to cultural influences. As a classless society, merit basically determines who achieves leadership positions in Japan. Up-and-coming leaders must do well in selective schools that channel students into particular roles. So anyone who succeeds in this environment, regardless of his or her background, can advance into leadership roles. But in other nations, business executives tend to emerge from powerful families or specific classes or strata in society. For instance, in some Arab countries, strong leaders typically come from successful tribal families with long histories of wielding power and influence.

Naturally, followers typically have beliefs about the attributes that successful business leaders should have. In the United States, leaders who are intelligent, self-confident, and decisive are often viewed positively by their subordinates—these are all attributes that are held in high regard within cultures valuing individual performance. Still, it would be wise to expect that the criteria for effective leadership will shift, at least somewhat, when cultural boundaries are crossed. But attitudes can change, and there is evidence that some universals have emerged, or are emerging, regarding what it takes to be an effective leader—regardless of the context.

For instance, one study asked senior managers from eight countries to pick the five most important leadership attributes. Some attributes, such as the ability to articulate a vision, appeared on the lists of managers from most countries. This implies that senior managers, regardless of where they are from, share certain challenges, particularly in large multinationals. But there were no identical lists of attributes across countries. Indeed, for specific pairs of countries, there was virtually no overlap on the top five attributes. Culture probably explains this, at least to an extent. For example, the focus on harmonious group work in Japan may help explain why only Japanese executives listed "empowering others" among the top three leadership attributes. Along the same lines, the tendency of American and British managers to rank "getting results" highly is consistent with the value placed on individual performance in Anglo cultures.

Combating Stereotypes and Making Better Sense of Culture

Needless to say, our discussion to this point underscores both the pervasive impact and the complexities associated with culture. We have tried to make sense of all this by presenting a variety of culture frameworks and discussing some of the influence that culture can have on employee perceptions and attitudes. Nevertheless, it is important to remember that any discussion of culture involves generalizations, and therein is the slippery slope to trouble. After all, even if our views about culture are useful, as "sophisticated stereotypes" they may already be outdated and lag behind reality. While stable in the short run, cultures are constantly evolving and changing.[44]

Indeed, the stereotypes that some managers harbor about certain parts of the world can create huge problems if they are not contained or sidestepped. One CEO who wanted to build a plant in Mexico was surrounded by advisors who urged him not to. They argued that any money saved by having production in Mexico would be consumed by the "siesta culture" of the local workforce. The CEO brushed off this corrosive stereotype and made the right decision—the plant was built and yielded more than $1 billion in revenues in less than five years. That said, cultural stereotypes are often much more subtle, with managers carrying views that people in certain countries are good in some things or bad in others, regardless of the reality.[45]

To be truly effective around the world, international managers must effectively grasp how culture shapes the attitudes and behaviors of their employees. This begs the question, however, of how managers and the multinationals they work for can better develop an accurate understanding of the cultures they must operate in. Fortunately, we can offer some concrete advice for international managers toward that end, shown on page 66.

- **Engage with other cultures to test any "sophisticated stereotypes."** Think about any cultural stereotypes you might harbor and treat them as hypotheses that must be tested rather than truths. Effective international managers are open to changing their views of people.

- **Find help from cultural mentors.** Ideal mentors (1) really grasp a culture's nuances, paradoxes, and logic and (2) are eager to share their insights. The better you understand a culture, the more tolerant and effective a manager you will become.

- **Carefully analyze information that appears inconsistent with your cultural stereotypes.** Managers may stop learning if they do well initially when operating in other cultures. The key for managers is to always be open to deeper learning—by constantly seeking and analyzing information that appears paradoxical to what a culture supposedly stands for (e.g., why are many American managers so autocratic if the United States embraces equality and egalitarianism?).[46]

- **Develop mental maps that will improve your effectiveness.** Cultures can be thought of as complex roadmaps for understanding how people think and act. That does not mean you have to figure out everything about a culture and all of the rules, implicit and explicit, governing it. But a high priority should be placed on understanding the core values or major signposts that provide the foundation for the mental maps used in a culture.

To test some of these suggestions, consider an American manager being sent to Bangkok. While a cursory perspective on Thai culture and values can be gleaned from culture frameworks (such as Hofstede and GLOBE), these really just scratch the surface. Moreover, as the comparison of U.S. and Thai business values shown in Table 2.5 suggests, some values will come as surprises to most Americans—even after reading this chapter. Plus, values are shifting in Thailand, with traditional respect for elders and emotional reserve eroding, particularly among the younger generation.[47]

Finally, we want to offer advice for corporations interested in improving the cultural savvy of their management workforce:

- **Select people with cognitive complexity for international positions.** In a nutshell, avoid black-and-white thinkers; pick people who can handle alternative viewpoints and plenty of ambiguity.

- **Stress in-country training for people working abroad.** Too much cultural training happens in a classroom context at home and focuses on concepts instead of experience. People should be trained in the locations where they are going to work so they can be challenged to figure out answers to real cultural issues in the local environment.

Table 2.5
Comparing U.S. and Thai Business Values

Thai Culture	U.S. Culture
Buddhist values of giving more than taking, resisting material attachments	Need for achievement and material reward are signs of success
Desire to have trust in business relations built through traditional social networks over time	Need for rules, regulatory procedures, and laws
Desire for face-to-face business contact, based on trusted relationships	Need to use the increased productivity of e-commerce via the Internet and public displays of data/performance
Need to take care of employees, avoid layoffs, and protect investors from taking a "haircut" (thereby losing face)	Accelerate restructuring and cost cutting as needed
Be humble and very considerate of others' feelings	Not inconsiderate of others, but should stand out, speak up, and be yourself
A strong sense of hierarchy in government and business alike (knowing one's place)	Less position-driven respect accorded to those in power

Source: Adapted from Niffenegger, P., Kulviwat, S., & Engchanil, N. (2007). Conflicting cultural imperatives in modern Thailand: Global perspectives. In C. Rowley & M. Warner (eds.), Management in South-East Asia. New York: Routledge.

■ Evaluate cultural expertise among personnel already in foreign countries. Not everyone will be at the same point when it comes to their learning about culture—people will have different degrees of understanding. These differences may be a function of individual differences in skills or level of exposure to the local culture. Assessing cultural expertise can help companies decide how long people should stay in a location to develop the cultural understanding they need to be effective.

CHAPTER SUMMARY

Culture has a pervasive impact on human resource practices, strategy formation, conflict management, and leadership. Culture is a complex concept. The collective programming of the mind of a particular culture can have roots in historical events, geography, shared traditions, economic developments, language, and religion, among other things. Cultures are also constantly evolving.

We reviewed three prominent efforts to cluster countries by cultural values. Hofstede's work continues to be a valuable guide for international managers. He argued that all cultures could be described in terms of four basic dimensions. *Individualism–collectivism* reflects the extent to which people in a culture see themselves as individuals or as part of a group. *Masculinity–femininity* describes whether people in a culture place a higher priority on the acquisition of money and power or on good relationships with coworkers. *Power distance* reflects the extent to which people in a culture can accept large gaps in power across ranks in an organization. Finally, *uncertainty avoidance* reflects the level of tolerance people in a culture have for ambiguity.

By crossing pairs of dimensions, Hofstede produced valuable *cultural maps* that have many implications for managing employees in different countries. More recently, Hofstede has introduced a fifth cultural dimension, long-term versus short-term orientation. Recent efforts by Trompenaars and others to cluster countries by cultural values generally support Hofstede's views and have added to our knowledge about developing countries. In particular, the GLOBE dimensions provide a more contemporary approach while offering alternative methods and measurements to Hofstede's work. There are controversies associated with both Hofstede and GLOBE, and it remains to be seen which effort will be more influential in the long run—though Hofstede has had a tremendous impact for some 30 years. This is a record that GLOBE has yet to match.

We then illustrated how culture can impact work-related perceptions about people, events, and time. Cultural differences in perception of these can cause headaches for international managers in business interactions and negotiations. Also considered is the influence of culture on important workplace attitudes, including job satisfaction, organizational commitment, and how culture may affect an individual's view about leadership. We concluded the chapter with advice to help people move beyond the "sophisticated stereotyping" that comes with the limitations of culture frameworks. Specifically, to be more effective in different cultures, this includes approaching other cultures with the idea of testing such stereotypes, finding cultural mentors to help, and carefully assessing inconsistent information. For companies, our advice included selecting people with cognitive complexity for international positions, stressing in-country training, and capitalizing on cultural expertise among personnel already abroad.

DISCUSSION QUESTIONS

1. Describe the basic cultural dimensions proposed by Hofstede and GLOBE. What are their similarities, differences, and limitations? How might international managers use the information from these cultural dimensions?

2. What are some of the ways that culture can influence work-related perceptions and attitudes?

3. What is your own orientation toward time? Are you more monochronic or polychronic? What challenges might this present for you in an international business context?

4. How can companies and international managers go beyond the "sophisticated stereotyping" that a superficial understanding of cultures might produce?

Developing Your International Career

WHAT ARE YOUR ATTITUDES TOWARD INDIVIDUALISM AND COLLECTIVISM?

Purpose and Instructions

The goal of this exercise is to promote an enhanced understanding and grasp of your own attitudes about individualism and collectivism. First, assume that you are somewhere in North America and that you desire an outstanding career in a U.S. or Canadian multinational. Next, answer the questions that follow regarding your behavior in the workplace, placing the appropriate number from the scale below next to each question.

5	4	3	2	1
strongly agree	agree	not sure	disagree	strongly disagree

1. _____ I would offer my seat in a bus to my supervisor
2. _____ I prefer to be direct and forthright when dealing with people.
3. _____ I enjoy developing long-term relationships among the people with whom I work.
4. _____ I am very modest when talking about my own accomplishments.
5. _____ When I give gifts to people whose cooperation I need in my work, I feel I am indulging in questionable behavior.
6. _____ If I want my subordinate to perform a task, I tell the person that my superiors want me to get that task done.
7. _____ I prefer to give opinions that will help people save face rather than give a statement of the truth.
8. _____ I say no directly when I have to.
9. _____ To increase sales, I'd announce that the individual salesperson with the highest sales would be given a "Distinguished Salesperson" award.
10. _____ I enjoy being emotionally close to the people with whom I work.

11. _____ It is important to develop a network of people in my community who can help me when I have tasks to accomplish.
12. _____ I enjoy feeling that I am looked upon as equal in worth to my superiors.
13. _____ I have respect for the authority figures with whom I interact.
14. _____ If I want a person to perform a certain task, I try to show how the task will benefit others in the person's group.

Next, imagine that you are working in one of the countries listed below. Pick the country about which you have the most overall knowledge (e.g., thanks to overseas experience, reading, having friends or relatives from that country, or classes that you have taken).

Argentina	Peru
Brazil	Philippines
China	Spain
Greece	Taiwan
India	Thailand
Italy	Turkey
Japan	Venezuela
Mexico	

Now go back and answer the same fourteen questions—while imagining that you are working in the country you picked from the list. Imagine that you will be living in that country for a long period of time and want to have a good career in a corporation there. Use the same five-point scale that you used before.

1. _____	8. _____
2. _____	9. _____
3. _____	10. _____
4. _____	11. _____
5. _____	12. _____
6. _____	13. _____
7. _____	14. _____

Scoring

Scoring this exercise involves comparing two sets of numbers: your set of numbers for a career in North America and your set of numbers for a career in one of the other listed countries. Let's call the first time you answered the questions the "first pass" and the other time the "second pass." In scoring, give yourself one point according to the following guidelines.

Give yourself a point if...

Question 1:   your number in the second pass is higher than in the first pass.
Question 2:   your number in the first pass is higher than in the second pass.
Question 3:   your number is higher in the second pass.
Question 4:   your number is higher in the second pass.
Question 5:   your number is higher in the first pass.
Question 6:   your number is higher in the second pass.
Question 7:   your number is higher in the second pass.
Question 8:   your number is higher in the first pass.
Question 9:   your number is higher in the first pass.
Question 10:   your number is higher in the second pass.
Question 11:   your number is higher in the first pass.
Question 12:   your number is higher in the first pass.
Question 13:   your number is higher in the second pass.
Question 14:   your number is higher in the second pass.

If your total score was six points or more, you are sensitive to the cultural differences captured by the concepts of individualism and collectivism. You grasp that cultures that embrace individualism may require different behaviors to accomplish goals and to achieve career success than cultures that embrace collectivism.

Source: From Brislin, R. W., & Yoshida, T. (eds.), *Improving Intercultural Interactions: Modules for Cross-cultural Training Programs*. Copyright © 1994 by Sage Publications. Reprinted by permission of Sage Publications, Inc.

Making the Case for International Understanding

IS A CULTURE OF ENTREPRENEURIAL PROBLEM SOLVING KEY FOR INDIA?

India is a complex and chaotic place with hundreds of millions of poor citizens and a ramshackle infrastructure—particularly when compared to the gleaming new ports, highways, and airports that China has been building in recent years. Moreover, India has long been plagued by a notoriously inefficient, albeit democratic, government. But these challenges and barriers have arguably produced something remarkable in India—a problem-solving mentality that helps many Indians to quickly, cheaply, and cleverly invent new products and new ways of doing things.

Indeed, this mentality has caused multinationals the world over to flock to India, not just for backroom outsourcing but to tap some of the most innovative minds in the world. As a result, optimists are saying that India today is booming in many respects, with a variety of world-class firms such as Tata Motors and mobile phone provider Bharti Airtel. Not surprisingly, they predict that India's gross domestic product growth will pass China's in a few years. And by 2015, some estimate that another 460 million Indians will join the ranks of the middle class, bringing spending power with them. Small wonder that some predict that India, not China, will be the fastest growing big country in the world for the next quarter-century.

Interestingly, while China's approach to growth has been, for the most part, government driven, India's successes are more connected to the collective efforts of its nearly 50 million entrepreneurs. The unleashing of India's underlying entrepreneurial culture has been driven by several factors, including reforms that started 20 years ago (e.g., lower tariffs, friendlier rules for investment, and less business red tape). Another factor is the domestic market. While many Indian companies do a brisk export business in services, the local market is large and demanding, with customers wanting cheap products that work well from the start. And India's frugal innovators provide them what they want. In fact, some of what they have come up with is nothing short of mind-boggling. For instance, Tata Chemicals has developed a water filter that costs less than $1, needs no power, and provides 30 days of pure drinking water for a five-person family. And Indian scientists have developed a new laptop they hope to bring to market—one that costs just $35!

All of this is consistent with recent research about cultural values that seems to encourage entrepreneurship. Entrepreneurs function in a social context, and consequently societal culture can play a role in inhibiting or enhancing the entrepreneurial problem solving seen in India today. Specifically, cultural values that encourage helpfulness, cooperation, relationship building, and bootstrapping—particularly as mechanisms for overcoming obstacles in society—seem to help spur entrepreneurial innovation. And India generally scores high on these attributes—on what GLOBE refers to as humane orientation. Likewise, India scores highly on in-group collectivism, where strong family connections and ties dominate and define India's most prominent and entrepreneurial companies. Moreover, when entrepreneurship is touted as being socially desirable in a country, it can, over time, strengthen and support cultural values that encourage entrepreneurial activity.

But, as stated earlier, India is a complex place with plenty of built-in contradictions. Because of bureaucratic barriers and increasing domestic competition, some of India's best companies, such as Godrej Consumer Products, are looking abroad to places such as Africa to grow their revenues—where their efficient and inexpensive business models are well suited to create products tailored to local demands. Indeed, many companies feel that India remains a very challenging place to do business. Many Indian roads are abysmal, and some are slowed by checkpoints where officials demand bribes from truck drivers. Likewise, companies often must maintain their own backup power and sanitation systems given the lack of stable utilities. Moreover, while India has plenty of innovative entrepreneurs, it is woefully short on engineers and other trained professionals, has too few outstanding universities, and has a weak primary education system. The government is also somewhat unpredictable, and laws are routinely challenged in court, making it difficult for businesses to know what will happen next. One Western businessman noted that China was much easier to operate in compared to "the freewheeling chaos of India."

The big question, of course, is whether India's cultural support for its unique, problem-solving frugal innovators can continue to lift the country up faster and farther than its challenges and weaknesses hold it back. Will the optimists or the pessimists be right in the end about India? What do you think?[48]

ASSIGNMENT QUESTIONS

1. Perform an in-depth assessment of Indian culture. What specific elements of that culture support entrepreneurship? Are there elements that hinder it? Can you provide examples of how these cultural elements are manifested in successful Indian firms as well as firms that have struggled recently?

2. As an international manager for a foreign multinational, how would you try to make sense of and adapt to the Indian business and cultural environment if you were doing business there? How might you be able to take advantage of India's expertise in frugal innovation?

3. Overall, do you side with the optimists who believe that India's culture will help it leapfrog China in the next few decades or the pessimists who see India as facing daunting problems that will hold its growth back for years to come? Either way, fully explain your position.

NOTES

1. Lin, H. C., & Hou, S. T. (2010). Managerial lessons from the East: An interview with Acer's Stan Shih. *Academy of Management Perspectives*, 24, 6–16.

2. Lin, H. C., & Hou, S. T. (2010). Managerial lessons from the East: An interview with Acer's Stan Shih. *Academy of Management Perspectives*, 24, 6–16.

3. McFarlin, D. B., & Sweeney, P. D. (2011). *International Management: Strategic Opportunities and Cultural Challenges* (4th ed.). New York: Routledge; Osland, J. S., & Bird, A. (2000). Beyond sophisticated stereotyping: Cultural sensemaking in context. *Academy of Management Executive*, 14, 65–79.

4. Hofstede, G. (2010). The GLOBE debate: Back to relevance. *Journal of International Business Studies*, 41, 1339–1346; Sivakumar, K., & Nakata, C. (2001). The stampede toward Hofstede's framework: Avoiding the sample design pit in cross-cultural research. *Journal of International Business Studies*, 32, 555–574.

5. Hofstede, G. (1980). Motivation, leadership, and organization: Do American theories apply abroad? *Organizational Dynamics*, Summer, 42–63; Hofstede, G. (2001). *Culture's Consequences* (2nd ed.). Thousand Oaks, CA: Sage; Hofstede, G. (1984). *Culture's Consequences*. Newbury Park, CA: Sage; Hofstede, G. Cultural constraints in management theories. *Academy of Management Executive*, 7, 81–94; Hofstede, G. (1991). *Cultures and Organizations: Software of the Mind*. London: McGraw-Hill; Hofstede, G. (1996). An American in Paris: The influence of nationality on organization theories. *Organizational Studies*, 17, 525–537.

6. Gelfand, M. J., Erez, M., & Aycan, Z. (2007). Cross-cultural organizational behavior. *Annual Review of Psychology*, 479–514; Triandis, H. C., & Gelfand, M. J. (1998). Converging measurement of horizontal and vertical individualism and collectivism. *Journal of Personality and Social Psychology*, 74, 118–128.

7. Morris, M. W., Podolny, J. M., & Ariel, S. (2000). Missing relations: Incorporating relational constructs into models of culture. In P. C. Earley & H. Singh (eds.), *Innovations in International and Cross-cultural Management* (52–90). Thousand Oaks, CA: Sage.

8. Hofstede, G. (2001). *Culture's Consequences* (2nd ed.). Thousand Oaks, CA: Sage; Hofstede, G. (1993). Cultural constraints in management theories. *Academy of Management Executive*, 7, 81–94.

9. Hofstede, G. (2001). *Culture's Consequences* (2nd ed.). Thousand Oaks, CA: Sage.

10. Hofstede, G. (2001). *Culture's Consequences* (2nd ed.). Thousand Oaks, CA: Sage.

11. Hofstede, G. (2001). *Culture's Consequences* (2nd ed.). Thousand Oaks, CA: Sage.

12. Bond, M. H. (1991). *Beyond the Chinese Face*. Hong Kong: Oxford University Press; Hofstede, G. (1993). Cultural constraints in management theories. *Academy of Management Executive*, 7, 81–94.

13. Dowling, P. J., & Nagel, T. W. (1986). Nationality and work attitudes: A study of Australian and American business majors. *Journal of Management*, 12, 121–128; Lenartowicz, T., & Roth, K. (2001). Does subculture within a country matter? A cross-cultural study of motivational domains and business performance in Brazil. *Journal of International Business Studies*, 32, 305–325.

14. Hofstede, G., Van Deusen, C. A., Mueller, C. B., Charles, T. A., & The Business Goals Network. (2002). What goals do business leaders pursue? A study in fifteen countries. *Journal of International Business Studies*, 33(4), 785–803; Kirkman, B., Lowe, K., & Gibson, C. (2006). A quarter century of Culture's Consequences. *Journal of International Business Studies*, 37, 285–320; Leung, K., Bhagat, R., Buchan, N., Erez, M., & Gibson, C. (2005). Culture and international business. *Journal of International Business Studies*, 36, 357–378; McSweeney, B. (2002). Hofstede's model of national cultural differences and their consequences. *Human Relations*, 55, 89–118; Smith, P. (2006). When elephants fight, the grass gets trampled. *Journal of International Business Studies*, 37, 915–921; van Oudenhoven, J. P. (2001). Do organizations reflect national cultures? A 10-nation study. *International Journal of Intercultural Relations*, 25, 89–107.

15. Japanese firms in China: Culture shock. *The Economist*, July 10, 2010, 64; Linowes, R. G. (1993). The Japanese manager's traumatic entry into the United States: Understanding the American-Japanese cultural divide. *Academy of Management Executive*, 7, 21–40.

16. Trompenaars, F. (1993). *Riding the Waves of Culture*. London: Brealey; Trompenaars, F., & Hampden-Turner, C. (1998). *Riding the Waves of Culture: Understanding Cultural Diversity in Global Business* (2nd ed.). New York: McGraw-Hill.

17. Ali, A. (1988). A cross-national perspective of managerial work value systems. In R. N. Farmer & E. G. McGoun (eds.), *Advances in International Comparative Management*, Vol. 3 (151–170). Greenwich, CT: JAI Press; Trompenaars, F. (1993). *Riding the Waves of Culture*. London: Brealey.

18. McFarlin, D. B., & Sweeney, P. D. (2011). *International Management: Strategic Opportunities and Cultural Challenges* (4th ed.). New York: Routledge; Trompenaars, F., & Hampden-Turner, C. (1998). *Riding the Waves of Culture: Understanding Cultural Diversity in Global Business* (2nd ed.). New York: McGraw-Hill.

19. House, R., Hanges, P. J., Javidan, M., Dorfman, P. W., & Gupta, V. (2004). *Culture, Leadership, and Organizations: The GLOBE Study of 62 Societies*. London: Sage.

20. South Korea's industrial giants: The chaebol conundrum. *The Economist*, May 31, 2010. Available at www.economist.com/node/15816756; House, R., Hanges, P. J., Javidan, M., Dorfman, P. W., & Gupta, V. (2004). *Culture, Leadership, and Organizations: The GLOBE Study of 62 Societies*. London: Sage; Ihlwan, M. (2008). Samsung under siege: Allegations of governance abuses help shed light on how the founding family maintains its grip on the conglomerate. *Business Week*, April 28, 46–50.

21. House, R., Hanges, P. J., Javidan, M., Dorfman, P. W., & Gupta, V. (2004). *Culture, Leadership, and Organizations: The GLOBE Study of 62 Societies*. London: Sage.

22. Hofstede, G. (2010). The GLOBE debate: Back to relevance. *Journal of International Business Studies*, 41, 1339–1346; Maseland, R., & van Hoorn, A. (2010). Values and marginal preferences in international business. *Journal of International Business Studies*, 41, 1325–1329; Taras, V., Steel, P., & Kirkman, B. L. (2010). Negative practice–value correlations in the GLOBE data: Unexpected findings, questionnaire limitations and research directions. *Journal of International Business Studies*, 41, 1330–1338; Venaik, S., & Brewer, P. (2010). Avoiding uncertainty in Hofstede and GLOBE. *Journal of International Business Studies*, 41, 1294–1315; Venaik, S., & Brewer, P. (2010). GLOBE practices and values: A case of diminishing marginal utility? *Journal of International Business Studies*, 41, 1316–1324.

23. Hofstede, G. (2010). The GLOBE debate: Back to relevance. *Journal of International Business Studies*, 41, 1339–1346; Venaik, S., & Brewer, P. (2010). Avoiding uncertainty in Hofstede and GLOBE. *Journal of International Business Studies*, 41, 1294–1315.

24. Sarala, R. M., & Vaara, E. (2010). Cultural differences, convergence, and crossvergence as explanations of knowledge transfer in international acquisitions. *Journal of International Business Studies*, 41, 1365–1390; Stephan, U., & Uhlaner, L. M. (2010). Performance-based vs. socially supportive culture: A cross-national study of descriptive norms and entrepreneurship. *Journal of International Business Studies*, 41, 1347–1364.

25. Social media in Indonesia: Eat, pray, tweet. *The Economist*, January 8, 2010, 64; Ioffe, J. (2011). In Russia, Facebook is more than a social network. *Bloomberg Businessweek*, January 3–9, 32–33.

26. Bond, M. H., & Forgas, J. (1984). Linking person perception to behavioral intention across cultures: The role of cultural collectivism. *Journal of Cross-Cultural Psychology*, 15, 337–353.

27. Bryson, B. (2000). The land down where? *Wall Street Journal*, September 15, A18.

28. Bond, M. H., Wan, K. C., Leung, K., & Giacalone, R. A. (1985). How are responses to verbal insult related to cultural collectivism and power distance? *Journal of Cross-Cultural Psychology*, 16, 111–127.

29. Forgas, J. P., & Bond, M. H. (1985). Cultural influences on the perceptions of interaction episodes. *Personality and Social Psychology Bulletin*, 11, 75–88.

30. Miyamoto, Y., Nisbett, R. E., & Masuda, T. (2006). Culture and the physical environment: Holistic versus analytic perceptual affordances. *Psychological Science*, 17, 113–119; Nisbett, R. (2003). *The Geography of Thought: How Asians and Westerners Think Differently...and Why*. New York: Free Press; Begley, S. (2003). East vs. West: One sees the big picture, the other is focused. *Wall Street Journal*, March 28, B1.; Masuda, T., & Nisbett, R. E. (2001). Culture and attention to object vs. field. *Journal of Personality and Social Psychology*, 83, 922–934.

31. Alon, I., & Brett, J. M. (2007). Perceptions of time and their manifestations in Arabic-speaking Islamic and Western cultures. *Negotiation Journal*, January, 55–73.

32. Levine, R. V., & Wolff, E. (1985). Social time: The heartbeat of culture. *Psychology Today*, March, 28–35; Levine, R. (1997). *A Geography of Time: The Temporal Misadventures of a Social Psychologist, or How Every Culture Keeps Time Just a Little Bit Differently*. New York: Basic Books.

33. Levine, R. V., & Bartlett, K. (1984). Pace of life, punctuality, and coronary heart disease in six countries. *Journal of Cross-Cultural Psychology*, 15, 233–255.

34. Saunders, C., Van Slyke, C., & Vogel, D. R. (2004). My time or yours? Managing time visions in global virtual teams. *Academy of Management Executive*, 18, 19–31; Yong, A. (2008). Cross-cultural comparisons of managerial perceptions of profit. *Journal of Business Ethics*, 82, 775–791.

35. Hall, E. T. (1983). *The Dance of Life*. Garden City, NY: Anchor Press.

36. Hall, E. T., & Hall, M. R. (1990). *Understanding Cultural Differences*. Yarmouth, ME: Intercultural Press.

37. Lincoln, J. R. (1989). Employee work attitudes and management practice in the U.S. and Japan: Evidence from a large comparative survey. *California Management Review*, Fall, 89–106; Lincoln, J. R., & Kalleberg, A. L. (1990). *Culture, Control, and Commitment: A Study of Work Organization and Work Attitudes in the U.S. and Japan*. Cambridge, England: Cambridge University Press; Near, J. P. (1986). Work and nonwork attitudes among Japanese and American workers. *Advances in International Comparative Management*, 2, 57–67; Near, J. P. (1989). Organizational commitment among Japanese and U.S. workers. *Organization Studies*, 10, 281–300.

38. Azumi, K., & McMillan, C. J. (1976). Worker sentiment in the Japanese factory: Its organizational determinants. In L. Austin (ed.), *Japan: The Paradox of Progress* (215–229). New Haven, CT: Yale University Press; Cole, R. E. (1979). *Work, Mobility and Participation*. Berkeley: University of California Press; Hattrup, K., Mueller, K., & Aguirre, P. (2007). Operationalizing value importance in cross-cultural research: Comparing direct and indirect measures. *Journal of Occupational and Organizational Psychology*, 80, 499–513; Kunungo, R., & Wright, R. (1983). A cross-cultural comparative study of managerial job attitudes. *Journal of International Business Studies*, 14, 115–129; Lincoln, J. R., Hanada, M., & Olson, J. (1981). Cultural orientations and individual reactions to organizations: A study of employees of Japanese-owned firms. *Administrative Science Quarterly*, 26, 93–115; Naoi, A., & Schooler, C. (1985). Occupational conditions and psychological functioning in Japan. *American Journal of Sociology*, 90, 729–752; Pascale, R. T., & Maguire, M. (1980). Comparison of selected work factors in Japan and the United States. *Human Relations*, 33, 433–455; Warr, P. (2008). Work values: Some demographic and cultural correlates. *Journal of Occupational and Organizational Psychology*, 81, 751–775.

39. Huang, X., & Van de Vliert, E. (2004). Job level and national culture as joint roots of job satisfaction. *Applied Psychology: An International Review*, 53, 329–348; Hui, C. H., Yee, C., & Eastman, K. L. (1995). The relationship between individualism-collectivism and job satisfaction. *Applied Psychology: An International Review*, 44, 276–282; Paton, N. (2009). India and Brazil crack employee engagement, www.management-issues.com, April 20, 1–2.; Kenexa. (2009). www.kenexa.com/kri/insight-reports.

40. Diener, E., Oishi, S., & Lucas, R. E. (2003). Personality, culture, and subjective well-being: Emotional and cognitive evaluations of life. *Annual Review of Psychology*, 54, 403–425; Huang, X., & Van de Vliert, E. (2003). Where intrinsic job satisfaction fails to work: National moderators of intrinsic motivation. *Journal of Organizational Behavior*, 24, 159–179; Judge, T. A., Parker, S. K., Colbert, A. E., Heller, D., & Ilies, R. (2001). Job satisfaction: A cross-cultural review. In N. Anderson, D. S. Ones, H. K. Sinangil, & C. Viswesvaran (eds.), *Handbook of Industrial, Work, and Organizational Psychology* (25–52). Thousand Oaks, CA: Sage; Gelfand, M. J., Erez, M., & Aycan, Z. (2007). Cross cultural organizational behavior. *Annual Review of Psychology*, 58, 479–514.

41. Lincoln, J. R., & Kalleberg, A. L. (1990). *Culture, Control, and Commitment: A Study of Work Organization and Work Attitudes in the U.S. and Japan*. Cambridge, England: Cambridge University Press; Luthans, F., McCaul, J. S., & Dodd, N. G. (1985). Organizational commitment: A comparison of American, Japanese, and Korean employees. *Academy of Management Journal*, 28, 213–219; Randall, D. M. (1993). Cross-cultural research on organizational commitment: A review and application of Hofstede's value-survey module. *Journal of Business Research*, 26, 91–110.

42. England, G. W., & Misumi, J. (1986). Work centrality in Japan and the United States. *Journal of Cross-Cultural Psychology*, 17, 399–416.

43. Gomez-Mejia, L. R. (1984). Effect of occupation on task-related, contextual, and job involvement orientation: A cross-cultural perspective. *Academy of Management Journal*, 27, 706–720; Hattrup, K., Mueller, K., & Aguirre, P. (2008). An evaluation of the cross-national generalizability of organizational commitment. *Journal of Occupational and Organizational Psychology*, 81, 219–240; Meyer, J. P., Stanley, D. J., Herscovitch, L., & Topolnytsky, L. (2002). Affective, continuance, and normative commitment to the organization: A meta-analysis of antecedents, correlates, and consequences. *Journal of Vocational Behavior*, 61, 20–52.

44. Greenberg, J., & Baron, R. A. (2000). *Behavior in Organizations* (7th ed.). Englewood Cliffs, NJ: Prentice Hall; Hofstede, G. (1993). Cultural constraints in management theories. *Academy of Management Executive*, 7, 81–94; Yukl, G. (2009). *Leadership in Organizations* (7th ed.). Upper Saddle River, NJ: Prentice Hall.

45. Laurent, A. (1983). The cultural diversity of Western conceptions of management. *International Studies of Management and Organization*, 13, 75–96.

46. Ali, A. (1988). A cross-national perspective of managerial work value systems. In R. N. Farmer & E. G. McGoun (eds.), *Advances in International Comparative Management*, Vol. 3 (151–170). Greenwich, CT: JAI Press; Bass, B. M. (1990). *Stogdill's Handbook of Leadership: A Survey of Theory and Research*. New York: Free Press.

47. Ayman, R., Kreicker, N. A., & Masztal, J. J. (1994). Defining global leadership in business environments. *Consulting Psychology Journal*, 46, 64–73; Dorfman, P. (1996). International and cross-cultural leadership. In B. J. Punnett & O. Shenkar (eds.), *Handbook for International Management Research* (267–350). Cambridge, MA: Blackwell; House, R., Hanges, P. J.,

Javidan, M., Dorfman, P. W., & Gupta, V. (2004). *Culture, Leadership, and Organizations: The GLOBE Study of 62 Societies*. London: Sage.

48. A bumpier but freer road. *The Economist*, October 2, 2010, 75–77; House, R., Hanges, P. J., Javidan, M., Dorfman, P. W., & Gupta, V. (2004). *Culture, Leadership, and Organizations: The GLOBE Study of 62 Societies*. London: Sage; Srivastava, M. (2010). The untold wealth of unknown cities. *Bloomberg Businessweek*, October 4–10, 9–11; Srivastava, M., & Sharma, S. (2010). Corporate India finds greener pastures—in Africa. *Bloomberg Businessweek*, November 8–14, 61–62; Stephan, U., & Uhlaner, L. M. (2010). Performance-based vs. socially supportive culture: A cross-national study of descriptive norms and entrepreneurship. *Journal of International Business Studies*, 41, 1347–1364.

Communicating Effectively Across Cultures

He who speaks has no knowledge, and he who has knowledge does not speak.

—Japanese proverb

Nothing done with intelligence is done without speech.

—Greek proverb

In Chapter 2, the foundation was set for much of the rest of the book. Several major perspectives on culture, which are valuable tools for interpreting international behavior in organizations, were presented. After all, trying to make sense of the many different ways in which we act, especially across hundreds of cultures and countries, is an extremely complex task. One way to handle this complexity is to isolate a core set of values shared by a specific set of countries. This is precisely what researchers have done—including Hofstede, the GLOBE Research Group, and others reviewed in Chapter 2. In that chapter, it was concluded that a big plus of knowing how cultures and countries cluster together is that it helps companies customize their management practices. This customization, in turn, makes international business easier and more productive.

In the process of describing these models, we looked at how value differences could help us to understand how others perceive events differently. This can also explain varying cross-cultural attitudes resulting from those perceptions. Chapter 2 concluded by highlighting some important cross-cultural challenges posed by such cultural differences. Chapter 3 picks up right where Chapter 2 left off. That is, once you perceive and interpret the behavior of another person, you often need to communicate your feelings or reactions. And that is where your prowess and insight into others' ways of thinking is critical, especially in an international environment.

In this chapter and the ones to follow, reference is made to the models of culture reviewed in Chapter 2, with special application to communication. And even though it may be self-evident to some, along the way we will touch on the importance of communication to cross-cultural understanding and business success. If communication is important, then what are the forms we should be aware of, and how do they impact intercultural commerce? Finally, we will discuss some barriers to understanding and methods to use that will help minimize—but never eliminate—mistakes in communication.

GOOD COMMUNICATION IS CRUCIAL IN INTERNATIONAL BUSINESS

There are many different ways that communication savvy can pay dividends in international business—perhaps limited only by the thousands of distinct languages spoken around the globe. There is no doubt that managers appreciate some of these differences and the value of effective cross-cultural communication. To say otherwise would suggest a poor view of both international managers and the firms they represent. Yet despite this recognition of importance, significant communication issues and barriers continue to impede better interaction. So if nonrecognition of the importance of communication does not explain these continuing problems, what does?

We believe the reasons are more complex and multifaceted. For one, while communication has a high value in the abstract, in the heat of practice, other things might get in the way. We have all had the experience of such good intentions being set aside. In international business, this is easy to understand. After all, managers face project deadlines that must follow import/export regulations and requirements, which in turn means that they need to navigate governmental entities in at least one other country (as well as their own), which in turn affects production and financing. So while managers value communication in the abstract, in the heat of battle, communication can take a backseat to more urgent issues. In addition to these everyday business pressures, experts point to another reason for communication problems: a general underappreciation of the fact that communication comes in many different forms. Managers sometimes get into trouble by assuming that communication is the same everywhere—language differences aside. Yet there are many subtleties, not often understood as communication, that can play a big role in cross-border interaction. For example, to an American, a silent pause in conversation is often seen as an opportunity (or obligation) to respond. Long gaps are uncomfortable and create a desire to fill in the silence. But in Finland and Japan, longer periods of silence in conversation are normal, even expected. Pauses may actually be a communication tool—one that signals that you are carefully mulling over what has been said. In fact, in these countries and others like them, responding too fast can be seen as offensive. It could indicate that you either did not listen or that you gave little thought to a proposal.[1]

A third reason some serious problems continue is that even when speaking the same language, you can hit some speed bumps. The examples already mentioned refer to cross-language problems, yet business interactions are regularly affected by cultural background and experiences. This explains why there are mistakes—sometimes of consequence—that occur between nationals of Australia, the United Kingdom, and the United States. Among other things, there seem to be differences in the English that is spoken in each country. For example, to table a proposal can mean to open it up for discussion in the United Kingdom, whereas it means suspending or removing a proposal from discussion in the United States. Likewise, Americans heavily salt their business communications with sports analogies, often not well understood by all (such as to "cover all the bases," "step up to the plate," or the need to "hit a home run"). Interestingly, the former CEO of DaimlerChrysler, Dieter Zetsche, a German national born in Turkey and fluent in

English, had such an experience with a baseball analogy. Once, during an interview with an American reporter, he was told he was about to get a question from "left field." After pausing a second, the savvy Zetsche replied, "Okay...as long as you don't throw me a curve ball." Unfortunately, many others fail to understand such references, and, worse yet, the communicator may not know that the message is unclear. The effect is that many can "strike out" when communicating with foreign business partners.[2]

Nonverbal communication matters, too, and further highlights the point that even language-savvy managers can undervalue communication. For example, leaning back or sitting low in your seat is acceptable in the United States, especially if you want to convey a relaxed and familiar atmosphere, but in some other countries, it would be viewed as irritating or offensive. This form of communication is discussed in more detail below. For now, however, we do note it as an underappreciated form of sending messages. The bottom line, as one expert put it, is that "what blows deals is a failure to understand communication styles."[3]

The good news here, however, is that multinational firms do seem increasingly interested in both spoken language and in more subtle stylistic issues. And, as is often the case when a clear market need arises, a set of smaller, entrepreneurial firms emerge to fill this need. Below we will document that there is little doubt that many people across the globe wish to master English. And, as a result, numerous small to medium-sized firms have arisen to serve these demands. McKinsey & Co., a large and influential consulting firm, estimates that more than 300 million Chinese are studying English and that the foreign language business in China is worth over $2 billion each year. But, as we noted, it is not just language per se. The CEO of one of these language training firms in China has said that "a lot of people start by thinking they need grammar practice, when what they really need is management skills."[4]

In other words, sometimes the actions and cultural context surrounding communication affect its meaning. Consider the so-called charm schools found all over China, with the goal to teach businesspeople how to better interact with and sell to Westerners. The founder of one such training firm, Jack Ma, has said that he is impressed with the shrewdness of Chinese businessmen, but that they "need to learn to be more polished" in Western ways. He told the *Wall Street Journal* that when he attended the World Economic Forum in Beijing, he was taken aback by the communication and behavior in business situations. Many Chinese smoked constantly (about 65% of the male population smokes) and held loud cell phone conversations during meetings. Ma's firm teaches businesspeople to avoid these mistakes as well as how to write polite business letters, understand Western etiquette, listen during meetings, and to be aware of PowerPoint and Internet style preferences. "We not only teach them how to do business, we teach them how to be charming," said Ma.[5]

Yet another sign of the global importance of business communication is the entry of the Walt Disney Corporation into the foreign language instruction business in China. Parents in China spend $1,000 per year to send their children to twice-a-week English classes conducted by Disney because they "want their kids to be international" and because Disney is a "familiar and trustworthy brand."[6] All this certainly suggests that language and other communication factors are worthy of time spent—many benefits could accrue to large and small firms alike.

VERBAL/SPOKEN COMMUNICATION

The single most important way that humans communicate is through language, both spoken and written. First, let's look at the role that spoken language plays in intercultural communication.

Features of the World's Languages

Some experts believe that there are thousands of distinct languages currently spoken in the world. This estimate does not include the even larger number if offshoots or dialects of languages are taken into consideration. At the same time, however, most of these dialects are spoken by relatively few people. In fact, only about 6% of all languages have more than 1 million speakers.[7] And, even more significantly, about 10 languages account for most of the communication on the planet (see Table 3.1). Keep in mind that experts disagree on the exact numbers presented in Table 3.1—estimates can vary up to 10% or more, especially for complexities in Chinese and Arabic. This table shows that there are over 1.12 billion Mandarin speakers, only a fraction of whom reside outside of China. It also shows that English and Spanish are more likely to spoken by nonnative speakers than is Mandarin.

This last point raises the issue of the impact of language. After all, one could argue that a language spoken almost entirely by one people—even if that population is over 1 billion people—has less influence than it could otherwise. And on the surface, this seems to be the case—some languages have widespread influence across borders, such as Spanish and English, while others are largely limited to only one nation, such as Polish, Japanese, and Greek. Table 3.2 provides some data that address language impact more directly. There, you will see several measures of impact, including the number of countries where a language is spoken, and an interesting index of overall influence of a language. These data show that English has a wide impact across the globe. Some have even argued that the use of language on the Internet is a good indicator of a language's

Table 3.1
**Widely Spoken and Influential Languages
Used Around the World**

Language	Approximate Number of *Native* Speakers (in millions)	Language	Approximate Number of *Native* and *Secondary* Speakers (in millions)
Mandarin Chinese	1,100	Mandarin Chinese	1,120
English	330	English	480
Spanish	300	Spanish	320
Hindi/Urdu	250	Russian	285
Arabic	200	French	265
Bengali	185	Hindi/Urdu	250
Portuguese	160	Arabic	221
Russian	160	Portuguese	188
Japanese	125	Bengali	185
German	100	Japanese	133

Source: Adapted from Weber, G. (1997). Top languages: The world's 10 most influential languages. *Language Today*, 3, 12–18.

influence. Research there shows that about 30% of all Internet content is in English, 15% in Chinese, 9% in Spanish, and 8% in Japanese.[8] Others have said that the Internet is "augmented" language, as it is accompanied by much graphical content that eases interpretation and so its impact may be less than we think. Either way, the preponderance of data across measures makes it clear that English, French, and Spanish are widely influential.[9]

Nevertheless, the dominant language in any one country or region has a great effect on and can even define a particular culture and its impact. An interesting case in point has been the Chinese government's efforts to promote Mandarin as the official national language—in a country that arguably has the most linguistic diversity on earth. Used by over 70% of the population, Mandarin is the most common language group in China.[10] But Mandarin is hard for people from Shanghai and its surrounding provinces to understand. There, various dialects of Wu are common. Some have said that the eight main languages of China are as different as Spanish is from French.[11]

Table 3.2
Indices of Global Language Influence

Language	Number of Countries in Which Language Was Spoken	Language	Overall Influence of Language
English	115	English	37
French	35	French	23
Arabic	24	Spanish	20
Spanish	20	Russian	16
Russian	16	Arabic	14
German	9	Chinese	13
Mandarin	5	German	12
Portuguese	5	Japanese	10
Hindi/Urdu	2	Portuguese	10
Bengali	1	Hindi/Urdu	9

Source: Adapted from: Weber, G. (1997). Top languages: The world's 10 most influential languages. *Language Today*, 3, 12–18.

Note: Number of countries includes core countries (language has full legal/official status), outer core countries (some legal or official status and is influential minority language—such as English in India), and fringe countries (no legal status, but influential in trade, tourism, and preferred language of the young—such as French in Romania). Overall influence is defined as the weighted sum of six factors (e.g., number of total speakers, economic power of countries using the language, socioliterary prestige, etc.)

Speaking (and Not Speaking) Other Languages

Language Challenges in Business

The large number of languages across the globe presents several challenges to international managers. One the one hand, it is great to be fluent in a second (or third) language. But to study it, you have to commit to that particular language. What if you are assigned to Bangkok or Seoul instead of Santiago or Madrid for an extended assignment? How can you use the Spanish you studied since grade school? On the other hand, being fluent in another language does signal to others that you are open to cultural experiences and appreciate languages and their value. Plus, there may be native Spanish speakers in the Seoul office anyway, and you would be a resource for communication with Santiago.

Americans and Foreign Languages

Regardless of whether you are lucky enough to work in a country in whose language you are fluent, most agree that to be effective, communication and negotiation in that country's language is important. You will probably need to speak pieces of it, understand it, or be willing to place enormous trust in a translator. Americans speak relatively few second or third languages. About 80% of U.S. households speak *only* English at home.[12] What accounts for Americans' lack of interest in other languages? Some say it is because the United States is relatively isolated geographically and thus has had no great need for additional languages. This explanation, however, does not hold up well in the face of the millions of immigrants and ethnic minorities within the United States—numbers that have increased over the last four decades. Indeed, nearly 8 million foreign nationals came to the United States from 2001 through 2005—more than came during any other five-year period in history. Considering that this occurred post–September 11, 2001, and in light of much tighter immigration scrutiny, the numbers are especially significant. The isolation argument does not pass the technology test either. Rapid transmission of information is a given now, rendering the notion of isolation more illusory than in the past.

Others who are more critical suggest that part of the reason for Americans' lack of foreign language proficiency may be ethnocentrism. This tendency to be more inwardly focused on one's own culture could be the cause of the relatively low importance that Americans attach to this skill. Some experts predicted that after September 11, the study of Arabic in U.S. universities would jump dramatically. Yet data show that only 70 total degrees in Arabic were awarded in 2008. Globally, however, Arabic is an influential language. Having said all this, there are some promising signs that students in the United States are taking a greater interest in studying languages. Nearly 1.4 million college students are currently studying a language (more than 50% study Spanish), more U.S. students are traveling abroad than ever before, and there is greater awareness of the importance of language. A major study abroad group, for example, has set a U.S. goal of having more than 1 million students traveling abroad every year to study. According to a survey by the language training firm Rosetta Stone, 58% of Americans said that they believe the lack of language skills in the United States will lead to foreigners taking higher-paying jobs. So perhaps we will see more Americans studying foreign languages in the coming years.[13]

Global Impact of English

One factor that has made it easy for Americans to be complacent about being monolingual is that the rest of the world uses English increasingly in business interactions. English is the language for international air traffic, regardless of city of departure or arrival; it is the most common language on the Internet; and universities and academia around the world use English for research and teaching. Peruse French job ads and you will find that most management and professional positions require *anglais courant*. English is the official language of oil firm Total S.A., one of the ten largest firms in the world and the largest in France—this in a country that historically protects its language fiercely. In fact, France has created a government ministry of culture, in part to foster the French language and culture. Why then is English becoming more pervasive in international business circles, even in France? There seem to be several reasons:[14]

- The sheer size of the U.S. economy and the global reach of U.S. multinationals has effectively made using English good business sense.
- U.S. higher education is very influential around the globe, arguably having world market share. University admission in the United States, and its attendant success, require English.
- Much business on the Internet has a U.S. connection, and U.S. firms were early adopters. As a result, the Internet is exposing many people to the English language. While the percent of Internet content in English has steadily declined (from 75% in 1999 to 30% in 2007), it is still the most common Internet language.
- English is fairly simple, grammatically speaking, and consequently makes for a relatively easy common tongue to use in international business.

For these reasons and more, English has been impactful within global commerce for decades now. In China, estimates are that more than 350 million people are learning English, with perhaps 150 million already speaking the language. Consider the European Union (EU), where many languages are spoken. Experts say that over half of the population is reasonably conversant in English, that it is the most commonly studied language at school in the EU, and even more people agree that they "should speak English." The Dutch already do: 80% are conversant in English. Countries such as South Korea have reemphasized their already high commitment to English, having just developed plans to recruit 23,000 new English teachers. Currently, there is even some contentious debate about whether national competitiveness would be strengthened if English was made the country's official language. In Singapore, the percentage of households speaking Mandarin and other local dialects has steadily declined over the last two decades, whereas the percentage of households speaking English has dramatically increased. Overall, English is the most popular second language in Europe, Africa, Japan, and China, among other places. Consequently, it is probably no exaggeration to consider English the language of international business—lingua franca.[15]

Of course, as one expert has said, "every language is the most important language in the world—to its speakers."[16] There is tremendous pride about one's native language, and some individuals are taking steps to protect their language and culture. For example, like the French before them, some German officials worry about the intrusion of English into their culture. One member of the German parliament decried the trend, calling it a "flood of Anglicisms descending on us from the media, advertising, product descriptions, and technology."[17] When people adopt a second language, it is often because it is useful in business interactions. In China, for instance, speaking English means better jobs, better pay (often double), and foreign travel opportunities. No wonder teaching English is big business, with up to $3 billion being spent annually on English language training in Asia alone.[18] This global trend seems likely to continue, including in Japan, which has long had a reputation of being relatively closed, culturally speaking. Some Japanese firms are providing extensive training in foreign languages and even making English the required language for all business transactions and meetings—even those that take place in the home country. In the accompanying *Global Innovations* box, we present what the online retail giant Rakuten is doing in this regard.

That said, other languages really are not going away, in business or otherwise. And what does competence in English, or any other language, really mean? In fact, there is no one definition, but there is little doubt that many people overestimate their language skills. Plus, as noted, perception and understanding are linked to cultural values regardless of what language is spoken. So communication in international business is likely to have plenty of rough edges to it, even when a common language is used. Those rough edges can often create real problems, and sometimes even danger. Consider air travel, where the most common cause of accidents is pilot error (about 70% of accidents). Some accidents have been directly tied to communication problems, as was a crash of a KAL flight near Cheju, South Korea. Flight data recorders clearly indicate that the instructions of the English pilot were misunderstood by the Korean first officer. The result was that the plane crashed and burst into flames. Very fortunately, none of the 157 people on board

GLOBAL INNOVATIONS

They Have Ways of Making You Talk: A Japanese Firm Requires English

As noted, English is the most popular language to study in the world. Many people already speak it, and millions more are studying it this moment. If we needed a sign of this trend, we could turn to Japan for proof. Japan is considered relatively isolated and slow to adopt the conventions of other cultures, including language. Yet in corporate Japan, there is a huge movement toward the adoption of English in the conduct of commerce.

Consider the Rakuten Corporation, the largest online retailer in Japan. Every Monday morning, about 2,000 employees in its Tokyo headquarters meet for an *asakai,* or company meeting. Since March 2010, those meetings, as well as corporate officer meetings and board meetings, have been held in English. Megumu Tenefusa, vice president of public relations, said that the firm is increasing the number of foreign nationals. And, he said, "in order to globalize the company, everyone from top management to regular employees should be able to speak English." Most current employees are Japanese, although hiring will likely increase the number of non-Japanese employed by the firm, which is 300 employees currently. Despite this, even if the meeting included all Japanese, soon even those meetings will be held in English.

This Japanese rival to Amazon, the U.S. online retailer, has big plans. Already a nearly $4 billion company, recent acquisitions in the United States and Europe will be followed by even more acquisitions in the near future. And Rakuten says that its English-only policy is "crucial to its goal of becoming a global company." The firm's employees seem to be okay with this move—or they are at least taking it in stride. Rakuten provides in house English lessons for employees. The firm declined to say how they assess English competence of employees, but management did say that English proficiency is necessary for promotion. In the meantime, the company has changed signs in the cafeteria to English; employees need to be able to understand and order "tofu hamburg steak curry" in English if they want the company-provided free meals. More significantly, CEO Hiroshi Mikitani, who has an MBA from Harvard University and is fluent in English, recently gave the earnings report entirely in English. Japanese reporters present for the report asked questions (in Japanese), and Mikitani answered in English, with an accompanying translation.

A few Japanese firms have more or less adopted English. Sony, for example, conducts many meetings in English, as does Nippon Sheet Glass Company, but each has no official policy. And Nissan Motor Co., as well as some other firms that have been acquired by foreign companies, has made English a common language. But it is rare for a company such as Rakuten, which is dominated by Japanese management, to take such a step (all 16 Rakuten board members are Japanese). The extreme approach by Rakuten has resulted in some rare public criticism by observers and by other Japanese firms. At a recent press conference, for example, Takanobu Ito, CEO of Honda, said that forcing Japanese workers to speak to each other in English is "stupid." Others within the company lament that this policy is the first step toward the disappearance of the mother tongue—and, ultimately, the fall of Japan.

These arguments do not faze Mikitani, even along with criticisms that his English leaves something to be desired. Instead, his response is that lack of English speaking is a huge problem for the country: "Japan is the only country with many well-educated people who can't speak English." Indeed, data support his statement. According to the International Monetary Fund, Japan had the lowest scores of the TOEFL test (an exam required for foreign students studying in the United States and other countries) of all 34 of the advanced-economy countries. The last word, however, might be Mikitani's if Rakuten's tremendous growth is any judge.[19]

was killed. This was not an isolated incident, and some expect that we may see more such misunderstandings. After all, pilot training is expensive and time-consuming and airlines cannot keep up with demand—especially in Asia.[20]

Language competence pays dividends in international business. And that is why a U.S. reliance on the English language represents a competitive disadvantage that will continue to cause problems into the future. Data show that U.S. firms continue to underplay the value of multilingual employees. One study showed that, although American managers felt that cross-cultural understanding was important, they also felt that foreign language skills were not as important because that could be dealt with by hiring foreign nationals and translators.[21] Given this chapter's discussion, it is not surprising that yet another survey shows that the United States has the lowest foreign language proficiency of any major trading nation in the world.[22] Unfortunately, this also seems to translate into little knowledge of foreign cultures as well—at least in the eyes of the United States' foreign business partners. In a survey of more than 10,000 businesspeople from more than 40 countries around the world, the United States received the lowest rating of intercultural understanding and language knowledge. On a 10-point scale, the United States received a rating of 2.8, with the next lowest developed country being the United Kingdom, which received a 4.1 rating on average. Most of the Nordic countries received ratings of over 7 (e.g., Sweden received a rating of 7.2), and Belgium received the highest rating (7.7).[23]

Communicating in Foreign Languages: Plenty of Room for Error

Lack of foreign language skills is a disadvantage in international business. But assuming that you speak Mandarin, English, and/or Russian, your problems are far from over. Even with great proficiency, many problems can arise in verbal communication. Because of these challenges, international managers must be sensitive to the possibility that what they *intended* to communicate was not what was *understood*. Many a firm and expatriate have experienced this problem. A large U.S. telecommunications company, for example, replaced its expatriate managers in Thailand and other Asian countries with American-born Thais and American-born Chinese. The company's intentions were good—it felt that the replacements would be more culturally attuned to doing business in Asia. But these Americans of varied ethnicity made mistakes. They often assumed that they were communicating well, and thus they did not make any special efforts to check with foreign colleagues and subordinates to see if this was true.

This was not arrogance, but simply an assumption that a message was getting through. As experienced expatriate managers have said, often these problems can't be solved solely by expanding one's vocabulary. We should not assume that nuances or common phrases will be understood. After all, even more concrete items, such as a deadline, can be confused. Consider the experience of a Western manager at Reuters Group, a financial information provider. He told his Thai colleagues that he would like a project to be done by a certain date. When it was not completed, he was upset. Yet the problem here was not a lack of motivation or the wrong use of vocabulary, but instead a cultural interpretation. The Thais had taken this request as a preference rather than a demand or order (as in "I'd *like* some water"). Similarly, a Swedish banker was advised that during a presentation to a recently acquired Estonian bank, he should be more assertive. The banker's language use was fine. He was told, however, that the Estonians would respond better to a more forceful communication style—something not as common in Sweden. The Swedish leader was advised, for example, to change "it is good" to "it is vitally important" and to directly address the fears of the acquired bankers rather than to sidestep their feelings. Similarly, some Japanese firms are training employees to be more "rude" (more direct, less formal)—traits that Japanese seem to show less than many other cultures. And, interestingly, the Japanese firms have found that English helps accelerate this effect. One Japanese journalist says that English allows him to be more direct. Instead of conducting interviews in Japanese, in which responses to even simple questions are often obscure and veiled in courtesies, he sometimes conducts them in English so that even Japanese feel more comfortable answering yes or no.[24]

Of course, it is possible to make a major communication error, even after having given a message due consideration. Perhaps you have heard of the mistake made by the Swedish-owned firm Electrolux, which once used the phrase "nothing sucks like an Electrolux" in ads to promote its vacuum cleaners. Besides being vaguely obscene, this phrasing could be interpreted as something less than a rousing evaluation of the product! Table 3.3 presents other out-and-out blunders committed by companies as they tried to communicate internationally, including both translation mistakes and cultural ones. If you think such errors are only committed by smaller, less experienced firms, read about the mistakes Microsoft made with the translation of its Word™ program. And consider the fact that Microsoft, as well as some of the companies discussed in Table 3.3, hired professionals to work on and translate their ads or products but still had problems.[25]

Most of the mistakes shown in Table 3.3 happened despite the time that the communicators had taken to think through and prepare their messages. Imagine the mistakes that could be made in real-time communications, where preparation is sketchy and discussions are more spontaneous. Personal communication such as this is likely to produce more problems.

For example, imagine a meeting between American and Japanese managers. Even if we assume accuracy in the translation of words, the actual meaning can vary considerably. As mentioned earlier, in Japan, it is generally considered inappropriate to say no in a blunt or direct fashion. The Japanese tend to avoid saying no to others—it is a sign of politeness and a way to avoid direct confrontation, which

Table 3.3
Language Blunders Abroad

Examples of Translation Errors

- Microsoft had shocking errors in the Spanish version of its popular Word™ program. It likened Indians to man-eating savages and provided the Spanish word for bastard as a substitute for people of mixed race. The thesaurus had suggested that *maneater, cannibal,* and *barbarian* were all substitutes for the Spanish term for people of African heritage.

- A foreign airline operating in Brazil advertised plush "rendezvous lounges," which in Portuguese implies a room for making love.

- One German translation of the phrase "Come alive with Pepsi" literally meant "Come alive out of the grave with Pepsi."

- A sign on the elevator in a Romanian hotel read: "The lift is being fixed. For the next two days we regret that you will be unbearable."

- A sign in a Japanese hotel read: "You are invited to take advantage of our chambermaid."

- A Bangkok dry cleaner tagline read: "Drop your trousers here for best results."

Examples of Failing to Appreciate Local Norms
and Cultural Values When Communicating

- One U.S. firm operating in Europe handed out fake coins with "$1 billion" emblazoned on them. Instead of spreading goodwill, this was largely seen as a reflection of U.S. pomposity and superiority.

- In Britain, General Mills used a breakfast cereal package that showed a clean-cut child saying, "See kids, it's great!" Although this was a prototypical U.S. ad, the product received a poor reception; it failed to appreciate that English families are less child centered than U.S. families when making food purchases.

- A foreign appliance company used an ad in Middle Eastern markets that showed a refrigerator full of food, including a large ham.

- Listerine was introduced in Thailand with an ad that showed a boy and a girl, obviously enthralled with one another. After learning that the public depiction of romantic relationships was objectionable, the ad was revised to show two girls discussing bad breath and was more effective.

Sources: Adapted from Ricks, D. A. (1983). *Big Business Blunders: Mistakes in Multinational Marketing.* Homewood, IL: Dow Jones Irwin; Clark, D. (1996). Hey, #!@*% amigo, can you translate the word "gaffe"? *Wall Street Journal,* July 6, B6.

is generally considered rude. Instead, the Japanese rely on a variety of indirect ways to say no. A person not savvy about such cultural norms may not understand that "I will consider your proposal" could actually mean no. It is so common for the Japanese to avoid direct negatives that the Japan Export Trade Organization

Table 3.4
How to Say No in Japanese

Phrase That Really Means No	A Common but Incorrect U.S. Interpretation
"That would be very hard to do."	Some adjustments are needed, but the deal is still possible.
"It is very difficult."	The matter is difficult but not impossible.
"I will consider it."	The issue is under consideration for future use.
"We shall make efforts."	Energy will be put into exploring options.
Silence or delay in response	The other party is thinking about the topic or is offended by our message; time is being wasted.
"I'll think about it."	The issue is still alive and under consideration.
"Yes, but . . . "	Conditional agreement

Source: Adapted from Imai, M. (1975). *Never Take Yes for an Answer*. Tokyo: Simul Press; Ueda, K. (1978). Sixteen ways to avoid saying "no" in Japan. In J. C. Condon & M. Saito (eds.), *Intercultural Encounters with Japan. Communication—Contact and Conflict* (185–195). Tokyo: Simul Press.

provides a pamphlet for foreigners to help them understand the difference between a yes and a no.[26] Table 3.4 presents some common phrases that actually mean no but allow for the bad news to be cushioned. Apparently, even the structure of the language seems to be designed in part to preserve interpersonal accord. In Japanese, the verb comes at the end of a sentence. A communicator can present the subject and object first and then alter the verb after gauging the reaction. Further, the speaker can easily add a negative at the end of a sentence that entirely changes the meaning in order to avoid discord.[27]

Some researchers have gone even further with this point—suggesting that language might be a good indicator of underlying cultural values, such as individualism or collectivism. Consider, for example, that languages vary in the freedom they give to drop pronouns in a sentence. In English, for instance, it is not proper to drop the subject in a sentence such as "I went to a movie last night." In Japanese and other languages, however, communicators are likely to drop the subject, making the same sentence "Went to the movie last night." In a study of 39 languages spoken in over 70 cultures, it was found that when the main language permits pronouns to be dropped, those countries were much more likely to be individualistic. This effect was replicated in a later study in which the researchers also showed that pronoun drop improved the ability to predict the degree of individualism or collectivism of a country, even after controlling for factors such as a country's degree of affluence (e.g., its gross domestic product). Dropping pronouns (such as I, he, or she) deemphasizes the importance of the person or subject of action, whereas requiring the pronoun makes individuals a prominent focus of attention.[28] It could be that language itself reinforces important values (e.g., *inter-* or *in*dependence with others) salient in people's minds. As shown in the accompanying *Culture Clash* feature, new research seems to support the belief that language may actually guide, or direct, the thinking about and processing of information that reinforces culture.[29]

Forms of Verbal Communication

It can be difficult for people in some cultures to directly address an issue or confront another person. In some cultures, people can be easily irritated when they

---

CULTURE CLASH

What's in a Word across Cultures?

A Rose in a Different Language May Not Smell as Sweet

Long ago, Shakespeare suggested that what matters is what something actually *is,* not what it is *called.* In *Romeo and Juliet,* he said, "What's in a name? That which we call a rose by any other word would smell as sweet."[30] In other words, the names we give things or the languages we use to describe reality do not matter—only what things actually *are* matters. This perspective has great appeal and seems to say much about human behavior— particularly that which occurs across cultures. This suggests that there may be some fundamental similarities among people, even among those who speak very different languages.

Recent research in social science has taken this question head on. Do the languages we speak simply express our thoughts, or do languages and their structures actually shape the thoughts themselves? This question went unexamined for a long time and was largely dismissed among researchers in the 1960s and 1970s, when Chomsky's theory of language held the day. Chomsky suggested that languages do not differ from one another in significant ways. If so, then there is no reason to think that language itself led to varying modes of thinking. Research on language universals yielded significant findings over the decades, yet, as one prominent researcher claimed despite this body of research, not one single universal has stood the test of time. Instead, lots of differences were uncovered. Take, for example, the nursery rhyme that begins "Humpty Dumpty sat on a wall..." In English, the verb would change to reflect tense (*sat* instead of *sit*). In Indonesian, you cannot change the verb to reflect tense. In English, you have discretion in identifying gender ("Yesterday I saw someone fall from a wall"), but you cannot avoid gender in French or German. Russians, too, flag gender; the verb would change if Humpty was a man or woman. Indonesian would not be concerned with grammatical gender, as the same word is generally used for *she* and *he* and *his* and *her.* Turks would mark the verb to show how they got the information—seeing the fall and hearing about Dumpty's fall would be expressed differently.

Of course, just because different people express things differently does not mean that they think differently. The real question is, do Turks, Russians, the English, or Indonesians know things differently and act differently because of their unique languages? The answer seems to be yes, according to a set of relatively new research studies. Take, for example, the Pormpuraaw, an Aboriginal people from Australia. They do not use terms like *left* or *right* but instead make reference to absolute direction (as in "the sandal on your southeast foot" or "please move your plate to the north-northwest"). Researchers have shown that, as a result of a language that relies on absolute directions (there are many), people become very good at knowing where they are located and where they are going. Researchers from Stanford University traveled to Australia to study the Pormpuraaw's approach to related topics. They presented sets of pictures showing a progression of events over time (e.g., a person at different ages of life and different stages of a banana being eaten). The Pormpuraawans arranged the pictures from east to west—wherever they sat, they intuitively knew the absolute direction they faced. The researchers repeated the task using Stanford undergraduates and found that they always portrayed time as moving from left to right. Other cultures are different still: in Mandarin, the future can be below and the past above; other cultures see the future behind and the past in front.

There are features other than time and space that show these language differences; views about the cause of events also seem tied to language. It is common in English to describe events in terms of people as the causal agents. For example, "Paul broke his phone" even if it was accidental. Yet, in Spanish or Japanese, this might be expressed in a more benign way, such as "the phone was broken." What impact do these differences have on cross-cultural behavior? This question was addressed in a study that had English, Spanish, and Japanese speakers watch an odd video. The video featured several people popping balloons, breaking eggs, and spilling drinks—some on purpose and others by accident. When the participants watching the video were later asked to recall the events, interesting results were found: the Japanese and Spanish subjects had a more difficult time recalling the cause of the accidental events relative to the English participants. Since Japanese and Spanish language patterns do not code the cause of accidents, this was the pattern predicted by researchers. The effects can be even more subtle. Researchers had English speakers watch the famous Janet Jackson wardrobe malfunction with Justin Timberlake during the Super Bowl halftime show in 2004. Some media outlets used a brief and understated causal phrase ("ripped the costume") while others used a brief but ambiguous phrase ("the costume ripped"), which presented two different ways of viewing the situation, to two different sets of people watching the video. Even here, language mattered. Despite watching the same brief video snippet, those who read "ripped the costume" were more likely to blame Timberlake than those who read a noncausal version of the phrase and believed it was a wardrobe malfunction.

So what does this all mean for cross-cultural communication? Communication patterns matter, and these patterns are often built into the language structure itself. Such patterns, in effect, act as filters that shape what we might see, how we see it, and our subsequent actions that might result. These subtle differences can have palpable effects on the way speakers view events, people, and other organizations as they attempt to make sense of these events as they navigate international business across borders. Mind you, there is no evidence that any language *prevents* a communicator from thinking something. Of course, even though some Australian aborigines use only cardinal directions (east, west, north, south), clearly they understand what "in front" means. So, instead, it is best to say that language acquisition creates habits of thought that shape our experience in significant ways. Shakespeare said, "'Tis but thy name that is my enemy."[31] But research seems to show this isn't the case—a rose may not automatically be seen as a rose in another language. And this could be the source of culture clash in doing business across borders.[32]

feel they are being strung along or not given a straight answer when the news is bad.[33] In the previous example of the Japanese reluctance to say a direct no, the problem is that a savvy partner *should* be hearing a no but is not. Said differently, it is not that the Japanese are insincere. They may be working very hard to maintain harmony and to show consideration for the feelings of others when communicating bad news. A flat-out refusal would certainly be the worst option for many Japanese. And, conversely, many Japanese perceive the communications of German, Americans, Swiss, and others as blunt, too insensitive, overly critical, or just plain prying. Of course, it would behoove both sides to gain a better understanding of the other.[34]

Toward that end, please see Table 3.5, which compares various forms of verbal communications in individualistic and collectivist cultures. The table presents various communication situations that everyone commonly encounters. One way to gain better cross-cultural understanding is to listen to others and to note features about them that you admire—probably a good communication tool in any culture. Yet it is interesting to observe that methods of smoothing interpersonal interaction—such as *compliments*—differ across culture. For instance, research shows that Americans praise each other much more frequently than do the Japanese. Americans are also much more likely to commend personal traits and physical appearance than are Japanese. Why these differences? The value placed on the individual self in U.S. culture—so much so that there is great difficulty in accepting a mistake and apologizing—may lead many Americans to be especially solicitous of compliments that make themselves feel better or otherwise stand out. Conversely, the Japanese are more likely to compliment interpersonal accomplishments and are more likely to offer apologies because of the collective preferences in that culture.[35]

Features shown in Table 3.5 are generally characteristic of individualistic and collectivist cultures. But there are also differences across cultures in terms of how often praise is given, what is praised, and how people respond. For instance, Egyptians tend to have a complimenting culture. While they may not compliment as much as Americans, their salutations tend to be longer and have more depth. For example, on one occasion, a host complimented an Egyptian dinner guest on his

Table 3.5
Differences in the Approach to Common Communication Issues

Communication Dimension	Individualistic	Collectivistic
General approach	Blunt, to the point, explicit, direct; not great at picking up cues from others; more self-focused	Subtle, point is made deftly, implicit, indirect references; much better at monitoring others and oneself in relation to others
Compliments	Praise is frequent; often public or in front of others	Praise is not common, especially among others; less personal when it does occur
Criticism	More direct criticism; directed at individuals, occasionally with anger but also constructive suggestions	Passive criticism (reference to third parties), ambiguous causal statements
Embarrassment	More likely to involve out-group members (acquaintances, friends of friends, strangers); temporary awkwardness	Involves in-group interactions (with family, friends, coworkers); more likely to feel longer-lasting shame
Apology/regret	Apologies done directly but not as intense as Japanese and with justifications and explanations offered for behavior	Apologies also done directly and extensively, without offering explanations and reasons for actions
Forgiveness	Forgiveness emphasizes personal; sought as personal redemption	Forgiveness is more common; is interpersonal; provided as reintegration to social group

Sources: Adapted from Imai, M. (1975). *Never Take Yes for an Answer.* Tokyo: Simul Press; Ueda, K. (1978). Sixteen ways to avoid saying "no" in Japan. In J. C. Condon & M. Saito (eds.), *Intercultural Encounters with Japan. Communication—Contact and Conflict* (185–195). Tokyo: Simul Press.

necktie. The Egyptian promptly took off the tie and gave it to his host, who politely refused the gift but found it neatly folded on the couch after the party was over.[36] Along the same lines, American children are often told that "sticks and stones may break my bones, but names will never hurt me." Interestingly, Egyptians have a nearly opposite saying: "A sharp tongue cuts deeper than the sword." Clearly, there are differences in compliments, often linked to underlying cultural norms.[37]

The opposite of compliments are *criticisms*, and, as shown in Table 3.5, differences across cultures are also apparent. Americans are much more apt to criticize directly but also to provide constructive suggestions. Japanese are much more indirect, with reference to third parties to deflect blame. It appears that the need for group harmony in collectivist cultures impacts how people deliver critical comments. Even more direct criticism, such as delivering insults, seems to be tied to culture. Researchers have found that people in individualistic cultures focus their insults on the other person (e.g., "*You* are stupid," "I hope *your* project fails"), whereas insults in collectivist cultures brought in other considerations to the insult ("I wish a financial failure on you and your firm"). Criticism is delivered less frequently in collectivist cultures. Causing someone to lose face in this manner is something that is to be avoided.[38]

But what happens once offense is taken or a loss of face occurs as a result of an insult or by other means? Part of the answer was provided in one study of Japanese and Americans who were asked to recall and describe a recent embarrassing situation. Japanese participants in the survey mentioned embarrassment involving in-group interactions (e.g., with family, friends, and coworkers). American respondents, however, were more likely to mention relations that happened with out-group members (e.g., acquaintances, friends of friends, and strangers).[39]

An interesting follow-up is how people overcome this embarrassment, especially if it was caused by one's own actions. One tactic is to *apologize* for our part in creating the social problem. For example, Japanese and Americans react differently in situations in which one person harms another—physically or psychologically. Earlier, we presented the communication problems that contribute to commercial airline accidents. When these accidents occur, there is always a major effort made to determine the cause. Some years ago, a Japan Airlines (JAL) flight crashed into Tokyo Bay; 24 people died and many others were hurt. After the accident, the president of JAL publicly apologized, bowing deeply during the televised press conference. He also personally visited each family affected by the tragedy and offered up his resignation. American management in a similar situation would certainly work hard to uncover the cause of the accident, but it is unlikely that such a personal apology would be delivered.

Research shows that Japanese prefer to apologize directly and extensively (as in the airline example), without offering explanations or reasons for their actions. Interestingly, Americans, while not quite as direct as the Japanese, also generally prefer to apologize directly. American apologies are not as intense but include many more justifications and attributions to explain behavior. The Japanese were highly sensitive to lapses in their social obligations and went to great lengths to try to make amends. The American tendency to provide many explanations for social failure may reflect the higher value placed on the self in an individualistic culture. In turn, this may make the admission of failure or guilt much more difficult. Such was the case in an Alaska Airlines accident near Seattle, where all aboard were killed when an MD-83 aircraft nose-dived into the Pacific (after two separate harrowing free falls). Many causes were cited, including faulty stabilizers, a possible Boeing defect, Boeing's countercharge of poor maintenance by Alaska Airlines, and more. Eventually, both Boeing and Alaska Airlines admitted liability and settled all 88 lawsuits out of court.[40]

One lesson to take from this effect and the others described above is that international companies should help their employees understand that the type of apologies and explanations provided by people are driven by culture-specific attitudes. Managers who fail to adjust communication strategies risk provoking conflict and creating misunderstandings in cross-cultural situations such as daily teamwork, regular interactions with employees and clients, as well as performance appraisals.[41]

This raises another question: how well are apologies accepted? Are people commonly *forgiven*? Like many differences we discuss, there are great individual differences, but broad cross-cultural differences have also been studied. One study compared views of forgiveness in the Congo and France. Researchers found that willingness to forgive was more common in the Congo (collectivist culture) and that forgiveness could be more widely encompassing (group based) than in more individualistic France. The Congolese view the offender as being cut off from society, so the justice system's goal is to integrate him or her back into society. In France, personal sanction is at the core of the judicial system, with neither apology nor forgiveness being of special concern. Rehabilitation is a goal of the U.S. penal system, but even to the degree that this is true, that approach is largely personal, exemplified by the common idea of serving one's time. Interestingly, many Americans were taken aback by the Truth and Reconciliation Commission of South Africa, conducted after the end of apartheid (legal, and violent, racial segregation). There, people who were responsible for many terrible acts asked for, and were granted, forgiveness by the tribunals. There was criticism of the commission from within South Africa, as well as globally, but the work of forgiveness did move ahead.[42]

WRITTEN COMMUNICATION

One way to avoid all these potential language understanding problems is to communicate in writing—via letter or e-mail, for example. If you do not speak the language well, you can at least hire someone with writing expertise and knowledge of the language to transcribe thoughts and directions. Another option is to take the time to carefully craft the message yourself before sending it. In today's technology age, it may seem appealing to forego an attempt at communicating verbally, but it is not as simple as it seems on the surface. For one thing, hiring writing help is impractical much of the time given the volume of written communication often required in business settings and circumstances. Second, it can be expensive, as managers would need to find a trustworthy and competent translator willing to put in the time and effort needed to ensure a job well done. And, third, it still requires additional effort to stay on top of the message content and related processes, especially electronically delivered messages.

Electronically Delivered Messages

According to experts, one estimate finds that the average corporate e-mail user can expect to receive 50 to 60 new messages each day—a figure that we have found to be grossly underestimated. For international managers, the e-mail volume can be much higher. In fact, the growth of international business may account for a good chunk of the rising use of e-mail, with estimates ranging from 25% to 50% of office time spent on e-mail. Studies show that there are different rates of use for various electronic media, including e-mail, texting, and more. In one study, for example, researchers found that students varied in their willingness to experiment with technology. Those from the high uncertainty avoidance countries of Hofstede's study were less willing to adopt those new communication methods. Likewise, executives from high uncertainty avoidance and power distance countries found various information systems less useful, rating them less favorably than their counterparts from countries low in these dimensions.[43] A similar finding was also reported for Internet adoption rates in the United States, Japan, and a number of other countries. Adoption frequency was negatively correlated with degree of country collectivism, uncertainty avoidance, and power distance.[44] Apparently, the tendency to embrace new communication venues is more likely for those in cultures that are (a) willing to take chances, (b) not particularly status oriented, and (c) individualistic in focus.

A more recent study compared the preferences of Chinese and Australian managers for a variety of communication methods, including instant messaging (IM), e-mail, and telephone. Researchers found that Chinese respondents preferred the telephone and IM over other communication methods. This was predicted because of the Chinese tendency toward higher power distance and avoiding uncertainty—in addition to their high context style. High context, in particular, would suggest that this background information could be conveyed better in a richer environment in which nuances and subtleties could be accomplished (e.g., the telephone). Australians are more low context and thus were found to be more comfortable with lean communication methods such as e-mail. E-mail is more formal and offers few, if any, nonverbal cues—an arm's-length communication method.

We should note, however, that while culture did play a significant role in the study results, the researchers found that other variables present in all cultures (such as gender, age, and experience) were more important than culture itself in predicting communication preference. For example, younger people in both cultures were comfortable with most methods, including the use of social media such as Facebook and Twitter. Nevertheless, this study underscores the point that extensive communication—even if only virtual—has cross-cultural complications.[45] Nearly 70,000 people from 238 global companies were asked the question: "What method is the hardest for you to handle in English?" Even though the telephone is a rich form of communication and preferred by some, if English is the lingua franca, it still presents problems. The phone was cited as the hardest to handle in English by 77% of the respondents, with face-to-face meetings (64%) and e-mails (63%) also being mentioned.[46] Studies of intercultural e-mail show that the use of jargon, such as common American informal greetings and slang, is the most common problem for international clients. The ability to understand the urgency of requests and issue importance are equally common problems.[47]

Constructing Written Communications

E-mail and web content allow for quick, convenient, and, at times, elaborate communication. But volume of communication and convenience of sending does not inevitably make for *good* communication.[48] Think about how you could construct a letter, an e-mail, or web content to get a point across. If you are an American, you probably would: (1) use English, (2) keep the text short and to the point, (3) stress the use of the personal tone (by using personal pronouns), and (4) avoid flowery or exaggerated language.[49] If you were French, however, you would probably: (1) use French, (2) be less concise (maybe the letter would spill onto a second page), (3) stress third person, and (4) use more formal and polite openings and endings. Americans might perceive these parts of the letter to be old fashioned or too formal.[50]

Some researchers have approached this empirically by asking 100 major U.S. corporations for sample letters that they sent to foreign firms, and the letters that were received in response. Letters were collected from more than 20 countries (e.g., Brazil, Mexico, Italy, Thailand, India, Caribbean countries) and were coded for various features. The results in Table 3.6 show that the letters sent by Americans tend to use an informal, casual tone and sharply contrast with the more formal letters received in response from other countries. Likewise, Americans appear to avoid exaggerated courtesy and compliments that other cultures are likely to consider important.[51]

NONVERBAL COMMUNICATION

As discussed in previous sections, cross-cultural communication is not easy. There are many challenges associated with getting your message across and understanding the messages of others, either technologically or verbally. But nonverbal communication presents even more challenges. Nonverbal communication is the

Table 3.6
An Analysis of Letters Written to and Received from Foreign Countries

Writing Element	Foreign Letters Received Using Writing Element (%)	U.S. Letters Sent Using Writing Element (%)
Use of personal tone (personal pronouns, informal language, etc.)	25	37
Impersonal tone (formal, passive voice)	25	6
Exaggerated courtesy	44	19
Obvious compliments	16	6
Words omitted from sentences	38	6

Source: Adapted from Kilpatrick, R. H. (1984). International business communication practices. *Journal of Business Communication*, 21, 33–44.

transmission of messages without the use of words or writing. This is a recognition that goes beyond what is being said; often *how* it is said provides valuable information. Nonverbal behavior includes features about your appearance (e.g., facial expressions, posture, and eye contact) as well as how you may communicate (what words or topics you emphasize, vocal characteristics, etc.). We will discuss how nonverbal communication can vary across countries and cultures and how it can importantly affect your communication and that of the receiver.

Interpersonal Space and Gestures

One important type of nonverbal behavior is the amount of physical space that we prefer to have between us and others in social interaction, referred to as personal space by most researchers. You may not have reflected on this much before, but we regularly make very subtle choices about how much physical space to allow between us and another person during interaction. For instance, women tend to have a closer interpersonal space than men do, while friends often stand physically closer to one another during interaction than do strangers. For our purposes, it is important to understand that cross-cultural messages are communicated by these space differences (or violations of space). Researchers have systematically observed people engaged in business conversations and found large differences across cultures. North American and Northern European business space seems to be about three feet apart on average, whereas about one and a half feet apart is common in Latin cultures. Conversations in Arab cultures are conducted in even closer proximity (often one foot or so apart). Whether intended or not, messages are communicated by space choices. And you can imagine the potential impact that violations of these norms have. It is possible that a German unfamiliar with these norms might view a Latin business partner as pushy during discussions. Conversely, the Latin business partner might infer that the German business partner's preference for greater distance apart reflects a standoffish attitude—or worse.[52]

While we have characterized space as a choice, it is more often than not done automatically, based on little or no thought. Gestures, however, are usually more direct and deliberate and are designed to amplify a message. Thus, gestures serve as a separate form of communication by themselves, even if they become automatic over time. Examples might include a shoulder shrug, a thumbs-up sign, a head nod, or many other, sometimes country-specific gestures. Native speakers of a given language have an ability to rapidly size up these valuable signals and their meaning, but they are a much bigger challenge for second-language speakers. One study videotaped a series of real and fake gestures and then asked a group of nonnative students in the United States to rate their meaning. The students' accuracy in interpretation of a gesture was correlated with the length of stay within the United States and with ratings of their intercultural competence.[53]

Emotions and Touch

Closely related to the concept of gestures are the emotions people express across their interpersonal space. Facial expressions of emotion can be a common communication method across cultures. Research has shown that facial expressions of basic emotions such as anger, happiness, and sadness can be recognized reasonably well across cultures. On the other hand, studies have also shown that our accuracy in figuring out the various emotions gets worse as the cultures become more dissimilar. It is common, for example, for a Western manager to wonder why an Asian employee might be smiling during a performance appraisal meeting. Smiling does not signal enjoyment or arrogance, but instead often discomfort in that social situation.[54]

Related research suggests that there may even be the equivalent of nonverbal accents among cultural groups. Just as linguistic accents (such as pronunciations) can provide clues to one's ethnic or country origin, various features of emotions can act as clues to one's origins. One study asked a set of people to look at photos of Japanese Americans and Japanese nationals expressing emotions. Observers were able to detect subtle cues and difference among the individuals and thus were better at identifying the person's culture (American or Japanese). When Australians and Americans were photographed showing happy expressions and when videotaped while walking or waving in greeting, observers were also able to spot their respective nationalities. These studies and others suggest that we might have faint nonverbal accents that communicate features about us to others.[55]

It has been observed that when people express emotion, they often reach out to others. This use of touch, also called *haptics*, can be a powerful nonverbal communication tool—and one that varies cross-culturally. Touching in France, for example, is a natural and expected part of social interaction and communication. In other countries and cultures, such as in the United States, people do not use touch very often to communicate, except among individuals who have already formed a personal relationship. To examine this issue, researchers conducted a simple study: they observed people as they sat in outdoor cafés located in four different countries. Their data show that within random one-hour periods, on average, they observed 180 touches in San Juan, Puerto Rico; 110 in Paris, France; 1 in Gainesville, Florida; and none in London, England.[56]

It is valuable to reflect on what might be communicated with culturally specific touching styles. Consider a meeting between an Arab, who tends to use a lot of touching (and other nonverbal behavior), and someone from the United Kingdom, who generally avoids touch. A typical interaction might leave an Arab feeling that the British are aloof and distant, while many British might wonder why Arabs are so interpersonally aggressive and invasive. Perhaps an even more important point to consider is whether we can adopt another's style and then communicate better. A recent study tried to do just that. Researchers trained a group of Britons to use nonverbal behaviors appropriate to Arab culture, such as extensive touching during a meeting to emphasize a point or belief. Then they had these businesspeople and a control group who did not receive training interact with the Arab businesspeople. The results clearly showed that Arabs expressed more liking for the culturally trained Britons. For example, Britons were trained to use a gesture that puts their hand over their heart—a sign of respect in Arab culture—and to employ strong and intense eye contact during conversations. These behaviors were clearly noticed by Arab partners.[57]

Vocal Qualities as Nonverbal Communication

Research shows that vocal qualities such as speed and the loudness of one's voice can also communicate a message in and of itself, sometimes adding or changing what was explicitly said. One set of researchers compared the impression transmitted by identical messages that were delivered either quickly or slowly to Koreans and Americans. Groups of each nationality watched a video about smoking. Even though the content was always the same, the presentation was varied. The message was delivered at either a slow, normal, or fast rate, using a technology that retained the natural sound of the speaker. Interesting differences emerged in the ratings of both the communicator and the message. Americans thought that a relatively fast voice conveyed power and competence, whereas the Koreans felt that more power and competency was shown in slow delivery. The researchers suggested that because Koreans live in a more collective culture and, as a result, are more concerned with measuring their words carefully so as not to offend others, they gave more credibility to the slow message.[58]

CONTEXT

While nonverbal behavior can provide background for understanding what someone is communicating, an even more subtle form of influence on perception is exerted by *context*. Almost all evaluations occur within some kind of context. For instance, an identical statement could mean dramatically different things, depending, of course, on the context. Many of us know this intuitively, and maybe you have experienced this firsthand if you have been quoted out of context. The need for context is relatively universal. Nevertheless, some researchers claim that various cultures are more or less reliant upon context in the perceptions and interactions with others.

Table 3.7 shows how some cultures differ in their general reliance on context. In *low-context* cultures, such as the United States and Australia, the interpretation of people and behavior importantly depends on what is actually said or written. And these messages are often precise, with the words themselves carrying most of the real message, silence being uncomfortable, and great attention paid to details and clarification.

In relatively *high-context* cultures—ones that often approach a business event very differently—the context provides people with information that they can use to interpret what might otherwise be an ambiguous event. Put simply, people may not require or expect detailed, explicit information about an event. Instead, verbal or written information can take a backseat to what is generally understood via the context. High-context cultures also tend to be concerned with long-term relationships, a person's word or reputation, and establishing trust over time. In contrast, people from low-context cultures tend to be concerned with getting the entire context up front. They tend to be concerned about the details of an arrangement and want to be clear about the rules for conducting business. As a result, people from low-context cultures are likely to prefer explicit agendas for meetings and exhaustive legal documents to establish clarity about business deals as opposed to relying on trust or relationships. Not so for those from high-context cultures, where people are generally more comfortable with silence, feel that details can be worked out later, and engage in more complex and indirect communication.

Table 3.7
Comparing High- and Low-Context Cultures

Culture	Context
Chinese	HIGH
Korean	■ What is unsaid but understood carries more weight than
Japanese	written and verbal comments.
French	■ Relies on trust for agreement.
Arab	■ Personal relations add to business.
Greek	
Spanish	
Italian	
English	
	LOW
U.S.	■ Focus on specifics of what was said or written.
Scandinavian	■ Handshake is insufficient.
German	■ Trust secured with legal agreement; personal relations
Swiss	detract from business.

Source: Adapted from Hall, E. T. (1976). *Beyond Culture*. Garden City, NY: Anchor Press.

Let's consider in more detail the degree to which each type of culture prefers written or verbal communication. In low-context cultures such as Germany and the United States, people tend to rely on written communication because that medium allows for a permanent and explicit record of a message. In high-context cultures such as Japan, however, people may prefer verbal and face-to-face communications because these modes are more dynamic and allow for greater subtlety than written messages. Indeed, experts warn that international managers need to understand that many Japanese are reluctant to communicate via letters.[59]

But whether we are writing or not, context seems to affect our communication style. Indeed, one study found that Japanese business communications were indirect and relied on an intuitive style. In contrast, Americans and Canadians were much more direct and relied on a rational, fact-based approach. There are many examples of companies using this understanding of context to their benefit, one being a well-crafted advertisement by the Chinese detergent producer Nice. Its deep understanding of the Chinese consumer was illustrated in a successful ad showing a young girl helping her mother, who had just been laid off from her job, do the family laundry. The ad strongly connected with the Chinese concept of *dongshi*—what happens when a child starts to appreciate family and societal responsibilities, an extremely gratifying aspect of parenthood in China. Many experts pointed to this use of context as a key factor for the success of the ad and product.[60]

In a low-context culture, however, it is less common to use these nonverbal features—mostly because it is wise not to beat around the bush. Communication will be more effective if concrete, specific, and logical statements are made. Because of these contrasting approaches, it is rare to see a message that simultaneously communicates well to both cultures. One writer, however, described a sign that he saw in Switzerland that was translated into three languages—German, English, and French. The words were modified to reflect the varying context of these three countries. In German, the sign read "Walking on the grass is forbidden"—a direct, unambiguous message for this low-context country. The English version read "Please do not walk on the grass"—a message softened a bit from the German to reflect the somewhat higher context. Finally, the French version read "Those who respect the environment will avoid walking on the grass"—a much higher-context message reflective of that cultural tendency in France.

In summary, researchers argue that differences in context may explain common cross-cultural problems that arise in international business. All in all, the basic lesson for us is that it is important to know when and how to use context to your advantage. Obviously, you need to keep in mind who you are dealing with and how much context might be necessary. Consider the following example. A German manager working for a French company was terminated within a year because his performance fell short. The German was shocked, especially since "nobody told me what they wanted me to do." A French employee who resigned from a German company had the opposite experience. The French employee became fed up with being constantly told what to do by his German boss. He felt both his pride and intelligence were threatened. What we have here is a failure due to context. The French tend to be high context and would typically expect the German employee to pick up on the message. The low-context German employee, in contrast, would usually expect intervention and direction by the French manager. Unfortunately, that intervention either never came or came too late.[61]

CHAPTER SUMMARY

The focus of this chapter was on the strategic importance of good communication. Communication comes in many forms, yet managers sometimes mistakenly assume that it is similar across many geographic borders—actual language differences aside. One of the most important modes of communication is the spoken word, and it is widely recognized that being multilingual is a valuable asset for international business. Some countries, however, such as the United States, are in large part monolingual. Indeed, Americans' foreign language skills rank among the weakest in the world. Yet some American firms feel that these skill deficits are not as large a problem as they could be, since English seems to be the de facto language of world business. Despite this, myriad communication problems can emerge even among those speaking the same language—let alone different ones.

Written communication, in several different forms, offers the promise of increased message clarity. A communicator can take more time to carefully craft a letter or e-mail, and it can be referred to repeatedly by the recipient—in contrast to the fleeting nature of verbal communication. Finally, as if communication isn't hard enough, we cannot overlook nonverbal communication. This is the transmission of messages without the use of words or writing and includes topics such as interpersonal space, touch, vocal features, and context interpretation.

International managers need to be aware of the complex ways that cross-cultural differences can manifest themselves in communication. This can affect a wide range of messages we seek to convey to others, including compliments, criticism, and apologies. Increasingly, multinational firms are getting more savvy about their communication processes and are willing to devote resources to making sure they work. All in all, it might be best to consider the suggestion of experts in international communication and follow their advice as a starting point for becoming an effective intercultural communicator:

- Assume that people are different, not similar.
- When experiencing a lot of conflict, look for communication problems as the first source.
- Delay judgment; emphasize description of events, not evaluation or interpretation.
- Practice putting yourself in other people's shoes when communicating—be patient and understanding.
- Treat your interpretations as temporary and subject to further analysis.[62]

DISCUSSION QUESTIONS

1. Explain why both spoken and written communication present many challenges to cross-cultural communication.
2. How might various dimensions *of* culture (e.g., collectivism, power distance, and uncertainty avoidance) affect various forms of communication *across* cultures?
3. How would a country's standing on the context aspect of nonverbal behavior affect its communication patterns? Would high-context cultures prefer written or spoken language as a communication medium? What about the preferences of those from low-context cultures?

Developing Your International Career: Researching a Foreign Language

PURPOSE AND INSTRUCTIONS

The goal of this exercise is to examine a few basic elements of a language with which you are not familiar and to recognize problems that foreign nationals might have as they apply their basic language tools to English.

First, select a language with which you are not at all familiar. Research some basics about this language and prepare a few statements and greetings from the language to present to class (more detail is provided below). Your instructor might want to assign individual students or groups to various languages to make sure that several different ones are covered as well as to make sure that the groups have no familiarity with the language basics. Either way, we recommend looking at the following website, which provides briefings on many languages spoken throughout the world: www.123world. com/languages/index.html. It is unlikely, for example, that many students (or professors) are very familiar with languages such as Afrikaans, Arabic, Dutch, Farsi, Hindi, Japanese, Russian, Swahili, Turkish, or many others, and this site will provide many such choices.

Once you choose a language, you should begin to gather information that will give you a bit of insight into some basic features of the language and those individuals who speak it. In particular, we recommend that you discover the following (with possible supplements provided by your instructor):

- Where is the language spoken as the primary language? How many people speak it? Where else has it been adopted (if at all)?
- What are the origins of the language? How is it related to other families of language?
- What is unique or specific to the language (e.g., its grammar, syntax, accent marks, etc.)?
- What are several basic phrases in that language you could present to the class or in your report? If the report is given verbally, you should try to pronounce those phrases or use some of the sources provided below to present the phrases to the class (several websites offer .wav files that almost any classroom computer can read so that the phase can be heard in a native tongue).
- What types of challenges might native speakers of this language face when communicating to English speakers? That is, what are some transfer issues if they tried to speak in English (e.g., their tones, accents, sounds that are wildly different) and if their communication was translated into English by others?
- Do you have any recommendations for communication training or a possible set of guidelines or advice for speakers of this language?

Once you've chosen a language and considered the above questions, you can begin your research. There are several good sources to begin your work on this assignment (please also see the www.123world.com/languages/index.html site mentioned above):

- *The Linguist List* (http://linguistlist.org/sp/Dict.html)—This super site, run by Eastern Michigan University and Wayne State University, presents an amazing number of bilingual and multilingual dictionaries and translation tools. Some of the nearly 200 such dictionaries offer complete translation of phrases that you enter in English.
- *The Linguist List Subpage* (http://linguistlist.org/sp/LangAnalysis.html#25)—This page is also part of The Linguist List, but it could be missed in the wealth of information provided on the site. So we draw your attention here also. Presented here are many links to language families and many language meta-sites. Some of these will be helpful for the background research required in this assignment.
- *Language Page of GlobalEdge, of the CIBER at Michigan State* (www.globaledge.msu.edu/acaemy/languages).
- *Ethnologue: Languages of the World* (www.ethnologue.com)—A large and authoritative source of information about languages.
- *I Love Languages, Guide to Languages on the Web* (www.ilovelanguages.com/index.php?category = Languages).
- *Yamada Language Guides* (http://babel.uoregon.edu/)—Another site with a large amount of information about languages and language groups.

Making the Case for International Understanding

IMPROVING INTERNATIONAL COMMUNICATION AT TEKNOVUS INC.

In 2007, the board of a relatively new California-based chip designer, Teknovus Inc., began looking for someone who understood the attributes of different cultures and who could manage across those cultures. The firm was facing a big set of challenges, some of which dealt with communication among its increasingly far-flung operations. Teknovus sold most of its semiconductors to customers in Asia from the company's headquarters in Petaluma, a small community north of San Francisco.

The communication challenges were formidable, many centering on the need to respond better to clients' needs. International management expert Mary Brannen, a professor at the prestigious INSEAD Business School, located in France, has advised companies such as Cisco on multicultural problems such as these faced by Teknovus. Her experience suggests that many integration problems in cross-national operations are exacerbated by the mistrust and frustration that comes with long-distance communications across different languages. The Teknovus experience seemed to fit the mold. Firm executives targeted customers in Japan, South Korea, and China for their semiconductors because of the importance of the product in the advanced telecom systems of these countries. To jump-start the business, Teknovus hired sales managers in those countries. But contact between the customers themselves, as well as with the firm's engineers back in Petaluma, was minimal and limited. Increasingly, customers were dissatisfied, especially as they raised specification issues and requested customized applications to meet their network needs. It was not uncommon for Teknovus's customers to interact mostly with sales managers assigned to their region and to only occasionally problem-solve with their engineers. Yet, because of the nature of the product application (fiber-optic communication networks), it was necessary for the Asian telecom staff and the local carriers that operate the networks to seek help from Teknovus's engineers. Tensions rose on both sides, especially among the engineers at headquarters who expressed frustration over repeated changes made to the technical specs from the various overseas offices in Korea and China, among others. The engineers did not understand the reason for the requests—requests that required significant attention and time and that could have been avoided in the initial design phase. As a result, when overseas customers requested new features or bells and whistles, Teknovus engineers sometimes resisted. For example, when Japanese customers sought detailed reports for problems that they experienced, U.S. engineers were puzzled and irritated.

Communication was in a state of disarray. So the board put a premium on finding a CEO who not only knew the business inside and out but who was also sensitive to these increasingly critical intercultural communication issues. They hired Greg Caltabiano as the new CEO and are happy that they did. Caltabiano is an engineer by training, having spent 14 years based in China and Japan, most recently as a general manager for a telecom firm. Thus, Caltabiano fit the position specs well. But it was not the technical side per se where changes were made by the new CEO. Indeed, over the last two years, he has begun building communication bridges between Teknovus employees and customers and staff overseas. The effects seemed to have already taken root: sales have more than doubled in the past three years to $50 million; market share in China has increased; and some Japanese customers include the firm early in their product planning. All of these are very positive signs.

ASSIGNMENT QUESTIONS

1. Given what you know from reading this chapter, what do you think Caltabiano did to improve communications, and which had these positive effects on firm performance?
2. Try to mention several specific and tangible ways that intercultural communication could be improved among the Teknovus offices and with customers as well.
3. In your answer to Question 2, please consider the different communication modes (written, verbal, and nonverbal) as sources of both the communication problems and the possible solution.

Source: Adapted from Dvorak, P. (2009). Frequent contact helps bridge interaction divide. Chip-designer Teknovus improves Asian ties by raising status of overseas offices, encouraging staff visits. *Wall Street Journal*, June 1, B4.

NOTES

1. Adair, C. (2000). Don't get into cultural hot water. *Toronto Star*, August 9, G6; Jandt, F. E. (2001). *Intercultural Communication: An Introduction*. Thousand Oaks, CA: Sage; Tung, R. L. (1984). How to negotiate with the Japanese. *California Management Review*, 26, 62–77.

2. Adapted from and quotes taken from Jones, D. (2007). Do foreign executives "balk" at sports jargon? *USA Today*, March 30, 1, 4.

3. Adair, C. Don't get into cultural hot water. *Toronto Star*, August 9, G6.

4. Dvorak, P. (2007). Plain English gets harder in global era. *Wall Street Journal*, November 5, B1.

5. Fong, M. (2004). Chinese charm school: Seminars help businessmen conform to Western manners. Tip: Always answer e-mail. *Wall Street Journal*, January 13, B1.

6. Areddy, J. T., & Sanders, P. (2009). Chinese learn English the Disney way. *Wall Street Journal*, April, 20, B1.

7. *Ethnologue: Languages of the World*. (2011). Available at www.ethnologue.com/ethno_docs/distribution.asp?by = size.

8. *Internet World Users by Language*. Internet World Statistics, June 20, 2007. Miniwatts Marketing Group. Available at www.internetworldstats.com/stats7.htm.

9. Weber, G. (1997). Top languages: The world's 10 most influential languages. *Language Today*, 3, 12–18. Available at www2.ignatius.edu/faculty/turner/languages.htm.

10. *Ethnologue: Languages of the World*. (2011). Available at www.ethnologue.com/ethno_docs/distribution.asp?by = size.

11. Chinese whispers. *The Economist*, January 30, 1999. 77–79.

12. U.S. Census Bureau, 2007, http://factfinder.census.gov; They all speak English: As bilingualism becomes the norm worldwide, the future of English has moved. *The Economist*, December 13, 2006, 4–6; Americans breaking out of their English-only shells: Better resources, opportunities encourage U.S. foreign language students. (2009). Available at www.america.gov/st/washfile-english/2006/March /20060302142421ajesrom0.4190485.html #ixzz0JBQD0RQn&C.

13. 10 U.S. institutions awarded bachelor's degrees in Arabic. *Chronicle of Higher Education*, April, 23, 2010, A3; God's worst linguists: If the world is learning English, why on earth should the British learn the world's languages? *The Economist*, December 13, 2006, 1–3; They all speak English: As bilingualism becomes the norm worldwide, the future of English has moved. *The Economist*, December 13, 2006, 4–6; Dulek, R. E., Fielden, J. S., & Hill, J. S. (1991). International communication: An executive primer. *Business Horizons*, 34, 20–25; 1.4 million students studying foreign language. *MLA Newsletter*, Winter-Spring 2004; Commission on the Abraham Lincoln Study Abroad Fellowship Program. (2005). *Global Competence and National Needs: One Million Americans Studying Abroad*. Washington, DC. www.lincolncommission.org; Mandarin's great leap forward. *The Economist*, November 20, 2010, 72.

14. Graddol, D. (2008). *English Next: Why Global English May Mean the End of English as a Foreign Language*. British Council. Available at www.britishcouncil.org; Multilingual website widens the way to a new online world. *Financial Times*, February 7, 2001, 1; *Internet World Users by Language*. Internet World Statistics, June 20, 2007. Miniwatts Marketing Group. Available at www.internetworldstats.com/stats7.htm.

15. Fox, J. (2000). The triumph of English. *Fortune*, September 18, 209–212; Graddol, D. (2008). *English Next: Why Global English May Mean the End of English as a Foreign Language*. British Council. Available at www.britishcouncil.org; Song, J. A. (2008). South Koreans step up to learn English. *Financial Times*, April 3, 19; Boone, J. (2006). Native English speakers face being crowded out of market. *Financial Times*, February 15, 8; English is still on the march. *The Economist*, February 24, 2001, 50–51; Tietze, S. (2008). *International Management and Language*. New York: Routledge. See also Charles, M. (2007). Language matters in global communication. *Journal of Business Communication*, 44, 260–282.

16. Weber, G. (1997). Top Languages: The World's 10 Most Influential Languages. *Language Today*, 3, 12–18. Available at www2.ignatius.edu/faculty/turner/languages.htm.

17. Dvorak, P. (2007). Plain English gets harder in global era. *Wall Street Journal*, November 5, B1.

18. Dvorak, P. (2007). Plain English gets harder in global era. *Wall Street Journal*, November 5, B1; Boone, J. (2006). Native English speakers face being crowded out of market. *Financial Times*, February 15, 8; Halpern, J. W. (1983). Business communication in China: A second perspective. *Journal of Business Communication*, 20, 43–55; Ling, C. (2001). Learning a new language. *Wall Street Journal*, March 12, R18; Zong, B., & Hildebrandt, H. W. (1983). Business communication in the People's Republic of China. *Journal of Business Communication*, 20, 25–32.

19. This box is based on the following articles: Matsutani, M. (2010). Rakuten to hold all formal internal meetings in English. *Japan Times Online*, May 18. Available at http://search.japantimes.co.jp; Wakabayashi, D. (2010). English gets the last word in Japan. *Wall Street Journal*, August 6, B1, B2. Matsutani, M. (2010). Rakuten's all-English edict a bold move, but risky too. *Japan Times Online*, July 16. Available at http://search.japantimes.co.jp.

20. Ling, C. S. (2010). So many Asian flights—and so few pilots. *Bloomberg Businessweek*, October 18–24, 24–26; Korean airlines faulted on safety by internal study. *Wall Street Journal*, April 8, 1999, A1; Glain, S. (1994). Language barrier proves dangerous in Korea's skies. *Wall Street Journal*, October 4, B1.

21. Fixman, C. S. (1990). The foreign language needs of U.S.-based corporations *Annals of the American Political and Social Science Association*, 511, 25–46.

22. Dulek, R. E., Fielden, J. S., & Hill, J. S. (1991). International communication: An executive primer. *Business Horizons*, 34, 20–25.

23. *Global Competitiveness Report 2002*. Geneva, Switzerland: World Economic Forum.

24. Barnes, W. (2008). Tricky feats of cross-cultural communication. *Financial Times*, August 7, 18; Dvorak, P. (2007). Plain English gets harder in global era. *Wall Street Journal*, November 5, B1; Boone, J. (2006). Native English speakers face being crowded out of market. *Financial Times*, February 15, 8; Flintoff, J. P. (2001). Sayonara to ceremony: The Japanese are having to learn to be more rude and are using English to help them. *Financial Times*, May 5, 1. See also the following website for case study examples of similar problems experienced by many other companies: www.globalenglish.com/m/successful_results/case_studies/.

25. Victor, D. A. (1992). *International Business Communication*. New York: Harper Collins.

26. Victor, D. A. (1992). *International Business Communication*. New York: Harper Collins.

27. Koide, F. (1978). Some observations on the Japanese language. In J. C. Condon & M. Saito (eds.), *Intercultural Encounters with Japan: Communication, Contact and Conflict* (173–179). Tokyo: Simul Press; Weitz, J. R., Rothbaum, F. M., & Blackburn, T. C. (1984). Standing out

and standing in: The psychology of control in America and Japan. *American Psychologist*, 39, 955–969.

28. Kashima, Y., & Kashima, E. S. (2003). Individualism, GNP, climate, and pronoun drop: Is individualism determined by affluence and climate, or does language use play a role? *Journal of Cross-Cultural Psychology*, 34, 125–134; Kashima, E. S., & Kashima, Y. (1998). Culture and language: The case of cultural dimensions and personal pronoun use. *Journal of Cross-Cultural Psychology*, 29, 461–486.

29. Kemmelmeier, M., & Cheng, B. Y. (2004). Language and self-construal priming: A replication and extension in a Hong Kong sample. *Journal of Cross-Cultural Psychology*, 35, 705–712; Gardner, W. L., Gabriel, S., & Lee, A. Y. (1999). "I" value freedom, but "we" value relationships: Self-construal priming mirrors cultural differences in judgment. *Psychological Science*, 10, 321–326; Trafimow, D., Silverman, E. S., Fan, R. M.-T., & Law, J. S. F. (1997). The effects of language and priming on the relative accessibility of the private self and the collective self. *Journal of Cross-Cultural Psychology*, 28, 107–123.

30. *William Shakespeare's Romeo and Juliet*. Folger Shakespeare Library. New York: Simon & Schuster, 2004.

31. *William Shakespeare's Romeo and Juliet*. Folger Shakespeare Library. New York: Simon & Schuster, 2004.

32. Boroditsky, L. (2010). Lost in translation: New cognitive research suggests that language profoundly influences the way people see the world. *Wall Street Journal*, July 24–25, W3; Deutscher, G. (2010). Does your language shape how you think? *New York Times*, August 26, 1–9. Available at www.nytimes.com/; Birner, B. (2010). Does the language I speak influence the way I think? *Linguistic Society of America*. Available at www.lsadc.org/info/pdf_files/Does_language_influence.pdf; Augustin, S. (2010). Language and experience: Language influences experience of the world. *Psychology Today*, October 3, 3–4. Available at www.psychologytoday.com.

33. Barnlund, D. C. (1989). Public and private self in communicating with Japan. *Business Horizons*, 32, 32–40; Tung, R. L. (1984). How to negotiate with the Japanese. *California Management Review*, 26, 62–77.

34. Barnlund, D. C. (1989). Public and private self in communicating with Japan. *Business Horizons*, 32, 32–40; Haneda, S., & Shima, H. (1982). Japanese communication behavior as reflected in letter writing. *Journal of Business Communication*, 19, 19–32.

35. Barnlund, D. C., & Araki, S. (1985). Intercultural encounters: The management of compliments by Japanese and Americans. *Journal of Cross-Cultural Psychology*, 16, 9–26.

36. Almaney, A., & Alwan, A. (1982). *Communicating with Arabs*. Prospect Heights, IL: Waveland Press, cited in Nelson, G. L., El Bakary, W., & Al Batal, M. (1993). Egyptian and American compliments: A cross-cultural study. *International Journal of Intercultural Relations*, 17, 293–313.

37. Copeland, L., & Griggs, L. (1985). *Going International*. New York: Random House.

38. Semin, G. R., & Rubini, M. (1990). Unfolding the concept of person by verbal abuse. *European Journal of Social Psychology*, 20, 463–474; Gudykunst, W. B., & Nishida, T. (1993). Interpersonal and intergroup communication in Japan and the United States. In W. B. Gudykunst (ed.), *Communication in Japan and the United States* (149–214). Albany: State University of New York Press.

39. Imahori, T. T., & Cupach, W. R. (1994). A cross-cultural comparison of the interpretation and management of face: American and Japanese responses to embarrassing predicaments. *International Journal of Intercultural Relations*, 18, 193–219; Sueda, K., & Wiseman, R. L.

(1992). Embarrassment remediation in Japan and the United States. *International Journal of Intercultural Relations*, 16, 159–173.

40. Barnlund, D. C., & Yoshioka, M. (1990). Apologies: Japanese and American styles. *International Journal of Intercultural Relations*, 14, 193–206.

41. Tata, J. (2000). Toward a theoretical framework of intercultural account-giving and account evaluation. *International Journal of Organizational Analysis*, 8, 155–178; Dvorak, P. (2000). Japanese dairy pours on the apologies: Snow brand puts humility first after big recalls. *Wall Street Journal*, July 12, A21; Gilovich, T., Wang, R. F., Regan, D., & Nishina, S. (2003). Regrets of action and inaction across cultures. *Journal of Cross-Cultural Psychology*, 34, 61–71.

42. Kadiangandu, J. K., Gauche, M., Vinsonneau, G., & Mullet, E. (2007). Conceptualizations of forgiveness: Collectivist-Congolese vs. Individualist-French viewpoints. *Journal of Cross-Cultural Psychology*, 38, 432–437; Sandage, S. J., & Williamson, I. (2005). Forgiveness in cultural context. In E. L. Worthington (ed.), *Handbook of Forgiveness* (41–56). New York: Routledge.

43. Thatcher, J. B., Srite, M., Stepina, L. P., & Liu, Y. (2003). Culture, overload and personal innovativeness with information technology: Extending the homological net. *Journal of Computer Information Systems*, 44, 74–81; Leidner, D. E., Carlsson, S., Elam, J., & Corrales, M. (2000). Mexican and Swedish managers' perceptions of the impact of EIS on organizational intelligence, decision making, and structure. *Decision Sciences*, 30, 633–661.

44. LaFerle, C., Edwards, S. M., & Mizuno, Y. (2002). Internet diffusion in Japan: Cultural considerations. *Journal of Advertising Research*, 42, 65–79.

45. Guo, Z., Tan, F. B., Turner, T., & Xu, H. (2008). An exploratory investigation into instant messaging preferences in two distinct cultures. *IEEE Transactions on Professional Communication*, 51, 396–415, Grace-Farfaglia, P., Dekkers, A., Sundararajan, B., Peters, L., & Park, S. (2006). Multinational web uses and gratifications: Measuring the social impact of online community participation across national boundaries. *Electronic Commerce Research*, 6, 75–101.

46. Survey data cited in Dvorak, P. (2007). Plain English gets harder in global era. *Wall Street Journal*, November 5, B1.

47. Davis, A. S., Leas, P. A., & Dobleman, J. A. (2009). Did you get my e-mail? An exploratory look at intercultural business communication by e-mail. *Multinational Business Review*, 17, 73–98.

48. Hymowitz, C. (2000). Flooded with e-mail? Try screening, sorting, or maybe just phoning. *Wall Street Journal*, September 26, B1.

49. Kilpatrick, R. H. (1984). International business communication practices. *Journal of Business Communication*, 21, 33–44.

50. Varner, I. I. (1988). A comparison of American and French business correspondence. *Journal of Business Communication*, 25, 55–65; Haneda, S., & Shima, H. (1982). Japanese communication behavior as reflected in letter writing. *Journal of Business Communication*, 19, 19–32; Johnson, J. (1980). Business communication in Japan. *Journal of Business Communication*, 17, 65–70.

51. Kilpatrick, R. H. (1984). International business communication practices. *Journal of Business Communication*, 21, 33–44.

52. Hall, E. T. (1983). *The Dance of Life*. Garden City, NY: Anchor Press; Hall, E. T., & Hall, M. R. (1990). *Understanding Cultural Differences*. Yarmouth, ME: Intercultural Press.

53. Molinsky, A. L., Krabbenhoft, M. A., Ambady, N., & Choi, Y. S. (2005). Cracking the nonverbal code: Intercultural competence and gesture recognition across cultures. *Journal of Cross-Cultural Psychology*, 36, 380–395. See also McCarthy, A., Lee, K., Itakura, S., & Muir,

D. W. (2008). Gaze display when thinking depends on culture and context. *Journal of Cross-Cultural Psychology*, 39, 716–729.

54. Matsumoto, D., & Willingham, B. (2006). The thrill of victory and the agony of defeat: Spontaneous expressions of medal winners of the 2004 Athens Olympic Games. *Journal of Personality and Social Psychology*, 91, 568–581; Ekman, P. (1997). What we have learned by measuring facial behavior. In P. Ekman & E. L. Rosenberg (eds.), *What the Face Reveals: Basic and Applied Studies of Spontaneous Expression Using the Facial Action Coding System (FACS)* (469–485). New York: Oxford University Press; Elfenbein, H. A., & Ambady, N. (2002). On the universality and cultural specificity of emotion recognition: A meta-analysis. *Psychological Bulletin*, 128, 203–235; Mesquita, B., Frijda, N. H., & Scherer, K. R. (1997). Culture and emotion. In J. W. Berry, P. R. Dasen, T. S. Saraswathi, Y. H. Poortinga, & J. Pandey (eds.), *Handbook of Cross-cultural Psychology*, Vol. 2. *Basic Processes and Human Development* (2nd ed., 255–297). Boston: Allyn & Bacon.

55. Marsh, A. A., Elfenbein, H. A., & Ambady, N. (2007). Separated by a common language: Nonverbal accents and cultural stereotypes about Americans and Australians. *Journal of Cross-Cultural Psychology*, 38, 284–301; Marsh, A. A., Elfenbein, H. A., & Ambady, N. (2003). Nonverbal "accents": Cultural differences in facial expressions of emotion. *Psychological Science*, 14, 373–376.

56. Knapp, M. (1980). *Essentials of Nonverbal Communication*. New York: Holt, Rinehart and Winston; Barnlund, D. C. (1975). *Public and Private Self in Japan and the United States: Communication Styles of Two Cultures*. Tokyo: Simul Press; Barnlund, D. C. (1989). Public and private self in communicating with Japan. *Business Horizons*, 32, 32–40.

57. Collett, P. (1971). Training Englishmen in the nonverbal behavior of Arabs: An experiment on intercultural communication. *International Journal of Psychology*, 6, 209–215.

58. Lee, H. O., & Boster, F. J. (1992). Collectivism–individualism in perceptions of speech rate: A cross-cultural comparison. *Journal of Cross-Cultural Psychology*, 23, 377–388; Peng, Y., Zebrowitz, L. A., & Lee, H. K. (1993). The impact of cultural background and cross-cultural experience on impressions of American and Korean male speakers. *Journal of Cross-Cultural Psychology*, 24, 203–220.

59. Limaye, M. R., & Victor, D. A. (1991). Cross-cultural business communication research: State of the art and hypotheses for the 1990s. *Journal of Business Communication*, 28, 277–299; Haneda, S., & Shima, H. (1982). Japanese communication behavior as reflected in letter writing. *Journal of Business Communication*, 19, 19–32.

60. Kume, T. (1985). Managerial attitudes toward decision-making: North America and Japan. In W. B. Gudykunst, L. P. Steward, & S. Ting-Toomey (eds.), *Communication, Culture, and Organizational Processes* (231–251). Beverly Hills, CA: Sage; Williamson, P., & Zeng, M. (2004). Strategies for competing in a changed China. *Sloan Management Review*, 45, 85–91.

61. Hall, E. T. (1976). *Beyond Culture*. Garden City, NY: Anchor Press; Hall, E. T., & Hall, M. R. (1990). *Understanding Cultural Differences*. Yarmouth, ME: Intercultural Press.

62. Dvorak, P. (2009). Frequent contact helps bridge interaction divide. Chip-designer Teknovus improves Asian ties by raising status of overseas offices, encouraging staff visits. *Wall Street Journal*, June 1, B4; Skapinker, M. (2008). A word in your ear: Keep it slow and simple. *Financial Times*, August 26, 9.

Chapter 4

Managing Conflict and Conducting Effective Negotiations

Seldom, very seldom, does complete truth belong to any human disclosure; seldom can it happen that something is not a little disguised, or a little mistaken.

—Jane Austen, *Emma*

Chapter 3 made it clear that it is no easy task to communicate well. Messages get distorted, confused, or missed altogether when transmitted across cultures, making good communication more illusion than reality. This puts a measurable value on cross-cultural communication skills. Yet, in the heat of the international business battle, development (and sometimes appreciation) of these skills can take a backseat to more pressing business needs. All in all, therefore, we have got a breeding ground for conflict. Conflict occurs when disagreements and friction arise in the course of social interaction because of opposing interests, cultural differences in communication styles, and misunderstandings.

This chapter reviews some of the causes of conflict—in addition to poor communication. Not all conflict is bad, and there is value in recognizing and understanding it. If the underlying conflict is understood, you can more effectively manage it, especially in an international context. One vital management tool here is negotiation: the process of resolving conflict and differences between individuals or groups. As you will see, the view of negotiation—the process itself as well as the tactics that are used—is the result of many factors. Undoubtedly, some negotiation skills transcend culture, but many skills are context dependent and culture specific. Failing to understand and customize your negotiation style and processes could cause even further conflict instead of reducing the existing level you sought to overcome in the first place. Accordingly, the chapter will finish with some practical advice and information about international negotiation.

CONFLICT IN INTERNATIONAL MANAGEMENT

Causes of Conflict

Prevalence of Conflict

It is probably a fair statement to say that there has always been conflict among people—and most likely, that there always will be. While conflict has often resulted in violent interaction throughout human history, there are also many examples of successful resolution of conflict, offering hope for all of us. A recent example is the situation in Northern Ireland. Several decades ago, violence resulted in many deaths (thousands since 1970 alone). Many said that because of its link to centuries-long enmity among religious and political factions, the situation was intractable and would never be solved. Yet with persistent attempts at resolution, we have seen a cease-fire that has by and large held for 15 years, as well as talks and movement toward shared political power, a change in governments, and an improved business environment.

Cross-Cultural Conflict

Fortunately, managers generally do not have to deal with violence or terrorism, or the conflict that is at the root of such extreme conflicts. Their tasks, however, are still difficult. Compounding the communication problems and other challenges common today is that international managers and employees are more like diplomats than ever before, with an increasingly burdensome set of missions to carry out that can stir up serious disagreements. For example, international managers may have to handle foreign labor strife, manage suppliers, lobby governments, and soothe relations with outside pressure groups over environmental or other issues—all while somehow convincing employees with conflicting interests to work together.[1] That is a lot to expect. Plus, consider that one good reason that firms send expatriates abroad, at least for the short or medium term, is to head off or fix a problem or conflict.

It is important to note, however, that not all conflict is bad, even though it may prove challenging and even though some cultures try to avoid it. In fact, sometimes conflict focuses people's attention on getting things done. Conflict between environmental groups and multinationals has increased awareness of sustainability around the world and has built green business opportunities. Confrontations between social responsibility advocates and business interests have also improved working conditions in developing countries. At a personal level, while disagreement can be uncomfortable, it also leads to better understanding in some instances. Most performance reviews these days are two-way encounters, with employees providing input that can counter a manager's evaluation. Conflict can result in better reviews and better performance on both parts in the future. Conflict is very common. It has been estimated that U.S. managers spend about 20% of their time at work dealing with conflict situations.[2] And, given all the cross-cultural communication problems reviewed in the previous chapter, it is not surprising to learn that conflict occupies an even greater portion of time for managers with international responsibilities. Not only do expatriate managers face the same sources of conflict as domestic managers, but they must also grapple with many other interpersonal (e.g., language) and organizational (e.g., structure, reporting lines) conflicts as they try to keep a toehold in their host country.

Understanding Sources of Conflict

Given these stakes, international managers need a good understanding of the basic causes of conflict. As noted, *language* difficulties represent one major contributor to conflict. A poor translation could cause confusion and even anger on both sides. Differing *cultural norms* may give rise to conflict, especially when each side lacks an appreciation or understanding of the other's typical frame of reference. More than one U.S. manager has been greatly offended to be kept waiting well beyond a scheduled appointment time in a foreign country, with some even storming out at this perceived offense.[3] The resulting conflict could have been avoided had the U.S. manager been aware that he or she was bringing a monochronic orientation about time into a polychronic culture.[4] Of course, if the meeting had actually taken place, a host of potential sources of conflict could have emerged. As just one example, different norms about the directness of communication (e.g., low versus high context) can easily provoke frustration and resulting conflict. A German manager might provide unambiguous performance feedback to his or her Thai subordinate, highlighting positive and negatives, as might be done in Germany. But such directness violates the norms of Thai culture and can create performance issues or even turnover of an otherwise excellent employee.

The *decision-making* approach that a company uses is another potential source of conflict, especially if there is a mismatch with employee values. For example, some international firms prefer structures that are highly centralized. When the power and decision-making control is concentrated in just a few people at the top, speed of overall decision making can be slower but with better understanding and consensus among a team. Other firms, however, operate in a more dispersed fashion, with decision-making control decentralized and pushed down into lower ranks. Negotiators from countries with these decentralized styles might wonder about the seriousness of the other side if those at the table need approval for every tiny step. Likewise, some firms may experience conflict when they try to extend their decentralized decision-making style to operations in other countries. These efforts can backfire when they are not consistent with decision-making norms, as shown in Table 4.1. The conflict felt in this table could have been avoided if the U.S. manager had understood the Greek general preference for centralized over participative decision making.

Approaches to Conflict

An additional and important cause of conflict is the propensity for individuals in a given culture to be involved with conflict in the first place. Some cultures go to great lengths to avoid friction between individuals and groups, whereas others approach conflict head-on. In collectivist cultures, various social mechanisms are in place to make direct conflict less likely to occur in the first place. One example is the Japanese tendency to use indirect ways to say no as a way to smooth interpersonal relations. Yet paradoxically this tendency can be extremely frustrating and conflict provoking when used across cultures. The risk of damaging conflict may be highest when a cultural mismatch occurs, such as between a

Table 4.1
The Road to Conflict Is Paved with Misinterpretation:
A Conversation between a Greek and an American

Words Spoken	Perception/Interpretation by Each Party
AMERICAN: How long will it take you to finish the report?	AMERICAN: I asked him to participate.
	GREEK: Her behavior makes no sense. She is the boss. Why doesn't she tell me?
GREEK: I don't know. How long should it take?	AMERICAN: He has refused to take responsibility.
	GREEK: I asked her for an order.
AMERICAN: You are in the best position to analyze the time requirements	AMERICAN: I press him to take responsibility for his actions.
	GREEK: What nonsense—I'd better give her an answer.
GREEK: Ten days.	AMERICAN: He lacks the ability to estimate his time; this estimate is totally inadequate.
AMERICAN: Take 15 days. Is it agreed? You will do it in 15 days?	AMERICAN: I offer a contract.
	GREEK: These are my orders: 15 days.

Source: Triandis, H. C. (1977). *Interpersonal Behavior.* Pacific Grove, CA: Brooks/Cole Publishing Company, a division of International Thomson Publishing, Inc. Reprinted by permission.

Japanese manager, who believes that indirect confrontation of conflict is best, and a Dutch manager who thinks that conflict should be addressed openly and aggressively. Although a tendency to be open and blunt may be seen as up-front and effective by many Dutch, few qualities are more off-putting to the Japanese. The same is largely true in other collectivist cultures, such as in China, Singapore, and Thailand. In Thai culture, for example, children are taught at a young age to be *sam ruam*—to keep their feelings inside. Conflict in the form of outward expression of anger is seen as ignorant, crude, and immature. In fact, one study found that Thais are so sensitive to the negative comments of others that they do not look as favorably upon interaction with others, feeling that they are less supportive and helpful. Americans, however, when viewing the same behavior, do not have the same reaction.[5] Table 4.2 presents features about conflict that are common in five different countries. Keep in mind that these are general tendencies. As in most cultures and countries, there is a great degree of variation among people.

Table 4.2

Examples of Differences in Approaches to Conflict in Five Countries

Views of Conflict	Country				
	China	Germany	Japan	Saudi Arabia	United States
Avoid Conflict	Yes	No	Yes	Yes/no	No
Degree of Directness	Indirect	Direct	Indirect/subtle	Indirect; face-related concerns are high	Direct
Use of Third Party/ Mediation	Preferred (but a familiar mediator)	Not first choice but as a way to break deadlock	Can be used but not common	Yes; go-between can often smooth relations and air difficulties	Not first choice, but when used, mediator unfamiliar with parties to conflict
Face-Saving Tendency	High	Low	High	High	Low
Common Reaction to Conflict	Discomfort, embarrassment, redirection	Can disagree openly and be blunt. Initial discomfort but willing to mix it up/represent themselves	Discomfort, embarrassment, silence	Discomfort; undaunted by lack of progress due to social issues; will stay the course	Initial discomfort, but willing to mix it up/ represent themselves

Managing Conflict Effectively: Stylistic Differences Across Cultures

Let's assume that conflict does raise its head, as it often does, even in societies that prefer to sidestep conflict. A case in point was the antigovernment unrest, violence, and looting in conflict-avoidant Thailand in 2009–2010—including the firebombing of the stock exchange. If conflict is nearly inevitable in international business, how can it be managed effectively to minimize the damage or to even capitalize on the benefits of confronting opposing interests? There is considerable research on how people react to conflict once it does occur.

Conflict Styles

Conflict management research often focuses on what managers do once conflict does arise.[6] There seem to be at least five unique styles of handling conflict once it occurs, and these are shown in Figure 4.1. This model contrasts two key elements. First is cooperativeness, which refers to our degree of concern about outcomes that others might receive. This dimension is crossed with the degree of assertiveness shown in your reaction to conflict—your degree of concern for outcomes that you might receive. When these two features are considered simultaneously, the result is the recognition of the five distinct styles that each of us could use to handle conflict. There has been plenty of research done on these styles, although most studies focus on U.S. employees. In general, studies show that people adopt a relatively consistent style and stick with it—often requiring training to be able to react differently to conflict. Research also shows that, even within a culture, some big differences exist among individuals in conflict preference. For example, there are people who like to confront conflict head-on (competition) and others who try to ignore it altogether (avoidance). We all probably know people who regularly give in to others in a conflict situation (accommodation) and many who give up something in order to reach a mutual resolution (compromise). Finally, a mutually beneficial style (collaboration) is perhaps the hardest and least common style to have—within and across cultures. This integrative approach has often been called a win-win style where both parties gain (without great compromise) because someone thought of a new, inventive solution.

Culture-Specific Use of Styles

Research shows that some general, culture-based tendencies exist that can distinguish how groups of people tend to handle conflict. For instance, it appears that many Americans like a good argument. One study compared Japanese and Americans on a scale that measured the tendency to either embrace or avoid arguments. The results showed that the Japanese were less inclined to argue in the first place,

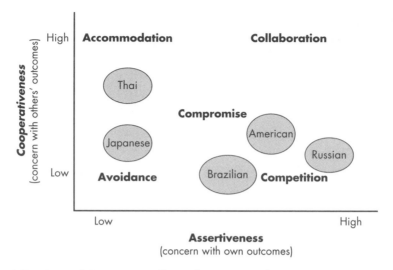

FIGURE 4.1 A Typology of Common Conflict Styles Across Cultures

but once involved, their degree of argumentativeness was less than that of the Americans.[7] Based on this and other studies, some experts have gone so far as to say that Americans feel stimulated by an argument, with many perhaps even enjoying the intellectual challenge it provides.[8] Whether or not that is true, the same cannot be said for the Japanese and several other Asian cultures. The Japanese are not fond of open conflict to say the least. If it does occur, they can even feel mortified, and they tend to worry that it could disturb group interaction. Based on these findings, it is reasonable to conclude that Americans tend toward the competitive conflict management style, while Japanese tend to fall in the avoidance area shown in Figure 4.1. We remind you, though, that these generalizations might not apply to individual Americans or Japanese.[9]

Other studies have compared the conflict styles of Americans with people from many other countries. In general, this research finds that people from collectivist cultures tend to prefer an avoidance style, while people from individualist cultures tend to prefer a direct, competitive style of dealing with conflict. Examples of countries with a collectivist orientation include China, Japan, Korea, and Mexico; the United States has been the primary individualist culture studied.[10] From a Western, and specifically U.S., viewpoint, a basic assumption is that conflict is something that should be approached. If a conflict is avoided, or if an individual fails to approach it head-on, individuals can be labeled passive-aggressive by colleagues. Yet, in many cultures, avoiding conflict is the better part of valor—at least among one's own in-group, a preferred set of people with whom you have regular and valued interactions. One researcher examined this issue in a study of young adults in Hong Kong and the United States. The young adults were asked to read about a conflict situation and then to make judgments about what actions they might personally take if they were involved. Both groups indicated that they would be more likely to pursue the conflict if the stakes were high and/or if the other party was an out-group member (not part of one's work group, strangers, etc.). Importantly, though, the Chinese participants were less likely to engage in the conflict with an in-group member and more likely to engage with an out-group member than were the U.S. respondents.[11] So as suggested earlier, Americans prefer more active, confrontational approaches, while Chinese tend to use more avoidance-type approaches when handling conflict.[12]

Meaning of Conflict

It is important to point out that avoidance could mean different things in individualist and collectivist cultures.[13] In collectivist cultures, for example, a high concern for others often drives the preference for avoidance, whereas in individualist cultures avoidance is believed to reflect low concern with others (see the cooperativeness dimension in Figure 4.1). One study, for example, found that Australians (individualists) rated the competitive style higher and the avoidance style lower than did Chinese students. Yet, when their reputation was threatened, respondents from both countries preferred to use direct, assertive approaches to defend themselves.[14] Newer research shows that it is the type of conflict and why it arose in the first place that distinguishes a culture. As an example, what would you do if someone asked you to do something but without a good reason? What if you were making photocopies and someone came in and, nearly out of breath, asked, "Can I use this machine because I have to make copies?" Of course, the person has to make copies—that is why you are there and obviously why he or she is there, too. Why should you stop what you are doing so that another individual can step in? Would you say no, would you sidestep the request, or would you do the person a favor? In four studies, researchers found that both Americans and Chinese rejected requests from others when they were asked without a good reason. Both groups agreed to the request when it was presented with a very good reason. For the previous example, a very good reason would be if your coworker explains that his or her boss needs a memo copied and sent out urgently in order to make an unexpected deadline. It was only in conditions of having a moderately good reason when the Americans were more assertive in rejecting the requests. It appears that under these conditions, when a reason for a request was provided, Americans' sense of self and the Chinese sense of others are more likely to be activated. This seems to account for more assertive responses by Americans.[15]

Parties to Conflict Situations

Experts point out that conflict preferences may vary depending on *who* is party to the conflict. For instance, some might be surprised to hear that managers from

Turkey and Jordan tend to use a general conflict-handling style that is not all that different from their U.S. counterparts. This preference for a competitive style changes, however, when peers become involved. Then, the Turkish and Jordanian managers tend to avoid conflict. Yet with their subordinates, they take a much more forceful approach when conflict erupts.[16]

A similar, situation-specific finding was observed in another study, this time with Chinese, Japanese, and U.S. managers. Researchers studied how these managers, as a third party to a disagreement, might react to disputes that become embroiled. A simulation was used whereby a dispute between two managers occurred and in which a third manager (the study participant) was consulted and involved. Respondents were then asked to predict features of the conflict resolution (e.g., What was the final outcome? Who decided it?). While the results are complex, they do point to the impact of cultural values in third-party conflict resolution. Briefly, the researchers found that U.S. and Japanese managers acted in ways we might predict, given their typical cultural values (Japan being more hierarchical and traditional than the United States). The Chinese managers in the study, however, were much more sensitive to situational cues (e.g., the status of those involved in the conflict) as evidenced by their conflict resolution actions. So, in addition to underscoring the impact of cultural values, these studies also suggest that this is not the full answer in working through conflict across culture. A detailed understanding of norms and context seems to help predict conflict resolution behavior as well.[17]

But it goes both ways. Norms can emerge from cultural preferences. Conflict preferences are deeply rooted within culture and extend to a variety of different areas. Consider a relatively common organizational exercise, such as dividing up resources (e.g., raises, promotions), often on an annual basis. This situation can engender conflict, both within and across cultures. For instance, people in individualist cultures often prefer an *equity* norm when dividing up organizational resources.[18] In determining pay raises, for example, individual contributions should be closely related to the eventual raise for these individualists (people should get what they've earned or deserve). In nations with individualist cultures (such as the United Kingdom or Australia), equity is the natural way of operating—it is the norm for figuring out who deserves what. In collectivist cultures (such as South Korea and Colombia), however, people have a tendency to prefer an *equality* norm, in which every group member gets a more or less equal share of rewards.[19]

These preferences may, in part, result from inherent cultural differences in dealing with conflict. As the Japanese say, the first person to raise his or her voice loses the argument. In other words, displaying a direct, out-in-the-open conflict style is an ineffective approach in Japan. In the United States, however, there are many myths and stories that celebrate rugged individualists who conflict with the majority ("the squeaky wheel gets the grease"). Clearly, then, there are cultural prescriptions about how to deal with conflict. While individualism may be a virtue for Americans, it can have negative connotations (e.g., selfishness) in other cultures, even serving as a challenge to one's self-esteem.[20]

The Role of Face in Conflict Prevention and Reactions

What Is Face?

The concept of "face" is closely related to the contrasting issues of interpersonal conflict on the one hand and decorum among people on the other. Face has a lot to do with the need to obtain and maintain both self-respect and the respect of others. One expert sets face squarely in the area of conflict and negotiation while defining it as "the interaction between the degree of threats or consideration one party offers to another, and the degree...of respect put forth by the other party."[21] If there is any concept that might cut across most cultures, it could be that of face. After all, pride and the respect of others are of great importance to most people.

There are many ways that face can be lost, including inflicting personal insult (whether intended or not), forcing unnecessary concessions, highlighting a failure, mocking cultural values, and damaging a relationship that has been cultivated over time (among many other causes). But the ways that face plays out, in and across cultures, are different. It appears that some cultures may value this respect of others more than others. One of the sharper contrasts that can be drawn across cultures is that between some Asian cultures and the general U.S. set of behaviors associated with face. The accompanying *Culture Clash* box illustrates this and provides some advice to all about being careful and respectful to those in other cultures—even if it may be more nuanced than is portrayed.

CULTURE CLASH

Face the Nation: The Importance of Respect across Cultures

While the need for the respect of others, or face, is important in all cultures, it is particularly important in many Asian cultures. One authority claims that "to speak or act in a way that causes an Asian to lose face is tantamount to physical assault in the West." Since many Asian cultures are interdependent, they also try to save face for others. In fact, in a study of one hundred Chinese managers, all of them said that respect was mutual—that it should be returned when given.[22] For example, if you were to ask an Asian for directions to the post office, he or she may actually take you there, even if it is out of the way. If the person does not know where the post office is, he or she may still point and say, "That way." To not know is to lose face. Likewise, the person may not provide you feedback if that information is, or could be, viewed as critical of you.

The concept of face can explain why some Westerners perceive Asians as indirect.[23] Americans pride themselves on how direct, frank, and honest they are, and they expect similar behavior when dealing with others. Yet these features are a big source of loss of respect for other cultures, including many in Asia. Asians are also very honest people. The clash occurs in how each culture expresses itself. The social demands in China, both within the culture and in terms of interactions with foreigners, prescribe ways to communicate information. Schooled in that culture, many implicitly understand how and when to communicate mistakes or bad news. Ditto for Americans: this news should be delivered with little latency and directly to those affected.

How does one resolve this culture clash? The solution for Americans is somewhat complex and difficult to enact. One technique is to try to use a more indirect approach to conveying information or resolving conflict. For example, a Western product engineer might ask for any suggestions regarding product design that an Asian may be asked to build. That way, the Asian does not feel compelled to avoid discussing problems or issues with the design—something he or she might otherwise do to preserve the reputation of the American. Thus, the face of all parties is preserved. Another option might be to work through a third party to convey or solicit news that affects the face of others. The third party could be carefully chosen to be of appropriate status and to be someone with the time and background to craft the feedback.

Regardless of the tactics used, the general rule to follow is: do not mistake a smile as a solid connection with your business contact. Quite the contrary—it is actually easy for an American to create resentment and even not pick up on it. If you did offend, it is not likely that you will be told, since no one wants you to lose face. Alternatively, you might be told in such a subtle fashion that you miss the message anyway. For example, you will find that things will slowly become more difficult, no one will seem very cooperative, and not much will be accomplished. We present good advice within the text, but here we will share one suggestion for Westerners that will go a long way toward helping all maintain face and smooth interactions. This expert says, "go slow, be calm, never loud. Listen more than you talk." This is probably good advice for doing business anywhere—but especially in Asia.

Social Complexities of Face

To be sure, we are simplifying here—the effects of culture are often more complex than they seem at first blush. Even within cultures, certain social triggers can make face more (or less) important. For example, research has shown that even the Chinese—who are often portrayed as being among the most concerned about face—when confronted with situations involving individuals of differing status (such as a supervisor or a subordinate) are more likely to arouse concern for face. One recent study looked at this in accounting firms—a setting where information sharing is vital. Researchers looked at the degree to which information about errors was shared when a supervisor was, or was not, present at a meeting. The study compared Chinese managers to those from Chile. China and Chile were chosen because they are very similar on their degree of collectivism, power distance, and other features. The results showed little difference between the countries when supervisors were not present at the meeting, but much less information was shared by the Chinese when their supervisors were present at the meeting.[24] It appears that the presence of a superior activates a stronger need to maintain face—perhaps for both the managers and their supervisors.

Practical Advice about Face

Overall, research paints a more complex picture of what face is and how to give it, get it, and keep it. This makes applying these concepts a daunting task in practice, especially for Westerners not used to doing business in Asia. Fortunately, experts have provided some general suggestions to keep in mind when navigating around problems with face in conflict and negotiation situations:[25]

- Frankness in Asia is almost always rudeness; subtler, high-context communication is the norm.
- Compliment but never criticize; even if presented with a situation in which a critique or honest negative opinion is seemingly required, stay as positive as possible.
- Asians are likely to laugh at awkward situations in order to save face; they laugh in order to change the subject or to move forward.
- If you ask a question that goes unanswered, wait until you are able to ask it again privately, away from the group; a lack of initial response typically means that the answer is offensive to, or demeaning of, the culture.
- Never show anger, even if you feel it. Public displays of emotion are unusual and not generally accepted well.
- Do not be in a rush, because it is an attack on the face of others. To Asians, your sense of hurry says that they are not important enough to spend time with and that you have better places to be.

Some of these suggestions, such as taking your time and focusing attention on your company, are good advice in any culture, because it displays behavior that is polite and considerate. But some claim that obeying such social rules is akin to capitulating to the demands of the Asian partner. Parts of both positions are likely true. But acknowledging differences does not mean that you have to be a pushover. In fact, you could use face to your advantage. Sometimes simply saying, "I would lose face at home if I were to agree to this deal" will carry more weight than a rational, numbers-based argument. Nevertheless, one expert advises those doing business in Asia to "be firm, but avoid obstinacy and rudeness. A calm and relaxed stubbornness is advised. Be persuasive in a gentle way."[26]

Other Responses to Conflict

The previous section discussed face and the impact that it can have on creating conflict and accentuating conflict's effects. What other reactions could people have when conflict arises? If the conflict is egregious enough, people might hold a grudge or look for ways to strike back at one another. In one study, researchers looked at what happened when conflict did occur. Comparisons were conducted between Chinese and Americans, this time managers of real firms. All participants read a brief story that asked them to imagine themselves in a conflict situation with a colleague. The conflict resulted from that colleague taking the participant's idea and presenting it to the boss as his or her own. Interestingly, Americans and Chinese were about equally as likely to express a desire to get back at the perpetrator of the head-on conflict (the colleague). There were differences, however, in the approach to this revenge. The Americans were more likely to choose a direct approach, such as confronting the colleague or reporting the colleague to a boss. The Chinese chose an indirect approach, such as criticizing the colleague to others. The Chinese were also more bent on teaching a moral lesson and shaming in comparison to the U.S. approach.[27]

Instead of getting even, as just described, one might try to involve a third party to resolve a conflict that has come out into the open. Earlier in this chapter, we mentioned a study that looked at how third parties might react to disputes in which they become involved. There, traditional values within the culture predicted the reactions to conflict among third parties well. Indeed, the issue of traditional values raises larger questions such as whether the likelihood of seeking out third parties or mediators is more likely in individualist cultures than in collectivist cultures. After all, given the attention paid to referees and umpires in professional sports in many Western countries, and the well-documented tendency for collectivist cultures to underplay conflict, why would we expect people in Eastern cultures to bring more attention to conflict by involving external, third parties?

The answer is surprising—the Chinese have a very long social tradition of using mediation. What are more interesting and instructive, however, are the types of mediators preferred and chosen by Americans versus Chinese. The Anglo-American tradition is to seek third parties who are dispassionate and disconnected from disputes, which one U.S. observer stated should be "a eunuch from Mars."[28] The belief that someone with little interest or connection to the conflict would render the best judgment is at the heart of this preference—this is what contrasts sharply with the Chinese view. The Chinese prefer mediators who are involved and knowledgeable about the situation. Unlike the neutrality preferred in the United States, this understanding and knowledge of the disputants is valued among Chinese for mediators.[29]

UNDERSTANDING INTERNATIONAL NEGOTIATION

Knowing how to manage conflict—either to stop it from occurring in the first place or to suppress any negative effects after it does arise—is a valuable skill in the global and domestic work environment. One extremely important, but complex, set of skills that is just as valuable is the ability to negotiate well. Negotiations that reach an impasse or are fraught with conflict need to be understood and explained, hopefully to avoid those problems in the future.

Negotiation is perhaps one of the best ways to avoid conflict or to at least keep it to a minimum. Negotiation is the process of communicating back and forth with another person or group with the explicit purpose of working toward a joint decision or agreement about a particular issue or dispute. All negotiations have three key elements:

1. Several sides (two or more) are involved.
2. Motives often conflict across those sides, but there are shared interests as well.
3. Each side shows some movement from its position over time in an effort to reach an agreement.[30]

Approaches to Negotiating

Because negotiation is so common in international business, it is one of the most heavily researched topics around. Many approaches can be classified into one of two well-established perspectives, briefly reviewed here.[31]

First is the *macro strategic* approach, which focuses on how negotiation outcomes are affected by larger, strategic issues, such as the relative bargaining power of the parties involved in the situation. For instance, consider a situation where a U.S. multinational wants to set up operations in a developing country—say, Tanzania. The U.S. firm may end up in a series of negotiations with the Tanzanian government (along with other officials) before locating there. In fact, the course of discussion may shift from initial entry to site location or acquisition and then to ongoing operations. As this process unfolds, the relative power of the parties may also shift. The impact of the U.S. firm tends to decrease after the initial investment is made, with a likely shift to the Tanzanian government, because government officials are responsible for enforcing local codes and rules, with the U.S. firm required to answer to them.

The second perspective is the *comparative* model, which is more concerned with what actually happens when negotiators from different cultures sit down across from one another and negotiate face-to-face, as well as how those interactions (and the ones preceding the cross-table discussions) shape the results. This approach suggests that we pay attention to the role of cultural factors and their impact on how the negotiation process unfolds between individuals or small groups of negotiators.[32] A compelling illustration—one with life-and-death consequences—is the latest thinking and research on negotiations with terrorists and other criminals who may hold hostages. In the accompanying *Global Innovations* box, we apply the low-context and high-context concepts introduced in chapter 3 to this important topic in today's volatile world.

GLOBAL INNOVATIONS

Out of Harm's Way: Cross-Cultural Hostage Negotiation

Violence in its many forms is a worldwide menace that has only recently been studied in some depth. Researchers on terrorism have been able to classify terrorist acts and those who commit them into several categories. One is called an *absolute terrorist,* which refers to those who commit heinous, self-contained acts of violence that end when the act is completed. These terrorists, such as suicide bombers and the like, are generally beyond the point of negotiation. Other forms and other types are amenable to negotiation because they seek some outcome, such as money for kidnapped executives or some sort of political gain.

Officially, most governments and companies say that they do not negotiate with terrorists. Yet, in practice, most do.[33] There is reason to believe that they should attempt to negotiate, as studies continue to show that more people have died from raids or assaults committed by authorities than at the hands of terrorists in these situations. It is true that there are several prominent examples of little or no loss of life in assaults on hostage takers (e.g., the Israeli raid in Uganda to free Israeli citizens kidnapped by the Popular Front for the Liberation of Palestine). But these examples are more than offset by tragedies resulting from such actions (e.g., Israel's efforts at the 1972 Olympics and Russian efforts to free 900 hostages taken in a Moscow theater by Chechen rebels). So it is good to negotiate, and many general rules have been developed to improve success. Recent research, however, suggests that some culturally based suggestions should play a role in those negotiations.

Consider, for example, the August 2002 kidnapping of a Dutch citizen and medical aid volunteer in Dagestan, a Russian Federation Republic. The Dutch negotiators conversed with the Russian kidnappers for many months, with a positive result: the aid volunteer was released after 600 days in captivity. Observers said that the Russian criminals were very oblique in their negotiating style, often seeming very ambiguous to the Dutch authorities. And they expected a similar type of discussion with the Dutch, who used a more direct and up-front style that is common in the Netherlands.

This example shows that while the negotiation was successful, resulting in no loss of life, the process used by both parties was complicated by the varying culture styles. One recent study took this a big step further. Researchers meticulously coded transcripts of 25 different crisis negotiations in which police interacted with perpetrators from a different culture. The sample was unique in that many audiotapes and subsequent transcripts created about the incidents were available—including statements by the criminals who held hostages and/or who kidnapped others. In all, nearly 7,000 separate turns of speaking across the 25 crises were coded—with about an equal number from the police and the perpetrators.

Importantly for purposes here, the researchers classified the hostage takers as being from low- or high-context societies. In earlier chapters, we said that people in low-context (LC) cultures commonly use direct communication methods—ones in which the meaning of the exchange is accurately reflected in what people say or write. People in high-context (HC) cultures are more likely to use indirect messages or messages that are best interpreted within the framework of one's culture. Most cultures and countries use both HC and LC communication, but in some cases one of the approaches is more common. In individualist cultures, LC is more common, whereas HC messages are more common in collectivist cultures.

Researchers found that across a number of hostage negotiation situations (some involving kidnapping, others extortion, and more) around the world, LC perpetrators of the crime were more likely than HC perpetrators to use persuasive arguments during their negotiations (e.g., "You just said you have the money available, so why can't you bring it to me right away?"). And these LC criminals were more likely to respond to persuasive arguments of negotiators with compromises. The research also showed that LC perpetrators were more likely than HC criminals to communicate direct threats—especially early in the negotiation (e.g., "I will kill the hostage if I don't get the money soon."). These cultural effects were more likely to occur in the later phases of negotiation—when the initial crisis had given way to the more common cultural styles. Plus, there was some evidence that those from HC cultures were more flexible in their styles and may have adapted more to their police counterparts. Indeed, the police tended to compromise more when they negotiated with an HC criminal than they did when they negotiated with one from an LC culture.

Given the discussions in both this and the previous chapter, it is interesting to speculate how negotiations might proceed between Westerners (LC cultures typically) and Asians (much more HC in orientation). What sort of touch points in the style of each could come into play in negotiations involving these two types of cultures? We know that Westerners are more likely to value directness and provide definitive answers or replies. Asians, however, will likely be more reserved and cautious during such negotiations. Given the Western orientation toward negotiations, little time will be spent on background information, and instead they will get right to the persuasion phase—and likely take a win–lose orientation. We know from research that the Japanese are much more likely to seek a win-win approach in their negotiations. We also know from Hofstede's research discussed in

Chapter 2 that Asians might be significantly less receptive to risk than would a Westerner. All these differences and more could dramatically impact the course of negotiations—examination of actual hostage and related negotiation has shown this to be the case. Of course, many other variables are involved in these terrible situations; they are extremely volatile and complex, with luck regularly playing a role in success. Nevertheless, this and other research suggests that negotiators who are sensitive to the cultural backgrounds of those involved in the crisis might end up with better outcomes for all.[34]

It is important to recognize that negotiation is a process, and a fairly elaborate process at that. A more common, but incorrect, view of the essence of negotiation is that it is really all about the jockeying back and forth across a conference table, the result being an agreement reached by both parties. Those who take this view of negotiation are more likely to fail than those who recognize that it as a process. In fact, those taking this narrow view will likely prepare a lot less because they do not see the value of extensive preparation. Instead, they are more likely to place emphasis on less important parts of the negotiation process. It is absolutely critical to prepare well in advance of the cross-table banter typically seen as the heart of negation. Doing your homework on the business culture of your partner will produce real value. The same is true for following the advice of experts on things such as allowing more time than you might otherwise expect for negotiations; not to go it alone, but instead to work with colleagues and others; and to consider possible training in advance. The more due diligence you engage in, the better off you will be. For now, let's assume that you have followed all of these suggestions. Now we can move on to the four-stage model of negotiation.

International Negotiation: A Four-Stage Process

Many experts believe that negotiation involves a regular sequence of actions. Although there is professional disagreement about the number of stages involved and what happens in each stage, one popular model divides the process into four main phases.[35]

The first stage of negotiation is called *nontask sounding*. This stage is comprised of efforts to establish a rapport with one's business partner and to get to know the other party better. Interactions during this stage are not directly related to what some normally think of as negotiation. Nevertheless, this is the first stage—one whose function is to sound out the other party. The length of this stage can vary dramatically, from minutes to months depending on the culture.

The second stage involves the task-related *exchange of information*. Interactions here commonly entail an exchange of the two parties' needs and preferences and are often accompanied by clarification of background issues relevant to the negotiation. Following this is the *persuasion* stage of negotiations, in which, as the label implies, there are overt attempts to modify each other's positions.

These lead to the last stage—the *agreement* phase—in which bargains are agreed upon and perhaps contracts signed. A good deal of research has compared cultures across these four stages, and we will present some of that work here.[36]

Stage 1: Nontask Sounding

Nontask sounding is a common occurrence in most social interactions, especially when meeting someone for the first time. In fact, the effort to establish rapport while getting to know someone is typical within and across cultures. But that doesn't mean that nontask sounding unfolds the same way everywhere. In fact, there often are great differences between cultures in how people approach this particular stage.

One important variable in the nontask sounding stage is simply the amount of time spent on this stage. In reference again to the concept of context, it is common for HC cultures to spend considerable time in this stage. They would want to know about you and the company you represent in great detail. For example, you might be asked about how long you have been with the firm, what you have done during that time and positions you have held within the company, your education and other qualifications, as well as details about your personal background. This conversation could be extended over days and in different places (e.g., banquets, golf courses, tours, etc.). In contrast, while getting to know a business partner is important in LC cultures too, the process is typically a lot shorter in length. In fact, it could be quite brief, perhaps even over a breakfast the day of the scheduled negotiation.

From an American's perspective, if this work can be done over breakfast, why is there a need for meeting after meeting before talk about contract elements can even begin? In other words, what to an American might seem to be discussions about irrelevant personal details or tangential issues often means a great deal to an Indonesian negotiator. In fact, it might be vital from the Indonesian perspective to have such discussions early on. Again, remember that people from low-context cultures like the United States generally do not want a lot of personal background before undertaking negotiations. It might even be fair to say that the goal is to end up with a contextless contract—one that is explicit and in writing. If this is the case, then spending enormous amounts of time to get to know the other party in the negotiation is not only unimportant but also possibly an impediment to reaching the goal. The general view of those from HC cultures such as Indonesia, China, Japan, or Mexico is often very different, and this explains why individuals from these cultures feel that it is important to spend a significant amount of time on nontask sounding. The personal and organizational information that they seek across various settings provides context that is critical for understanding messages in their culture. Table 4.3 summarizes this and other differences that might be observed between high- and low-context cultures in the nontask sounding stage.

The amount of time spent on what Americans might consider meaningless interaction can vary dramatically across cultures. And in HC cultures, it really does matter in ways that impact final outcomes. For example, one study showed that for Brazilian and Japanese negotiators, interpersonal comfort was much more likely to lead to outcomes that satisfied the negotiating partner than it was for Americans. This finding underscores the role of nontask sounding in building the personal relationships that are essential for successful negotiations in HC cultures.[37]

Table 4.3
Behavior in the Stages of Negotiation: Differences Across Low- and High-Context Cultures

Stage of Negotiation	Low-Context Culture	High-Context Culture
Stage 1: Nontask Sounding	■ Brief exchange of social niceties ■ Will get to the point (stage 3) quickly ■ Not especially concerned with status of other group	■ Will want to know all about the other parties and their companies ■ Long presentations, meetings to get to know other parties ■ Give careful attention to age, rank, status of other negotiators
Stage 2: Task-Related Exchange of Information	■ Relatively brief stage ■ Young, ambitious likely to do well	■ Among the longer stages ■ Advantage given to older, higher-status team members
Stage 3: Persuasion	■ Argumentative ■ Most important stage ■ To-the-point negotiating style ■ Cost-benefit approach; face saving not very important	■ Declarative ■ Least important stage ■ More guarded style ■ Face saving very important
Stage 4: Concession/ Agreement	■ Favor or require detailed written contract ■ Decision/agreement is impersonal ■ Profit motive determines agreement	■ Less emphasis on long contracts ■ Deal is sealed on the basis of the contextual variables ■ Good setting necessary for final agreements

But nontask sounding goes well beyond simply the time factor—the substance of that sounding also differs across cultures. Consider that information about the professional status of the participants is often sought out and is yet another sign of work being done during this getting-to-know-you stage. And some research suggests different approaches across cultures. For example, studies show that in LC cultures such as Australia or Canada, negotiations among those equal in status is more common than in HC cultures. Negotiators in the United States often downplay status in any number of ways (e.g., by using first names, dressing casually, and soliciting input from all team members). But in Mexico and many HC cultures, title and status are very important and interactions are more formal.[38] It would be rare, for example, for an HC negotiator to address the other party by his or her first name. For instance, the French are relatively HC and are aware of and attuned to status differences on negotiation teams; they prefer to negotiate with the head executive of the foreign company.[39] This is also an apparent preference among Japanese, Saudi, and Mexican negotiators, among others.[40]

Status or position provides background to upcoming negotiations for HC negotiators, but it is less important in LC cultures. To illustrate this point, one study had groups of English, French, Germans, and Americans participate in a simulated negotiation. The study found that the French (i.e., the highest-context country on average of the four groups participating) were most interested in, and affected by, the status of other negotiation team members. Another study involved observations from more than 700 business people from 11 different cultures. The cultures ranged from very LC (e.g., Germany, Switzerland, Sweden) to very HC (e.g., Korea, China, Taiwan). This study found that high status and personal relations mattered more to people from HC cultures. In Japan, for example, status distinctions can be based on age, gender, and relative position in the firm. So if you are older, male, and hold a position higher up in the firm, the odds are that it will impress a Japanese bargainer.[41] In the low-context United States, however, Americans often want to establish equality between people, even where it clearly does not exist.[42]

Stage 2: Task-Related Exchange

The previous section noted that a clash could occur among those who need to spend more time sounding out the other and those who need little such time. Let's assume, however, that this issue was overcome; if so, the negotiation might move on to the second phase. Here, the parties might begin an exchange of needs, interests, and preferences—an important step. In HC cultures such as some in the Middle East, long and in-depth explanations of the parties' initial bargaining positions should be expected. This exchange and the meetings that go along with it will be time-consuming, with many questions offered to the other party.

The long-term approach taken by HC cultures also means that you are likely to see an initial offer that is not very favorable. The belief is that a poor initial offer will leave plenty of room to maneuver in later stages of the negotiation process. This was verified in a study involving groups of businessmen from the United States, Japan, and Brazil who participated in simulated negotiations. The Japanese asked for higher profit outcomes in their initial offer than their U.S. and Brazilian counterparts. The U.S. negotiators, however, were more likely to offer a price that was closer to the eventual terms agreed upon by both parties. And the Americans and Brazilians were irritated at the Japanese for what were perceived as their greedy initial offers.

A second study with the same three cultural groups found that U.S. bargainers could reduce this irritation and improve their outcomes by stretching out this second stage of negotiations. In particular, the more that Americans encouraged information exchange from their bargaining partners—something that they typically shortchange—the better their financial outcomes were in the end.[43] This finding was underscored by a study of the negotiation transcripts of Japanese and U.S. businesspeople. Early first offers generated higher gains for the Japanese and lower ones for U.S. negotiators. But exchange of information prior to the first offer resulted in a turnaround of this effect—U.S. negotiators received higher gains.[44] In general, experts suggest that the probability of success in international negotiation increases as the negotiators are motivated to search for new information and are flexible in their approach during the process.[45] Time spent in this exchange phase, therefore, is time well spent. This is not new advice, yet data seem to show that LC negotiators still often give sparse attention to a detailed task-related information exchange—often dramatically less time than some from HC cultures. Instead, it has been said that a slight glance at the wristwatch is enough to move an American onto the next stage of negotiations. One reason for rushing through the task-related exchange is that they are anxious to get to the third stage.

Stage 3: Persuasion

The persuasion stage involves explicit attempts to modify each other's positions. To Americans, this is the most important step in the negotiating process and one that a lot of LC negotiators see as being at the heart of negotiation. But how the persuasion stage unfolds in other cultures may end up surprising many Americans, Finns, and Germans.

Consider the amount of time spent at this stage—LC negotiators expect to spend much more time here than their HC counterparts. This may be one reason they view the earlier stages as digressive and not of direct value. Other cultures, such as the Japanese, take the time to sound each other out earlier, and therefore they spend relatively less time engaging in the kind of overt persuasion that many Americans are used to. In some cases, a lot of persuasion just may not be necessary because of the time spent earlier.

Then there are the actual tactics used to persuade. As you might expect, many LC people believe that this stage is where the real negotiating takes place. Americans, for example, typically pay very close attention to the interactions that occur here. They will often compromise and make modifications to their initial bargaining position. Concessions are common throughout all stages of negotiations for most Americans. Unlike U.S. bargainers, however, Japanese negotiators tend to wait until toward the end of negotiations before making any concessions.[46] Consequently, Americans engaged in international negotiations may go too far and give too much away in an effort to compromise in this persuasion stage.[47] Interestingly, while Americans may be among the best in the world at compromising, the meaning of the word *compromise* and related terms can differ dramatically across cultures. In the Middle East, compromise carries with it many negative connotations (e.g., "his virtue was compromised"). The Farsi word for mediator translates to "meddler." And in many Latin cultures, such as in Mexico, compromise raises issues of personal honor and face and is touchy ground. Finally, conceding a point, even while receiving another, could suggest an influence of their will to a Russian that could lead to confrontational negotiation.[48]

In the persuasion stage, an LC negotiator is now ready to lay the cards on the table (another sign that this is where LC communicators believe the real negotiation takes place). Americans, for example, often give and expect to receive in return frank information during this stage of negotiations. Research has shown that Americans often believe that the ideal position for both parties should be put on the table. Then progress can be made—often on an issue-by-issue basis and often toward some kind of compromise. One study reported that Americans were more likely to share information directly with negotiation partners (e.g., "we pay suppliers $35 per subcomponent part and need to recover this cost") than were those from five other countries: Brazil, France, China, Japan, and Russia. Those from Russia, Japan, and China (Hong Kong) were more likely to use indirect strategies to communicate in negotiations (e.g., "supplier costs can be high and unpredictable").[49] Another study looked at the appropriateness of various bargaining methods and found that Americans were less likely to endorse tactics such as bluffing and feigning threats than were Brazilians. It is clear that cultural background impacts much of what goes into such a decision, including the larger legal environment, the firm's code of ethics, firm goals, and views of the other party.[50]

But being up front aside, this U.S. style often does not mesh well with the bargaining approaches used in other countries and cultures. Apparently, this U.S. approach to negotiation stems from an idealistic moral philosophy rather than a focus on the relative consequences of specific actions. For instance, Saudis tend to embrace a more relativist philosophy that affords them more freedom in their negotiating style.[51] Another example of this effect is when a Chinese negotiator makes sudden demands that he or she presents as nonnegotiable. Such demands often place Westerners at a disadvantage or throw them off if they are not well prepared.[52] Similarly, another study using a simulated bargaining session found that Chinese negotiators used more competitive approaches (such as persuasive communication, threats, etc.) and fewer cooperative methods (such as multiple offers/attempts, focus on long-term outcomes, etc.).[53] With some patience and flexibility, however, research shows that Americans might find that concessions will appear from the Chinese side and other HC negotiators, occasionally at the last minute.[54]

Table 4.4 presents some elements of what might be considered the stereotypic U.S. negotiating style. Many of these elements are relevant to the persuasion phase, but they can also operate in the other stages. Put simply, the prototypical U.S. style is that of the frontiersman or cowboy in the old West. These behaviors might work well within the United States, but these classic features of U.S. individualism can be received poorly in a foreign setting. Even in the United States it pays to be flexible and it is probably rare for any one successful negotiator to consistently use more than a couple of the behaviors presented in the table. After all, negotiation is by definition interdependent and some of the most successful negotiation training in LC countries is more long-term oriented with a focus on both parties benefiting (win-win).[55] Having said this, however, interdependence has not been a major emphasis in U.S. culture. Consideration of the behaviors comprising this U.S. stereotype in Table 4.4, whether completely accurate or not, can benefit potential negotiators.[56]

So what can happen when the typical U.S. negotiator meets another culture—say Japanese? Let's follow this through with some possible outcomes. First, Americans might quickly present a complex set of arguments. They may conclude their presentation with an offer that is not too far from what they eventually expect. The Japanese might be surprised by the abruptness of the offer but will probably consider it. They may know that Americans like to get to the point. What they may not know, however, is that the U.S. offer is pretty close to their ideal offer. In fact, almost everywhere else in the world, bargainers leave themselves plenty of room to maneuver. Accordingly, the Japanese may counter by asking for a lot, which makes perfect sense in light of what they typically do. But Americans may react angrily, something that can harden positions.[57] This is exactly what happened in another study based on a simulated negotiation session. U.S. negotiators initially asked for a fair price—one closer to their final offer—whereas Japanese negotiators initially asked for much higher profit options, a position that upset the Americans.[58] Nevertheless, Americans would probably press on by trying to deal with one issue at a time. But this could become another point of friction. The Japanese typically do not like dealing piecemeal with issues—this explains why their concessions are bunched toward the end of the negotiation process. Second, even if Americans are very persuasive, they may get a silent response—which the Americans may interpret as stonewalling. A cultural analysis shows the source of frustration here. The Americans may have used their on-the-spot latitude to grant a concession. But the Japanese may not have the same amount of discretion at their disposal. Instead,

Table 4.4
Some Elements of the Stereotypical U.S. Negotiating Style

U.S. Style	Prescriptions for Use in Other Countries
1. **Just call me John:** Americans downplay status and titles as well as other formalities such as lengthy introductions.	1. **Follow local customs:** U.S. informality is out of place in most other cultures; foreign clients are more comfortable when Americans follow their customs.
2. **Get to the point:** Americans want to dispense with the small talk and get down to business.	2. **Get down to business:** This is defined differently across cultures; getting to know the other party is important in many countries.
3. **Lay your cards on the table:** We expect honest information at the bargaining table ("You tell me what you want, and I'll tell you what I want").	3. **Hold something back:** Foreign executives seldom lay everything on the table; the negotiating process is expected to take time with concessions made along the way.
4. **Don't just sit there, speak up:** Americans don't deal well with silence: they get into trouble by feeling pressured to fill in silence with possible concessions.	4. **Silence can be a powerful negotiating tool:** Consider its use, but also be aware of its use against you.
5. **Don't take no for an answer:** Americans are taught to be persistent and not to give up; negotiation is mostly persuasion.	5. **Minds are often changed behind the scenes:** If an impasse is reached, ask more questions; take a recess; try a more subtle approach.
6. **One thing at a time:** Americans approach a negotiating task sequentially ("Let's settle the quantity issue first and then discuss price").	6. **Postpone concessions:** Wait until you've had a chance to get all issues on the table; don't measure progress by the number of issues that have been settled.
7. **A deal is a deal:** When Americans make an agreement, they give their word. They expect to honor the agreement no matter the circumstances.	7. **The meaning of commitment varies:** Commitment means different things in Tokyo, Rio, and Riyadh; deals—particularly new ones—are more uncertain than Americans are used to.

Source: Adapted from Graham, J. L., & Herberger, R. A. (1982). Negotiators abroad—Don't shoot from the hip. *Harvard Business Review,* July–August, 160–168.

the Japanese decision-making style is to take time among themselves to discuss an offer and, in the process, reach a consensus. This approach is more common in high-power-distance countries (e.g., Mexico, India, and Japan to a somewhat lesser degree). Consequently, the Japanese negotiators are not likely to react immediately to an offer.[59]

If they are frustrated at this point, Americans may counter with a very aggressive tactic. They might tell the Japanese, "If you can't lower your price, we'll just go with another supplier." This may be the worst thing the Americans could do, because the directness of this approach might offend the Japanese. This option is much better presented through a third party. Or the Americans might be a little more indirect while still getting across the point (e.g., "lowering per-unit prices on your part would go a long way toward our not having to consider other options.") Other tactics, such as repeating the explanation of your position, asking questions, playing dumb, or even silence, also can be effective.[60]

Indirect approaches, however, are neither the first choice nor a forte of Americans. Yet, in dealing with others from around the world, indirectness works. Consider this situation: You are with a U.S. firm that has a contract with a Chinese manufacturer of bicycles. You have received convincing data that this producer has had some quality problems in the past and that the bikes in your order have an annoying rattle. The bulk of the order is supposed to ship to Hong Kong next week. What option would you choose?

A. You fly tomorrow to the plant to see the quality problem yourself. You tell the plant manager that the rattling has to be fixed before shipping.
B. You go to the plant and test some bikes. You take the plant manager for a ride near the factory and afterward ask: "Do all the bikes rattle? Will the rattling be a problem for buyers?" And then you leave.[61]

If you are like most Americans, your gut probably told you to choose option A. This brief but true story actually ended well when the American took the indirect approach (option B). Gently asking about the buyer's view helped—the bikes arrived on time with no rattle. This indirect confrontation is more common in collectivist cultures; it does not imply blame or make the problem personal. The issue does not morph from a problem with rattling *bikes* to the *people* who made the rattling bikes. For those from HC cultures, this indirect approach effectively leaves personalities out of the equation—it gets across the message without communicating disrespect. This tendency to be flexible in style is something that defines what some experts call a culturally intelligent negotiator. Researchers measured cultural intelligence prior to a negotiation and found that it was related to measures such as joint profit increases for both sides. This concept has a great deal of promise in the area of international negotiation.[62]

Stage 4: Agreement

As the heading says, often negotiations result in an agreement being reached. But in most cultures, an agreement is only as good as the follow-through. In other words, all the considerable time and effort you invest in the previous three stages could be wasted if both parties do not behave in ways that are consistent with the agreement. Recognizing this fact, it is common for firms embracing an LC culture to insist that formal contracts be signed that bind each party to details of the agreement. As common as this might seem to someone from such a culture, signing a contract is sometimes resisted in HC cultures. Or, if a contract is signed, it is not seen as written in stone but continually negotiable. Instead, they hope that the ties that they spent so much time building and strengthening in the earlier stages of the process will now pay off. The hope is that the general trust established in the nontask sounding stage will allow a much more general agreement to be operational for each party.[63] As you might guess, most firms nowadays expect a lengthy formal contract to be requested if they are negotiating with U.S. or other culturally similar companies. But, others, such as the Chinese, prefer broad agreements about general principles rather than a long, meticulous contracts Some say the Chinese want broad agreements because they believe that if all parties agree to the principles, the details can be worked out later by people of good intention.[64] Conversely, Americans and other Westerners often take the position that if trust exists, then the Chinese should be willing to make clear commitments. Who is right probably depends on the specific case. One thing, however, is certain: Americans tend to slight the process of establishing broad principles. To Americans, these principles are similar to the corporate philosophies that are all the rage these days—they are nice words, but in practice they can be unimportant, if not meaningless. Oddly, research shows that U.S. firms are more likely to have such ethical codes, with negotiation stipulations included, than some of their foreign partners and competition.

What many Americans fail to realize, however, is that these principles are the standards that the Chinese use to evaluate future agreements. As a result, Americans often consent to them with little input. Ultimately, this may be the right thing to do anyway, since general items can be interpreted to support your position. Nevertheless, experts recommend that Western firms provide serious input into this process, including laying out their ideas on business concepts such as quality products, profit, and shareholder return instead of just going through the motions.[65] Table 4.5 summarizes some common features observed across five sample countries in the stages of negotiation and beyond.

An agreement is only good if it is kept. Whether other parties live up to their end of the agreement depends, at least in part, on the potential long-term impact. This impact, in turn, is determined by the trust we have in the other parties and our satisfaction with the agreement. Making sure the other parties feel they also got a good deal, therefore, pays off in the long run.[66] Global competition is so fierce today that general principles are probably worth abiding by in order to communicate effectively and negotiate a lasting agreement.

Table 4.5
Examples of Differences in Negotiating Features in Five Countries

Element of Negotiation	China	Germany	Country Japan	Saudi Arabia	United States
Nontask Sounding (rapport)	Extensive time spent in this stage; very useful for progress in latter stages	Short time period; little weight placed on this stage; time is of the essence	Extensive time period; rely on this information in latter stages	Long period; until trust established; hospitable and gracious; status important	Very short; little weight; can be bothered by length of this stage
Exchange of information	Arguments presented, but more generally and indirectly	Presentation of logical arguments; details reviewed	Extensive; emphasis on receiving and gathering information	Less emphasis on technical elements; more emphasis on background information	Systematic and large volume; emphasis on providing
Persuasion	Conducted with combination of flexibility and firmness	Considered counterarguments and ready to rebut; will tell you your proposal stinks	Reviewing points, sometimes several times	Use of go-betweens most effective; emphasis on interpersonal treatment	Put cards on the table in this stage; expect others to as well; frank about negotiation elements
Close approach	Decisions made outside negotiation room	Don't concede easily; look for common ground	Flexibility more evident between meetings; won't be rushed; team consensus	Team makes recommendation to senior manager	Flexibility, as representatives often provided with on-the-spot discretion over negotiations.
Postagreement	Look to satisfy general principles of mutual interest	Stick to what they agreed; details important	Expect both parties to live up to spirit and letter of agreement	Personal relationships are the key to success	Expect to live by specific contractual conditions and requirements on both sides
Typical number involved	Larger number, with a senior leader	Small number	Teams often represent different functional areas; membership can grow	Small to medium number of participants	Small team

CHAPTER SUMMARY

Conflict seems to occur all too often across the globe, so much so that some experts believe it is inevitable. Thus, it is important to understand the cause of conflict across borders and cultures. Important causes of conflict include varying cultural norms, decision-making styles, and the characteristic cultural tendency to engage in or avoid conflict in the first place. Understanding conflict is important and can head off its occurrence in cross-cultural business settings; yet if it is so common, prevention itself will not suffice. We need ways to reduce conflict once it does raise its head. There are many different styles that people in a number of cultures use to deal with conflict issues once they arise. An important way to avoid, or at least minimize, conflict is through negotiation. A four-stage model was presented as a way to present key cross-cultural differences that occur in the negotiation process. Different cultures put varying levels of importance on each stage. These stages include: (1) nontask sounding, (2) task-related exchange of information, (3) persuasion, and (4) agreement. Even if you complete the last stage, an agreement is only as good as the actions of each partner.

DISCUSSION QUESTIONS

1. List and briefly explain as many negative aspects to cross-cultural conflict as you can think of. Can you also think of some positive impacts of conflict that might result from cultural interaction?

2. How might each of the following characteristically deal with conflict? What is the typical style of each, and what are the parts of the style that might rub the other cultures the wrong way?
- Asians
- Latinos/Latinas
- Middle Easterners
- North Americans

3. What would you guess is the perceived order of importance of each of the four stages of negotiation for the following:
- an American
- a Mexican
- a Saudi

4. If you have traveled to a foreign country, try to determine the typical style in that country—what stages might be emphasized there?

Developing Your International Career

CHARACTERISTIC NEGOTIATION STYLES AROUND THE GLOBE

Purpose and Instructions

The purpose of this exercise is to become knowledgeable about how people in different cultures and countries negotiate as well as why they seem to prefer a particular style. The answers to the why question can help avoid difficulty in negotiation or, if it occurs, can help you manage your way out of that trouble.

For this exercise, your instructor will divide you into small groups of two to five people. A member of each group will pull a note from a hat to select a culture or country to study. This will ensure that a large number of cultures will be investigated. In meetings outside of class with your group, split up the research work that you will need to do. In particular, please work to find at least three important cultural values that are said to characterize your country. Try to find some specific behaviors that follow from these values—behaviors you could observe if you visited that country. These values and behaviors may drive some of the negotiation tactics used by businesspeople in your assigned culture. Try to list as many of these as you can while you tie them to underlying cultural values.

Several websites might be useful in your research. Your instructor might suggest sites at which to find information. Consider the following:

- *Global Negotiator* (www.globalnegotiator.com/). This is a useful site for those interested in studying cross-cultural negotiation. It reviews more than 50 countries and provides specific information regarding country characteristics and values that might impact negotiation.
- *U.S. Department of State Country Background Notes* (www.state.gov). Like most pages maintained by the Department of State, this one is informative and well organized and can provide a good bit of useful background information for this assignment.
- *The Economist Country Profiles* (www.economist.com/countries/). *The Economist* magazine is well known, but its Intelligence Unit—while less well known—is an invaluable resource for anyone interested in international business.
- *CIA World Factbook* (https://www.cia.gov/library/publications/the-world-factbook/). This is a complete and detailed source of information about all countries on the globe—useful for this exercise and others as well.

Based on your research, each group should:

- Meet to discuss the cultural values of your location and some of the possible behaviors these values might produce in a negotiation setting.
- Make some predictions about how negotiators from that culture act as a result.

- Make predictions about how this style might mesh with those of business people from the United States (or your own home country).
- Finally, come up with a strategic negotiating response for each of the predicted negotiating behaviors.

Your instructor might ask your group to present its research findings and suggested negotiating strategy in class or in a written report.

Source: Adapted from Whatley, A. (1979). *Training for the Cross-Cultural Mind*. Washington, DC: SIETAR.

Making the Case for International Understanding

CONFLICT CROSSES THE BORDER: NEGOTIATIONS BETWEEN MEXICANS AND AMERICANS[67]

Two companies were vying for a lucrative contract from the Mexican government. Both firms—one from the United States and one from Sweden—had already jumped several hurdles to get the business. Each was invited to Mexico City to present proposals to ministry officials and start the process of negotiating the terms of the proposed deal.

The Americans put a lot of effort into producing an impressive high-tech and hard-hitting presentation, working hard to assemble a team of senior technical experts, lawyers, and interpreters from the New York office. Their bottom line was clear: "We can give you the most technically advanced equipment at a price the others can't match." The team met several times with senior management before the presentation to discuss possible concessions, and they were given latitude to make decisions on the spot if need be. The team flew to Mexico City for a week and stayed at one of the top hotels in the city.

Arrangements for a fancy hotel conference room were made so that they could make the best possible presentation to the ministry officials. In a demonstration of due diligence and to impress their potential customer, they brought all the necessary equipment with them and had mailed outlines of the presentation to officials two weeks ahead of time. They also proposed a detailed schedule and other arrangements in a memo to the officials along with the presentation. The Mexican officials dutifully thanked the Americans for their information and said they looked forward to meeting with them and finding out more about their proposal and their firm. They provided information about the history of their agency and the top members of the current ministry.

The Americans arrived early the day before the meeting to avoid problems with their flight. And all team members met at the conference room very early to set it up and make sure all was a go for the meeting later that day. Finally, at the agreed time, the Americans were all ready to present and impress. Unfortunately, the Mexican ministry officials were not—in fact, no one from the ministry was there yet! Instead, various ministry officials arrived gradually over the next hour. They offered no apologies to the perplexed Americans, but instead began to chat amiably about a variety of non–contract-related matters. The U.S. team leader was feeling pressure from both the situation and his team members— should he act leaderly and get the meeting organized, or should he let the Mexican officials provide the right signal? Finally, after about an hour of glancing at his watch and scanning nervously, the team leader assertively suggested that the meeting should start. The Mexicans seemed surprised but politely agreed and took their seats that were set up ahead of time by the Americans.

The presentation began with informal introductions of the team members by the presenter. The presentation itself was flawlessly delivered, thanks to endless practice. About 20 minutes into the presentation, the minister himself, with an entourage of other officials, walked in. When he figured out what was going on, his demeanor turned unpleasant. Angrily, he asked the Americans to start the presentation over. They complied and started again. Once more, the presentation was going for about 10 minutes, and then an aide arrived with a message for the minister that was delivered in hushed tones. Not wanting to anger him again, the U.S. presenter stopped to wait until the message was delivered. But the minister signaled for him to continue, so he did. A few minutes later, a number of audience members were talking among themselves. By this time, the Americans were frustrated, but they slogged on and finished. At the end, when the audience was invited to ask questions, the minister's only comment was to wonder why the Americans had focused so much on the technical details—why had they told the Mexicans so little about their firm's history?

Later during lunch, the Americans felt that they had to be very forceful about keeping the conversation focused on the topic at hand—the contract and any outstanding issues or problems they could address. Most of the conversation was again seemingly casual, having little or nothing to do with the business at hand—not unlike what happened earlier during the presentation. The Americans were surprised by the many questions about their individual backgrounds and personal experience—including their qualifications. The minister breezed in during the lunch, had a brief but casual conversation with the U.S. team leader, and then left, not to return.

Over the next several days of their time in Mexico City, the Americans repeatedly contacted the Mexican officials for follow-up. Were there additional questions about the specs? How about the technical features of their implementation? What were the initial reactions? Was more information needed? They reminded ministry officials of the schedule they shared ahead of time and the fact that they needed to return to New York soon. In short, they wished to start the negotiation process. The Mexican response was the same to all these forays throughout the rest of the week: "We need time to examine your proposal among ourselves here first." The Americans got more and more angry; at the end of the week, this turned to plain frustration. After all, the ministry officials had had the proposal for several weeks before the meeting and had multiple opportunities for elaboration of the specs and other elements. The team left Mexico empty-handed. Later they found that the contract was awarded to the Swedish firm.

ASSIGNMENT QUESTIONS

1. Summarize how the reactions of each side may have been influenced by cultural differences, including the culture issues at work here and the typical Mexican and U.S. approaches to this issue. Put differently, what is your diagnosis of the problems here and the reasons for the breakdown in the process.
2. Provide suggestions about how each side could respond better and adapt to the other side in a more functional way.
3. How could each side have been better prepared for the negotiation?
4. Given the problems that emerged, what could the parties have done to keep them to a minimum or reduce their impact so that process could be made? Could the Americans have done anything to salvage the situation—even after the minister took offense.

NOTES

1. Saner, R., Yiu, L., & Sondergaard, M. (2000). Business diplomacy management: A core competency for global managers. *Academy of Management Executive*, 14, 80–92.
2. Thomas, K. W., & Schmidt, W. H. (1976). A survey of managerial interests with respect to conflict. *Academy of Management Journal*, 10, 315–318.
3. Ricks, D. A. (1983). *Big Business Blunders: Mistakes in Multinational Marketing.* Homewood, IL: Dow Jones Irwin.
4. Alon, I., & Brett, J. M. (2007). Perceptions of time and their impact on negotiations in the Arabic-speaking Islamic world. *Negotiation Journal*, January, 55 73.
5. McCann, R. M., & Giles, H. (2006). Communication with people of different ages in the workplace: Thai and American data. *Human Communication Research*, 32, 74–108.
6. Thomas, K. W. (1976). Conflict and conflict management. In M. D. Dunnette (ed.), *Handbook of Industrial and Organizational Behavior* (889–935). Chicago: Rand McNally.
7. Prunty, A. M., Klopf, D. W., & Ishii, S. (1990). Argumentativeness: Japanese and American tendencies to approach and avoid conflict. *Communication Research Reports*, 7, 75–79.
8. Klopf, D. W. (1991). Japanese communication practices: Recent comparative research. *Communication Quarterly*, 39, 130–143.
9. Niikura, R. (1999). Assertiveness among Japanese, Malaysians, Filipino, and US white collar workers. *Journal of Social Psychology*, 139, 690–699; Fao, A., Hashimoto, K., & Rao, A. (1997). Universal and culturally specific aspects of managerial influence: A study of Japanese managers. *Leadership Quarterly*, 8, 295–312.
10. Holt, J. L., & DeVore, C. J. (2005). Culture, gender, organizational role, and styles of conflict resolution: A meta-analysis. *International Journal of Intercultural Relations*, 29, 165–196; Ting-Toomey, S., Gao, G., Trubinsky, P., Yang, Z., Kim, H. S., Lin, S. L., & Nishida, T. (1991). Culture, face maintenance, and styles of handling interpersonal conflict: A study in five cultures. *International Journal of Conflict Management*, 2, 275–296; Tse, D. K., Francis, J., &

Walls, J. (1994). Cultural differences in conducting intra- and inter-cultural negotiations: A Sino-Canadian comparison. *Journal of International Business Studies*, Autumn, 537–555.

11. Leung, K. (1988). Some determinants of conflict avoidance. *Journal of Cross-Cultural Psychology*, 19, 125–136.

12. Posthuma, R. A., White, G. O., Dworkin, J. B., Yanez, O., & Swift, M. S. (2006). Conflict resolution styles between co-workers in US and Mexican cultures. *International Journal of Conflict Management*, 17, 242–260; Tinsley, C. H., & Brett, J. M. (2001). Managing workplace conflict in the United States and Hong Kong. *Organizational Behavior and Human Decision Processes*, 85, 360–381; Morris, M. W., Williams, K. Y., Leung, K., Larrick, R., Mendoza, M. T., Bhatnagar, D., Li, J., Kando, M., Luo, J. L., & Hu, J. C. (1998). Conflict management style: Accounting for cross-national differences. *Journal of International Business Studies*, 29, 729–748; Kirkbride, P. S., Tang, S. F. Y., & Westwood, R. I. (1991). Chinese conflict preferences and negotiating behavior: Cultural and psychological influences. *Organization Studies*, 12, 365–386.

13. Tinsley, C. H., & Brett, J. M. (2001). Models of conflict resolution in Japanese, German, and American cultures. *Journal of Applied Psychology*, 83, 316–323.

14. Brew, F. P., & Cairns, D. R. (2005). Styles of managing interpersonal workplace conflict in relation to status and face concern: A study with Anglos and Chinese. *International Journal of Conflict Management*, 15, 27–56.

15. Cheng, C., & Chun, W. Y. (2008). Cultural differences and similarities in request rejection: A situational approach. *Journal of Cross-Cultural Psychology*, 39, 745–764. See also Gelfand, M. J., Major, V. S., Raver, J. L., Nishii, L. H., & O'Brien, K. (2006). Negotiating relationally: The dynamics of the relational self in negotiations. *Academy of Management Review*, 31, 427–451; Ohbuchi, K. I., Fukushima, O., & Tedeschi, J. T. (1999). *Journal of Cross-Cultural Psychology*, 30, 51–71.

16. Kozan, M. K. (1989). Cultural influences on styles of handling interpersonal conflicts: Comparisons among Jordanian, Turkish, and U.S. managers. *Human Relations*, 42, 787–799.

17. Brett, J. M., Tinsley, C. H., Shapiro, D. L., & Okumura, T. (2007). Intervening in employee disputes: How and when will managers from China, Japan, and the USA act differently? *Management and Organization Review*, 3, 183–204.

18. Leung, K., & Iwawaki, S. (1988). Cultural collectivism and distributive behavior. *Journal of Cross-Cultural Psychology*, 19, 35–49.

19. McFarlin, D. B., & Sweeney, P. D. (2001). Cross-cultural applications of organizational justice. In R. Cropanzano (ed.), *Justice in the Workplace: From Theory to Practice*, Vol. 2 (67–95.). Mahwah, NJ: Lawrence Erlbaum.

20. Victor, D. A. (1992). *International Business Communication*. New York: HarperCollins.

21. Ting-Toomey, S. (1990). *A Face Negotiation Perspective Communicating for Peace*. Thousand Oaks, CA: Sage; Cardon, P. W. (2009). A model of face practices in Chinese business culture: Implications for Western businesspersons. *Thunderbird International Business Review*, January/February, 51, 19–36.

22. Redding, S. G., & Ng, M. (1983). The role of "face" in the organizational perceptions of Chinese managers. *International Studies of Management and Organization*, 11, 92–123; Ho, D. Y. (1994). Face dynamics: From conceptualization to measurement. In S. Ting-Toomey (ed.), *The Challenge of Facework: Cross-Cultural and Interpersonal Issues* (269–286). Albany: State University of New York Press; Cardon, P. W. (2006). Reacting to face loss in Chinese business culture: An interview report. *Business Communication Quarterly*, December, 439–443.

23. Reeder, J. A. (1987). When West meets East: Cultural aspects of doing business in Asia. *Business Horizons*, January–February, 69–74.

24. Schulz, A. K. D., Salter, S. B., Lopez, J. C., & Lewis, P. A. (2009). Reevaluating face: A note on differences in private information sharing between two communitarian societies. *Journal of International Accounting Research*, 8, 57–65.

25. Reeder, J. A. (1987). When West meets East: Cultural aspects of doing business in Asia. *Business Horizons*, January–February, 69–74.

26. Reeder, J. A. (1987). When East meets West: Cultural aspects of doing business in Asia. *Business Horizons*, January–February, 69–74.

27. Tinsley, C. H., & Weldon, E. (2003). Responses to normative conflict among American and Chinese Managers. *International Journal of Cross-Cultural Management*, 3, 183–194.

28. Fu, H. Y., Morris, M. W., Lee, S., & Chiu, C. Y. (2002). Why do individuals follow cultural scripts? A dynamic constructivist account of American–Chinese differences in choice of mediators to resolve conflict. *Academy of Management Proceedings*, D1–D6.

29. Fu, H. Y., Morris, M. W., Lee, S., & Chiu, C. Y. (2002). Why do individuals follow cultural scripts? A dynamic constructivist account of American–Chinese differences in choice of mediators to resolve conflict. *Academy of Management Proceedings*, D1–D6.

30. Weiss, S. E. (1996). International negotiations: Bricks, mortar, and prospects. In B. J. Punnett & O. Shenkar (eds.), *Handbook for International Management Research* (209–265). Cambridge, MA: Blackwell.

31. Weiss, S. E. (2006). International business negotiation in a globalizing world: Reflections on the contributions and future of a (sub) field. *International Negotiation*, 11, 287–316.

32. Sebenius, J. K. (2002). The hidden challenge of cross-border negotiations. *Harvard Business Review*, March, 76–85; Graham, J. L. (1983). Brazilian, Japanese, and American business negotiations. *Journal of International Business Studies*, 14, 47–62; Weiss, S. E. (1996). International negotiations: Bricks, mortar, and prospects. In B. J. Punnett & O. Shenkar, *Handbook for International Management Research* (209–265). Cambridge, MA: Blackwell.

33. See a special issue of the journal *International Negotiation* published in 2004 and edited by William Zartman (Vol. 8, issue 3 of the journal) that was focused on terrorism and features about such crimes. In particular, background information on negotiating with terrorists, especially in regard to hostages, was based on Faure, G. O. (2004). Negotiating with terrorists: The hostage case. *International Negotiation*, 8, 469–494.

34. Giebels, E., & Taylor, P. J. (2009). Interaction patterns in crisis negotiations: Persuasive arguments and cultural differences. *Journal of Applied Psychology*, 94, 5–19; Salacuse, J. (2009). Negotiating: The top ten ways that culture can affect your negotiations. *Ivey Business Journal*, September/October, 1–6.

35. Graham, J. L., & Sano, Y. (1986). Across the negotiation table from the Japanese. *International Marketing Review*, 3, 58–71.

36. Graham, J. L. (1985). The influence of culture on the process of business negotiations: An exploratory study. *Journal of International Business Studies*, 16, 81–96.

37. Graham, J. L., & Mintu-Wimsat, A. (1997). Culture's influence on business negotiations in four countries. *Group Decision and Negotiation*, 6, 483–502; Li, J., & Labig, C. E. (2001). Negotiating with Chinese: Exploratory study of relationship building. *Journal of Managerial Issues*, 13, 342–348.

38. Herbig, P. A., & Kramer, H. E. (1992). Dos and don'ts of cross-cultural negotiations. *Industrial Marketing Management*, 21, 287–298.

39. Banthin, J., & Steizer, L. (1988/1989). "Opening" China: Negotiation strategies when East meets West. *Mid-Atlantic Journal of Business*, 25, 1–14; Tung, R. L. (1982). U.S.–China trade negotiations: Practices, procedures, and outcomes. *Journal of International Business Studies*, Fall, 25–37.

40. Campbell, N. C. G., Graham, J. L., Jolibert, A., & Meissner, H. G. (1988). Marketing negotiations in France, Germany, the United Kingdom, and the United States. *Journal of Marketing*, 52, 49–62; Tung, How to negotiate with the Japanese. *California Management Review*, 26, 62–77.

41. Trompenaars, F., & Hampden-Turner, C. (1998). *Riding the Waves of Culture: Understanding Diversity in Global Business*. New York: McGraw-Hill.

42. Campbell, N. C. G., Graham, J. L., Jolibert, A., & Meissner, H. G. (1988). Marketing negotiations in France, Germany, the United Kingdom, and the United States. *Journal of Marketing*, 52, 49–62; Graham, J. L., Mintu, A. T., & Rodgers, W. (1994). Explorations of negotiation behaviors in ten foreign cultures using a model developed in the United States. *Management Science*, 40, 72–95.

43. Graham, J. L. (1983). Brazilian, Japanese, and American business negotiations. *Journal of International Business Studies*, 14, 47–62; Tung, R, (1984). How to negotiate with the Japanese. *California Management Review*, 26, 62–77.

44. Adair, W., Weingart, L., & Brett, J. (2007). The timing and function of offers in U.S. and Japanese negotiations. *Journal of Applied Psychology*, 92, 1056–1068; Adair, W., Brett, J., Lempereur, A., Okumura, T., Shikhirev, P., Tinsley, C., & Lytle, A. (2004). Culture and negotiation strategy. *Negotiation Journal*, January, 87–111.

45. Brett, J. M. (2000). Culture and negotiation. *International Journal of Psychology*, 35, 97–104.

46. Graham, J. L. (1988). Negotiating with the Japanese: A guide to persuasive tactics (Parts I and II). *East Asian Executive Reports*, 10, November v. 6, 19–21; December v. 8, 16–17.

47. Barnum, C., & Wolniansky, N. (1989). Why Americans fail at overseas negotiations. *Management Review*, October, 56–57.

48. Herbig, P. A., & Kramer, H. E. (1992). Dos and don'ts of cross-cultural negotiations. *Industrial Marketing Management*, 21, 287–298.

49. Adair, W., Brett, J., Lempereur, A., Okumura, T., Shikhirev, P., Tinsley, C., & Lytle, A. (2004). Culture and negotiation strategy. *Negotiation Journal*, January, 87–111.

50. Volkema, R. J. (1999). Ethicality in negotiations: An analysis of perceptual similarities and differences between Brazil and the United States. *Journal of Business Research*, 45, 59–67; Rivers, C. (2009). Negotiating with the Chinese: EANTs and all. *Thunderbird International Business Review*, 51, 473–489; Rivers, C., & Lytle, A. (2007). Lying, cheating foreigners!! Negotiation ethics across cultures. *International Negotiation*, 12, 1–28; Ma, Z. (2010). The SINS in business negotiations: Explore the cross-cultural differences in business ethics between Canada and China. *Journal of Business Ethics*, 91, 123–135.

51. Al-Khatib, J. A., Malshe, A., & AbdulKader, M. (2008). Perception of unethical negotiation tactics: A comparative study of US and Saudi managers. *International Business Review*, 17, 78–102.

52. Stewart, S., & Keown, C. F. (1989). Talking with the dragon: Negotiating in the People's Republic of China. *Columbia Journal of World Business*, 24, 68–72.

53. Liu, M. (2009). The intrapersonal and interpersonal effects of anger on negotiation strategies: A cross-cultural investigation. *Human Communication Research*, 35, 148–169.

54. Sheer, V. C., & Chen, L. (2003). Successful Sino-Western business negotiation: Participants' accounts of national and professional cultures. *Journal of Business Communication*, 40, 50–85; Weiss, J. (1988). The negotiating style of the People's Republic of China: The future of Hong Kong and Macao. *Journal of Social, Political and Economic Studies*, 13, 175–194.

55. Fisher, R., & Ury, W. (1982). *Getting to Yes: Negotiating Agreements without Giving In*. New York: Random House.

56. Graham, J. L., & Herberger, R. A. Negotiators abroad—Don't shoot from the hip. *Harvard Business Review*, July–August, 160–168.

57. Liu, M. (2009). The intrapersonal and interpersonal effects of anger on negotiation strategies: A cross-cultural investigation. *Human Communication Research*, 35, 148–169.

58. Graham, J. L. (1985). The influence of culture on the process of business negotiations: An exploratory study. *Journal of International Business Studies*, 16, 81–96; Graham, J. L., & Herberger, R. A. Negotiators abroad—Don't shoot from the hip. *Harvard Business Review*, July–August, 160–168.

59. Graham, J. L. (1988). Negotiating with the Japanese: A guide to persuasive tactics (Parts I & II). *East Asian Executive Reports*, 10, November v. 6, 19–21; December v. 8, 16–17; Graham, J. L., & Herberger, R. A. Negotiators abroad—don't shoot from the hip. *Harvard Business Review*, July–August, 160–168.

60. Graham, J. L. (1988). Negotiating with the Japanese: A guide to persuasive tactics (Parts I & II). *East Asian Executive Reports*, 10, November v. 6, 19–21; December v. 8, 16–17.

61. Negotiation scenario taken from Brett, J. M., & Gelfand, M. J. (2005). Lessons from abroad: When culture affects negotiating style. *Negotiation*, January, 3–5.

62. Brett, J. M., & Gelfand, M. J. (2005). Lessons from abroad: When culture affects negotiating style. *Negotiation*, January, 3–5; Imai, L., & Gelfand, M. J. (2010). The culturally intelligent negotiator: The impact of cultural intelligence (CQ) on negotiation sequences and outcomes. *Organizational Behavior and Human Decision Processes*, 112, 83–98.

63. Oh, T. K. (1984). Selling to the Japanese. *Nation's Business*, October, 37–38.

64. Banthin, J., & Steizer, L. (1988/1989). "Opening" China: Negotiation strategies when East meets West. *Mid-Atlantic Journal of Business*, 25, 1–14.

65. Pettibone, P. J. (1990). Negotiating a joint venture in the Soviet Union: How to protect your interests. *Journal of European Business*, 2, 5–12; Choi, C. J. (1994). Contract enforcement across cultures. *Organization Studies*, 15, 673–682.

66. Adler, N. J., Graham, J. L., & Gehrke, T. S. (1987). Business negotiations in Canada, Mexico, and the United States. *Journal of Business Research*, 15, 411–429.

67. Fox, C. (2006). International negotiator. *British Journal of Administrative Management*, June/July, 20–22; Posthuma, R. A., White, G. O., Dworkin, J. B., Yanez, O., & Swift, M. S. (2006). Conflict resolution styles between co-workers in U.S. and Mexican cultures. *International Journal of Conflict Management*, 17, 242–260; Heydenfeldt, J. A. G. (2000). The influence of individualism/collectivism on Mexican and U.S. business negotiation. *International Journal of Intercultural Relations*, 24, 383–407. See also www.globalnegotiationresources.com/cou/Mexico.pdf.

Part 2

Leading People and Teams Across Cultural Boundaries

Motivating Employees Across Cultures

Character consists of what you do on the third and fourth tries.

—John Michener

To handle yourself, use your head; to handle others, use your heart.

—Donald Laird

If you put good people in bad systems you get bad results. You have to water the flowers you want to grow.

—Stephen Covey

As illustrated by the collection of quotes above, there are some wide differences in views about motivation. Some people believe that motivation is all about effort or persistence (Michener). Some people believe that it has a lot to do with the ability to inspire others (Laird), whereas yet others believe that structure can impede or foster inherently high motivation (Covey). If anything can be confidently said about motivation, it is this: there is no dearth of thinking about it. There are people all over the globe thinking and theorizing about motivation. As a result, there are many different perspectives about what gets people motivated or disheartened.

ONE SIZE FITS SOME

This great amount of attention to the topic underscores what most people think about motivation—that it is an important topic and companies need motivated employees to succeed.[1] Ultimately, motivation might have been most accurately described by Dwight Eisenhower: "Motivation is the art of getting people to do what you want them to do because they want to do it."[2] This focus on the outcome of motivation might be the most common perspective. It is one thing to recognize this general point, though, and it is quite another to implement a motivation program. The devil, quite often, is in the details. As a result, the issue of *how* to motivate employees can be a frustrating exercise for many managers.

MOTIVATION ACROSS BORDERS

Motivating across borders or cultural contexts complicates matters and makes motivation an even bigger challenge. And, while you would be able to find plenty of advice for U.S. and some Western audiences, cross-cultural recommendations are harder to come by and tougher to apply. Western approaches to motivation typically reflect person-focused and goal-driven beliefs—features that created and shaped those cultures in the first place. This, in turn, may severely limit their applicability among employees who embrace different values. Many experts believe that the features that produce motivated employees, as well as how those employees respond to direction and feedback along the way, may vary dramatically along cultural lines.[3] Views about the very nature of work can vary greatly. Some feel that work is a money-for-effort transaction, while others see it as an inherent good in and of itself, with still others viewing work as an opportunity to be part of something important. While many unanswered questions remain about the way motivation works across cultures, one thing is clear: what works in one place is unlikely to work well everywhere, at least not without some adaptation.[4]

It is useful to first explain how culture may limit the applicability of popular Western approaches to motivation. To be effective, managers need to know which motivation strategy works best for their employees and what sort of culture-specific adaptation might be required (assuming a perspective is effective at all in a particular culture).[5] Few cross-cultural universals exist when it comes to motivation. Even if the notion of what motivates extends across borders, the way in which managers implement a merit pay system, for example, sometimes has to be tweaked to match local cultural norms. Research shows that managers in most countries would prefer to rely less on formal authority and more on trust and intrinsic factors to motivate their employees.[6] Employees everywhere want to be trusted by their superiors and fairly compensated. But *how* managers should delegate authority, build trust, and define fair pay may vary considerably from place to place.[7] Not surprisingly, cultural values also may have a big impact on leadership styles, a related topic addressed in the next chapter.

International managers must understand how cultures can shape employee motivation in a given country and then be able to gauge employee response to a particular program within that country, within that company. Complicating everything is that some experts believe that cultures and countries are constantly in the process of changing and adapting. And, importantly, approaches to motivation that run counter to the prevailing culture may still work, especially if given enough time or if focused on a receptive segment of the population. For example, Japan is now aging at a faster rate than any country in history. The working-age population will shrink so quickly that by 2050, it will be smaller than it was in 1950, before Japan's economic boom that saw it rise to the world's second largest economy. Younger people are now more likely to lose out on better jobs held by older citizens and are said to want to live more in the moment than for the future.[8] This will likely impact motivational methods commonly used in Japan, if it has not already. International managers may also face important regional differences in values *within* countries that impact motivation and business performance.[9]

WESTERN MOTIVATION CONCEPTS APPLIED TO OTHER CULTURES

Now we will look at some motivational theories that have been popular and widely applied in workplaces throughout the United States and other Western companies.

In particular, we will examine the cross-cultural applicability and limitations of these popular approaches.[10] Content-based theories are outlooks that focus on the substance of employees' thinking as the key driver of motivation. Two examples of these content perspectives are Maslow's *hierarchy of needs* and Herzberg's *two-factor theory*—both of which focus on explaining what needs and thoughts actually energize employee behavior.

Process-based theories are viewpoints that focus on how motivation unfolds over time and the processes involved. As might be expected, experts disagree on what the most important process is, so there are many competing approaches. Process theories are much preferred by practicing managers because they specify steps for increasing motivation. They can be retraced and fixed if something goes wrong. It is harder to do the same, however, when considering the content of people's thought. Three of the most popular process theories help explain this viewpoint: the reward process (*reinforcement theory*), interpretations about rewards and goals (*expectancy theory*), and the fairness of organizational rewards and outcomes (*equity theory*).

Maslow's Hierarchy of Needs

Psychologist Abraham Maslow claimed that we are all motivated by five distinct needs. These needs are organized in pyramid-like structure in our heads and we pursue them sequentially.[11] At the bottom of the pyramid are the most basic, physiological needs such as food and shelter. Once these needs are met, by earning a decent wage for example, then employees set their sights higher. They now become motivated by safety needs, such as life insurance and retirement benefits. Next are social needs. These are satisfied when employees feel that they belong to a given work group, company, or their family. Even higher up the structure are esteem needs, which are met when employees have achieved self-respect and confidence. Finally, at the top of the pyramid, the point at which employees are the most highly motivated and perform at peak levels, are the self-actualization needs. It is rare for people to reach and stay at this, our maximum potential, partially because all other needs must be met first. Challenges to the lower-order needs present concerns that need our attention. There is some research to support this notion of hierarchy, but overall the data show that needs are not always triggered in the order specified by Maslow. It is quite possible for someone to be simultaneously grappling with a physical challenge or family problem (social need) while still performing at very high levels in his or her work.[12]

Cross-Cultural Applicability

We might expect that the motivation to pursue higher-order needs (such as self-actualization) could be strongest in developed countries since, by definition, people are wealthier and have higher standards of living. Those in developing countries have greater challenges with lower-order survival needs, which are more prominent in their lives. Put simply, many workers in poor countries may be less interested in self-actualization if their survival or safety is in question. This same pattern may also exist within countries. For instance, in one survey, wealthy citizens in rapidly developing nations such as India, China, Russia, and Brazil were much more positive about how things were going in their countries (and presumably better positioned to self-actualize) than were people in the general (and poorer) population at large. This point calls attention to a primary finding about Maslow's theory—that cultural values and societal context may impact which needs are pursued most strongly. Moreover, the way in which employees view motivation features, such as competition or social needs, are shaped by a complex set of factors, including not only culture but also an employee's position in society and the firm.[13]

For example, the desire for cooperative coworkers and other social needs may rank above self-actualization for some Chinese employees or those from other collectivist societies.[14] Other studies find that employees in individualist societies (e.g., the United States) are more likely to be interested in pursuing personal accomplishment than are employees in more collectivist societies (e.g., Japan, Mexico). They are also less interested in esteem needs than employees in societies embracing feminine values (e.g., Sweden; see Chapter 2).[15] For example, Swedish employees are more likely to value time off with family and other quality-of-life experiences than would those from the United Kingdom or Australia.

Earlier it was noted that the motivation methods used by organizations change as society changes. What is also interesting is that patterns of motivation are sometimes very slow to change, even in the face of large-scale social upheavals. For instance, Germans raised in the formerly communist eastern part of the country may still focus more on simple existence needs and be less concerned with personal achievement than Germans raised in the western half of the country. For decades, subservience to the state was taught in schools throughout East Germany, something that shaped work-related values.

Despite the fact that East Germany collapsed some two decades ago, the effects of the country's nearly 40-year separation still linger, slowing fading with the passage of time. As proof, consider a recent Gallup survey that compared Western and Eastern European countries. The results showed that a clear majority of employees in Western European countries see their supervisor as a "partner who involves them in decisions and provides some 'self-actualizing'" autonomy rather than an autocratic boss who is uninterested in their opinions. The opposite was true in most Eastern European nations, which is most likely a reflection of their previous heritage as communist members of the old Soviet bloc. Perhaps the years under this characteristically heavy-handed, top-down management style took their toll on motivational preferences. Table 5.1 summarizes these results by country. Not included in this table is another thought-provoking result. Eastern European employees who were fortunate enough to work for a supervisor-as-partner reported

Table 5.1
Partner or Boss? How Employees in European Countries View Their Supervisors

Eastern European Nations	Most Employees View Supervisors as . . .
Belarus	Autocratic boss
Czech Republic	No clear majority
Estonia	Autocratic boss
Hungary	No clear majority
Latvia	Autocratic boss
Lithuania	No clear majority
Moldova	Autocratic boss
Poland	Autocratic boss
Romania	Partner
Russia	Autocratic boss
Slovakia	Autocratic boss
Slovenia	Autocratic boss
Ukraine	Autocratic boss

Western/Northern European Nations	Most Employees View Supervisors as . . .
Austria	Partner
Belgium	Partner
Denmark	Partner
Finland	Partner
France	Partner
Germany	Partner
Greece	Partner
Ireland	Partner
Netherlands	Partner
Norway	Partner
Portugal	Partner
Spain	Partner
Sweden	Partner
Switzerland	Partner
United Kingdom	No clear majority

Source: Adapted from Brown, I. T. (January, 2009). In Western Europe, more partners than bosses. Available at www.gallup.com/poll/114076/western-europe-partners-bosses.aspx.

being more satisfied with their jobs than their counterparts toiling under a more autocratic boss.[16]

Research on Maslow's ideas is clear: needs do not operate in a fixed hierarchy across borders.[17] In essence, the hierarchy is a philosophy that may reflect *U.S.* values. Its emphasis on higher-order growth needs is popular in the United States because key values in U.S. culture include individualism, personal achievement, risk taking, and other growth needs. All in all, this personal focus may not fit with some other cultures that are more likely to place great emphasis on the group or the needs of society as a whole. Even self-actualization might be achieved in the service of society in non-Western cultures. To underscore this point further, even the word *achievement* is extremely difficult to translate into other languages. Overall, to the extent that individuals or nations evolve toward a set of similar values, we would expect more receptiveness to higher-order growth needs.[18]

Herzberg's Two-Factor Theory

Frederick Herzberg suggested that without a minimum level of so-called *hygiene* factors, such as good pay and working conditions, employees will be unhappy and unmotivated. But just because these hygiene needs are attended to does not mean that employees will be highly motivated. If firms want highly motivated employees, Herzberg suggests that management must be aware of and work to provide *motivators* such as challenge, responsibility, and autonomy for their employees.[19] Hygiene factors are often extrinsic to the job (such as conflict with coworkers, pay, and poor supervision) and should be dealt with to improve the workplace. In addition, however, considerable effort should be put into those motivators that deal more directly with doing the job itself—*intrinsic* factors. Providing these key motivators is often referred to as job enrichment and is a popular approach in the United States.

Cross-Cultural Applicability

While Herzberg's ideas are interesting and thought-provoking, research has produced mixed results. One study found that workers in Zambia generally matched Herzberg's two-factor approach, with growth needs more strongly associated with high motivation and bad working conditions more highly correlated with dissatisfaction. Similar two-factor predictions were supported in studies conducted in Japan, Romania, and Israel. At the same time, different studies suggest that Herzberg's ideas do not fit other cultures precisely and may work best in a U.S. context. It is this context in which efforts to increase individual opportunity and performance are often very attractive to employees.[20]

For instance, another study found that French managers were more interested in responsibility and autonomy than were British managers. British managers were less interested in security, fringe benefits, and good working conditions than were French managers. This implies that job enrichment efforts might be easier to implement in Britain than in France.[21] Generally, the more a culture tends to value individualism, risk taking (low uncertainty avoidance), and is performance oriented (masculinity), the more likely Herzberg's motivators will spur personal achievement. Many employees in the United States and Britain fit this description. On the other hand, employees in Sweden commonly embrace individualism while also being very relationship oriented (feminine). In these circumstances, efforts to improve interpersonal harmony in the workplace may be more motivating than would job enrichment efforts aimed at fostering individual achievement.[22]

Herzberg's motivators may also face some cultural impediments in developing countries such as Indonesia, India, and Pakistan. These countries tend to be collectivist, high in uncertainty avoidance and power distance, and low in masculinity. Employees who tend to avoid uncertainty and believe in high power distance may be reluctant to make decisions involving risk, ambiguity, or independent initiative. Likewise, workers who are more collectivist in their views may also react poorly to efforts aimed at enriching jobs on an individual basis. And when feminine values hold sway, job enrichment efforts that focus narrowly on the job itself, without concern for personal relationships in and out of the workplace, may backfire since employees' obligations to family or community are often a priority.[23]

That said, the worldwide trend toward increasingly complex, or enriched, jobs and the responsibility that goes with them remains popular. Yet employees' willingness to embrace such jobs may depend in part, on their cultural values.[24] Fortunately, many experts believe that cultural obstacles preventing the implementation of job enrichment efforts can be overcome. The first step for international managers is to learn about the local cultural environment in depth before attempting any job enrichment effort. Once they understand how local values may impact any job enrichment methods under consideration, managers can sidestep cultural barriers while leveraging local values in other ways to improve employee motivation.[25]

The French electronics corporation, Thomson, is a case in point with its customized approach. It improved motivation and performance at a plant in Morocco by convincing employees to take on greater responsibilities and to make decisions independently of management. In doing so, openness and trust also increased dramatically. While this sounds like a typical Western job enrichment effort, these motivation changes were accomplished in a careful, culture-specific way.

Morocco is a high-power-distance context, one in which senior executives often expect to wield authority in a supreme and authoritative manner. Consequently, Thomson management decided to lead by example, using culturally appropriate leverage. In enacting a new quality program, senior managers rolled up their sleeves and worked on tasks previously reserved for junior employees (e.g., waiting in line, cleaning work areas, entering data). Company efforts to improve motivation were described as a new "moral code" that everyone would live by. Moreover, this new code was linked to Islamic values that are pervasive in Moroccan life. Management encouraged employees to embrace greater responsibility as a way of living Islam's emphasis on openness, honesty, and respect for the contributions of others. So the manner of implementing enrichment involved not only widely applied tools but was customized to local tastes.[26]

It is important to call attention to the impact that hygiene factors alone can have, under certain conditions, on producing highly motivated employees. Job security and pay often act as motivators in developing countries.[27] Hygiene factors, however, may also be very motivating in industrialized nations. According to one survey, Danish employees are the most satisfied workers in the world—perhaps because of outstanding relations between labor and management, including good pay, another hygiene factor. This subject of getting along is a common theme within the toymaker Lego, perhaps Denmark's best-known company. The firm's name is derived from two Danish words that mean "play well."[28] But the approach used in Denmark can clash with the values of other countries. Consider how the hygiene factor of money is a big motivator for some Russian women by reading the following *Culture Clash* box.

CULTURE CLASH

Money Drives Russian Women Working for Mary Kay and Avon

Mary Kay Cosmetics and Avon, both U.S. firms, have been successful in Russia for years. Thanks to burgeoning demand for cosmetics, Russia ranks high among the more than 35 countries in which Mary Kay operates. Likewise, some 70% of Avon's revenue comes from developing nations—Russia is one of its three biggest foreign markets. A key to Mary Kay's and Avon's success is their sales forces of Russian women, and for most of them, money is a key motivator. Mary Kay provides sales training and sells its products to Russian sales representatives discounted from retail prices. Representatives then sell them at full price, preferably to small groups of customers. Women in Mary Kay's Russian sales force typically make several hundred dollars per month, while top performers, many of whom have their own offices and administrative staff, rake in thousands. Either way, Mary Kay's sales force exceeds the average monthly wage in Russia by a considerable margin, which may explain why turnover among Mary Kay's Russian sales force is so low. Avon's experience is similar, and the company prides itself on helping its representatives get started, including offering low-cost loans.

Mary Kay and Avon are attractive to Russian women because they offer financial independence, something that remains relatively rare in Russia. Some women feel that Russia's economic development has left them behind, as the majority of Russia's unemployed are women, and some Russian organizations still reserve certain jobs for men. When they are employed, women in Russia are often trapped in low-paying jobs and are the first to be laid off. Ironically, these same attitudes toward gender in Russia make being a Mary Kay or Avon sales representative a socially acceptable job for Russian women—one that can pay very well indeed.[29]

Overall, it might be simpler just to assume that what motivates employees varies from place to place more often than not. Implementing enriched jobs that provide autonomy and opportunities for achievement is likely to foster deeper motivation and commitment more quickly in places where individualist and masculine values are strong (e.g., the United States). In contrast, it may be better to improve working conditions and relations with workers if managers want to create a motivated and committed workforce in places where collectivism (e.g., Japan) or feminine values tend to hold sway (e.g., Sweden).[30]

Reinforcement Theory: The Process of Connecting Behavior and Rewards

The central idea behind reinforcement theory is that the best way to motivate is to clearly link valued consequences to desired behaviors.[31] For example, managers such as those at Mary Kay (as discussed in the *Culture Clash* feature) can improve employee performance by applying positive reinforcers (e.g., big bonuses, time off, other rewards). Conversely, poor performance can be eliminated by carefully applying punishment (e.g., a pay cut, demotion, or more).[32]

Culture, Context, and Reinforcement Techniques

Managers need to know what employees value in order to use positive reinforcement effectively. Culture and societal context, however, make this more challenging than it seems on the surface. In South Africa, for instance, many black employees are more motivated when their firm works to remove the social inequalities such as inferior housing that is a continuing legacy of apartheid, the infamous policy of racial discrimination against non-European groups in South Africa. This connection between work and life outside of work also reflects African cultural values that emphasize the importance of community and family. Such values are less common in Western management approaches.[33]

Culture may also affect how employees interpret feedback that they receive about their performance. For instance, while employees everywhere react more favorably to positive feedback than to negative feedback, this pattern is more pronounced in collectivist cultures. Moreover, employees in individualist cultures tend to respond more to individualized performance feedback rather than group performance feedback, with employees in collectivist cultures being more responsive to group-based feedback. Narrowing our focus to U.S. employees, they tend to prefer positive feedback and will often take steps to explain away or dismiss negative feedback. In contrast, while Japanese employees tend to react even more strongly to negative feedback than Americans, they tend to be more open to it as well as more likely to change their behavior as a result of the feedback. It is likely that these tendencies are rooted in cultural and societal circumstances. Many Americans like to revel in their triumphs, especially individual ones, while finding failure threatening to their self-worth as individuals. In collectivist Japan, Indonesia, or the Philippines, however, critical evaluations may help people maintain a humble posture toward the wider group as well as offer suggestions for improving overall group performance.[34]

Similarly, U.S. and Mexican workers may react differently to positive performance feedback.[35] Americans may see praise as suggesting that even better performance is possible, while Mexicans may see it as recognition that their current performance is good, or good enough. Mexican workers are also less likely to exceed the informal performance norms and work pace of their work groups regardless of the feedback they receive from a supervisor. Compared with Americans, Mexican employees are more collectivist and tend to pay close attention to group norms.[36]

Cultural values also present hurdles for reinforcement strategies. For instance, performance-based pay, such as a bonus or other discretionary reward, may not motivate workers in cultures that are high in uncertainty avoidance. Because pay is put at risk with performance-contingent rewards, bonus systems may not be as useful in uncertainty-avoidance cultures. Using large bonuses or big pay increases alone may also prove difficult in feminine cultures since loyalty to the boss, company, or coworkers can be prized above a short-term indicator of performance. India is an example of a country in which cultural values may limit reinforcement strategies. In fact, pay systems in some Indian companies violate reinforcement principles. Compensation may reflect employee seniority as opposed to being awarded contingent on behavior. Performance appraisal may also be rudimentary, making merit pay seem arbitrary. This may reinforce the resigned fatalism and indifference to good performance (a state referred to as *chalega*) that some Indians already embrace because of their upbringing. Instead, Indian employees' efforts may be directed to activities aimed at strengthening relationships with supervisors who offer valued rewards.[37]

Managers must be willing and able to scale what is often a formidable learning curve to understand what works best in a particular cultural context. This does not necessarily mean that U.S. managers have to avoid Western approaches to reinforcement. What it does mean, however, is that to be accepted by employees, reinforcement approaches may have to be modified to fit local sensibilities.[38]

Expectancy Theory: Tying Goals to Rewards

Expectancy theory pulls together many of the ideas about motivation that we have presented so far. The expectancy approach assumes that three factors determine employee effort in a given situation.[39] First, employees must believe that working hard will result in good performance. If employees feel that it is impossible to reach production goals that have been set, they will not exert much effort. Employees must also believe that rewards are forthcoming in response to good performance. If this is not the case, then overall motivation will suffer. Finally, the available rewards must be valued, because motivation and effort will suffer if the rewards employees receive are unimportant to them. Thus, this approach builds on reinforcement theory—which, in large part, assumes that we're all motivated by similar rewards.

Cultural Assumptions of Expectancy Theory

Clearly, expectancy theory makes some now-familiar cultural assumptions, emphasizing individualist and masculine values, such as focus on tasks rather than on relationships. It also assumes that individual workers are rational and control their lives by altering their level of effort. All of this fits U.S. culture quite well, but many Chinese, for example, believe that fate helps determine events. Similarly, many Mexicans feel that being from the appropriate family is a real key to success. Many Saudis believe that what happens at work is a reflection of God's will. In each case, external forces are important factors not commonly considered in this model.[40]

Because rewards must be valued to produce motivation, expectancy theory suggests that the rewards provided should reflect cultural values. For instance, in one study, U.S. managers felt that bonuses should be closely connected to performance. This fits the theory's assumption that people are achievement oriented and can tolerate risk. But French and Dutch managers in the study were less interested in money and were more skeptical about linking bonuses to performance. In reality, the bonuses earned by French and Dutch managers were smaller and varied less than did those of Americans. Compared with their U.S. counterparts, the Dutch tend to have a more feminine orientation and are less individualist. As a consequence, Dutch managers are less likely to use pay as a way to track individual achievement. Similarly, managers in high-uncertainty-avoidance cultures, such as France, may be leery of reward systems with large, highly variable performance bonuses.[41]

These cultural differences help explain why the outrage threshold for executive compensation is generally lower in Europe than in the United States. The issue of excesses in executive pay packages is much more salient in the minds of most Europeans. In particular, these differences might affect the second key element of expectancy theory noted above: the belief that rewards are tied to good performance. Indeed, European executives in major firms earn only about 40% of what their U.S. counterparts take home. (For more compensation comparisons between the United States and Europe, see Table 5.2.) Moreover, legal restrictions on executive pay, bonuses, golden parachutes, and stock options tend to be more severe in Europe than they are in the United States. As a result, it is not surprising that the $14 million pay package earned by the CEO of giant Swiss pharmaceutical Novartis in 2007 sparked significant negative commentary about excessive compensation in Europe a few years ago over a sum that would be unlikely to provoke a similar reaction in the United States. In fact, this figure was only a fraction of the nearly $100 million earned that year by American Larry Ellison, CEO of Oracle. That said, pay packages for U.S. executives will and do produce outrage if they are seen exorbitant by U.S. standards and are not perceived to be strongly linked to performance.[42]

Sensibilities about pay change. Indeed, some of the outrage in Europe regarding huge executive pay packages reflects a shift toward U.S.-style compensation. Between 1998 and 2008, for instance, CEO pay, while still lagging at U.S. levels, jumped dramatically as European firms tried to keep up in the worldwide search for talent. In fact, foreigners now run the show in several major German and French companies, with U.S.-type incentives and bonus plans much more common across the board. After losing talent to U.S. and British rivals in recent years, Deutsche Bank and Bayerische Vereinsbank began offering U.S.-style performance bonuses that can increase total compensation by 50% or more. Yet many German banks remain uneasy, relying on smaller bonuses than their U.S. counterparts, with some

Table 5.2
Pay Up: Total Compensation for U.S. and European CEOs in Large Firms

Country	Approximate Annual Median CEO Compensation
United States	13,000,000
Britain	6,000,000
France	6,000,000
Europe-wide median	5,000,000
Germany	4,000,000
Netherlands	3,000,000

Source: Adapted from Executive pay in Europe: Pay attention. *The Economist*, June 14, 2008, 77–78.

even making part of the bonus contingent upon an employee's ability to work well with colleagues. This underscores the fact that pay differences do persist across European nations, as Table 5.2 illustrates. Northern European countries (e.g., the Netherlands, Norway, Sweden, and Germany) tend to have more egalitarian values than the United Kingdom and France, which could account for their tendency to pay CEOs less.[43] At the same time, consider Japan, which seems to cling to many workplace customs, sometimes in the face of challenges that demand a need for change. Yet even in tradition-rich Japan, some firms are experimenting with reward systems and trying to innovate. See the *Global Innovations* box for a closer look at how performance–reward linkages are evolving in Japan.

GLOBAL INNOVATIONS

Global Dining Cooks Up New Approach to Rewards for Its Japanese Employees

The United States' cutthroat capitalism is a tough sell for many Japanese. Contentious disputes about pay and performance are rare in Japan, at least in many traditional companies. But Japanese firms such as Global Dining may provide a peek into the future. This restaurant chain embraced three innovations that are shocking for many Japanese: (1) plenty of conflict, (2) do-or-die competition between employees, and (3) brutally honest individual performance feedback. How brutal? One cook sat in front of a group of bosses and peers to demand a large pay increase. They immediately shouted criticisms—that his cooking was uneven and sales on his shift were lousy. A quick vote was taken, and the humiliated cook was rebuffed and sent back to his work station.

In fact, all employees at Global Dining, from senior leaders to dishwashers, are evaluated against performance criteria in such face-to-face meetings. Employees who miss their performance targets get no bonuses. Managers who foul up are quickly demoted or fired. But excellent performers are rewarded incredibly well. One young restaurant manager made over $150,000—more than even a typical midcareer executive working for a large Japanese firm. Global Dining's CEO summed up the system's philosophy this way: "Just as sharks need to keep swimming to stay alive, we only want people who are constantly craving challenges."[44]

The willingness to embrace this demanding approach is part of a broader debate in Japan about traditionally cushy relationships between employees and big firms that often had little to do with performance (e.g., lifetime employment, seniority-based raises). Japan's prolonged economic difficulties have been driving that debate in part, while the crushing natural calamities that the country faced in 2011 present even more such challenges. Yet Global Dining is not alone. Companies such as electronics giant Sony, clothing chain Fast Retailing, and machine parts firm Misumi Corporation are among some of the big Japanese companies that have aggressively recruited younger managers willing to live with the ups and downs of tough pay-for-performance schemes. Thanks to bonuses, one young Misumi manager pulled in almost $530,000—a sum that eclipsed the pay of the company president.

But some workers at Global Dining worry about the pressures under such a ruthless performance management system. Even waiters watch each other closely since employees vote on raises and bonuses for everyone else. Global Dining employees may have the last word, something that is also extremely innovative for a Japanese firm. One sign of this is that the evaluation system actually encourages criticism of superiors, right up to the CEO. In fact, at one point, employees complained to the CEO about the bonus formula. Feeling that their voices were not heard, employees eventually demanded a vote on the issue. The CEO lost, and the formula was modified. One manager who left Global Dining to start his own restaurant said that while performance management was a good thing, his system would be less ruthless. As he put it, "There's a saying, 'Too much is as bad as too little.'"[45]

The opposite of the Global Dining approach is the growing percentage of younger Japanese who are considered slackers—people perfectly content with hum-drum jobs. These workers, labeled by the Japanese as *hodo-hodo zoku* ("so-so folks"), deliberately avoid working hard and refuse to accept more responsibilities, promotions, and even pay raises. As unusual as it may seem in workaholic Japan, only 3% of Japanese employees said they were giving their jobs full effort in a recent 18-nation survey—the lowest of any country. Critics suggest that Japan's crumbling traditions of lifetime employment and generous benefits are causing younger workers to do the minimum and threatening Japanese productivity in the process. But, many of these so-so employees watched their parents commit themselves totally to their jobs and companies, putting in extraordinarily long hours—only to see them rewarded with layoffs and pay cuts during recessions in the 1990s and 2000s. As one hodo-hodo zoku employee put it, "That's definitely not the life I want." Consequently, companies as diverse as Sanyo Electric and Dai-ichi Mutual Life Insurance are having a hard time just finding employees who are willing to be promoted into management, even with their more traditional approaches to compensation.

Perhaps the answer for these companies is to take the Global Dining approach and offer more radical alternatives to employees—where there are plenty of risks but also plenty of bigger rewards. That might entice younger Japanese into signing up if they believe big rewards will really follow working hard, unlike their parents' experience in the slow, seniority-based promotions and small raises found in traditional Japanese firms. Yet it remains to be seen whether younger Japanese will gravitate more toward hodo-hodo zoku thinking, the cutthroat capitalism embraced by Global Dining, or something else entirely. Regardless, it will be a change from their parents'—and traditional Japanese—attitudes toward work.[46]

As interesting as these Japanese examples are, major shifts in attitude about motivation do not happen overnight. For instance, in recent years Japanese workers have been seeking out foreign companies for employment in ever-increasing numbers. In most cases, this attraction is based on the belief that, relative to Japan-based firms, foreign firms demand fewer hours of employees and are more willing to pay for individual performance and to promote based on personal achievement. That said, the percentage of Japanese in the workforce who are employed by foreign companies is small (less than 3%) and trails the percentage in other industrialized nations by a considerable margin (e.g., over 5% in both the United States and Germany).[47] So, while change is occurring, the starting point is low and the rate of change unclear. In general, the perceived link between effort and performance remains stronger for Americans than for Japanese. The longer history of performance-contingent reward systems in the United States may help explain this. Finally, Americans still tend to see pay increases, promotions, and personal recognition as more desirable than do many of their foreign counterparts, including the Japanese. Cultural values that emphasize individual performance and achievement in the United States and group cohesion in Japan may account for this difference. Consequently, how fast and to what extent Japanese society (or other societies for that matter) may become more individualist remains to be seen. But the Japanese government apparently wants to move in that direction. A few years ago, Japan launched a new education policy designed to help children become more independent and individually oriented.[48]

Equity Theory: You Should Get What You Deserve

Equity theory proposes that if employees perceive that they have been treated unjustly, they are motivated to restore a sense of fairness.[49] This happens when employees compare themselves to other employees and peers in terms of job outcomes such as pay and job inputs such as effort. When the comparison of outcomes to inputs is balanced, employees should feel that they have been fairly treated by their organization. If it is not balanced, employees will try to restore the balance.[50]

Applying Equity Concepts across Cultures

How different cultures define, interpret, and assess fairness can vary considerably, often in ways that are not well understood. Moreover, national culture is not the only factor impacting employee views about equity. The corporate context (e.g., firm norms, nature of the industry) can also shape employee acceptance of equity concepts. For instance, over time a strong merit pay system, in which higher pay is linked to individual performance, may influence employee attitudes. Supporting this perspective is the fact that as multinational corporations continue to push abroad, they are acting to shape workforce values in the places where they do business. One study found that Chinese employees working for international joint ventures involving Western firms were increasingly accepting of company norms that distributed rewards based on their performance. This flies in the face of the fact that distributing rewards more equally among workers would be more consistent with traditional Chinese values. Yet how fast and how far such changes will permeate the broader Chinese workforce remains to be seen.[51]

In general, international managers would be wise to consider the impact of cultural values when it comes to equity concepts, even if that consideration suggests that, say, Swedes are very open to equity-based pay decisions and less on a natural tendency toward equality as a yardstick for fairness judgments. Workers in cultures that highly value individualism may still be more motivated by equity and deservingness than employees elsewhere. In such cultures, individual performance (inputs) is important and should be rewarded accordingly based on deservingness (outcomes). On the other hand, in collectivist cultures, there may be more openness to seeing rewards distributed equally, regardless of performance, to preserve group harmony and cohesiveness.[52]

Multinational firms and managers sometimes forget that their approaches to motivation reflect a particular combination of values not always shared by others. Consequently, introducing those approaches in places where other norms hold sway can be problematic, especially if companies have not taken steps to prepare employees or to modify their approaches to begin with. A case in point happened in a joint-venture operation in Shanghai. New U.S. plant managers on the scene gave leather jackets to a small group of Chinese employees who had come up with some good suggestions for improving operations. This reward was designed to recognize and encourage employee initiative. But instead of serving as a positive example, the jacket gesture sparked backlash. After hearing about the jackets, Chinese employees throughout the plant wanted to know why they did not receive one. Management's explanation that the jackets were a reward for good performance went nowhere. Chinese employees continued complaints, asking for equal treatment. At one point, local government officials called the firm to inquire about the issue. Sensing that things were getting out of hand, the U.S. management decided to give all 700 Chinese employees a jacket.

How can something as commonplace to U.S. managers as rewarding superior performance create problems in China? Historically, Chinese employees expected to be taken care of by their bosses and offered obedience in return. Tying rewards to performance was rarely part of that equation. Chinese companies also typically gave workers benefits such as housing and food in addition to job security. Until recently, foreign companies that fired employees for lousy performance would expect to be grilled by local officials concerned about the social problems caused by displaced workers. While China is changing dramatically and the use of performance-based rewards is rising, vestiges of the old "iron rice bowl" approach remain. And that is something to consider when it comes to motivating Chinese workers, especially if the employees being managed embrace traditional values such as in a state-owned enterprise or a joint venture.[53]

Clearly, the link between culture and equity-based rewards is both complex and evolving. Some studies suggest that employees in collectivist cultures are less likely to apply equity concepts when distributing rewards than employees in individualist cultures.[54] Other experts, however, suggest a more nuanced view, pointing out that research has found that employees in collectivist cultures may be more likely to use equity norms when rewarding efforts to promote *group cohesiveness* (a more collective outcome/value). And still other studies suggest that in-group versus out-group differences may complicate matters in collectivist cultures (e.g., China), with *equality* norms being preferable when distributing rewards to in-group members and *equity* or performance-based norms being preferable when rewards are divvied up to out-group members. Finally, some studies have suggested power distance can impact equity–equality preferences. The research shows that low-power-distance employees prefer equality, whereas high-power-distance employees prefer equity as the fairest way to distribute rewards.[55]

An alternative perspective emerging on equity theory in an international context is that less focus should be placed on broad fairness rules and instead we should concentrate on understanding what goes into the mental equation employees solve when judging fairness in different parts of the world. There may be fewer differences than we think across cultures when it comes to preferences for equity or equality norms. Culture may have a bigger impact on what employees consider to be relevant work inputs and outcomes—as well as how important they are. While everyone may understand and have similar views about broad norms such as equity, how these are implemented may be shaped to a large extent by culture. An indirect example of how this might be manifested in the workplace is shown in Table 5.3. It shows the results of a survey of nearly 90,000 employees across 18 countries (five example countries are shown in the table). The employees were asked to rank features that attract them to a company as well as features that engage them, such as willingness to contribute to company success, once they are at the firm. There is both some consistency in the items ranked highly and some unique elements that motivate within some countries.

Hopefully, researchers will be able to sort this out in the years ahead and then offer more concrete advice to international managers in the process. Cultures are not static, however, but are moving targets, complicating our efforts at understanding. And the pace of change may vary considerably across countries as a consequence of local circumstances. For instance, although we mentioned the notion of shifts in equity perspectives among Chinese employees, there is also evidence to suggest that Chinese managers have been slower to adopt Western equity rules to distribute material rewards than their Russian counterparts. Russian employees and managers alike seem very open to these pay methods.[56]

So what do these complex findings on an equity approach to motivation mean for international managers? Our advice is that managers should:

1. Think through how their own cultural values might affect their use of equity rules in doling out rewards.
2. Take the time needed to understand how their subordinates' cultural values might affect their assessment of equity rules when they are used (e.g., what inputs and outcomes do employees consider and why?).

Table 5.3
What Drives Attraction to a Firm and Engages Employees Once They Are There?

Country	Top Three Attraction Drivers	Top Three Engagement Drivers
Brazil	Competitive base pay Career advancement opportunity Challenging work	Organization rewards outstanding customer service Improvement of my skills over last year Senior management sincerely interested in employee well-being
China	Learning and development opportunity Career advancement opportunity Competitive base pay	Excellent career advancement opportunities Organization encouraged innovative thinking Organization reputation for financial stability
India	Career advancement opportunity Challenging work Learning and development opportunity	Input into decision making Senior management actions consistent with values Organization's reputation for social responsibility
South Korea	Competitive benefits Competitive base pay Reputation of organization as good employer	Senior management ensures organization's long-term success Unit has skills needed to succeed Organization supports work–life balance
United States	Competitive base pay Competitive health care benefits Vacation/paid time off	Senior management sincerely interested in employee well-being Organization's reputation for social responsibility Improvement of my skills over last year

Source: Adapted from Closing the engagement gap: A road map for driving superior business performance. *Tower Perrin Global Workforce Study*, 2008. Available at www.towersperrin.com/tp/showhtml.jsp?url=global/publications/gws/index.htm&country=global.

Note: Results from a survey of nearly 90,000 employees in 18 countries. Attraction refers to things about a firm that grab an employee's attention; engagement drivers refer to items that motivate employees once they join the firm. Items are presented in the order of average importance.

As countries evolve, traditional values and practices may change in ways that affect how rewards should be allocated. Again, consider China. In the recent past, firms operating on the coast of China could keep their workers from the interior of the country reasonably satisfied with low pay and small or no raises (sometimes for years). They could do this because job prospects elsewhere in the country were slim—the very reason these workers migrated from other provinces. But this has been changing as the country develops and opportunities spread. Good employment opportunities within the inner provinces now exist, such as those in Chongqing, a massive city in the southwest province of Sichuan. This city of over 28 million people is a huge manufacturing hub for the country, with many state- and foreign-owned employers. Additionally, many low-paid employees in China already feel pangs of inequity as they compare themselves to others who seem better off. They do not have to look hard or far to see plenty of signs that many other Chinese are better off. This provides ample opportunities for social comparisons suggested by equity theory.[57] As noted in earlier chapters, in the late 2000s, this resulted in significant worker protests and is at least partially responsible for ethnic strife in some Chinese provinces.

CONCLUSIONS ABOUT MOTIVATION ACROSS CULTURES

International managers would be well-served to take culture and related factors into account when designing and implementing motivation strategies for use abroad. This is no small challenge, especially since cultural values are constantly changing and managers may not recognize how their own values affect the motivation strategies they use.[58] Consequently, international managers should rely on motivation approaches and tactics that *complement* rather than *conflict* with the specific cultures involved. They should strive for cultural synergy in their motivation efforts. This can be done in five basic, but difficult-to-implement, steps:

1. *Describe the motivation situation.* How does the manager view the motivation issue(s)? What perspectives do subordinates have? The purpose of this first step is to discover whether different perspectives exist and whether they create conflict.
2. *Identify cultural assumptions about motivation.* The next step is to uncover the cultural values that explain why different perspectives on motivation exist. The goal is to be able to reverse perspectives and see things from another culture's point of view.
3. *Determine where cultural overlaps exist.* The key here is to determine where similarities as well as differences exist between the specific cultures in the work environment.

4. *Generate culturally synergistic alternatives.* Once cultural assumptions have been identified, the next challenge is to develop motivation strategies that blend elements of the cultures involved or even go beyond them.

5. *Select, implement, and then refine a synergistic strategy.* The final step involves picking what appears to be the best motivation strategy and implementing it. A key here is to have all parties observe the strategy from their own cultural perspective. The chosen strategy may need to be fine-tuned based on any feedback received.

These steps may seem mushy to a student in business, because they do not parallel definitive actions that they are taught in capital budgeting or net present value. Yet they reflect the reality faced in using management methods across cultures. Accomplishing these steps may require conversations with foreign employees as well as future involvement of those employees in the development and implementation of specific motivation strategies. To increase the chances of success in these efforts, managers and employees must possess both cultural self-awareness (i.e., awareness of their own values) and cross-cultural awareness (i.e., awareness of others' values). Having both types of awareness increases the odds that the chosen strategy can be implemented in a way that reflects the best of the specific cultures involved. But, first, underlying values and cultural frames of reference must be identified. This will foster an appreciation for alternative perspectives, which can then be used to generate motivational approaches that accomplish management goals in ways that are sensitive to local cultures.[59] Even if you march through these steps and get it wrong, it could be beneficial for your next effort and, at the least, is not a knee-jerk application of something you take for granted in your home country

CHAPTER SUMMARY

In this chapter, we discussed the challenge of understanding what motivates employees and management across cultural boundaries.

There are relatively few universal approaches when it comes to motivation. But even if the underlying principles used are the same, how they are framed and presented needs to reflect local values to be effective, at least to an extent. For instance, something as simple as feedback designed to reinforce good performance can have very different effects when applied elsewhere.

Overall, managers should explicitly take cultural variables into account while designing reward systems and motivational strategies. We presented a series of action steps that international managers can take to develop synergistic solutions to motivation issues. These can be hard work and involve efforts by managers to understand their own value systems, as well as employees', before tackling motivation issues. Identifying underlying values and cultural frames of reference should create an appreciation for alternative perspectives, which can then be used to generate motivational approaches that accomplish management goals in ways that are sensitive to local cultural values and dynamics.

DISCUSSION QUESTIONS

1. What problems might a manager face when using the various motivations approaches discussed in this chapter?
2. What specific concerns might come up if managers were trying to motivate employees from Spain, from Indonesia, or from Australia?
3. What approaches should you consider to construct a culturally synergistic approach to motivation? And what difficulties might you encounter in trying to implement those steps?

Developing Your International Career

HOW ARE YOUR CROSS-CULTURAL MOTIVATION SKILLS?

Purpose and Instructions

The purpose of this exercise is to learn more about the challenge of motivating people from different cultures. Six short situations are presented about Egyptian, Chinese, Japanese, and U.S. subordinates, along with alternative possibilities for motivating them.

Think about and select an answer for each situation—either ahead of time or in class, depending on what your instructor prefers. Your instructor may ask you to break into small groups of four to six students to come up with a consensus answer for each example in class. Your group can then make a brief presentation (five minutes) about your answers and rationales. Your instructor can then lead a discussion about the most appropriate answers for each situation.

MOTIVATION SITUATIONS

1. You would like to have a Saudi Arabian colleague's help so that you can finish a major assignment. You are most likely to get that help if you say:
   a. "In the name of God, please help me."
   b. "If you help me, I'll buy you dinner."
   c. "My friend, I need your help."
   d. "Let's be the first to finish this assignment."

2. You are a department manager in China. Which of the following would probably work best to motivate your production supervisor to improve performance?
  a. "If our department increases output by 20%, you'll get a 5% bonus."
  b. "I'm planning to reorganize the department, and I'm thinking of promoting you if production increases."
  c. "If your team doesn't meet the quotas, you're fired."
  d. "Why don't you put in some overtime to help make the production quotas?"

3. You are a manager about to conduct a series of performance appraisals on your U.S. subordinates. To motivate them, you will probably want to focus on recognizing the Americans'...
  a. promptness.
  b. creativity.
  c. directness and openness.
  d. accomplishments.

4. Last month your Japanese team hit all production targets. Which of the following would be the best way to acknowledge their achievement?
  a. Treat them to a dinner where you give special recognition to the team leader.
  b. Don't mention it, because meeting targets is their job.
  c. Call the oldest team member aside and thank him or her.
  d. Thank the group at your next meeting and ask them to increase production even more.

5. You are managing a factory in Egypt. One supervisor's group is not meeting your production expectations. Which of the following might be the best way for you to draw the supervisor's attention to this problem?
  a. "Increase your group's productivity or you're fired."
  b. "Do you need any help with your group?"
  b. "You'd better take care of your group, or I may have to move you to another job."
  c. "Why don't you hold a meeting with your group to find out what's wrong?"

6. You are a manager in a large international company and are about to begin an important project. Mr. Hiro has been assigned to work for you on this project. Because Mr. Hiro is Japanese, which of the following is likely to motivate him?
  a. Being part of a strong, leading international firm
  b. A good raise in his annual salary
  c. A promotion to group leader and a better title
  d. A trip to Hawaii for him and his wife after the project is completed

Making the Case for International Understanding

FIRING UP THE BEAR: HOW SHOULD WESTERN FIRMS MOTIVATE RUSSIAN EMPLOYEES?

Since the 1990s, Russia has been transforming itself economically. And while there have been ups and downs in the process, Russia has changed in many ways in the last 20 years. Indeed, today the trappings of Western consumerism are ubiquitous in Russian cities, with shopping malls, supermarkets, car dealerships, fast-food restaurants, and movie theaters that would not be out of place in New York, London, or Munich. You would not have to look hard for familiar brand names such as BlackBerry, Coach, Coca-Cola, McDonald's, Nestlé, Pizza Hut, Sony, Tag Heuer, and Volkswagen on shopping excursions in Russia

But appearances can be deceiving. It would be a mistake to ignore Russia's long history of autocracy and paternalism—in both government and business. That history has proven hard to shake and lingers just under Russia's modern economic facade. As one U.S. ambassador put it, "Russia seems more similar to our culture than it really is."

There is little doubt that most Western firms operating in Russia would agree with this assessment, especially since many of them have faced serious challenges in motivating Russian employees. Those challenges have increased in recent years as more foreign companies set up shop in Russia, hiring locals to staff their operations instead of relying on planeloads of expensive expatriates.

This underscores the need to figure out what works best to motivate Russian employees. It also raises questions about whether Western motivation approaches can work in Russia. Fortunately, we have begun to get some answers now thanks to a number of recent studies. For example, one study pitted three Western motivation programs against each other in a Russian cotton mill.

- Program 1 was based on the reinforcement concept of providing contingent rewards. It involved giving Russian employees extrinsic rewards (e.g., valued consumer goods, bonuses) in exchange for improvements in performance.
- Program 2 was also based on reinforcement ideas but focused instead on behavior management tactics. These tactics were used to shape employee behavior using verbal feedback. For instance, Russian supervisors were trained to praise workers when they improved their performance and to offer corrective suggestions when negative behaviors were displayed.
- Program 3 used a job enrichment approach that relied on employee participation. Here employees were asked for suggestions about how their jobs might be changed and improved, without Russian supervisors being present. For instance, employees were asked to provide their ideas for improving work procedures, increasing worker autonomy, and developing additional skills. Employees also were empowered to im-

plement their suggestions, with the idea that doing so would improve their motivation and subsequent performance.

Think about which of these programs would work best to improve the motivation and performance of Russian employees and why. Do some research on how Russian history and culture might affect work motivation. Your instructor may lead a discussion about the research team's findings and the conclusions you all reach in your research on this topic.

ASSIGNMENT QUESTIONS

1. Which of these motivational programs is the most compatible with Russian norms? Why do you believe this is the case?
2. Which program do you think would work best to improve the motivation and performance of the Russian employees?
3. Be sure to provide *specifics* to justify your answers in both Question 1 and Question 2 above.
4. Taking everything into consideration, how likely is it that any of these programs will work in the Russian culture (as you understand it)? Given your knowledge of Russian cultural values, describe any methods you might think would work *better* than those described here.

Sources: Based on Welsh, D. H. B., Luthans, F., & Sommer, S. M. (1993). Managing Russian factory workers: The impact of U.S.-based behavioral and participative techniques. *Academy of Management Journal*, 36, 58–79; Elenkov, D. S. (1998). Can American concepts work in Russia? *Academy of Management Review*, 40, 133–156; Fey, C. F., & Shekshnia, S. (2007). How to do business in Russia. *Wall Street Journal*, October 27–28, R4.

NOTES

1. Thomas, D. C. (2008). *Cross-Cultural Management: Essential Concepts* (2nd ed.). Thousand Oaks, CA: Sage.
2. *The American President: A Reference Resource*. University of Virginia, Miller Center for American Politics, 2011. Available at http://millercenter.org/president.
3. Alder, N. J., & Gundersen, A. (2008). *International Dimensions of Organizational Behavior* (5th ed.). Mason, OH: Thompson-South-Western; Communal, C., & Senior, B. (1999). National culture and management: Messages conveyed by British, French, and German advertisements of managerial appointments. *Leadership and Organizational Development Journal*, 20, 26–35.
4. Gelfand, M. J., Erez, M., & Aycan, Z. (2007). Cross-cultural organizational behavior. *Annual Review of Psychology*, 58, 479–514; Huang, X. (2008). Motivation and job satisfaction across nations. In P. B. Smith, M. F. Peterson, & D. C. Thomas (eds.), *The Handbook of Cross-Cultural Management Research* (77–93). Thousand Oaks, CA: Sage; Thomas, D. C., Au, K., & Ravlin, E. C.

(2003). Cultural variation and the psychological contract. *Journal of Organizational Behavior*, 24, 451–471.

5. Rodrigues, C. (1990). The situation and national culture as contingencies for leadership behavior: Two conceptual models. In B. Prasad (ed.), *Advances in International Comparative Management*, 5, 51–68. Greenwich, CT: JAI Press.

6. Bass, B. M. (1990) *Stogdill's Handbook of Leadership: A Survey of Theory and Research*. New York: Free Press.

7. d'Iribarne, P. (2002). Motivating workers in emerging countries: Universal tools and local applications. *Journal of Organizational Behavior*, 23, 243–256.

8. The dearth of births: Why are so few young Japanese willing to procreate? *The Economist*, November 20, 2010, 14–15; Into the unknown: A special report on Japan. *The Economist*, November 20, 2010, 1–16; Rowley, I., & Hall, K. (2007). Japan's lost generation. *Business Week*, May 28, 40–41; Yukl, G. (2010). *Leadership in Organizations* (7th ed.). Upper Saddle River, NJ: Prentice Hall.

9. Lenartowicz, T., & Roth, K. (2001). Does subculture within a country matter? A cross-cultural study of motivational domains and business performance in Brazil. *Journal of International Business Studies*, 32, 305–325; Perlaki, I. (1994). Organizational development in Eastern Europe: Learning to build culture-specific OD theories. *Journal of Applied Behavioral Science*, 30, 297–312.

10. Hofstede, G. (1996). An American in Paris: The influence of nationality on organization theories. *Organizational Studies*, 17, 525–537.

11. Maslow, A. H. (1970). *Motivation and Personality* (2nd ed.). New York: Harper & Row.

12. Greenberg, J., & Baron, R. A. (2001). *Behavior in Organizations* (7th ed.). Englewood Cliffs, NJ: Prentice Hall.

13. Where money seems to talk. *The Economist*, July 14, 2007, 63–64; Alder, N. J., & Gundersen, A. (2008). *International Dimensions of Organizational Behavior* (5th ed.). Mason, OH: Thompson-South-Western; Gelfand, M. J., Erez, M., & Aycan, Z. (2007). Cross-cultural organizational behavior. *Annual Review of Psychology*, 58, 479–514; Hayward, R. D., & Kemmelmeier, M. (2007). How competition is viewed across cultures. *Cross-Cultural Research*, 41(4), 364–395; Peterson, M. F., & Wood, R. E. (2008). Cognitive structures and processes in cross-cultural management. In P. B. Smith, M. F. Peterson, & D.C. Thomas (eds.), *The Handbook of Cross-Cultural Management Research* (15–58). Thousand Oaks, CA: Sage; Thomas, D. C. (2008). *Cross-Cultural Management: Essential Concepts* (2nd ed.). Thousand Oaks, CA: Sage.

14. Shenkar, O., & Von Glinow, M. A. (1994). Paradoxes of organizational theory and research: Using the case of China to illustrate national contingency. *Management Science*, 40, 56–71.

15. Alder, N. J., & Gundersen, A. (2008). *International Dimensions of Organizational Behavior* (5th ed.). Mason, OH: Thompson-South-Western; Sagie, A., Elizur, D., & Yamauchi, H. (1996). The strength and structure of achievement motivation: A cross-cultural comparison. *Journal of Organizational Behavior*, 17, 431–444.

16. Borg, I., & Braun, M. (1996). Work values in East and West Germany: Different weights, but identical structures. *Journal of Organizational Behavior*, 17, 541–555; Brown, I. T. (2009). In Western Europe, more partners than bosses. Available at www.gallup.com/poll/114076/western-europe-partners-bosses.aspx?; Frese, M., Kring, W., Soose, A., & Zempel, J. (1996). Personal

initiate at work: Differences between East and West Germany. *Academy of Management Journal,* 39, 37–63.

17. Alder, N. J., & Gundersen, A. (2008). *International Dimensions of Organizational Behavior* (5th ed.). Mason, OH: Thompson-South-Western; Ronen, S., & Shenkar, O. (1985). Clustering countries on attitudinal dimensions: A review and synthesis. *Academy of Management Review,* 10, 435–454.

18. Ronen, S. (2001). Self actualizational vs. collectualization. In M. Erez, U. Kleinbeck, & H. Thierry (eds.), *Work Motivation in the Context of a Globalizing Economy* (341–368). Mahwah, NJ: Erlbaum. Hofstede, G. (2001). *Culture's Consequences* (2nd ed). Thousand Oaks, CA: Sage.

19. Herzberg, F. (1966). *Work and the Nature of Man.* Cleveland, OH: World.

20. Alder, N. J., & Gundersen, A. (2008). *International Dimensions of Organizational Behavior* (5th ed.). Mason, OH: Thompson-South-Western; Machungwa, P. D., & Schmitt, N. (1983). Work motivation in a developing country. *Journal of Applied Psychology,* 68, 31–42.

21. Kanungo, R. N., & Wright, R. W. (1983). A cross-cultural comparative study of managerial job attitudes. *Journal of International Business Studies,* 14, 115–129.

22. Hofstede, G. (2001). *Culture's Consequences* (2nd ed). Thousand Oaks, CA: Sage.

23. Mendonca, M., & Kanungo, R. N. (1994). Motivation through participative management. In R. N. Kanungo & M. Mendonca (eds.), *Work Motivation: Models for Developing Countries* (184–212). Thousand Oaks, CA: Sage; Robert, C., Probst, T. M., Martocchio, J. J., Drasgow, F., & Lawler, J. J. (2000). Empowerment and continuous improvement in the United States, Mexico, Poland, and India: Predicting fit on the basis of the dimensions of power distance and individualism. *Journal of Applied Psychology,* 85, 643–658.

24. Huang, X., & Van De Vliert, E. (2003). Where intrinsic job satisfaction fails to work: National moderators of intrinsic motivation. *Journal of Organizational Behavior,* 24, 159–179; Schaubroeck, J., Lam, S. S. K., & Xie, J. L. (2000). Collective efficacy versus self-efficacy in coping responses to stressors and control: A cross-cultural study. *Journal of Applied Psychology,* 85, 512–525.

25. Randolph, W. A., & Sashkin, M. (2002). Can organizational empowerment work in multinational settings? *Academy of Management Executive,* 16, 102–115.

26. d'Iribarne, P. (2002). Motivating workers in emerging countries: Universal tools and local applications. *Journal of Organizational Behavior,* 23, 243–256.

27. Mendonca, M., & Kanungo, R. N. (1994). Motivation through effective reward management in developing countries. In R. N. Kanungo & M. Mendonca (eds.), *Work Motivation: Models for Developing Countries* (49–83). Thousand Oaks, CA: Sage.

28. A survey of management: The return of von Clausewitz. *The Economist,* March 9, 2002, 18–20; Boyle, M. (2001). Nothing is rotten in Denmark. *Fortune,* February 19, 242.

29. Ding dong! Empowerment calling. *The Economist,* May 30, 2009, 70; Banerjee, N. (1995). For Mary Kay sales reps in Russia, hottest shade is the color of money. *Wall Street Journal,* August 30, A8. Also see www.marykay.com/company/aroundtheworld/default.aspx.

30. Gelade, G. A., Dobson, P., & Auer, K. (2008). Individualism, masculinity, and the sources of organizational commitment. *Journal of Cross-Cultural Psychology,* 39(5), 599–617.

31. Skinner, B. F. (1969). *Contingencies of Reinforcement.* New York: Appleton-Century-Crofts.

32. Sweeney, P. D., & McFarlin, D. B. (2002). *Organizational Behavior: Solutions for Management.* Burr Ridge, IL: Irwin/McGraw-Hill.

33. Mangaliso, M. P. (2001). Building competitive advantage from Ubuntu: Management lessons from South Africa. *Academy of Management Executive*, 15, 23–33; McFarlin, D. B., Coster, E. A., & Mogale-Pretorius, C. (1999). Management development in South Africa: Moving toward an Africanized framework. *Journal of Management Development*, 18, 63–78.

34. Bailey, J. R., & Chen, C. C. (1997). Conceptions of self and performance-related feedback in the U.S., Japan, and China. *Journal of International Business Studies*, 28, 605–625; Gelfand, M. J., Erez, M., & Aycan, Z. (2007). Cross-cultural organizational behavior. *Annual Review of Psychology*, 58, 479–514.

35. Podsakoff, P. M., Dorfman, P. W., Howell, J. P., & Tudor, W. D. (1986). Leader reward and punishment behaviors: A preliminary test of a culture-free style of leadership effectiveness. In R. N. Farmer (ed.), *Advances in International Comparative Management*, Vol. 2 (95–138). Amsterdam: Elsevier Ltd.

36. Hofstede, G. (2001). *Culture's Consequences* (2nd ed.). Thousand Oaks, CA: Sage.

37. Mendonca, M., & Kanungo, R. N. (1994). Motivation through effective reward management in developing countries. In R. N. Kanungo & M. Mendonca (eds.), *Work Motivation: Models for Developing Countries* (49–83). Thousand Oaks, CA: Sage.

38. d'Iribarne, P. (2002). Motivating workers in emerging countries: Universal tools and local applications. *Journal of Organizational Behavior*, 23, 243–256.

39. Porter, L. P., & Lawler, E. E. (1968). *Managerial Attitudes and Performance*. Homewood, IL: Irwin; Vroom, V. H. (1964). *Work and Motivation*. New York: Wiley.

40. Alder, N. J., & Gundersen, A. (2008*). International Dimensions of Organizational Behavior* (5th ed.). Mason, OH: Thompson-South-Western; Shenkar, O., & Von Glinow, M. A. (1994). Paradoxes of organizational theory and research: Using the case of China to illustrate national contingency. *Management Science*, 40, 56–71; Thomas, D. C. (2008). *Cross-Cultural Management: Essential Concepts* (2nd ed.). Thousand Oaks, CA: Sage.

41. Pennings, J. M. (1993). Executive reward systems: A cross-national comparison. *Journal of Management Studies*, 30, 261–279.

42. Executive pay in Europe: Pay attention. *The Economist*, June 14, 2008, 77–78; Reilly, D., Ball, D., & Ascarelli, S. (2003). Europe's low pay-rage threshold. *Wall Street Journal*, September 10, A8, A9.

43. Executive pay in Europe: Pay attention. *The Economist*, June 14, 2008, 77–78; Steinmetz, G. (1995). German banks note the value of bonuses. *Wall Street Journal*, May 9, A18; Stewart, M. (1996). German management: A challenge to Anglo-American managerial assumptions. *Business Horizons*, 39, 52–54; Walker, M. (2002). Deutsche Bank finds that it has to cut German roots to grow. *Wall Street Journal*, February 14, A1, A10.

44. Ono, Y. (2001). A restaurant chain in Japan chops up the social contract. *Wall Street Journal*, January 17, A1, A19.

45. Ono, Y. (2001). A restaurant chain in Japan chops up the social contract. *Wall Street Journal*, January 17, A1, A19.

46. Ono, Y. (2001). A restaurant chain in Japan chops up the social contract. *Wall Street Journal*, January 17, A1, A19; Tabuchi, H. (2008). Slacker nation? Young Japanese shun promotions. *Wall Street Journal*, November 1–2, A1, A6.

47. Sayonara salaryman. *The Economist*, January 5, 2008, 68–70; Foreign firms in Japan. *The Economist*, October 26, 2002, 58.

48. Dubinsky, A. J., Kotabe, M., Lim, C. U., & Michaels, R. E. (1994). Differences in motivational perceptions among U.S., Japanese, and Korean sales personnel. *Journal of Business Research*, 30, 175–185; Ono, Y. (2002). Rethinking how Japanese should think. *Wall Street Journal*, March 25, A12, A14.

49. Adams, J. S. (1965). Inequity in social exchange. In L. Berkowitz (ed.), *Advances in Experimental Social Psychology*, Vol. 2 (267–299). New York: Academic Press.

50. Allen, R. S., Takeda, M., & White, C. S. (2005). Cross-cultural equity sensitivity: A test of differences between the U.S. and Japan. *Journal of Managerial Psychology*, 20, 641–662; McFarlin, D. B., & Frone, M. R. (1990). Examining a two-tier wage structure in a non-union firm. *Industrial Relations*, 29, 145–157; Sweeney, P. D., & McFarlin, D. B. (2002). *Organizational Behavior: Solutions for Management*. Burr Ridge, IL: Irwin/McGraw-Hill.

51. Choi, J., & Chen, C. C. (2007). The relationships of distributive justice and compensation system fairness to employee attitudes in international joint ventures. *Journal of Organizational Behavior*, 28, 687–703; Fischer, R., Smith, P. B., Richey, B., Ferreira, M. C., Assmar, E. M. L., Maes, J., & Stumpf, S. (2007). How do organizations allocate rewards? The predictive validity of national values, economic and organizational factors across six nations. *Journal of Cross Cultural Psychology*, 38(1), 3–18; Morris, M. W., & Leung, K. (2000). Justice for all? Progress in research on cultural variation in the psychology of distributive and procedural justice. *Applied Psychology: An International Review*, 49, 100–132.

52. Gelfand, M. J., Erez, M., & Aycan, Z. (2007). Cross-cultural organizational behavior. *Annual Review of Psychology*, 58, 479–514; Hofstede, G. (2001). *Culture's Consequences* (2nd ed). Thousand Oaks, CA: Sage.

53. Bond, M. II. (1991). *Beyond the Chinese Face*. Hong Kong: Oxford University Press; Shenkar, O., & Von Glinow, M. A. (1994). Paradoxes of organizational theory and research: Using the case of China to illustrate national contingency. *Management Science*, 40, 56–71.

54. Kim, T., Weber, T. J., Leung, K., & Muramoto, Y. (2010). Perceived fairness of pay: The importance of task versus maintenance inputs in Japan, South Korea, and Hong Kong. *Management and Organization Review*, 6, 31–54; Bond, M. H., Leung, K., & Wan, K. C. (1982). How does cultural collectivism operate? The impact of task and maintenance contribution on reward distribution. *Journal of Cross-Cultural Psychology*, 13, 186–200.

55. Gelfand, M. J., Erez, M., & Aycan, Z. (2007). Cross-cultural organizational behavior. *Annual Review of Psychology*, 58, 479–514; Kim, K. L., Park, H. J., & Suzuki, N. (1990). Reward allocations in the U.S., Japan, and Korea: A comparison of individualistic and collectivistic cultures. *Academy of Management Journal*, 33, 188–198; Thomas, D. C. (2008). *Cross-Cultural Management: Essential Concepts* (2nd ed.). Thousand Oaks, CA: Sage.

56. Fischer, R. (2008). Organizational justice and reward allocation. In P. B. Smith, M. F. Peterson, & D. C. Thomas (eds.), *The Handbook of Cross-Cultural Management Research* (135–150). Thousand Oaks, CA: Sage; Giacobbe-Miller, J. K., Miller, D. J., Zhang, W., & Victorov, V. I. (2003). Country and organizational-level adaptation to foreign workplace ideologies: A comparative study of distributive justice values in China, Russia, and the United States. *Journal of International Business*, 34, 389–406.

57. Wonacott, P. (2002). China's secret weapon: Smart, cheap labor for high-tech goods. *Wall Street Journal*, March 14, A1, A6; Chen, C. C. (1995). New trends in rewards allocation preferences: A Sino-U.S. comparison. *Academy of Management Journal*, 38, 408–428.

58. Gomez-Mejia, L., & Welbourne, T. (1991). Compensation strategies in a global context. *Human Resource Planning*, 14, 29–41.

59. Schneider, S. C., & Barsoux, J. L. (2003). *Managing across Cultures* (2nd ed.). Harlow, England: Pearson Education; Thomas, D. C. (2008). *Cross-Cultural Management* (2nd ed.). Thousand Oaks, CA: Sage.

Chapter 6

Effective Leadership in a Multicultural Environment

All of the great leaders have had one characteristic in common: it was the willingness to confront unequivocally the major anxiety of their people in their time. This, and not much else, is the essence of leadership.

—John Kenneth Galbraith

Leadership is among one of the most studied topics in all of social sciences. And rightfully so because leaders can influence, persuade, and inspire members not only of their organizations but also a whole country. There is no dearth of thinking about what leadership is and how it operates—including Galbraith's view illustrated in the opening quote. The thousands of studies completed by researchers in organizational behavior and psychology are also accompanied by practical advice. If you visit the Barnes & Noble bookstore website and type in "leadership" as your search term, you will have nearly 70,000 books to buy for your nightstand. Most of this literature is new, with the great majority written in the last 40 years. Perhaps there is more to leadership than what Galbraith suggests above. But, more importantly for our purposes, much of this work was conducted among and about leaders in the United States and Western Europe.

GLOBALIZATION OF LEADERSHIP

Fortunately, in the last decade, attention to cultural influences on leadership behavior has expanded greatly. This attention might be at the most opportune time. The impact of globalization on world economies, and all that comes with it (e.g., demographic patterns; flows of capital and goods, expanding supply chains), presents daunting challenges for today's leaders. Whether it is coordinating virtual teams from 10,000 miles away to leading a foreign subsidiary as an expatriate, to running a multicultural department in their home countries, it is tough to be a leader. Consequently, effective leadership in international companies requires openness, an appreciation of cultural differences, and the ability to bridge differences quickly in order to develop culturally synergistic solutions to international management challenges.[1] As one expert suggests, globalization has presented several new challenges for effective leadership:

- Leaders increasingly need to be able to influence people from different cultures.
- Successful persuasion and influence is built on a good cultural understanding.
- To be maximally effective, leaders need to understand how their actions are viewed by others, especially across cultures.[2]

In this chapter, therefore, we will review the current thinking about leadership in general, its applicability across cultures, and how this thinking can be used by practicing managers.

EFFECTIVE LEADERSHIP IN AN INTERNATIONAL CONTEXT

Leaders set things in motion in their organizations—they guide the development of the firm's vision and they enable employees to accomplish goals that lead to achievement of that vision. Yet what leadership means in practice can become blurry once borders are crossed. One reason is that perspectives on leadership vary, including views about what characteristics leaders must possess to be effective. Regardless, we know that leaders exist in every culture. But how are various attributes about leadership viewed across cultures? Some features are viewed as positive contributions to leader effectiveness in most countries. Likewise, some attributes are widely seen as detractors from leader success across borders. Still other traits and behaviors are viewed differently depending on the culture in which they're enacted. Table 6.1 presents some examples of leader attributes that are positive in most places, negative in most places, and interpreted very differently across cultures. Being decisive, honest, and positive are valued features about leaders across borders. Leaders in countries as varied as Austria, Iran, Kazakhstan, Singapore, South Africa, and Zimbabwe are expected to be decisive, honest, and fair. Conversely, egocentric behavior and leaders who freely express irritation and anger are frowned upon among people across most borders and cultures.

Because of its practical significance, research on the importance of various leadership attributes across cultures has continued. One recent study showed that self-awareness, an attribute often seen as critical to leadership effectiveness in the United States, may not travel well. Americans seem to embrace the open sharing of inner thoughts and feelings. This self-awareness is widely seen among Americans as helpful in improving managers' use of feedback they receive from others. Many other cultures, however, place great value on saving face (as discussed in previous chapters). As a result, direct communication or feedback is a far less acceptable management tool (see Chapters 2 and 3), and less important for leadership success.

But even when attributes are generally seen as good or bad in most cultures, how those attributes are manifested varies considerably depending on the cultural context. For example, it has already been noted that being decisive is widely viewed as positive. But, in the Netherlands, employee participation and consultation has a long tradition. A decisive leader who ignores this can pay a price. Even if certain types of leadership behaviors are common in a culture, this does not mean that an international manager should automatically emulate or copy those behaviors. An expatriate manager may actually enjoy more latitude in performing actions that counter the typical cultural tendencies. This is because employees know the manager is a foreign national with different styles and norms, and they may be more open to a counter-culture technique used by that manager. Some foreign managers may even capitalize on that latitude early in their tenure. A new approach may be exactly what's needed and could be more effective in the long run.[3] This strategy, however, should be used

Table 6.1
Leadership Attributes across Cultures: Examples of the Good, the Bad, and the Different

Common View of Leadership Attribute	Leader Attributes
Viewed as good in many cultures	Decisive
	Good communicator
	Honest
	Intelligent
	Has integrity
	Positive
	Trustworthy
Viewed as bad in many cultures	Dictatorial
	Egocentric
	Irritable
	Ruthless
Viewed differently across cultures	Ambitious
	Enthusiastic
	Individualistic
	Logical
	Sensitive
	Willing to take risks

Sources: Adapted from Frost, J., & Walker, M. (2007). Cross-cultural leadership. *Engineering Management*, June/July, 27–29; Dorfman, P. W., Hanges, P. J., & Brodbeck, F. C. (2004). Leadership prototypes and cultural variation: The identification of culturally endorsed implicit theories of leadership. In R. J. House, P. J. Hanges, M. Javidan, P. W. Dorfman, & V. Gupta (eds.), *Leadership, Culture, and Organizations: The GLOBE Study of 62 Societies*, Vol. 1 (343–394). Thousand Oaks, CA: Sage.

thoughtfully. Too often, expatriates do not take the time to learn cultural features, and then, when faced with everyday production pressures, they revert to their familiar home country approach. Leaders need to do their cultural homework. Do managers behave differently across cultures in leadership roles? Do certain situations require similar leadership behaviors, regardless of culture? Can corporate culture override or weaken other cross-cultural effects with respect to leadership? The next section will offer some answers to these and other important questions.

LEADER BEHAVIOR ACROSS CULTURES AND TIME

Complicating matters even further is the fact that leadership concepts, values, and styles continue to evolve around the world—especially in global business circles. We cannot assume that what was a valued leader attribute 20 years ago will be the same today. For example, an evolutionary shift in leader behaviors can be seen in the Czech Republic, Poland, Romania, and other countries in Eastern Europe. The stodgy, status quo leader of the old days could not withstand the great social and economic upheaval experienced in recent years in these countries.[4] Yet tension between old and new ways of leading has not gone away completely. And it is not limited to former members of the Soviet bloc. South Korea, for example, has produced some remarkable success stories in recent years, with many Korean brands such as Hyundai, LG, and Samsung now household names in the United States and other Western markets. There is little doubt that some of this success reflects the impact of shifting leadership cultures in some of the top South Korean firms, a point we ask you to consider more closely in the chapter closing case.

How Do Leaders Behave?

A common distinction drawn by Western researchers is that two basic types of leader behavior exist. First, leaders engage in *task-oriented behavior* when they work to clarify performance expectations and specific procedures to be followed. Other task-related examples include planning, scheduling, providing technical help, and setting goals. In contrast, *relationship-oriented behavior* includes showing concern for feelings, needs, and the well-being of subordinates. Other examples include expressing empathy, warmth, encouragement, consideration, and trust toward subordinates. While there seems to be general agreement on these two main forms of leader actions, which type of behavior produces the best performance? In which countries? There is really no simple answer. On the one hand, leaders in collectivist cultures (e.g., Chile) may tend to use relationship-oriented behaviors more than leaders in individualist cultures (e.g., Australia). On the other hand, when relationship-oriented behaviors are used, employees across a wide variety of cultures tend to respond positively. Reactions to task-oriented behavior, however, tend to be more variable across cultures. The bottom line is that depending on the circumstances—which may include cultural factors, organizational context, and employee characteristics—leaders may need to use different combinations of task-oriented and relationship-oriented behaviors to be effective.[5]

Alternative Views of Leader Behavior

Non-Western experts have proposed some interesting alternatives to simplistic distinctions between task- and relationship-oriented leader behaviors. Take India as an example—it presents a challenging leadership environment. This chapter's *Culture Clash* feature describes what might be an emerging, indigenous leadership style, done the Indian way.

Japan has also produced some interesting ideas about leadership. For example, the *PM leader* is a leadership style that combines complementary concern about problem solving and motivation of group performance (performance leadership) with behavior designed to promote interdependence, avoid conflict, and maintain harmony within the group (maintenance leadership). On the surface, these behaviors resemble the distinction between task- and relationship-oriented behaviors drawn by U.S. researchers. But implementation in Japan makes it clear that both sets of behaviors are different because of their grounding in this different cultural context. For instance, a Japanese leader discussing a subordinate's family problems with other employees would likely be seen as very high in maintenance leadership. The same behavior in the United States, however, would most likely be viewed as inappropriate and not very leaderly at all. Similarly, performance leadership behaviors that would be seen as positive in Japan, such as being strict about following company policies or urging employees to work to their utmost as a group, would likely be uncomfortable or off-putting to many U.S. employees. These divergent reactions likely reflect cultural differences. U.S. employees typically view leadership as an individual process, wanting leaders to make tough calls and to take charge. In contrast, traditional Japanese leadership tends to have a more communal quality, focusing on group performance. Decision making in Japan is typically much slower, involving plenty of consultation with and concern for peers.[6]

Lumping everything into two behavioral dimensions can mask important cross-cultural differences. For instance, the relationship-oriented behavior described by Western scholars is colder and more egalitarian than the paternalistic Indian version.[7] A paternalistic version of relationship-oriented behavior may, in fact, produce positive reactions from employees in places such as India, the Middle East, and parts of Latin America. Consequently, international managers may get themselves into trouble if they limit leadership to Western versions of task-oriented and relationship-oriented behaviors.[8]

A survey of Iranian employees illustrates this point. Employees were asked whether their direct supervisor showed various forms of task-oriented and relationship-oriented behaviors. The results indicated that there were no noticeable correlations between the task- and relationship-oriented ratings and either the actual performance of the Iranian managers or with subordinate satisfaction. Instead, the results showed that Iranian supervisors who acted in a benevolent and paternalistic way had the best performance ratings from subordinates. These findings certainly imply that Western definitions of leader behavior may not fit Middle Eastern cultures. In Iran, the boundary between work and family relationships is often ambiguous. The warm but firm father figure who plays such a prominent role in Iranian society translates into the supervisor who is directive but still shows respect for subordinates.[9]

Leadership style must be understood in terms of both its general underlying structure (something less easy to see and understand) as well as the tangible behaviors actually observed. For example, U.S. and Japanese leaders might agree that being supportive (relationship-oriented behavior) is important for success. In the individualist United States, a manager might express support by showing respect for subordinates' ideas. In collectivist Japan, however, a manager might express support by spending more time with subordinates as a group.[10]

In fact, a study comparing managers from the United States, United Kingdom, Japan, and Hong Kong found that while there was agreement on basic aspects of leadership style, the specific expression of these behaviors varied across the four countries.[11] These differences may explain why managers often have problems in foreign contexts. For instance, U.S. and Japanese managers often encounter enormous difficulties leading in each other's home environment. Overcoming this may require a blending of leadership strategies that parallel our synergistic recommendations on motivation.[12]

CULTURE CLASH

Vineet Nayar: Changing the Leadership Culture, 1.2 Billion at a Time

India is a large and rapidly developing country with a number of features shared by the United States. For example, India is the world's largest democracy, with the rule of law firmly established. It nurtures a free press, a strong judiciary, and well-educated business leaders who operate in open markets. Yet there are significant differences, too—ones that can create a culture clash if you are not well schooled on each culture. Likewise, even within a country as large as India, clashes can occur between old and new. This might be especially the case in India, where personal relations are critical and complexities abound due to culture, religion, caste, and family ties, just to name a few.

This unique mix may have led to an indigenous and unique leadership style. Many Indian experts have suggested that a nurturing style of leadership that mixes empathy and concern for subordinates with an emphasis on getting the job done often works best in many Indian work contexts. Researchers asked Indian executives about this and related leadership issues. Leaders of the 100 largest publicly listed companies were asked to order their priorities in running their businesses. The responses were compared to those of U.S. executives. A distinctive feature of the Indian approach was the high priority that leaders placed on investing in and power given to their employees. This ranked well above maximizing shareholder value, which was the highest priority voiced by U.S. executives.[13]

Given this priority, it is no surprise that interesting and unique leadership ideas are coming out of India. There is no doubt that large portions of India remain impoverished, but in the growing tech sector, Indian companies are fighting hard to attract and retain talented and highly skilled employees who are among the world's best. At HCL Technologies, the fifth largest information technology outsourcing firm in India, even throwing money, perks, and fancy benefits at employees was not enough to stem a high attrition rate. So HCL's CEO, Vineet Nayar, decided to focus on his people. First, he deployed a 360-degree feedback system that collected assessments of over 1,500 managers worldwide (including Nayar himself) from their peers, bosses, subordinates, customers, and more. As Nayar said, "Our competitive differentiation is that we are more transparent than anybody else in our industry . . . [employees and customers] like us because there are no hidden secrets." HCL routinely puts the results of these 360-degree reviews on the firm's intranet for all to see—including Nayar's own evaluation. Instead of determining who gets bonuses or promotions, the goal of the system is to encourage democracy. And in a reversal of the usual truism (as Nayar puts it), our goal is "to get the manager to suck up to the employee."

Other new approaches include an online employee complaint system, which employees can use for any issue. Nayar also spends his weekends personally responding to the 50 or so questions he receives from employees every week and posting his responses for all to see. Nayar claims that a traditional command-and-control orientation at HCL is giving way to collaborative management. But he is not content to let this take its own course; Nayar has pushed for more rapid evolution. In any one year, he spends upward of half his time in town hall meetings with employees, sharing his views and vision and taking questions. He has a personal goal of shaking every employee's hand every year, with the goal (self-stated) of "destroying the office of the CEO" in five years. On his public blog (also titled "Destroying the Office of the CEO") he explains that he wants decision making pushed out of the C suite and into where the company meets the client.

Overall, these unique employee-focused approaches may be consistent with the nurturing style of leadership described above. Either way, it has gotten people's attention. And while a variety of Western firms have visited India to learn about HCL's leadership ideas, none have adopted its 360-degree system so far. Nayar's explanation is simple: "It's too radical for most of them."[14] It is easy to see why Vineet Nayar's well-understood motto is "Employee first, customers second."

Culture and the Impact of Leader Behavior

Culture also may be a driving force for the impact of leader behavior on employee commitment and performance. In collectivist, high-power-distance cultures such as Taiwan or Thailand, task-oriented behaviors may have a stronger positive impact on employees than in individualist, low-power-distance cultures such as the United States. The criticism that Japanese managers often aim at subordinates would likely seem punitive to many Americans, even though it works well in Japan. In their high-power-distance, collectivist context, Japanese managers will often balance criticism with plenty of supportive behaviors and go to great lengths to minimize status symbols. On the other hand, Americans are more likely to use status symbols such as a large office to project authority.[15]

Leadership knowledge, however, may be especially important when working within another culture. Accordingly, what might happen when U.S. subordinates work under Japanese leadership at a facility in the United States, as they do in Illinois, Ohio, and California, among other locales? In one study, Japanese managers had less of an impact on their U.S. subordinates than on their Japanese subordinates and had less influence overall than did the U.S. supervisors. U.S. subordinates, however, performed better when a Japanese supervisor was friendly and supportive but worse when a U.S. supervisor did basically the same thing. So supervisors' nationalities may affect how their behavior is *interpreted* by subordinates in specific contexts. In this case, friendliness by a U.S. supervisor may imply weakness or maybe even phoniness, while the same behavior from a Japanese supervisor may be seen as a desire to get things done.[16]

Are there leader behaviors that produce the same positive effects across cultural contexts? Yes, at least according to experts testing Likert's System 4 model. Likert argued that there are four basic systems of leadership. In an *exploitative authoritative* organization (System 1), decision making is reserved by upper management, communication is top-down, and punishments are used to motivate. The *benevolent authoritative* organization (System 2) is also autocratic, but managers are more paternalistic, interested in employees' needs, and allow some limited decision-making freedom for employees. In a *consultative* organization (System 3), employees are even more involved in communicating, decision making, and working with managers, with management reserving the right to make the final decision. And in a *democrative* organization (System 4), employees are heavily involved in decision making on important issues, while managers are supportive, the use of teams is widespread, and employees communicate laterally as well as vertically.[17]

Likert suggested that all companies should move toward the more participative System 3 and System 4 approaches, because they tend to result in better employee performance and morale. This suggestion is supported by research that examines U.S. companies. We would predict that participative approaches (Systems 3 and 4) are a good match for low-power-distance cultures such as the United States. But would a paternalistic, autocratic leadership approach fit better, and result in more productive workers, in a high-power-distance culture? The answer seems to be yes. One study did a careful comparison of managers in production plants in Mexico and the United States, both owned by the same U.S. firm and producing the same product. The results revealed several interesting findings. Mexican managers were more paternalistic and autocratic than their U.S. counterparts. Overall, the Mexicans used System 2, whereas the Americans were more likely to use System 3. Yet both plants were equally productive and efficient. Apparently, the more paternalistic Mexican style was a good match for the high-power-distance culture in Mexico. Likewise, the more participative System 3 approach was a good fit for the U.S. plant and its U.S. values.[18]

The broader implication is that foreign outposts can match the level of performance in U.S. facilities without having to use a strictly U.S. approach to leadership.

Consider the U.S.–Mexico comparison in more detail. Many of the initial production problems facing the now hundreds of U.S.-owned plants in Mexico may be due to the use of management techniques inconsistent with Mexican cultural values. These differences surface when U.S. multinationals send poorly prepared Americans to manage Mexican workers. Table 6.2 describes some of the divergent expectations that may separate U.S. and Mexican managers. For example, Mexican workers may sometimes appear passive to Americans. Compared to the United States, Mexico is less individualist but higher in power distance and uncertainty avoidance. Many Mexicans feel that conformity, respect, and personal loyalty to supervisors are important and should be rewarded. Indeed, for many Mexican employees, viewing the organization as an extended family makes sense. Just like in a family, people should work cooperatively but within prescribed roles. The value that Americans place on individual achievement and power sharing may strike many Mexican employees as inconsistent with this view. Mexican employees might expect managers to make decisions affecting their work life. Because of their high-power-distance viewpoints, Mexican followers expect leaders to use their power instead of delegating it. A participative workplace or program, therefore, would be harder to implement in Mexico than the United States. In fact, in the GLOBE study described in Chapter 2, Mexicans rated participative leadership fifty-ninth among the lowest of all 62 countries that participated in the study. Yet there are also signs of change. Even though they rate alternative leader styles low, Mexicans simultaneously say they believe there should be less power and status differences in their society. More such change in Mexico may be seen in the near future.[19]

Regardless of whether such changes take place, U.S. managers need to be sensitive to such differences when interacting with Mexican employees. For instance, honoring the status of others is a key part of Mexican business practice. At a plant in Mexico, the ranking union leader was insulted when the U.S. plant manager failed to introduce him to visiting executives. Formality is one way that many Mexicans recognize status differences, and this can clash with the U.S. tendency toward informality. For example, a U.S. manager in Mexico tried to reduce status differences by wearing jeans and dropping titles, but instead he appeared unsophisticated to Mexicans. Distance between management and labor is expected. Indeed, Mexican workers often see autonomy as less important and may respond best to formal but empathetic managers who supervise them closely. Historically, Mexican supervisors are used to being listened to—having to explain an order is seen as weakness. This can also explain why U.S. efforts to share power and encourage problem solving can be misunderstood by some other cultures. Some studies suggest that this can be addressed by training that relies on culturally familiar concepts to encourage change, such as relating to each other as family in the workplace or conceptions of loyalty to a specific manager (not a set of policies).[20]

Table 6.2
Crossing the Leadership Border: Differences between U.S. and Mexican Managers

Leadership Issue	Management Expectations and Attitudes	
	U.S. Managers	**Mexican Managers**
Valued subordinate behaviors	Initiative, achievement	Obedience, harmony
Key to subordinate evaluation	Performance	Personal loyalty
Leadership style	Loose/informal, communicative, power sharing possible	Close/formal, empathetic, use of directives, little power sharing
Basis of discipline/ justice	Uniform application of rules and procedures	Personal relationships
Work environment model	Competitive team	Cooperative family

Source: Adapted from de Forest, M. E. (1994). Thinking of a plant in Mexico? *Academy of Management Executive*, 8, 33–40.

Aligning Leadership Behavior with the Cultural Context

Global managers may need to alter and adapt their leadership style to expectations in specific countries. To illustrate, consider a common cultural mistake made by U.S. managers in Japan—giving portions of projects to different individuals instead of handing it off to one group. In the United States, giving clear, specialized assignments to each employee is often seen as the best way to organize work. In Japan, however, it would be better to give the entire project to a group of subordinates, letting them tackle it as they see fit. The Japanese view is that interaction among employees provides the structure for organizing work.[21]

Nevertheless, many Americans continue to believe that if they are good managers in Chicago or Austin, they can export their style overseas with great success. One study debunked this idea by comparing Americans managing in Hong Kong and the United States on 12 different leader behaviors. As expected, the U.S. managers behaved similarly in both places. But the relationship between behavior and performance was quite different. While eight of the leader behaviors were correlated with overall performance in the United States, only one behavior was correlated with performance for the Americans in Hong Kong. In short, the same behaviors that worked in the United States had little impact in Hong Kong.[22]

Americans are not the only ones who have trouble adapting to a foreign business context. Unfortunately, they are joined by many other nationalities in these actions. For example, consider some of the trouble experienced by managers from Siemens, the huge German conglomerate. Siemens has subsidiaries and plants in the United States with thousands of U.S. employees. One complaint heard from the U.S. side is that German leadership is too autocratic, inflexible, slow, and bureaucratic. Americans cite the many decisions requiring approval from Germany. At Siemens, a management board meets in Munich to make decisions about a variety of strategic and operational issues. When major decisions are involved, the supervisory board (consisting of both employees and shareholders) has to step in and approve the decision made by the management board before the firm can proceed. As you might suspect, many Americans view this leadership approach as inefficient and as one that tends to shut out local input and initiative.[23]

TRANSFORMATIONAL LEADERSHIP: DOES IT WORK ACROSS CULTURES?

In this section we consider *transformational leadership*, a recent and increasingly popular perspective in the United States. While transformational leaders might be good at showing key task- and relationship-orientated behaviors, their skills go far beyond those. A transformational leader is said to be able to galvanize employees, even turning poorly performing companies into winners in a relatively short time. This happens when the transformational leader creates an emotional bond with employees—something that inspires intense loyalty and outstanding performance. This bond is the result of four features about a leader:

1. *Charisma*—arouses intense emotions among followers based on faith in and identification with the leader.
2. *Use of inspirational appeals*—communicates a clear and compelling vision for the future with very high performance expectations for employees.
3. *Intellectual stimulation*—challenges subordinates to think about new ways to do things, overcome problems, and design products as they pursue the leader's vision.
4. *Individualized consideration*—offers subordinates personal attention, empathy, and communication.[24]

In U.S. firms, transformational leaders can have positive effects on the effort, performance, and satisfaction of subordinate employees. Additionally, the charisma they possess increases the perception of leader effectiveness. This often requires a willingness to cede control to the leader, which is more likely when subordinates feel vulnerable, such as during a business downturn or other external threat. Indeed, transformational leaders seem to have their greatest impact during a crisis.[25]

But does this mean that international business, with its rapid changes and competitive threats, is tailor-made for transformational leadership? Some experts say that the most successful international managers are transformational leaders. Supporting this view are studies showing the positive impact of transformational leadership in places as diverse as Israel, New Zealand, Germany, and Singapore. Indeed, a large-scale study of leadership and its effects in many countries found that behaviors associated with transformational leaders, such as charisma, confidence, and trust, are widely accepted as key leader attributes. It is important to note that this finding cuts across cultures widely viewed as very different, including some in Asia and the West.[26]

Still, broad statements about the global value of transformational leadership should be treated cautiously for several reasons.[27] First, the nature of the positive impact of transformational leadership can vary from place to place. Most studies done in Western cultures find improved job satisfaction to be one of the benefits of transformational leadership—something that does not seem to be the case in the Middle East or India. Second, research suggests that regardless of the type of positive impacts, they are driven by different aspects of transformational leadership in different cultures. Sometimes they result from unique, culture-specific aspects. For instance, research has found that doing one's duty (*dharma*) is a key component of transformational leadership in India, whereas in China, showing good moral character and sensitivity to others are important parts of transformational behavior. Further, attributes such as risk taking and ambition are more valued in Western countries, whereas leaders who display self-effacement, sensitivity, and compassion are more influential in some East Asian countries.[28]

Other research suggests that the behavior of transformational leaders can actually have negative effects on innovation in an international management context, as it did for research and development alliances between U.S. and Japanese firms. This highlights the impact of international context (in this case, a complex, research-oriented alliance) on leadership effectiveness. But we need more research about how transformational leadership works and under what circumstances.[29]

For now, the appeal of transformational leadership may be somewhat limited in collectivist cultures where group harmony is highly prized. In countries such as South Korea and Indonesia, for instance, a charismatic leader who tries to galvanize individual performance could be seen as destructive to group cohesiveness. In such cultures, tweaking a transformational approach to focus on group performance may be a better bet. Regardless, implementing a transformational approach to leadership will likely be more difficult in Korea than in the United States. Yet most research on transformational leadership does not study foreigners or expatriates using transformational styles with local employees.

As discussed earlier, U.S. employees may react differently to Japanese managers than they would to U.S. managers, even when managerial behavior is similar. This has made some wonder whether a Japanese executive would have been seen as successful in taking over Nissan as Carlos Ghosn, who is of Lebanese decent, was a few years ago. Seen as heroic by many Japanese, Ghosn came from Renault and turned struggling Nissan around. Ghosn was born in Brazil and raised in France. His tactics were decidedly non-Japanese: he closed unproductive plants and fired employees while pushing for bold new products. Ghosn's own words—in this case, on product design—speak to his inspirational vision and intellectual stimulation of employees, both hallmarks of transformational leaders: "We are unleashing the imagination of our designers as part of our strategy for the market. You are going to see revolutionary designs from Nissan."[30] A foreigner such as Ghosn might have an easier time enacting a transformational style than would an indigenous Japanese.

CROSS-CULTURAL LEADERSHIP EFFECTIVENESS: PULLING EVERYTHING TOGETHER

There is no shortage of thinking about leadership. Unfortunately, when it comes to a comprehensive framework that can account for a variety of individual, organizational, and situational factors—including culture—there is still a long way to go. Nevertheless, this discussion concludes by presenting several leadership viewpoints that will help pull things together in a practical way.[31]

International managers are busy people who already have a tougher road to travel than domestic-only managers. So, while they may appreciate the processes by which effective international leadership might unfold, they inevitably will ask for practical guidance about leadership effectiveness in different parts of the globe. To address these needs, two frameworks are presented that summarize the impact of culture on international leadership. These are not meant to be easy checklists of advice to follow, and they should not preclude international managers from thinking critically about their specific leadership situations. They can, however, provide some important initial guidance for international managers to consider.

The first is the GLOBE approach that comes from the impressive research effort discussed in Chapter 3 involving scholars from more than 60 countries. The GLOBE project uncovered six basic leadership dimensions, pinpointed because they are potential drivers of leadership effectiveness. The study also suggested where these leadership features would be most and least likely to be displayed. Table 6.3 summarizes these findings. Overall, the researchers discovered that two leadership dimensions—charismatic/value-based and team-oriented—were positive contributors to effectiveness, while one dimension—self-protective—was generally negative. This finding generally held across countries and cultures. We would expect, however, that there may still be differences in how a leader would behave in order to be charismatic or team-oriented in a specific culture. Regardless of how a leader might tweak his or her behavior to convey leadership dimensions to employees, a leader is the one who has the most consistent impact on effectiveness across countries and cultures. So it is worth one's time to investigate these dimensions fully to find out

Table 6.3
Leader Behavior Dimensions: Effectiveness and Prevalence across Cultural Boundaries

Leader Behavior Dimension	Description of Behavior	Effective across Countries/ Cultures?	Where Is Dimension Most and Least Prevalent?
Autonomous	Encourages individualist and independent behavior	Depends—ranges from facilitating to impeding effectiveness	Most prevalent in Eastern Europe; least prevalent in Latin America
Charismatic/value based	Motivates/inspires, high expectations; driven by beliefs	Generally facilitates leader effectiveness	Most prevalent in Anglo nations; least prevalent in Middle East
Humane orientation	Supportive, generous, considerate, compassionate	Modestly facilitates leader effectiveness but has little impact in some places	Most prevalent in South Asia; least prevalent in Nordic countries
Participative	Involves others in making decisions	Generally positive impact on leader effectiveness but considerable variation	Most prevalent in Germanic countries; least prevalent in Middle East
Self-protective	Concerned with safety, security, face saving	Generally negative impact on leader effectiveness	Most prevalent in South Asia; least prevalent in Nordic countries
Team oriented	Focuses on team building, common goals among team members	Generally facilitates leader effectiveness	Most prevalent in Latin America; least prevalent in Middle East

Source: Adapted from House, R. J., Hanges, P. J., Javidan, M., Dorfman, P. W., & Gupta, V. (eds.). (2004). *Culture, Leadership, and Organizations: The GLOBE Study of 62 Societies*. Thousand Oaks, CA: Sage.

how charismatic/value-based leadership operates in Indonesia, Kuwait, or Canada when on assignment there. For the remaining dimensions (autonomous, humane oriented, participative), the results were mixed, with effectiveness much more a function of the cultural context (again, see Table 6.3). In short, in the right cultural environment, these dimensions could prove moderately to highly effective.[32]

A second model that might provide good advice to leaders is one that is arguably the most proscriptive of all, and one that has been tailored to include cultural variables. The *path-goal leadership* approach predicts that leadership effectiveness is contingent on matching leadership style to a particular business situation. So, for example, a research and development division might require a different leader style than one in which customer service is the primary function. To understand this approach, it is important to know the four basic leadership styles:

- *Directive.* This is a common leadership style that occurs when leaders provide clear procedures and rules for subordinates to follow when doing their jobs.
- *Supportive.* Here the leader focuses on subordinates' needs and overall well-being to maintain positive relationships.
- *Participative.* Leaders exhibiting this style consult with their subordinates, solicit their opinions, and otherwise involve them in decision making.
- *Achievement oriented.* This style focuses on actions leaders take to maximize subordinate performance by setting lofty goals, providing challenges, and emphasizing excellence.

A key prediction of the models is that leaders are most effective when they use the style that best fits the demands of a particular situation. In fact, several elements may shape which style produces the highest motivation and performance among employees. For example, tasks that are poorly defined or unpredictable may require more directive leadership. On the other hand, tasks that are well defined with clear guidelines for performance may be a better fit for participative leadership. Similarly, employees who lack experience may benefit from directive leadership, while employees who have well-developed skills may benefit from achievement-oriented leadership.[33]

Some experts have also factored in cultural dimensions (see the discussion of Hofstede in Chapter 3) into the path-goal approach. In effect, these become other situational elements that should be considered when adopting a more effective leader style. For example, participative leadership should work best in low-power-distance cultures, such as Canada, while directive leadership should work best in high-power-distance societies, such as the Philippines. Countries with moderate levels of power distance may find leadership that combines participation with some supportive behavior most attractive. A hybrid style, combining both supportive and directive behaviors, should work best in collectivist societies. Individualist societies, which are often associated with low power distance, should embrace participative leadership. Finally, strong-uncertainty-avoidance cultures may prefer directive leadership, while in cultures that are more tolerant of ambiguity, participative and achievement-oriented styles might be better received. These suggestions are presented in Table 6.4. It is important to remember that these are generalizations. International managers need to consider factors besides culture, such as local laws, division goals, and so on, to arrive at the leadership approach that will work best in their specific situation.[34]

Table 6.4
Adding Cultural Contingencies to Path-Goal Theory:
Identifying Compatible Leadership Styles

Culture	Country Example	Most Compatible Leadership Style			
		Directive	Supportive	Participative	Achievement
Small PD	Sweden			X	
Large PD	France	X			
Moderate PD	United States		X	X	
Collectivist	Taiwan	X	X		
Individualist	Denmark			X	
Moderate individualist	Argentina			X	
Strong UA	Greece	X			
Weak UA	England			X	X
Moderate UA	Germany			X	X

Source: Adapted from Rodrigues, C. (1990). The situation and national culture as contingencies for leadership behavior: Two conceptual models. In B. Prasad (ed.), *Advances in International Comparative Management*, Vol. 5 (51–68). Greenwich, CT: JAI Press.

Note: PD = power distance. UA = uncertainty avoidance.

LEADERSHIP DEVELOPMENT IN MULTINATIONALS

The leadership challenges discussed in this chapter are daunting and add to an already difficult job. After all, leaders are not exactly welcomed with open arms and showered with positive feedback in their own countries, let alone while working in a foreign culture. Presented in Figure 6.1 are the results of a study of nearly 30,000 employees who rated their senior management on five attributes. Ratings included features such as the leader's ability to deal with company challenges and their people-management skills. The highest-rated leaders were from China and India—over 70% of employees rated leaders as effective in those countries. Overall, however, the average score given to leaders across the 21 countries was only 55%, with Japan bringing up the rear. Japanese leaders received awful ratings—only 35% of employees in Japan rated leaders as effective—a dramatic fall from the late 1980s, when Japanese leaders drew wide praise for their various management techniques. (These data were collected before the recent sequence of tragedies that occurred in early 2011 in Japan.) Consistent with the predictions of path-goal theory, the study also showed that ratings of effectiveness varied across a number of situational circumstances, such as government versus private settings and high-tech versus low-tech firms.

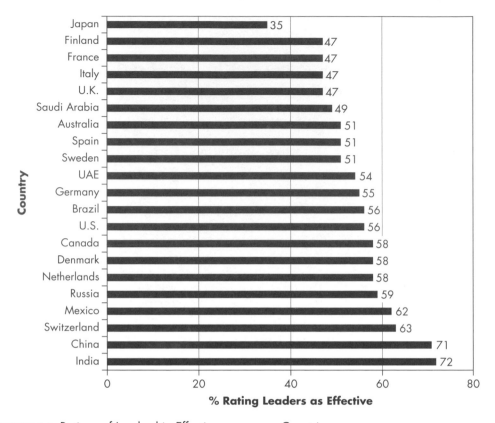

FIGURE 6.1 Ratings of Leadership Effectiveness across Countries

Many multinationals undoubtedly hope that the increasing similarity of companies around the world in terms of structure, technology, and strategy will weaken or overcome cross-cultural differences and make their job a little easier. But these convergent forces may be offset by factors that continue to maintain, or even accentuate, cultural differences, as discussed below. Consequently, a safe assumption is that a manager's effectiveness will continue to depend, at least in part, on how well he or she adapts approaches to the cultural circumstances. In fact, some U.S. (e.g., General Electric), European (e.g., Nokia), and Japanese (e.g., Sony) multinationals have created comprehensive programs to develop more effective international managers. Some experts have gone so far as to say that multinationals also need training programs to help local employees interact more effectively with their international managers—again, because of cultural differences.[35]

Other multinationals work hard to embed their corporate values into the local values that they encounter in various countries. Employers such as Wal-Mart believe that by emphasizing a common set of corporate values, a more homogeneous international workforce can be created. This, in turn, allows managers to use similar leadership strategies everywhere the firm does business. This assumes, of course, that employees are willing to accept corporate values at the expense of their own. Some successful examples of this approach are FedEx and McDonald's.

Building a global workforce with a common set of values, however, is very difficult. Simply working for a multinational may accentuate local cultural values. In one study, cultural differences were more pronounced among employees working for a multinational than for employees working in their own countries for a local firm. Apparently, the contrast accentuates differences that might otherwise blend in better. So, for example, Italians acted more Italian when they worked for foreign firms than when they worked for an Italian firm. The same was true for the other nationalities in the study.[36] Resistance is also likely when multinationals push foreign employees to embrace corporate values that explicitly conflict with local values. For example, a U.S. multinational's effort to encourage participative decision making among European managers backfired—merely reinforcing the differences between corporate and local values. The conclusion reached by management was "horses for courses," or that some situations and cultures are more amenable to participative leadership than others.[37]

Developing International Leadership Skills

As suggested, the best option for multinationals may be training and development programs aimed at building international leadership skills throughout the corporation. But that is just part of the story. Companies need to identify aspiring international managers early, using valid and reliable methods.[38] Once on an international leadership track, it takes managers time to acquire the skills they need to be effective. As the CEO of one international search firm put it, "cultural sensitivity doesn't always come naturally, so developing global executives often requires helping people to see their own biases." Doing that means more than simply plugging managers into a foreign outpost. Rotating people through international work assignments is just one part of a systematic and proactive effort to design a career plan that takes managers' experience and skills, as well as the company's needs, into account.[39]

Some firms are using distinctive training programs for international leaders. PricewaterhouseCoopers (PwC) started a development program in 2000 that it called Ulysses, the purpose of which was to build a network of global leaders for the firm. It involved sending promising leaders overseas to gain experience in cultural diversity and is the subject of the accompanying *Global Innovations* box. At IBM, the most promising international managers participate in similar programs. IBM managers are sent in small groups for one-month stints abroad to help solve social and economic problems in developing countries. This Peace Corps–type approach is aimed at teaching managers how the world works and exposes them to everything from installing water wells in Filipino villages to battling malaria in Ghana. Many managers return recognizing the need to change their leadership styles.[40]

GLOBAL INNOVATIONS

It Takes a Village: Developing an International Leadership Cadre at PricewaterhouseCoopers

Alain Michaud was reflecting on the time he spent in Paraguay and what he learned there. Tahir Ayub talked about his experiences in the Namibian outback. And Jennifer Chang was wowed by her trip and time in Belize—great experiences all. But Chang wasn't reflecting on one of those exotic eco-tourism vacations that are all the rage now. Nor were the others sharing great get-away experiences they found out about in *Travel* magazine. Instead, they were commenting on the impact of an innovative leadership training program called Ulysses that they had participated in with their firm, PricewaterhouseCoopers (PwC).

In 2000, PwC started Ulysses to build a network of global firm leaders. The goal was to send promising senior managers overseas to gain experience in cultural diversity and to better equip them to work and lead in a global stakeholder society. So Ayub, a PwC partner, worked in a Namibian village to help leaders there deal with their community's AIDS crisis. The cultural disconnect was huge—something that PwC was looking for in this and other assignments, like Chang's in Belize, where she lived among residents in dirt-floored houses and terrible poverty. Ayub and two colleagues had to lose the BlackBerry and the PowerPoint presentations and work from the break of dawn to nightfall (often there was no electricity) to provide help to the community. Others completed similar projects in their eight-week stints.

Does this walk-a-mile-in-someone-else's-shoes approach make for an effective leader development tool? PwC thinks so. The results are hard to quantify, but they point to the tangible benefits the firm has noticed among participants. Among other things, increased understanding of others, deeper listening skills, and the value of trust in interactions have all been cited by participants.

Likewise, Genesis Park is a related program deployed by the firm. This is a ten-week assignment also designed to develop leadership and innovation. Burgeoning leaders are nominated by their managers to work on real-life problems in multicultural teams with input from other diverse leaders. The problems are strategic rather than technical and ones that PwC's clients are likely to encounter (e.g., how do PwC and others enter a new market?). The teams collaborate, get necessary information, throw around innovative and creative solutions, evaluate, and then prepare recommendations to PwC leadership. The teams live in close quarters during their ten weeks together and are pushed hard. At the start, they're told that they'll be challenged "physically, emotionally, professionally, and intellectually." The expected results are surprisingly nontangible, especially for an accounting firm: leaders become more creative, innovative, better able to understand client and firm problems and wider personal, political, and global realities. PwC is careful to monitor and build on the benefits accrued from these and other global leadership development programs.

Thinking about the image of public accounting firms may conjure up images of staid, conservative approaches to problems and managers who are more reactive than proactive. Yet, in our opinion, accounting firms are often at the vanguard of modern human resource practices, and these innovative leadership programs mentioned are just a couple of examples of the global innovation that we have seen.[41]

Regardless of how they acquire it, international managers should have a perspective on cultural issues that is not limited to a particular country or region. The continuing globalization of business is increasing the variety of cross-cultural relationships that managers must contend with. As a result, a country-based or regional set of experiences and skills is insufficient over the long haul. Ultimately, managers need *transnational leadership skills* to be effective; these are listed in Table 6.5.

Table 6.5
Comparing Transnational and Traditional Skills for International Managers

Skill/Development Area	A Transnational Manager...	A Traditional International Manager...
Worldview	Understands the business environment from a global perspective	Focuses on managing relationships between headquarters and a single foreign country
Culture knowledge	Learns about a variety of cultures	Becomes an expert on a single culture
Approach to learning	Learns from many cultures simultaneously, creates a culturally synergistic workplace	Works with people in each foreign culture separately or sequentially, integrates foreigners into parent firm culture
Ability to adapt	Able to transition effectively to living in a variety of foreign cultures	Able to adapt to living in a single foreign culture
Cross-cultural interaction	Uses cross-cultural interaction skills daily	Uses cross-cultural interaction skills mainly on foreign assignments
Collaboration	Interacts with foreign managers as equals	Interacts within defined hierarchies of cultural and structural dominance
Foreign experience	Views foreign experience as critical for career and company development	Views foreign assignments as a mechanism for getting a job done

Source: Adapted from Adler, N. J., & Bartholomew, S. (1992). Managing globally competent people. *Academy of Management Executive, 6,* 54.

With some exceptions, such as PwC and IBM, relatively few multinationals have made a sustained effort to develop managers with transnational leadership skills. But we expect that this will continue to change for the better, with more substantial leadership development programs replacing the limited, modest efforts undertaken by most firms.[42] Chapters 11 and 12 will consider international employees in more detail and illustrate how firms can link leadership development to their international business objectives. Some general suggestions for a transnational leadership development strategy are summarized in Table 6.6 and include

Table 6.6
Suggestions for Individuals and Corporations for Developing Transnational Leadership Skills

Suggestions for Individuals	Description/Explanation
Be open emotionally and intellectually to new international experiences	A key skill to develop is tolerance for ambiguity—consequently, treat international experiences as learning opportunities
Avoid making assumptions or forcing your cultural values onto others	Focusing on what others want and feel in an international context will help you recognize and bridge cultural differences
Do your cross-cultural homework	Putting time into researching the cultures you are working with is essential—read as much as you can and find mentors to help
Grab opportunities to meet foreign colleagues face-to-face	Video conferences save money, but there's no substitute for face-to-face interaction, either in learning or building relationships
Reflect on your limitations	Understanding your own strengths and weaknesses will help you make the most out of any international development experiences

Suggestions for Corporations	Description/Explanation
Emphasize overseas experience for managers	Work experience is a key for developing international managers
Make sure leadership development and key human resource practices are aligned	Building international skills into appraisal and promotion processes reinforces the value of international development
Create support mechanisms for development	This helps track careers and development activity effectiveness
Make senior executives responsible for international leadership development	Top management is in the best position to build visible and influential support for international development efforts

Sources: Adapted from Conner, J. (2000). Developing the global leaders of tomorrow. *Human Resource Management, 39*, 147–157; Frost, J., & Walker, M. (2007). Cross-cultural leadership. *Engineering Management*, June/July, 27–29.

both suggestions for individuals as well as corporate training and human resource management programs. Companies that are serious about preparing managers for international leadership challenges will take these ideas to heart.[43]

CHAPTER SUMMARY

This chapter discussed the challenge of leading across cultural boundaries. A key feature of this review is that most leadership research was done by Americans with all their accompanying cultural baggage. If managers need to know which approaches and techniques work well overseas, then what passes for common wisdom in the United States may be inappropriate in other countries. A number of models and research findings that show how leadership behavior and styles are effective (and expected) in the United States are suspect in their cross-cultural applicability. What makes for effective leadership in an international context can vary in both quantitative and qualitative ways.

In the process of reviewing different approaches to leadership, it is concluded that leadership behavior can vary across cultures and that a manager's international effectiveness can be increased by awareness of this fact. Indeed, what constitutes *effective* leadership behavior and style also differs across cultures to some degree. Leadership frameworks that may help guide international managers are discussed, and, in doing so, attention is brought to the fact that understanding the basic process of leadership is important, as is recognizing that factors other than culture may impact leader effectiveness. Six basic leadership dimensions emerged from the GLOBE project that contribute to leadership effectiveness and where this is so. Modified versions of the path-goal approach to leadership are also discussed, suggesting that to be as effective as possible, leaders should use the style that best fits the demands of a particular situation and culture. The chapter concludes by examining cross-cultural leadership development from a multinational company perspective. It is suggested that multinationals need leaders with *transnational skills* throughout their ranks.

DISCUSSION QUESTIONS

1. How might a typical Western style of leadership differ from one used in Asia or the Middle East?
2. What difficulties might managers encounter as they lead in another culture? What problems might emerge when expatriate managers use their common leader style in a foreign country?
3. Describe Likert's System 4 approach. How can it explain why different leader behaviors can have the same positive effects across cultures?

4. How can corporations identify and develop managers with transnational leadership skills?

Developing Your International Career

THICK AS A BRIC: LEADERSHIP MIND-SETS IN THE NEW ECONOMIC POWERHOUSES

Purpose and Instructions

The purpose of this exercise is to conduct a detailed analysis of how leadership approaches have evolved in the BRIC countries (Brazil, Russia, India, and China). These countries have all experienced rapid economic growth in recent years. Russia and China also have had long experience with authoritarian leadership. All four countries are expected to continue to play increasingly large roles in the global economy in the years ahead. It is quite likely that sometime during your (international) career, you may be assigned to work in one of these countries. Consequently, assessing the business leadership approach commonly used will likely have great value. Researching these styles will help you better understand these countries as well as their associated strengths or weaknesses.

Your instructor may ask you to complete this assignment in a group (ideally four to six students) or individually. Either way, the basic task will be to research and compare basic country/cultural approaches to leadership in and outside of class. In particular, please consider the following items (that may be augmented by your instructor):

1. Determine the key features about the (dominant) business leadership approaches used in the four BRIC countries *and* your home country.
2. Elaborate on these key features with examples of how they might be seen by everyday employees (e.g., if Russian managers prefer a directive style, how might this be seen in an assignment you receive?).
3. How does each prototypical style stack up on the six leader behavior dimensions identified by the GLOBE study (see Table 6.3 and references below)?
4. Present an analysis of any changes in leadership and management practices that could be made to position any country as a more formidable global competitor. In particular, can your home country import a leader behavior or technique that could be of use (or could you use those methods when managing in one of those foreign settings)? Likewise, could you export an indigenous method to any of the BRIC countries?
5. Finally, what suggestions might you have to overcome any barriers to import or export of potentially useful leader methods (i.e., how could changes in leadership values and management practices be specifically encouraged or developed)?

Your instructor may ask each group or individual to make a presentation (roughly 10 minutes long) about your findings to the class. This could be followed by a discussion about common and unique leadership themes in the BRIC countries as well as the role of cultural values. If your instructor decides to make this an individual assignment, be prepared to take part in a general class discussion on the issues raised—especially on any different techniques suggested by any of the other groups or individuals.

RESEARCH TIPS

To get started with your research, you may want to consult the websites below for background information and profiles about BRIC countries. These websites should help you refine your research efforts and act as a gateway to articles, reports, and other websites about leadership issues and management practices in your assigned country:

- *CIA World Factbook* (https://www.cia.gov/library/publications/the-world-factbook/index.html). This widely used resource provides in-depth information about every nation on the planet and is used by diplomats and business people alike.
- *International Monetary Fund* (www.imf.org/external/country/index.htm). This is also a widely used resource by business professionals and others and provides country-specific economic background information.
- *World Bank* (www.worldbank.org). Again, a useful source on most countries around the globe. See the "Data and Statistics" page for country-specific information.

Then we suggest obtaining one or more articles that compare leader behavior and style across countries and cultures. For example, the GLOBE research team has produced many empirical research studies on cross-country differences. Please see the bibliography at the end of this book for example studies. On the home page of the GLOBE research group (www.thunderbird.edu/sites/globe/) are many resources that could be of help with this project. Plus, we have provided a reference to get your research started on GLOBE. You will also be able to easily find more GLOBE and other resources in your library or via electronic resources that your university provides.

- Good introductory article on GLOBE: Javidan, M., et al. (2006). In the eye of the beholder: Cross cultural lessons in leadership from Project GLOBE. *Academy of Management Perspectives, 20,* 67–90.

Making the Case for International Understanding

CAN SOUTH KOREAN COMPANIES LOOSEN UP THEIR LEADERSHIP?

Many Western companies want leaders who encourage ideas, innovation, and speedy decision making. But leadership in Asia conjures up words like order, paternalism, and formality. That certainly describes the leadership approach in many large Korean companies over the past 50 years. Over this half century of great economic success, the power to make key decisions was concentrated at the top of rigidly bureaucratic corporate structures. And these structures were themselves tied to larger interrelated and co-owned conglomerates—the Korean *chaebol* system. These massive industrial groups are often run by rich, inscrutable families who live much like royalty in South Korea. For example, the Lee family is the head of Samsung Electronics—a group whose products account for nearly 20% of the country's gross domestic product. Other major company groups include Hyundai and Lucky Goldstar (LG).

These massive firms, and the hierarchical and closed leadership style they employ, seem ideally suited for Korean culture. From them flowed a traditional approach to leadership based on Confucian values that emphasize family, seniority, and loyalty. This is supported by South Korea's standing on some of the value dimensions discussed in earlier chapters. For example, South Korea scores very high on uncertainty avoidance. South Koreans work to create a society that reduces uncertainty and increases control and predictability—the chaebol structure follows directly from this. Far-flung chaebol interests are held together by the family autocrat or *taipan*. This person provides a focus for power and decision making that coordinates activity. According to some experts, the taipan are determined and aggressive in overcoming obstacles (*pae-gi* in Korean). And, above all, a strong work ethic is supported by its famously in-a-hurry population. Apparently, the words *ppalli-ppalli* ("fast fast") are sometimes the first words learned by foreigners upon arrival in the country.

This authoritarian nature allows South Korean firms to move decisively and quickly. But it also stifles creativity and creates problems. At each level of management, subordinates are often prohibited from questioning their superiors, much less allowed to communicate with other executives further up the line. Some experts think this approach stunted growth, putting many Korean companies in danger of falling behind foreign competitors and producing failure. In the Asian financial crisis of the late 1990s, the chaebol were widely blamed by the public for the crisis, and they failed in droves. After Daewoo collapsed in 2000, more than half of the other 30 conglomerates followed in bankruptcy. Massive corruption schemes came to light, many involving the highest government officials and the chaebols. Lee Kun-Hee, chairman of Samsung Electronics, was himself convicted of tax evasion. Like many other corporate leaders, however, he evaded prison time by paying massive fines (more than $1 billion alone for Chung Mong-koo, chairman of Hyundai, who was convicted of bribery and embezzlement). The paternalistic and authoritarian leader style promoted by this clan or family system clearly produced a top-down decision system in these Korean firms and, some believe, a potential liability going forward for Korean firms.

So what are Korean firms to do in today's environment? In late 2010, the *Wall Street Journal* raised key questions for the country. The special report, called "The Miracle Is Over: Now What?" gave ample credit to the successful country-level business strategy that brought South Korea into the upper echelon of world economies. But the report was also critical of current leadership and advocated a tough and important self-examination—along the lines suggested by our discussion above. For example, it cited the many successes that have made Samsung the largest technology company in the world. And it detailed some of the innovations of the global conglomerates LG and SK Telecom.

ASSIGNMENT QUESTIONS

1. Do you think a new approach to leadership is necessary in the new South Korea? Or should Koreans stick to their traditional approach that brought them to where they are? Note that Lee Kun-Hee of Samsung (see above) has been brought back from disgrace to again lead the firm. And he's clear about the issue: "We're in a crisis now. No one knows what will become of Samsung. Most of our products will be obsolete in 10 years. We must begin anew." In 1992, Lee used the same rhetoric as a harbinger of his traditional style ("Samsung is a second class company...employees should change everything but their wife and children"). Samsung has taken sides on this issue, with a clear preference for the traditional leader-emanating style. What's your view?

2. Not all Korean firms have kept a traditional leadership approach. Others are starting to use nontraditional approaches. What sort of options might firms like LG and SK Telecom have at their disposal?

3. What specific things could these firms import from other countries to unfreeze this purported stodgy, hierarchal, family-style leadership?

4. Importing a different style is far from a panacea. As discussed in this chapter, a different style can be prone to problems when applied poorly across cultures. What are some of these problems that could be anticipated if a more Western style is used?

5. How might LG and SK Telecom work to overcome the resistance to new styles should they choose to use these? (Investigate these firms a bit to answer this question.)

Sources: Adapted from The miracle is over: Now what? *Wall Street Journal* (Special Journal Report), November 8, 2010, R1–R14; Return of the overlord. *The Economist,* April 3, 2010, 71–73; Weisbart, M. (2010). So fast, so dynamic, yet still hierarchical. *Wall Street Journal,* November 8, R6.

NOTES

1. Alder, N. J., & Gundersen, A. (2008). *International Dimensions of Organizational Behavior* (5th ed.). Mason, OH: Thompson-South-Western; Aycan, Z. (2008). Cross-cultural approaches to leadership. In P. B. Smith, M. F. Peterson, & D. C. Thomas (eds.), *The Handbook of Cross-Cultural Management Research* (219–238). Thousand Oaks, CA: Sage; Gupta, A. K., &

Govindarajan, V. (2002). Cultivating a global mindset. *Academy of Management Executive*, 16, 116–126.

2. Yukl, G. (2010). *Leadership in Organizations* (7th ed.). Upper Saddle River, NJ: Pearson Education.

3. Atwater, L., Wang, M., Smither, J. W., & Fleenor, J. W. (2009). Are cultural characteristics associated with the relationship between self and others' ratings of leadership? *Journal of Applied Psychology*, 94(4), 876–886; Aycan, Z. (2008). Cross-cultural approaches to leadership. In P. B. Smith, M. F. Peterson, & D. C. Thomas (eds.), *The Handbook of Cross-Cultural Management Research* (219–238). Thousand Oaks, CA: Sage; Frost, J., & Walker, M. (2007). Cross-cultural leadership. *Engineering Management*, June/July, 27–29; House, R. J., Hanges, P. J., Javidan, M., Dorfman, P. W., & Gupta, V. (eds.). (2004). *Culture, Leadership, and Organizations: The GLOBE Study of 62 Societies.* Thousand Oaks, CA: Sage.

4. Banai, M., & Teng, B. S. (1996). Comparing job characteristics, leadership style, and alienation in Russian public and private enterprises. *Journal of International Management*, 2, 201–224; Geppert, M. (1996). Paths of managerial learning in the East German context. *Organization Studies*, 17, 249–268; Kostera, M., Proppe, M., & Szatkowski, M. (1995). Staging the new romantic hero in the old cynical theatre: On managers, roles and change in Poland. *Journal of Organizational Behavior*, 16, 631–646; Kets De Vries, M. F. R. (2000). A journey into the "wild East": Leadership style and organizational practices in Russia. *Organizational Dynamics*, 28, 67–81; McCarthy, D. J., & Zhuplev, A. V. (1996). Meeting of the mindsets in a changing Russia. *Business Horizons*, 40, 52–59.

5. Thomas, D. C. (2008). *Cross-Cultural Management: Essential Concepts* (2nd ed.). Thousand Oaks, CA: Sage; Wendt, H., Euwema, M. C., & van Emmerik, I. J. H. (2009). Leadership and team cohesiveness across cultures. *Leadership Quarterly*, 20, 358–370; Yukl, G. (2010). *Leadership in Organizations* (7th ed.). Upper Saddle River, NJ: Prentice Hall.

6. Misumi, J. (1985). *The Behavioral Science of Leadership: An Interdisciplinary Japanese Research Program.* Ann Arbor: University of Michigan Press; Dvorak, P. (2006). Making U.S. management ideas work elsewhere. *Wall Street Journal*, May 22, B3; Peterson, M. P., Brannen, M. Y., & Smith, P. B. (1994). Japanese and U.S. leadership: Issues in current research. In S. B. Prasad (ed.), *Advances in International Comparative Management*, Vol. 9 (57–82). Greenwich, CT: JAI Press; Thomas, D. C. (2008). *Cross-Cultural Management: Essential Concepts* (2nd ed.). Thousand Oaks, CA: Sage.

7. Bhagat, R. S., Kedia, B. L., Crawford, S. E., & Kaplan, M. R. (1990). Cross-cultural issues in organizational psychology: Emergent trends and directions for research in the 1990s. In C. L. Cooper & I. T. Robertson (eds.), *International Review of Industrial and Organizational Psychology*, 5, 59–99.

8. Pellegrini, E. K., & Scandura, T. A. (2008). Paternalistic leadership: A review and agenda for future research. *Journal of Management*, 34(3), 566–593.

9. Ayman, R., & Chemers, M. M. (1983). Relationship of supervisory behavior ratings to work group effectiveness and subordinate satisfaction among Iranian managers. *Journal of Applied Psychology*, 68, 338–341.

10. Doktor, R. H. (1990). Asian and American CEOs: A comparative study. *Organizational Dynamics*, 18, 46–57.

11. Smith, P. B., Misumi, J., Tayeb, M., Peterson, M., & Bond, M. (1989). On the generality of leadership style measures across cultures. *Journal of Occupational Psychology*, 62, 97–109.

12. Tolich, M., Kenney, M., & Biggart, N. (1999). Managing the managers: Japanese strategies in the U.S.A. *Journal of Management Studies*, 36, 587–607.

13. Cappelli, P., Singh, H., Singh, J., & Useem, M. (2010). The India way: Lessons for the U.S. *Academy of Management Perspectives*, May, 6–24; McGregor, J. (2007). The employee is always right. *Business Week*, November 19, 80–82; Sinha, J. B. P. (1980). *The Nurturant Task Leader: A Model of Effective Executive*. New Delhi: Concept; Sinha, J. B. P. (1984). A model of effective leadership styles in India. *International Studies of Management and Organization*, 14, 86–98; Singh, N., & Krishnan, V. R. (2007). Transformational leadership in India. *International Journal of Cross-Cultural Management*, 7(2), 219–236; Out of India: A briefing on the Tata group. *The Economist*, March 5, 2011, 75–78.

14. McGregor, J. (2007). The employee is always right. *Business Week*, November 19, 80–82; Cappelli, P., Singh, H., Singh, J., & Useem, M. (2010). The India way: Lessons for the U.S. *Academy of Management Perspectives*, May, 6–24.

15. Dorfman, P. W., & Howell, J. P. (1988). Dimensions of national culture and effective leadership patterns: Hofstede revisited. In R. N. Farmer & E. G. McGoun (eds.), *Advances in International Comparative Management*, Vol. 3 (127–150). Amsterdam: Elsevier Ltd.; Peterson, M. P., Brannen, M. Y., & Smith, P. B. (1994). Japanese and U.S. leadership: Issues in current research. In S. B. Prasad (ed.), *Advances in International Comparative Management*, Vol. 9 (57–82). Greenwich, CT: JAI Press.

16. Peterson, M. P., Brannen, M. Y., & Smith, P. B. (1994). Japanese and U.S. leadership: Issues in current research. In S. B. Prasad (ed.), *Advances in International Comparative Management*, Vol. 9 (57–82). Greenwich, CT: JAI Press; Thomas, D. C. (2008). *Cross-Cultural Management: Essential Concepts* (2nd ed.). Thousand Oaks, CA: Sage.

17. Bass, B. M. (1990). *Stogdill's Handbook of Leadership: A Survey of Theory and Research*. New York: Free Press; Likert, R. (1967). *The Human Organization*. New York: McGraw-Hill; Morris, T., & Pavett, C. M. (1992). Management style and productivity in two cultures. *Journal of International Business Studies*, 23, 169–179; Pavett, C. M., & Morris, T. (1995). Management styles within a multinational corporation: A five country comparative study. *Human Relations*, 48, 1171–1191.

18. Morris, T., & Pavett, C. M. (1992). Management style and productivity in two cultures. *Journal of International Business Studies*, 23, 169–179.

19. Pellegrini, E. K., & Scandura, T. A. (2008). Paternalistic leadership: A review and agenda for future research. *Journal of Management*, 34(3), 566–593; Morris, T., & Pavett, C. M. (1992). Management style and productivity in two cultures. *Journal of International Business Studies*, 23, 169–179; Nicholls, C. E., Lane, H. W., & Brechu, M. B. (1999). Taking self-managed teams to Mexico. *Academy of Management Executive*, 13, 15–25.

20. d'Iribarne, P. (2002). Motivating workers in emerging countries: Universal tools and local applications. *Journal of Organizational Behavior*, 23, 243–256; de Forest, M. E. (1994). Thinking of a plant in Mexico? *Academy of Management Executive*, 8, 33–40; Gowan, M., Ibarreche, S., & Lackey, C. (1996). Doing the right things in Mexico. *Academy of Management Executive*, 10, 74–81; Stephens, G., & Geer, C. R. (1995). Doing business in Mexico: Understanding cultural differences. *Organizational Dynamics*, 24, 39–55.

21. Keys, J. B., Denton, L. T., & Miller, T. R. (1994). The Japanese management theory jungle revisited. *Journal of Management*, 20, 373–402; Maruyama, M. (1992). Changing dimensions in international business. *Academy of Management Executive*, 6, 88–96.

22. Black, J. S., & Porter, L. W. (1990). Managerial behaviors and job performance: A successful manager in Los Angeles may not succeed in Hong Kong. *Journal of International Business Studies*, 21, 99–112.

23. Karnitschnig, M. (2005). Too many chiefs at Siemens? *Wall Street Journal*, January 20, A12; Karnitschnig, M. (2003). For Siemens, move into U.S. causes waves back home. *Wall Street Journal*, September 8, A1, A8.

24. See Yukl, G. (2010). *Leadership in Organizations* (7th ed.). Upper Saddle River, NJ: Prentice Hall.

25. Bass, B. M. (1990). *Stogdill's Handbook of Leadership: A Survey of Theory and Research*. New York: Free Press; Likert, R. (1967). *The Human Organization*. New York: McGraw-Hill; Yukl, G. (2010). *Leadership in Organizations* (7th ed.). Upper Saddle River, NJ: Prentice Hall.

26. House, R. J., Hanges, P. J., Javidan, M., Dorfman, P. W., & Gupta, V. (eds.). (2004). *Culture, Leadership, and Organizations: The GLOBE Study of 62 Societies*. Thousand Oaks, CA: Sage.

27. Bass, B. M., & Avolio, B. J. (1992). Developing transformational leadership: 1992 and beyond. *Journal of European Industrial Training*, 14, 21–27; Brodbeck, F., Frese, F., & Javidan, M. (2002). Leadership made in Germany: Low on compassion, high on performance. *Academy of Management Executive*, 16, 16–30; Koh, W. L., Steers, R. M., & Terborg, J. R. (1995). The effects of transformational leadership on teacher attitudes and student performance in Singapore. *Journal of Organizational Behavior*, 16, 319–333; Popper, M., Landau, O., & Gluskinos, U. (1992). The Israeli Defence Forces: An example of transformational leadership. *Leadership and Organization Development Journal*, 31, 3–8; Singer, M. S. (1985). Transformational versus transactional leadership: A study of New Zealand company managers. *Psychological Reports*, 57, 143–146.

28. Aycan, Z. (2008). Cross-cultural approaches to leadership. In P. B. Smith, M. F. Peterson, & D. C. Thomas (eds.), *The Handbook of Cross-Cultural Management Research* (219–238). Thousand Oaks, CA: Sage.

29. Osborn, R. N., & Marion, R. (2009). Contextual leadership, transformational leadership and the performance of international innovation seeking alliances. *Leadership Quarterly*, 20, 191–206; Rossant, J. (2002). The fast fall of France's celebrity CEOs. *Business Week*, April 1, 48; Yukl, G. (2010). *Leadership in Organizations* (7th ed.). Upper Saddle River, NJ: Prentice Hall.

30. Aycan, Z. (2008). Cross-cultural approaches to leadership. In P. B. Smith, M. F. Peterson, & D. C. Thomas (eds.), *The Handbook of Cross-Cultural Management Research* (219–238). Thousand Oaks, CA: Sage; Taylor, A. (2003). Nissan shifts into higher gear. *Fortune*, July 21, 98–104.

31. Aycan, Z. (2008). Cross-cultural approaches to leadership. In P. B. Smith, M. F. Peterson, & D. C. Thomas (eds.), *The Handbook of Cross-Cultural Management Research* (219–238). Thousand Oaks, CA: Sage.

32. House, R. J., Hanges, P. J., Javidan, M., Dorfman, P. W., & Gupta, V. (eds.). (2004). *Culture, Leadership, and Organizations: The GLOBE Study of 62 Societies*. Thousand Oaks, CA: Sage.

33. House, R. J. (1971). A path-goal theory of leader effectiveness. *Administrative Science Quarterly*, 16, 321–339; House, R. J., & Mitchell, T. R. (1974). Path-goal theory of leadership. *Contemporary Business*, 3, 81–98.

34. Rodrigues, C. (1990). The situation and national culture as contingencies for leadership behavior: Two conceptual models. In B. Prasad (ed.), *Advances in International Comparative Management*, Vol. 5 (51–68). Greenwich, CT: JAI Press.

35. Chhokar, J. S., Brodbeck, F. C., & House, R. J. (eds.). (2007). *Culture and Leadership across the World: The GLOBE Book of In-Depth Studies of 25 Societies.* Mahwah, NJ: Erlbaum; Gupta, A. K., & Govindarajan, V. (2002). Cultivating a Global Mindset. *Academy of Management Executive*, 16, 116–126; Herrmann, P., & Werbel, J. (2007). Promotability of host-country nationals: A cross-cultural study. *British Journal of Management*, 18, 281–293; Tichy, N. M. (1993). Global development. In V. Pucik, N. M. Tichy, & C. K. Barnett (eds.), *Globalizing Management: Creating and Leading the Competitive Organization* (206–226). New York: Wiley.

36. Alder, N. J., & Gundersen, A. (2008). *International Dimensions of Organizational Behavior* (5th ed.). Mason, OH: Thompson-South-Western; Laurent, A. (1983). The cultural diversity of Western conceptions of management. *International Studies of Management and Organization*, 13, 75–96.

37. McFarlin, D. B., Sweeney, P. D., & Cotton, J. C. (1992). Attitudes toward employee participation in decision-making: A comparison of European and American managers in a U.S. multinational company. *Human Resource Management*, 31, 363–383.

38. Judge, T. A. (2009). Core self-evaluations and work success. *Current Directions in Psychological Science*, 18, 58–62; Adler, N. J., & Bartholomew, S. (1992). Managing globally competent people. *Academy of Management Executive*, 6, 52–65; Caligiuri, P., & Tarique, I. (2009). Predicting effectiveness in global leadership activities. *Journal of World Business*, 44, 336–346; Spreitzer, G. M., McCall, M. W., & Mahoney, J. D. (1997). Early identification of international executive potential. *Journal of Applied Psychology*, 82, 6–29.

39. Meiland, D. (2003). In search of global leaders. *Harvard Business Review*, August, 44–45.

40. Hamm, S. (2009). The globe is IBM's classroom. *Business Week*, March 23, 56–57.

41. Please see the PwC page on the Genesis Park program for more details on its operation: www.pwc.com/gx/en/genesis-park/index.jhtml. Hempel, J., & Porges, S. (2004). PricewaterhouseCoopers tests partners by sending them to work in poor nations: It takes a village—and a consultant. *Bloomberg Businessweek*, September 6, 76.

42. Tichy, N. M., Brimm, M. I., Charan, R., & Takeuchi, H. (1993). Leadership development as a lever for global transformation. In V. Pucik, N. M. Tichy, & C. K. Barnett (eds.), *Globalizing Management: Creating and Leading the Competitive Organization* (47–60). New York: Wiley.

43. Alder, N. J., & Gundersen, A. (2008). *International Dimensions of Organizational Behavior* (5th ed.). Mason, OH: Thompson-South-Western; Frost, J., & Walker, M. (2007). Cross-cultural leadership. *Engineering Management*, June/July, 27–29.

Chapter 7

Managing Diversity and Ethical Dilemmas in an International Context

I hope that someday it will be more colorful and prettier, too.

> —Deutsche Bank chief executive Josef
> Ackermann's joking remark in discussing
> the bank's desire to add women to its
> all-male executive committee

Whoever wants it to be more colorful or prettier should go to a flower meadow or a museum. I wish Mr. Ackermann were as ambitious regarding the advancement of women as he is regarding issuing returns [on the bank's stock].

> —Ilse Aigner, Germany's minister
> for consumer protection[1]

As you might suspect, Ackermann's attempt at humor fell flat, unleashing plenty of criticism. The backdrop for his comment was a debate in Germany over whether to require corporate boards to reserve some seats for women. Granted, big German firms have a lousy track record in this regard—in 2011, only three women served on the executive boards of the country's 30 top companies. Other European countries, including France, Norway, and Spain, have all passed laws requiring that a certain number of board seats be filled by women. On the other hand, the United Kingdom debated board quotas for women but passed no laws requiring such quotas. And it is unlikely that legalizing quota requirements for women board members will ever gain traction in the United States. Issues related to diversity are viewed differently across countries. Moreover, diversity issues are sensitive and complex. Indeed, managing diversity in a cross-cultural context includes (among other things) assessing the impact of heterogeneity in national, cultural, and ethnic backgrounds on employee morale, cohesiveness, and communication. It also includes determining how to best promote women and their careers in the workforce as well as establishing bias-free human resource management systems (recruiting, promotion, and retention). Finally, managers must grapple with building a corporate culture where various types of diversity are accepted. Yet an international context raises the stakes, as managers must decide how to communicate and frame important and sensitive issues related to diversity across cultural boundaries. With Ackermann, we imagine he wishes that he could retract his comment about building a "more colorful and prettier" executive board at Deutsche Bank![2]

In the sections that follow, we will tackle issues associated with managing diversity abroad. The chapter takes on some associated challenges, including understanding and managing conflict and dealing with ethical dilemmas in culturally complex and diverse environments. Chapter 8 expands and elaborates on these topics by discussing how multicultural groups and teams, as well as firm-level collaborations such as joint ventures, can be managed effectively.

MANAGING DIVERSITY: SENSITIVE AND DIFFICULT CHALLENGES

When companies cross borders, they may run afoul of cultural norms related to diversity. On the other hand, international companies may sometimes be able to hire better local employees because of local sensibilities about diversity. Consider, for instance, gender issues related to diversity in Japan compared to Europe and the United States. Japan is a country where women have traditionally been considered subordinate to men. In the United States, women hold nearly half of all managerial positions versus just over 10% in Japan. Gender discrimination has been illegal in Japan for more than two decades, but laws are not rigorously enforced. This is not terribly surprising, given widely held attitudes in Japan. According to one survey, some 60% of Japanese women feel that their role is to raise children and run the household while men's role is to be the family's breadwinner. Much lower percentages of women in North America and Europe endorse such views. For instance, in the United States, less than 25% of women feel that it is the role of men to be the primary breadwinner. Moreover, among college-educated Japanese women, nearly 75% eventually leave their jobs voluntarily at some point during their careers (compared to just 31% of comparable U.S. women). While raising children is the biggest reason U.S. women quit their jobs, for Japanese women, the top reason is feeling undervalued by their employers, thanks, in many cases, to being pushed into dead-end positions by often-sexist bosses.[3]

Indeed, foreign multinationals see a vast pool of talented women in Japan waiting to be utilized and placed in professional positions. Consequently, the Japanese outposts of drugmaker Bristol-Meyers Squibb and tech giant IBM have deliberately been focusing on women in hiring and promotion efforts. Conversely, when Japanese firms operate in the United States, they run into trouble if they fail to take U.S. attitudes and laws regarding gender discrimination seriously. That may be the situation with Toshiba's U.S. business unit, which was slapped with a $100 million gender discrimination lawsuit in 2011. The lawsuit alleged that inside the firm, systematic gender discrimination took place against women workers in the United States. While the lawsuit specified that this included wage and promotion practices that were biased against women, it also noted that "[i]f a female employee does not conform to typical gender stereotypes or is not submissive towards male employees, she is labeled insubordinate, criticized, and retaliated against." To the extent that this was indeed the case at Toshiba, it begs the question about the role of top managers in the firm's U.S. subsidiaries, all of whom are, as of this writing, Japanese.[4]

DIVERSITY CHALLENGES FACING EXPATRIATES

Of course, struggles with diversity issues are not unique to foreign companies that set up outposts within the United States. Indeed, U.S. firms face plenty of diversity challenges in doing business abroad. First, the laws that make it illegal for U.S. companies to discriminate against Americans on the basis of sex, race, ethnicity, religion, or national origin also apply to U.S. citizens working overseas. The only situation in which U.S. firms are not bound by these requirements is if obeying U.S. law results in a local law's violation. More typically, however, cultural rather than legal differences are what complicate U.S. firms' efforts to offer equal opportunities to potential expatriates. For instance, the U.S. perspective that all employees deserve equal opportunities to develop and advance is fundamentally a cultural value. And it is a value that is not held everywhere—or at least not interpreted in the same way. U.S. consumer product giant Colgate discovered this some years ago when it had to change a company survey being used in Brazil after employees there did not understand the phrase "equal opportunity" in the survey they were asked to complete.[5]

Moreover, some U.S. and European managers believe that they should not send women to certain foreign locations as expatriates because of a perception that the cultural environment in some nations makes it very difficult for them to be effective in expatriate roles. To be sure, there are places in the world where extreme local norms are likely to fuel such concerns. For instance, many Saudi Arabian men would not seriously consider doing business with Saudi women. Businesswomen in Saudi Arabia must deal with travel inconveniences since it is illegal for women to drive there, despite recent protests to lift the ban. On the other hand, managers' reluctance may simply reflect their own stereotypes (e.g., that most women are not as interested in expatriate assignments as men because of family concerns or other "hardships"). A woman who coveted an expatriate assignment in Indonesia noted that when her name was put in front of her boss, "he said, 'she wouldn't want to go that far away, would she?' My boss couldn't see me in that role, so I never got the chance."[6]

Clearly, there are many countries where expatriates from the United States or Western Europe could find themselves facing traditional local attitudes that place women subordinate to men. This is the case in many African nations as well as in Russia, where few women have reached top management positions and roughly 75% of the unemployed population is female. Likewise, women account for just 25% of all managers in Latin America despite constituting over half of the workforce (the global average for women in management is about 40%).[7]

Nevertheless, the reluctance of some U.S. firms to send women or minorities into "harm's way" as expatriates comes with risks relative to U.S. law, particularly if the stated reason is simply to avoid clashes with local sensibilities. Of course, underneath these public reasons may be little more than sexism—a form of discrimination that is hardly exclusive to the United States, equal opportunity laws notwithstanding. For instance, thanks to such discriminatory attitudes, European women sometimes find it harder to land expatriate assignments compared to men counterparts with similar backgrounds and skills.[8]

Yet women are a growing part of the expatriate population globally (perhaps 25% today compared to 10–15% in years past). While this trend may continue, there is little doubt that some women will continue to be passed over for expatriate opportunities merely because their bosses follow stereotypes or overstate the risks of sending them to "difficult" foreign locations. Studies suggest that women expatriates are typically viewed as foreigners first and as women second, meaning that their foreignness tends to overshadow sexist attitudes, allowing them to be viewed as more unique and to be taken more seriously than might otherwise be the case. In short, expatriate women tend to encounter fewer problems in business contexts than their local counterparts. This does not mean that foreign women will not experience sexism or discrimination overseas. But female may actually provide an advantage to women who are expatriates in foreign countries because their uniqueness makes them more visible. Indeed, foreign business partners may be curious about women expatriates and want to learn more about their roles within the company and the knowledge that they bring to the table.[9]

Of course, the role of senior management is critical when it comes to helping women succeed abroad in expatriate roles. Here are four sets of suggestions for managers to consider, not just for women, but for any potential expatriates who might encounter diversity-related issues abroad due to race, ethnic background, or religion:

- *Avoid stereotypical assumptions when choosing expatriates.* Never assume people are disinterested in foreign postings or that they will be crippled by local perspectives. For instance, women should receive serious consideration for foreign assignments. These steps will help eliminate inaccurate perceptions about placing women expatriates in harm's way.
- *Provide appropriate training.* Management should provide training that educates individuals about local attitudes and how to respond. For women, training should focus on gender issues and how they can leverage their unique position to improve their effectiveness. Moreover, accompanying spouses or family members should participate in this training, because they may face similar challenges or at least serve as a support system for the expatriate abroad. Firms would also be well served to include local employees in any training about diversity issues and perspectives.
- *Offer ongoing support overseas.* Too often, company support ends with predeparture training. Instead, training on diversity and related issues should continue for at least several months into the foreign posting. Women expatriates can use such training as a platform to present especially difficult problems or unexpected challenges. Likewise, firms should help women expatriates by providing mentors and a support network of other expatriates and managers. Introducing new, diverse expatriates in positive terms also helps establish their credibility with local employees, officials, and customers.
- *Leverage expatriates as role models.* Once they return, expatriates are invaluable assets as role models for other employees. For instance, former (or current) women expatriates should be made available to other women being considered for foreign assignments to share their experiences. This will provide positive

evidence that women can, and do, succeed in expatriate roles, particularly in challenging foreign posts.[10]

Many multinational companies operate in countries that have traditionally embraced male-dominate attitudes and where finding talented employees is no small challenge. Indeed, in such places, finding and retaining talented women requires creative management thinking, particularly in societies in which women are typically expected to stay home and care for children, if not an entire extended family. For examples of what managers at multinational firms in India are doing to attract and retain talented women, read the accompanying *Global Innovations* box.

GLOBAL INNOVATIONS

Family-Friendly Perks Keep Indian Women on the Career Ladder

Women in India make up just 34% of the national workforce. And even if they have college degrees and career aspirations, women in India are often pressured to put children, husbands, and elderly parents first. Indeed, leaving work to care for elderly relatives knocks many Indian women out of the workforce just as they are ready to step into senior management. Not surprisingly, the gender gap in India grows wider as management levels are scaled. As one human resource expert put it, "The measures of daughterly guilt are much higher in India than in the West."

Combined with a rapidly growing economy (8–9% annually the past several years), a shortage of talented professionals, and the personnel needs of multinationals, the result is a perfect storm when it comes to attracting and holding women employees. But a number of multinationals are proving that they can think outside the box to get results.

U.S.-based Ernst & Young has some 4,000 employees in India, and half are women. Company management doggedly pursues its goal of having gender diversity in India. And there is no better example of that than how the firm reacts when professional women leave work to have children, especially after investing a lot of money in their training. After the women leave, the company stays in touch, communicating monthly to see how they are faring. Next, the company entices women to return with highly flexible hours (sometimes just a few hours per week) and a company nursery. It encourages women to gradually increase their workloads, eventually resuming full-time employment. Likewise, Indian information technology giant Infosys offers extended maternity leaves and sabbaticals to women and special training after they return to work. The company also tracks how women are treated by male managers after returning to ensure they are assigned value-added work. As one Infosys human resource executive noted, "A lot of men believe maternity is a disease, and we have to teach them." Today, nearly 90% of the firm's women employees return to work after having children versus just 30% several years ago.

Other companies have come up with other creative family-friendly perks. Google, for example, keeps taxis on standby for employees, something women find especially attractive when a family member becomes sick and they have to rush home. And since Indian families often disapprove when young women travel alone, German pharmaceutical firm Boehringer Ingelheim allows employees to bring their mothers on extended business trips—and picks up the tab.

Overall, Ernst & Young came to the conclusion that if you want to keep women happy and on the job in India, it pays to keep their families happy too. The firm hosts visits by the parents and in-laws of its women employees so they can eat, tour, and schmooze with senior executives. The goal is to help families better understand the work that their daughters do and how important they are to the company. Sounds like a winning strategy for maintaining gender diversity in India.[11]

CORPORATE-LEVEL APPROACHES TO MANAGING DIVERSITY

The creativity of multinationals responding to gender issues in India begs the question of how these firms cope with various diversity issues across literally dozens of nations. Indeed, multinational firms face the challenge of managing cross-national diversity (as employees from the parent country and other countries interact) as well as intranational diversity (as employees from the same country who represent different races, ethnic groups, and so on interact). For instance, the continuing flow of immigrants into Western European job markets has increased the diversity challenges that firms doing business there must deal with. The stakes are high since diversity offers tremendous benefits if managed properly, along with damaging costs if it is not. These potential benefits and costs are summarized in Table 7.1.[12]

Recent evidence suggests that few senior executives are proactive when it comes to managing diversity issues. One study of over 4,000 executives in nearly 150 multinationals found that roughly 90% fell short of being proactive on diversity in their firms. Most executives did little to promote inclusiveness or to bridge gaps related to diversity across groups of employees. Instead, they typically paid more attention to diversity metrics (such as ensuring that people from different backgrounds are hired) than on creating a culture of inclusiveness. This can allow unconscious biases to creep into management practices that detract from inclusiveness. For example, managers may fail to include individuals who represent otherness in terms of race and gender in discussions, meetings, and so on. Consequently, executives in multinationals should embrace synergistic multiculturalism, which requires the firm to seek positive aspects within all cultures and to explore differences to benefit the company. This is obviously complicated to carry out at times and demands considerable training to identify and leverage the positives associated with cultural diversity

Table 7.1
Diversity: Benefits and Costs for Multinationals

Potential Benefits of Diversity	**Potential Costs of Diversity**
Organizational benefits: Greater openness to new ideas, expanded perspectives and interpretations; expanded alternatives thanks to increased creativity, flexibility, and problem-solving ability	*Organizational costs*: Increased ambiguity, confusion, and complexity; miscommunication more likely; agreement on specific actions more difficult to reach
Location-specific benefits: Better understanding of local staff, customers, and markets; better understanding of local cultural, economic, legal, political, and social environment	*Location-specific costs*: Risk of overgeneralizing the use of company policies, practices, procedures, and strategies in the local context; ethnocentrism that ignores potential diversity benefits

Source: Adapted from Alder, N. J., & Gundersen, A. (2008). *International Dimensions of Organizational Behavior* (5th ed.). Mason, OH: Thomson South-Western, 102.

while minimizing the negatives. Consequently, few international executives adopt this approach or execute it well. Much more common are managers who respond to cultural diversity by embracing parochialism (i.e., diversity is essentially ignored) or ethnocentrism (i.e., managers attempt to instill corporate values to reduce differences between employees). Table 7.2 summarizes approaches to managing cultural diversity as well as the strategies and outcomes that typically accompany them.[13]

While synergistic multiculturalism is not common, some multinationals have done well implementing it. Colgate, the U.S.-based consumer products giant that operates in more than 200 countries, is one such example. Company executives take a broad perspective on cultural diversity, going well beyond typical diversity aspects (e.g., gender, nationality) to include differences that are less obvious (e.g., sexual orientation, family situations, life experiences). Moreover, Colgate's leadership believes that an inclusive culture is essential if the firm is to benefit from diverse perspectives and ideas. To convert these beliefs into action, Colgate managers attend a training program called Valuing Colgate People that focuses on how to value differences to achieve firm goals. This program emphasizes Colgate's global values, such as caring for employees, and tackles specific diversity issues that commonly pop up in particular countries. For countries such as the United States, managers are taught how to address issues such as racial discrimination, while managers posted to Middle Eastern countries might learn how to grapple with class or

Table 7.2
Three Approaches to Managing Cultural Diversity

Firm Approach to Diversity and Associated Perceptions	Strategies Often Used with Each Diversity Approach	Most Likely Outcomes for Each Diversity Approach	How Frequently Diversity Approach Is Used
Parochial (our way is the only way): Cultural diversity is perceived to have no impact on companies	Ignore differences and the impact that diversity can have on companies	Problems surface, but are not linked by management to issues associated with cultural diversity	Very frequently
Ethnocentric (our way is the best way): Cultural diversity is perceived to create problems for companies	Attempt to minimize the sources and impact of cultural diversity by socializing employees worldwide to embrace corporate values	May succeed in reducing costs associated with diversity (e.g., ambiguity), but will likely erase or ignore potential benefits	Frequently
Synergistic multiculturalism (leveraging our differences may work best): Cultural diversity is believed to have both benefits and costs for companies	Managers are trained to identify and then use various cultural differences in ways that create benefits and advantages for the company	Likely to succeed at tapping the benefits of diversity while still experiencing some problems and costs that require ongoing management	Comparatively rare

Source: Adapted from Alder, N. J., & Gundersen, A. (2008). *International Dimensions of Organizational Behavior* (5th ed.). Mason, OH: Thompson South-Western, 108.

religious discrimination. The idea is to tailor training to diversity barriers that managers experience in specific locations. Valuing Colgate People also assesses whether company procedures promote respect. As a result, managers' performance reviews now include an assessment of how well they model respect to subordinates.[14]

CULTURAL DIVERSITY IN TEAMS: CHALLENGES AND SOLUTIONS

Some of the thorniest diversity challenges that international managers face involve teams of employees from a variety of cultures and countries. Managers often must lead teams consisting of foreign nationals, immigrants, expatriates, and members of racial and ethnic minorities—even when working in their home country. Regardless of whether they are working in their home country or are posted abroad, one of the biggest mistakes that managers can make is to automatically assume that everyone in a team will eventually behave similarly and share the same attitudes. This homogeneity perspective implies that with enough interaction, the employees in a team will blend their many different perspectives into one. This quintessentially U.S. viewpoint (the *e pluribus unum* motto on U.S. coins illustrates this, as it means "out of many, one") resonates well with employees in the United States. But such melting-pot beliefs may not exist elsewhere. Consequently, it may be more appropriate to assume that teams are characterized by cultural and other forms of diversity, at least at the start.[15]

Pros and Cons of Diversity in Teams

Managers responsible for developing effective multicultural work teams face huge challenges. Communication is more difficult in multicultural teams, and confusion, ambiguity, and conflict are more common. The benefits of team diversity take longer to manifest, partially because diversity increases the time that teams need to function effectively and make decisions. That said, in the long run, teams that are culturally diverse should make better decisions, develop better ideas, and relate more easily to foreign clients and customers. Think about two teams working on a new computer chip design. One team consists of U.S. scientists. This team will undoubtedly experience some problems as these relatively homogeneous employees learn to work together. But the second team, comprised of U.S., German, and Japanese scientists, has a much bigger challenge and will face additional problems since each culture has different ways of working and of leading. Sorting this all out will take more time given the different norms, values, and languages of the team members. Yet the cultural diversity of this team may eventually lead to a more innovative chip design. The following *Culture Clash* box presents just such a situation in more detail.[16]

CULTURE CLASH

Science Project: Overcome Barriers in Multicultural Teams

Some years ago, nearly 100 U.S., German, and Japanese scientists were brought together and formed into a cluster of work teams at an IBM facility in New York. Their goal was to create a new computer chip. Once the project was under way, management began to worry that the teams' cultural diversity would create problems—and they were right.

The Germans were shocked when their Japanese counterparts closed their eyes and apparently slept through parts of key meetings. Yet this is common behavior when Japanese employees realize that the current discussion does not center on them or their specific talents, especially because they tend to work in large teams. The Japanese had their own concerns, as they found it very uncomfortable to sit around in small, individual offices and to speak English. Consequently, they retreated whenever possible to the more comfortable confines of all-Japanese groups. The U.S. scientists thought that the Germans spent way too much time planning and that the Japanese, who were constantly reviewing proposals, could not make decisions quickly. The Germans and the Japanese both complained that the Americans did not make much of an effort to get to know them, either at work or at social events.

All of these perceptions resulted in a work climate characterized by misunderstanding and mistrust. Hardly the type of environment that would lead to breakthrough chip designs! So what went wrong here? Theoretically, putting diverse and intelligent people into groups should pay creative dividends. But this did not work, at least initially, because the scientists were allowed to retreat back into their separate cultural subgroups. Eventually, management realized that while they had paid considerable attention to the technical and logistical aspects of the project, little effort had been made to ensure effective group interaction and team building, particularly in the face of the significant cultural diversity in the groups they formed.

Despite these obstacles, the scientists said they learned a lot from working in their multicultural teams, particularly about how to interact cooperatively with people from around the world. Doing so required an understanding of the three cultures involved. For instance, Americans were characterized as using a "hamburger style" when leveling criticisms. They started gently, with how's-the-family small talk—the top of the hamburger bun. Then they went to the meat of the matter—the criticisms—followed by more bun (i.e., words of encouragement). In contrast, when dealing with the Germans, it was all meat (i.e., they were very direct), and with the Japanese you had to learn to smell the meat (i.e., they were very indirect).[17]

Using Cultural Diversity to Your Advantage

In general, the composition of a diverse team tends to impact its initial performance— the greater the diversity (based on characteristics such as gender, age, and/or culture), the more difficulty the team will have. More diverse teams have bigger headaches while communicating, more difficulty building unit cohesion, and more trouble setting up an effective structure than less diverse or homogeneous teams. Nevertheless, over the long run, diverse teams often perform best, particularly with novel problems, because they bring many perspectives to bear, which fosters greater innovation. Indeed, one study of top management teams found that cultural diversity was responsible for higher team performance. There is also evidence that having national diversity on top management teams impacts strategic choices made when entering foreign markets. There is a greater preference for more collaborative and complex forms of entry with shared ownership, such as international joint ventures. In essence, having nationality diversity at the top may make it easier to grasp and manage the complexities associated with entry choices involved in shared ownership.[18]

Other studies have found that homogeneous teams initially outperformed more diverse teams but were surpassed later on. Part of the challenge with diverse teams is that people from different cultural backgrounds have divergent views on what it means to work in a group or team. For example, one study found that workers from several countries had different metaphors in mind when they thought about working in groups. Workers from individualist countries such as the United States tended to use competitive sports metaphors when referring to groups (e.g., "people who focus and work as a team win championships"). In countries where power distance was high, such as the Philippines, groups were associated with family metaphors (e.g., "a work team is like a big family"). And since various cultures attach different meanings to teams, it is likely that the behaviors expected from individual team members for success are also different. Consistent with this expectation, another study found that Mexican workers thought that supportive behaviors among members (such as offering coworkers compliments) were important for team success, while U.S. workers thought that if team members focused on the task at hand, they would be successful.[19]

The following are some guidelines for managing diverse multicultural teams:

- *Select the right people.* Do not choose members of a multicultural team based solely on their ethnicity or cultural background. Instead, pick members who have high ability levels and who will bring diverse attitudes and perspectives to the team.
- *Explicitly recognize cultural differences.* Do not minimize or overlook cultural differences. Instead, encourage team members to recognize and embrace such differences. This will help team members move toward greater understanding and, eventually, openness to what different cultural perspectives can contribute to the tasks at hand. That said, this technique must be used with care, because it may exacerbate existing differences and create fault lines within the team.
- *Create a clear a vision and mission.* Since team members come from diverse backgrounds, they may disagree about how to focus their efforts. Consequently, time spent to clearly define the team's vision and mission in advance will help bridge individual differences and increase the odds of success.
- *Avoid creating power and status gaps on the team.* Power differences among team members can undercut the creativity of multicultural teams. While it

is common among international teams to have an employee from the parent company serve as leader, that person may end up dominating the group—especially if many people are from countries high in power distance. A strong norm of deferring to an officially designated leader may suppress team members' willingness to contribute.

- *Provide feedback.* Culturally diverse teams often have trouble agreeing on the merits of various ideas because members use different criteria to assess the options under consideration. Giving members frequent feedback will help them, over time, to develop shared yardsticks for evaluating ideas and speed up idea generation.

- *Recognize that reactions to training may differ around the world.* While providing diversity training can help multicultural teams succeed, firms should understand that team members may respond differently to training because of their cultural values. For instance, people from individualist countries tend to be more accepting of diversity training and willing to embrace trainers from different backgrounds. On the other hand, people from collectivist nations seem to respond best to trainers from collectivist cultures. In short, care needs to be taken when introducing training to multicultural teams to produce maximum acceptance.[20]

DIVERSITY AND CONFLICT MANAGEMENT

Earlier we noted that one of potential costs of cultural diversity is increased ambiguity and miscommunication. As discussed in Chapter 4, messages that are confused or missed often lead to conflict. In the context of this chapter, conflict can occur between employees because of divergent interests and cultural differences. Compounding matters is the fact that international managers must juggle many conflict-provoking issues, including dealing with foreign labor unions, negotiating with overseas vendors, soothing dissatisfied clients, and convincing employees with conflicting cultural perspectives to work together.

Consequently, to capitalize on diversity, it is important for international managers to learn to cope with conflicts that are the result of these perspectives. One important way to accomplish this is by using accounts effectively. An account is simply an explanation a manager can use to smooth over a perceived slight or to mitigate problems resulting from diverse perspectives. Figure 7.1 provides an overview of the account-giving process. In terms of diversity and conflict management, the final two steps in the account-giving sequence matter most. Since conflict is likely when conducting international business, how managers use accounts to understand and guide different viewpoints can be critical for preserving effective working relationships among groups.[21]

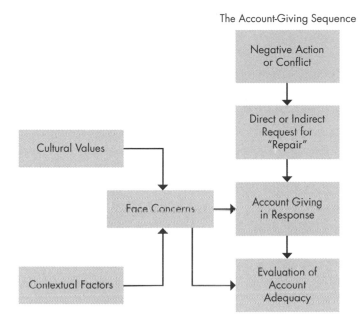

FIGURE 7.1 Managing International Conflicts with Accounts

Source: Adapted from Tata, J. (2000). Toward a theoretical framework of intercultural account-giving and account evaluation. *International Journal of Organizational Analysis, 8,* 158.

Several types of accounts exist. Mitigating accounts are aimed at lowering tensions caused by an initial action, thereby reducing or staving off subsequent conflict. For instance, a concession is a type of mitigating account in which someone takes responsibility for giving offense and offers an apology (e.g., "It was my mistake to use words that upset you. Please know that I am very sorry"). A justification is an account involving an admission that, although an offensive action occurred, it was unintentional or unavoidable given the circumstances (e.g., "I was late for our meeting because a car accident caused a big delay"). An ideological account involves owning up to actions taken while claiming that it was legitimate to do so given the circumstances (e.g., "The low performance evaluation I gave you will make you a better employee in the long run"). Finally, a refusal is an account likely to exacerbate rather than reduce conflicts. Here, a person either denies the existence of a negative action or declines to explain why it occurred (e.g., "I will not approve your request and let's leave it at that").[22]

Unfortunately, we do not yet have a management road map explaining how cultural values specifically connect to diversity-related conflicts and which accounts work best to mitigate them. Part of the problem is the existence of a variety of vexing complexities. For instance, when Americans adopt the interaction rules used in collectivist societies (e.g., Japan), it may be viewed as a sign of respect. But if foreigners attempt to adopt the interaction patterns found in individualist societies such as the United States (e.g., being interpersonally assertive), it may backfire. In an individualist cultural context, such efforts may be perceived as inauthentic—a failure to present the self honestly.

Another interesting complexity is that culture impacts work–family conflicts. For instance, employees in the individualist United States tend to place a higher value on personal family time than employees in more collectivist China. Generally speaking, Americans put self-interest (e.g., family time) above collective interest (e.g., work), and Chinese do the opposite. Americans tend to view their careers in terms of individual achievement (hence, chasing a career should not destroy the quality of family life), while Chinese tend to see careers as a way to bring prosperity and honor to their families. Consequently, Chinese tend to view working long hours as a sacrifice made for the family instead of a selfish statement about personal ambition. The upshot is that family demands appear to cause more work conflicts in the United States than they do in China. Of course, young professionals in China (a growing group) may have different views on the work–family balance than their elders.[23]

In any case, while we lack a definitive road map about how managers can use accounts to defuse diversity-related differences, Figure 7.2 represents a step in the right direction and brings to bear some of our earlier discussion about face from Chapter 4. The exhibit links two cultural dimensions (individualism–collectivism and masculinity–femininity) to the concerns that diverse employees are likely to have about face and how certain accounts may be received. You will recall that

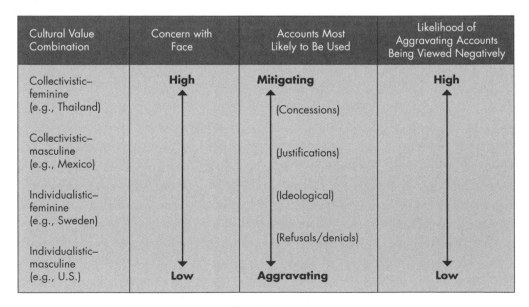

Cultural Value Combination	Concern with Face	Accounts Most Likely to Be Used	Likelihood of Aggravating Accounts Being Viewed Negatively
Collectivistic–feminine (e.g., Thailand)	**High**	**Mitigating**	**High**
		(Concessions)	
Collectivistic–masculine (e.g., Mexico)		(Justifications)	
Individualistic–feminine (e.g., Sweden)		(Ideological)	
		(Refusals/denials)	
Individualistic–masculine (e.g., U.S.)	**Low**	**Aggravating**	**Low**

FIGURE 7.2 Matching Cultural Values to Effective Use of Accounts

Source: Adapted from Tata, J. (2000). Toward a theoretical framework of intercultural account-giving and account evaluation. *International Journal of Organizational Analysis*, 8, 169.

masculine cultures typically stress values such as autonomy, achievement, and assertiveness, while feminine cultures emphasize relationships and cooperation.[24]

MANAGING ETHICS IN AN INTERNATIONAL CONTEXT: THE ROLE OF CULTURE

Knowing how to manage accounts effectively in a cross-cultural context is a valuable skill for international managers to have. The ability to handle accounts well may be especially useful when managers have to explain the decisions they make about the difficult ethical dilemmas they often face in the international arena. The final section of this chapter will consider some of these ethical challenges as well as offer guidance to international managers.

To many, the concept of business ethics is about as murky as it gets when borders are crossed. Culture clearly impacts what people in various countries feel is ethical behavior for businesses and their employees. Naturally, these views end up shaping behavior and the decisions that managers make about everything from bribery to the treatment of employees. The discussion of ethical dilemmas begins with two basic approaches to ethics: universalism and cultural relativism. Each approach offers divergent guidance for international managers.[25]

UNIVERSALISM AND CULTURAL RELATIVISM

Universalism takes the position that objective moral guidelines exist and that they should be followed by everyone everywhere. Proponents argue that virtually every culture sees certain behavior as wrong (e.g., harming others) and that certain principles for doing business are widely accepted (e.g., nearly every country prohibits bribery and stealing in business activity). Critics claim, however, that some of these laws are weak, poorly enforced, or riddled with loopholes.[26]

Yet many believe that there are rules for doing business that everyone should follow. Moreover, proponents of universalism have been active in articulating universal guidelines for behavior, including global codes of ethical conduct (e.g., covering workers' rights to nondiscriminatory treatment, among other things).[27]

But the implementation of universal principles is not easy. Because such principles tend to be broad, they come with ambiguity that leads to different interpretations and inconsistent implementation (e.g., what does "all employees should enjoy good working conditions" mean exactly?). As a result, cultural relativism has proven a popular alternative to universalism. Proponents feel that the definition of ethical behavior in a country is shaped by its culture, laws, and business practices. Consequently, if common practice is to offer a small payment (i.e., a bribe) to a public official to process export paperwork, then it is the right thing to do, even if it would be seen as wrong elsewhere. This when-in-Rome perspective argues that doing otherwise disrespects the culture in which you are doing business. In short, international managers should mimic local practices when doing business in different countries.[28]

Cultural values also shape the extent to which people embrace universalism or cultural relativism in the first place. One study examining marketing ethics found that Americans were more likely than Chinese to endorse universalism and less likely to endorse relativism. This also extends to the corporate level—as the next section on corporate social responsibility shows.[29]

ETHICS AND CORPORATE SOCIAL RESPONSIBILITY

In many firms, making ethical decisions is a balancing act. If management tilts toward cultural relativism, it does not mean that it thinks using prison labor in factories and employing young children are moral activities because they happen in Rangoon instead of Miami. Similarly, adopting a universalist code of conduct for the company and its employees worldwide does not necessarily translate into action. Strong enforcement of such codes requires time, commitment, and money. Yet multinational firms have been increasingly asked to inject public interest issues into their corporate decision making (e.g., to behave in ways that promote the triple bottom line of people, planet, and profits). This is the essence of corporate social responsibility (CSR).[30]

Critics say CSR detracts from the fundamental profit-making role of business, encourages superficial efforts to keep watchdog groups happy, and provides yet another grandstanding opportunity for CEOs to brag (e.g., about their passion for the environment and the like). Still, management attitudes toward CSR are changing for the better. In a recent survey of over 1,000 international executives, 60% said that CSR was a high priority in their companies—up from 35% a few years before. And only 4% of these executives thought that CSR activities were a waste of time. Indeed, nearly 60% said that CSR activities were a necessary cost of doing business that also distinguished their firm in the market and improved decision making.[31]

Indeed, the impact of CSR can be significant, both for the company and the countries where it does business. A study of Anglo-Dutch giant Unilever's CSR activities in Indonesia found that the firm supported the equivalent of 300,000 jobs, paid $130 million in taxes, and pumped roughly $600 million into the Indonesian economy. A review of more than 160 studies suggests a modest link between CSR activities and firm performance, while another recent investigation found that the companies most engaged in CSR in developing countries were also the most profitable. Overall, it's likely that CSR activities will continue to grow in the years ahead.[32]

ETHICAL DIFFERENCES ACROSS COUNTRIES

Yet when it comes to specifics, it is clear that perspectives on ethics vary across countries. In one study, U.S. managers were more likely to see employee theft and other personnel matters as ethical issues than either Austrians or Germans. Conversely, Austrian and German managers were more likely to view local politics through an ethics lens. Americans tend to be individualist and feel that individuals are the primary source of ethical values. Germans and Austrians are also generally individualist but tend to be more community oriented and see ethics playing out through the relationship between businesses and their local environments.[33]

Another interesting study compared how U.S., French, and German managers reacted to several ethical scenarios, including offering bribes to obtain business. In most cases, Americans were least likely to pay a bribe. When asked about their reasoning, nearly half of the U.S. managers said that bribery was unethical, illegal, or against company policy. Just 15% of the French and 9% of the German managers stated these reasons. Instead, both groups were more inclined to say that competitive pressures made bribery necessary. Overall, U.S. managers were more concerned about ethical issues than their European counterparts.[34]

This may explain why the U.S. government has continued to snare European companies in bribery scandals in recent years (any firm traded on U.S. stock exchanges can be prosecuted according to the Foreign Corrupt Practices Act; more on this below). For instance, companies from Sweden (Panalpina), the Netherlands (Royal Dutch Shell), and Germany (Siemens) have all paid large fines in recent years to settle bribery and related charges.[35]

In any case, research also shows that even if views about ethical issues are similar across countries, they may result from different moral reasoning processes. And cross-national differences in moral reasoning or ethical perspectives are unlikely to change in the short term, even when social, political, and economic conditions have shifted. Indeed, as suggested, corporations may reflect, if not reinforce, cross-national differences in ethics. For instance, compared to European firms, U.S. companies are more likely to have ethics codes in place to guide management decisions.[36]

Of course, ethics codes do not mean much if they are not enforced. Some experts believe that the claims management makes about the impact of these codes, particularly in developing nations, are exaggerated—and if management fails to respond effectively to enforcement complaints, real damage can be done to the firm and its reputation.[37]

Take Nike as an example. In the 1990s, media stories highlighted allegations that Nike's foreign contract manufacturers were ignoring the company's code of conduct, employing children and allowing horrific working conditions in places such as Vietnam. Other critics lambasted Nike for relying on a code that allowed foreign contractors to merely follow weak local labor laws in places such as Indonesia. Such criticism, along with boycotts and anti-Nike protests, led CEO Phil Knight at one point to admit that Nike's corporate image was sullied and associated with the abuse of foreign workers. In response, the company toughened its code of conduct and strengthened enforcement efforts. Despite these changes, however, workplace conditions for employees in Nike contract facilities still leave much to be desired according to some, presenting Nike with ongoing challenges—and criticism. That said, Nike's efforts to be more transparent with its stepped-up enforcement of conduct codes and greater scrutiny of supplier relationships may put pressure on other multinationals to do the same.[38]

BRIBES AND QUESTIONABLE PAYMENTS

How to treat employees around the world provides fertile ground for discussion about the merits of universalism versus cultural relativism. But so does the issue of how to deal with questionable payments in different countries—which include bribery, extortion, and "grease payments" to bureaucrats and business leaders. Bribery has a long history in international business and is relatively common in much of the world. Nearly every language in the world has a word for bribery. In addition to cash, bribery can include providing pricey gifts, free trips, and lavish entertainment.[39]

For example, in Turkey *baksheesh* refers to a questionable payoff that businesses might offer to officials to protect themselves from an imperfect legal system. In Mexico, the comparable term *la mordida* ("the bite") may reflect a similar sense of powerlessness with government bureaucracies. Indeed, euphemistic and evocative imagery is often used to describe bribery, including the Italian *bustarella* ("little envelope") and the French *pot au vin* ("jug of wine").[40]

Almost all countries ban bribery of its own officials, and many prohibit company representatives from offering bribes abroad. Indeed, in recent years, countries as diverse as the United Kingdom, Saudi Arabia, Russia, Indonesia, India, and China have either passed new antibribery laws or strengthened existing ones. Yet nations vary considerably in terms of how much corruption is actually tolerated in practice, laws notwithstanding. For example, an expatriate offering a bribe in Indonesia would face little risk of local prosecution since payoffs are common, if not expected. A recent survey of Indonesians found that over 65% of households indicated that public officials had asked them for unofficial payments at some point, and over 50% stated that teachers had asked for payments to ensure a child could enroll in school. Moreover, half of the Indonesian officials in the survey acknowledged receiving under-the-table payments.[41]

To put bribery in perspective, Table 7.3 presents annual results from a recent survey conducted by Transparency International (a nonprofit group that tracks

Table 7.3
Frequency of Bribe Paying Reported by People around the World in 2010

Region	Percent Who Paid Bribe in Prior 12 Months	Examples of Countries in the Region
Sub-Saharan Africa	56	Cameroon, Kenya, Nigeria, Senegal, Zambia
Middle East and North Africa	36	Iraq, Israel, Lebanon, Palestine
Newly Independent States and Russia	32	Armenia, Belarus, Georgia, Ukraine
Latin America	23	Argentina, Brazil, Chile, Mexico, Peru
West Balkans and Turkey	19	Bosnia and Herzegovina, Croatia, Kosovo, Serbia
Asia/Pacific	11	China, India, Pakistan, Thailand, Indonesia
European Union	5	Bulgaria, France, Hungary, Poland, Spain
North America	5	Canada, United States

Source: Adapted from Riano, J., Heinrich, F., & Hodess, R. (2010). *Global Corruption Barometer 2010.* Berlin: Transparency International. Available from www.transparency.org. Table entries are based on nearly 92,000 people surveyed by Transparency International.

corruption worldwide). Based on responses from nearly 92,000 people around the world, the table displays the percentage of people in specific regions who reported paying a bribe in the prior 12 months. Transparency International reports that bribery and other forms of corruption have generally increased over the past few years. Table 7.3 shows that bribery is most common in Africa and the Middle East and least common in the European Union and North America.[42]

The Impact of the Foreign Corrupt Practices Act

Ironically, while most countries have laws prohibiting bribery, relatively few make it illegal for their citizens to bribe foreign officials. In short, the when-in-Rome perspective applies—common local practices should be followed by citizens when doing business in foreign nations. And up until fairly recently, German, French, and Swiss laws allowed bribes to be deducted from corporate tax burdens. At a minimum, such laws were a tacit endorsement of corruption.[43]

The U.S. government started taking bribery more seriously after some embarrassing high-level cases in the 1970s. One of the most infamous examples involved payments made by a Lockheed executive to Japanese officials and agents to secure a large contract. Several bribes were paid totaling $12.5 million. While such illicit payments were not an uncommon business practice in Japan, public disclosure of the Lockheed case created a firestorm in that country as well. The Japanese officials involved were criminally charged and one committed suicide.[44]

As it turned out, however, the Lockheed case was not unique. Further investigations revealed that nearly 450 U.S. firms made inappropriate payments to foreign officials or companies during the mid-1970s. An outraged public demanded action, and the U.S. Congress responded by passing the Foreign Corrupt Practices Act (FCPA) in 1977. Since then, the FCPA has been amended a number of times to clarify ambiguous provisions.[45]

Under the FCPA, it is illegal for U.S. firms to offer bribes to foreign officials in an effort to gain business. Foreign companies whose stock is traded on U.S. exchanges are also subject to the FCPA. Penalties for violators can include hefty fines and imprisonment (e.g., in 2011, one U.S. telecom representative was given a 15-year prison term for paying out bribes totaling $900,000). Interestingly, the FCPA does not prohibit all questionable payments—it distinguishes between bribes to gain business and facilitating payments designed to grease the wheels of business. Specifically, the FCPA permits grease payments to foreign officials if the goal is to encourage them to perform the normal functions of their jobs—functions that may impact business. Overall, it's estimated that over $1 trillion in bribes of all sorts are paid worldwide every year.[46]

Indeed, in some countries it is wise to make small payments to customs officials so they do what they are supposed to do anyway (e.g., to allow shipments of imported parts to pass through customs). Without making grease payments, companies may find their shipments held up for an inordinate amount of time. Other examples of grease payments that are permitted under the FCPA include: (1) giving gifts to overcome bureaucratic red tape, such as having electricity turned on in your plant more quickly; (2) making modest payments to supplement poorly paid officials' low salaries in exchange for services performed, such as having the installation of phone lines by a local utility sped up; and (3) making small payments to facilitate the issuing of paperwork needed to conduct business or run equipment, such as an occupancy permit for a hotel or license to operate restaurants or factories. Compared to bribes aimed at landing new business, grease payments are small and only offered to secure services that companies are entitled to anyway (such as processing an application for an import license). Some view this as a distinction without a difference.

Because of the FCPA, managers at many U.S. firms have developed clear guidelines about illegal payments and communicate them to employees. According to one estimate, nearly 80% of U.S. multinationals now have such guidelines. Some guidelines, like heavy-equipment manufacturer Caterpillar's, give detailed advice about what payments are permitted and which are not. Other corporate guidelines take a strong ethical stance. For example, IBM forbids managers from even making the facilitating payments permitted under the FCPA. But even specific guidelines with clear ethical imperatives may not be enough. IBM decided to do even more after paying a $10 million fine in 2011 to settle charges that more than 100 employees had paid bribes to officials in Asian countries over a period of years to land business contracts. While not admitting guilt, IBM said that it would improve controls that monitor employee behavior against company guidelines, especially overseas. IBM's experience notwithstanding, most corporate guidelines dealing with bribery and other questionable payments are somewhat vague and tend to advise managers about what they should not do rather than what they should do.[47]

Consequently, some suggest that U.S. multinationals need to do more to actively enforce and support their own guidelines, such as establishing ethics hotlines that employees can call anonymously. Another suggestion is that U.S. multinationals should redouble their efforts to persuade foreign multinationals and their governments to take a stronger stand against bribery and other corrupt practices. In general, however, this is a challenging proposition, even when managers work directly with U.S. government officials to lobby foreign organizations. Nevertheless, some countries seem to be doing more to combat bribery—even in China, where the practice has been common. It is unclear how far such changes will spread and how meaningful they will be. The track record of prosecutions for bribery—including in countries that recently passed new or tougher laws such as the United Kingdom and several countries in the Middle East—is relatively modest. In contrast, enforcement of the FCPA has become much more aggressive in recent years. For example, from 2007 to 2010, the U.S. government sharply increased the number of major FCPA enforcement actions it pursued against both U.S. and foreign companies, collecting hundreds of millions of dollars in fines each year in the process. Whether this enforcement will continue remains to be seen.[48]

CHAPTER SUMMARY

We examined the issue of managing both cross-national and intranational diversity in international firms. Firms are sometimes reluctant to send women and minorities to certain countries because of local biases. Such concerns, however, are typically overstated. On a broader level, the most functional approach for managing cultural diversity issues is synergistic multiculturalism, which involves being open to the positive aspects of all cultures and leveraging cultural differences in ways that benefit the firm. Relatively few executives embrace this approach; multinationals are more likely to use a parochial or ethnocentric approach to deal with cultural diversity.

The chapter also discussed cultural diversity in groups and how managers can effectively respond to the challenges it presents by using different types of accounts (e.g., from mitigating to aggravating). Understanding how to use accounts can help managers better deal with diversity-related conflict. A related impact of diversity is that it can elevate the already important topics of ethics and corporate social responsibility and explain why they are approached and understood in such different ways.

For example, universalism argues that there are common ethical values that should be applied everywhere. Many international and corporate codes of conduct have been developed based on this perspective, despite the fact that universal principles are often vague and difficult to implement. On the other hand, cultural relativism embraces the idea that countries have different sets of ethical values that are shaped by their own unique laws and practices. Most research regarding cross-national differences in ethical perspectives suggests that Americans tend to be more concerned with ethical issues than their counterparts in Europe, Asia, and other parts of the world. U.S. multinationals are also more likely to have written codes of conduct in place that spell out what is considered unethical behavior than are European multinationals.

International companies need to confront issues associated with bribery and other questionable payments. Most nations have laws that prohibit the bribery of officials. Few, however, actually outlaw bribes that their citizens may pay to foreigners. In many nations, in fact, bribery is commonly seen as part of the cost of doing business. Scandals in the 1970s led to the eventual passage of the Foreign Corrupt Practices Act (FCPA), which made it illegal to pay foreigners bribes in an effort to win business. It does allow for facilitating payments that will ensure that foreign officials do what they are supposed to do, given their job responsibilities. The FCPA has prompted many U.S. multinationals to adopt guidelines about bribery and other forms of questionable payments.

DISCUSSION QUESTIONS

1. What are some of the major approaches that companies can take to managing diversity? Which approach has the best chance of success in your view? Explain.

2. In discussing diversity-related conflict, we sometimes focus too much on negative implications. Can you think of any *positive* effects that might result from this concept?

3. What role does universalism and relativism play for international managers? Which approach to ethics makes the most sense in your view? Why?

4. How should multinationals deal with demands for bribes abroad? What about other questionable practices? Do you agree with the basic tenets of the FCPA? Explain your position.

Developing Your International Career

ASSESSING DIVERSITY: A REAL-WORLD AUDIT IN AN INTERNATIONAL FIRM

Purpose and Instructions

The purpose of this exercise is to demonstrate how cultural diversity concepts and ideas play out in a real organization as well as to develop your cultural diversity assessment skills and your ability to evaluate different levels of cultural diversity commitment across companies.

Your instructor will divide the class into teams of four to six people. Each team will be required to research cultural diversity efforts at a specific organization and make recommendations for changes or improvements. Unless otherwise directed by your instructor, doing so will involve both primary and secondary research. Each team will also be expected to: (1) produce a 15- to 20-page report and (2) present its findings in class with a 15-minute PowerPoint presentation. Your instructor will provide additional guidance on company selection (emphasizing firms with international business or operations), report structure, and presentation parameters.

1. Start by deciding what constitutes the criteria for effective cultural diversity management in international organizations.

2. Select an organization that operates internationally, has international customers, and/or has hired foreign employees.

3. Next, do *secondary research* on the chosen firm—review company web pages, documents (e.g., annual reports), press releases, and articles written about the company, focusing on any efforts to promote cultural diversity or address the problems that are associated with it (e.g., conflict, decision-making challenges). Use the information uncovered to generate a list of follow-up questions about cultural diversity that can be put to company representatives.

4. Do primary research on the organization by visiting company facilities, touring operations, and interviewing company officials. Collect any additional materials that you

think might be relevant while on-site (firm newsletters, policy manuals, etc.). If possible, try to make interview appointments with multiple company officials who are in a position to know something about cultural diversity efforts (e.g., human resource managers, trainers, foreign employees, managers in charge of international divisions).

5. Evaluate everything you have discovered about your target company against the effectiveness criteria you originally established for cultural diversity. After conducting your research, you may want to add other criteria not present on your original list. Be alert for disconnects in analyzing your information. For example, are there inconsistencies between what the company says it is doing to foster and take advantage of cultural diversity versus what is actually happening? Are there things the firm could be doing better? Differently? Are the action steps currently being taken seriously or do they appear to be superficial?

6. Prepare your report and presentation following the parameters noted above and those supplied by your instructor.

Source: Adapted from Harvey, C. P. (2002). Evaluating diversity in the real world: Conducting a diversity audit. In C. Harvey and M.J. Allard (eds.), *Understanding and Managing Diversity: Readings, Cases, and Exercises* (2nd ed., 285–286). Upper Saddle River, NJ: Pearson.

Making the Case for International Understanding

SAP'S GOAL TO BE MORE DIVERSE AND "LESS GERMAN" PRODUCES CROSS-CULTURAL CONFLICTS

Founded in 1972, SAP is Germany's largest software company. The firm grew through the 1980s and 1990s, with most software created by tight-knit groups of developers at company headquarters in Walldorf, Germany. Consequently, SAP's software had a distinctly German flavor. It took a year or more to perfect programs, with developers troubleshooting with teammates at coffee bars strategically placed in SAP's Walldorf facility. Complex and expensive, SAP's software systems often took months to install and debug. Clearly, SAP software products worked well and offered a one-stop shop for corporate customers. At the time, the fact that SAP products did not integrate well with other firms' software wasn't a big problem.

But in the late 1990s, businesses started focusing more on interconnectedness and integration, thanks to the Internet. This became a problem for SAP's stand-alone software model. Moreover, companies were backing away from buying pricey, complex software suites every five years, turning instead to more flexible web-based software offered by SAP's competitors. After tinkering with its business model, SAP decided in 2003 that the answer to these challenges was to become "less German." Implementing this strategy over the next several years produced plenty of change and conflict.

SAP co-CEOs Hasso Plattner and Henning Kagermann felt that their cautious approach to competitive threats had been holding back the firm, especially in the U.S. market. An injection of innovation was needed to shake up the company. This didn't come easily since Kagermann (an ex-physics professor) and Plattner (a hot-tempered tech guru) were both known for their cautious management styles. But they acquired a diverse chunk of non-German innovation in one fell swoop by purchasing an Israeli firm that developed web-based applications. This firm was led by Shai Agassi, a young entrepreneur with a brash style that CEOs Plattner and Kagermann took to. They gave Agassi tough management roles and made him responsible for hundreds of SAP programmers. Along the way, Agassi continued to pitch ideas for different and innovative products to his German bosses, despite being repeatedly rebuffed. Finally, one idea caught the eye of Plattner and Kagermann—an idea that became SAP's NetWeaver, a web-based software tool more flexible than traditional SAP software. Agassi was promoted and given more control at SAP.

While SAP was becoming less German thanks to Agassi, it was also becoming more diverse by hiring thousands of programmers from different parts of the world, particularly the United States and India. These programmers were put into development teams to tackle key projects that previously would have been given to German employees in Walldorf. Agassi also insisted on changing the official language of the company to English, even in SAP's German headquarters. Soon non-Germans occupied 50% of top executive positions at SAP. The hope was that this injection of newcomers would increase diversity in SAP and quicken the pace of innovation.

But these moves also created conflict, especially in Walldorf. Most firms start to globalize by building sales or manufacturing units first while keeping research and development and the development of company strategy close to home. SAP did not follow this model. Instead, it tried to globalize away from its German roots from top to bottom—something that came as a big shock to German employees embedded in the insular SAP culture at Walldorf. For instance, Agassi took major development projects away from German teams at Walldorf. SAP's Palo Alto office was assigned to handle the look and feel of products, and Indian programmers were given responsibility for analytical tools. Walldorf developers were relegated to doing hard-core coding.

Not surprisingly, veteran German developers at Walldorf complained about being shut out of all phases of the software development process. Others clashed with Agassi about how SAP units in countries were modifying "their" software. Agassi recalled German developers basically stating "they don't tell us what to do—we tell them what to build." Of course, this attitude was exactly what Agassi and his German superiors wanted to change. In response, SAP made the non-German Agassi responsible for SAP's traditional software operations in Walldorf as well as all SAP product strategy—moves Agassi later described as "punishment."

Yet Agassi took his newest assignment to heart and hired hundreds of programmers from Silicon Valley competitors, putting some in senior positions. From California, he created a plan to develop new products in 100 days, later dropping the target to 50 days. He pinpointed German managers whose opposition could threaten these changes and created a list of people to personally win over. To demonstrate that faster product development was possible, he created a showcase project that tasked 10 developers to produce 100 programs in 12 weeks, much quicker than would have been possible with SAP's traditional approach. The developers, however, pushed back and asked the goal to be set at 30 programs instead. Agassi refused, and they ultimately completed the project.

But the German grousing continued—about the quality of the products SAP was now turning out and that Palo Alto, rather than Walldorf, now called the shots on company strategy. While SAP's CEOs supported Agassi's changes and pointed out that employment at Walldorf was higher than ever, German veterans were having none of it. They complained about their loss of autonomy and the Americanization of SAP. One German noted, "We used to be kings," and pointed to the fact that Agassi pushed key product development teams into eight centers around the world, all directed from California.

More conflict surfaced at a series of meetings between Agassi and Walldorf developers that were called by SAP's CEOs. Agassi was hammered by German employees about his goals, jobs at Walldorf, and the behavior of foreign managers. At a subsequent set of town hall meetings in Walldorf, SAP executives heard more concerns about the Americanization of the company. The German media then swooped in, with a national newspaper publishing an article entitled "SAP & Globalization: March of the Americans." A German manager noted, "It's clear that Agassi would like to get as many functions to the U.S. as possible," while Agassi said that SAP was simply looking for the best talent it could find.

Eventually, SAP sponsored cultural sensitivity training to mitigate these problems. The training sessions revealed that Indian developers preferred a great deal of attention and supervision, while Germans would rather be left alone to do their work. Differences were also uncovered in how feedback was delivered—differences that could be off-putting or send inconsistent messages. For instance, Americans tended to be more effusive with their praise—an American would be more likely to compliment a piece of work by describing it as "excellent" than a German, who would be more likely to describe the same work as "good." Foreign managers hired by SAP were also advised during training about how to interact more effectively with German developers—part of the answer was to work hard and impress them.

But these efforts were apparently too little and too late for Agassi, who had become increasingly frustrated with all the conflict inside SAP. He decided to resign. During a subsequent interview with reporters, CEO Kagermann stated that he would continue his efforts to persuade and convince employees that SAP could not go back to its old Walldorf-centric ways. When asked about Agassi's departure, Kagermann noted, "it's not easy to manage."[49]

ASSIGNMENT QUESTIONS

1. What was the nature of the diversity-related conflicts that unfolded at SAP? Why did they occur? What cultural differences might be responsible?

2. What is your assessment of the efforts that SAP made to tackle these internal conflicts? Were they sufficient? If not, what mistakes were made? Could anything have been done differently to prevent things from reaching this point? Why?

3. If you were advising CEO Kagermann, how would you suggest he deal with the continuing problems and internal problems he faced? Can this situation be salvaged?

NOTES

1. Stevens, L. (2011). German CEO's call for a "prettier" board flops. *Wall Street Journal*, February 8, A9.

2. Cox, T. H., & Blake, S. (1991). Managing for cultural diversity: Implications for organizational competitiveness. *Academy of Management Executive*, August, 45–56; Stevens, L. (2011). German CEO's call for a "prettier" board flops. *Wall Street Journal*, February 8, A9.

3. Land of the wasted talent. *The Economist*, November 5, 2011, 80; Dunung, S. P. (1995). *Doing Business in Asia: The Complete Guide.* New York: Lexington Books; Fackler, M. (2007). Career women in Japan find a blocked path. *New York Times*, August 6. Available at www.nytimes.com/2007/08/06/world/asia/06equal.html; Reitman, V. (1995). Japan: She is free, yet she's alone in the world. *Wall Street Journal*, July 26, B1, B12; Thomas, P. (1995). United States: Success at a huge personal cost. *Wall Street Journal*, July 25, B1, B12.

4. Bray, C. (2011). Toshiba's U.S. unit faces discrimination suit. *Wall Street Journal*, February 1, B5; www.toshiba.com/tai/about_us_companies.jsp.

5. Feltes, P., Robinson, R. K., & Fink, R. L. (1993). American female expatriates and the Civil Rights Act of 1991: Balancing legal and business interests. *Business Horizons*, March–April, 82–85; Solomon, C. M. (1994). Global operations demand that HR rethink diversity. *Personnel Journal*, July, 40–50.

6. Copeland, A. P., & Meckman, S. (2004). Women expatriates: A view of their own. Available at www.expatica.com/hr/story/women-expatriates-a-view-of-their-own10532.html; Feltes, P., Robinson, R. K., & Fink, R. L. (1993). American female expatriates and the Civil Rights Act of 1991: Balancing legal and business interests. *Business Horizons*, March–April, 82–85; Mackey, R. (2009). A year later, a Saudi woman still waits to drive legally. *New York Times News Blog*, http://thelede.blogs.nytimes.com/2009/03/12; Scheibal, W. (1995). When cultures clash: Applying Title VII abroad. *Business Horizons*, September–October, 4–8; www.guardian.co.uk/world/2011/jun/17/saudi-arabia-women-drivers-protest.

7. Erwee, R. (1994). South African women: Changing career patterns. In N. J. Adler & D. N. Izraeli (eds.), *Competitive Frontiers: Women Managers in a Global Economy* (325–342). Cambridge,

MA: Blackwell; Hollway, W., & Mukurasi, L. (1994). Women managers in the Tanzanian civil service. In N. J. Adler & D. N. Izraeli (eds.), *Competitive Frontiers: Women Managers in a Global Economy* (343–357); Herrera, J. M., & Erdener, C. (2009). Western ethical theories and their relevance to HRM in Latin America. In A. Davila & M. M. Elvira (eds.), *Best Human Resource Practices in Latin America* (157–169). New York: Routledge; Kishkovsky, S., & Williamson, E. (1997). Second-class comrades no more: Women stoke Russia's start-up boom. *Wall Street Journal*, January 30, A12; Prada, P. (2010). Women ascend in Latin America. *Wall Street Journal*, December 24, A10.

8. Linehan, M., & Walsh, J. S. (2000). Beyond the traditional linear view of international managerial careers: A new model of the senior female career in an international context. *Journal of European Industrial Training*, 24, 178–189; Scheibal, W. (1995). When cultures clash: Applying Title VII abroad. *Business Horizons*, September–October, 4–8.

9. Global relocation trends show future expat growth. (2009). Available at www.goinglobal. com/newsletter/march09corp_general_global.asp; Expatriate workforce demographics. *HR Magazine* (2006). Available at http://findarticles.com/p/articles/mi_m3495/is_5_51/ai_ n26865604/; Alder, N. J., & Gundersen, A. (2008). *International Dimensions of Organizational Behavior* (5th ed.). Mason, OH: Thomson South-Western; Briscoe, D. R., Schuler, R. S., & Claus, L. (2009). *International Human Resource Management* (3rd ed.). New York: Routledge; Jordan, M. (2001). Have husband, will travel. *Wall Street Journal*, February 13, B1, B12; Taylor, S., & Napier, N. (1996). Working in Japan: Lessons from women expatriates. *Sloan Management Review*, Spring, 76–84.

10. Briscoe, D. R., Schuler, R. S., & Claus, L. (2009). *International Human Resource Management* (3rd ed.). New York: Routledge; Copeland, A. P., & Meckman, S. (2004). Women expatriates: A view of their own. Available at www.expatica.com/hr/story/women-expatriates-a-view-of-their-own10532.html; Taylor, S., & Napier, N. (1996). Working in Japan: Lessons from women expatriates. *Sloan Management Review*, Spring, 76–84.

11. Srivastava, M. (2011). Keeping women on the job in India. *Bloomberg Businessweek*, March 7–13, 11–12.

12. Alder, N. J., & Gundersen, A. (2008). *International Dimensions of Organizational Behavior* (5th ed.). Mason, OH: Thomson South-Western; Ante, S. E., & Magnusson, P. (2003). Too many visas for techies? *Business Week*, August 25, 39; MacDonald, A. (2011). Multiculturalism loses its allure. *Wall Street Journal*, February 10, A16; Tung, R. L. (1993). Managing cross-national and intranational diversity. *Human Resource Management*, 32, 461–477.

13. Alder, N. J., & Gundersen, A. (2008). *International Dimensions of Organizational Behavior* (5th ed.). Mason, OH: Thompson South-Western; Kwoh, L. (2011). Study: Executives could do better on diversity. *Wall Street Journal*, November 21, B7; Tung, R. L. (1993). Managing cross-national and intranational diversity. *Human Resource Management*, 32, 461–477.

14. Solomon, C. M. (1994). Global operations demand that HR rethink diversity. *Personnel Journal*, July, 40–50. Also see material from Colgate website: www.colgate.com/app/Colgate/ US/Corp/LivingOurValues/CoreValues.cvsp.

15. Alder, N. J., & Gundersen, A. (2008). *International Dimensions of Organizational Behavior* (5th ed.). Mason, OH: Thomson South-Western.

16. Cramton, C. D., & Hinds, P. L. (2005). Subgroup dynamics in internationally distributed teams: Ethnocentrism or cross-national learning? *Research in Organization Behavior*, 26, 231–263; Houlder, V. (1996). How to get ideas to hatch. *Financial Times*, September 9, 10;

Von Glinow, M., Shapiro, D. L., & Brett, J. M. (2004). Can we talk, and should we? Managing emotional conflict in multicultural teams. *Academy of Management Review*, 29, 578–592.

17. Browning, E. S. (1994). Computer chip project brings rivals together, but the cultures clash. *Wall Street Journal*, May 3, A1, A8; Salk, J. E., & Brannen, M. Y. (2000). National culture, networks, and individual influence in a multinational management team. *Academy of Management Journal*, 43, 191–202.

18. Dalton, M., Ernst, C., Deal, J., & Leslie, J. (2002). *Success for the New Global Manager: How to Work across Distances, Countries, and Cultures*. San Francisco: Jossey-Bass; Earley, P. C., & Mosakowski, E. (2000). Creating hybrid team cultures: An empirical test of transnational team functioning. *Academy of Management Journal*, 43, 26–49; Elron, E. (1997). Top management teams within multinational corporations: Effects of cultural heterogeneity. *Leadership Quarterly*, 8, 393–412; Gelfand, M. J., Erez, M., & Aycan, Z. (2007). Cross-cultural organizational behavior. *Annual Review of Psychology*, 58, 479–514; Guzzo, R. A., & Shea, G. P. (1992). Group performance and intergroup relations in organizations. In M. D. Dunnette & L. M. Hough (eds.), *Handbook of Industrial and Organizational Psychology*, Vol. 3 (2nd ed.). Palo Alto, CA: Consulting Psychologists Press; Harrison, D. A., Price, K. H., Gavin, J. H., & Florey, A. (2002). Time, teams and task performance: Changing effects of surface- and deep-level diversity on group functioning. *Academy of Management Journal*, 45, 1029–1045; Jehn, K. A., Chadwick, C., & Thatcher, S. M. B. (1997). To agree or not to agree: The effects of value congruence, individual demographic dissimilarity, and conflict on workgroup outcomes. *International Journal of Conflict Management*, 8, 287–305; Nielsen, B. B., & Nielsen, S. (2011). The role of top management team international orientation in international strategic decision-making: The choice of foreign entry mode. *Journal of World Business*, 46, 185–193; Thomas, D. C. (1999). Cultural diversity and work group effectiveness: An experimental study. *Journal of Cross-Cultural Psychology*, 30, 242–263; Uday-Riley, M. (2007). Eight critical steps to improve workplace performance with cross-cultural teams. *Performance Improvement*, 45, 28–32; Watson, W. E., Kumar, K., & Michaelson, L. K. (1993). Cultural diversity's impact on interaction process and performance: Comparing homogeneous and diverse task groups. *Academy of Management Journal*, 36, 590–602.

19. Ayoko, B. O., Hartel, C. E., & Callan, V. J. (2002). Resolving the puzzle of productive and destructive conflict in culturally heterogeneous workgroups: A communication accommodation theory approach. *International Journal of Conflict Management*, 13, 165–195; Earley, P. C., & Mosakowski, E. (2000). Creating hybrid team cultures: An empirical test of transnational team functioning. *Academy of Management Journal*, 43, 26–49; Gibson, C. B., & Zellmer-Bruhn, M. E. (2001). Metaphors and meaning: An intercultural analysis of the concept of teamwork. *Administrative Science Quarterly*, 46, 274–303; Harstone, M., & Augoustinos, M. (1995). The minimal group paradigm: Categorization into two versus three groups. *European Journal of Social Psychology*, 25, 179–193; Sanchez-Burks, J., Nisbett, R. E., & Ybarra, O. (2000). Cultural styles, relational schemas and prejudice against outgroups. *Journal of Personality and Social Psychology*, 79, 174–189.

20. Alder, N. J., & Gundersen, A. (2008). *International Dimensions of Organizational Behavior* (5th ed.). Mason, OH: Thomson South-Western; Earley, P. C. (1999). Playing follow the leader: Status-determining traits in relation to collective efficacy across cultures. *Organizational Behavior and Human Decision Processes*, 80, 192–212; Holladay, C. L., &

Quinones, M. A. (2005). Reactions to diversity training: An international comparison. *Human Resource Development Quarterly*, 16, 529–545.

21. Tata, J. (2000). Toward a theoretical framework of intercultural account-giving and account evaluation. *International Journal of Organizational Analysis*, 8, 155–178.

22. Tata, J. (2000). Toward a theoretical framework of intercultural account-giving and account evaluation. *International Journal of Organizational Analysis*, 8, 155–178.

23. Chen, K. (2005). China's growth places strains on a family's ties: Brothers with different goals split over business venture, as father feels ignored. *Wall Street Journal*, April 13, A1, A15; Coffey, B. S., Anderson, S. E., Zhao, S., Liu, Y., & Zhang, J. (2009). Perspectives on work–family issues in China: The voice of young urban professionals. *Community, Work and Family*, 12, 197–212; De Cieri, H., & Bardoel, E. A. (2009). What does "work–life management" mean in China and Southeast Asia for MNCs? *Community, Work and Family*, 12, 179–196; Mortazavi, S., Pedhiwala, P., Shafiro, M., & Hammer, L. (2009). Work–family conflict related to culture and gender. *Community, Work and Family*, 12, 251–273; Yang, N., Chen, C. C., Choi, J., & Zou, Y. (2000). Sources of work–family conflict: A Sino–U.S. comparison of the effects of work and family demands. *Academy of Management Journal*, 43, 113–124.

24. Pornpitakpan, C., & Giba, S. (1999). The effects of cultural adaptation on business relationships: Americans selling to Japanese and Thais. *Journal of International Business Studies*, 30, 317–338; Tata, J. (2000). Toward a theoretical framework of intercultural account-giving and account evaluation. *International Journal of Organizational Analysis*, 8, 155–178.

25. Business ethics: Doing well by doing good. *The Economist*, April 22, 2000, 65–67; Cohen, J. R., Pant, L. W., & Sharp, D. J. (1992). Cultural and socioeconomic constraints on international codes of ethics: Lessons from accounting. *Journal of Business Ethics*, 11, 687–700; Schlegelmilch, B. B., & Robertson, D. C. (1995). The influence of country and industry on ethical perceptions of senior executives in the US and Europe. *Journal of International Business Studies*, 26, 859–879.

26. Bribery: Supply side. *The Economist*, November 5, 2011, 12; DeGeorge, R. T. (1993). *Competing with Integrity in International Business*. New York: Oxford University Press.

27. Buller, P. F., Kohls, J., J., & Anderson, K. S. (1991). The challenge of global ethics. *Journal of Business Ethics*, 10, 767–775; Frederick, W. C. (1991). The moral authority of transnational corporate codes. *Journal of Business Ethics*, 10, 165–177; Donaldson, T. (1989). *The Ethics of International Business*. New York: Oxford University Press; Velasquez, M. (1995). International business ethics: The aluminum companies in Jamaica. *Business Ethics Quarterly*, 5, 865–881.

28. Baron, D. P. (1996). *Business and Its Environment*. Upper Saddle River, NJ: Prentice Hall.

29. Singh, J. J., Vitell, S. J., Al-Khatib, J., & Clark, I. (2007). The role of moral intensity and personal moral philosophies in the ethical decision making of marketers: A cross-cultural comparison of China and the United States. *Journal of International Marketing*, 15, 86–112.

30. Kaltenheuser, S. (1995). China: Doing business under an immoral government. *Business Ethics*, May/June, 20–23; Kelly, M. (1996). Is Pizza Hut Burma's keeper? *Business Ethics*, July/August, 73–75.

31. Just good business: A special report on corporate social responsibility. *The Economist*, January 19, 2008, 3–24; Yong, A. (2008). Cross-cultural comparisons of managerial perceptions of profit. *Journal of Business Ethics*, 82, 775–791.

32. Egri, C. P., & Ralston, D. A. (2008). Corporate responsibility: A review of international management research from 1998 to 2007. *Journal of International Management*, 14, 319–339;

Kaufmann, L., Reimann, F., Ehrgott, M., & Rauer, J. (2009). Sustainable success: For companies operating in developing countries, it pays to commit to improving social and environmental conditions. *Wall Street Journal*, June 22, R6; Lund-Thomsen, P. (2008). The global sourcing and codes of conduct debate: Five myths and five recommendations. *Development and Change*, 39, 1005–1018.

33. Schlegelmilch, B. B., & Robertson, D. C. (1995). The influence of country and industry on ethical perceptions of senior executives in the US and Europe. *Journal of International Business Studies*, 26, 859–879.

34. Becker, H., & Fritzsche, D. J. (1987). A comparison of the ethical behavior of American, French, and German managers. *Columbia Journal of World Business*, 22, 87–95.

35. Scannell, K., & Catan, T. (2010). Settlements near in bribery case. *Wall Street Journal*, October 15, A1, A2; Searcey, D. (2010). Watergate-era law revitalized in pursuit of corporate corruption. *Wall Street Journal*, October 15, A2.

36. Husted, B. W., Dozier, J. B., McMahon, J. T., & Kattan, M. W. (1996). The impact of cross-national carriers of business ethics on attitudes about questionable practices and forms of moral reasoning. *Journal of International Business Studies*, 27, 391–411; Langlois, C. C., & Schlegelmilch, B. B. (1990). Do corporate codes of ethics reflect national character? Evidence from Europe and the United States. *Journal of International Business Studies*, 21, 519–539; Moore, R. S., & Radloff, S. E. (1996). Attitudes towards business ethics held by South African students. *Journal of Business Ethics*, 15, 863–869.

37. Clifford, M. L. (1996). Keep the heat on sweatshops. *Business Week*, December 3, 90; Holmes, S. (2003). Free speech or false advertising: Nike's sweatshop statement case hits Supreme Court. *Business Week*, April 28, 69–70; Singer, A. W. (1996). Levi Strauss' global sourcing guidelines come of age. *Ethikos*, May/June, 4–12.

38. Bernstein, A. (2003). Sweatshops. Finally, airing the dirty linen. *Business Week*, June 23, 100–102; Levenson, E. (2008). Citizen Nike: A decade ago the shoe giant was slammed as a sweatshop operator. Today it's taking responsibility to heart. Will it work? *Fortune*, November 24, 165–170; Montero, D. (2006). Nike's dilemma: Is doing the right thing wrong? *Christian Science Monitor*, December 22, 1–2, www.nikeresponsibility.com.

39. Jacoby, N. H., Nehemkis, P., & Eells, R. (1977). *Bribery and Extortion in World Business. A Study of Corporate Political Payments Abroad.* New York: Macmillan; Noonan, J. (1984). *Bribes.* New York: Macmillan.

40. Jacoby, N. H., Nehemkis, P., & Eells, R. (1977). *Bribery and Extortion in World Business: A Study of Corporate Political Payments Abroad.* New York: Macmillan.

41. Bribery: Supply side. *The Economist*, November 5, 2011, 12; Borsuk, R. (2003). In Indonesia, a new twist on spreading the wealth: Decentralization of power multiplies opportunities for bribery, corruption. *Wall Street Journal*, January 29, A16.

42. See www.transparency.org.

43. Bribery: Supply side. *The Economist*, November 5, 2011, 12; Czinkota, M. R., Ronkainen, I. A., Moffett, M. H., & Moynihan, E. O. (1995). *Global Business.* New York: Dryden Press; Gold, R., & Crawford, D. (2008). U.S., other nations step up bribery battle. *Wall Street Journal*, September 12, B1, B6.

44. Cohen, J. A. (1976). Japan's Watergate. *New York Times Magazine*, November 21, 104–119; DeGeorge, R. T. (1993). *Competing with Integrity in International Business.* New York: Oxford University Press; Singer, A. W. (1991). Ethics: Are standards lower overseas? *Across the Board*, 28, 31–34.

45. Boulton, D. (1978). *The Grease Machine.* New York: Harper & Row; Kotchian, C. A. (1977). The payoff: Lockheed's 70-day mission to Tokyo. *Saturday Review,* July 9, 7–16.

46. Bribery: Supply side. *The Economist,* November 5, 2011, 12; Roberts, D., & Blum, J. (2010). Bribery is losing its charm in China. *Bloomberg Businessweek,* July 12–18, 11–12.

47. Calderon, R., Alvarez-Arce, J. L., & Mayoral, S. (2009). Corporation as crucial ally against corruption. *Journal of Business Ethics,* 87, 319–332; Schlegelmilch, B. (1989). The ethics gap between Britain and the United States: A comparison of the state of business ethics in both countries. *European Management Journal,* 7, 57–64; Holzer, J., & Raice, S. (2011). IBM settles bribery charges. *Wall Street Journal,* March 19–20, B1, B3.

48. Operating an ethics hotline: Some practical advice. *Ethikos,* March/April 1996, 11–13; Graham, G. (1993). US seeks OECD foreign bribes ban. *Financial Times,* December 6, 3; Holzer, J., & Raice, S. (2011). IBM settles bribery charges. *Wall Street Journal,* March 19–20, B1, B3; Keatley, R. (1994). U.S. campaign against bribery faces resistance from foreign governments. *Wall Street Journal,* February 4, A6; Searcey, D. (2010). Watergate-era law revitalized in pursuit of corporate corruption. *Wall Street Journal,* October 15, A2.

49. Dvorak, P., & Abboud, L. (2007). Difficult upgrade: SAP's plan to globalize hits cultural barriers; software giant's shift irks German engineers, U.S. star quits effort. *Wall Street Journal,* May 11, A1.

Chapter 8

Managing Multicultural Teams and International Partnerships

Johnson Controls and Saft have a fundamental disagreement about the future direction and appropriate scope of the joint venture.

—Alex Molinaroli, president of Johnson Controls Inc.'s Power Solutions unit

Saft has made a number of constructive proposals to try to reach a compromise agreement with JCI and avoid any legal procedure. These proposals have been rejected by JCI.

—Saft Groupe SA statement[1]

These quotes underscore the challenges associated with managing international joint ventures as well as other cross-national partnerships and alliances. U.S.-based Johnson Controls and its French partner Saft Groupe SA formed a joint venture to manufacture batteries for hybrid and electric vehicles. But after five years, Johnson Controls was not happy with the partnership and began proceedings to dissolve the joint venture in 2011. Although we do not know precisely what led up to this point, it is likely that the gap between U.S. and French management cultures compounded the firms' differences regarding the strategic direction of the joint venture. In the end, the two international companies had to agree to disagree, with one partner seeing significant problems with the joint venture and the other partner thinking things were just fine.[2]

Any type of cross-cultural working relationship has plenty of potential for disagreement. Firm-level tie-ups, including international joint ventures, are complex to set up in the first place—challenges made all the more difficult when different cultures and management styles are thrown into the mix. Firm-level relationships and how they can be effectively managed are addressed later in this chapter. Specifically, we will explore what executives need to think through when setting up international partnerships as well as the headaches that may result in managing them.

Before tackling such partnerships, however, we build up to them by first discussing how to effectively manage smaller multicultural teams that work in the trenches day-to-day. In doing so, the next section picks up where Chapter 7 left off, broadening the presentation of cross-cultural team issues.

...ULTICULTURAL TEAMS

...locks of organizations. There are work teams
...going basis, cross-functional teams that dis-
..., and management teams that grapple with
...setting strategic direction. Of course, many
...tual teams that can handle a variety of tasks
...ms is simple—they tap the pooled knowl-
...which, generally speaking, results in better
...ervice delivery, more efficient production).
...ces working in teams. While teams have
...ith challenges. Chapter 7 addressed some
...multicultural teams, but we broaden our
...sequent sections. In essence, management
...stage so that the promise of teams can be
...er and calling them a team is naïve and ul-
...of misunderstandings, disagreements, and
...etween people. Naturally, these problems
...ms, where employees from different na-

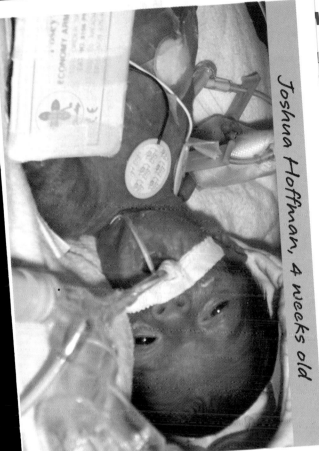

Joshua Hoffman, 4 weeks old

... Team Behavior

...multicultural work teams may eventually yield benefits (e.g., more
creative problem solving), their diversity also comes with costs, including higher
task conflict (i.e., disagreements between team members over how work should be
done). These costs are often driven by cultural differences among team members
that can impact, among other things, how they perceive teams, how accepting
they are of power distance, how motivated they are to avoid uncertainty, and how
much context matters in their communications. In other words, cultural differences can dramatically complicate, if not compromise, the effectiveness of multicultural teams.[3]

For example, group goals tend to be more important than individual goals in
collectivist cultures, while the opposite is the case in individualist societies, where
individual achievement and self-reliance are prized. Moreover, people who embrace individualist values generally look at everyone through the same values lens,
while collectivists tend to use different yardsticks when dealing with their in-
groups and out-groups. For many collectivists, groups are not the same. For some,
family comes first (e.g., many Chinese); for others, the company comes first (e.g.,
many Japanese). Regardless, collectivists draw sharper boundaries between their
in-groups and out-groups than do most individualists. In short, the process of team

interaction in the workplace may vary significantly when individualists and collectivists are involved.[4]

These interaction differences appear early. One study examined group interaction patterns among children working on a task. Chinese children used cooperative, group-enhancing approaches to complete the task, while U.S. children used self-enhancing, competitive approaches. These differences underscore the emphasis in U.S. society on individual achievement, as well as the traditional Chinese saying, "Friendship first and competition second." Understanding how employees from different cultures approach group work can help international managers create and maintain more effective multicultural teams.[5] The following are four specific areas in which culturally driven barriers can hinder multicultural teams:

1. *Decision-making norms that diverge or conflict.* Multicultural team members may have different views about how much analysis needs to be done before decisions are made. As a result, some members may be inclined to make decisions quickly, becoming impatient when others want to take more time to gather information, build a consensus, and so on. These differences have cultural roots in many cases. For instance, individualistic Americans tend to be quick decision-makers, focusing more on efficiency and getting the job done. In contrast, their more collectivistic Japanese and Korean counterparts tend to be willing to spend more time making decisions to solicit input from all team members, thereby preserving solidarity and cohesiveness.

2. *Different views about hierarchy.* Members from different cultures may have attitudes about status that lead to divergent expectations about how team members should be treated. For example, team members from low-power-distance cultures such as Australia may want to treat everyone the same, while team members from high-power-distance cultures such as Korea may think it is important to defer to people with more status in the firm. These differences can produce embarrassment, anger, and loss of credibility when expectations collide. For example, a Korean team member's deference toward higher-status members may be interpreted by Australians on the team as signaling lack of confidence, indecisiveness, or incompetence.

3. *Explicit (low-context) versus implicit (high-context) communication styles.* Team members from low-context cultures, such as Germany, use direct words to convey views and deliver feedback. In contrast, members from high-context cultures, such as Indonesia, tend to be more concerned about group harmony, reflecting a stronger collectivistic orientation. Consequently, they tend to be indirect to avoid giving offence—asking questions, using examples, or telling stories to make points implicitly and embedded in context. Naturally, these stylistic differences can lead to problems. For instance, Germans may react negatively to implicit communication, feeling like they cannot get straight answers from foreign teammates. Consider two Germans on a multicultural product team

who discover a technical glitch. The Germans would likely provide specific corrective feedback to the Indonesian engineers on the team about what needed to be fixed. Taking such a direct approach would likely be interpreted as placing blame and would embarrass the Indonesians, causing them to pull back from future interactions with the Germans. A better approach would be for the Germans to pose a question about what would happen if the technology in question did not work and discuss any implications, despite knowing that it is flawed.

4. *Language fluency problems.* Culture is also linked to team members' primary language. It is likely that team members who are not fluent in the primary language used by the team will have trouble getting their points and knowledge across. This can create feelings of incompetence and frustration as well as preclude the team from tapping valuable expertise from all its members.[6]

Of course, all of this begs the question of what managers can do to effectively respond to common challenges seen within multicultural teams. Naturally, one idea would be to construct teams consisting of members who are all fluent in the primary language that will be used. Ideally, all members should also possess high cultural intelligence—the capability to adapt to new cultural environments, such as a multicultural team.[7]

Clearly, it may not be possible to select such team members or to spend the time needed on training or experience building to raise their cultural intelligence. Consequently, teams—and particularly the managers that they report to—must be prepared to tackle cross-cultural challenges themselves. Table 8.1 summarizes some common problems found in multicultural teams along with four approaches that managers (and employees, in some cases) can use to combat them. The table also highlights the conditions under which each problem-solving approach tends to work best as well as some of their associated costs and complications.

It is important that managers carefully assess both the problems confronting a particular multicultural team and the background conditions accompanying it. Such assessments are critical for determining which approach has the best chance to succeed given the circumstances. Indeed, assessing context differences is also essential for shaping the nature of broader interventions aimed at instituting high-performance work systems across cultures.[8]

Here, in more detail, is each approach for solving problems in multicultural teams:

■ *Adaptation.* This involves modifying the attitudes, processes, and practices found in the team without disturbing the makeup of the members or altering the assignment being tackled. A major advantage of adaptation is that it is something that the team can do on its own in many cases—sometimes without any management involvement. By stepping up and solving their problems, team members learn how to make changes inside the team while avoiding destructive conflict. That said, adaptation takes considerable time and energy, which may be in short supply depending on the objectives of the team. Adaptation tends

Table 8.1
Managing Common Problems in Multicultural Teams

Common Team Problem	Typical Negative Consequences	Possible Management Approach	When Best to Use Approach (and Costs or Complications)
Decision-making norms that diverge or conflict	Frustration, conflict, impatience, inability to be effective	**Adaptation:** find ways to work with or around culture gaps without changing team itself	Members have high cultural awareness, feel problems are due to culture, not personalities (can be time-consuming to execute)
Different views about hierarchy	Anger, embarrassment, lost credibility, inability to tap members' skills	**Management Intervention:** make decisions for the team without their input	Teamwork is stalled, high negative emotion exists (risks creating dependency on management)
Explicit versus implicit communication styles	Embarrassment, mistrust, uncertainty, lost credibility, conflict	**Structural Intervention:** reorganize team or team processes to reduce tensions	Team/tasks can be subdivided, members are clinging to negative stereotypes (subgroups may exacerbate differences)
Language fluency problems	Miscommunication, frustration, inability to tap members' skills	**Exit:** remove one or more team members	Some team members can't adjust, too much damage already done, team is permanent (costs to train, develop exited member are lost)

Sources: Adapted from Brett, J., Behfar, K., & Kern, M. C. (2006). Managing multicultural teams. *Harvard Business Review,* November, 84–91; Brett, J. (2007). *Negotiating Globally: How to Negotiate Deals, Resolve Disputes, and Make Decisions across Cultural Boundaries* (2nd ed.). San Francisco: Jossey-Bass.

to work best with savvy team members who are able to recognize and acknowledge cultural differences while being motivated to bridge them. For example, consider a U.S.–Japanese software development team whose members recognize their different decision-making norms. Rather than always push ahead fast in the typical U.S. fashion (which would mortify the Japanese), or spend an enormous amount of time in discussions to build consensus on every issue (which would frustrate the Americans), the team could adapt and compromise. Specifically, the team could decide that pushing ahead more quickly was appropriate in some areas of the project, while moving more slowly to solicit support from inside and outside the team was more important in other areas.

■ *Management intervention.* This occurs when a manager steps in to make a decision to solve or prevent problems in multicultural teams. When teams reach an impasse and have a great deal of pent-up anger and negative emotion, it can be quite effective to have a manager enter the fray and impose a way forward. The downside of such an intervention is that team members may not learn all that much and may eventually become dependent on management to solve their problems. Consequently, managers may want to preempt this by intervening early in the life of a multicultural team to establish norms and expectations. This stage-setting can prevent some cultural differences from spiraling into major problems later. For instance, a manager could inform a newly formed Australian–Malaysian marketing team that they were selected because of their skills as marketers rather than their rank or seniority and that they should ignore any perceived differences in status or power while working together.

■ *Structural intervention.* This type of intervention involves management introducing changes that modify the structure of the team or its work methods. The goal is typically to eliminate sources of conflict or reduce tensions between team members. A good example of a structural intervention would be to break a team into smaller subgroups to either tackle portions of the work or to address issues that the team as whole has trouble dealing with because of friction between certain members. Of course, structural intervention makes the most sense when: (1) tensions already exist; (2) there are logical ways to subdivide the team's work; and (3) cliques on the team (based on nationalities, affiliation with a foreign subsidiary versus headquarters, etc.) have negative influence that could be weakened by mixing up members. That said, subgroups can create problems later if isolated members harden their attitudes, causing flare-ups when the larger team eventually reconvenes to finish its work.

■ *Exit.* In temporary teams (e.g., ad hoc groups formed to solve near-term challenges), members may be able to put up with (if not smooth over) cross-cultural differences. In more permanent teams, however, removing team members may be a viable option if emotions are running too high, too much face has already been lost, or certain members are unwilling to change their negative behavior. While regrettable, allowing individuals who are too upset or who have personalized their negative interactions to stay on the team is a recipe for disaster. In removing team members, management must come to terms with the fact that the money invested in those individuals (e.g., for training and development) is essentially lost.[9]

Cultural Differences in Social Loafing

Another fascinating, culturally driven phenomenon that occurs in groups and defies easy categorization is social loafing. Studies conducted in the United States have repeatedly shown that people are more productive when working alone than when working in groups. This is the essence of social loafing. People assume that, because of the group, the work will get done at some point—with multiple people working on the same set of tasks, the assignment will certainly be completed. Hence, an individual can attend to his or her own goals, even if that means taking a break while being part of the group. Apparently people loaf or slack off because they assume the group will get the job done anyway and because they can then redirect effort toward their own goals, be it relaxation or something else.[10]

But is social loafing just a U.S. phenomenon? After all, U.S. culture stresses individuality, while other cultures (e.g., Japanese) seem to find it much easier to embrace teamwork. Consistent with this finding, studies show that, unlike Americans, Japanese perform better in groups than on their own. Other studies have found that social loafing happens among Americans (individualists) but not among Chinese (collectivists).[11]

Yet group effects do not always reveal an advantage for collectivist employees. For instance, communication may be surprisingly weak between collectivist employees who are members of *different* in-groups. Consider two collectivist employees on different work teams who both see their team as an in-group since it is important to them. Communication between the two employees is likely to be weaker than communication between each employee and other members of their respective work teams. One study actually found that collectivists were more competitive than individualists when interacting with members of out-groups in their firm (i.e., groups that employees feel unattached to or are otherwise of little importance to them, such as a work team in another part of the company).[12]

Moreover, the type of group seems to impact when social loafing occurs, particularly among collectivists. One study assessed U.S., Chinese, and Israeli managers working alone and in two different group situations (in-group and out-group). The in-group scenario was created by suggesting to managers that they shared characteristics that often lead to close friendships. In contrast, the out-group scenario was created by telling managers that they had little in common with other group members, who came from very different backgrounds and had very different characteristics. The study replicated the common finding that there was an overall reduction in group performance (i.e., more loafing) for the individualistic Americans but not for the more collectivistic Israeli and Chinese managers. But the Israelis and Chinese did engage in social loafing when working with an out-group, reducing their effort on a team that was unimportant to them. When these collectivists worked with an in-group, however, there was no social loafing found—likely a testament to their desire to preserve group harmony and cohesion by pulling their weight when working in a group that mattered to them.[13]

Social loafing research has important implications for international managers. For instance, it suggests that managers must be careful when introducing group-based incentives with teams in collectivistic cultures. Since the type of group in which collectivists work seems to impact their performance, it would be best to form teams around natural collections of employees (i.e., existing in-groups) to maximize the effects of group incentives in collectivistic environments. That might mean forming groups around collectivistic employees who are already working together or who already have established relationships with each other. In the United States, efforts to organize work around teams have increased dramatically in recent years. Of course, the emphasis on individualism in U.S. culture presents difficulties for making team-based approaches work well. The United States is also becoming more culturally diverse, thanks, in part, to immigration—which creates further challenges when diverse employees are put into teams, at least in the short run. How to sort out social loafing effects from other problems otherwise facing multicultural teams is a challenge going forward for both managers and researchers alike.[14]

In the meantime, one area in which it is extremely important to have teams working at peak performance is in the airline business. Problems in flight crews can literally have life-or-death consequences. The following *Global Innovations* box illustrates some of the challenges in training flight crews from different cultures.

GLOBAL INNOVATIONS

Care in the Air: Cultural Challenges and Flight Crew Training

Operating large commercial jets safely depends on a team of experienced professionals. A flight crew on a large jet may include more than a dozen people, all of whom have important operational and safety roles. More than two-thirds of all commercial aviation accidents are due to flight crew behavior, not equipment failure. As a result, flight crew communication, decision making, and leadership have been carefully studied to reduce accidents—especially given the critical impact of culture.

Since commercial aviation is highly regulated, flight crews perform similar tasks in similar environments everywhere. Consequently, differences in attitudes across flight crew members from different countries are likely to be culturally based. One study asked pilots and flight attendants from several nations to complete a survey about ideal behavior on the flight deck. Interestingly, members of Asian flight crews had more similar attitudes than their U.S. counterparts, perhaps reflecting the need for social harmony in collectivistic cultures.

The findings also revealed that U.S. flight attendants preferred flight officers who encouraged questions but took charge in emergencies. U.S. pilots tended to have highly individualistic attitudes reminiscent of the solo flyers of old—more than any other group.

Asian flight attendants and pilots preferred autocratic but communicative flight officers in virtually all circumstances.

These cross-cultural differences present challenges for the most common training approach for modern flight crews. This approach, called *crew resource management* (CRM), stresses acceptance, recognition, and, importantly, the free flow of information among the flight crew. Since CRM seems to reflect collectivism and low power distance, this could either create problems or be a big asset depending on the cultural values of the flight crew members being trained. For instance, individualistic U.S. pilots have to put aside their solo flyer images and work more as a team. Although this may be difficult for U.S. pilots, CRM training can also take advantage of the fact that the United States is a low-power-distance culture. In other words, it shouldn't be hard for U.S. flight officers to embrace sharing information in the cockpit or elsewhere.

Conversely, while Asian flight crews would, at least on the surface, appear to be more in sync with the strong team orientation of CRM training, their high-power-distance orientation can discourage information sharing. In fact, CRM training that advocates assertive action by junior flight officers during emergencies may rub Chinese and other Asian flight crews the wrong way, at least initially. Likewise, the CRM concept of soliciting group input may be too hard for some U.S. pilots to accept. In the final analysis, U.S. and Asian flight crews may both have cultural assets and liabilities when it comes to training and handling emergencies. The challenge for crew resource management is to ensure that all aspects of training are eventually embraced by flight crews from all cultures.

Fortunately, CRM training efforts ultimately seem to help overcome cultural barriers that impede peak flight crew performance. Not only is air travel relatively safe to begin with, global airline safety has been improving significantly over the past few decades—including a drop in the percentage of accidents due to flight crew errors. There is little doubt that CRM training, along with improvements in equipment, has played a role in increasing commercial flight safety worldwide.[15]

INTERNATIONAL PARTNERSHIPS: MANAGING COMPLEXITY AND COORDINATION

This section takes our examination of multicultural relationships further, addressing the complexities and cultural challenges associated with international partnerships between firms. In doing so, however, it is important to remember that people must manage the relationship between partnering firms. Consequently, the role of culture is again front and center. Before examining specific types of partnerships (everything from acquisitions to joint ventures to marketing alliances), we begin with some stage-setting about the management decision-making processes that lead to the formation of new partnerships and alliances, as well as the developmental stages that international firms often go through along the way.

Bridging Barriers in International Decision Making

Formal and Informal Mechanisms

Management processes that facilitate strategic decision making are critical if international firms are to respond quickly to the competitive environments they face. For instance, firms can bring together managers from different countries to make decisions impacting operations worldwide. Such management teams can bridge cultural and geographic barriers to develop and effectively implement complex international strategies. Likewise, a key competitive advantage for firms is to have international management teams that identify important capabilities (e.g., one factory's ability to make new computer chips faster than anyone else in the world), which are then diffused across boundaries via sophisticated informal networks.[16]

Indeed, both formal and informal coordination mechanisms are important tools that multinational firms use to develop their strategies and knit together (at times) far-flung corporate empires while bridging cultural differences. Formal mechanisms, such as strategic planning teams, are specifically created by firms to serve coordination and related needs. Many types of formal coordination mechanisms exist. Some multinationals, for instance, put together teams of managers from various units to coordinate efforts across countries and improve information exchange. Others may assign managers to serve as liaisons between business areas and geographic areas. Informal mechanisms are also powerful and can be tapped to coordinate firm activities—common examples include the networks of relationships that exist between employees as well as corporate culture. For instance, McDonald's uses its strong training and culture—which reinforce company values of efficiency and cleanliness among all employees—as informal coordination mechanisms that help it outperform competitors around the globe.[17]

In recent years, experts have urged multinationals to develop lateral communication networks. This informal coordination mechanism is essentially the interpersonal relationships between managers in different units of a multinational. Put simply, when problems pop up in one unit, managers can turn to their informal network—a quick, flexible, and effective way to exchange information. These networks can be leveraged to spread expertise and knowledge across the organization, especially in large multinationals with formidable bureaucracies. In fact, some believe that informal interunit networking is even more important than formal structures. Building informal networks, however, is difficult. Some multinationals encourage managers to use technology to nurture international relationships (e.g., video conferencing) while also bringing people together from outposts around the world to interact face-to-face. Companies that have done much to encourage informal networks include S. C. Johnson and Unilever, among others.[18]

Creating Buy-In with the Strategy Development Process

Many multinationals have trouble making their coordination mechanisms, whether formal or informal, work well. This difficulty often can be traced back to mistrust between headquarters and subsidiaries around the globe—something that top-down strategy development tends to exacerbate. This can be avoided if firms use processes perceived to be fair when creating international strategy. A fair process ensures more cooperation from local subsidiary employees (who must implement company strategies anyway) and helps strengthen relationships over time, especially when a new strategy involves change. To have a fair process, executives from headquarters must: (1) make significant efforts to familiarize themselves with foreign operations; (2) ensure two-way communication while the strategy is being developed; (3) be consistent across foreign subsidiaries in making decisions; (4) encourage local employees to challenge them; and (5) fully explain decisions once they are made to local employees. Figure 8.1 illustrates in more detail how this process works. By engaging local employees, fully explaining decisions, and clarifying expectations, executives can improve local employee trust in headquarters management. And when employees trust the firm, they are more likely to behave in ways that ensure company success abroad.[19]

Institute a Fair International Strategy Development Process
- **Engagement** (ask local employees impacted by strategic changes for input, encourage dissent)
- **Explanation** (fully lay out how and why strategic decisions are being made as they are)
- **Expectation Setting** (describe how behaviors will have to change with a new strategy and how employees will be judged)

Trust and Commitment Improves
- Local employees feel their opinions are being listened to
- Local employees feel that their views are valued and help shape company direction

Behavior Reflects Improved Commitment
- Local employees voluntarily engage in cooperative behavior consistent with new strategy
- Local employees are willing to "go above and beyond" in doing their jobs

Successful Strategy Execution
- Subsidiary performance exceeds expectations
- Local employees do whatever is necessary to ensure strategic success

FIGURE 8.1 How a Fair Decision-Making Process Improves Strategic Success in Foreign Subsidiaries

Source: Adapted from Kim, W. C., & Mauborgne, R. A. (2005). *Blue Ocean Strategy: How to Create Uncontested Market Space and Make the Competition Irrelevant*. Boston: Harvard Business School Press.

Toward Partnerships and Alliances: Stages in International Development

Of course, many of the important decisions that companies make involve how to grow their international operations. Consequently, it is useful to first understand how firms develop internationally over time. Historically, firms gradually expand their international reach in distinct stages as their overseas experience, capabilities, and markets grow.[20]

Many small firms first enter foreign markets by exporting since the capital requirements are low (e.g., no need to build overseas plants). Of course, foreign facilities may become necessary as companies grow. Some firms develop in a series of gradual, sequential stages while others do not. Indeed, manufacturers are more likely to evolve gradually. For instance, Toyota began by exporting cars from Japan, then slowly expanded overseas by building plants in other countries. In contrast, service companies cannot start slowly in setting up operations abroad. Instead, they have to jump in with both feet. For example, GE Capital, the financial services arm of parent General Electric, has become adept at setting up foreign operations quickly by building them from scratch or rapidly integrating foreign acquisitions. There are different perspectives about how to define the stages that firms evolve through as they become more sophisticated internationally. What is clear is that firms can be successful at any stage and that the time required to move through stages varies. Table 8.2 presents a framework that highlights six developmental stages that firms may evolve through—we will consider the stages next.[21]

Table 8.2
Typical Stages in International Development

Stage 1:   Export

Stage 2:   Sales subsidiary

Stage 3:   International division

Stage 4:   Multinational

Stage 5:   Global or transnational

Stage 6:   Alliances, partners, and consortia

Source: Adapted from Briscoe, D. R. (1995). *International Human Resource Management*. Englewood Cliffs, NJ: Prentice Hall.

Stage 1: Exporting

Many domestic firms begin internationalizing by exporting. They may rely on an export manager or use consultants to provide the expertise needed for many export-related activities (e.g., dealing with letters of credit). For instance, L. L. Bean was a Stage 1 firm for many years. The firm began in 1912 by serving only the U.S. market but later began exporting clothes to foreign customers. It now sends products to customers in more than 160 countries.[22]

Stage 2: Sales Subsidiaries

As foreign sales grow, firms may start using distributors or representatives abroad to promote products and provide service. For instance, L. L. Bean moved to Stage 2 in 1992, when it established customer service operations in Japan to help local customers. Likewise, U.S. motorcycle maker Harley-Davidson moved to Stage 2 once growth in overseas markets prompted the firm to set up foreign offices and retail outlets to provide better sales support.[23]

Stage 3: International Division

Today, Harley-Davidson is in Stage 3, which involves assembly or manufacture of products overseas. Harley-Davidson's first foreign plant was in Brazil, where the company shipped motorcycle kits for assembly and sale. While most Harley-Davidson motorcycles are still made in the United States, the company's move to assemble products in Brazil represents a common progression. Having an international division means that a more sophisticated structure exists to manage foreign business and support expansion.[24]

Stage 4: Multinational

The final three stages involve complex multinational operations that may develop over time. Firms in Stage 4 understand that while headquarters must shape strategic direction, foreign outposts often do best when run by employees who grasp the local environment. Indeed, foreign subsidiaries in Stage 4 firms generally serve the markets where they are located. But balancing local demands with headquarters imperatives is easier said than done. Harley-Davidson, for instance, bought Italian motorcycle maker MV Agusta Group in 2008, only to sell it a year later. Harley-Davidson concluded that the money and effort spent on running the Italian company was too distracting. JCPenney had more luck when it bought a Brazilian department store chain. It kept the local brand name as well as local managers—the backbone of the Brazilian chain's success. And Wal-Mart changed some of its headquarters-knows-best attitudes after stumbling abroad, including in Germany (where Wal-Mart eventually pulled out) and Japan (where its cultural snafus included pushing Japanese employees to be assertive with customers). Today, Wal-Mart does more to listen and adapt its retail approach when outside the United States.[25]

Stage 5: Global or Transnational

Some firms never reach the point of being truly global or transnational. But Stage 5 firms ignore geographic boundaries—they build product, source materials, and hire talent wherever it helps reduce costs and maximize returns. Computer peripherals maker Logitech International has two headquarters (Silicon Valley and Switzerland) but locates its senior manufacturing executive in Taiwan so that faster decisions can be made about component sourcing (Taiwan is a hub of low-cost component suppliers). Needless to say, managing in this environment requires flexibility, the ability to bridge cultural differences, interdependence across units, and a global perspective that still allows for location-specific tailoring of products or services. And at large, diverse companies such as General Electric, each business unit (e.g., plastics, medical imaging, etc.) must decide just how locally tailored its products have to be in order to beat out competitors.[26]

Stage 6: Alliances, Partners, and Consortia

Increasingly, firms are forming relationships with each other to leverage their respective strengths or combine resources. Indeed, firms that have established partnerships such as joint ventures are often in Stage 6. For example, automobile corporations Daimler, Mitsubishi, and Hyundai set up a partnership to jointly develop a new engine, sharing key technologies and minimizing costs in the process. But alliances and partnerships are not limited to manufacturers. Wal-Mart created a joint venture with local market expert Bharti Enterprises Ltd. in opening its first store in India. Bharti's expertise helped Wal-Mart navigate India's complex retail environment.

Despite the popularity of such firm-level relationships, building and maintaining trust is a tall order, especially when cultural differences are involved. Yet it can be done. U.S. suppliers developed greater trust with Japanese automakers operating in the United States thanks, in part, to the Japanese firms' willingness to help, such as sending in consultants without charge. The overall lesson is that in order to build trust in partnerships, give it (trust) first.[27]

Multinationals from Developing Countries: An Alternative Road

We have already said these international development stages will not apply to every firm. Indeed, many multinationals from developing countries have traveled a different evolutionary road. They internationalize fast and come from countries with lousy business infrastructures, weak intellectual property protection, and opaque legal systems. Coming from tough home markets may better equip these multinationals to cope with challenges in developing nations than multinationals coming from countries like the United States, Germany, and Japan. These developing country market firms are typically more nimble, too, lacking the bureaucracy and entrenched cultures that can hamstring more established multinationals. They often improve their competitive capabilities by buying into or forming alliances with more sophisticated multinationals. Just in the past few years, for instance, Chinese energy companies such as Sinopec have been trying to acquire foreign energy firms from Argentina to Norway.[28]

International Partnerships: Making Choices and Managing Challenges

How do companies decide which foreign firms will make the best partners in the first place? And should that partnership be in the form of an acquisition, a joint venture, or some other type of alliance? How should the partnership be run, and what management and cultural challenges might exist? Table 8.3 presents some of the considerations that management must grapple with in answering these questions. To begin, management must determine whether a partnership or alliance makes sense given the trade-offs. While leveraging the competencies of potential partners is attractive, doing so must be weighed against the costs as well as the dependencies and management challenges they often create.

Choosing (Carefully) International Partners

Once a firm decides to set up an international partnership, it must select a collaborator. Picking a foreign partner with similar business practices and management styles may reduce collaboration difficulties. But this can be a tall order in an international context, especially given the complex impact of cultural differences—both national and corporate. Instead, it may be best to take a complementary approach—choosing foreign partners because they bring needed competencies, talent, or resources to the table. Naturally, choosing mutually beneficial partners will take time. But it is time well spent, especially if a degree of trust between potential partners can be built in the process—something that is particularly important for establishing business relationships in certain countries (e.g., China). Even so, international partners must often tackle thorny management and cultural challenges once they begin working together in earnest.[29]

Indeed, a key reason why international partnerships have a fairly low survival rate is that many partnering firms fail to monitor their relationship closely. While it is

Table 8.3
Thinking about an International Partnership? Issues to Consider

Issue	Description
Determining whether a partnership makes sense in the first place	Identify when, where, and why to form a partnership; are the costs (e.g., time, less control) worth it (acquired learning)?
Deciding which international firm to partner with	Select partners that maximize benefits and minimize risks (consider compatibility of management and culture, level of trust, and extent of complementary needs and assets)
Deciding how to best structure a partnership	Create a structure that provides incentives for success (contract or equity based)
Developing awareness of partnership dynamics and how to manage them	Understand that management adjustments may be needed as partnerships evolve
Recognizing partnership limits	Partnerships can have organizational constraints, lead to strategic gridlock, and create dependence

Source: Adapted from Gomes-Casseres, B. (1993). *Managing International Alliances*. Publication No. 793–133. Boston: Harvard Business School Publishing.

understandable for firms to focus on the business end of things, not addressing cultural differences and any potential friction that results risks undermining the relationship. In many cases, little advance preparation occurs for such issues, leaving problems to be dealt with on the fly. This can prove vexing, especially for firms engaged in several partnerships at once. For instance, multinationals such as Toshiba and Corning Glass are serial partners. Each firm has a portfolio of different partnerships that offer them competitive advantages at a lower cost. The key to managing multiple partnerships effectively starts at the top. Senior executives' personal involvement and commitment to relationship building is critical for establishing trust—which can be leveraged to deal with any problems that arise between partnering firms. For example, Corning Glass executives have made a point to take the time to develop personal relationships with their counterparts in partner firms with face-to-face visits and interactions.[30]

Ending Partnerships

Eventually, most partnerships end. So before multinationals jump *into* a partnership, they should think through how to get *out* of them. Partnerships can end for many reasons: partnering firms run into financial trouble; firms find better partners that will bring in more business and greater revenue; or management decides to pursue new strategic directions. Of course, another set of reasons has to do with managers of the partnering firms simply being unable to bridge their differences about how to run the partnership, how to interact with each other, and what they consider important—differences that often have cultural roots. It is important to avoid a costly and unfriendly "divorce." A prior relationship helps—if partners have worked together before and have developed some mutual trust, ending the partnership is more likely to be cooperative. To protect themselves, multinationals can include exit clauses in partnership agreements that specify: (1) the conditions that allow each firm to dissolve the partnership; (2) how assets will be divided up when the partnership ends; and (3) how disputes will be resolved.[31]

Acquisition Challenges

Acquisition is a common way multinationals partner with foreign companies—while maintaining control at the same time. This is a complicated process, particularly when the acquisition target is a state-owned firm. In the past few decades, many countries (such as Russia and China) have sold off state-owned enterprises to private buyers. China, for example, privatized many state-owned businesses that were simply too weak to survive against foreign competition. But turning broken-down state firms into world-class competitors is not easy or cheap—often the acquiring firm must spend significant amounts of money in the process (e.g., to upgrade outdated equipment and retrain employees). With China, many of its stronger state-owned firms are also acquirers (e.g., Chinese energy companies such as Sinopec). They buy foreign companies to gain access to technology, management expertise, and markets. For instance, Beijing Auto (owned by Beijing's municipal government) sought to acquire foreign carmakers to obtain technology and market access. In 2009, Beijing Auto offered to buy a controlling interest in GM's European operations (Adam Opel GmbH). GM refused because of worries it would later have to compete in China against a Beijing Auto armed with Opel technology. Obtaining technologies, capabilities, and market access are the main motivations for acquisitions made by newer multinationals emerging from developing economies such as Russia, Malaysia, India, and China.[32]

Completing a foreign acquisition, however, is often just the beginning of the challenges that the buyer faces. Acquiring a foreign firm means acquiring all of its problems too, such as inferior products and tense labor-management relations. Moreover, cultural and stylistic gaps often separate the buyer and the foreign firm that it has acquired. These can be tough to overcome. While the buying company often struggles to integrate its acquisition, employees in the acquired firm may suffer too. These employees can be dismayed by the management styles of their foreign acquirers, especially if large cultural differences exist. This is the case for some Westerners adapting to new Chinese owners. Problems often center on the deferential behavior expected by Chinese managers (especially those with little experience outside China) and the lack of clarity about how decisions are really made in the parent company. One European manager felt that the office environment was tense because executives from the new Chinese owner frowned on open discussion. As he put it, "Nobody contests what their immediate superior says. Never, never, never…the decisions are taken somewhere else."[33]

Yet research shows that over the long term, it is actually better for firm performance when there is a large cultural distance between the acquirer and the foreign firm being acquired. Management may do more homework and act more cautiously before making acquisitions in culturally distant locations. More preparation means fewer mistakes. In addition, acquiring a foreign company that operates in a significantly different cultural context entails more management learning—which can help the acquirer build strengths that in turn improve competitiveness. So, if culture clashes happen in foreign acquisitions, it does not always mean that they will be debilitating over the long haul. Indeed, in some cases, cultural differences across acquisition partners can prove complementary and promote the flow of knowledge and information across the firms involved. Sometimes the firms in an acquisition can successfully integrate their management styles and cultures to create a new way of doing things that promotes information sharing, especially if a reservoir of trust exists.[34]

Still, it is important not to underestimate the challenges (including cultural differences) that foreign acquisitions present to management in the short to intermediate term. For example, some years ago U.S. Steel acquired a former state-owned steelmaker in Slovakia. In doing so, it inherited outdated equipment, corrupt bosses, a bloated workforce, and opposition to the U.S. business culture that was exacerbated by cultural stereotypes and nationalistic chest-thumping. Likewise, when a U.K.-based firm bought Kazakhstan's Karmet steelmaking complex, it inherited more than just old equipment and an oversized workforce of 38,000. Adding to management's headaches were hundreds of employees who came to work drunk each day and an ornery local union demanding huge pay increases from the "rich" new owners.[35]

Joint Venture Challenges

Unlike acquisitions, joint ventures are a partnership involving shared ownership. Joint ventures are set up as separate legal entities and represent a particular type of alliance between two companies. Ownership in joint ventures can be split equally or one firm can hold a dominant stake. Companies that seek a 50% share or more do so to have tighter control over the joint venture.[36]

Multinationals with cutting-edge technology often want a controlling stake in joint ventures to protect their intellectual property, especially if the partner is a local firm whose main asset is expertise about local markets. That is increasingly the case with Western multinationals seeking Chinese partners, and was the approach that U.S. appliance maker Whirlpool took to move into Asian markets. Whirlpool set up six joint ventures with Chinese and Indian firms with a controlling stake in each to maximize control. However, the cost of this expansion, along with management headaches and formidable local competitors (e.g., China's Haier), led Whirlpool to pursue cheaper alternatives a few years later. Today, multinationals with technology to protect in places like China want their own managers to run joint venture operations or at least control the intellectual property, especially if a majority stake isn't possible.[37]

Indeed, a common purpose behind many international joint ventures is to produce and distribute a product in a particular country or region. In many cases, the partners include a multinational and a smaller local company—an arrangement attractive to both. The multinational brings technological expertise to the local company, which in turn offers the multinational insights into local culture and business practices. Cost and risk sharing are also important motivations behind international joint ventures in many cases, especially for firms wanting a foothold in tough emerging markets. For instance, U.S. giant United Technologies' early joint venture with Russia's Aviadvigatel to put its Pratt and Whitney engines on Russian jets was also designed to position the U.S. firm to tap into expected future growth in Russia's airline industry.[38]

Of course, cultural and managerial conflicts can hinder joint ventures. For instance, different cultural values and business practices may cause partners to clash when it comes to making decisions about what goals to set, how to run the joint venture, and how to evaluate performance. Underscoring this is recent research suggesting that 10 or more decision factors shape joint venture performance— many of which are complex, impacted by cultural differences, and centered on how the partners interact with each other in managing their relationship. Clearly, effectively managing the relationship and making good decisions in multiple areas are key if the joint venture is to perform well over time.[39]

One tactic for minimizing conflict between international joint venture partners is to use a delegated arrangement to manage things. In essence, the partners agree to step back from directly managing joint venture operations and put a new management team in place, consisting of executives hired from outside or reassigned from the partners. Naturally, this is not foolproof since conflict may erupt about who should be hired or reassigned. Executives must think through all of the steps involved in setting up joint ventures and answer important questions in each part of the process. These steps and the questions that accompany them are presented in Table 8.4.[40]

Many of the questions in Table 8.4 reflect concerns about control. Indeed, one of the biggest disadvantages of joint ventures has to do with control issues. Decision making can be slowed because joint ownership makes consultation imperative,

Table 8.4
Creating a Joint Venture: Process Steps and Key Questions

Steps in Joint Venture Creation	Key Questions to Address
Evaluating the rationale for a joint venture	■ What are our goals? Are we in this for the long haul or the short term?
	■ What resources are needed to achieve our goals, and how do we get them?
	■ Is a joint venture really our best option? Are the benefits worth the cost?
	■ What are our partner's goals and are they aligned with ours?
Choosing the best partner	■ Does the partner have the resources we need, and will they provide them?
	■ Does the partner have any international joint venture experience?
	■ What are the partner's motives, and are we compatible as companies?
	■ What cultural differences might get in the way of working well together?
	■ What is best for the joint venture, and is our management supportive?
Negotiating terms of the joint venture	■ What are the business practices like where the joint venture will be?
	■ Who will manage the joint venture? How will performance be assessed?
	■ What equity split is appropriate? What is most important to each partner?
	■ Are all assumptions on the table? Are any unresolved issues remaining?
	■ How should we handle disputes and the potential need to renegotiate terms?
Implementing/managing the joint venture	■ How can we bridge any cultural differences that cause conflicts or undercut trust between the partners?
	■ If performance is poor, how do we improve? Under what circumstances should the joint venture be terminated?
	■ Are we learning, and can the parent firm leverage any new capabilities?

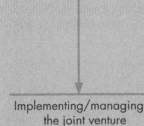

Source: Adapted from Beamish, P. W., & Lupton, N. C. (2009). Managing joint ventures. *Academy of Management Perspectives,* 23(2), 88.

especially on important issues where the partners have different culture-driven perspectives. And while having majority control makes things easier, it is no cure-all. Sometimes foreign partners resist taking a minority stake in the first place. Nevertheless, having a majority stake in joint ventures in places such as China can be worth the additional cost to protect technology and give managers from the majority partner more clout over critical decisions. U.S. managers in U.S.–China joint ventures seem to agree, feeling that these partnerships are more successful when the U.S. side has majority control.[41]

That said, it is dangerous for executives to fantasize about running things as they see fit with a foreign joint venture partner as mere add-on. Actually doing so means ignoring the local partner's perspective and losing any learning opportunities that come with it—one of the major reasons for setting up a joint venture to start with. Over time, multinationals risk disaster if they ignore foreign joint venture partners or don't pay attention to managing the relationship and bridging cultural differences, even if they hold a dominant stake. The accompanying *Culture Clash* box focuses on Danone's joint venture in China, offering a potential cautionary tale and a case in point.[42]

CULTURE CLASH

No Laughing Matter: Danone's Joint Venture in China Goes Sour

In 1996, France's Groupe Danone SA created a 51% joint venture with China-based Hangzhou Wahaha Group to supply juices, soft drinks, and milk products to increasingly affluent Chinese citizens. Danone's 51% stake was worth over $500 million at the time, included more than three dozen operations, and ensured access to Wahaha's market-leading brand name in China.

Danone went public with complaints about Hangzhou Wahaha. This was a very unusual move—in China disputes are generally dealt with behind closed doors to save face for all sides. What followed were a slew of back-and-forth charges and lawsuits. Finally, in 2009 Danone announced it was done with Hangzhou Wahaha and was exiting the joint venture after reaching a settlement. In the process, Danone apparently lost $100 million and had to restart operations in China from scratch. Danone launched a yogurt product on its own via a new, wholly owned subsidiary—without access to its former partner's large distribution network in China.

Why did this joint venture fall apart? To be sure, managing joint ventures in China is no easy task. For one thing, the partners' motives often diverge, with the foreign multinational seeking profits and market access and the Chinese partner wanting to create more jobs and gain access to superior technology. Many foreign joint venture partners have raised issues about theft of technology and the inability or unwillingness of Chinese courts to take action to stop it.

In this case, Danone claimed that Hangzhou Wahaha's founder, Zong Qinghou, had established parallel operations to make Wahaha drinks outside of the joint venture. Danone argued that the joint venture agreement stipulated that it was owed 51% of the profits from all products labeled with the Wahaha brand. The problem was that Danone wasn't receiving any money from these parallel Wahaha facilities. Zong's response was testy and made three basic points: (1) that Danone gave him permission to establish these plants, (2) that the joint venture's terms were "outdated" regardless, and (3) that the French were only interested in making a quick profit.

From the outside, part of the breakdown of the joint venture appears to be traceable to a couple of key factors. First, Danone had embarked on a partnership with a Chinese firm that was already successful, tapping into the impressive Wahaha brand and distribution network that Zong had created. On top of that, however, Danone's managers just didn't seem to be paying much attention. Apparently, Danone was happy to have Hangzhou Wahaha run the joint venture, taking on little, if any, management role for itself in China. One analyst noted that to create and operate joint ventures successfully in China, the partnering firms need to work closely together to build their relationship and their business from the ground up. That apparently was not the case with Danone, even though the firm had a 51% majority stake in the joint venture. In essence, Danone gave Zong the freedom to operate joint venture facilities with virtually no supervision, oversight, or review. And while the breakup of this joint venture was painful and no laughing matter, the former partners have since moved on, with neither continuing to cry much over spilled milk.[43]

Other Types of Alliances

International partnerships do not always involve whole or shared ownership. Table 8.5 presents four other types of alliances that we will briefly examine in this section. For any alliance to be successful, trust between partners and the formation of clear goals are essential. It also helps if management grasps "the contradiction between synergy and identity," as Nissan's visionary CEO Carlos Ghosn puts it. In essence, each partner should keep its unique identity while embracing common objectives for the alliance. Managerial and cultural differences still must be bridged. For instance, when Northwest Airlines formed its alliance with KLM Royal Dutch Airlines in the 1990s, incompatible management styles created considerable distrust and plenty of conflict. The more aggressive style of Northwest's U.S. management conflicted with the understated style of Dutch managers at KLM. The result was a bitter battle for control, with charges and countercharges being lobbed back and forth for years. While the alliance bruised egos and went to the brink of collapse on several occasions, it continues to this day, albeit in

Table 8.5
More than Joint Ventures: Other Types of International Alliances

Alliance Type	Goals of the Alliance Partners
Production alliance	Acquire complex manufacturing expertise and know-how from partners, reducing the costs of production.
Research and development alliance	Conduct joint research that will lead to development of new products, services, or technologies (i.e., pooled resources are more likely to result in breakthroughs).
Financial alliance	Reduce financial exposure with particularly expensive and risky projects by sharing the costs involved (e.g., jointly building a $1 billion computer chip manufacturing facility).
Marketing alliance	Share services or expertise in marketing-related areas in ways that generate additional profits for the partners.

different form. The Northwest brand no longer exists, thanks to its merger into Delta. And KLM is now part of Air France KLM. But Delta and Air France KLM continue as alliance partners.[44]

The types of alliances described in this section are more limited than joint ventures—they are often narrower in scope, less formal, and may not be legally independent of the partnering firms. They are created when multinationals feel their own interests in some area are best served by entering into a cooperative agreement with another firm. Such alliances have grown in popularity because they can make market entry easier, allow for risk sharing, and help firms gain new "invisible skills" that require close observation. These skills often evolve from a particular cultural context, such as Honda's expertise in developing small engines—a blend of know-how in manufacturing, quality control, and product development.[45]

Production Alliances

Obtaining such expertise may be part of the motivation behind production alliances—where firms agree to manufacture products or deliver services in shared facilities either built or owned by one of the partners. Another reason for production alliances is to lower costs. For example, at one point executives at U.S.-based food giant H. J. Heinz asked their counterparts at foreign competitors Nestlé and Unilever to share production facilities as a way to cut manufacturing costs.[46]

Research and Development Alliances

These alliances help partner firms stay on the cutting edge of rapidly changing technology as well as involve joint research to develop new services or products. The partners typically agree to share any new technologies that are developed so that all sides benefit. Hewlett-Packard's 25-year partnership with Japan's Canon Corp. to develop and leverage new printer-related products and technologies is a case in point. Among other things, Canon brought its expertise in imaging software to the table, while Hewlett-Packard brought its know-how in ink-jet technology that allowed images to be converted into a printable format.

Financial Alliances

Formed when partners want to reduce the financial risks associated with specific projects, financial alliances are typically used in capital-intensive industries where large investments are required to develop and manufacture products. Such was the case when IBM and Toshiba formed a financial alliance to share the cost of building expensive new computer chip manufacturing plants.[47]

Marketing Alliances

These alliances are created when firms pool resources to gain access to partners' markets. Marketing alliances are now standard practice for airlines worldwide, with most major carriers belonging to one of the three large global alliances: Oneworld, Sky Team, or Star Alliance. Each of these alliances includes code-sharing agreements so that members can sell tickets that stitch together flights from different carriers. This gives airlines in an alliance access to each others' route structures, while offering customers an integrated trip experience. For example, customers flying from Detroit to Moscow via New York and Rome would fly on one ticket, despite the fact that Delta would get them to New York, Alitalia would fly the leg to Rome, and Aeroflot would handle the final hop to Moscow. While efficiency is a key aspect of airline alliances, the main benefit is brand marketing. The Sky Team alliance, for instance, says it provides members superior brand recognition.[48]

CHAPTER SUMMARY

Multicultural teams face many challenges. Research shows that cultural differences have the potential to both cause problems and offer benefits on such teams. Groups are more important in collectivistic cultures than in individualistic cultures—and in a collectivistic culture, in-groups and out-groups vary dramatically in their value.

We reviewed four common problems that can occur in multicultural teams as well as several management approaches for dealing with them effectively. Social loafing, a common effect in individualistic countries, tends to occur among collectivists but *only* in groups that are unimportant to them (out-groups). Collectivistic employees are likely to pitch in wholeheartedly when working in groups that are important to them (in-groups).

Strategic direction and other firm-level issues are also important to understand, again through the lens of cultural differences. Formal and informal mechanisms can be used by international firms to make key decisions and diffuse information across their far-flung corporate empires. Indeed, multinationals must realize that if the processes used to make strategic decisions are seen as fair, managers worldwide are more likely to behave accordingly and follow through to support them. To create fairness, managers should make significant efforts to familiarize themselves with local operations and ensure two-way communication with local employees when developing their international strategies.

Many firms go through six stages as they develop their international operations. In Stage 1, domestic firms begin internationalizing by exporting. Stage 2 firms have opened overseas offices or sales subsidiaries. Next, Stage 3 involves the establishment of more significant operations abroad. In Stage 4, firms have embraced a multinational perspective, recognizing that, while headquarters must lead on strategic decisions, foreign operations are best run locally. Firms with a more global or transnational orientation have moved into Stage 5, and Stage 6 is characterized by firms linking up to leverage their combined resources in partnerships and alliances.

It is important to consider management and cultural issues associated with specific types of partnerships, as there are major questions that companies must address when setting up international partnerships as well as issues that must be dealt with in managing them. Acquisitions offer more control, but the buyer is also acquiring all of the problems in the acquired firm, while joint ventures are set up as a separate legal entity with ownership split between the partnering firms. Regardless, cultural and other management challenges can plague joint venture and other types of alliances.

DISCUSSION QUESTIONS

1. What might happen when Americans, Indians, and Brazilians are put together on a team to develop a new product? What difficulties might such a group encounter that would make it hard for them to complete this project in a creative fashion? What could be done to ensure that the group can function more effectively?

2. What types of mechanisms can multinational companies use to make more effective firm-level strategic decisions and to better coordinate units worldwide?

3. What are the different stages that companies may pass through as they develop internationally? Discuss examples of firms that have progressed through all the stages.

4. Describe the different types of international partnerships and alliances that may exist between firms. What are some of the major management and cultural headaches associated with each type?

Developing Your International Career

DEVELOPING CULTURAL INTELLIGENCE: JAPANESE GROUP DECISION MAKING

Purpose and Instructions

The purpose of this exercise is to give you the opportunity to evaluate your own level of cultural intelligence and your ability to adapt across cultures as well as to give you the opportunity to experience the Japanese approach to consensual decision making. You should compare personal experiences with group decision making against the Japanese approach to better understand how group processes might differ across cultures.

Take a few minutes to complete the Cultural Intelligence instrument below. The instrument provides subscores on cognitive, behavioral, and motivational aspects of cultural intelligence. Higher scores indicate higher levels of cultural intelligence. Write the appropriate number in the space next to each statement to reflect your level of agreement or disagreement.

1	2	3	4	5
Strongly	Disagree	Disagree	Neutral Agree	Strongly Agree

1.____ It is easy for me to change my body language (e.g., eye contact, posture) to suit people from a different culture.

2.____ I can alter my expressions when a cross-cultural encounter requires it.

3.____ I modify my speech style (e.g., accent and tone) to suit people from a different culture.

4.____ I can easily change the way I behave when a cross-cultural encounter requires it.

____ **Behavioral subscore (add items 1 through 4)**

5.____ Before interacting with people from a new culture, I ask myself what I want to achieve.

6.____ When I encounter something unexpected while in a new culture, I use this experience to figure out better ways to interact with other cultures in the future.

7.____ I think about how I am going to interact with people from another culture before I meet them.

8.____ When in a new cultural context, I can sense right away if things are going well or not.

____ **Cognitive subscore (add items 5 through 8)**

9.____ I am confident that I can interact well with people from different cultures.

10.____ I am certain that I can befriend people from different cultural backgrounds.

11.____ I can adapt to the lifestyles of other cultures with relative ease.

12.____ I am confident that I can deal with unfamiliar cultural situations.

____ **Motivational subscore (add items 9 through 12)**

____ Total Cultural Intelligence Score (add Behavior + Cognitive + Motivational subscores; range = 12 to 60, with higher scores indicating higher cultural intelligence).

After completing the Cultural Intelligence instrument, your instructor will move on to the Japanese decision-making portion of the exercise. He or she will explain the processes of Ringi and Nemawashi before splitting the class into groups of four to six people. Groups will include leaders (Kacho) and student managers (Bucho). The challenge for each group is to design a final exam format that will prove to be a valuable learning tool and a fair way of evaluating your performance in the class (20 minutes).

Next, your instructor will divide the class again into new groups of four to six people (the Kacho groups). These new groups will continue working on the exam task, using the results of the first group as a starting point. After that, groups can choose their own venue for future meetings outside of class—these will occur at the initiation of the group and student leaders (20 minutes).

Later, the whole class will generate a Ringi document that specifies the content of the exam—it must be signed by all students in the class. Your instructor will discuss what problems, if any, the Ringi document might cause. To conclude the exercise, the entire class will discuss the following questions:

1. How much did your experience resemble the descriptions of Ringi and Nemawashi provided by your instructor?

2. What difficulties did you encounter? Were those difficulties likely to be present in the Japanese context? If so, how would they probably be managed?

3. After this experience, would you change the way you filled out the Cultural Intelligence instrument if you had to do it over again? Which scores might go up or down? Why?

Sources: Adapted from Earley, P. C., & Mosakowski, E. (2004). Cultural intelligence: Knowing what makes groups tick is as important as understanding individuals. *Harvard Business Review*, October, 139–146; Van Buskirk, W. (1994). Japanese decision-making exercise (Ringi/Nemawashi). In D. Marcic and S. Puffer (eds.), *Management International: Cases, Exercises, and Readings* (52–53). Minneapolis: West Publishing.

Making the Case for International Understanding

GENERAL ELECTRIC POWERS UP JOINT VENTURES IN CHINA

GE sees China as a key market and has been selling its products there for more than 20 years. Especially important to GE's efforts are turbines that are used to generate electricity since power demand in China is rising thanks to strong economic growth. GE turbines were in place in 2009, when China opened its largest biogas energy plant. The company also has a wholly owned wind turbine assembly plant facility in China.

Some of the most important technology for GE's wind turbines is being jointly developed with local partner Nanjing High Speed and Accurate Gear Company (NGC). GE brought technical prowess to the table and flew NGC managers to the United States for leadership development. Yet GE's experience in China also highlights some of the challenges multinationals face in the Chinese market. GE's turbine customers in China are mostly regional utilities and energy-producing firms. Because cutting-edge power turbines are complex pieces of technology, GE's primary competitors in China are world-class multinationals such as Germany's Siemens and Japan's Mitsubishi. In that sense, the competitive landscape for GE in China seems relatively simple.

But in trying to win a lucrative contract to provide power turbines to regional utilities, GE ran into Chinese negotiators who demanded that the company hand over 100% of the technology it used to develop cutting-edge turbines. Indeed, China's approach in key industries has been to grant market access to foreign multinationals if they agree to transfer critical technologies to Chinese companies. GE was torn. While the contract was attractive, the Chinese technology transfer demand was a bitter pill, particularly since GE spent $500 million developing its most advanced turbine technology. The unenviable trade-off for GE was to either seek short-term gain at the expense of enabling Chinese firms to become formidable competitors later on or to keep its technology and lose a lucrative contract in China. To deal with such dilemmas, many Western multinationals (e.g., Motorola, Nokia) have either formed joint ventures with Chinese firms or set up research centers in China to provide technology access. Indeed, GE also went the joint venture route, as the earlier example of its partnership with a Chinese company to develop wind turbine technology suggests.

GE decided, in this specific case, to take a middle position. In doing so, it eventually won a $900 million contract to supply power turbines to Chinese utilities. Put simply, GE agreed to share some of the technology needed to manufacture the most advanced power turbines. As part of the deal, GE also agreed to establish two joint ventures where it held the majority stake. One joint venture was with Harbin Power Equipment Ltd., a state-owned company that would assemble GE turbines in an existing plant. The other joint venture, with Shenyang Liming Aero-Engine Group Corp., would make some turbine blades using GE technologies in metallurgy and combustion systems. But GE held back its most critical technologies, such as the manufacturing processes needed to produce certain blades used in advanced turbines. In the joint venture contract, GE produced parts using its most sophisticated technologies in the United States and then shipped them to Harbin in China, where they were installed in the final product.

GE felt that transferring some of its technology to Chinese firms was not enough to turn them into serious competitors in the short run, because they lacked the staff expertise needed to put it to full use. Indeed, in the telecom industry, after their joint ventures with multinationals such as Nokia ended, Chinese companies still could not produce cutting-edge equipment given rapid advances in technology. GE's experiences were similar—it had previously licensed some turbine technology to Chinese firms, reasoning that they would figure out how to obtain this technology regardless. Moreover, in the 1980s, GE and other multinationals had set up joint ventures with Chinese companies to make smaller and simpler power turbines—which involved technology transfers. Their Chinese partners did finally master the production of these steam-driven turbines, but by the time they did, the turbines were no longer state-of-the-art. In short, the Chinese were unable to keep up with the technical advances made by GE and others.

Overall, GE believes it can maintain its edge in technology and still land big contracts in China. It aims to keep developing more sophisticated turbines while potential Chinese competitors struggle to produce older versions. The Chinese know that, for now, they must rely on GE for key components and technology. One official noted, "The foreigners are now agreeing to tell us how and where to dig a hole, but we still do not know why to dig a hole there."

Yet things can change quickly in China. In 2010–2011, China stepped up its emphasis on "indigenous innovation." In essence, utilities and other government entities were encouraged to buy from firms that produce new technologies locally. This could eventually hit GE hard, either precluding it from winning future contracts in China's energy sector or forcing it to turn over more technology to local partners. And fighting back is a complicated proposition for GE, given acute Chinese sensitivities about foreign companies and China's national objective to be a global technology powerhouse. So whether GE can continue using its balanced joint venture approach in China remains to be seen. Given China's push for indigenous innovation, Chinese companies may be able to learn faster and catch up to GE and other foreign multinationals more quickly. And while they may still trail GE in product sophistication, Chinese competitors have clearly been improving. In the past few years, Shanghai Electric and Dongfang Turbine both won equipment contracts from power plants in Belarus and India—just one more international challenge for GE to grapple with in the future.[49]

ASSIGNMENT QUESTIONS

1. What is your assessment of GE's future in China, especially given Chinese demands for transferring technology? Are there ways that GE can make its case without provoking a destructive cycle of conflict when negotiating with potential partners or the Chinese government?

2. How might GE structure future joint ventures with Chinese companies to better protect its intellectual property? What cultural and managerial differences might complicate this effort and how might they be overcome?

3. Present some alternatives to the joint venture approach that GE has chosen in China. Describe the managerial challenges associated with each. Which option makes the most sense in your view? Why?

NOTES

1. Ramsey, M. (2011). Johnson Controls aims to quit venture. *Wall Street Journal*, May 19, B4.
2. Ramsey, M. (2011). Johnson Controls aims to quit venture. *Wall Street Journal*, May 19, B4.
3. Brett, J., Behfar, K., & Kern, M. C. (2006). Managing multicultural teams. *Harvard Business Review*, November, 84–91; Stahl, G. K., Maznevski, M. L., Voigt, A., & Jonsen, K. (2010). Unraveling the effects of cultural diversity in teams: A meta-analysis of research on multicultural work groups. *Journal of International Business Studies*, 41, 690–709.
4. Triandis, H. C. (1988). Collectivism v. individualism: A reconceptualism of a basic concept in cross-cultural social psychology. In G. K. Verma & C. Bagley (eds.), *Cross-Cultural Studies of Personality, Attitudes, and Cognition* (60–95). New York: St. Martin's Press.
5. Bond, M. H., & Hwang, K. (1986). The social psychology of the Chinese people. In M. H. Bond (ed.), *The Psychology of the Chinese People* (213–266). Hong Kong: Oxford University Press; Domino, G. (1992). Cooperation and competition in Chinese and American children. *Journal of Cross-Cultural Psychology*, 23, 456–467; Earley, P. C., & Mosakowski, E. (2004). Cultural intelligence: Knowing what makes groups tick is as important as understanding individuals. *Harvard Business Review*, October, 139–146.
6. Brett, J., Behfar, K., & Kern, M. C. (2006). Managing multicultural teams. *Harvard Business Review*, November, 84–91.
7. Early, C. P. (2002). Redefining interactions across cultures and organizations: Moving forward with cultural intelligence. In B. M. Staw & R. M. Kramer (eds.), *Research in Organizational Behavior*, Vol. 24 (271–299). Oxford, England: Elsevier; Ng, K., Van Dyne, L., & Ang, S. (2009). From experience to experiential learning: Cultural intelligence as a learning capability for global leader development. *Academy of Management Learning and Education*, 8, 511–526.
8. Brett, J., Behfar, K., & Kern, M. C. (2006). Managing multicultural teams. *Harvard Business Review*, November, 84–91; Lawler, J. J., Chen, S., Wu, P., Bae, J., & Bai, B. (2011). High performance work systems in foreign subsidiaries of American multinationals: An institutional model. *Journal of International Business Studies*, 42, 202–220; Stahl, G. K., Maznevski, M. L., Voigt, A., & Jonsen, K. (2010). Unraveling the effects of cultural diversity in teams: A meta-analysis of research on multicultural work groups. *Journal of International Business Studies*, 41, 690–709.
9. Brett, J., Behfar, K., & Kern, M. C. (2006). Managing multicultural teams. *Harvard Business Review*, November, 84–91.
10. Liden, R. C., Wayne, S. J., Jaworski, R. A., & Bennett, N. (2004). Social loafing: A field investigation. *Journal of Management*, 30, 285–304.
11. Earley, P. C. (1989). Social loafing and collectivism. *Administrative Science Quarterly*, 34, 565–581; Gabrenya, W. K., Latane, B., & Wang, Y. (1985). Social loafing on an

optimizing task: Cross-cultural differences among Chinese and Americans. *Journal of Cross-Cultural Psychology*, 16, 223–242; Matsui, T., Kakuyama, T., & Ongltco, M. L. U. (1987). Effects of goals and feedback on performance in groups. *Journal of Applied Psychology*, 72, 407–415.

12. Earley, P. C. (1993). East meets West meets Mideast: Further explorations of collectivistic and individualistic work groups. *Academy of Management Journal*, 36, 319–348; Espinoza, J. A., & Garza, R. T. (1985). Social group salience and inter-ethnic cooperation. *Journal of Experimental Social Psychology*, 23, 380–392; Triandis, H. C. (1988). Collectivism v. individualism: A reconceptualism of a basic concept in cross-cultural social psychology. In G. K. Verma & C. Bagley (eds.), *Cross-Cultural Studies of Personality, Attitudes, and Cognition* (60–95). New York: St. Martin's Press.

13. Earley, P. C. (1993). East meets West meets Mideast: Further explorations of collectivistic and individualistic work groups. *Academy of Management Journal*, 36, 319–348.

14. Work team trivia. *Competitive Edge*, March/April 1992, 12; Dumaine, B. (1990). Who needs a boss? *Fortune*, May 7, 52–60; Earley, P. C. (1994). Self or group? Cultural effects of training on self-efficacy and performance. *Administrative Science Quarterly*, 39, 89–117.

15. Statistical summary of commercial jet airplane accidents: Worldwide operations, 1959–2008. Seattle, WA: Boeing Corp, 2009. Available at www.boeing.com/news/techissues/pdf/statsum.pdf; Merritt, A. C., & Helmreich, R. L. (1996). Human factors on the flight deck: The influence of national culture. *Journal of Cross-Cultural Psychology*, 27, 5–24.

16. Bartmess, A., & Cerny, K. (1993). Building competitive advantage through a global network of capabilities. *California Management Review*, 35, 2–27; Snow, C. C., Snell, S. A., Davison, S. C., & Hambrick, D. C. (1996). Use transnational teams to globalize your company. *Organizational Dynamics*, 24, 50–67.

17. Hill, C. W. L. (2009). *International Business* (7th ed.). Burr Ridge, IL: McGraw-Hill/Irwin.

18. Ghoshal, S., Korine, H., & Szulanski, G. (1994). Interunit communication in multinational corporations. *Management Science*, 40, 96–110.

19. Kim, W. C., & Mauborgne, R. A. (2005). *Blue Ocean Strategy: How to Create Uncontested Market Space and Make the Competition Irrelevant*. Boston: Harvard Business School Press; Kim, W. C., & Mauborgne, R. A. (1991). Implementing global strategies: The role of procedural justice. *Strategic Management Journal*, 12, 125–143; Making global strategies work. *Sloan Management Review*, Spring 1993, 11–25.

20. Guillen, M. F., & Garcia-Canal, E. (2009). The American model of the multinational firm and the "new" multinationals from emerging economies. *Academy of Management Perspectives*, 23(2), 23–35.

21. Cavusgil, S. T., Knight, G., & Riesenberger, J. R. (2008). *International Business: Strategy, Management, and the New Realities*. Upper Saddle River, NJ: Prentice Hall; Negandhi, A. (1987). *International Management*. Boston: Allyn & Bacon; Milliman, J., Von Glinow, M. A., & Nathan, M. (1991). Organizational life cycles and strategic international human resource management in multinational companies: Implications for congruence theory. *Academy of Management Journal*, 16, 318–339; Rohwer, J. (2000). GE digs into Asia. *Fortune*, October 2, 165–178 (see also www.gecapital.com); Shirouzu, N. (2003). As Toyota pushes hard in China, a lot is riding on the outcome. *Wall Street Journal*, December 8, A1, A12; Welch, L. S., & Luostarinen, R. (1988). Internationalization: Evolution of a concept. *Journal of General Management*, 14, 55–71.

22. Black, J. S., Gregersen, H. B., & Mendenhall, M. E. (1992). *Global Assignments: Successfully Expatriating and Repatriating International Managers*. San Francisco: Jossey-Bass. See also www.llbean.com.

23. Aeppel, T. (2009). Harley-Davidson profit plunges. *Wall Street Journal*, October 16, B5. See www.llbean.com and www.harley-davidson.com.

24. See www.harley-davidson.com.

25. Aeppel, T. (2009). Harley-Davidson profit plunges. *Wall Street Journal*, October 16, B5 (also see www.harley-davidson.com); Bellman, E. (2009). Wal-Mart exports big box concept to India. *Wall Street Journal*, May 28, B1; Bianco, A., & Zellner, W. (2003). Is Wal-Mart too powerful? *Business Week*, October 6, 100–110; Landers, P. (2001). Penney blends two business cultures. *Wall Street Journal*, April 5, A15, A17; Smith, G. (2002). War of the superstores. *Business Week*, September 23, 60; Zimmerman, A., & Fackler, M. (2003). Wal-Mart's foray into Japan spurs a retail upheaval. *Wall Street Journal*, September 19, A1, A6.

26. Hamm, S. (2003). Borders are so 20th century. *Business Week*, September 22, 68–72; Rohwer, J. (2000). GE digs into Asia. *Fortune*, October 2, 165–178.

27. Ball, J., Zaun, T., & Shirouzu, N. (2002). Daimler explores idea of "world engine." *Wall Street Journal*, January 8, A3; Bellman, E. (2009). Wal-Mart exports big box concept to India. *Wall Street Journal*, May 28, B1; Briscoe, D. R. (1995). *International Human Resource Management*. Englewood Cliffs, NJ: Prentice Hall; Dyer, J. H. (2000). Examining interfirm trust and relationships in a cross-national setting. In P. C. Earley & H. Singh (eds.), *Innovations in International and Cross-cultural Management* (215–244). Thousand Oaks, CA: Sage; Tse, D. K., Pan, Y., & Au, K. Y. (1997). How MNCs choose entry modes and form alliances: The China experience. *Journal of International Business Studies*, 28, 779–803.

28. Guillen, M. F., & Garcia-Canal, E. (2009). The American model of the multinational firm and the "new" multinationals from emerging economies. *Academy of Management Perspectives*, 23(2), 23–35; Poon, A. (2009). Chinese oil firms bid $17 billion to expand. *Wall Street Journal*, August 11, B1, B2.

29. Arino, A., Ozcan, P., & Mitchell, J. (2009). KLM: Gaining altitude via alliances. *IESE Insight*, October, 1–3. Available at http://insight.iese.edu; Ren, H., Gray, B., & Kim, K. (2009). Performance of international joint ventures: What factors really make a difference and how? *Journal of Management*, 35, 805–832; Teegen, H. J., & Doh, J. P. (2002). U.S./Mexican alliance negotiations: Cultural impacts on trust, authority, and performance. *Thunderbird International Business Review*, 44, 749–775.

30. Dyer, J. H., Kale, P., & Singh, J. (2001). How to make strategic alliances work. *Sloan Management Review*, Summer, 37–43.

31. Co, H. C., & Banro, F. (2009). Stakeholder theory and dynamics in supply chain collaboration. *International Journal of Operations and Production Management*, 29, 2–22; Ryall, M. D., & Sampson, R. C. (2009). Formal contracts in the presence of relational enforcement mechanisms: Evidence from technology development projects. *Management Science*, 55, 906–925; Serapio, M. G., & Cascio, W. F. (1996). End-games in international alliances. *Academy of Management Executive*, 10, 62–73; Stahl, G. K., Maznevski, M. L., Voigt, A., & Jonsen, K. (2010). Unraveling the effects of cultural diversity in teams: A meta-analysis of research on multicultural work groups. *Journal of International Business Studies*, 41, 690–709.

32. Red tape and blue sparks. *The Economist*, June 2, 2001, 9–10; Shirouzu, N. (2009). Beijing auto maps out a global expansion. *Wall Street Journal*, October 9, B4; Kumar, N. (2009). How

emerging giants are rewriting the rules of M&A. *Harvard Business Review*, May, 115–121; Wonacott, P. (2001). China's privatization efforts breed new set of problems. *Wall Street Journal*, November 1, A15.

33. Being eaten by the dragon. *The Economist*, November 13, 2010, 81–83; Hill, C. W. L. (2008). *Global Business Today*. New York: McGraw-Hill/Irwin; Olie, R. (1994). Shades of culture and institutions in international mergers. *Organizational Studies*, 15, 381–405.

34. Calori, R., Lubatkin, M., & Very, P. (1994). Control mechanisms in cross-border acquisitions: An international comparison. *Organizational Studies*, 15, 361–379; Chakrabarti, R., Gupta-Mukherjee, S., & Jayaraman, N. (2009). Mars–Venus marriages: Culture and cross-border M&A. *Journal of International Business Studies*, 40, 216–236; Hill, C. W. L. (2008). *Global Business Today*. New York: McGraw-Hill/Irwin; Olie, R. (1994). Shades of culture and institutions in international mergers. *Organizational Studies*, 15, 381–405; Sarala, R. M., & Vaara, E. (2010). Cultural differences, convergence, and crossvergence as explanations of knowledge transfer in international acquisitions. *Journal of International Business Studies*, 41, 1365–1390; Schweiger, D. M., Csiszar, E. N., & Napier, N. K. (1993). Implementing international mergers and acquisitions. *Human Resource Planning*, 16, 53–70.

35. Allen, M. (1995). What is privatization anyway? *Wall Street Journal*, October 2, R4; Barkema, H. G., Bell, J. H. J., & Pennings, J. M. (1996). Foreign entry, cultural barriers, and learning. *Strategic Management Journal*, 17, 151–166; Filatotchev, I., Hoskisson, R. E., Buck, T., & Wright, M. (1996). Corporate restructuring in Russian privatizations: Implications for U.S. investors. *California Management Review*, 38, 87–105; Matthews, R. G. (2000). U.S. Steel's plunge into Slovakia reflects urgent need to grow. *Wall Street Journal*, October 12, A1, A10; Ramamurti, R. (2000). A multilevel model of privatization in emerging economies. *Academy of Management Journal*, 25, 525–550; Pope, K. (1996). A steelmaker built up by buying cheap mills finally meets its match. *Wall Street Journal*, May 2, A1, A6.

36. Griffin, R. W., & Pustay, M. W. (2005). *International Business* (4th ed.). Upper Saddle River, NJ: Pearson Education.

37. Blodgett, L. L. (1991). Partner contributions as predictors of equity share in joint ventures. *Journal of International Business Studies*, 22, 63–73; Ghemawat, P., & Ghadar, F. (2000). The dubious logic of global megamergers. *Harvard Business Review*, 78, 64–72; Mattioli, D. (2010). In China, Western firms keep secrets close. *Wall Street Journal*, August 30, B9; Rose, R. L. (1996). For Whirlpool, Asia is the new frontier. *Wall Street Journal*, April 25, B1, B4.

38. Hill, C. W. L. (2008). *Global Business Today*. New York: McGraw-Hill/Irwin; Ingrassia, L., Naj, A. K., & Rosett, C. (1995). Overseas, Otis and its parent get in on the ground floor. *Wall Street Journal*, April 21, A6.

39. Hill, C. W. L. (2008). *Global Business Today*. New York: McGraw-Hill/Irwin; Ren H., Gray, B., & Kim, K. (2009). Performance of international joint ventures: What factors really make a difference and how? *Journal of Management*, 35, 805–832.

40. Griffin, R. W., & Pustay, M. W. (2005). *International Business* (4th ed.). Upper Saddle River, NJ: Pearson Education; Hill, C. W. L. (2008). *Global Business Today*. New York: McGraw-Hill/Irwin; Ren H., Gray, B., & Kim, K. (2009). Performance of international joint ventures: What factors really make a difference and how? *Journal of Management*, 35, 805–832; Weiss, S. E. (1987). Creating the GM–Toyota joint venture: A case in complex negotiations. *Columbia Journal of World Business*, 22, 23–38; Yan, A., & Gray, B. (1994). Bargaining power,

management control, and performance in United States–China joint ventures: A comparative case study. *Academy of Management Journal*, 37, 1478–1517.

41. Newman, W. H. (1992). Launching a viable joint venture. *California Management Review*, 35, 68–80; Osland, G. E., & Cavusgil, S. T. (1996). Performance issues in U.S.–China joint ventures. *California Management Review*, 38, 106–130; Phatak, A. V. (1997). *International Management: Concepts and Cases*. Cincinnati, OH: South-Western.

42. Blumenthal, J. (1995). Relationships between organizational control mechanisms and joint-venture success. In L. Gomez-Mejia & M. Lawless (eds.), *Advances in Global High-Technology Management*, Vol. 5, part B (115–134). Greenwich, CT: JAI Press.

43. Areddy, J. T. (2009). Danone pulls out of disputed China venture. *Wall Street Journal*, October 1, B1.

44. Arino, A., Ozcan, P., & Mitchell, J. (2009). KLM: Gaining altitude via alliances. *IESE Insight*, October, 1–3. Available at http://insight.iese.edu; Kiley, D. (2008). Ghosn hits the accelerator. *Business Week*, May 12, 48–49; Matlack, C. (2008). Carlos Ghosn's Russian gambit. *Business Week*, March 17, 57–58; Tully, S., & Eiben, T. (1996). The alliance from hell. *Fortune*, June 24. Available at http://money.cnn.com/magazines/fortune/fortune_archive/1996/06/24/213761/index.htm. See also www.klm.com/corporate/en/about-klm/index.html.

45. Honda Aero breaks ground for HQ, jet engine plant. December 3, 2007. Available at www.aviationtoday.com; Blumenthal, J. (1995). Relationships between organizational control mechanisms and joint-venture success. In L. Gomez-Mejia & M. Lawless (eds.), *Advances in Global High-technology Management*, Vol. 5, part B (115–134). Greenwich, CT: JAI Press; Gillespie, K., & Teegen, H. J. (1995). Market liberalization and international alliance formation: The Mexican paradigm. *Columbia Journal of World Business*, 30, 59–69; Serapio, M. G., & Cascio, W. F. (1996). End-games in international alliances. *Academy of Management Executive*, 10, 62–73.

46. Baker, S. (1996). The odd couple at Heinz. *Business Week*, November 4, 176–178; Hamel, G. (1991). Competition for competence and inter-partner learning within international strategic alliances. *Strategic Management Journal*, 12, 83–103.

47. Bremner, B., Schiller, Z., Smart, T., & Holstein, W. J. (1996). Keiretsu connections: The bonds between the U.S. and Japan's industry groups. *Business Week*, July 22, 52–54. See www.hp.com/hpinfo.

48. Done, K. (2003). New bonding could mean altered shape for alliances. *Financial Times*, October 1, 18; Esterl, M. (2009). Star draws 2 airlines closer. *Wall Street Journal*, October 27, B1, B5; Takahashi, Y. (2009). Japan airlines to cut jobs, pursue alliance. *Wall Street Journal*, September 16, B3. See also www.oneworld.com; www.skyteam.com; www.staralliance.com.

49. The long arm of the state. *The Economist*, June 25, 2011 (Special report on China), 14–15; Selling foreign goods in China: Impenetrable. *The Economist*, October 17, 2009, 73–74; Brown, A., & Dean, J. (2010). Business sours on China. *Wall Street Journal*, March 17, A1, A6; Kahn, G., Bilefsky, D., & Lawton, C. (2004). Burned once, brewers return to China—With pint-size goals. *Wall Street Journal*, March 10, A1, A8; Kranhold, K. (2004). China's price for market entry: Give us your technology, too. *Wall Street Journal*, February 26, A1, A6; Pruitt, A. (2009). Making power out of chicken waste in China. September 29. Available at www.energyboom.com; Roberts, D. (2010). Closed for business? *Bloomberg Businessweek*,

April 5, 32–37; Stein, M. A. (2009). Going clean. *Wall Street Journal*, October 19, R7; Ueno, T. (2009). *Technology Transfer to China to Address Climate Change Mitigation*. Issue Brief 09-09, August. Resources for the Future. Available at www.rff.org/RFF/Documents/RFF-IB-09–09.pdf. See also www.freedoniagroup.com/Turbines-In-China.html; www.gepower.com.

Part 3

Building and Managing a Global Workforce

Chapter 9

Selecting and Evaluating International Employees

For years, people you saw in bars in Burma were executives. Now, you see all kinds of people—computer nerds, people setting up cable systems. They aren't hairy-chested danger seekers—all are expats that need to be protected.

—Robert Pelton,
International Security Consultant

Chapter 8 looks at how multinationals can improve their competitive positions by using multicultural teams, alliances, and partnerships. There are some significant challenges and opportunities offered by these structures. One important challenge we did not discuss is the selection of employees that comprise those teams and then the appraisal of their work. We will turn our attention in this chapter to a strategic overview of employee selection options. Chapter 10 will follow with global compensation and reward methods. A discussion of the details and intricacies of staffing and the important issues of appraisal and evaluation of international employees is presented in Chapter 11.

To start this discussion, it is important to note that all human resource managers are global in the sense that they hire foreign nationals, use multicultural teams, and compete with other multinationals in their local markets. Human resource professionals in medium to large multinationals have broader and deeper challenges than their domestic counterparts. Among other things, those who work in international human resource management (IHRM) must grapple with a wider variety of complex environments (e.g., legal and economic systems), a more diverse mix of employees, and a larger portfolio of human resource functions and activities (e.g., supporting employees and their families, compensation difference). For these and other reasons, many experts believe that human resource executives should be involved in most phases of international strategy and goal development.[1]

When they are involved, IHRM professionals can help address and handle problems. They can be instrumental in getting top executives to understand and value different cultures in the workforce and beyond, provide advice about structure and coordination across borders, and train employees in key cross-cultural skills that can impact the bottom line.[2] Consider a firm that wants to enter a country that is in the process of converting from state-owned operations to market-based ones. As shown in Chapter 8, market-entry choices such as buying local firms, building new plants, or establishing joint ventures can place a firm knee-deep in big human resource problems that could potentially impact productivity. Among other things, productivity could be improved by careful consideration of staffing, compensation, and communication of firm policies. For example, maybe it would be best for the firm to centralize IHRM functions for employees from the home country or a third country but then delegate decisions about host-country nationals to their local units.[3] Quality human resource management can be a real competitive advantage—one that could be more difficult for competition to duplicate than even an advantage gained from buying technology or securing capital.[4]

SORTING OUT STAFFING OPTIONS

Selection of Employees

This section provides an overview of some of the options for staffing international operations—getting the right employee who will succeed on the job. It is also important to examine how to develop an employee's management skills once he or she is selected and how firms provide feedback about those skills and the resulting performance.

The strategic choices that firms make to compete internationally should be supported by a set of matching IHRM practices. For instance, a company that earns a sizable amount of its revenue in foreign countries could benefit from being led by senior executives who have a firsthand understanding of foreign markets, cultures, and business practices. In recent years, U.S. multinationals have focused on hiring and promoting top managers with international experience, and they have worked to make sure that other rising managers are offered international development opportunities.[5]

At the same time, many U.S. multinationals have more work to do at home. Some companies are seemingly multinational in name only—at least when it comes to the percentage of board members who have international work experience.

Of course, board membership is only a rough proxy for a firm's international posture, and not all international experience is the same. Some knowledge might be better suited to one or another international assignment. This makes what is already a tough job for the human resource department all the more difficult and the whole notion of staffing international operations very complex. There is a dizzying array of choices for types of employees that can help run international operations. Some of these employee categories overlap, and not all employee options will be used by any one company. To give you a better sense of the options, we focus here on a few prominent types of employees that are commonly used by multinationals.[6]

A common option is to recruit *parent-country nationals* (PCNs) for top management and important technical positions in foreign subsidiaries. PCNs have citizenship in the country in which the hiring multinational is headquartered (and are thus sometimes called home-country employees, too). Once posted abroad for at least a year, PCNs are often referred to as *expatriates*. These employees are well known to top management and can more easily carry out the organization mission than other types of international staff.[7] On the other hand, sending a PCN abroad is typically the most expensive option. Adding to the expense is that success rates for expatriate assignments are variable—and by no means assured. Estimates for failure rates vary considerably (from under 5% to about 70%).[8] Perhaps the biggest risk in sending PCNs overseas is their often limited grasp of local cultures and business practices, especially early in the assignment.[9]

This latter problem is a main reason why many companies turn to *host-country nationals* (HCNs)—especially to fill lower- and middle-level management jobs. HCNs are individuals from the foreign country where a multinational has set up operations. Some firms are reluctant to put HCNs in top management positions, fearing it may dilute their control over foreign operations or corporate culture. Still, HCNs offer some potential advantages over PCNs. Typically, HCNs have a superior grasp of the local culture, business practices, and language. HCNs are also less expensive to employ since the use of expatriates usually involves expensive relocation costs and higher salaries. Plus, going local to staff foreign operations can bring public relations benefits and relieve government pressures to create jobs.[10] Yet filling positions with HCNs is not as easy as these advantages might make it seem. For example, while the labor force is large and seemingly plentiful in China, consider some of the problems that multinationals face in locating—and holding onto—Chinese HNCs. This situation is described in the accompanying *Global Innovations* box.

GLOBAL INNOVATIONS

Setting Your Sights on Foreign Employees: Hiring the Best Means Hard Work

Hiring the top employees in science and technology fields is tough going for some U.S. firms. One approach those firms have taken is to find, screen, and hire foreign professionals with those critical skills. U.S. household names such as Hewlett-Packard, Microsoft, Texas Instruments, and Pfizer have all hired foreigners in increasing numbers to fill key positions in the United States in recent years.

Screening potential foreign hires is not easy, however, and presents special challenges, above and beyond the U.S. visa requirements that must be met. For instance, assessing qualifications for foreign job candidates whose educational credentials were earned outside the United States is difficult. There is no doubt that many overseas universities provide a great education, and increasingly so this last decade as the U.S. world market share is starting to be challenged. The problem is that decisions about quality aren't easy for most U.S. human resource professionals. Foreign universities often have different standards, courses, and grading systems than their U.S. counterparts, making direct comparisons difficult. Some firms use their own in-house tests to appraise the skills of foreign applicants. A more common approach is to rely on consulting firms, such as World Education Services Inc. (www.wes.org), to assess foreign education credentials.

The challenge does not stop there. Assessing the work experience of foreign job applicants can be difficult and is slowed by the complexities in conducting background checks. Moreover, language barriers often come into play when contacting foreign references or "gatekeepers" (e.g., administrative assistants) because of language differences. Consequently, it is best to conduct background checks in the relevant language—something that is a big challenge in itself and again best done by consulting firms with the expertise and overseas contacts necessary to size up a candidate.

Let's look at the screening process for past criminal behavior to illustrate potential problems. First, since legal systems vary across nations, what is considered a crime in the United States may not be viewed as such elsewhere—or vice versa. Also, many foreigners hired to work temporarily in the United States eventually want permanent resident status. To pursue this, foreigners must present documents from their home countries describing whether they have a criminal history. Depending on that history, the U.S. firm could lose its foreign hire. Conversely, foreigners with clean records in their home countries may be barred from working in the United States because they have admitted behavior that is illegal under U.S. law. Finally, criminal records and databases are poor in certain countries, making background checks more difficult.

Cultural differences also may make screening foreign candidates a challenge. Communication styles, expectations about performance feedback, and work values may all act to cloud the screening process. For instance, body language and nonverbal communication styles vary considerably across countries and are easily misinterpreted or overinterpreted. The expectations that U.S. recruiters have for firm handshakes and direct eye contact, for example, may put foreign candidates from certain Asian cultures at a comparative disadvantage. U.S. human resource professionals should do their homework about these cultural differences prior to interviewing foreign candidates. They should also be prepared to explain the company's values and behavioral expectations to candidates. This preparation helps recruiters assess whether a foreign job candidate can successfully adapt and will improve the chances of a successful selection process.[11]

Another related and common staffing option is the use of *third-country nationals* (TCNs), either to work in foreign subsidiaries or at multinational headquarters. These international employees work in countries where they are not citizens; nor are they citizens of the multinational's parent country. These employees are hired when a multinational wants someone with expertise in local culture and business practices to fill a management position in a foreign subsidiary. PCNs may have plenty of management experience but lack local knowledge. And, while HCNs understand local conditions, they may lack relevant technical skills. As a result, a TCN may be the best option, especially if the goal is to groom someone for a top management position in a foreign subsidiary. If there are needs for someone to effectively run operations in countries that lack homegrown management talent, then they fit the bill, too. For instance, a U.S. firm setting up manufacturing operations in Costa Rica may find appropriate candidates in Mexico, a country with a large pool of Spanish-speaking management talent.

PCNs, HCNs, and TCNs represent the most common staffing categories, but others do exist. Interestingly, some experts urge international firms to have PCNs, HCNs, TCNs, and other types of employees working side by side wherever possible. The rationale is that a diverse work environment improves innovation and learning, outcomes that ultimately raise subsidiary performance. The role for IHRM professionals in this context is to select the right people and to ensure that the advantages of staff diversity are not overwhelmed by its accompanying disadvantages (e.g., more conflict and coordination difficulty).[12] This can be accomplished by appropriate selection, socialization, and training efforts that make employees aware of staffing goals while they also improve their international skills.[13]

Selecting and Developing International Employees

Identifying the types of possible international employees is one thing, but how do firms decide which type is best for a specific overseas position? Experts advise that such decisions should be made with a firm's international business strategy in mind, taking into account its competitive environment, overseas sophistication, level of internationalization, and the foreign market in which the position will be based. In short, it is a complex decision and easy to get wrong—but very important to get right. One study of a U.S. financial services firm found that overseas branches with higher proportions of U.S. expatriates offered more complex services for their customers. In these locations, expatriates could offer more insights about customer needs than could their local counterparts. On the other hand, branches in foreign countries (places in which local knowledge was critical) with fierce local competition had more HCNs and fewer expatriates.

The degree to which IHRM is included in a firm's strategic decision making, as well as the specific selection tactics and training approaches used, varies across countries. This suggests that national culture impacts human resource activities. One example is the Chinese emphasis on business contacts that rely on reciprocal obligation (known as *guanxi*), which seeps into the hiring practices, training approaches, and career development activities of many firms in ways not seen elsewhere. There is pressure to reciprocate a favor, and this could extend to one with human resource implications. This type of local, cultural knowledge often needs to be developed in PNCs and even TCNs and should be part of a firm's development programs. The ability to put this knowledge into play can, as we will see in the second part of this chapter, be included in a performance evaluation. Table 9.1 summarizes some of the skills that international managers need to succeed. While this is a formidable list of skills, research shows that even mastering several of these goes a long way toward improving managerial effectiveness.[14]

Cultural Differences in Selection and Development Procedures

Many business researchers are now focusing on the connections between cultural values and staffing decisions, especially when it comes to expatriate deployment.

Table 9.1
Think You Have the Right Stuff? A Skill Profile for International Managers

Skill Area	Thumbnail Sketch of Desired Competencies
Multidimensional perspective	Has extensive multifunctional, multicountry, and multienvironment experience
Line management proficiency	A successful track record in overseas projects and assignments
Decision making	Successful in making strategic decisions across a variety of situations
Resourcefulness	Has skills to be accepted by host country's government and business elite
Cultural adaptability	Can quickly adapt to foreign cultures, with diverse cross-cultural experience
Cultural sensitivity	Deals effectively with people from many cultures, races, nationalities, and religions
Team building	Can create culturally diverse working groups that achieve organizational goals
Mental maturity	Has the endurance needed for the rigors of foreign posts
Negotiation	Has track record of successful business negotiations in multicultural contexts
Delegation	Has track record of ability to delegate in cross-cultural contexts
Business practices	Can conduct business across borders successfully in a global environment
Change agent	Has track record of successfully initiating or implementing organizational changes
Vision	Can quickly spot and respond to threats and opportunities in the host country

Sources: Adapted from Briscoe, D. R., Schuler, R. S., & Claus, L. (2009). *International Human Resource Management* (3rd ed.). New York: Routledge; Howard, C. G. (1992). Profile of the 21st-century expatriate manager. *HR Magazine*, June, 93–100.

How cultural values shape the selection, development, and placement of international staff has already been alluded to above. For instance, U.S. and U.K. multinationals tend to use somewhat different procedures to select and manage expatriates than do managers in German and Japanese firms.[15] One way to illustrate effects of these differences is to look at what happens when one method meets the other.

Consider what an American experienced when he was interviewed and hired by South Korean firm Samsung to help set up a plant in New Jersey:

> The hiring process was unique. Many people attended the interviews. Side conversations in Korean were the norm. Decision making inched forward as consensus was painstakingly achieved. The senior people did not commit themselves to a position until their respective staffs had fully and freely expressed their support or concerns for my candidacy. Personal issues were critical. Those items went beyond my wife and me. They penetrated into realms of what my father had done for a living, whether or not my mother worked outside of the home, and what my brothers and sister were doing. They all seemed to have a significance I could not fathom.[16]

This American was dumbfounded by a hiring process that differed wildly from what normally happens in the United States. His admitted ignorance of Korean culture and hiring practices prevented him from fully understanding what was happening at the time. Likewise, Samsung's Korean managers were clearly unaware that Americans would find their personal questions to be shocking and off limits. In the United States, such questions are perceived as irrelevant, discriminatory, and possibly illegal. Many other countries either do not have the same types of legal protections in place when it comes to forms of discrimination (e.g., Thailand) or do not enforce them as consistently (e.g., Mexico) as is done in the United States. In any case, it is no surprise that foreign managers may be unaware of U.S. legal and cultural restrictions or may not grasp that what is commonly seen as a fair selection procedure varies across countries. But from their perspective, the Korean managers in this example likely felt that they couldn't make a good hire without understanding the candidate's background, including home life, religious orientation, and family.[17]

Selection procedures can, of course, be customized and modified. For example, traditional U.S. procedures can be adapted to better fit cultural values that Japanese firms want to emphasize in their U.S. plants. In one auto parts plant, the Japanese management wanted to stress team skills, consensus building, harmonious relationships, and other typically Japanese values in their hiring interviews. Yet these values sharply contrast with the common U.S. practice of openly comparing individual applicants. This is uncomfortable for some Japanese. U.S. managers, in contrast, generally feel their role is to pick the best candidate for the job. This makes comparisons between people necessary. Clearly, U.S. and Japanese approaches to selection are different.

Fortunately, the selection system developed at this Japanese plant in the United States cleverly blended both approaches. In this hybrid system, groups of job applicants assemble windshield wiper motors. Employee performance within groups is assessed by trained evaluators who arrive at a final score for each person using a consensus process. All applicants who reach a predetermined cutoff score are considered qualified and are hired to staff the plant. This system combines individual assessment (U.S.) with consensus decision making (Japanese) to reach an overall evaluation. It also allows Japanese managers to gauge what are critical issues for them—such as an applicant's ability to work well in a team.[18]

Finally, the success of any selection or training program depends in part on how well it matches the values and culture of the employees being trained. For most U.S. managers, *self-focused* training improves performance more than *group-focused* training. The opposite is true for many Chinese managers. Americans generally find information about their ability to succeed at a task (self-focused training) more useful than information about the ability of a group to which they belong (group-focused training). Self-focused information is valued in individualist cultures in which performance is usually viewed as the result of a single person's actions. In contrast, Chinese managers may pay more attention to information that describes how a group they belong to should approach a task. As you know by this point in the book, people in collectivist cultures tend to view themselves as members of a group first and as individuals second. As a result, performance is a function of shared responsibilities, making information about group behavior more valuable. In sum, firms should take the cultural values of employees into account when designing training programs.[19]

EMPLOYEE PERFORMANCE APPRAISAL: THE GLOBAL CHALLENGE

Selection and development of employees is complicated enough. But to gauge the success of these approaches, and to ensure organizational performance as a whole, leaders must evaluate job performance. Thus, we now turn our attention to the companion topic of performance evaluation and the provision of feedback to employees.

Managing employee performance is always challenging. But for multinationals, the difficulty is compounded by having employees scattered all around the world—many of whom embrace different cultural values and localized practices for performance management. The headaches multiply when you consider the thorny issue of how to evaluate and manage the performance of expatriates. There is no doubt that employee performance evaluation is more costly and complex for a multinational than for firms with single-country operations—by a significant margin. Accordingly, it is important to keep in mind the core questions facing multinationals when it comes to managing and appraising employee performance:

- Should multinationals rely on a standardized set of policies, procedures, and practices for appraising employee performance worldwide?
- Should multinationals rely on a dispersed set of systems that are aligned with local business and management practices in the countries where it does business?

■ Should multinationals take a blended approach to performance appraisal and management—one that relies on a combination of standardized practices and local latitude aimed at keeping some local practices intact?

These questions have been asked and have been location-tested by many a company. The bottom line is that there are no simple answers. And while some multinationals have moved toward a blended method over the years, this is also the approach that is usually the hardest to manage. A key is to keep the global workforce focused on company goals and executing the firm's strategy, and performance appraisal systems are an important mechanism for doing just that. Yet this all has to be done against a background of employees in different places who vary in how they interpret performance, react to feedback, and generally view their jobs.[20]

Receiving a performance appraisal is not likely to be high on employees' list of favorite things to do. Likewise, conducting performance appraisals is one of the things many managers dislike most about their jobs. Performance appraisal, after all, is inherently difficult, and few managers enjoy giving employees direct performance feedback, especially when that input is negative.

Imagine you have six employees reporting to you in your firm's London headquarters—your job as a manager is to determine how well they performed their jobs and give them performance appraisals on an annual, semiannual, or even more frequent basis. Unless you took extensive notes on each employee as the year unfolded, you would need to recall the accomplishments, limitations, and setbacks of each person. Then, somehow you would sum up these pros and cons over the evaluation period, hopefully in a consistent and accurate way, trying not to be overly influenced by recent or overly salient events. Next, you may want to compare these appropriately weighted evaluations across your six people and rank-order them so you can distribute your limited pool of rewards and demonstrate to your superiors that you have the fortitude to distinguish between employees and can give someone a negative evaluation if they deserve it. Finally comes what is often the hardest part for managers—following the company's procedures to meet with each person to give them feedback and tell them what level of rewards you think they deserve.

As if that is not a lot already, now imagine if one of the subordinates you had to evaluate was an expatriate posted to Mexico City. First, your office is in London, and even if you visited Mexico City during the year, it is not likely that you would have had a chance to assess the expatriate's performance in any detailed manner. (Although some jobs, such as sales, might be easier than others to evaluate.) Moreover, imagine that you have never worked in Mexico and do not know much about the environment there, including any differences in culture or business practices. You would probably have great difficulty grasping how you could possibly appraise the expatriate's performance, especially from thousands of miles away. The last half of this chapter tackles problems just like this—when managers must confront the pitfalls that can occur in conducting performance evaluations of expatriates and foreign nationals.

Multinationals and Performance Evaluation for Expatriates

Evaluating expatriates can prove daunting. That is especially the case for large multinationals, because they often have employees scattered across dozens of countries in which they do business. While it has been noted that these firms face considerable range in employee attitudes and values across countries, it is also true that multinationals themselves vary (sometimes considerably) in how they approach performance appraisal in the first place.

For instance, in our London example, some underlying assumptions are apparent—including that performance appraisal is focused on individual performance, with the best performers getting the biggest share of available rewards. This winner-takes-all orientation is more common among firms based in the United States and the United Kingdom. In Northern European countries (such as Sweden), however, corporations face more state regulation of compensation and associated performance management systems. This may be a reflection of egalitarian values that discourage wide compensation differences and punitive performance appraisal (see Chapter 10). Likewise, compared to their U.S. or British counterparts, Japanese multinationals evolved in a more collectivist environment. They tend to emphasize loyalty to the company in their performance appraisal procedures, with length of service carrying relatively more weight and individual performance relatively less. It is important to remember that most multinationals are in part a product of the home environment where they evolved. Although they are always evolving, it is not uncommon for those roots to run deep and to reflect firms' philosophies and practices related to performance appraisal feedback.[21]

Research shows that, regardless of their roots, when multinationals tailor performance appraisal and other IHRM practices to the local context, their foreign subsidiaries tend to perform better—largely because employees become more motivated and skilled, with their performance improving as a result. Nevertheless, some experts argue that multinationals should apply IHRM best practices globally, particularly those that help firms implement their international strategies or preserve corporate values deemed important for all employees to embrace.[22]

Some multinationals take a blended approach, insisting on some common practices everywhere while also allowing for considerable tailoring in local units. Interestingly, a number of factors seem to impact how much local tailoring takes place. For instance, as the number of expatriates increases, the amount of local IHRM tailoring tends to decrease. In essence, more expatriates make it easier for multinationals to directly transfer parent company knowledge and practices, including about IHRM, to foreign subsidiaries. The nature of the foreign location itself, however, may also impact how much, or how little, local IHRM adaptation takes place. For example, consider Western multinationals operating in both China and India. One study found that, compared to their Chinese subsidiaries, Indian subsidiaries were seen as playing a stronger strategic role for the firm while also using more localized IHRM practices. This may reflect India's greater exposure to Western influence (i.e., due to the British presence for many years) as well as the more common use of English—factors that may make it easier for both the parent company and the subsidiary to create blended IRHM practices.[23]

The goals of gaining additional skills and a more global perspective are among the key reasons that multinationals send expatriates abroad. These goals are often met. At least one study showed that expatriation increased the ability to manage cultural differences and understand international operations and even made expats more open-minded and flexible.[24] While these growth experiences benefit the employee as well as the company, few are part of a domestic performance appraisal. If they are considered, such experiences are tough to evaluate (how do you assess "open-mindedness"?), especially without observing the employee over a long period of time and from a distance—whether geographic or cultural.

Nevertheless, most multinationals routinely evaluate the performance of their expatriates, regardless of their country of origin or their assignment location. Consequently, the remainder of this section will discuss several important questions about performance appraisal for expatriates: (1) *Who* should evaluate their performance? (2) *When* or how often should they be evaluated? (3) *What* aspects of performance should be evaluated?

Who Should Evaluate Expatriate Performance?

Multinationals have a variety of options for evaluating expatriates. First, expatriate evaluations can be conducted in the host country, the home country, or both. Moreover, any number of potential evaluators can be involved in this process in addition to the expatriate's supervisor—including peers, subordinates, and human resource professionals. Research shows that, in practice, a mix of home- and host-country personnel is commonly used to conduct the evaluation process. All of this suggests some sophisticated evaluation systems, but the reality is that most expatriate evaluations are anything but. Instead, they are often conducted on a relatively informal basis. While expatriate evaluations frequently follow the outlines of domestic performance appraisal processes, an irony is that fewer evaluators may be involved. According to one survey, domestic performance evaluations involved twice as many evaluators as international performance evaluations. Despite this, it is still more challenging to evaluate expatriates than it is to evaluate domestic employees.[25]

For example, while a U.S. manager assigned to the Netherlands may have a Dutch boss, he or she may also still have a boss in the United States—and may be evaluated by both. Part of the frustration for multinationals is that little hard evidence exists as to what the best practices are with respect to evaluating expatriates. For instance, there is considerable controversy about which evaluator is better—a host-country manager or a home-country manager. The pros and cons of each of these are discussed in turn.[26]

Evaluations by Host-Country Professionals

Having host-country professionals involved in expatriate evaluation is a popular option (about 71% of firms report doing so). This is more common among bigger multinationals—those with a large number of expatriates to manage. Presumably, the advantages associated with host country evaluation increase with numbers. A larger number of expatriates makes it more difficult for home-country managers to collect the information needed to perform adequate reviews on their far-flung workforces. Plus, host-country professionals are physically closer to the actual work being done, so they are more likely to be familiar with the expatriate's work and performance, particularly given local cultural norms. That is important, because the quality of the expatriate's job may revolve around how culturally savvy he or she is. Consequently, having expatriates evaluated by their host-country supervisors or other professionals at the foreign location makes a great deal of sense. This leads many experts to suggest that these are the only people who are in a position to closely observe and understand the context of the expatriate's work over a long period of time.[27]

Relying on host-country managers to evaluate expatriate performance is not without its drawbacks. For instance, while local professionals are knowledgeable about their environment, they also bring their own cultural frames of reference to the table, and this can cause problems. One U.S. expatriate working in India pressed his subordinates for their ideas about a project—consistent with participative management techniques that work well in the United States. But his host-country supervisor frowned on this behavior and gave him negative feedback in an evaluation. The local supervisor's reactions are not surprising, given that Indian culture tends to be higher in power distance than U.S. culture, making autocratic forms of leadership more suitable. The expatriate nevertheless paid the price—after returning home, this negative evaluation was one of the reasons he was denied a promotion.

One reaction to this incident is that the U.S. expatriate may have gotten what he deserved—he should have been cognizant of the local demands. On the other hand, what if the U.S. parent company had wanted the expatriate to instill openness to participative management in its Indian workforce? Regardless of the wisdom of such an approach, should the expatriate be punished for following instructions? Or perhaps the blame could also be placed on the home office for failing to provide the appropriate cultural training needed to go about infusing more appreciation for participation in an Indian-appropriate manner. Regardless of where the blame lies, this underscores some of the dangers associated with having host-country professionals evaluate expatriate performance.[28]

Other potential problems emanate from language differences—the host-country professional may simply be unable to clearly communicate feedback to the expatriate. Perhaps more important, however, is that dimensions of performance considered important may vary significantly between the local context and the home country. Some of this may stem from cultural differences. Whatever the reason, factors that are important to the host-country professionals evaluating expatriates will likely be weighted heavily in the evaluation. Problems can occur, however, when expatriates do not realize that the evaluation criteria used in the home country are not aligned with those used locally. An expatriate in Thailand, for example, may have to learn over time to show considerable restraint in sharing his or her feelings, even if he or she is upset with a subordinate. That restraint may count positively for a local Thai manager, while it could be viewed as not leader-like in the United States.[29] While one might hope that the home office would recognize and understand what the expatriate has done, this is far from certain. In some ways, the expatriate may be ahead by shrugging off the feedback and focusing on the future.[30]

Differences in criteria may be subtle and not directly related to performance per se; instead, they may reflect differences in interaction norms. As a result, even if a multinational uses the same performance appraisal system everywhere, the results might be different because of these norms. Naturally, expatriates parachuting into a new environment may not be aware of these norms and may make mistakes as a result. For instance, consider Indian expatriates posted to a U.S. subsidiary. Because of common interaction norms in their home country, these Indian expatriates might make an effort to develop a relationship with their bosses. After all, in India, having a supervisor like you may positively impact performance evaluations. However, U.S. supervisors, often trained to separate personal feelings from performance goals and targets, are less likely to be swayed by this. Indeed, they may wonder why the Indian expatriates spend so much time on relationship building instead of doing their jobs. Conversely, U.S. expatriates posted to an Indian subsidiary may not realize the importance of building a positive personal relationship with their immediate supervisor. Failing to do this may be seen as rude and result in supervisory dislike that spills over to the expatriates' evaluation. In short, the evaluations of both the Indian and U.S. expatriates are likely to suffer. This is something that could be alleviated by training that is directed to expatriates as well as to the evaluators in host countries.[31]

Overall, the use of host-country professionals to evaluate expatriate performance has both pluses and minuses. Consequently, multinationals may want to use home-office personnel for performance evaluations of expatriates for greater control and continuity.

Evaluations by Home-Country Professionals

There are some clear advantages to having home-country professionals evaluate expatriates. For one, these managers are usually more familiar with expatriates' experiences, work history, and performance track record. Plus, they usually speak the same language and share the same basic cultural roots. This could be an advantage over host-country professionals when it comes to communicating feedback. Shared perspectives make it easier for the home-country manager to help the expatriate learn and develop from the feedback he or she receives.

Using home-country professionals to evaluate expatriates can also have its shortcomings. Distance is often an impediment. Home-country professionals cannot observe expatriates and their performance in the foreign locations where they work, or they only see small slices of behavior. Add to this that they typically receive little feedback or information from the host country about the expatriates they have to evaluate. Consequently, a major challenge for home-country professionals is gaining access to the information they need to make a quality evaluation. Studies show that most expatriates have relatively little quality contact with home-office personnel during their overseas assignments, including their direct home country supervisor. When there is contact, it is often initiated by the expatriates.

Granted, e-mails and video conferencing have made it easier to connect with the home office, but this kind of contact is no substitute for extended on-the-job observations; nor does it mean that home-office personnel really understand what is happening on the ground in the foreign subsidiary. As a result, they may not understand expatriate pressures or the appropriate standards to use when evaluating expatriate performance.[32]

Table 9.2 summarizes the pros and cons associated with home- and host-country professionals who conduct performance evaluations of expatriates. Naturally, this begs the question of what the best solution is for multinationals trying to do the right thing. The answer is that it really depends on a host of variables. Among other things, evaluators must consider their goals, the number of expatriates involved, where they are posted, and the nature of their work. Some multinationals have capitalized on the respective strengths of home- and host-country professionals by involving both in the evaluation process for expatriates. This may translate into home-office professionals playing a supporting rather than leading role in the appraisal process. For example, AT&T and 3M Corporation developed a "career sponsor" program to link expatriates to the corporate office. Sponsors keep the expatriate in touch with what is going on at home and act as mentors. They also conduct performance evaluations using the cultural perspective of the home office. Assessments of such programs show that they work, as one study of U.S. firms

Table 9.2

Pros and Cons of Home-Country versus Host-Country Evaluation of Expatriates

	Performance Evaluation Done by Home-Country Professional	Performance Evaluation Done by Host-Country Professional
Pros	■ Typically has a better understanding of overall corporate goals and objectives	■ In the best position to observe expatriate's behavior and performance over a long period of time
	■ Has more background on expatriate's work history and track record	■ Has excellent understanding of local context, practices, and values and how they relate to performance
	■ Typically shares expatriate's values and language, making transmission of performance feedback easier	
Cons	■ May have little knowledge or understanding of local context or culture	■ Evaluations will likely be shaped by local values and perspectives, which may create problems with company objectives
	■ Has little or no direct observation of expatriate performance or effectiveness in foreign location	■ Less familiar with overall company strategies and objectives
	■ May have weak grasp of criteria important for performing well in local context	■ May have more difficulty communicating because of language and cultural differences

Sources: Adapted from Briscoe, D. R., Schuler, R. S., & Claus, L. (2009). *International Human Resource Management* (3rd ed.). New York: Routledge; Oddou, G., & Mendenhall, M. (1991). Expatriate performance appraisal: Problems and solutions. In M. Mendenhall & G. Oddou (eds.), *International Human Resource Management* (364–374). Boston: PWS-Kent.

found when a balanced set of raters from both the home and host country increased the accuracy of performance evaluations.[33]

When Should Expatriate Performance Be Evaluated?

The next question to address is when expatriate evaluations should be performed. U.S. firms have historically evaluated employees—domestic and international—once or twice per year. Experts, however, have argued that this is too infrequent and forces evaluators to rely on shaky memories or the most recent events. They suggest that evaluations be completed more often, taking into consideration features such as the tasks or projects involved as well as the role of the evaluator.[34]

Given the complexities associated with evaluating expatriates, it makes sense to have local supervisors or professionals conduct evaluations as major projects or milestones are completed. Home-country professionals, in contrast, might perform less frequent or calendar-based evaluations of performance given their distance from the work (such as on a six-month schedule). Again, this may vary depending on the expatriate's work role, rank, and experience. It may be premature to conduct a formal performance appraisal during the first six months of a foreign assignment, as expatriates and their families need time to adjust to their foreign surroundings. On the other hand, if it is obvious that things are not going well, management—in either the host or home country—should let the expatriate know and take steps to help out as soon as possible.[35]

This underscores the need to be flexible about the timing of expatriate evaluations. Early on in their assignments, it might be best to give expatriates informal feedback, waiting until after the first six months abroad before conducting anything more formal. Naturally, the cycle of task or project completion may impact the precise timing of evaluations, particularly those done locally. Still, multinationals would be wise to expect and plan for problems, many of which we have already discussed. For example, obtaining home-office support may be difficult if visits are infrequent or short term (i.e., limited to brief e-mails, phone calls, or video conferences). Plus, a key principle of any feedback is that sensitive information is best conveyed in a personal, face-to-face context—something that is by nature more difficult for home-office professionals to do. Depending on where the expatriate is posted, it also may be culturally difficult for local managers or professionals to provide informal feedback. For example, in high-power-distance cultures, where it is common for managers to separate themselves from employees, informal feedback is more difficult to share. Overall, the best time to evaluate expatriates depends on what is right given the nature of the overseas assignment.[36]

Context Variables That Impact Evaluations of Expatriates

As suggested, one of the thorniest questions about evaluating expatriates has to do with what areas or criteria should be considered in the evaluation process. At least three important features about the *context* of the assignment should be kept in mind when evaluating expatriate performance: (1) the *environment* in which the job is done, (2) the *task* or tasks themselves, and (3) the *personal characteristics* of the expatriate.[37]

Environmental Variables

The circumstances under which any job is performed can be more or less demanding. Working in a mine is more physically demanding than working in an office, which, in turn, would have its own challenges. Consequently, the extent to which the environment presents special challenges should be taken into account when determining performance criteria. Of course, posting expatriates to a foreign location can present unique environmental challenges. In other words, for an American, working for a mining company in Zimbabwe will probably be more difficult than working for one in Montana.

The full impact of environmental variables is difficult to appreciate from a distance. For example, imagine that the expatriate running a plant in Mexico reports a productivity level much lower than a comparable plant running in the United States (the firm's home country). Should the expatriate be given a negative evaluation as a result? Experts would say probably not—this outcome reflects peculiarities of the Mexican context. An internal comparison could very well show that the expatriate's employees were much more productive than their average Mexican counterparts. In short, the expatriate manager is dealing with the constraints of working in Mexico, not the relative advantages of managing in South Korea, Germany, or Japan.[38]

Task Variables

It might be important to consider the nature of the work itself in a performance appraisal. For instance, an important job factor in many expatriate roles is how much interaction will be required with locals. Expatriates whose roles—and performance—rely on effective interactions with locals should have performance evaluations that include such task criteria. Naturally, displaying cultural savvy will be more important with some types of work than it will be in other assignments. A software engineer, for example, is less likely to need the same level of cultural awareness to perform successfully than an expatriate in a marketing role. The latter is more likely to need to effectively interact with (or at least understand) large numbers of foreign nationals. Likewise, on foreign assignments, U.S. expatriates who are middle-level managers might need to have more interactions with government officials overseas than they would in comparable roles back in the United States.[39]

Personal Characteristics

Finally, there are simply inherent differences among individuals in their abilities to handle a foreign assignment—either because of experience, temperament, or other personal features. For instance, a personality trait such as flexibility is a characteristic that helps expatriates adjust to their overseas location and to succeed at their jobs. Consequently, features about one's personality, such as openness and a willingness to tolerate ambiguity, are personal characteristics that can predict success or failure on expatriate assignments. Screening on these and other traits can be taken into consideration, particularly during the process of choosing whom to send.

ADDITIONAL CHALLENGES WITH CROSS-BORDER PERFORMANCE EVALUATIONS

Even if a firm has considered these three important constraints on performance overseas, measuring an expatriate's performance can still be challenging. While it might seem straightforward to evaluate an expatriate who is leading a business unit using financial measures, the overseas context complicates matters. First, business laws and tax rules will be different than they are in the home country, making it more difficult to calculate things such as profitability. Moreover, there may be challenges associated with currency conversion and profit repatriation—issues that can prove especially vexing when currency values shift suddenly or nations create hurdles for getting money out of the country. The regulatory environment in China, for example, is burdensome and complex. It is easy to see how jumping through all of the bureaucratic hoops required in China could make it harder to figure out how well an expatriate leading a multinational's Chinese subsidiary is actually doing from a financial perspective. These conditions are clearly beyond the control of any expatriate, but they can influence financial performance and, in turn, a manager's evaluation.[40]

Moreover, because of tax law and currency differences, multinationals often take a variety of steps to minimize taxes and avoid losses from currency fluctuations. As a result, the true performance of a foreign subsidiary—and the leadership team running it—can be obscured and very difficult to manage. Instead, it may be more practical to follow some general guidelines for effectively evaluating expatriate performance.[41]

General Guidelines for Expatriate Evaluation

A set of general practical advice regarding the performance appraisal of expatriates, combined from previous discussion, follows.

Rate the Assignment Difficulty

A firm might consider buying (from providers) or conducting a thorough assessment in advance regarding how difficult specific foreign assignments will be for their expatriates. Difficulty scores can then be applied to weight the normal process used to evaluate performance. For example, if an expatriate will be posted to a very difficult assignment, his or her usual evaluation could be multiplied by 1.5. If the foreign posting is moderately difficult, then the process could be weighted by 1.25, and so on.

The challenge for human resource personnel is to figure out which assignments are more difficult than others as well as the specific weights to be applied—a topic that researchers have reflected on.[42] One factor contributing to assignment difficulty is the extent of necessary *language adjustment*. All things equal, a U.S. expatriate posted to a location where the primary business language used is English (e.g., India) will have an easier time than if he or she is sent to a place where English use is less pervasive (e.g., Vietnam) and where many local languages or dialects exist (e.g., China). Closely related to language usage, the degree of *cultural toughness* can also affect the difficulty of an assignment. An assignment in London or Munich would be easier for most U.S. expatriates than would one in Quito, Ecuador, or Jakarta, Indonesia.

Finally, *economic and political stability* are factors that would determine difficulty. While this is a complex topic, here we simply note that the political and economic problems in a country can be very difficult for an expatriate manager to cope with, much less overcome. Expatriates who do well in such places are most likely performing at very high levels. For example, one U.S. expatriate was instrumental in stopping a strike in the firm's Chilean plant—which would have shut down the plant and soured relations with the home office. Stopping the strike was an important accomplishment, especially in a country that is used to such strikes occurring regularly. Clearly, the expatriate demonstrated a good deal of cultural acumen and insight. Unfortunately, while the labor situation was unfolding, volatile exchange rates in Chile caused demand for the plant's product to temporarily drop 30%. Rather than recognizing the expatriate for averting the strike, the parent company focused on the negative sales figures. As a result, the expatriate received a lackluster performance evaluation.[43]

Additional Suggestions for Expatriate Evaluation

After assessing the general difficulty of an expatriate assignment, experts suggest additional considerations for evaluating expatriates. While many recommend that multiple home- and host-country evaluators be involved in expatriate assessment, a common suggestion is to place greater weight on evaluations performed by host-country managers, since they are in a better position to observe an expatriate's actual daily performance. A related idea, especially if the home office is responsible for expatriate evaluation, is to involve another person who has experience in the country to which expatriates are posted. This increases the local expertise that can be brought to bear when the home office is evaluating expatriates. Conversely, if host-country personnel have primary responsibility for conducting expatriate evaluations, they should seek input from the home office before sharing any feedback with expatriates. This has the twin benefits of helping local professionals understand how parent company values should shape the performance evaluation as well as any corporate norms about delivering performance feedback.

Often overlooked in the evaluation process are expatriates themselves. Regardless of how performance is going to be evaluated, it is important that multinationals:

- Communicate early on with expatriates about the performance criteria likely to be used by host- and home-country managers—and what defines success relative to those criteria.
- Fully explain how the appraisal process will work for expatriates—ideally integrating it into expatriates' assignment plans.
- Conduct training for both the evaluators and expatriates about the role played by their respective frames of reference.
- Emphasize that evaluations will be conducted more frequently given the challenges of expatriate assignments, with an early delay for adjustment.[44]

Evaluating Foreign-Born Employees

Parent country expatriates are not the only type of employee that needs to be managed successfully. There is also a need to manage foreign nationals in the parent country (e.g., a Korean national posted to the headquarters of a Swiss multinational) as well as host-country nationals working for expatriates in foreign subsidiaries. These examples highlight two common performance evaluation scenarios for multinational firms and illustrate that effectively delivering feedback, regardless of whether the news is good or bad, is not easy.

Complicating matters is the fact that business environments everywhere are changing and evolving. As countries develop economically, they seem to move more toward Western-style approaches to performance evaluation and feedback. That said, there are plenty of variations in speed of adoption across both countries and companies. In developing countries such as China and India, large swaths of the business landscape still embrace local or traditional methods. This may reflect both the influence of cultural values and variations among firms from developing countries. The number of state-owned enterprises in China continues its precipitous decline, but their assets are still huge. In those public firms, appraisals tend to involve more evaluators and include moral dimensions (such as honesty) compared to private firms. Foreign multinationals operating in China tend to be the most common users of individual performance evaluations—something that Chinese employees appear to generally accept. Overall, like much in China, performance evaluation and feedback practices are in flux. Nevertheless, it is fair to assume that some cultural differences exist that may impact the effectiveness of evaluation and feedback methods used with foreign-born employees.[45]

Compared to the United States, performance evaluation systems in Middle Eastern countries are usually more informal, with less use of evaluation metrics, forms, and documentation. Feedback is therefore more subjective and informal, with an emphasis on the interpersonal aspects of performance. It is less likely to see completed forms change hands or written evaluations filed away for future reference. This presents an interesting situation, because some multinational firms simply export their formal and explicit performance appraisal forms to their foreign subsidiaries. This combination of an implicit and informal culture and an explicit and formal performance evaluation system can create a clash.[46]

Even the feedback method may be moderated by culture. For example, given the strong emphasis on collectivist values in Japan, it should come as no surprise that performance evaluations are much more likely to be conducted in a group setting in Japan than they are in Europe or the United States. And while team-based work is popular in some Western countries, performance evaluations are still primarily done at the individual level. Interestingly, since 2000, Japanese firms have been slowly shifting toward a greater emphasis on individual performance evaluations—despite the potential disruption to group harmony (a trend Japanese refer to as "performance-ism" or *seikashugi*).[47]

Home-country values can also shape how foreign employees react to performance feedback and various types of delivery mechanisms. Consider Great Britain—a country that has the outward appearance of being culturally similar to the United States. One study found that British and U.S. employees react somewhat differently to performance feedback. Americans became more productive after receiving either praise or criticism. In general, the more feedback they received, the higher their subsequent performance. This finding was observed for British employees *only* after they received praise for their behavior—they did not respond well to criticism.[48] Other research finds differences in reactions to feedback between individualist countries to the more face-conscious and collectivist orientations found in many Asian countries. It would be a mistake to lump these sets of nations together and assume that reactions to feedback will be the same across Asia or Western Europe.[49] Indeed, there can be wide differences in reactions to performance appraisals across Asian countries (e.g., Indonesia, Malaysia, the Philippines, and Thailand).

To conclude this section, Table 9.3 summarizes performance appraisal characteristics often found in four different countries, particularly in local firms. Clearly, differences persist in how performance evaluations are conducted, though practices continue to evolve. In the United States, for example, the general emphasis in the appraisal is on evaluation, not on development or improvement per se. Criticism is direct, with relatively little concern with face-saving of the employee. In other countries, however, the process of providing feedback is monitored much more carefully for its effect on the recipient. In South Korea, feedback is often more indirect, with considerable concern for saving face. This chapter's *Culture Clash* offers some general guidelines for providing feedback to foreign employees that are worth considering.

Table 9.3
Differences in Performance Evaluation Systems: A Four-Country Snapshot

		Country		
Characteristic	**United States**	**Saudi Arabia**	**South Korea**	**China**
General purpose	Evaluation of performance	Evaluation, coaching	Coaching	Financial reward, retention
Feedback from superiors	Considerable amount	Considerable amount	Relatively little	Little, but may receive some from peers
Face-saving concern	Low	High	High	High
Employee involvement	Medium to high	High	Low	Medium; self-evaluation is expected
Type of feedback	Criticism is direct	Criticism is less direct	Criticism is mostly indirect	Criticism is mostly indirect
Level of formality	Formal; probably written	Informal; not written	Informal; not written, but this is changing	Largely informal
Determinants of positive appraisal	Performance criteria	Seniority, connections	Seniority, but ability and performance becoming important	Age and seniority, but becoming more performance oriented

Sources: Adapted from Cooke, F. L. (2008). Performance management in China. In A. Varma, P. S. Budhwar, & A. DeNisi (eds.), *Performance Management Systems: A Global Perspective* (193–209). New York: Routledge; Harris, P. R., & Moran, R. T. (1991). *Managing Cultural Differences* (3rd ed.). Houston: Gulf; Yang, H., & Rowley, C. (2008). Performance management in South Korea. In A. Varma, P. S. Budhwar, & A. DeNisi (eds.), *Performance Management Systems: A Global Perspective* (210–222). New York: Routledge.

CULTURE CLASH

Do Not Necessarily Give as You Expect to Be Given: Advice for Providing Performance Feedback to International Employees

Sage advice for U.S. managers is to reward in public and criticize in private. Yet this advice may not always be the best for foreign-born employees. Instead, experts suggest some useful guidelines for sharing performance feedback to those from a different culture. These recommendations do not fit every culture or employee, but they are good starting points for conveying important feedback:

- *Give feedback through a third party.* In many countries, receiving direct feedback from a superior—even if it is positive—can be uncomfortable. That is especially true for employees who embrace collectivist values and find the prospect of being singled out for feedback disconcerting. Consequently, feedback may often be best delivered through a trusted third party.

- *Communicate to the whole group.* Another way to blunt the effect of direct feedback to individuals is to provide feedback on a group basis. A work group can be gathered together and the messages delivered that management thinks reflect the group's performance. This tactic may be particularly appropriate if tasks are performed in teams or groups—and can work well even in more individualist cultures.

- *Change the form of feedback.* In most cases, the same message can be delivered in several different ways. Trying several different approaches, even if employees give the appearance of grasping what they are being told, increases the odds that the core message will be understood.

- *Simplify the feedback.* This recommendation can apply to anyone but is especially important for foreign-born employees. Messages can almost always be shortened and simplified to improve clarity. For example, managers can eliminate or replace needless words. The phrase "in spite of the fact that…" could be simplified to *although.* (Other examples: "the reason why is that" can be shortened to *because,* and "this is a subject that" can be restated as *this subject.*) Shorter, simpler messages increase comprehension.

- *Avoid slang.* Phrases such as "the bottom line," "they'll eat this one up," "the home stretch," "I'm all ears," "we need to make some plays," and "let's get rolling" are often very difficult to interpret across cultural boundaries. Although these phrases are common and carry obvious meaning for U.S. managers, foreign employees may have little or no cultural and experiential context in which to interpret what is really being said. Naturally, this does not just apply to Westerners—it is best to avoid slang terms and phrases, regardless of their origin, when delivering feedback in an international management context.[50]

CHAPTER SUMMARY

Few managers enjoy conducting performance evaluations. Adding foreign employees into the mix only makes the task more complex and burdensome. There are many problems associated with the appraisal of expatriate performance and they are not easily overcome. These basic questions loom large: *who* will evaluate the expatriate, *how often* will the evaluation be done, and most importantly, *what* will be evaluated and *how*. The "who" question involves making tradeoffs between whether the evaluation is conducted by a local manager or the home office. Some of the pros and cons of both options were presented, as were general guidelines for delivering feedback in an international context. We also addressed the role culture can play in how feedback is both given and received.

Chapter 10 takes up one of the major consequences of the appraisal decision—an international employee's level of compensation

DISCUSSION QUESTIONS

1. What are some of the problems in evaluating employee performance, and how are these problems complicated in an international setting?
2. Describe the trade-offs and challenges associated with appraising the performance of expatriates.
3. How can a firm better understand the foreign context of an expatriate's job performance?
4. What are some key features to keep in mind when providing feedback about performance levels to employees in different locations with different cultural values?

Developing Your International Career

GIVING NEGATIVE PERFORMANCE FEEDBACK ACROSS CULTURES

Purpose and Instructions

The goal of this exercise is to explore the important task of providing performance feedback to employees and to develop the skills needed to do this effectively across cultures.

Assume that your multinational company has instituted a 360-degree feedback performance evaluation, a system that involves getting feedback from many people in the work setting (boss, subordinate, customers, etc.). One of your jobs as a manufacturing division manager is to meet with subordinates individually to go over their results. You are about to meet with a manufacturing supervisor who has been with the company for seven years. A review of his past performance evaluations indicates an employee who has been reliable and has had above-average productivity. Results from his 360, however, have a definitely negative consistency—he avoids trying new ideas, uses coercion with peers and subordinates, does not listen well, ignores feedback, often fails to return phone calls or other inquiries, blames mistakes on others or tries to cover them up, and is often unavailable when questions arise.

PART A: EVALUATION OF A U.S. SUPERVISOR

Assume that the manufacturing supervisor described above is an American based at a company facility outside of Atlanta. Your instructor will put you into groups of three to six students and ask you to prepare an action plan regarding this situation that will help the supervisor improve. Your instructor may ask you to assign someone to speak for the group in summarizing your plan to the class. The instructor may also ask a member of your group to role-play the meeting with the supervisor. Consider some or all of these questions as you work on the plan:

1. How should the manager approach the meeting with the supervisor? What problems might come up? How can the manager ensure that any messages will be heard?
2. How can the manager and the supervisor listen to one another without becoming confrontational or defensive?
3. How clear are the goals of the action plan? Why will it be helpful?
4. How should the manager proceed if the goals set with the supervisor are met? What if he fails to meet them?

PART B: CROSS-CULTURAL EVALUATION OF A TURKISH SUPERVISOR

In this section of the exercise, you will again prepare a plan to communicate performance feedback to the manufacturing supervisor with the same 360 report described above. Only this time, assume that the supervisor is a Turkish national who is based at a plant outside Istanbul. On your visit to the plant, you have the chance to meet with this supervisor. As you prepare your action plan, consider these questions:

1. What might need to be done differently given that the supervisor is Turkish with Istanbul as the context?
2. What are the key differences between this plan and the one you devised for the U.S. employee? What underlying cultural differences or concerns are reflected in your plan?

Source: Adapted from French, W. (1998). *Human Resources Management* (4th ed.). Boston: Houghton Mifflin, 362–363.

Making the Case for International Understanding

MULTINATIONALS FIND THAT RECRUITING AND RETAINING CHINESE TALENT IS TOUGH BUSINESS[51]

China presents many challenges for foreign companies. Perhaps one of the most surprising is that finding, and retaining, talented Chinese employees is tough business indeed. The reasons have to do with the thousands of foreign companies that establish themselves in China annually—a trend that has been going on for years. Simply put, there are too few Chinese who have the experience and quality education that multinationals desire. Only about 6% of the massive Chinese population has a college degree, and most universities in China (while turning out millions of graduates every year) lag behind their Western counterparts in areas such as accreditation and hands-on training. Plus, many highly skilled Chinese would rather work for a local firm (where the promotion odds are seen as better). This shrinks the pool of talent available to multinationals even further.

Even if a multinational is somehow able to lure top Chinese employees, it is often difficult to hold onto them despite offers of plenty of training and perks added into the mix. In skilled positions, many multinationals in China report turnover rates above 30% annually. It has reached the point at which multinationals would be pleased with a 15% retention rate—a shockingly high rate in most Western countries. As one human resource expert said in describing the situation in China, "If you are in your 30s, have English skills, you can walk right out of one job and into another without breaking a sweat."

Moreover, raising salaries has created bidding wars. Small wonder, then, that salaries in China are estimated to be rising at a 15% annual clip for talented, English-speaking Chinese. For the most part, the salary hikes have not done much to stem attrition or help firms attract top talent. Chinese employees, especially in technical areas, often jump ship to become entrepreneurs or to work in up-and-coming Chinese firms, even for lower salaries. Increasingly desperate multinationals needing technical help in China are doing more hiring right out of college, even though most Chinese engineering graduates have weak English skills and little experience.

An increasingly large number of multinational firms are locked in a talent war with Chinese companies—many of which also now do business abroad. Both sets of firms are after the same pool of young, college-educated Chinese with good English skills and a bit of experience to fill jobs in marketing, finance, manufacturing, and a variety of technical fields. The big question remains how to win in this tough recruiting game, especially since continuing to raise salaries ever higher clearly is not the answer. Of course, the manager charged with dealing with all of this may be a foreign expatriate posted to China, making things doubly tough given the cultural backdrop that is quite different from the United States or Europe.

DISCUSSION QUESTIONS/ASSIGNMENT

Please consider the following general questions and any specific additional ones provided by your professor:

1. If you were in the position described above, what would you do? What tactics might help you recruit and hold the Chinese talent that will be the key to your success as a multinational firm in China?
2. One clue is that other things besides money seem to be increasingly important to skilled Chinese employees. A search firm manager in China put it this way: "Money is a less important reason to change jobs than the potential to grow and have close working relationship with your boss."
3. You can get some ideas by searching for stories in the popular press about how forward-thinking multinationals, such as Motorola, Tyson Foods, and others, are making interesting moves in response to recruiting challenges in China. Borrow or build on some of these ideas in your analysis (and report if required by your instructor).
4. You may also wish to see what the Chinese firms that are competing for potential employees are doing. Companies such as Sohu.com (http://corp.sohu.com) and the popular Chinese search engine Baidu.com seem to be very aggressive recruiters of top talent. Your advice for multinationals could be sharpened by investigating what the competition is doing.

NOTES

1. Briscoe, D. R., Schuler, R. S., & Claus, L. (2009). *International Human Resource Management* (3rd ed.). New York: Routledge; DeCieri, H., Cox, J. W., & Fenwick, M. (2007). A review of international resource management: Integration, interrogation, imitation. *International Journal of Management Reviews*, 9, 281–302; Roberts, K., Kossek, E. E., & Ozeki, C. (1998). Managing the global workforce: Challenges and strategies. *Academy of Management Executive*, 12, 93–106.
2. Briscoe, D. R., Schuler, R. S., & Claus, L. (2009). *International Human Resource Management* (3rd ed.). New York: Routledge; Fey, C. F., & Bjorkman, I. (2001). The effect of human resource management practices on MNC subsidiary performance in Russia. *Journal of International Business Studies*, 32, 59–75; Wright, P. M., McMahan, G. C., & McWilliams, A. (1994). Human resources and sustained competitive advantage: A resource-based perspective. *International Journal of Human Resource Management*, 5, 301–326.
3. Bartlett, C., & Ghoshal, S. (1989). *Managing across Borders: The Transnational Solution*. Boston: Harvard Business School Press; Schuler, R. S., & Florkowski, G. W. (1996). International human resources management. In B. J. Punnett & O. Shenkar (eds.), *Handbook for International Management Research* (351–401). Cambridge, MA: Blackwell; Schuler, R. S., Fulkerson, J. R., & Dowling, P. J. (1991). Strategic performance measurement and management in multinational corporations. *Human Resource Management*, 30, 365–392; Taylor, S., Beechler, S., & Napier, N. (1996). Toward an integrative model of strategic international human resource management. *Academy of Management Review*, 21, 959–985.
4. Porter, M. E. (1985). *Competitive Advantage: Creating and Sustaining Competitive Advantage*. New York: Free Press, 43; Briscoe, D. R., Schuler, R. S., & Claus, L. (2009). *International Human Resource Management* (3rd ed.). New York: Routledge.

5. Carraher, S. M., Sullivan, S. E., & Crocitto, M. M. (2008). Mentoring across global boundaries: An empirical examination of home- and host-country mentors on expatriate career outcomes. *Journal of International Business Studies*, 39, 1310–1326; Dickmann, M., & Doherty, N. (2008). Exploring the career capital impact of international assignments within distinct organizational contexts. *British Journal of Management*, 19, 145–161; Cascio, W., & Bailey, E. E. (1995). International human resource management: The state of research and practice. In O. Shenkar (ed.), *Global Perspectives of Human Resource Management* (15–36). Englewood Cliffs, NJ: Prentice Hall; Hymowitz, C. (2003). European executives give some advice on crossing borders. *Wall Street Journal*, December 2, B1.

6. Reiche, S. B., & Harzing, A. W. K. (2009). International assignments. In A. W. K. Harzing & A. Pinnington (eds.), *International Human Resource Management*. London: Sage.

7. Downes, M., & Thomas, A. S. (2000). Managing overseas assignments to build organizational knowledge. *Human Resource Planning*, 20, 33–48.

8. Carraher, S. M., Sullivan, S. E., & Crocitto, M. M. (2008). Mentoring across global boundaries: An empirical examination of home- and host-country mentors on expatriate career outcomes. *Journal of International Business Studies*, 39, 1310–1326; Hsieh, T. Y., Lavoie, J., & Sarnek, R. A. P. (1999). Are you taking your expatriate talent seriously? *McKinsey Quarterly*, 3, 71–83.

9. Briscoe, D. R., Schuler, R. S., & Claus, L. (2009). *International Human Resource Management* (3rd ed.). New York: Routledge; Phatak, A. V. (1995). *International Dimensions of Management* (4th ed.). Cincinnati, OH: South-Western; Ready, D. A., & Conger, J. A. (2007). How to fill the talent gap. *Wall Street Journal*, September 15–16, R4.

10. Briscoe, D. R., Schuler, R. S., & Claus, L. (2009). *International Human Resource Management* (3rd ed.). New York: Routledge; Phatak, A. V. (1995). *International Dimensions of Management* (4th ed.). Cincinnati, OH: South-Western.

11. Alsop, R. (2007). How students from abroad learn to talk the talk. *Wall Street Journal*, November 6, P11; Bachler, C. J. (1996). Global inpats—Don't let them surprise you. *Personnel Journal*, June, 54–64; Greengard, S. (1996). Gain the edge in the knowledge race. *Personnel Journal*, August, 52–56; Hira, R. (2009). H-1B visas: It's time for an overhaul. *Business Week*, April 13, 63–64; West, L. A., & Bogumil, W. A. (2000). Foreign knowledge workers as a strategic staffing option. *Academy of Management Executive*, 14, 71–84.

12. Latta, G. W. (1998). Global staffing: Are expatriates the only answer? *HR Focus*, July, S1, S2; Woodruff, D. (2000). Distractions make global manager a difficult role. *Wall Street Journal*, November 21, B1, B18.

13. Gong, Y. (2003). Toward a dynamic process model of staffing composition and subsidiary outcomes in multinational enterprises. *Journal of Management*, 29, 259–280.

14. Brewster, C., Wood, G., & Brookes, M. (2008). Similarity, isomorphism or duality? Recent survey evidence on the human resource management policies of multinational corporations. *British Journal of Management*, 19, 320–342; Brewster, C., & Mayrhofer, W. (2008). Comparative human resource management policies and practices. In P. B. Smith, M. S. Peterson, & D. C. Thomas (eds.), *Handbook of Cross-Cultural Management Research* (353–366). Thousand Oaks, CA: Sage.

15. Peterson, R. B., Napier, N. K., & Shul-Shim, W. (2000). Expatriate management: Comparison of MNCs across four parent countries. *Thunderbird International Business Review*, 42, 145–166.

16. Dimmick, T. G. (1995). Human resource management in a Korean subsidiary in New Jersey. In O. Shenkar (ed.), *Global Perspectives of Human Resource Management* (63–70). Englewood Cliffs, NJ: Prentice Hall.

17. Cascio, W., & Bailey, E. E. (1995). International human resource management: The state of research and practice. In O. Shenkar (ed.), *Global Perspectives of Human Resource Management* (15–36). Englewood Cliffs, NJ: Prentice Hall; Daspro, E. (2008). An analysis of U.S. multinationals' recruitment practices in Mexico. *Journal of Business Ethics*, 87, 221–232; Scroggins, W. A., Benson, P. G., Cross, C., & Gilbreath, (2008). Reactions to selection methods: An international comparison. *International Journal of Management*, 25, 203–216.

18. Love, K. G., Bishop, R. C., Heinisch, D. A., & Montei, M. S. (1994). Selection across two cultures: Adapting the selection of American assemblers to meet Japanese job performance demands. *Personnel Psychology*, 47, 837–846.

19. Brewster, C., & Mayrhofer, W. (2008). Comparative human resource management policies and practices. In P. B. Smith, M. S. Peterson, & D. C. Thomas (eds.), *Handbook of Cross-Cultural Management Research* (353–366). Thousand Oaks, CA: Sage; Briscoe, D. R., Schuler, R. S., & Claus, L. (2009). *International Human Resource Management* (3rd ed.). New York: Routledge; Earley, P. C. (1994). Self or group? Cultural effects of training on self-efficacy and performance. *Administrative Science Quarterly*, 39, 89–117.

20. Briscoe, D. R., Schuler, R. S., & Claus, L. (2009). *International Human Resource Management* (3rd ed.). New York: Routledge.

21. Marin, G. S. (2008). National differences in compensation: The influence of the institutional and cultural context. In L. R. Gomez-Mejia & S. Werner (eds.), *Global Compensation: Foundations and Perspectives* (19–28). New York: Routledge.

22. Fey, C. F., Margulis-Yakushev, S., Park, H. J., & Bjorkman, I. (2009). Opening the black box of the relationship between HRM practices and firm performance: A comparison of MNE subsidiaries in the USA, Finland, and Russia. *Journal of International Business Studies*, 40, 690–712.

23. Bjorkman, I., Budhwar, P., Smale, A., & Sumelius, J. (2009). Human resource management in foreign-owned subsidiaries: China versus India. In M. Warner (ed.), *Human Resource Management with "Chinese Characteristics": Facing the Challenges of Globalization* (195–208). New York: Routledge.

24. Oddou, G., & Mendenhall, M. (1991). Expatriate performance appraisal: Problems and solutions. In M. Mendenhall & G. Oddou (eds.), *International Human Resource Management* (364–374). Boston: PWS-Kent.

25. Briscoe, D. R., Schuler, R. S., & Claus, L. (2009). *International Human Resource Management* (3rd ed.). New York: Routledge.

26. Tung, R. I. (2008). Expatriate selection and evaluation. In P. B. Smith, M. S. Peterson, & D. C. Thomas (eds.), *Handbook of Cross-Cultural Management Research* (367–378). Thousand Oaks, CA: Sage.

27. Briscoe, D. R., Schuler, R. S., & Claus, L. (2009). *International Human Resource Management* (3rd ed.). New York: Routledge.

28. Oddou, G., & Mendenhall, M. (1991). Expatriate performance appraisal: Problems and solutions. In M. Mendenhall & G. Oddou (eds.), *International Human Resource Management* (364–374). Boston: PWS-Kent.

29. Briscoe, D. R., Schuler, R. S., & Claus, L. (2009). *International Human Resource Management* (3rd ed.). New York: Routledge.

30. Oddou, G., & Mendenhall, M. (1991). Expatriate performance appraisal: Problems and solutions. In M. Mendenhall & G. Oddou (eds.), *International Human Resource Management* (364–374). Boston: PWS-Kent.

31. Varma, A., Pichler, S., & Srinivas, E. S. (2005). The role of interpersonal affect in performance appraisal: Evidence from two samples—The US and India. *International Journal of Human Resource Management*, 15(11), 2029–2044.

32. Briscoe, D. R., Schuler, R. S., & Claus, L. (2009). *International Human Resource Management* (3rd ed.). New York: Routledge.

33. Cascio, W., & Bailey, E. (1995). International human resource management: The state of research and practice. In O. Shenkar (ed.), *Global Perspectives of Human Resource Management* (15–36). Englewood Cliffs, NJ: Prentice Hall; Gregersen, H., Hite, J., & Black, J. S. (1996). Expatriate performance appraisal in U.S. multinational firms. *Journal of International Business Studies*, 27, 711–738.

34. Briscoe, D. R., Schuler, R. S., & Claus, L. (2009). *International Human Resource Management* (3rd ed.). New York: Routledge.

35. Cascio, W., & Bailey, E. (1995). International human resource management: The state of research and practice. In O. Shenkar (ed.), *Global Perspectives of Human Resource Management* (15–36). Englewood Cliffs, NJ: Prentice Hall; Gregersen, H., Hite, J., & Black, J. S. (1996). Expatriate performance appraisal in U.S. multinational firms. *Journal of International Business Studies*, 27, 711–738.

36. Briscoe, D. R., Schuler, R. S., & Claus, L. (2009). *International Human Resource Management* (3rd ed.). New York: Routledge; Tung, R. I. (2008). Expatriate selection and evaluation. In P. B. Smith, M. S. Peterson, & D. C. Thomas (eds.), *Handbook of Cross-Cultural Management Research* (367–378). Thousand Oaks, CA: Sage.

37. Dowling, P. J., & Schuler, R. S. (1990). *International Dimensions of Human Resource Management*. Boston: PWS Kent.

38. Briscoe, D. R., Schuler, R S., & Claus, L. (2009). *International Human Resource Management* (3rd ed.) New York: Routledge; Garland, J., & Farmer, R. N. (1986). *International Dimensions of Business Policy and Strategy*. Boston: PWS-Kent.

39. Dowling, P. J., & Schuler, R. S. (1990). *International Dimensions of Human Resource Management*. Boston: PWS-Kent.

40. *China Overview—Part 2: Establishing a Presence*. LaSalle Bank/ABN AMRO publication, 2006. Available at www.fpsc.com/RBS/GlobalTradeAdvisor/PDF/China-Establishing_Presence.pdf; www.china-briefing.com; Dowling, P. J., & Schuler, R. S. (1990). *International Dimensions of Human Resource Management*. Boston: PWS-Kent; Webb, L. (2003). Corporate dilemma: Profits idle in China. *Asia Today Online*, January 12, Available at www.asiatoday.com.au/feature_reports.php?id = 38.

41. Evans, P., Pucik, V., & Barsoux, J. L. (2002). *The Global Challenge: Frameworks for International Human Resource Management*. New York: McGraw-Hill/Irwin.

42. Oddou, G., & Mendenhall, M. (1991). Expatriate performance appraisal: Problems and solutions. In M. Mendenhall & G. Oddou (eds.), *International Human Resource Management* (364–374). Boston: PWS-Kent.

43. Oddou, G., & Mendenhall, M. (1991). Expatriate performance appraisal: Problems and solutions. In M. Mendenhall & G. Oddou (eds.), *International Human Resource Management* (364–374). Boston: PWS-Kent.

44. Briscoe, D. R., Schuler, R. S., & Claus, L. (2009). *International Human Resource Management* (3rd ed.). New York: Routledge; Oddou, G., & Mendenhall, M. (1991). Expatriate performance appraisal: Problems and solutions. In M. Mendenhall & G. Oddou (eds.), *International Human Resource Management* (364–374). Boston: PWS-Kent.

45. Cooke, F. L. (2008). Performance management in China. In A. Varma, P. S. Budhwar, & A. DeNisi (eds.), *Performance Management Systems: A Global Perspective* (193–209). New York: Routledge; DeNisi, A., Varma, A., & Budhwar, P. S. (2008). Performance management around the globe: What have we learned? In A. Varma, P. S. Budhwar, & A. DeNisi (eds.), *Performance Management Systems: A Global Perspective* (254–261). New York: Routledge.

46. Ali, A. (1988). A cross-national perspective of managerial work value systems. In R. N. Farmer & E. G. McGowen (eds.), *Advances in International Comparative Management* (151–169). Greenwich, CT: JAI Press; Arvey, R. D., Bhagat, R. S., & Salas, E. (1991). Cross-cultural and cross national issues in personnel and human resources management: Where do we go from here? *Research in Personnel and Human Resources Management*, 9, 367–407; DeNisi, A., Varma, A., & Budhwar, P. S. (2008). Performance management around the globe: What have we learned? In A. Varma, P. S. Budhwar, & A. DeNisi (eds.), *Performance Management Systems: A Global Perspective* (254–261). New York: Routledge.

47. Allen, L. A. (1988). Working better with Japanese managers. *Management Review*, 77, November, 55–56; Morishima, M. (2008). Performance management in Japan. In A. Varma, P. S. Budhwar, & A. DeNisi (eds.), *Performance Management Systems: A Global Perspective* (223–238). New York: Routledge.

48. Bolino, M. C., & Feldman, D. C. (2000). The antecedents and consequences of underemployment among expatriates. *Journal of Organizational Behavior*, 21, 889–911; Early, P. C. (1986). Trust, perceived importance of praise and criticism and work performance: An examination of feedback in the U.S. and England. *Journal of Management*, 12, 457–473; Morton, C. (1988). Bringing manager and managed together. *Industrial Society*, September, 26–27.

49. Vance, C. M., Paik, Y., Boje, B. M., & Stage, H. D. (1993). *A Study of the Generalizability of Performance Appraisal Design Characteristics across Four Southeast Asian Countries: Assessing the Extent of Divergence Effect*. Paper presented at the Academy of Management conference, Atlanta.

50. Stull, J. S. (1988). Giving feedback to foreign-born employees. *Management Solutions*, 33, 42–45.

51. Sovich, N. (2006). Western firms find hiring, retention in China surprisingly tough. *Wall Street Journal*, August 11, A4; Wozniak, L. (2003). Companies in China struggle to train, retain qualified managers. *Wall Street Journal*, December 30, A8; Conlin, M. (2007). Go-go-going to pieces in China. *Business Week*, April 23, 88; Hymowitz, C. (2005). Recruiting top talent in China takes a boss who likes to coach. *Wall Street Journal*, April 26, B1; Zhu, C. J., Cooper, B., De Cieri, H., Thomson, S. B., & Zhao, S. (2009). Devolvement of HR practices in transitional economies: Evidence from China. In M. Warner (ed.), *Human Resource Management with "Chinese Characteristics": Facing the Challenges of Globalization* (71–85). New York: Routledge.

Rewarding and Compensating International Employees

> Multinational companies whose employees move from country to country face predictable but widespread and daunting compensation challenges.
>
> —Mercer Worldwide Consulting[1]

International business can be tough going. This chapter reviews all the vagaries and difficulties faced by expatriates. There's the constant travel, little contact with friends or family, trouble in understanding others, difficulty in getting one's favorite foods, and even getting used to driving—just to name a few. Adding poor compensation to this list might be just too much to take for many employees. Conversely, being properly compensated for tough overseas duty might be one of the saving graces for this tough job of expatriate.

REWARDS AND COMPENSATION IN THE MULTINATIONAL FIRM

Managing employee performance is challenging, a task much compounded by having employees scattered all around the world—many of whom embrace different cultural values and who experience localized practices for performance management that vary considerably. This makes the already painful process of performance appraisal and the provision of feedback all the more distasteful.

One of the main reasons that multinationals spend time on performance evaluation is that it helps set and manage compensation levels around the world. This is a complex and dynamically changing task that is difficult for managers and firms to administer and conduct. One reason is that reward and compensation systems are varied, complex, and often customized to a firm, let alone a country or location. Regardless, if there is one universal, it is that fair compensation is necessary for the long-term success of the firm.

This process is full of challenges. One is that compensation includes everything that the firm does to recognize and reward employees for their performance. While a casual observer might think this involves only pay or promotions, this is not the case. In fact, employees closely watch the many different outcomes distributed by their firm and received by their peers and others. As shown in Chapter 5, a dizzying number of rewards are possible: office space; parking; training opportunities; preferred assignments; various incentive plans; living allowances; and more tangible rewards such as pay, benefits, and other perks. As employees rise in the firm, compensation may also include perquisites such as extra vacation time, stock options, and retirement contributions. All of this compensation must be accurately juggled and divvied up consistent with corporate policy.

What is more challenging for multinationals is that their systems need to account for the fact that living costs, attitudes about pay, and laws governing compensation can vary considerably from country to country. Multinationals must account for all the variety in human resource practices that exist across the locations where they do business and have employees. Companies must also deal with the special compensation challenges associated with sending expatriates abroad, a topic addressed later in this chapter. Overall, the compensation systems used by multinationals are typically designed and implemented with several key goals in mind:

- Attract and retain the best people to staff positions worldwide.
- Ease the transfer of people to various firm locations.
- Maintain consistent and fair compensation levels for all employees wherever they are, taking local differences into account.
- Maintain compensation levels that align well with competitors while also closely watching costs.[2]

Meeting these goals is a task that confronts managers in most industries and fields. It is central to employee life in and out of the workplace. This is a complex process, with great need for communication and coordination.[3]

The Meaning of Compensation

One of the many challenges in doing business across cultures is breaking through language barriers—something already discussed in Chapter 3. But even when a language is mastered, there is often a culture barrier that needs to be bridged. Even the most tangible topics can have a special cultural twist. So it might be for compensation—views of what this means and entails vary across cultures.

Compensation in the United States is often seen as a swap—employees provide effort and output while receiving wages and benefits in return. While this exchange model of compensation is more common in Western cultures, differences in perspective remain nevertheless. For instance, in Germany the word for compensation also implies achievement. Apparently, the word originated among shoemakers who custom-fit shoes to the buyer's feet. Shoes that "measured up" were ones that deserved compensation. In contrast, the Japanese word for "compensation" suggests protection, consistent with a more traditional, paternalistic Japanese employment system. Japanese employees may see entitlement and obligation as important components of the compensation they receive from employers. Indeed, the Swedish word for compensation means "making equal." Sweden has a considerable number of laws that regulate wages. One expert suggests that decisions about pay in Sweden are effectively taken out of the hands of the organization and placed in the hands of regulators. As a result, many Swedish organizations have very similar pay systems.[4] These are just a few examples, and there is variation within each country. Overall, however, this suggests that firms and managers need to be aware of differences in expectations about the employment relationship that may come with doing business across borders.[5]

Employee Pay Across Borders

There are big differences in compensation amounts and types across borders. Multinational firms have been keenly aware of this and may be partly responsible for an increase in the outsourcing of professional service jobs and others. For example, between 2003 and 2008, McKinsey (a large global consulting firm) estimated that an additional 2.6 million offshored service jobs were created globally. Most of these were in low-wage countries such as India, Hungary, and the Philippines.[6] Granted, some have reversed outsourcing decisions because of unanticipated or newly risen logistical and control challenges that actually increase costs. Other firms, however, will continue to move their work abroad because of wage differentials and other factors. In June 2010, for instance, Whirlpool closed a plant in Indiana (wiping out 1,100 jobs) and moved the work to Mexico. Whirlpool cited the need to "reduce excess capacity and improve costs," noting some $275 million per year would be saved by the move. While the company did not break out labor savings, it is likely that less expensive Mexican workers played a role in Whirlpool's move. While direct compensation comparisons should be made with caution, Mexican manufacturing workers earn, on average, roughly 11.5% of their U.S. counterparts.[7]

There are many nations where workers earn just a fraction of the wages typically offered in the United States. In Sri Lanka, for example, the average hourly rate is only 2.5% of U.S. rates. There are also many countries with roughly similar wage rates to the United States, at least in manufacturing (e.g., Canada, France), as well as many whose wage rates are much higher (e.g., Germany, Norway). Table 10.1 lists examples of average wage rates for manufacturing workers in many countries (in U.S. dollars). While these data paint only part of the cost picture for firms interested in foreign relocation, these wage rates are instructive. Labor cost differences do not just help explain the actions of U.S. firms, but they also help explain why some foreign firms seek lower-priced talent elsewhere. Germany's BMW, for example, has built factories in the United States. German manufacturing wage rates are 153% of comparable U.S. wages. For U.S. companies, the much lower costs in Mexico for labor, combined with easy access to the U.S. market, are among the reasons why thousands of firms (many of U.S. origin) have established *maquiladoras*—plants set up right across the U.S. border in Mexico.[8] Wage differentials can also explain why some high-paying and prestige professions, such as law and accounting, are also being outsourced.[9]

Average wage data, however, are not very precise if companies are trying to understand compensation patterns in specific industries. Even within countries, large differences in compensation rates exist (e.g., between northern and southern

Table 10.1
Hourly Compensation Costs for Manufacturing Workers in Different Countries

Country/Region	Average Hourly Rate in U.S. Dollars (as of December 2007)
The Americas	
United States	$25.27
Brazil	$ 5.96
Canada	$29.08
Mexico	$ 2.92
Europe	
Belgium	$35.45
Czech Republic	$ 8.20
Denmark	$42.29
France	$28.57
Germany	$38.63
Hungary	$ 6.60
Ireland	$29.04
Netherlands	$34.07
Norway	$48.56
Poland	$ 6.21
Portugal	$ 7.70
Spain	$20.98
Sweden	$36.03
United Kingdom	$30.18
Asia/Pacific Rim	
Australia	$30.17
Hong Kong	$5.78
Japan	$19.75
New Zealand	$17.27

(Continued)

Table 10.1 (Continued)

Country/Region	Average Hourly Rate in U.S. Dollars (as of December 2007)
South Korea	$1.13
Singapore	$8.47
Sri Lanka	$0.61
Taiwan	$6.58

Source: Adapted from U.S. Department of Labor, Bureau of Labor Statistics, Office of Productivity and Technology. (2007). *Hourly Compensation Costs for Production Workers in Manufacturing.* December 14. Available at ftp://ftp.bls.gov/pub/special.requests/ForeignLabor/pwind3133naics.txt.

U.S. states). Moreover, estimates vary about true wage differences across countries. For example, some estimates place Mexican wage rates closer to their U.S. counterparts (approximately 40% of U.S. wages) compared to the 11.5% figure shown in Table 10.1. The higher estimates might include bonuses that are distributed. There is a commonly observed custom in Mexico of paying a Christmas bonus equivalent to one month's pay. Mexico also requires firms to distribute a share of their pretax profits to employees and mandates that workers be paid 365 days a year. Nevertheless, even when wages are adjusted by these factors, they continue to yield significant savings for companies from more expensive labor markets such as the United States—everything else being equal.[10]

Senior Executive Compensation Across Countries

Cross-national differences also emerge when we consider the compensation of executives of U.S. firms relative to their peers in foreign companies. The United States has earned a reputation for paying its senior leaders more than other countries anywhere else. In Chapter 5, we showed that CEO total compensation in the United States was twice as high as the next closest country (Britain). Part of this reflects differences regarding how senior executive compensation is structured. These are connected to underlying cultural values in a society (e.g., individualist, performance-oriented norms in the United States) and how compensation is viewed as a result.[11]

In U.S. firms, senior executive compensation is often heavily weighted to variable performance measures connected to stock prices (e.g., stock options)—with performance bonuses and base salary being smaller slices. According to one survey, roughly 60% of a top executive's compensation in the United States comes from such longer-term incentives, with base salary and performance bonuses accounting for the remaining 40%. This can produce some mind-boggling results. For instance, not long ago, one U.S. CEO took home a "small" base salary of $4.6 million while also pocketing over $650 million in long-term compensation. In contrast, almost 60% of the compensation earned by executives in Nordic countries comes from base salary, while in Germany this figure is about 80%, with relatively little exposure to performance-based incentives.[12] In recent years, there has been a backlash in the United States against heavy reliance on such incentives and bonuses for executives, particularly in the wake of a deep recession and financial crisis. Some U.S. firms have scaled back their compensation packages. But whether this makes a long-term dent in the compensation advantage that U.S. executives have traditionally enjoyed over their foreign counterparts remains to be seen.[13] Indeed, early data on executive earning as the economy began to improve after the recession suggests that they are back in the highly paid cloud.

Perks and Other Compensation

Although typically not large enough to make up for the compensation lead enjoyed by executives at U.S. companies, foreign companies often provide a variety of perks to help offset the bite taken by taxes. Perks are typically nonmonetary forms of compensation that are given to executives in recognition of their status or performance. For example, consider the package received by Portuguese executives, which may include a maid, a gardener, and a washerwoman. In addition, executives will probably have a company car (with gas allowance), company-provided housing, a monthly expense allowance, and paid utilities. A Mexican executive may receive a company car and chauffeur, along with a certain amount of groceries and liquor delivered to his or her home twice a month. In Japan, high tax rates mean that firms sometimes pay up to 50% of mortgage interest for all employees, and, as they move up the ladder, they get more. Executives may also have a chauffeured car at their disposal, a larger expense account, and paid memberships at exclusive golf and social clubs (known in Japan as "castles"). An American working in Japan said this about one of his Japanese colleagues: "Each time he got promoted, he moved to a better house. And as his expense account grew, the bars he'd visit would get better."[14] As the economic challenges of the last decade mount for Japanese firms, these packages have declined.

Vacation Time: Less in the United States, More in Europe

Another important part of compensation packages is vacation time, and this, too, varies considerably from country to country. Workers in the United States and Canada have among the fewest paid days off of any country in the world. Table 10.2 shows that many countries offer their experienced employees 30 to 40 paid days off (combining paid vacation days and paid public holidays) compared to the 25 days workers in similar positions enjoy at large U.S. firms. Moreover, U.S. companies are not required by law to give workers a minimum number of days off—paid or unpaid. On a regional basis, Table 10.2 also reveals that European, Middle Eastern, and African countries tend to be the most generous with vacation time, whereas firms in North America provide the least. In between are companies in the Asia-Pacific region, although wide variability also exists across nations there, with some providing large amounts of vacation time (Japan) and others less (Thailand).[15]

Table 10.2
Paid Days Off Provided by Firms in Countries around the World

Country/Region	Paid Vacation Days (Minimum)	Public Holidays (with Pay)	Total Days Off
The Americas			
United States[a]	15 (typical large firm)	10 (typical large firm)	25 (typical large firm)
Canada	10	10 (average)	20
Asia/Pacific			
Hong Kong	14	12	26
India	12	19	31
Indonesia	12	13	25
Japan	20	15	35
Pakistan	14	14	28
Philippines	5	14	19
Singapore	14	12	26
South Korea	19	11	30
Taiwan	14	11	25
Thailand	6	13	19
Vietnam	14	8	22
Europe/Scandinavia			
Belgium	20	10	30

Table 10.2 (Continued)

Country/Region	Paid Vacation Days (Minimum)	Public Holidays (with Pay)	Total Days Off
Bulgaria	20	12	32
Czech Republic	20	11	31
Denmark	25	10	35
France	30	10	40
Germany	24	10	34
Greece	25	12	37
Hungary	23 (if > 21 yrs old)	10	33
Ireland	20	9	29
Italy	20	11	31
Lithuania	28	12	40
Poland	26	10	36
Spain	22	14	36
Sweden	25	11	36
United Kingdom	20	8	28
Middle East/Africa			
Egypt	21	16	37
Israel	24	16 (avg.)	40
Lebanon	15	18	33
Morocco	21	19	40
South Africa	21	12	33
UAE	30	9	39

Sources: Adapted from Sahadi, Jeanne. (2007). Who gets the most (and least) vacation. June 14. Available at www.CNNMoney.com; Employee statutory and public holiday entitlements: Global comparisons. (2009). Available at www.mercer.com.

[a]Numbers for the United States reflect common practice among big companies. Unlike in most countries, U.S. federal law does not require employers to provide a minimum number of vacation days and holidays off, either unpaid or paid. In contrast, the European Union requires paid public holidays plus a minimum of 20 paid days off annually. For comparison purposes, data are for employees with 10 years of experience.

Just because workers have vacation time does not mean that they will take that time off. Americans and Japanese are known for either not taking allotted vacation time or cashing it out instead. Likewise, South Koreans work more hours on average than any of the other 30 highly industrialized countries, including Japan and the United States. Yet South Koreans are generally loath to take their allotted vacation time. Years of government efforts to inculcate a national sense of urgency regarding the economy, combined with some cultural tendencies, can explain this. The *Making the Case for International Understanding* box picks up this issue and asks you to investigate and compare work norms around the globe. You will see that the South Korean government is now working overtime to try to convince workers to take time off, in part because of a national-level problem regarding productivity.

Explaining Compensation Differences Across Countries

Overall, a working understanding of a specific country's laws and customs is needed to fully grasp the compensation costs associated with doing business there.[16] Some evidence suggests, however, that there is increasing similarity in compensation practices among countries with similar cultures. In fact, one study found that cultural grouping (e.g., Asian, Latin, and European) explained compensation practices much better than did country-level customs and laws.[17]

Cultural values may partly explain some compensation differences seen across countries that persist despite evidence of convergence of other human resource practices such as performance-based pay. Given the desire of many firms to simplify and better manage their compensation systems globally, it is surprising that such differences still exist. Indeed, while some studies suggest that up to half of multinationals manage aspects of employee performance appraisal on a global basis, 75% or more allow pay, bonuses, and perks to be administered locally. This suggests the strength and longevity of culture-driven nuances in compensation around the world. Consequently, multinationals that abandon local or regional practices may do so at their peril.[18]

In the United States, compensation is commonly viewed as an exchange based on deservingness—greater contributions should result in greater compensation. In essence, this is an equity norm, a value strongly embraced in U.S. culture and therefore by U.S. firms. As discussed in chapter 5, U.S. firms are more likely to operate on this equity principle than firms in any other country.

In those countries where equity norms are weaker or where other cultural values are more prominent than in the United States, compensation has evolved differently. Consider France and its norms of equality and workers' rights to speak up. The traditional bonus system used by many French companies is an approach not tied closely to performance. Many employees receive an extra month's salary before vacation time in July or August and again before Christmas. This pattern leads many French employees to think in terms of net pay. In fact, when they are offered a monthly salary, new French employees may be quick to ask, "Is it net or gross?" and "How many times a year do I get this salary?" Many French employees have become used to these bonuses and consider them as part of base pay. This has caused problems for French companies trying to implement performance-based bonuses. For example, a performance-based bonus was paid by one firm for two straight years because the company did well. The third year, however, saw a drop in performance and no bonus was paid. French workers did not accept this and threatened to close down the plant. The bonus had become viewed as an expected benefit. The company eventually relented and paid the bonus.[19]

Mexico carries this practice a step further by systematizing worker acquisition of compensation extras. Mexico has an acquired rights law, which mandates that if a bonus or benefit is given at least two years in a row, it becomes the employee's right to receive it in the future.[20] The Japanese view is traditionally paternalistic as well as egalitarian—slowly increasing rewards are provided for length and extent of service and for skill acquisition rather than for performance. Wage increases are more graduated and a higher percentage of total compensation is fixed (up to 80%) than in the United States. One research study asked managers to distribute pay raises to employees described as low and high performers. The data showed that U.S. managers gave bigger raises to the high performers and lower raises to the poor performers than did Japanese managers. Japanese managers gave roughly twice as much of a raise to low performers and about 80% less to high performers than did the Americans. This restriction in range of pay likely reflects the cultural influence noted above. Stated differently, the results show a stronger link between perfor mance and pay decisions for U.S. than Japanese managers.[21]

Although traditional practices persist in Japan and other Asian countries, the pressures for change also exist. How far and how fast things change, however, remains to be seen. And as we have said, some local and regional practices will persist and perhaps thrive—even in multinationals. Nevertheless, a recent survey of Japanese human resource managers shows that the relative impact of seniority versus merit in determining pay raises has been dropping over the past generation. Top Japanese firms such as Toshiba and Toyota have been offering higher salaries and larger incentive packages to younger employees, including raising the proportion of compensation that is at risk via its tie to performance. The labor market in China is also significantly different than it was only a decade ago.[22] Research shows that new pay for performance methods resulted in greater personal job responsibility (consciousness) among Chinese professionals (engineers). On the other hand, the data also showed a negative effect on more traditional views such as commitment to the organization and even level of interpersonal helping on the job.[23]

Speaking of Toyota, management there has been shaking things up for the past decade or so—sometimes in ways inconsistent with Japanese traditions. The following *Culture Clash* details these leadership-driven changes at Toyota and illustrates that Japanese who advocate equity as the basis of compensation can still attract considerable attention, if not resistance.

CULTURE CLASH

The Nail That Stuck Out at Toyota

Hiroshi Okuda led Toyota Motor Company as it slowly, but continuously, transformed itself into what many feel was, and still is, the best car company in the world. Okuda joined the fledgling company in 1955, rising to president and later chairman before stepping down to become a senior advisor to the board in 2006. But that road to power was neither easy nor quiet.

The Japanese have a saying that "the nail that sticks out gets hammered down." And, indeed, from the start of his career, Okuda seemed to be that nail. He was the antithesis of the quiet, cautious Japanese business executive. To start with, his six-feet-plus frame made him stand out in a crowd—whether he was in Detroit or Tokyo. He was also very outspoken, frank, and fluent in English. Regularly, he would challenge, push, and—heresy of heresies—publicly criticize. For example, a question from a U.S. journalist once prompted Okuda to openly criticize the styling of a Ford vehicle. Similarly frank comments about the superiority of Toyota's Lexus plant in Japan over a plant in Kentucky also drew attention. Toyota's flustered public relations department muttered off record that if you stick out all over the place, you are going to get hammered down. Even a friend said of Okuda, "He sticks out all over the place."

There is no doubt that he stuck out at Toyota. Okuda was the first person outside the Toyoda family to run the company. He changed many things about Toyota in an effort to avoid what he called "big company disease." Indeed, Toyota was due for a shakeup, given its erratic performance in the years leading up to Okuda's taking over. Beyond the many problems with the Japanese economy, Toyota was also dealing with managers who were not up to the task of reshaping and redirecting the company. One observer noted that Okuda's predecessor "was very civilized but a lousy businessman." Toyota by then had become big and lethargic, qualities the company has been accused of possessing again recently.

Part of Okuda's solution to this problem was to change entrenched management attitudes. He believed that only younger executives had the vigor and imagination to run a big company like Toyota. Accordingly, he announced a new policy that took titles away from general managers at age 55 and managers at age 50. They were allowed to stay on with the firm, but with greatly reduced responsibilities. Needless to say, this ruffled some feathers.

The steps taken by Okuda completely overhauled Toyota's traditional seniority-based promotion system, which was replaced with a new emphasis on merit. "I had no choice," he said. "Employing young people is vital to any company." Okuda also cleared away the dead wood from the board of directors and retired about a third of Toyota's top executives. These moves are rare in most companies, let alone in traditional Japanese companies that revere seniority. Nevertheless, younger executives were put in place, some jumping several grades with one promotion.

Okuda was driven by his strategic assessment of the automotive industry and where it was headed. And pushing Toyota to be more efficient was not going to be enough to keep the firm growing. Instead, it had to push into new territory, often in the face of industry skeptics. It was on his watch that Toyota not only perfected its world-class assembly methods using the Toyota Production System but also started building cars in the United States. Plus, it launched the Prius—the first mass-market hybrid in the world, sold first in 1997 in Japan and then released around the world in 2001. Since then, more than 1 million have been sold in the United States, and Toyota has produced a variety of other hybrid electric vehicles that have helped make the company a leader in green technologies. As Okuda put it, "We need to continue innovating." Sounds like good advice for Toyota and other firms—now and in the years ahead.[24]

Table 10.3 summarizes many of the compensation system differences referenced throughout this chapter by presenting how cultural values in specific countries are linked to their compensation practices. This table does not capture all the differences that exist across countries with respect to compensation, nor does it reflect the ongoing evolution of those practices as countries, economies, and values develop. Instead, Table 10.3 serves as a reminder that taking the time to identify where and why differences exist will pay dividends for international managers. Data support this view that expatriate compensation preferences are tied to cultural environment and that it is possible to strike a balance between standardization and the needs of a far-flung and heterogeneous set of employees.[25]

THE CHALLENGES OF EXPATRIATE COMPENSATION

We turn our attention now to a complicated and important issue for multinationals: how to construct compensation and benefit packages for a key group of employees—expatriates. Chapter 11 will discuss many important issues associated with using these home-country employees in overseas operations, but for now we focus on only the compensation challenges for expatriates.

Grappling with Expatriate Costs... and Employee Comparisons

Not only do multinationals have to grapple with a host of cross-national differences such as laws, taxes, and compensation practices, they also need to ensure

Table 10.3
Selected Compensation Practices across Cultures and Countries

Cultural Dimension	Sample Countries	Characteristics of Compensation System
Strong individualism	United States, Canada, New Zealand, United Kingdom	Performance-based Equity used to distribute compensation Rewards given for individual efforts
Strong collectivism	Indonesia, Japan, Korea, Singapore	Nonperformance variables (e.g., seniority) matter in raises Group compensation schemes often are successful Equality/need are important norms
Low power distance	United States, United Kingdom, Denmark, Australia	Wage gap between lower and higher jobs often not that great Profit sharing likely to be successful
High power distance	Malaysia, Mexico, Philippines, Spain	Compensation tied to place in the social structure Large salary gap between workers and management
Low uncertainty avoidance	Singapore, Sweden, Canada, United States	High level of variable/contingent compensation Bonuses/pay at risk depending on performance
High uncertainty avoidance	Greece, Japan, Korea, Portugal	Highly structured, lock-step compensation plans Centralized decision making/evaluation Discretionary pay minimized

Sources: Adapted from Gomez-Mejia, L. R., & Welbourne, T. (1991). Compensation strategies in a global context. *Human Resource Planning, 14*, 29–41; Hodgetts, R. M., & Luthans, F. (1993). U.S. multinationals' compensation strategies for local management: Cross-cultural interpretations. *Compensation and Benefits Review, 25*, 42–48.

that their employees around the world believe that the various compensation and benefits packages they have are fair. Multinationals do not want expatriates to feel cheated by virtue of being sent from an affordable home-office location in Columbus, Ohio, to London, England, or Chongqing, China. Firms know that their expatriates will engage in comparisons of their compensation packages. After all, a foreign assignment is not like taking a flight to Los Angeles, where you might pay several hundred dollars more than the person sitting next to you, simply based on when and where you purchased your ticket. In that situation, it is unlikely you will feel deprived or that you will be interested or able to compare your ticket price to what others paid. The expatriate, however, has both opportunity and motive to compare. A strong sense of unfairness can result when they compare their compensation with other expatriates and find that what they receive relative to their peers for this tough assignment is subpar. This is not a trivial or isolated concern. According to one study, nearly 80% of the expatriates surveyed were unhappy with their compensation and benefits package.[26]

Nor do multinationals relish the thought of local employees bristling at overpaid expatriates who seem to parachute in from the parent company with fat salaries and plenty of special perks. One study found that local employees working for foreign expatriates in China felt that the huge pay gap between the two groups was unfair. Moreover, this had negative effects on Chinese employees' morale and commitment to the firm. To blunt this, experts recommend that expatriates work hard to build trust with local employees and to redirect comparisons to other local employees (who are often paid less).[27]

Overall, firms must juggle very real cost differences (e.g., Beijing is more expensive than Indianapolis) and the fairness comparisons made by employees (both inside and outside of the firm). Some firms are tackling this problem by moving away from packages that are tied to its home country. Such firms now believe that they can offer less in the way of inducements to recruit expatriates to start with, or they simply want to reduce large pay gaps between expatriates and local employees with whom they will work side by side. Either way, the high cost issue can explain why firms are constantly on the lookout for new ways to compensate expatriates. For instance, according to one survey, the cumulative net additional cost of sending one expatriate abroad (accompanied by a spouse and children) for three years averages around $750,000. In some expensive locations, the total additional cost for three years may run $1 million or more. Generally speaking, an international relocation costs up to five times as much as a domestic move for most companies.[28]

These figures are sky high and beg the question of what accounts for all these costs. There are the usual things involved in any move, including interviewing and hiring and actual moving costs. Each of these factors is more expensive, sometimes greatly so, for an expatriate than for a domestic relocation. But that is only part of the story. Most multinationals go well beyond this by providing an assortment of costly benefits (e.g., housing allowances, food supplements, cars, drivers, and insurance). Costs jump further because of financial increments and assistance with acclimating to the foreign culture. Table 10.4 provides detailed examples of these additional expatriate costs—some of which we will discuss in more detail later.

Multinationals should first focus on creating a consistent and comprehensive compensation and benefits policy for expatriates that will help educate and inform all employees about company goals and what expatriates can expect. This would

Table 10.4
Potential Sources of Costs Associated with Expatriation

Direct Payments/Reimbursements	Support for Adjustment to Global Assignment
Tax reduction/equalization	Home leave (4–6 weeks)
Housing allowance	Emergency leave
Furnishing allowance	Personal security
Education allowance	Car/driver
Hardship/foreign service premium	Domestic help
Currency protection	Spouse employment
Goods and services differential	Child care provider
Temporary living allowance	Language/translation services
Car/transportation allowance	Cultural training
Assignment completion bonus	Repatriation assistance
Extension bonus	Social club fees
Help renting U.S. home	Imported food and other goods

Source: Adapted from Milkovich, G. T., & Newman, J. M. (2004). *Compensation*. Chicago: Irwin.

include how much customization across locations is allowed while also communicating that expatriates will not profit more by going to one place over another. These are tough issues to balance. Regardless, an effective compensation plan for expatriates will likely include the following:

- Some form of incentive for an employee to accept an expatriate assignment (e.g., money, benefits, career mobility/advancement)
- Maintenance of a reasonable/comparable standard of living
- Support for any trailing family members
- Plans to repatriate the employee back into the home country after the foreign assignment concludes (see Chapter 11 for these details)[29]

METHODS FOR COMPENSATING EXPATRIATES

These recommendations for expatriate compensation plans raise the question of exactly how multinationals can go about constructing those plans in the first place. Fortunately, a variety of options exist. We will review the most popular approaches next, including the ad hoc, localization, and balance sheet methods. These are not mutually exclusive, and, depending on the circumstances, multinationals may use all of them in different situations. But in choosing between these methods, multinationals should factor in concerns such as how long the assignment will last, where and why the expatriate is going, and the expatriate's level within the firm.[30]

The Ad Hoc Approach

This method has serious drawbacks, especially for larger multinationals with many expatriates. Indeed, it tends to be used more by smaller or emerging multinationals with little experience overseas and who must often send an expatriate to fix problems abroad. That can mean doing a quick search and then paying whatever is necessary to entice an employee to go. In operation, the ad hoc method is simple—the company and its expatriates negotiate on a case-by-case basis to cover the costs inherent in a foreign assignment.[31] Its virtues are clear: it is quick, you do not need a lot of expert advice, and you can get on with things quickly. But, while the ad hoc method has some merit, there are a few specific drawbacks whose effect can be considerable. One such drawback is that there is high potential for unfair treatment across expatriates. Some may be better negotiators or communicators than others. A relatively naïve employee can thus accept the arrangement in good faith but find out later that his or her expenses in London are way beyond expectation. Likewise, there could be negative firm-level effects, including an inability to systematically track pay and benefit packages and a lack of organizational learning about the country (e.g., taxes, cost of living, type of housing); mistakes are repeated and good practices not noted.

A company may come out ahead in the short run by successfully negotiating down its costs with individual expatriates, but this requires skills and due diligence on the firm's part. Still, if employees later find out later that their overseas costs are much higher or that others negotiated a much better deal, there is the potential for trouble, which is hardly conducive to good morale, much less good performance.[32] For these reasons, firms have considered several other methods.

The Localization Method

This more systematic method involves paying the expatriate essentially the same as local employees in similar positions. Localization may be especially useful when expatriates want to extend their stay in particular locations or are interested in being permanent expatriates who travel from assignment to assignment. In both cases, the expatriate is less likely to use home-country wage standards in evaluating his or her compensation. Localization is much easier to apply when the expatriate moves to a country with a higher standard of living (e.g., from Mexico to the United States). If, for example, expatriates are moving to Vietnam from Europe or the United States, it may be much more difficult for them to accept a lower level of compensation. Localization, however, is rarely used in its entirety or in only this way. Variations of this approach, with adjustments (e.g., to base pay, allowances, retirement, etc.) are often applied, which in effect render it a hybrid (of localization and ad hoc).[33]

While these adjustments are practically useful, they make localization subject to the same problems suffered by the ad hoc approach. The use of the localization model continues to rise in hyper-developing markets such as China—where local talent, especially at senior levels, is in short supply and where labor market dynamics are volatile. As living conditions in China have improved and the country is often viewed as a great place for career development, expatriates are increasingly interested in extending their stays. We recently spoke to one such person, who, reflecting on the changes in Beijing over the last five years, said he loves to travel there now and could see himself being stationed there. These attractive features, combined with a desire to reduce costs, have led many multinationals to use the localization method for their expatriates in China. In a 2009 survey of Asia-based multinationals, 57% of respondents were considering localization for expatriates in China (up from 39% in 2008). Likewise, just over a quarter of the Western multinationals responding were considering localization in China.

Granted, there are complexities associated with localization. For example, foreigners typically cannot participate in local pension plans or the Chinese versions of social security programs found in the United States and Europe. Moreover, being posted in China may preclude expatriates from participating in their home-country retirement plans. Consequently, multinationals will sometimes make extra payments to compensate for this, enroll expatriates in third-country pension plans, or, if possible, retain them on the home-country pension system. Clearly, this offsets some of the cost advantages of localization—including the savings from paying expatriates at local wage rates. Multinationals will need to carefully weigh the outcomes expected from a localization strategy.[34]

The Balance Sheet Model

The most common approach to expatriate compensation is the balance sheet model. Nearly three-quarters of firms who responded to a recent global survey said that they use this approach. The key aim of the model is that expatriates should not suffer a loss as a result of an international assignment—any loss should be built back up. The resulting package should provide the expatriate with roughly the same purchasing power in the foreign location as they would enjoy at home. In other words, the objective is to balance out the cost differences between the expatriate's home country lifestyle and his or her foreign assignment location. If the lifestyle can be roughly duplicated, and the firm keeps the expatriate "whole," most firms and employees are more satisfied. Because the balance sheet model is by far the most common approach, the remainder of this chapter details this approach.[35]

In practice, many multinational firms go beyond efforts to ensure a standard of living and purchase power for the expatriate that resembles that of home. Some also provide additional incentives to entice employees to accept assignments or to compensate them for the hardship of being assigned abroad. In recent years, though, costs have escalated, and some multinationals have backed away from adding on extra incentive pay and perks. One recent survey showed that between 25% and 30% of multinationals either do not offer expatriates any additional incentive pay or are in the process of phasing those out. And even if they still offer those incentives, the efforts have been to make only the necessary living cost adjustments. Others have added strong encouragement to expatriates to adapt to local lifestyles and standards whenever possible. We will review more specific cost-saving measures below. In the meantime, first consider how the balance sheet method works.[36]

The balance sheet method starts the process of smoothing out cost of living and tax differences across countries by dividing expenses into four basic categories: (1) housing, (2) income taxes, (3) goods and services, and (4) savings reserve or discretionary component. Typically, expatriates would receive allowances to cover the increased taxes, more expensive housing, and higher living costs (e.g., for food, utilities, etc.) encountered abroad. No approach is perfect. The way that multinationals calculate these allowances is complex and somewhat controversial—if they calculate them at all. More often than not, multinationals rely on consulting firms such as AIRINC or Mercer to do this for them. These firms are more than willing to sell their services to help multinationals design a custom balance sheet approach, provide information on local compensation practices and living costs, secure housing and relocation support, provide tax services, and even administer the entire expatriate program. We will consider monetary incentives next before examining expatriate expense categories in more detail.[37]

Foreign Service Premiums, Hardship, and Danger Pay

One thing the balance sheet does not impact is the expatriate's base salary. Using the balance sheet method, salary is determined in the same way as it would be for domestic employees. That is, if domestic employees receive 4% average pay raises, then so would expatriates. Simply put, the particular economic conditions in the foreign location to which expatriates are assigned do not shape their base salary. Beyond base pay, however, the balance sheet can have a profound impact on expatriates' overall compensation abroad if multinationals are offering one or more of the following incentives: foreign service premiums, hardship, and/or danger pay.

Even at today's often reduced incentive levels, the total value of a package can be impressive. Some multinationals still pay a premium or incentive to the expatriate for taking the foreign assignment (often ranging between 10% and 30% of base pay). Expatriates may also receive hardship pay if they are posted to locations where living conditions are more difficult than in the home country (e.g., extreme weather, limited access to common goods and services, etc.). In locations where expatriates may be physically at risk (e.g., civil unrest, violence aimed at foreigners), additional danger pay may be stacked on top of foreign service premiums and hardship pay.[38]

It is difficult to make such hardship judgments, even for firms with extensive international experience. Consequently, many multinationals look to widely available rating schemes. The most referred to approach is the U.S. Department of State's *Hardship Post Differentials Guidelines*, which include allowances and benefits for personnel being posted abroad in difficult locations. Anyone can look up the specific incentives offered by the Department of State based on location (e.g., hardship pay or danger pay). The Department of State posts thousands of employees overseas and offers danger and hardship pay in 5% increments of base pay, starting at 0% and going up to 35%. For example, at the time of publication of this book, posts to Sydney, Australia, or Brussels, Belgium, would not yield extra danger or hardship pay. At the other extreme, however, posts in Rangoon, Burma, or Baghdad, Iraq, would provide a 70% premium to base pay (35% for hardship pay and another 35% for danger pay).[39]

Ensuring Similar Purchasing Power

Danger aside, the main goal of the balance sheet method is to smooth out expenses and protect the expatriate from incurring significant additional costs. Figure 10.1 illustrates this graphically. The first column on the far left in this figure presents the base costs in the home country—say, the United States. Moving from left to right, purchasing power at home can be translated into purchasing power abroad. Column 2 in the figure illustrates a common situation—one in which the host-country housing, taxes, and goods and services are all more expensive than at home. The model, therefore, would make adjustments (in Column 3), typically in the form of company-paid allowances, differentials, and extra payments. These would offset the higher costs and allow the expatriate to maintain his or her home lifestyle overseas—creating what is known as purchasing power parity. This resulting purchasing power

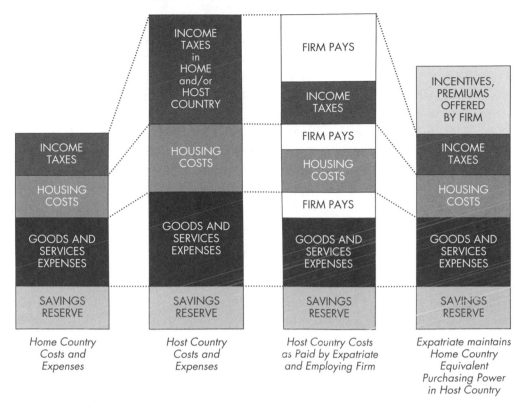

FIGURE 10.1 The Balance Sheet Approach to Expatriate Compensation: Keeping Employees "Whole"

Source: Adapted from Reynolds, C. (1994). *Compensation Basics for North American Expatriates: Developing an Effective Program for Employees Working Abroad.* ACA Building Block 15. Scottsdale, AZ: American Compensatio Association.

equivalence is shown in Column 4 in Figure 10.1, along with any premiums or incentive pay the company may provide on top of everything else.[40]

Housing Costs

In the United States, it is common to expect housing costs to be about 30% of take-home pay—one of the biggest outlays in a family budget. These costs can skyrocket internationally, and, therefore, they receive special consideration in the balance sheet model. Indeed, housing alone may account for 50% of the total additional compensation package. Overseas housing is typically rented and often covered by a shorter-term lease, thereby driving up prices. Likewise, expatriates— especially U.S. ones—often expect larger and more luxurious accommodations than their counterparts. Expatriates who come to the United States are often stunned by the size and low cost of U.S. housing. But for an American overseas, much smaller accommodations with fewer premium add-ons are still difficult to find and are more expensive once located in cities such as Tokyo, London, or Beijing.[41]

According to one survey, over 80% of multinationals provide either free expatriate housing or a location-specific housing allowance with some expected contribution by the expatriate. The same survey showed that Asian, Latin American, and European multinationals are more likely to provide free housing than housing allowances, while the reverse is true for U.S. firms. The cost for housing expatriates around the world can vary, but it is generally expensive. Consider that a one-bedroom apartment in Beijing could run from $8,000 to $12,000 per year, in Hong Kong from $30,000 to $60,000 per year, and about $35,000 per year in Dubai. If you want a three- or four-bedroom home in Beijing, expect to pay rent from $50,000 to $96,000 per year. This is a lot less than in Moscow, where the same would cost $120,000 per year, or Hong Kong, where a three-bedroom townhouse will run approximately $385,000 per year. Housing in many cities is very expensive, even for Americans transferring from large U.S. metro areas such as Chicago or Atlanta. Regardless, multinationals typically either pick up the cost of foreign housing for their expatriates, or provide a housing allowance designed to offset the additional foreign housing costs.[42]

Tax Expenses

A second major category of expenses addressed by the balance sheet method is income taxes (see Table 10.5). Again, the goals are to tie expatriates' tax burdens to their home countries regardless of where they are posted and simplify their reporting requirements (called tax equalization). This makes a good deal of sense, since tax laws and rates vary considerably from country to country and are in flux. Dealing with tax issues is probably the most complex aspect of the balance sheet method.[43]

Implementing tax equalization requires that multinationals first determine the total hypothetical income tax burden facing expatriates had they stayed home. Next, companies need to assess what the total tax obligation will likely be while expatriates are posted overseas. Once that is determined, multinationals will deduct an amount equal to what the expatriate's home-country income tax would be from his or her salary. These monies will be used to pay off taxes owed to the tax authorities in both the home and host countries. Alternatively, a firm may instead reimburse expatriates after they pay host-country taxes themselves. Either way, an end-of-year reconciliation is often needed to see if the firm owes tax equalization money to the expatriate or vice versa.[44]

The firm can easily get a handle on the cost of this portion of the balance sheet method. To illustrate, Table 10.5 presents the different personal income tax rates in

Table 10.5
Top Personal Income Tax Rates for Selected Countries by Region and Year

Region/Country	2003 Top Personal Income Tax Rate	2009 Top Personal Income Tax Rate
Asia-Pacific		
China	45%	45%
Hong Kong	15.5%	15%
India	30%	30%
Indonesia	35%	30%
Japan	50%	50%
Singapore	22%	20%
Taiwan	40%	40%
Europe		
Czech Republic	32%	15%
Denmark	59%	62.3%
Finland	35%	30.5%
France	48%	40%
Germany	48.5%	45%
Ireland	42%	46%
Netherlands	52%	52%
Norway	47.5%	40%
Poland	40%	32%
Russia	13%	13%
Sweden	57%	56.7%
United Kingdom	40%	40%
Middle East/Africa		
Bahrain	0%	0%
Egypt	34%	20%
Israel	50%	46%
Saudi Arabia	0%	0%

(Continued)

Table 10.5 (Continued)

Region/Country	2003 Top Personal Income Tax Rate	2009 Top Personal Income Tax Rate
South Africa	40%	40%
United Arab Emirates	0%	0%
North America		
Canada	29%	29%
Mexico	34%	28%
United States	35%	35%
South America		
Argentina	35%	35%
Brazil	27.5%	27.5%
Chile	40%	40%
Venezuela	25%	34%

Source: Adapted from KPMG. (2009). *KPMG's Individual Income Tax and Social Security Rate Survey 2009*. June. Available at www.kpmg.com/sitecollectiondocuments/individual-income-tax-rates-survey-2009_v2.pdf.

a few countries around the globe. The rates *do not* include other types of income-based taxes commonly found across borders (e.g., government-mandated social programs or plans, regional or provincial income taxes). Consequently, the true income tax burden in the countries listed in Table 10.5 will be higher in most cases. Incidentally, tax rates stayed the same in most countries between 2003 and 2009, with a few trending lower and a few higher. Generally speaking, countries in Western Europe and Scandinavia have the highest personal income tax rates, while at the other end of the spectrum, many oil-rich countries in the Middle East have no income tax.[45]

Agreements across countries that allow for tax equalization or the avoidance of double taxation for citizens posted to foreign countries can help reduce expatriates' tax exposure. The United States has such tax agreements with more than 65 countries. These provide Americans with exemptions or lower rates from foreign tax burdens (with the reverse also true for expatriates posted to the United States). Many countries tax not only income but also all allowances, adjustments, and incentives. France is a leader in making "totalization" agreements that excuse items such as housing, schooling, dividends, and capital gains and that eliminate social security taxes for expatriates in France.[46] In contrast, the United States is among the few countries that taxes expatriate income earned abroad (beyond an exempted amount of $92,000 in 2011).[47] As a result, even if a U.S. expatriate is paying relatively low taxes while living in Brazil, he or she may also owe tax in the United States. But this is exactly what the balance sheet method is designed to handle. Firms using this method will compensate the expatriate, directly or indirectly, for any additional taxes incurred.[48]

Goods, Services, and the Balance Sheet

Besides housing, no other piece of the expatriate compensation package causes more consternation for employees than allowances for goods and services. Multinationals— or the consultants that work for them— construct allowances by comparing the cost of a "market basket" of goods and services in the home country with the cost of a similar basket in the assignment country. The ratio of these two cost estimates provides the basis for paying expatriates a cost-of-living allowance (sometimes known as the goods and services differential) to help offset higher living costs that expatriates often encounter abroad. Again, the purpose of the allowance is to give expatriates the same purchasing power they enjoy at home.[49]

Included in the market basket are goods and service items such as food (prepared at home or bought in restaurants), alcohol and tobacco, personal care products (e.g., toothpaste, shampoo), domestic supplies (e.g., cleaning products), clothing, home services, transportation, utilities, and entertainment. As you might imagine, coming up with prices for all of these items, particularly across countries, not only can be time-consuming and tedious but also must be updated all the time. Prices are continually fluctuating, and they vary dramatically by location (e.g., the price of a loaf of bread or a pound of Starbucks ground coffee may vary considerably depending on where you buy it). On top of that, currency swings can play havoc with goods and services differentials—swelling the value of differentials when local currencies drop significantly and shrinking them when those currencies soar. Consequently, goods and services differentials should be monitored and periodically adjusted up or down as needed to take these changes into account. Sometimes multinationals pay expatriates in both the home and local currency for this reason (referred to as split pay)—working to even out currency fluctuations between countries.[50]

Despite these challenges, multinationals have many sources for estimates of goods and services prices worldwide as well as the differentials that may be necessary when sending expatriates to particular locations. For example, various consulting firms publish prices on hundreds of goods and services and provide cost-of-living indices for virtually every city in the world—based on data that are updated regularly. In the accompanying *Global Innovations* box, we present specifics on how this task is accomplished.

GLOBAL INNOVATIONS

What Do Zippers, Prozac, a Dozen Roses, and a Box of Titleists Have in Common? They Are All in a Day's Survey[51]

How do companies determine the level of compensation for international employees? What should they offer them in terms of per diems, reimbursements, and more for the expenses they incur while doing business overseas? Most companies want to be fair and treat their employees well, but they also are cost-conscious, especially these days. One solution to this problem is provided by the Cambridge, Massachusetts–based firm, AIRINC (Associates for International Research, Inc.), a large international survey research company. Among its other activities, the firm collects data on the prices of goods and services in countries all around the world. It sells this and other customized information to its clients—including many Fortune 500 companies—which use this information to calculate expatriates' cost of living, annual compensation, and other periodic adjustments. Demand for AIRINC's services is on the rise as employers try to keep close accounting of expatriate expenses.

Many firms put their trust in the data provided by AIRINC. One reason is that the firm goes on location to collect its own data rather than using estimates or self-reports of employees. These estimates can routinely be way off, either because memories of specific prices are a blur to those traveling to multiple countries in short bursts or because estimates might be inflated in comparison to vague memories of outdated home-country prices (what's the price of gasoline in Dallas?).

But getting price data directly from overseas retailers and others can be time-consuming and expensive. Plus, it is just hard work. It may be no surprise, therefore, that most of AIRINC's surveyors are in the 22 to 30 age range—young people with fewer roots and more wanderlust. Megan Lipman was a surveyor for seven years with AIRINC. Although she quickly grew to love the job, Lipman had little idea of what it entailed when she first applied. In fact, it never entered her mind that such a job even existed. After graduating from college with dual majors in art history and Spanish, and two years of experience as a translator, she responded to a newspaper ad: "job responsibilities include data collection, analysis, and preparation of various statistical data for cost-of-living analysis." It was the last sentence in the ad that made her send in a résumé: "Will spend at least one-third of time in international travel." The interviewers fired questions at her such as, "What would you do if you were stranded in a central African nation with three days until the next flight?" Her answer: "If there were no other safe ways to get out, I'd get as much work done on the phone as possible."

Lipman got the job and quickly began flying around the world from city to city for about six weeks at a time. Like the other young surveyors, she spent about half the year traveling to Qatar, the United Arab Emirates, Bangladesh, New Zealand, Cyprus, Venezuela, and dozens of other places. Once on site, she spent about three days pegging costs by visiting supermarkets, gas stations, theaters, and beauty salons—among other places. One trip to Malta involved tracking down prices for a 20-centimeter zipper, 20 milligrams of Prozac, a sleeve of Titleist golf balls, a 14-carat gold wedding ring, Tabasco sauce, a dozen red roses, and the cost of repairing a washing machine. She had a regular schedule of items to price, and the Malta list was not that unusual.

While it may be clear why they collect this data, *how* AIRINC surveyors get the data is another story. Consider Lipman's Malta trip. After settling in, she chose a setting such as a supermarket. She asked for the manager, presented her business card, and asked if she could carry out a pricing survey. She then headed up and down the aisles recording price after price. Most managers were very friendly and helpful. But in some shops, managers resent young foreigners nosing around the store, partly because they think the survey is being done by their competition. In those cases, AIRINC's surveyors often covertly wander the store with smaller notebooks and surreptitiously make their notes. While she was in a Malta pharmacy, one manager gruffly pulled Lipman aside and asked to have a word with her. Worried that she would be kicked out of the store and lose hard-earned data, she was relieved when he asked instead if his son could get an internship with AIRINC.

Lipman and other surveyors spend a good deal of time in many (luxury) hotel rooms, collecting even more data. There, hired translators use a phone directory to make calls to physicians, insurance and real estate agents, and repair shops for more prices. When the surveyors return home to Cambridge, the reams of data must be analyzed, average prices for various items must be determined, and continued tracking of prices to those of the last several surveys must be prepared. AIRINC then reports to and makes recommendations for clients (e.g., to raise or lower employee cost-of-living allowances).

Overall, surveyors such as Lipman like their jobs. They make a good salary, have very generous expense accounts, and generally enjoy the traveling. But before you Google AIRINC to find where to e-mail your application, consider the drawbacks. Travel hassles today abound (e.g., delays, cancellations, missed connections, etc.), and it involves a lot of time spent alone. It is also tough to maintain personal relationships, given the demanding travel schedule. But that is all in a day's survey!

Using this price data, multinationals can quickly get a sense of which foreign locations are the most or least expensive to send expatriates. You may see various lists published from time to time that lay out the 10 or 20 most expensive cities in the world in which to do business. These data fit into those calculations. For the last decade or so, Tokyo (one and a half times as expensive as New York), Moscow, and Geneva have been in the top 10. In 2011, for the first time ever, several African cities landed in the top 10, including the most expensive city in the world, Luanda, Angola, which wrested the dubious top spot away from perennial leader Tokyo. To give you a sense of various costs in Tokyo, consider these: an average movie ticket is $24, a beer is $11, and a quick lunch costs $27. You could eat at home, but eggs are $5.60 per dozen. A tube of toothpaste is $5.10. Different firms release these lists, so there will naturally be some variation. In 2011, no U.S. city (including New York City) appeared in the top 30 in any such list, thanks to a weak U.S. dollar.[52]

If all these prices are too hard to swallow, consider the Big Mac "economic index" that is constructed by the *Economist* magazine. The rationale of the index—partly tongue in cheek—is to provide a quick and "easily digestible" method that can be used to compare costs across countries. Table 10.6 presents U.S. dollar equivalent prices, as well as the cost in local currency, for a Big Mac in selected countries. While a Big Mac in Norway will cost $7.20, Thailand (at $2.17) and China ($1.95) offer relative bargains in comparison. While this is hardly a perfect index of purchasing power parity, it certainly is food for thought.[53]

Regardless of what index is used, goods and services will inevitably be more expensive in some countries than in others. Yet even in inexpensive countries, some expatriates tend to spend more anyway. Experts believe that, when overseas, some employees like to keep their relatively high-living home-country consumption tastes, even if it costs them more. They may be willing, for instance, to buy expensive imports from their home country, a habit that in turn drives expenses much higher than locally driven cost-of-living indexes would suggest. Some expatriates might expect to receive adjustments to their average domestic living expenses as a result, but firms are increasingly pushing back against these kinds of costs. Some companies calculate goods and services differentials using an *efficient purchaser index*. The prices in these calculations use cheaper or on-sale products and thereby encourage expatriates to become more efficient shoppers over time. Regardless, it can lead to smaller cost-of-living allowances for expatriates, saving their employers money. Other cost-saving steps include substituting cheaper transportation options or excluding pricier items altogether (e.g., imported alcohol).[54]

The Balance Sheet on Balance

All in all, the main goal of the balance sheet method is to treat expatriates fairly. The effect of many of the adjustments is to make a foreign posting less of a hardship, if not altogether pleasant. This is not to say, however, that the balance sheet approach is without problems. For one, it is complex, expensive, and difficult for multinationals to administer and explain. As noted, the balance sheet method requires either collecting or buying data on cost of living and housing. Likewise, the transfer of payments for the various adjustments is challenging to manage and monitor.[55]

Some practical problems also emerge when expatriates are sent to places where costs are generally *lower* than at home. In this case, housing as well as goods and services can produce negative differentials. In such cases, should the employee payments be reduced to reflect, for example, a lower cost of living in Mexico? While it would be entirely consistent with the balance sheet method to eliminate such windfalls to the employee, many multinationals choose not to do this. According to one survey, only about

Table 10.6
Do You Want Fries with That Foreign Assignment? The Big Mac in Various Countries

Country	Cost of Big Mac in Local Currency	Cost of Big Mac in U.S. Dollars
United States	$3.73	$3.73
Argentina	Peso 14.0	$3.56
Australia	A$4.35	$3.84
Brazil	Real 8.71	$4.91
Britain	£2.29	$3.48
Canada	C$4.17	$4.00
Chile	Peso 1,750	$3.34
China	Yuan 13.2	$1.95
Czech Republic	Koruna 67.6	$3.43
Hong Kong	HK$14.8	$1.90
Indonesia	Rupiah 22,780	$2.51
Japan	¥320	$3.67
Mexico	Peso 32.0	$2.50
Norway	Kroner 45	$7.20
Philippines	Peso 102	$2.19
Russia	Ruble 71	$2.33
Saudi Arabia	Riyal 10.0	$2.67
South Africa	Rand 18.5	$2.45
South Korea	Won 3,400	$2.82
Sweden	SKR 48.4	$6.56
Switzerland	CHf 6.50	$6.19
Taiwan	NT$75	$2.34
Thailand	Baht 70	$2.17
Turkey	Lira 5.95	$3.89

Source: Adapted from Burgernomics: When the chips are down. (2010). July 22. Available at www.economist.com,

Note: Prices and currency rates are as of July 21, 2010.

25% of firms deduct money or allowances from other parts of the expatriate package (e.g., from foreign service premiums) to compensate for negative differentials.[56]

More generally, what seems to be more popular among firms is to move away from thinking about foreign assignments as automatically deserving of a special premium. In fact, the number of firms that do not pay *any* incentive premium at all to work overseas has nearly doubled in recent years. As globalization increases, their rationale is that employees should relish an opportunity to work in important assignments overseas. If a firm makes the foreign assignment a significant part of its management development track, this is probably a reasonable position to take.[57]

CHAPTER SUMMARY

Compensation differs across borders and cultures. In the United States, compensation is seen as a swap, with employees providing effort and output and receiving wages and benefits in return. This may, in part, explain why U.S. executives are the highest paid in the world, with more of their pay tied to variable performance measures. Employees in other cultures may view compensation as an entitled benefit or company obligation rather than an exchange-driven process.

Multinationals need to be aware of these differences and partly drive multilevel decisions about performance appraisal and compensation. Overall, however, evaluations are more likely to be managed on a global basis, while pay and perks are more likely to be managed locally.

Expatriate compensation presents unique challenges. Several methods of compensation exist, including the *ad hoc* and *localization* approaches. The *balance sheet* method remains the most popular. Its goal is to maintain the same lifestyle for expatriates as they would have at home—without any significant additional expense. The balance sheet method keeps expatriates "whole" in terms of their lifestyles and purchasing power. In practice, however, the balance sheet method is complex to use. Recently, multinationals have taken steps to reduce costs, including cutting back on incentives for overseas assignments. There are many other important issues associated with expatriates—the subject of our next chapter.

DISCUSSION QUESTIONS

1. What are some problems in compensating employee performance, and how are these problems complicated by an international setting?
2. How might cultural beliefs regarding the basis for compensation affect an approach to rewarding expatriates and host-country/third-country nationals in the same firm?

3. What are some of the ways that employees and executives can be compensated for their international service?

4. How should expatriates be compensated? In your view, what is the best approach, and why?

Developing Your International Career

ASSEMBLING AN EXPATRIATE COMPENSATION PACKAGE

Purpose and Instructions

The purpose of this exercise is to help improve your understanding of how salary, tax, and living cost differentials across countries make it challenging to construct an expatriate compensation package and to possibly help you down the road in an international career.

Write a report that summarizes your research on the compensation of expatriates assigned to different countries. Your instructor may ask you to complete this assignment in small groups. Regardless, consider this setting: a U.S. multinational has plans to send four managers on expatriate assignments. Your instructor will indicate which pair of locations you will be assigned to research. Below are the pairs of foreign cities under consideration for each manager:

Manager 1: Cape Town, South Africa, or Frankfurt, Germany
Manager 2: Moscow, Russia, or Jakarta, Indonesia
Manager 3: Cairo, Egypt, or Mumbai, India
Manager 4: Santiago, Chile, or Shanghai, China

Assume that you work in human resources for this company and that your boss would like your advice about how to structure a compensation package for one of its managers. Unless your instructor specifies otherwise, you can assume that all four potential expatriates are based in Chicago, are married with two school-age children between the ages of 6 and 15, and have a base salary of $150,000. Of this amount, approximately 60% is spent on living expenses, about 30% goes to cover various taxes, and the remaining 10% is allotted to savings.

As noted in the chapter, living expenses are complex and vary dramatically from country to country. Your report will have to account for transportation, clothing, housing, food, school costs, and many other factors that could play a role in this category. Remember that the tax situation for many foreign assignments is complex, and this will have to be factored into your report.

All in all, how should the compensation packages differ across the two countries you are assigned to, if at all? In what areas might differences exist and why? What would your recommendations be for handling them, and why? Again, be sure to describe why there are differences across countries (or why not) in the specific aspects of the package.

In addition to the text and other reference sources, you may find many of the websites below useful for completing your report:

U.S. Department of State Foreign Allowances and Per Diem Pages

- http://aoprals.state.gov/Web920/allowance.asp?menu_id = 95
- http://aoprals.state.gov/web920/per_diem.asp
- www.state.gov/r/pa/ei/subject/

These links provide lists or drop-down menus for living, housing, and education allowances, among other things, by city/country.

International Tax and Accounting Site Directory

- www.taxsites.com/international.html#countries

This is an international tax site directory with country-specific information.

Organisation for Economic Co-operation and Development

- www.oecd.org

This site presents purchasing power parity data, permitting comparisons of the cost of a basket of consumer goods and services across countries. Other information is available as well, including details on tax treaties and income taxes.

Making the Case for International Understanding

TAKING A HOLIDAY FROM VACATIONS: WORKING OVERTIME TO CHANGE A NATIONAL HABIT[58]

The government of South Korea is cracking down on vacation time taken by workers. You may be thinking that this is an issue of mass fraud or of improperly reporting reimbursable time off. If so, you are wrong—the problem is that people are *not* taking enough vacation, if at all! Years of government pleading, combined with the cultural propensity of its people to sacrifice and to work hard for the future, has had a strong impact. In fact, according to the Organisation of Economic Co-operation and Development (OECD), South Koreans work more hours in one year than in any other developed country. Workers averaged about 2,300 hours of work per year, down from a historic high of 2,500 hours a decade ago but still well above the 1,768 average found among the 30 OECD countries (and the 1,794 average in the United States). If you consider an eight-hour-per-day work period over 52 weeks (no holidays or vacation factored in), Koreans work about 45 hours per week, compared to about 35 hours per week for Americans. Viewed differently, Koreans work an average of one and a quarter days per week more than do Americans.

Merely working more does not necessarily translate into greater productivity. For example, South Korea's productivity ranks below all but a few of the former Soviet bloc countries among all the OCED members. The government is trying to change this situation, and it thinks the solution may be taking time off to recharge before returning to work more vigorously and with creative juices flowing. The ministry in charge of human resources and personnel recently issued a request of the over 1 million government workers—it was directed to prepare a plan to take 16 days off the coming year and to submit that plan to their boss. This is a real challenge since the average worker was only taking *six* of his or her allotted 23 days.

In addition to previous government efforts to rally workers under the national advancement flag, there are also some cultural drivers of this workaholic attitude among employees. In Chapter 2, we studied the hierarchical nature of Korean society, and it seems to play a role in these numbers we have presented. In this society, superiors are greatly respected and are regularly followed and listened to. Yet many business and government leaders do not take *any* vacation at all—including a member of South Korean president Lee's cabinet, who was responsible for issuing the vacation directive mentioned above. When asked about this by the *Wall Street Journal*, he said, "I want them to take more time off...but as for me? I don't know." On top of all this, there are some government employees who received pay for their unused vacation days and who view this vacation push by leaders as a money-saving technique. Among the newer Korean companies, however, there is some sign of unfreezing of these attitudes. At LG, the average number of vacation days taken is 10 and, at SK Telecom, workers take between 5 and 15 of their 22 possible days off.

ASSIGNMENT QUESTIONS

1. Obtain additional data on hours worked in at least 10 countries, including South Korea and the United States. Try to choose your countries so that the cultural distance among them is great. Your instructor might assign specific countries or sets of countries (perhaps representing extremes of cultural dimensions of the approaches to classifying cultures that were discussed in chapter 2).

2. Add in additional data on gross domestic product, average worker pay, holiday and vacation leave averages, and a few other relevant economic and productivity markers for your chosen countries.

3. The feature provided some interesting detail about the reasons why hours worked in South Korea might be both culturally driven and result from concerted efforts on the part of the government. Choose three other countries in your data set and try to apply cultural explanations of their data on work hours and related features.

NOTES

1. *Mercer Expatriate Compensation Solutions: Helping You Solve International Compensation Issues.* Pamphlet published by Mercer Human Resource Consulting Group, 2011. Available at www.imercer.com/uploads/Europe/pdfs/Brochures/06-expatcompsolution_brochure.pdf.

2. Baeten, X. (2010). Global compensation and benefits management: The need for communication and coordination. *Compensation and Benefits Review*, 42, 392–402.

3. Milkovich, G. T., & Boudreau, J. W. (1997). *Human Resource Management.* Homewood, IL: Irwin.

4. Milkovich, G. T., & Boudreau, J. W. (1997). *Human Resource Management.* Homewood, IL: Irwin.

5. Milkovich, G. T., & Newman, J. M. (1996). *Compensation.* Chicago: Irwin.

6. Beshouri, C., & Farrell, D. (2005). *The Philippines' Offshoring Opportunity.* September. McKinsey & Company. http://www.mckinsey.com/Insights/MGI/Research/Labor_Markets/The_Philippines_offshoring_opportunity.

7. Engardio, P. (2009). Why NCR said, "Let's go back home." *Business Week*, August 24 and 31, 19; Jelter, J. (2009). Whirlpool to shut Indiana plant, cut 1,100 jobs. MarketWatch. Available at www.marketwatch.com.

8. Kras, E. S. (1989). *Management in Two Cultures: Bridging the Gap between US and Mexican Managers.* Yarmouth, ME: Intercultural Press. See wage data from ftp://ftp.bls.gov/pub/special.requests/ForeignLabor/industrynaics.txt.

9. Timmons H. (2011). Outsourcing firms are creating jobs for American lawyers. *Dayton Daily News*, June 5, B2.

10. Mexican labor's hidden costs. *Fortune*, October 1994, 17, 32; Milkovich, G. T., & Newman, J. M. (1996). *Compensation.* Chicago: Irwin.

11. Tosi, H. L., & Greckhamer, T. (2004). Culture and CEO compensation. *Organization Science*, 15(6), 657–670.

12. Attacking the corporate gravy train. *The Economist*, May 30, 2009, 71–73; Executive pay in Europe: Pay attention. *The Economist*, June 14, 2008, 77–78.

13. Attacking the corporate gravy train. *The Economist*, May 30, 2009, 71–73; Chief executives' pay as a multiple of manufacturing employees' pay. *The Economist*, September 30, 2000, 110; Bailey, E. K. (1995). International compensation. In O. Shenkar (ed.), *Global Perspectives on Human Resource Management* (147–164). Englewood Cliffs, NJ: Prentice Hall; Parker-Pope, T. (1996). Executive pay: So far away. *Wall Street Journal*, April 11, B12; Fryer, B. (2003). In a world of pay. *Harvard Business Review Case and Expert Commentary*, November, 31–40.

14. Mesdag, L. M. (1984). Are you underpaid? *Fortune*, March 19, 22–23.

15. Please see http://money.cnn.com/2007/06/12/pf/vacation_days_worldwide.

16. Bryan, S., Nash, R., & Patel, A. (2011). Law and executive compensation: A cross-country study. *Journal of Applied Corporate Finance*, 23, 84–97.

17. Townsend, A. M., Scott, K. D., & Markham, S. E. (1990). An examination of country and culture-based differences in compensation practices. *Journal of International Business Studies*, 21, 667–678.

18. Fay, C. H. (2008). The global convergence of compensation practices. In L. R. Gomez-Mejia & S. Werner (eds.), *Global Compensation: Foundations and Perspectives* (131–141). New York: Routledge.

19. Alis, D., Bournois, F., Croquette, D., & Poulain, P. Y. (2008). HRM in France: Changes in the corpus. In C. Scholz & H. Bohm (eds.), *Human Resource Management in Europe: Comparative Analysis and Contextual Understanding* (113–152). New York: Routledge; Hewitt Associates (1991). *Total Compensation Management: Reward Management Strategies for the 1990's.* Cambridge, MA: Basil Blackwell.

20. Flynn, G. (1994). HR in Mexico: What you should know. *Personnel Journal*, August, 34–44; Ramirez, J., & Zapata-Cantu, L. (2009). HRM systems in Mexico: The case of Novo Nordisk. In A. Davila & M. M. Elvira (eds.), *Best Human Resource Practices in Latin America* (97–112). New York: Routledge.

21. Beatty, J. R., McCune, J. T., & Beatty, R. W. (1988). A policy-capturing approach to the study of United States and Japanese managers' compensation decisions. *Journal of Management*, 14, 465–474; Marin, G. S. (2008). National differences in compensation: The influence of the institutional and cultural context. In L. R. Gomez-Mejia & S. Werner (eds.), *Global Compensation: Foundations and Perspectives* (19–28). New York: Routledge.

22. Marin, G. S. (2008). National differences in compensation: The influence of the institutional and cultural context. In L. R. Gomez-Mejia & S. Werner (eds.), *Global Compensation: Foundations and Perspectives* (19–28). New York: Routledge; Mroczkowski, T., & Hanaoka, M. (1989). Continuity and change in Japanese management. *California Management Review*, Winter, 39–52.

23. Du, J., & Choi, J. N. (2010). Pay for performance in emerging markets: Insights from China. *Journal of International Business Studies*, 41, 671–689.

24. Fackler, M., & Maynard, M. (2006). Chairman of Toyota steps down. *New York Times*, June 24. Available at www.nytimes.com; Taylor, A. (1996). Toyota's boss stands out in a crowd. *Fortune*, November 25, 116–122; Toyama, M., & Frederick, J. (2004). Hiroshi Okuda and Fuji Ocho: Toyota's tenacious twosome. *Time*, April 26. Available at www. time.com/time/magazine.

25. Warneke, D., & Schneider, M. (2011). Expatriate compensation packages: What do employees prefer? *Cross Cultural Management: An International Journal*, 18, 236–256.

26. Briscoe, D. R., Schuler, R. S., & Claus, L. (2009). *International Human Resource Management* (3rd ed.). New York: Routledge.

27. Leung, K., Zhu, Y., & Ge, C. (2009). Compensation disparity between locals and expatriates: Moderating the effects of perceived injustice in foreign multinationals in China. *Journal of World Business*, 44, 85–93. Also see an interesting article on perceived fairness in the eyes of host country nationals by Bonache, J., Sanchez, J. I., & Zarraga-Oberty, C. (2009). The interaction of expatriate pay differential and expatriate inputs on host country nationals' pay unfairness. *International Journal of Human Resource Management*, 20, 2135–2149.

28. Briscoe, D. R., Schuler, R. S., & Claus, L. (2009). *International Human Resource Management* (3rd ed.). New York: Routledge; Gould, C. (1999). Expatriate compensation. *Workforce*, September, 40–46; Mestre, C., & Traber, Y. (2009). Managing expatriates in unprecedented times: Containing international assignment costs. Available at www.mercer.com; Mervosh, E. M. (1997). Managing expatriate compensation. *Industry Week*, July 21, 13–18.

29. Briscoe, D. R., Schuler, R. S., & Claus, L. (2009). *International Human Resource Management* (3rd ed.). New York: Routledge.

30. Briscoe, D. R., Schuler, R. S., & Claus, L. (2009). *International Human Resource Management* (3rd ed.). New York: Routledge.

31. Reynolds, C. (1994). *Compensation Basics for North American Expatriates: Developing an Effective Program for Employees Working Abroad.* Scottsdale, AZ: American Compensation Association.

32. Briscoe, D. R., Schuler, R. S., & Claus, L. (2009). *International Human Resource Management* (3rd ed.). New York: Routledge.

33. Reynolds, C. (1994). *Compensation Basics for North American Expatriates: Developing an Effective Program for Employees Working Abroad.* Scottsdale, AZ: American Compensation Association.

34. Feng, S. (2009). Expatriate localization: A Chinese solution. Available at www.mercer.com.

35. Cordova, V. (2009). Reducing expatriate program costs under the balance sheet approach. *International HR Journal,* Summer, 10–14; Oemig, D. R. A. (1999). When you say, "We'll keep you whole," do you mean it? *Compensation and Benefits Review,* 31, 40–47.

36. Briscoe, D. R., Schuler, R. S., & Claus, L. (2009). *International Human Resource Management* (3rd ed.). New York: Routledge; Mestre, C., & Traber, Y. (2009). Managing expatriates in unprecedented times: Containing international assignment costs. Available at www.mercer.com.

37. Reynolds, C. (1994). *Compensation Basics for North American Expatriates: Developing an Effective Program for Employees Working Abroad.* Scottsdale, AZ: American Compensation Association. See also www.mercer.com.

38. Helms, M. (1991). International executive compensation practices. In M. Mendenhall & G. Oddou (eds.), *International Human Resources Management* (106–132). Boston: PWS-Kent; Infante, V. D. (2001). Three ways to design international pay: Headquarters, home country, host country. *Workforce,* January, 22–24.

39. For the most recent information about the U.S. Department of State foreign incentives, see http://aoprals.state.gov/content.asp?content_id=134&menu_id=75. Also see U.S. Department of State. (1999). *Indexes of Living Costs Abroad, Quarters Allowances, and Hardship Differentials.* Washington, DC: U.S. Government Printing Office.

40. Reynolds, C. (1994). *Compensation Basics for North American Expatriates: Developing an Effective Program for Employees Working Abroad.* Scottsdale, AZ: American Compensation Association. See also www.economist.com/research/Economics/alphabetic.cfm?letter = P.

41. Market rents. *Wall Street Journal,* January 24, 1997, B8; Briscoe, D. R., Schuler, R. S., & Claus, L. (2009). *International Human Resource Management* (3rd ed.). New York: Routledge; Sepede, M. L., & James, C. (2009). The challenge of expatriate housing—Managing costs and expatriates' expectations. January 29. Available at www.mercer.com.

42. Cordova, V. (2009). Reducing expatriate program costs under the balance sheet approach. *International HR Journal,* Summer, 10–14; Rosman, K. (2007). Expat life gets less cushy. *Wall Street Journal,* October 26, W1, W10.

43. Anderson, J. B. (1990). Compensating your overseas executives, Part 2: Europe in 1992. *Compensation and Benefits Review,* 22, 25–35; Briscoe, D. R., Schuler, R. S., & Claus, L. (2009). *International Human Resource Management* (3rd ed.). New York: Routledge; Klein, R. B. (1992). Compensating your overseas executives, Part 3: Exporting U.S. stock option plans to expatriates. *Compensation and Benefits Review,* 23, 27–38.

44. Briscoe, D. R., Schuler, R. S., & Claus, L. (2009). *International Human Resource Management* (3rd ed.). New York: Routledge; Cordova, V. (2009). Reducing expatriate program costs under the balance sheet approach. *International HR Journal,* Summer, 10–14; Goldberg, M. A., Kruth, C., & Miller, M. J. (2007). Management repercussions of the increased tax

on Americans working overseas. *International Business and Economics Research Journal*, 6(11), 31–38; Veliotis, S. (2008). The effect of the U.S. stimulus tax rebates on equalization programs. *Compensation and Benefits Review*, 40, 60–65.

45. See www.kpmg.com/sitecollectiondocuments/individual-income-tax-rates-survey-2009_v2.pdf.

46. Anderson, J. B. (1990). Compensating your overseas executives, Part 2: Europe in 1992. *Compensation and Benefits Review*, 22, 25–35. For U.S. tax treaties with other nations, see www.irs.gov/businesses/international/article/0,id = 96739,00.html.

47. What employees need to know about wages earned overseas. *Payroll Practitioner's Monthly*, January, 2011, 1–2.

48. Cordova, V. (2009). Reducing expatriate program costs under the balance sheet approach. *International HR Journal*, Summer, 10–14; Reynolds, C. (1994). *Compensation Basics for North American Expatriates: Developing an Effective Program for Employees Working Abroad*. Scottsdale, AZ: American Compensation Association. See also www.irs.gov/pub/irs-pdf/i2555.pdf.

49. Travelling more lightly. *The Economist*, June 24, 2006, 77–80; Prystay, C., & Herman, T. (2006). Tax hike hits home for Americans abroad. *Wall Street Journal*, July 19, D1, D2; Cordova, V. (2009). Reducing expatriate program costs under the balance sheet approach. *International HR Journal*, Summer, 10–14.

50. Shelton, T. (2008). Global compensation strategies: Managing and administering split pay for an expatriate workforce. *Compensation and Benefits Review*, January/February, 56–60; Briscoe, D. R., Schuler, R. S., & Claus, L. (2009). *International Human Resource Management* (3rd ed.). New York: Routledge; Traber, Y., Gibson, I., & Mestre, C. (2009). Setting and communicating competitive expatriate allowances. April. Available at www.mercer.com.

51. Silverman, R. E. (2000). Pricing zippers, Tabasco, Prozac in exotic locales. *Wall Street Journal*, June 13, B1, B14.

52. Wong, V. (2011). The world's most expensive cities, 2011, June 10th. Available at http://finance.yahoo.com; *Mercer's 2009 Cost of Living Survey Highlights—Global*. Updated July 7, 2009. Available at www.mercer.com.

53. Vachris, M. A., & Thomas, J. (1999). International price comparisons based on purchasing power parity. *Monthly Labor Review*, October, 3–12. Also see www.economist.com/markets/indicators/displaystory.cfm?story_id = 13055650.

54. Briscoe, D. R., Schuler, R. S., & Claus, L. (2009). *International Human Resource Management* (3rd ed.). New York: Routledge; Cordova, V. (2009). Reducing expatriate program costs under the balance sheet approach. *International HR Journal*, Summer, 10–14; Logger, E., Vinke, R., & Kluytmans, F. (1995). Compensation and appraisal in an international perspective. In A. Harzing & J. Van Ruysseveldt (eds.), *International Human Resource Management* (144–155). London: Sage; Wilson, L. E. (2000). The balance sheet approach to expatriate compensation: Still with us after all these years. *Relocation Journal and Real Estate News*, 14, 1–9.

55. Herman, T. (2007). U.S. expats get additional tax relief. *Wall Street Journal*, September 19, D3; Briscoe, D. R., Schuler, R. S., & Claus, L. (2009). *International Human Resource Management* (3rd ed.). New York: Routledge.

56. Rosman, K. (2007). Expat life gets less cushy. *Wall Street Journal*, October 26, W1, W10; Cordova, V. (2009). Reducing expatriate program costs under the balance sheet approach. *International HR Journal*, Summer, 10–14; Dwyer, T. D. (1999). Trends in global compensation. *Compensation and Benefits Review*, 31, 48–53; Milkovich, G. T., & Bloom, M. (1998). Rethinking international compensation. *Compensation and Benefits Review*, 30, 15–23.

57. Hollister, H. H. (2005). Expats face hurdles in saving up for a nest egg. *Wall Street Journal*, May 3, D2; Gould, C. (1999). Expat pay plans suffer cutbacks. *Workforce*, September, 40–46; Latta, G. W. (1999). Expatriate policy and practice: A ten-year comparison of trends. *Compensation and Benefits Review*, 31, 35–39; McGowan, R. (2003). The days of the "champagne lifestyle" expatriate assignments are numbered. *Mercer Human Resource Consulting*, January 29, 1–3; Reynolds, C. (1994). *Compensation Basics for North American Expatriates: Developing an Effective Program for Employees Working Abroad*. Scottsdale, AZ: American Compensation Association.

58. Ramstad, E., & Woo, J. (2010). South Korea works overtime to tackle vacation shortage. *Wall Street Journal*, March 1, A1, A22.

Chapter 11

Global Staffing Alternatives
Expatriates and Beyond

We need and seek employees who have the ability to seamlessly move between the world of the multinational and the India market.

> —Anjali Bansal, managing partner-India at executive recruiting firm Spencer Stuart on what foreign multinationals want from the managers they send to India[1]

Bansal's comment illustrates that international companies are increasingly looking for people with cultural fluency and flexibility when filling important positions overseas. This is particularly true in fast-growing nations such as India, China, and Brazil. Research shows that selecting the right people to serve as expatriates can enhance the performance of foreign subsidiaries, especially if those employees can improve the transfer of knowledge across cultural and organizational boundaries. Finding such talented people, however, is not easy. While traditional expatriates are a good option if they have the right skills, there are plenty of other—and sometimes better—choices. For example, an Indian national who immigrated to London years ago likely still retains tacit knowledge that could help British Petroleum (BP) with its operations in Mumbai. Likewise, an expatriate who has spent the better part of her career in overseas assignments might fit the bill presented by Bansal. Simply put, having multiple options is a good thing, because few people can shift easily across cultural boundaries, possess extensive knowledge of local markets, and have significant operational experience abroad.[2]

This point, briefly raised in Chapter 9, will be examined in detail in the first part of this chapter. Addressed next are the challenges associated with selecting, training, and repatriating expatriates. The chapter concludes with some advice for those seeking careers in international management.

OVERSEAS STAFFING: A WORLD OF CHOICES

The breadth of staffing options used by multinationals is often a function of how much revenue they earn abroad as well as practical and strategic issues. Generally speaking, the greater the percentage of revenue earned overseas, the more likely it is that firms will insist that their senior leaders possess significant international experience and a deep understanding of foreign cultures and markets. The German industrial giant Siemens, with over 275,000 employees outside of Germany, is a case in point. Among those employees are some 2,000 managers who are posted outside of their home country, roughly 60% of whom are German and are traditional expatriates. Because Siemens does business in over 190 countries, it is essential to have globally minded managers. Indeed, foreign experience is required to be promoted to the highest levels of Siemens's management. Many U.S. multinationals that depend on foreign markets have done more in recent years to create a development pipeline of international opportunities for lower-level managers while seeking to fill top positions with executives who have significant international experience.[3]

The composition of the board of directors also sends a signal about the extent to which international skills and expertise is taken seriously. Unfortunately, some U.S. multinationals appear to fall short in that regard. Less than 10% of board members possess either important foreign experience or are foreign born, a statistic that holds for firms that earn more than half their revenues overseas (e.g., Halliburton). Yet there are some internationally impressive boards at U.S. firms.

For instance, Colgate and Schlumberger both earn over 75% of their revenues in foreign markets, and both have internationally savvy boards (i.e., at least 50% of board members are either foreign nationals or U.S. executives with considerable foreign experience).[4]

In any case, staffing foreign operations is a complex proposition with a variety of choices. Table 11.1 presents the many types of employees that multinationals may want to consider. Of course, some of these employee categories overlap. A particular firm may not use all the different employee options available. Table 11.1 addresses a few of the more popular options.

A traditional option is to use *parent-country nationals* (PCNs) in senior executive and key technical roles overseas. PCNs are citizens of the country where the multinational is headquartered. If they are posted overseas for a year or more, PCNs are known as *expatriates*. Common reasons to send PCNs abroad long-term as expatriates include:

1. the belief that local employees in a foreign subsidiary lack relevant skills.
2. the belief that a PCN is the best way to monitor foreign operations and instill corporate values.
3. the desire to transfer knowledge about foreign markets back to headquarters.
4. the need to provide opportunities for high-potential employees to develop their cross-cultural expertise.

For example, Mexican multinational CEMEX had about 100 managers in expatriate roles in 2011. Most of this group was assigned abroad because of perceived skill deficits among local employees and to carefully install CEMEX corporate values—two of the reasons noted above.[5]

Despite the positive reasons for sending PCNs overseas, doing so is expensive, and failure is a real possibility. While precise figures are elusive, estimated failure rates vary from 5% to 70%. This range is large, but it is safe to assume that roughly 25% of expatriates fail, meaning that PCNs are ineffective in their jobs or return home prematurely because of adjustment challenges or other problems.[6]

A big risk associated with posting PCNs abroad as expatriates is that they often lack an understanding of the local business environment, particularly early on. Consequently, some multinationals target immigrants when recruiting, hoping to plug them into key company positions in their native countries. Known as *boomerangs*, these employees may face some unique challenges, as the following *Global Innovations* box illustrates.

If multinationals are really concerned about having local expertise in foreign markets, they often decide to hire *host-country nationals* (HCNs)—people native to the country where foreign operations exist. Korean giant Samsung believes in this approach. With almost 100,000 employees outside of South Korea (triple the number from a decade ago), the percentage of HCNs also keeps rising, approaching

Table 11.1
Types of International Employees

Type of Employee	Description
Parent-country nationals (PCNs)	Employees who are citizens of the country where the multinational is based
Traditional expatriates	PCNs who are sent on an overseas assignment for at least one year
Second-generation expatriates	Immigrants who are naturalized citizens of the multinational's home country and then posted abroad for at least one year to a country other than where they were born
Just-in-time expatriates	Expatriates hired as needed from outside the multinational to fill a specific role or particular assignment
Short-term international assignees	Employees sent on overseas assignments from a few weeks to a year—an increasingly popular option that doesn't require relocation
Frequent business travelers	Employees who must often travel internationally for their jobs, usually on trips lasting from a few days to a few months
Permanent expatriates	Employees who spend long stretches of years or even their entire careers in international assignments, going from one foreign posting to another
Host-country nationals (HCNs)	Local nationals hired to staff foreign operations in a specific country
Inpatriates	Typically, HCNs who are brought to the multinational's headquarters country to fill a temporary assignment lasting from months to two years
Third-country nationals (TCNs)	Employees who are hired to work in a foreign subsidiary or the headquarters of a multinational but who are citizens of another country
Domestic internationals	Employees who stay in their home country while performing remote international work (e.g., interacting with foreign customers by telephone or e-mail)
International commuters	Employees who live in one country but commute to work in another country
Boomerangs	Employees who are hired or chosen to return to their home countries to work for a multinational
Outsourced employees	Personnel who work for global employment firms hired by a multinational to provide workers or even entire staffs for a foreign outpost

Source: Adapted from Briscoe, D. R., Schuler, R. S., & Claus, L. (2009). *International Human Resource Management* (3rd ed.). New York: Routledge.

GLOBAL INNOVATIONS

Want an Alternative to Traditional Expatriates? Try "Boomerangs"

Traditional expatriates are nationals of the country where the parent company is head-quartered. But instead of posting expatriates to run operations in foreign countries, many multinationals are increasingly turning to *boomerangs*. They recruit an employee who emigrated abroad to return to their home country and run business operations there.

For instance, U.S. multinationals have frequently turned to Chinese boomerangs in recent years—often recruiting them while they are living in the United States and sending them back to China to run business units. The attractiveness of boomerangs is simple. Companies can fill key positions in important foreign markets with skilled professionals who also have a grasp of the local culture and business practices. Examples of U.S. firms using boomerangs include Marriott, McDonald's, and Payless Shoes—all of which have returned highly educated and well-trained immigrants to their home nations to offer service support or lead local operations.

Indeed, Payless Shoes sent a boomerang—a native El Salvadoran—to run a store in the Central American country and to lay the groundwork for further expansion in the region. This particular manager had left El Salvador at the age of 15 and eventually became a U.S. citizen. By posting her back to El Salvador at the age of 35, Payless Shoes had a boomerang manager in place who understood the local culture well and spoke Spanish fluently. Of course, there can be significant challenges. Boomerangs may struggle to adapt when they find themselves back in their home cultures. The reasons for these struggles vary but can include overestimating their understanding of the local culture after years spent elsewhere or their inability to change aspects of the local culture they find unappealing.

For instance, one Chinese executive who returned home after working for a number of Western multinationals found the traditional behavior of his subordinates frustrating. When he arrived to visit one branch office in China, the executive found employees waiting for him in a receiving line—a traditional courtesy designed to boost management egos. Peeved and embarrassed, he instructed the office manager to abolish receiving lines. He also had trouble persuading his managers not to run out to the airport to greet him when coming back from trips.

Boomerangs can also be surprised at the treatment they receive from local employees who may not perceive them as locals after so much time away. For example, one executive went back to Japan after more than two decades in the United States to run Apple Computer's Japanese operations. His Japanese colleagues felt he was "too American," and he left in frustration after just a year. Likewise, a management consultant returned to her Russian homeland after living for years in the United States. Despite her fluent Russian, she went back to the United States after less than two years, tired of Russian women who found her ambition and accomplishments off-putting.

Companies can help boomerangs overcome such obstacles and eventually succeed. One tactic that works well is to assign locals to serve as "cultural translators" for boomerangs to ease their adjustment back into their native cultures. Another option is cross-cultural training designed to help them reintegrate into their local cultures. Apparel giant Levi Strauss provides such training. One Peruvian Levi Strauss manager was educated in the United States but ran into trouble when she was sent to Mexico. During company training, she realized that her failure to use formal titles when addressing her Mexican colleagues was a key reason why they were being standoffish—they thought she was being rude. In any case, companies would be wise not to assume that boomerangs will automatically snap back into their native cultural environments without any difficulty, especially if they have been away for years.[7]

70% in 2011. One of Samsung's senior human resource (HR) executives explains: "This is a change from the past, when Samsung's overseas operations were mainly run by Korean expatriates." While some companies fear that HCNs lack knowledge about the corporate culture, the advantages of HCNs over PCNs are clear: HCNs usually have a better understanding of local business practices and culture. They are also cheaper—with none of the relocation costs or fancy pay packages associated with expatriates.[8]

Third-country nationals (TCNs) represent yet another staffing option. TCNs hold citizenship in a country other than where they are working (e.g., an Australian working in Indonesia). A TCN might be just the ticket for a firm in search of a manager of a foreign subsidiary with deep technical and cultural skills. While PCNs often have excellent technical skills, their knowledge of local culture may be limited. Similarly, while HCNs may have a deep grasp of the local environment, their technical skills may not be strong enough to solve thorny problems, such as a supply chain issue that's regularly encountered and solved at company headquarters. As a result, a TCN may be the best bet, particularly in a nation where local executive talent is thin and a multinational wants to develop leaders there. For example, a French firm with a new manufacturing plant in Nicaragua may want to look for excellent plant manager candidates in Mexico, a much larger country with a deep and talented pool of executives who are fluent in Spanish.

Beyond PCNs, HCNs, and TCNs, sophisticated multinationals often develop an *international cadre*—a set of managers they can send to any country to represent the firm and its values. This means that managers must be chosen based on their skills and potential, not their nationality, and then sent on different assignments abroad. Some international cadre members move from one overseas assignment to the next for most of their careers. Sometimes referred to as *permanent expatriates*, these employees may be posted abroad for multiple assignments over an extended period. This seems to work. Multinationals that use TCNs and regional transfers to develop international cadres perform better than multinationals relying on traditional expatriates.[9]

Then there are *inpatriates*, or foreign employees who are brought to the multinational's home country to fill a position at headquarters for months, or even a few years. U.S. multinationals operating in developing markets use inpatriates routinely, bringing high-potential employees from places such as Brazil, China, and India to the United States. The goal of this is typically to hone the skills of inpatriates, further socialize them to corporate values, and increase their commitment to the company. It is a two-way street, with multinationals also learning from their inpatriates about how to be more successful in foreign markets.[10]

STAFFING AND MANAGING INTERNATIONAL TALENT

How multinationals recruit and develop their international employees should reflect the firm's international strategy, the competitive environment, the availability of talent, and the challenges inherent in specific foreign markets. This general global talent management process and the desired outcomes that should result from it are summarized in Figure 11.1.

Forces Impacting Human Resource Practices in Multinationals
Work force demographics in different countries
Worldwide demand for employees with specific competencies and motivation
Ongoing globalization

International Staffing Challenges Facing Multinationals
Hiring people with the right skills, competencies, and motivation
Hiring an appropriate number of employees for specific positions and locations
Hiring employees at the right price

Key Human Resource Management Action Areas for Multinationals
Plan staffing needs for specific foreign locations
Attract and select outstanding international employees
Implement effective training and development programs for international staff
Implement effective retention efforts
Implement fair performance evaluation and compensation practices

Desired International Workforce Results
Successful positioning of talent (right people, right skills, right locations, right price)
Deeper pool of talent that can be called on in the future (greater "bench strength")
World-class international workforce that is a source of competitive advantage

FIGURE 11.1 A Process for Understanding the Selection and Development of International Employees

Source: Adapted from Schuler, R. S., Jackson, S. E., & Tarique, I. R. (2011). Framework for global talent management: HR actions for dealing with global talent challenges. In H. Scullion & D. G. Collings (eds.), *Global Talent Management* (19). New York: Routledge.

Clearly, several forces impact multinationals' efforts to develop their international workforces. These include globalization (which has deepened connections between economies), demographic trends (e.g., the shrinking, aging populations in developed countries versus the expanding, younger populations in developing nations), and the demand for skilled, flexible employees who are culturally sophisticated. For multinationals, the challenge is to have employees with the right skill sets in the right places at the right price. To accomplish this, firms must attract, develop, and retain outstanding employees, thereby creating a workforce that is a competitive advantage for the firm. Naturally, this requires trade-offs. For instance, because of the greater technical skills required of international workforces, it may be smart to rely on expatriates to staff overseas operations offering complex services or products. Here, the need for those sophisticated skills (e.g., in software, statistics) is great. On the other hand, in foreign markets where multinationals face fierce local competitors, key positions might be held by HNCs. They have greater knowledge of local competitors and the general business environment in their home country. Keep in mind, however, that these are generalizations that may not apply to what a specific employee might bring to the table. Nevertheless, they underscore the need for multinationals to make effective staffing decisions around the world.[11]

Sometimes multinationals embrace different staffing philosophies. Firms with a geocentric philosophy focus on ability when hiring international staff, regardless of nationality, with performance criteria being developed jointly by headquarters and foreign subsidiaries. The goal is to inculcate key corporate values and perspectives into managers who can be sent anywhere. At the other extreme are firms with an ethnocentric philosophy, where foreign subsidiaries have little say over headquarters decisions and key positions are always filled by PCNs.

In between are two other philosophies. Firms with a polycentric philosophy allow foreign subsidiaries to control their human resource management needs, with headquarters focusing on making strategic decisions. Consequently, HCNs typically occupy key positions in foreign subsidiaries and usually stay put, not moving beyond their home country. Finally, firms with a regiocentric philosophy move employees around within a particular region. While employees may be posted to several countries throughout their careers, they will generally not have the opportunity to hold positions at headquarters.[12]

Interestingly, the particular staffing approach taken by multinationals may also reflect cultural values. Everything else being equal, multinationals based in high-power-distance countries tend to rely on expatriates more, probably because national values reinforce the belief that higher levels of control are necessary overseas. Expatriates offer the strongest control, expense notwithstanding. This perspective may be exacerbated if firm headquarters and foreign subsidiaries have divergent views about authority. In short, if local values seem "threatening," it may increase the odds that expatriates will be sent. For instance, Korean and Japanese multinationals tend to use PCNs (traditional expatriates) in foreign subsidiaries more than European or U.S.

multinationals, in part because they value high power distance. As their experiences in foreign markets grows, however, Korean and Japanese firms often switch to using HCNs more in foreign subsidiaries. Samsung, for example, with considerable global reach and experience behind it, has shifted much more toward HCNs in recent years.[13]

DEVELOPING EMPLOYEES WITH INTERNATIONAL SKILLS

Many multinationals tilt toward a geocentric philosophy as their international operations become more sophisticated and far-reaching. Yet building an international workforce characterized by flexible, open-minded, and culturally savvy employees can take years. When multinationals have operations in dozens of countries, virtually everything they do involves some international contact. Consequently, international skills and experience can't be limited to just a few managers. Instead, the ideal would be for everyone in the company to grasp that cultural values and business practices change when borders are crossed, with implications for how business must be conducted in various foreign markets.

This begs the question of how multinationals can help large numbers of employees improve their international competencies. Some firms offer various training and development programs, such as moving promising employees through a series of foreign assignments over a period of years. This can give managers deep experience across multiple countries and circumstances (e.g., by establishing start-up operations in one country, managing an existing joint venture in a second location, and downsizing operations in a third). Procter & Gamble (P&G) stresses the cultivation of local talent worldwide. Employees with high potential are identified by their managers and then placed in regional talent pools as they gain the experiences and competencies needed to hold key positions in any location where P&G does business. P&G uses a computerized system to keep track of these employees globally, sorting them by competencies, experiences, and prior assignments. This makes it much easier and quicker for P&G to pick someone for international assignments when needed.[14]

Other options for improving the cultural skills and competencies of a workforce include recruiting foreign exchange students who decide to return to their home nations upon graduation. For this reason, their language and cultural expertise can come in handy for multinationals. Other firms identify employees who already speak multiple languages, who are open to new cultures, and who are interested in assignments overseas as criteria for inclusion in international development programs. For instance, some U.S. multinationals have enjoyed good results with programs that bring in promising managers from around the globe to tackle group projects together in a simulated context. These programs can help develop cross-national relationships and strengthen skills at solving culturally related problems. U.S.-based tech firm Motorola annually puts high-potential international managers in a weeks-long business simulation that is quite demanding, realistic, and involves making investment and other decisions with feedback. Likewise, IBM's Basic Blue program brings together managers from different countries and has been recognized by prominent publications and organizations. Among other things, it focuses on role playing as well as developing emotional intelligence and coaching skills via performance review simulations. Such simulations can prove quite effective—by using them to assess employees under consideration for foreign assignments, it took French food giant Danone SA just three years to reduce the percentage of expatriate managers who failed from 35% to 3%.[15]

Some multinationals with extensive foreign operations have created global training programs that cover large groups of employees. While they typically include training for expatriates who are headed to particular countries (more on this later), these programs tend to have broad goals, such as raising cultural awareness, making multicultural teams work well, and improving international communication competencies. Firms that have implemented global training programs successfully, with noticeable gains in cross-cultural awareness and group productivity, include Samsung, P&G, and Intel.[16]

EXPATRIATES: IMPROVING THE ODDS OF SUCCESS

Clearly, many multinationals have been trying to cut back on expatriates in recent years, partly because of the high cost. International firms are increasingly looking to hire HCNs or TCNs to staff their foreign operations and have been dispatching employees on shorter trips abroad and using technology, such as video conferencing, to keep people connected around the world.

Despite these trends, expatriates are not going to disappear anytime soon. Indeed, they will continue to play valuable roles for multinationals as technical experts, international managers, relationship builders—or all three. There is simply no better option than to send someone overseas for multiyear assignments in many cases. If anything, the expatriate population has actually been increasing in recent years, because more companies are engaging in international business than ever before, including multinationals rising up from developing markets such as Brazil, China, and India. Moreover, many established multinationals have expanded the number of countries in which they do business and have pushed heavily into emerging markets. This expanded need for expats can also explain their rising numbers. And those numbers are staggering. For example, in China, over 90% of companies on the Global Fortune 500 list operate there. Moreover, the number of foreign employees posted to China (more than 300,000) has doubled over the past several years.[17]

It goes without saying that many of the foreigners working in China are U.S. expatriates. Indeed, the number of Americans who work in foreign countries or travel abroad for business is astounding. About 6 million Americans work abroad in some capacity, and 7.5 million more go on business trips to foreign countries each year.

Roughly 1.3 million expatriates work for U.S. multinationals, 80% of whom have a partner or spouse that will accompany them. If we count children who accompany an expatriate parent, nearly 3 million people are somehow involved in expatriate assignments for U.S. multinationals alone. Some of the big multinationals support huge expatriate populations. For instance, energy giant Royal Dutch/Shell has more than 5,000 expatriates posted to 120 countries, while German conglomerate Siemens has roughly 2,000 expatriates posted to 190 countries.[18]

Balancing Risks and Rewards with Expatriates

All these figures notwithstanding, expatriates are a risky and pricey option. And when an expatriate fails for one reason or another (which can be caused by multinationals hiring the wrong person or providing inadequate training), the consequences can be severe. Table 11.2 illustrates this point.

Failure for expatriates can include having to come home early because of various difficulties, finishing the assignment but performing poorly, or leaving the company once a given assignment abroad is over. All of these result in negative outcomes that cost the company. Consider the expatriates who leave the firm upon returning to the home country. Even if they did a good job, they are now taking their wealth of experience gained from the firm's investment in them and using it elsewhere— likely with the competition. While failure estimates for expatriates vary, failure rates may have risen somewhat in the past few years. One recent survey reported that 34% of the expatriates in nearly 200 multinationals had failed. This high number may be due to the fact that expatriates are finding themselves increasingly posted to challenging countries such as Vietnam and Russia—places where living conditions can be harsh and far removed from the home culture. Interestingly, U.S. multinationals seem to have higher rates of expatriate failure (often 30% to 40%) than either European or Japanese firms (where failure rates are more typically around 10%). One possible explanation for this discrepancy is that Europeans live in an environment in which they are exposed to a wider variety of languages and intercultural experiences than their U.S. counterparts—something that may help them adapt to new cultures. While Japan is much more homogeneous than Europe or the United States, Japanese multinationals tend to send expatriates for longer overseas assignments. Longer assignments may help Japanese expatriates adjust, given that their culture is highly homogeneous.[19]

Still, expatriates are very expensive even when things go well. The total bill for all the extras during the first year of an overseas assignment—such as foreign service premiums, travel and relocation expenses, housing, tuition help for children, taxes, home leave, and extensive training—can easily cost three times that of an expatriate's annual salary. Indeed, the cost for a three-year expatriate assignment can cost a multinational corporation $1 million or more.[20]

Table 11.2
When Expatriates Fail: A Long List of Consequences

Consequences of Failure	Description and Implications
Returning home before assignment term is completed	Estimates of the percentages of expatriates who are told to come home early (or who request it) vary depending on the role and context. In any case, returning prematurely can jeopardize company effectiveness and the expatriate's career.
Wasted relocation expenses	Sending an expatriate overseas (plus partner, spouse, children, and/or belongings in many cases) is very expensive and can easily top $100,000.
Wasted preparation and support costs	Failure means the money spent on direct (e.g., training, overseas pay) and indirect (e.g., not getting the job done) costs to prepare and support expatriates are lost.
Other indirect costs	Failure hurts the careers and confidence of expatriates and damages relations with local employees, customers, and suppliers (which will take time to repair).
Poor or ineffective performance	If expatriates finish their assignments but have performed inadequately (e.g., making poor decisions, hurting local relations), it can cost the firm business.
Turnover following repatriation	When expatriates leave the firm after returning, the company receives no return on a $1 million-plus investment for a typical three-year posting.
Negative momentum for expatriate selection	When word about expatriates' challenges spreads, recruiting new expatriates becomes harder, undercutting firms' ability to seize overseas opportunities.

Sources: Adapted from Birdseye, M. G., & Hill, J. S. (1995). Individual, organizational/work and environmental influences on expatriate turnover tendencies: An empirical study. *Journal of International Business Studies, 41*, 787–806; Black, J. S., Gregersen, H. B., & Mendenhall, M. E. (1992). *Global Assignments: Successfully Expatriating and Repatriating International Managers.* San Francisco: Jossey-Bass; Carpenter, S. (2001). Battling the overseas blues. *Monitor on Psychology,* July/August, 48–49; Hauser, J. (1999). Managing expatriates' careers. *HR Focus,* February, 11–12; Poe, A. C. (2000). Destination everywhere. *HR Magazine,* October, 67–75.

Family disruptions are another factor that often gives potential expatriates pause—as do concerns about political strife, crime, and terrorism. Indeed, the perception is that the world is a more dangerous place now than in the past. Almost 30% of 240 overseas locations were recently ranked as high risk versus about 20% in 1998. Many people simply do not think that they would adjust well to daily life in a foreign country. If employees feel up to the challenge of an expatriate assignment, it is likely that the companies they work for will be interested. Multinationals increasingly want their managers to have plenty of foreign experience under their belts—especially if those employees want to become senior executives.[21]

Choosing People for Expatriate Assignments

In choosing expatriates, many factors should be considered in the selection and training process, including the assignment itself (e.g., which competencies are needed, how much interaction is required with local employees or customers), and features about the assignment location (e.g., cultural and socioeconomic differences present). Of course, what the potential expatriate also brings to the table in terms of motivation, skills, experience, and family situation should also matter a great deal. Yet, across countries and regions, multinationals weigh things differently or diverge altogether regarding the factors they use in selecting expatriates. For instance, U.S. firms tend to emphasize previous performance, technical skills, and desire to go when choosing expatriates, often because the assignment itself is aimed at fixing problems in overseas subsidiaries. Recently, U.S. multinationals have been paying more attention to personal fit and family circumstances when selecting expatriates. That is, screening on personal factors such as resilience, openness, and consideration of family motivation to travel have become important tools in the selection process. On the other hand, in Chinese firms, while managers take skills and performance into account when choosing expatriates, they may place more emphasis on their relationships with candidates. Chinese firms seem to be less interested in employee development when dealing with expatriate assignments. As a result, expatriate selection is driven by managerial authority, if not favoritism, in many Chinese firms.[22]

In contrast, European and Scandinavian firms tend to stress flexibility and cultural competencies more so than do multinationals from other parts of the world. Likewise, they tend to rely on a wider variety of evaluation methods than U.S.-based firms. This suggests that European and Scandinavian firms focus more on aligning candidate skills and attributes with the needs of a specific expatriate assignment. Many U.S. firms fail to systematically assess the extent to which location and assignment demands align with candidates' family situation, personal attributes, and "soft" skills. The most important factors for expatriate success include certain personal attributes (e.g., tolerance, emotional stability), soft competencies (e.g., motivation and ability to bridge cultural differences in building relationships), and family context (e.g., the accompanying spouse's or partner's ability or motivation to adapt).[23]

But how do multinationals actually evaluate candidates for expatriate assignments? As you might suspect, evaluation practices can vary, independent of the selection criteria used. Sophisticated Western multinationals may use talent information systems to track large groups of employees and build a pool of potential expatriates. P&G uses such a database to keep track of 13,000 managers all over the world, with variables that capture their experiences in foreign or cross-cultural contexts. From there, a variety of additional techniques can be employed to identify the best individual candidate for an expatriate position, including interviews (ideally incorporating spouses and partners), psychometric tests (measuring such traits as adaptability and emotional maturity), performance in assessment center training (where candidates are put through various real-world scenarios), and intensive reviews of past accomplishments relevant to the assignment. U.S. multinationals frequently use in-depth interviewing when picking expatriates. In addition to any job-relevant qualifications, such interviews are most productive if they examine individual attributes related to expatriate success. The key goal is to pick the person who best fits the requirements of the expatriate assignment.[24]

Interestingly, the precise factors that lead to success in expatriate assignments may also vary. Much will depend on how well expatriates adjust to their new cultural environment, the nature of the work they are doing overseas, and the interaction needs of their foreign colleagues. Individuals, however, bring different talents, skills, and experiences to the table. At the same time, firms will vary in terms of how much organizational and managerial support is provided to expatriates before and after they leave for an assignment. Consequently, how expatriates adjust to foreign assignments will differ. These variations in adjustment approaches may reflect differences in home cultures as well as the HR practices companies use to support expatriates.[25]

Regardless of how rigorous the selection process has been, an expatriate candidate may simply decline the assignment offer at the end of the day. To secure a yes from potential expatriates, the financial package will need to be attractive and the job itself interesting and rewarding (e.g., offering potential for advancement rather than a high risk of failure). Expatriate candidates may also decline assignments if their concerns or those of their family about the location are not assuaged. Few individuals would want to be assigned to a location that is viewed as politically unstable or physically unsafe. If there are meager job opportunities available for partners or spouses planning to accompany an expatriate or weak schools and education programs for any accompanying children, little incentive exists. Issues such as these can be particularly vexing. Not surprisingly, it is often difficult to convince an employee to consider an expatriate posting if the culture overseas does not provide for his or her family. Another deterrent is that expatriates themselves are more likely to be demoted rather than promoted after they finish an overseas assignment. Multinationals typically refuse (or are unable) to promise expatriates their old jobs back and instead often place them into open positions that are available after they return (often a de facto demotion). Naturally, multinationals should be clear about how expatriate assignments will develop employees' careers and specify how expatriates will be assigned a new position once they return home.[26]

Some multinationals have been taking additional steps to tackle common concerns of potential expatriates. About 25% of multinationals factor in the potential loss of a trailing spouse's or partner's job by including job search help, career counseling, or a cash bonus in the expatriate's assignment package. Approximately 90% of multinationals offer location visits before employees accept an assignment, and roughly 50% offer language or other training for family members who are accompanying the expatriate. For some of the most dangerous locations, extreme offers are made to lure expatriates. Several years ago, a U.S. company offered expatriates an annual $75,000 hardship bonus for working in Iraq. Firms may also give expatriates safety training before leaving, addressing emergency procedures, personal safety, and local politics as well as providing high-security housing within walled complexes guarded 24/7 by security personnel.[27]

Multinationals should have a systematic process for identifying and choosing expatriates that comprehensively evaluates candidates against the requirements of a particular foreign assignment. Firms would do well to follow the recommended process laid out in Figure 11.2—which begins by putting together a selection team and ends with the chosen expatriates preparing for their overseas assignments.

Selection teams should consist of home-country, host-country, and international HR professionals. The role of HR experts is to identify expatriate candidates and help the team use appropriate selection methods. Home- and host-country managers on the team are there to represent the needs of the parent company and foreign subsidiary, respectively. Once formed, the team should determine the job factors (e.g., nature of the work, skills required) and location factors (e.g., cultural differences) most relevant to the assignment. Next, the team should establish criteria for judging assignment success and then begin to build a pool of candidates (e.g., through job postings). Candidates should be carefully assessed on factors known to predict expatriate success and failure, including motivation to go, family dynamics, cross-cultural experience, personal attributes (e.g., tolerance), and appropriate competencies (e.g., assignment-specific technical and linguistic requirements). The team should use multiple methods and tools to conduct candidate screening (e.g., tests, interviews, exercises).[28]

After the candidate pool has been reduced to a handful of finalists, another set of interviews can be conducted that focus on assignment issues in greater depth. It would be wise at this point to include detailed information about what work and home life will be like in the host country as well as the specific implications of successful assignment completion for expatriates' careers. It is absolutely vital at this point to interview any trailing spouses, partners, or family members. Sending candidates and any trailing family members on preassignment trips to the host country may also help them grasp what life abroad will be like. This is also a good mechanism for fleshing out any potential lingering concerns held by the candidate or family members—these should be discussed at length and taken seriously. Once the selection team has had its assignment offer accepted (hopefully by the best-fitting candidate), the next step is to begin efforts to prepare the expatriate to succeed abroad.[29]

Create Selection Team
(team should include home and host country representatives, international HR experts)

**Determine Job/Firm Factors
Relevant to Assignment**

Nature of work
Technical/managerial skills needed
Level of interaction job required with locals
Nature of training available
Nature of on-site support available

**Determine Location Factors
Relevant to Assignment**

Extent of cultural differences with home context
Nature of political/social/business environment
Level of development and standard of living
Proximity to home country
Attitudes toward foreigners

Set Selection Criteria and Proceed to Recruit Candidates

Consider Individual Factors that Impact Expatriate Success or Failure

Ability and desire to go (e.g., for career or personal development purposes)
Family situation (are trailing spouse/partner, children in the mix?)
Educational background, international experience, technical skills, and language proficiency
Personal attributes—Tolerance, flexibility, openness, emotional stability, extroversion, agreeableness
"Soft" competencies—Relationship orientation, able to bridge home-host country practices

---

Apply Multiple Methods to Evaluate Candidates

Use assessment instruments that evaluate personal attributes and/or learned skills and competencies
Conduct formal reviews of past performance and experiences, especially in overseas contexts
Interview candidate and family members
Use assessment centers for simulations/exercises that evaluate candidate suitability

---

Potential Expatriate Accepts Assignment Offer

Transition New Expatriate into Training and Preparation Activities

FIGURE 11.2 Picking Right: Steps for Selecting Expatriates

Sources: Adapted from Black, J. S., Gregersen, H. B., & Mendenhall, M. E. (1992). *Global Assignments: Successfully Expatriating and Repatriating International Managers*. San Francisco: Jossey-Bass; Briscoe, D. R., Schuler, R. S., & Claus, L. (2009). *International Human Resource Management* (3rd ed.). New York: Routledge; Downes, M., & Thomas, A. S. (2000). Managing overseas assignments to build organizational knowledge. *Human Resource Planning*, 20, 33–48; Shaffer, M. A., Harrison, D. A., Gregersen, H., Black, J. S., & Ferzandi, L. A. (2006). You can take it with you: Individual differences and expatriate effectiveness. *Journal of Applied Psychology*, 91, 109–125.

Preparing Expatriates for Their Overseas Assignments

Effective preparation for expatriates should include activities before, during, and after the assignment. Many expatriates experience major adjustment problems and culture shocks both when they start their overseas assignments and again once they return home, making repatriation efforts critical. Many preparation activities are available, each with the goal of helping expatriates become effective overseas as quickly as possible while minimizing any adjustment issues experienced by expatriates and accompanying family members. And the scope of preparation activities can be quite broad. Besides training on culture and language, preparation may include briefings on the relocation itself. Issues considered include how to ship possessions overseas, navigating daily life overseas (e.g., tips on shopping, housing, etc.), employment options for spouses or partners, school choices for children, foreign business practices, health care, safety issues, and company history in the foreign location. Experts estimate that between 40% and 70% of companies offer no preparation or training of any significance before expatriates depart. It is likely that the percentage is closer to 70% (or even higher) for small to medium-sized firms. Regardless of the exact numbers, having so many firms do little to prepare expatriates is troubling since thoughtful training can improve their adjustment and performance once posted abroad.[30]

But if cross-cultural training should be a key part of efforts to prepare expatriates, what exactly should be included in that training? Stepping back for a moment, it is important to recognize that cross-cultural training produces learning through a series of steps. In the first step, expatriates begin to better understand how cultural differences might explain the attitudes and behaviors of foreigners. After that, expatriates must develop and retain knowledge about how to appropriately behave in particular cultural settings—developing a new mental framework for behavior that can serve as a guide and help prevent mistakes. Finally, expatriates must practice behaving in culturally appropriate ways, a process that improves confidence when dealing with foreign colleagues, customers, and so on.[31]

Cross-cultural training can run the gamut from brief, generic activities that take a couple of days to detailed, multifaceted programs that may take weeks or even months to complete. Table 11.3 presents different levels of training rigor along with some typical activities associated with each. Determining the proper level of rigor and choosing the right activities is no easy chore. Multinationals should take into account the nature of the assignment, its duration, and how much interaction expatriates must have with locals. For example, if an assignment requires sustained interactions with local businesspeople in the host country, then it would be wise to put the expatriate through a very rigorous training regimen. In essence, training rigor should reflect the *cultural toughness* of the assignment location. The bigger the difference

Table 11.3
Cross-Cultural Training: Rigor, Time, and Activities

Rigor	Typical Time Range for Completion	Typical Activities Involved
Very low to low	20 hours or less	Lectures, videos, area briefings
Moderate	Between 20 and 60 hours	Role-playing exercises, case analyses, and survival-level language training—in addition to everything above
High to very high	Between 60 and 180 hours or more	Detailed simulations and scenario exercises (often in an assessment center context), field trips abroad, and in-depth language training—in addition to everything above

Source: Adapted from Black, J. S., Gregersen, H. B., & Mendenhall, M. E. (1992). *Global Assignments: Successfully Expatriating and Repatriating International Managers*. San Francisco: Jossey-Bass, 97.

between the host-country culture and the expatriate's home culture, the more challenging the adjustment is likely to be. Consequently, training should be more rigorous when expatriates are sent to places high in cultural toughness for them. For example, U.S. expatriates may have more difficulty adjusting when posted to Africa, Asia, and the Middle East compared to Europe (where cultural values may feel less foreign). Cultural toughness has important implications for expatriate adjustment as well as employees' willingness to accept assignments. This chapter's *Culture Clash* takes another look at cultural toughness and related issues through the lens of two sets of expatriates—Westerners posted to China and Chinese posted to Western countries.[32]

Naturally, there are success stories out there about multinationals that have created sophisticated and effective training programs for their expatriates. A good example is Royal Dutch/Shell, which at one point surveyed 17,000 current, former, and potential expatriates plus their family members. The goal was to systematically evaluate important problems that surface when employees are posted abroad. The results from the firm's survey were used to create improved training programs. This kind of impressive and sustained effort tends to appear when senior executives at companies such as Royal Dutch/Shell, IBM, Unilever, and others, explicitly make international management development a top priority.[34]

In recent years, cross-cultural training programs veered away from superficial efforts to explain business practices and etiquette used in other countries. Today, training is more likely to stress open-mindedness, understanding, and respect—in part by directly challenging the attitudes, assumptions, and prejudices held about

CULTURE CLASH

Hardship Post or Comfortable Sojourn?

Western Expats in China and Chinese Expats in the West

Things have been looking up in recent years for Western expatriates on assignment in China. Rundown hotels, poor food, and weak education and hospitality services have given way to glitzy housing developments, fancy restaurants, and pricey private schools for children. China's rapid growth has made it the place to be for foreign expatriates, who are increasingly accepted within society and less likely to attract stares, even in far-flung Chinese provinces. Naturally, not everything is perfect. Air quality still leaves much to be desired in many Chinese cities, and traffic is often a chaotic nightmare. Censorship, opaque government rules, shifting regulations, restrictions on foreign companies, cultural differences, and complex relationships certainly create hassles for Western expatriates trying to run operations in China.

The movement of Western expatriates into China, however, is no longer a one-way street. Thanks to growing economic clout, Chinese companies are setting up shop and making deals all over the world. As a result, a flood of Chinese expatriates have been sent into places as diverse as Africa, Europe, and the United States. Yet the contrast between the context shift made by Western expatriates and their Chinese counterparts could not be starker. Western expatriates landing in China have left modern democracies with individualist values and slow-growing economies for a more collectivist place characterized by rapid growth and governed by an authoritarian regime. Of course, Chinese expatriates have done exactly the reverse. So are there differences in what each group of expatriates generally experiences? Which group might have the greater challenge making the adjustment?

While the answers to these questions are less than precise, anecdotally Chinese expatriates seem to have the shorter end of the stick. Part of the problem is that most Chinese expatriates fall well short of their Western counterparts when it comes to perks and pay. As a result, the much higher prices they often encounter in Western cities create hardships. Instead of having maids to cook and clean as they do at home, Chinese expatriates in Western countries find themselves having "to clean their own toilets," as one expatriate so aptly put it. Moreover, without having a generous expatriate package to lean on, most Chinese expatriates leave their families behind to cut costs. Many Chinese expatriates find their time in Western countries lonely—unless they are extroverted, single, and have outstanding language skills and are therefore able to communicate easily.

Beyond these challenges, Chinese expatriates may also encounter a variety of other difficulties. Back home, Chinese managers tend to be waited on and shown tremendous deference and respect, both in and out of the office. In Western countries, however, they are more likely to be greeted with a shrug, especially outside of the office. The entire atmosphere abroad as an expatriate may also be different for Chinese and Westerners. In Western multinationals, being picked for an expatriate assignment in China is a highly motivating event for many—an opportunity to learn a fascinating culture, make more money, and gain a de facto acknowledgement of being on the fast track to the top. But in China, winning promotions is often a function of cultivating close relationships with key superiors—and that is hard to do when you are on the other side of the world. Indeed, when Chinese managers are tagged for an expatriate assignment, it may signal that they are not well regarded by the company or have some important weaknesses. Moreover, unlike in most Western firms, Chinese who are employed by state-owned companies cannot refuse an expatriate assignment.

Then there are differences in attitudes and business practices that Chinese expatriates must deal with, including the fact that labor forces can often strike, stranding people at train stations and airports, particularly in Europe. While labor unrest occurs in China, it does not extend to public services because of tight government control. In addition, Chinese expatriates often start from behind, given that China's companies are not well known in most Western countries and the reputation of Chinese businesses in general is negative. Western customers often think that local firms will be much better than their Chinese counterparts, making penetrating Western markets difficult. Western directness tends to throw some Chinese expatriates for a loop. Being peppered with questions by potential customers in China would likely mortify a Chinese manager making a sales presentation, causing angst and feelings of rejection. Yet such behavior in Western countries is common and typically reflects a desire for more information as opposed to negative perceptions of the presenter.

Of course, there are some things about being posted to Western countries that Chinese expatriates see as positives. First, unlike China, society is relatively transparent and the regulations that businesses must abide by are clear. For example, instead of having to tap into your network of contacts or bribe someone to obtain a business license, one Chinese expatriate marveled that "you just download the form from the internet and apply." People in Western countries also tend to be friendly toward Chinese expatriates, with little evidence of hostility. And, finally, there is the air—it's cleaner in Western countries than in most Chinese cities. Consequently, while it may be challenging to be a Chinese expatriate in the West, at least taking a deep breath is easier.[33]

specific cultures. Motorola had those goals in mind when it opened a training center to help managers behave more effectively regardless of the cultural environment they found themselves working in.[35]

Some companies now do more to help expatriates deal with dual-career, family, and safety issues. This is a reaction to problems that have been challenging companies for some time and show no signs of disappearing anytime soon. One survey, for example, found that roughly 90% of companies in the Fortune 500 felt that dual-career issues would continue to complicate the selection and performance of expatriates for years to come. Underscoring this is the fact that family-related issues can be the most critical driver of expatriate success or failure—more important in many cases than job knowledge or cultural skills. By involving spouses, partners, and children in predeparture training, companies can boost the ability of expatriates and trailing family members to adjust to the host country, particularly if other forms of support are also in the mix (e.g., payments for lost spouse/partner income, assistance with job or education searches for spouses/partners).[36]

Looking ahead, companies may invest in some new directions for expatriate preparation that promise to increase expatriate success rates. Offering expatriates formal mentors is one such hopeful direction. Multinationals may want to institute a mentoring program that provides expatriates with both a home-country and host-country mentor for the duration of their assignments. The home-country mentor would offer support to help keep expatriates plugged in about developments in the home office—something that can improve expatriates' understanding of the company, job performance, and opportunities for promotion. And while they offer similar benefits, host-country mentors can also improve the extent to which expatriates share their knowledge, work effectively in teams, appreciate the host country, and feel integrated with host-country employees. Moreover, all of these represent career-enhancing benefits for expatriates. And that's especially critical given that many expatriates report that they end up taking a step back in their careers after coming home.[37]

Still, expatriates should not rely exclusively on their employers for assignment preparation and support. Instead, expatriates would be well served to take steps on their own to prepare, since companies rarely do everything possible to coach and support them. For example, expatriates can take university courses that may develop crucial skills that are not covered enough (if at all) in employer-provided training. Some beneficial courses might be in foreign languages, international management, and global marketing. Expatriates may also want to solicit second opinions from independent companies that provide international relocation help and cross-cultural training, such as U.S.-based Cartus (www.cartus.com). Other expatriates are a gold mine of potential information. If it's not something the employer provides, expatriates should consider making their own arrangements to visit the host country with any trailing family members before the assignment starts. This can help everyone know what to expect and settle in more quickly upon arrival. And once in the host country, expatriates can turn to other resources on their own for advice, support, and perhaps camaraderie (see www.talesmag.com).[38]

Coming Home: Repatriation Challenges

It would be a mistake to assume that once they complete their foreign assignments, expatriates are home free. If anything, a variety of potential challenges face expatriates once they are home. These *repatriation* issues are often responsible for the high turnover rate of expatriates after they return home. After years overseas, expatriates commonly run into these problems once they return:

1. Home feels foreign because changes in the home country have occurred (whether political, economic, or social).

2. Home feels foreign because the expatriate's values have changed while abroad.

3. Work feels foreign, and significant adjustment is needed because of changes in the headquarters office, which may include a new job (which may be a de facto demotion, a role not connected to the foreign assignment, or a dead end).

4. Expatriates may feel personally unappreciated by the company despite success abroad.

5. Home-country living conditions feel foreign because of a potential lower standard of living (thanks to higher costs and the loss of foreign service premiums or other expatriate benefits).[39]

Fortunately, many multinationals now understand how costly it is to ignore repatriation problems. Expatriates who have come home are a valuable resource for the firm—these are people who have gathered knowledge abroad, honed their cross-cultural skills, and created new ideas. This key resource will be lost, however, unless the company engages in successful repatriation efforts.[40]

Some multinationals tackle repatriation concerns well before expatriates even depart for their assignments. U.S.-based Monsanto, the agricultural/biotech firm, created a repatriation program to stem destructive levels of turnover among its expatriate population. These were driven in large measure by unmet expectations for promotion after returning home, so Monsanto started predeparture planning for the job expatriates would have after they returned. The company also provided a platform for expatriates to present their overseas experiences and accomplishments publicly after coming home and offered counseling help for expatriates' readjustment challenges. These and related programs have been shown to improve adjustment and boost the performance of expatriates after they come home.[41]

Another important issue for expatriates is their lack of visibility at headquarters while they are posted overseas. To combat this "out of sight, out of mind" challenge, some multinationals bring expatriates back to the home office multiple times annually to raise their visibility and to publicly thank them for their efforts overseas. During these home visits, expatriates can connect with key managers and mentors while also laying the groundwork for adjusting to life back home once their overseas assignments are finished. The more time expatriates spend abroad, the steeper the readjustment challenge will be when they return. One way that some multinationals address this is to increase the number of visits home as expatriates' return dates get closer, particularly for those who have been away for more than two years. For instance, U.S.-based Coherent, Inc. manufactures high-tech equipment (e.g., lasers) and operates in several European (e.g., France, Germany, United Kingdom) and Asian countries (e.g., China, Japan, Malaysia, Thailand). Coherent brings expatriates home for a few months just prior to their final return. During their time at home, expatriates complete small projects before going back to their foreign postings to wrap up their affairs for good. This visit back in the United States allows expatriates to re-engage with their colleagues in the home office and helps them catch up on bigger, ongoing projects. It also provides an extended pre-view of life back home. Coherent's program reduced the time it took expatriates to readjust once they returned. Table 11.4 presents further suggestions for firms to consider in the repatriation process.[42]

Table 11.4
Improving Repatriation: Suggested Activities Before and After Departure

Timing	Suggestions/Description
Before departure	• Clearly communicate reentry job options, create career development plan • Appoint home- and host-country mentors to support expatriate, set up home visits for visibility
6 to 9 months before return	• Narrow list of reentry job options, send expatriate job openings and listings • Conduct home office visits to facilitate adjustment, schedule job interviews
3 to 6 months before return	• Conduct briefings with employee and family about what they have learned • Describe home-country changes that may impact adjustment of expatriate and family • Ask expatriate to share return expectations to minimize misunderstandings • Explain firm's moving policies and repatriation programs
Immediately on return	• Assign employee/family to a welcome-home group consisting of former expatriates • Provide a home sponsor to review changes in firm (e.g., policies, products) • Provide returning spouse with career-related and job-search assistance • Offer counseling for more serious problems
3 to 6 months after return	• Provide training for reentry shock, any negative feelings about the return • Ask employee how new skills and experience can be better used by the firm • Reassess adjustment process to identify outstanding problems and offer assistance

Sources: Adapted from Shilling, M. (1993). How to win at repatriation. *Personnel Journal*, September, 40-46; Solomon, C. M. (1995). Repatriation: Up, down, or out? *Personnel Journal*, January, 28–37.

SEEKING AN INTERNATIONAL CAREER?

Our discussion of the hiring, development, and compensation of expatriates may have whetted your appetite for an international career. A thumbnail sketch of the competencies, characteristics, and experiences needed to succeed as a global manager in today's volatile and complex international business environment has been provided. In many companies, having significant international experience is no longer a luxury for advancement to the top—it is a necessity. Getting to the top in multinational firms, however, is a tall order in part because the rules of the game are not always clear. Multinationals from different parts of the world may look for different attributes in developing and promoting international managers. As an example, U.S. firms tend to weight ambition (as a sign of interest in leadership) heavily, while German firms tend to stress creativity in the approach to problems. And what constitutes significant international experience? In the past, the answer was simple—expatriate assignments. But thanks to cost-cutting pressures and technology such as video conferencing, some argue that it is possible to acquire significant foreign experience through a combination of shorter assignments (ranging from days to a year) and working with foreign colleagues who are living in your home country or interacting remotely (e.g., on virtual teams). That said, experience as an expatriate, particularly over multiple assignments, is likely to remain the gold standard for acquiring the skills and talent often needed to rise to senior management in a multinational firm.[43]

Consequently, it is interesting to look at what recent surveys of MBA students (specifically U.S., Canadian, and European students) from top-rated schools said about their level of interest in foreign assignments as a stepping-stone to an international career and top management. While interest in international assignments was high (roughly 80% wanted such an experience), interest in pursuing an international career was not as strong (about 50% of those surveyed expressed interest). Only about one-third of the MBA students surveyed wanted their first postgraduation job to be an international assignment.[44]

Equally interesting were the reasons that these MBA students gave for being either willing or unwilling to accept an expatriate assignment. Personal growth (i.e., learning about new cultures), being able to do interesting work, earning more money, and having better opportunities for advancement were the top four reasons that MBAs gave for being open to accepting an international posting. In contrast, the top four reasons cited for refusing an expatriate posting included a negative location (i.e., dangerous, unstable), an unattractive job (i.e., not challenging enough, high risk of failure, poor career move), the potential family problems it would create (i.e., dual-career issues, negative effect on children), and inadequate compensation for going abroad. Ironically, while today's up-and-coming managers may want to develop their international skills, they also seem keenly aware of the pros and cons associated with life as an expatriate. The good news is that because international experience is more valued these days, the career-related risk of accepting an expatriate assignment is lower than ever. In any case, please see the International Orientation Scale at the end of this chapter to assess your own level of interest in and suitability for an expatriate assignment.[45]

Pursuing International Career Paths

If you are committed to an international career and are willing to work for an extended period abroad, we offer some general advice to consider. First, do your homework. Identify multinationals that do an outstanding job of recruiting people into management development programs that include clear, well-defined international career paths. For example, Colgate, General Electric, Microsoft, P&G, and Schlumberger are just a few examples of U.S. multinationals known for their excellent international career opportunities. Colgate is particularly assertive about recruiting employees from the outside, offering eight different tracks for international careers (ranging from marketing to HR to supply chain management). Of course, in choosing a specific path, you should select something that aligns well with your interests, objectives, and experiences since requirements of particular paths can vary. The profile of desired attributes for Colgate's global marketing track are among the most stringent in terms of prior level of international skills and experiences (e.g., foreign language fluency and time spent living abroad are highly desirable if you want to join this track). This makes sense when you consider that, to be effective, the marketing function arguably is at or near the top when it comes to the need to deeply understand foreign markets and their consumers.[46]

While it is not possible to review every potential international option in detail, we do want to touch on human resource management as an area that, until recently, has not been thought of as a great place to build an international career. But that is changing thanks to the explosion of international business and the need for HR managers with international expertise. What is also shifting is the view that many Western multinationals have about Latin American or Asian subsidiaries as merely cheap export platforms. Instead, they are looking to develop products in and for emerging market customers. This shift places a premium on attracting and developing outstanding local employees who can also work well with the broader corporation. Many emerging market multinationals (e.g., from China and India) are experiencing the same challenges as they enter markets in developed countries. This is a huge obstacle that multinationals hope their international HR managers can surmount. For instance, in 2011, Indian technology giant Infosys sent an HR team to the United States to develop human resource policies that will help the company to better serve its large U.S. client base. U.K.-based cell provider Vodafone recently developed a fast-track career program for high-potential HR managers who want to work internationally to serve its growing global presence. Indeed, Indian, Chinese, and other emerging marketing multinationals represent career options for Western HR professionals, though significant cultural challenges can derail them. Nevertheless, the future looks bright for international HR as a career path.[47]

Multinationals recruiting for their international career development tracks sometimes require international experience just to get in the door. So it may be advisable to build your resume a bit before you try to land that plum job at a top multinational. On the other hand, you may already have decent international experience but lack the visibility and connections to get noticed—and hired. Table 11.5 presents tips for landing an overseas job, if not an international career. The exhibit is not exhaustive;

Table 11.5
Tips for Landing an Overseas Job

Tip	Explanation/Description
Learn additional foreign languages	Multilingual professionals are always in demand
For lower-level jobs, market any specialized skills you have	Specialized skills can provide an edge in lower-level jobs if marketed correctly
For higher-level jobs, network like crazy with key people	Focus on people who have clout where you want to go, develop good long-term relationships with executive recruiters
Seek out and get involved in international professional groups to raise your visibility	Attend international meetings, participate in global bulletin boards, and speak at international conventions—these provide opportunities to meet and impress people who might hire you for an overseas job
Raise your profile as an expert by getting noticed in the press about international issues	Volunteer to write articles, give reporters quotes for their stories about international business topics in newspapers or business publications—a reader with authority may notice and hire you
Seek introductions from foreign suppliers, customers, and officials	These people may be in a position to hire you (or to steer you to someone who can) in your desired location abroad
Keep track of former colleagues	They may now be working for a new employer in a foreign country and may be in a position to help
Offer to pay for recruiting costs	While offering to cover interview or even relocation costs is expensive, it may impress a hiring manager overseas and help you compete against local talent that is cheaper to recruit

Source: Adapted from Lublin, J. S. (2005). Job hopping overseas can enhance a career, but it takes fortitude. *Wall Street Journal*, June 7, B1.

for additional information, you may want to investigate job boards specifically designed for people seeking overseas jobs (e.g., www.anamericanabroad.com).[48]

CHAPTER SUMMARY

This chapter began with a detailed discussion of the options for staffing foreign operations, including *PCNs*, *HCNs*, and *TCNs*. Some multinationals develop an *international cadre* of managers who can be sent anywhere in the world, while others rely on *boomerangs* in foreign markets. Likewise, firms may identify high-potential foreign employees as *inpatriates*, bringing them to the parent country for developmental assignments.

Some companies follow specific selection philosophies in staffing their foreign operations. With a *geocentric* approach, ability is all that matters. On the other hand, an *ethnocentric* approach effectively means that key overseas positions are reserved for PCNs. And with a *polycentric* approach, human resource management control is in the hands of the foreign subsidiary, with headquarters still making key decisions. Finally, with a *regiocentric* approach, most foreign employees will not move into headquarters positions but can move from country to country in a particular region.

Next, issues associated with *expatriates* were discussed. Since the consequences of failed expatriate assignments are costly, firms should carefully develop a rigorous selection process, using criteria that predict expatriate success. Expatriates also need to be prepared to cope with the cultural and lifestyle changes they will encounter abroad. The nature and level of training should be driven, in part, by the *cultural toughness* of the foreign location. Preparation is also needed if employees are to be successfully *repatriated* back home. Many firms are creating more sophisticated repatriation programs that start before the expatriate has left for the foreign assignment.

The chapter concluded with a brief discussion about international career paths. While it may be possible to acquire significant foreign experience through a variety of mechanisms (e.g., brief trips abroad, working virtually with international colleagues), experience as an expatriate is likely to remain the gold standard for international careers. For individuals interested in an international career and willing to work for an extended period abroad, one important suggestion is to identify multinationals that do an outstanding job of recruiting people into substantial management development programs that include clear, well-defined international career paths.

DISCUSSION QUESTIONS

1. What are some of the pros and cons associated with using PCNs, TCNs, and HCNs?
2. What should the basic elements of a successful program to select, prepare, and repatriate employees destined for foreign assignments look like?

3. How can cultural toughness and family issues be managed effectively for expatriates?

4. Are you personally interested in an international career? Why or why not?

Developing Your International Career

YOUR INTERNATIONAL ORIENTATION: ARE YOU READY FOR AN EXPATRIATE ASSIGNMENT?

Purpose and Instructions

This exercise helps develop your insight about your cross-cultural skills as well as your experience with and interest in other countries. Consequently, it may offer you some valuable guidance about whether you would be attracted to and succeed in an expatriate or other foreign work assignment.

The items below come from the International Orientation Scale and include four dimensions (one attitudinal and three behavioral). Please answer each question using the various code keys provided and calculate a score for each dimension (the highest possible score for an individual dimension is 20 points).

Dimension 1: Your International Attitudes

Use the following code key to respond to Questions 1 through 4.

1   Strongly disagree
2   Disagree somewhat
3   Maybe or unsure
4   Agree somewhat
5   Strongly agree

1. _____ Foreign language skills should be taught in elementary school.
2. _____ Traveling the world is an important priority in my life.
3. _____ If my company offered me a year-long foreign assignment, it would be a fantastic opportunity for myself and my family.
4. _____ I am fascinated by other countries.
   _____ **Add up total score for Dimension 1** (scores will range from 4 to 20)

Dimension 2: Your Foreign Experiences

Use the code keys underneath each question.

1. _____ I have studied a foreign language.
   1. Never
   2. For less than a year
   3. For a year
   4. For a few years
   5. For several years

2. _____ I am fluent in another language.
   1. I don't know another language
   2. I am limited to very short, simple phrases
   3. I know basic grammatical structure and speak with a limited vocabulary
   4. I understand conversation on most topics
   5. I am very fluent in another language

3. _____ I have spent time overseas (e.g., traveling, studying abroad, on family trips, working)
   1. Never
   2. About a week
   3. A few weeks
   4. A few months
   5. Several months or years

4. _____ I was overseas before I turned 18
   1. Never
   2. About a week
   3. A few weeks
   4. A few months
   5. Several months or years

   _____ **Add up total score for Dimension 2** (scores will range from 4 to 20)

Dimension 3: Your Level of Comfort with Differences

Use the code key below for Questions 1 through 4.

1. Extremely similar
2. Mostly similar
3. Somewhat different
4. Quite different
5. Extremely different

1. _____ My friends' career objectives, interests, and educational backgrounds are...
2. _____ My friends' racial and ethnic backgrounds are...
3. _____ My friends' religious beliefs are...
4. _____ My friends' primary or first languages are...
   _____ **Add up total score for Dimension 3** (scores will range from 4 to 20)

Dimension 4: Your Participation in Cultural Events

Use the code key below to answer Questions 1 through 4.

1. Never
2. Rarely
3. Sometimes
4. Often
5. Always

1._____ I eat at a variety of ethnic restaurants (e.g., Greek, Indian, Thai, German).
2._____ I watch the major networks' world news programs.
3._____ I attend ethnic festivals.
4._____ I visit art galleries and museums.
_____ **Add up total score for Dimension 4** (scores will range from 4 to 20)

ASSIGNMENT QUESTIONS

1. Would you like to improve your international orientation? If so, what could you do to change or improve things?
2. Is an expatriate assignment something that is attractive to you? Why or why not? Do you think you are ready for an overseas assignment based on your scores?
3. Assuming that you are willing to go on an expatriate assignment, are there specific places in the world that you would be interested in going to? Places that you would not? Why?

Source: Adapted from Caligiuri, P. M. (1994). Self-assessment: International Orientation Scale. In D. Marcic & S. Puffer (eds.), *Management International: Cases, Exercises, and Readings* (165–167). Minneapolis/St. Paul: West Publishing.

Making the Case for International Understanding

SOUL-SEARCHING IN SEOUL: ONE U.S. EXPATRIATE'S CAUTIONARY TALE

Linda Meyer's experience in South Korea is a cautionary tale for any expatriate. She was very attracted to the opportunity to finally become an expatriate and accepted a management position in human resources at Seoul-based SK Telecom. This was an exciting prospect—to be an expatriate in Asia's fourth-largest economy while helping SK Telecom become a more global company. Meyers brought impressive credentials to her new employer, including years of experience as an expatriate consultant helping executives from top U.S. multinationals like ExxonMobil and Hewlett-Packard make successful transitions to their overseas assignments.

Yet soon after arriving in Seoul, Meyers began wondering if she had made a huge mistake. Despite experience in previous jobs requiring considerable overseas travel (including months-long stints in the Czech Republic and Ecuador) and her expertise as an expatriate consultant, Meyers was unable to grasp, much less operate effectively at, SK Telecom. During the next two years, Meyers came to realize that her direct style clashed with the formal and polite style of her Korean colleagues. She also learned that SK Telecom had few Western employees in general and only a handful of women in senior positions. Meyers discovered that she was, in effect, a trailblazer—one of the few U.S. women to serve in an executive capacity at any Korean company. Eventually, Meyers concluded that she and SK Telecom had divergent views about her role in the company. Meyers had become frustrated, demoralized, and exhausted—an outsider who was marginalized and precluded from having the impact she desired.

So what happened? The signs of things to come started early, when Meyers was initially e-mailed by an SK Telecom recruiter—who assumed she was a man. She obviously eventually took the job, feeling it was simply too good to pass up. Once she arrived in Seoul, Meyers was surprised that she received no official orientation or even much specific help from her bosses regarding how to adapt to her new surroundings. She was also struck by how homogeneous things were at SK Telecom and in South Korea more generally, where less than 3% of the population has foreign roots (versus roughly 20% or more in places like London, New York, and Singapore).

But Meyers was completely shocked by the struggles she had communicating with her Korean colleagues inside the company's hierarchical management structure. Her inability to speak Korean turned into a major impediment, and Meyers felt she had no choice but to ask for an interpreter to attend certain meetings. Getting information from Korean colleagues who did speak English also was difficult. Forced to ask questions to learn anything, Meyers felt that even her polite questions were interpreted as criticisms.

Nevertheless, after just four months on the job, SK Telecom promoted Meyers, asking her to lead SK Holding's Global Talent group. Meyers became frustrated, however, at her inability to push through any significant changes in HR policies and practices. This was especially vexing because Meyers saw herself as an agent of change for the company—a view that senior leadership at SK Holdings apparently did not share. Indeed, Meyers felt increasingly ostracized in her new job, hamstrung by the language barrier and what seemed to be a deliberate effort to exclude her from important conversations and meetings with top executives.

Things eventually got so bad that many of her colleagues simply would not speak with her. The other shoe finally dropped in 2009, when Meyers was told that her contract would not be renewed. While disappointed that she did not have the impact on the company that she would have liked, Meyers also felt a sense of relief that she would be leaving.

On reflection, Meyers felt she had made some important mistakes. One lesson was summarized by the phrase "easier said than done." The extensive experience that she had in prepping others for expatriate roles did not make it any easier to implement that advice herself. Moreover, much of the training she provided to other soon-to-be expatriates did not have much specific applicability to the SK Telecom environment in Seoul. Despite her own personal preparation efforts to read about and understand Korean business culture, Meyers estimated that, in hindsight, her efforts were superficial and missed about 80% of what she really needed to know. Another realization was that Meyers's view of progress and change did not align with her more conservative Korean bosses, something that she should have done more to clarify in advance.

In terms of her own style, Meyers also concluded that she should have been more patient when introducing changes to her Korean subordinates. For example, soon after arriving in Seoul, she tried to create a more informal environment by telling her Korean subordinates to stop using her title and address her as Linda. Unfortunately, this backfired: it caused her subordinates to lose respect for Meyers and to perceive her as weak. Likewise, Meyers admitted that she tended to jump to the conclusion that every misunderstanding she had with Korean colleagues was due to cultural differences or poor treatment because she was a foreigner. After one disagreement with a Korean manager, which she chalked up to a cultural misinterpretation, Meyers spoke to another colleague about how to handle the situation. The Korean manager was very embarrassed and upset when he found out that Meyers had consulted with another colleague about their misunderstanding.

After leaving SK, Meyers returned to her roots, again serving as a consultant to help other people prepare for their expatriate assignments. Her experience in Korea, Meyers believes, made her a better consultant. As she put it, "Those years in Seoul taught me to question my own actions and assumptions. I realized that my leadership style had been shaped by a particular environment and that my way was not always best."[49]

ASSIGNMENT QUESTIONS

1. What is your assessment of the situation that Linda Meyers found herself in? Who is responsible for her difficulties as an expatriate?
2. Does it surprise you that Meyers encountered so much trouble in Korea, particularly given her prior experiences and positions? Why did she struggle to respond more effectively? What is the implication of all of this?

3. If you had been advising Meyers, would you recommend that she take the SK Telecom job in the first place? Why or why not?

4. Were there additional steps that Meyers could have taken to better prepare for her role at SK Telecom (both before she accepted the job as well as after)?

NOTES

1. Lublin, J. S. (2011). Cultural flexibility is in demand. *Wall Street Journal*, April 11, B1, B9.

2. Lublin, J. S. (2011). Cultural flexibility is in demand. *Wall Street Journal*, April 11, B1, B9; Wang, S., Tong, T. W., Chen, G., & Kim, H. (2009). Expatriate utilization and foreign direct investment performance: The mediating role of knowledge transfer. *Journal of Management*, 35, 1181–1206.

3. Cascio, W., & Bailey, E. E. (1995). International human resource management: The state of research and practice. In O. Shenkar (ed.), *Global Perspectives of Human Resource Management* (15–36). Englewood Cliffs, NJ: Prentice Hall; Cook, F. L. (2011). Talent management in China. In H. Scullion & D. G. Collings (eds.), *Global Talent Management* (132–154). New York: Routledge; Dowling, P. J., & Schuler, R. S. (1990). *International Dimensions of Human Resource Management*. Boston: PWS-Kent; Geissler, C., Kuhn, L., & McGinn, D. (2011). Developing your global know-how. *Harvard Business Review*, March, 71–75; Hymowitz, C. (2003). European executives give some advice on crossing borders. *Wall Street Journal*, December 2, B1.

4. How global are you? *Business Week*, December 8, 2008, 12.

5. Downes, M., & Thomas, A. S. (2000). Managing overseas assignments to build organizational knowledge. *Human Resource Planning*, 20, 33–48; Geissler, C., Kuhn, L., & McGinn, D. (2011). Developing your global know-how. *Harvard Business Review*, March, 71–75.

6. Briscoe, D. R., Schuler, R. S., & Claus, L. (2009). *International Human Resource Management* (3rd ed.). New York: Routledge; Carraher, S. M., Sullivan, S. E., & Crocitto, M. M. (2008). Mentoring across global boundaries: An empirical examination of home- and host-country mentors on expatriate career outcomes. *Journal of International Business Studies*, 39, 1310–1326; Hsieh, T. Y., Lavoie, J., & Sarnek, R. A. P. (1999). Are you taking your expatriate talent seriously? *McKinsey Quarterly*, 3, 71–83; Phatak, A. V. (1995). *International Dimensions of Management* (4th ed.). Cincinnati, OH: South-Western; Ready, D. A., & Conger, J. A. (2007). How to fill the talent gap. *Wall Street Journal*, September 15–16, R4.

7. Browne, A. (2004). Chinese recruit top executives from abroad. *Wall Street Journal*, November 30, B1, B8; Lublin, J. S. (1996). Is transfer to native land a passport to trouble? *Wall Street Journal*, June 3, B1, B5; Millman, J., & Zimmerman, A. (2003). "Repats" help Payless Shoes branch out in Latin America. *Wall Street Journal*, December 24, B1, B2; Millman, J. (2000). Exporting management savvy. *Wall Street Journal*, October 24, B1, B18; Solomon, C. M. (1994). Global operations demand that HR rethink diversity. *Personnel Journal*, July, 40–50.

8. Briscoe, D. R., Schuler, R. S., & Claus, L. (2009). *International Human Resource Management* (3rd ed.). New York: Routledge; Geissler, C., Kuhn, L., & McGinn, D. (2011). Developing your global know-how. *Harvard Business Review*, March, 71–75; Phatak, A. V. (1995). *International Dimensions of Management* (4th ed.). Cincinnati, OH: South-Western.

9. Latta, G. W. (1998). Global staffing: Are expatriates the only answer? *HR Focus*, July, S1, S2; Woodruff, D. (2000). Distractions make global manager a difficult role. *Wall Street Journal*, November 21, B1, B18.

10. Alder, N. J., & Gundersen, A. (2008). *International Dimensions of Organizational Behavior* (5th ed.). Mason, OH: Thompson-South-Western; Briscoe, D. R., Schuler, R. S., & Claus, L. (2009). *International Human Resource Management* (3rd ed.). New York: Routledge; Schneider, S. C. (1991). National vs. corporate culture: Implications for human resource management. In M. Mendenhall & G. Oddou (eds.), *International Human Resource Management* (13–27). Boston: PWS-Kent.

11. Boyacigiller, N. (1990). The role of expatriates in the management of interdependence, complexity, and risk in multinational corporations. *Journal of International Business Studies*, 21, 357–381; Brewster, C., & Mayrhofer, W. (2008). Comparative human resource management policies and practices. In P. B. Smith, M. S. Peterson, & D. C. Thomas (eds.), *Handbook of Cross-Cultural Management Research* (353–366). Thousand Oaks, CA: Sage; Jeanquart-Barone, S., & Peluchette, J. V. (1999). Examining the impact of the cultural dimension of uncertainty avoidance on staffing decisions: A look at U.S. and German firms. *Cross-Cultural Management: An International Journal*, 6, 3–12; Peterson, R. B., Sargent, J., Napier, N. K., & Shim, W. S. (1996). Corporate expatriate HRM policies, internationalization, and performance in the world's largest MNCs. *Management International Review*, 36, 215–230; Schuler, R. S., Jackson, S. E., & Tarique, I. R. (2011). Framework for global talent management: HR actions for dealing with global talent challenges. In H. Scullion & D. G. Collings (eds.), *Global Talent Management* (17–36). New York: Routledge.

12. Briscoe, D. R., Schuler, R. S., & Claus, L. (2009). *International Human Resource Management* (3rd ed.). New York: Routledge.

13. Ando, N., Rhee, D. K., & Park, N. K. (2008). Parent country nationals or local nationals for executive positions in foreign affiliates: An empirical study of Japanese affiliates in Korea. *Asia Pacific Journal of Management*, 25, 113–134; Brock, D. M., Shenkar, O., Shoham, A., & Siscovick, I. C. (2008). National culture and expatriate deployment. *Journal of International Business Studies*, 39, 1293–1309; Geissler, C., Kuhn, L., & McGinn, D. (2011). Developing your global know-how. *Harvard Business Review*, March, 71–75.

14. Ready, D. A., & Conger, J. A. (2007). How to fill the talent gap. *Wall Street Journal*, September 15–16, R4; Roberts, K., Kossek, E. E., & Ozeki, C. (1998). Managing the global workforce: Challenges and strategies. *Academy of Management Executive*, 12, 93–106; Solomon, C. M. (1995). Navigating your search for global talent. *Personnel Journal*, May, 94–101; Stanek, M. B. (2000). The need for global managers: A business necessity. *Management Decision*, 38, 232–242.

15. Inkson, K., Arthur, M. B., Pringle, J., & Barry, S. (1997). Expatriate assignment versus overseas experience: Contrasting models of international human resource development. *Journal of World Business*, 32, 351–366; Solomon, C. M. (1995). Navigating your search for global talent. *Personnel Journal*, May, 94–101; Woodruff, D. (2000). Distractions make global manager a difficult role. *Wall Street Journal*, November 21, B1, B18.

16. Geissler, C., Kuhn, L., & McGinn, D. (2011). Developing your global know-how. *Harvard Business Review*, March, 71–75; Odenwald, S. (1993). A guide for global training. *Training and Development*, July, 23–31.

17. Expatriates and your global workforce. January 4, 2004. Available at www.hrspectrum. com/insightofweek.htm; 2002 worldwide survey of international assignment policies and

practices. January 4, 2004. Available at www.orcinc.com/surveys/wws2002.html; Briscoe, D. R., Schuler, R. S., & Claus, L. (2009). *International Human Resource Management* (3rd ed.). New York: Routledge; Feng, S. (2009). Expatriate localization: A Chinese solution. Available at www.mercer.com; Lublin, J. S. (2003). No place like home. *Wall Street Journal*, September 29, R7; Martins, A., & Lengre, J. (2007). Expat networking: Helping you improve the success of expat assignments. Available at www.expatwomen.com/tips/expat_networking_helping_improve_success.php.

18. Geissler, C., Kuhn, L., & McGinn, D. (2011). Developing your global know-how. *Harvard Business Review*, March, 71–75; Harzig, A. (2001). Of bears, bumble-bees, and spiders: The role of expatriates in controlling foreign subsidiaries. *Journal of World Business*, 36, 366–379; Harvey, M. (1997). Dual-career expatriates: Expectations, adjustment and satisfaction with international relocation. *Journal of International Business Studies*, 28, 627–659; Hsieh, T. Y., Lavoie, J., & Sarnek, R. A. P. (1999). Are you taking your expatriate talent seriously? *McKinsey Quarterly*, 3, 71–83; Lublin, J. S. (2003). No place like home. *Wall Street Journal*, September 29, R7; Shaffer, M. A., & Harrison, D. A. (2001). Forgotten partners of international assignments: Development and test of a model of spouse adjustment. *Journal of Applied Psychology*, 86, 238–254.

19. Briscoe, D. R., Schuler, R. S., & Claus, L. (2009). *International Human Resource Management* (3rd ed.). New York: Routledge; Martins, A., & Lengre, J. (2007). Expat networking: Helping you improve the success of expat assignments. Available at www.expatwomen.com/tips/expat_networking_helping_improve_success.php; Poe, A. C. (2000). Destination everywhere. *HR Magazine*, October, 67–75; Wederspahn, G. M. (1992). Costing failures in expatriate human resources management. *Human Resource Planning*, 15, 27–35.

20. Engen, J. R. (1995). Coming home. *Training*, March, 37–40; Hauser, J. (1999). Managing expatriates' careers. *HR Focus*, February, 11–12; Latta, G. W. (1999). Expatriate policy and practice: A ten-year comparison of trends. *Compensation and Benefits Review*, 31, 35–39.

21. Carpenter, M. A., Sanders, W. G., & Gregersen, H. B. (2000). International assignment experience at the top can make a bottom-line difference. *Human Resource Management*, 39, 277–285; Harris, N. (2002). Tools to protect traveling employees. *Wall Street Journal*, March 11, R8; Lublin, J. S. (2005). Job hopping overseas can enhance a career, but it takes fortitude. *Wall Street Journal*, June 7, B1; Lublin, J. S. (2003). No place like home. *Wall Street Journal*, September 29, R7.

22. Briscoe, D. R., Schuler, R. S., & Claus, L. (2009). *International Human Resource Management* (3rd ed.). New York: Routledge; Cooke, F. L. (2011). Talent management in China. In H. Scullion & D. G. Collings (eds.), *Global Talent Management* (133–154). New York: Routledge; Tung, R. L., & Varma, A. (2008). Expatriate selection and evaluation. In P. B. Smith, M. S. Peterson, & D. C. Thomas (eds.), *Handbook of Cross-Cultural Management Research* (367–378). Thousand Oaks, CA: Sage.

23. Carpenter, S. (2001). Battling the overseas blues. *Monitor on Psychology*, July/August, 48–49; Chen, G., Kirkman, B. L., Kim K., Farh, C. I. C., & Tangirala, S. (2011). When does cross-cultural motivation enhance expatriate effectiveness? A multilevel investigation of the moderating roles of subsidiary support and cultural distance. *Academy of Management Journal*, 53, 1110–1130; Hsieh, T. Y., Lavoie, J., & Sarnek, R. A. P. (1999). Are you taking your expatriate talent seriously? *McKinsey Quarterly*, 3, 71–83; Klaus, K. J. (1995). How to establish an effective expatriate program: Best practices in international assignment administration. *Employment Relations Today*, Spring, 59–70; Shaffer, M. A., Harrison, D. A.,

Gregersen, H., Black, J. S., & Ferzandi, L. A. (2006). You can take it with you: Individual differences and expatriate effectiveness. *Journal of Applied Psychology*, 91, 109–125; Tung, R. L., & Varma, A. (2008). Expatriate selection and evaluation. In P. B. Smith, M. S. Peterson, & D. C. Thomas (eds.), *Handbook of Cross-Cultural Management Research* (367–378). Thousand Oaks, CA: Sage.

24. Alder, N. J., & Gundersen, A. (2008). *International Dimensions of Organizational Behavior* (5th ed.). Mason, OH: Thompson-South-Western; Black, J. S., Gregersen, H. B., & Mendenhall, M. E. (1992). *Global Assignments: Successfully Expatriating and Repatriating International Managers.* San Francisco: Jossey-Bass; Briscoe, D. R., Schuler, R. S., & Claus, L. (2009). *International Human Resource Management* (3rd ed.). New York: Routledge; Carpenter, S. (2001). Battling the overseas blues. *Monitor on Psychology*, July/August, 48–49; Downes, M., & Thomas, A. S. (2000). Managing overseas assignments to build organizational knowledge. *Human Resource Planning*, 20, 33–48; Garonzik, R., Brockner, J., & Siegel, P. A. (2000). Identifying international assignees at risk for premature departure: The interactive effect of outcome favorability and procedural fairness. *Journal of Applied Psychology*, 85, 13–20; McDonnell, A., & Collings, D. G. (2011). The identification and evaluation of talent in MNEs. In H. Scullion & D. G. Collings (eds.), *Global Talent Management* (57–73). New York: Routledge; Nichols, C. E., Rothstein, M. G., & Bourne, A. (2002). Predicting expatriate work attitudes: The impact of cognitive closure and adjustment competencies. *International Journal of Cross-Cultural Management*, 2, 297–320.

25. Bolino, M. C., & Feldman, D. C. (2000). The antecedents and consequences of under-employment among expatriates. *Journal of Organizational Behavior*, 21, 889–911; Gelfand, M. J., Erez, M., & Aycan, Z. (2007). Cross-cultural organizational behavior. *Annual Review of Psychology*, 58, 479–514.

26. Schneider, S. C., & Asakawa, K. (1995). American and Japanese expatriate adjustment: A psychoanalytic perspective. *Human Relations*, 48, 1109–1127; Tung, R. L., & Varma, A. (2008). Expatriate selection and evaluation. In P. B. Smith, M. S. Peterson, & D. C. Thomas (eds.), *Handbook of Cross-Cultural Management Research* (367–378). Thousand Oaks, CA: Sage; Ward, C., & Rana-Deuba, A. (2000). Home and host culture influences on sojourner adjustment. *International Journal of Intercultural Relations*, 24, 291–306.

27. Alder, N. J., & Gundersen, A. (2008). *International Dimensions of Organizational Behavior* (5th ed.). Mason, OH: Thompson-South-Western; Black, J. S., Gregersen, H. B., & Mendenhall, M. E. (1992). *Global Assignments: Successfully Expatriating and Repatriating International Managers.* San Francisco: Jossey-Bass; Jordan, M. (2001). Have husband, will travel. *Wall Street Journal*, February 13, B1, B12; Latta, G. W. (1999). Expatriate policy and practice: A ten-year comparison of trends. *Compensation and Benefits Review*, 31, 35–39; Lublin, J. S. (2003). No place like home. *Wall Street Journal*, September 29, R7; Selmer, J. (1999). Corporate expatriate career development. *Journal of International Management*, 5, 55–71; Solomon, C. M. (1996). Expats say: Help make us mobile. *Personnel Journal*, July, 43–52; Swaak, R. A. (1995). Expatriate management: The search for best practices. *Compensation and Benefits Review*, 27, 21–29; Swaak, R. A. (1995). Today's expatriate family: Dual careers and other obstacles. *Compensation and Benefits Review*, 26, 21–26.

28. Alder, N. J., & Gundersen, A. (2008). *International Dimensions of Organizational Behavior* (5th ed.). Mason, OH: Thompson-South-Western; Black, J. S., Gregersen, H. B., & Mendenhall, M. E. (1992). *Global Assignments: Successfully Expatriating and Repatriating International*

Managers. San Francisco: Jossey-Bass, Briscoe, D. R., Schuler, R. S., & Claus, L. (2009). *International Human Resource Management* (3rd ed.). New York: Routledge; Caligiuri, P. (2000). The big five personality characteristics as predictors of expatriates' desire to terminate the assignment and supervisor-rated performance. *Personnel Psychology*, 53, 67–88; Carpenter, S. (2001). Battling the overseas blues. *Monitor on Psychology*, July/August, 48–49; Shaffer, M. A., Harrison, D. A., Gregersen, H., Black, J. S., & Ferzandi, L. A. (2006). You can take it with you: Individual differences and expatriate effectiveness. *Journal of Applied Psychology*, 91, 109–125.

29. Alder, N. J., & Gundersen, A. (2008). *International Dimensions of Organizational Behavior* (5th ed.). Mason, OH: Thompson-South-Western; Briscoe, D. R., Schuler, R. S., & Claus, L. (2009). *International Human Resource Management* (3rd ed.). New York: Routledge; Carpenter, S. (2001). Battling the overseas blues. *Monitor on Psychology*, July/August, 48–49; Sanchez, J. I., Spector, P. E., & Cooper, C. L. (2000). Adapting to a boundaryless world: A developmental expatriate model. *Academy of Management Executive*, 14, 96–106.

30. Black, J. S., Gregersen, H. B., & Mendenhall, M. E. (1992). *Global Assignments: Successfully Expatriating and Repatriating International Managers*. San Francisco: Jossey-Bass; Briscoe, D. R., Schuler, R. S., & Claus, L. (2009). *International Human Resource Management* (3rd ed.). New York: Routledge; Brislin, R. W., MacNab, B. R., & Nayani, F. (2008). Cross-cultural training. In P. B. Smith, M. S. Peterson, & D. C. Thomas (eds.), *Handbook of Cross-Cultural Management Research* (397–410). Thousand Oaks, CA: Sage; Deshpande, S. P., & Viswesvaran, C. (1992). Is cross-cultural training of managers effective: A meta analysis. *International Journal of Intercultural Relations*, 16, 295–310; Fitzgerald-Turner, B. (1997). Myths of expatriate life. *HR Magazine*, June, 1–7.

31. Black, J. S. (1992). Coming home: The relationship of expatriate expectations with repatriation adjustment and job performance. *Human Relations*, 45, 177–192; Black, J. S., Gregersen, H. B., & Mendenhall, M. E. (1992). *Global Assignments: Successfully Expatriating and Repatriating International Managers*. San Francisco: Jossey-Bass; Harrison, J. K. (1994). Developing successful expatriate managers: A framework for the structural design and strategic alignment of cross-cultural training programs. *Human Resource Planning*, 17, 17–35.

32. Alder, N. J., & Gundersen, A. (2008). *International Dimensions of Organizational Behavior* (5th ed.). Mason, OH: Thompson-South-Western; Aryee, S., Chay, Y. W., & Chew, J. (1996). An investigation of the willingness of managerial employees to accept an expatriate assignment. *Journal of Organizational Behavior*, 17, 267–283; Black, J. S., Gregersen, H. B., & Mendenhall, M. E. (1992). *Global Assignments: Successfully Expatriating and Repatriating International Managers*. San Francisco: Jossey-Bass; Briscoe, D. R., Schuler, R. S., & Claus, L. (2009). *International Human Resource Management* (3rd ed.). New York: Routledge; Parker, B., & McEvoy, G. M. (1993). Initial examination of a model of intercultural adjustment. *International Journal of Intercultural Relations*, 17, 355–379; Stroh, L. K., Dennis, L. E., & Cramer, T. C. (1994). Predictors of expatriate adjustment. *International Journal of Organizational Analysis*, 2, 176–192.

33. A tale of two expats. *The Economist*, January 1, 2011, 62–64.

34. Briscoe, D. R., Schuler, R. S., & Claus, L. (2009). *International Human Resource Management* (3rd ed.). New York: Routledge; Solomon, C. M. (1996). Expats say: Help make us mobile. *Personnel Journal*, July, 43–52.

35. Carpenter, S. (2001). Battling the overseas blues. *Monitor on Psychology*, July/August, 48–49; Hagerty, B. (1993). Trainers help expatriate employees build bridges to different cultures. *Wall Street Journal*, June 14, B1, B6.

36. Alder, N. J., & Gundersen, A. (2008). *International Dimensions of Organizational Behavior* (5th ed.). Mason, OH: Thompson-South-Western; Arthur, W., & Bennett, W. (1995). The international assignee: The relative importance of factors perceived to contribute to success. *Personnel Psychology*, 48, 99–114; Briscoe, D. R., Schuler, R. S., & Claus, L. (2009). *International Human Resource Management* (3rd ed.). New York: Routledge; Black, J. S., & Gregersen, H. B. (1991). The other half of the picture: Antecedents of spouse cross-cultural adjustment. *Journal of International Business Studies*, 22, 461–477; Swaak, R. A. (1995). Today's expatriate family: Dual careers and other obstacles. *Compensation and Benefits Review*, 26, 21–26.

37. Carraher, S. M., Sullivan, S. E., & Crocitto, M. M. (2008). Mentoring across global boundaries: An empirical examination of home- and host-country mentors on expatriate career outcomes. *Journal of International Business Studies*, 39, 1310–1326; Reiche, B. S., Harzing, A. W., & Kraimer, M. L. (2009). The role of international assignees' social capital in creating inter-unit intellectual capital: A cross-level model. *Journal of International Business Studies*, 40, 509–526.

38. Carpenter, S. (2001). Battling the overseas blues. *Monitor on Psychology*, July/August, 48–49.

39. Tu, H., & Sullivan, S. E. (1994). Preparing yourself for an international assignment. *Business Horizons*, 37, January–February, 67–70; Zaslow, J. (2003). The fourth without fireworks: Americans' quiet patriotism abroad. *Wall Street Journal*, July 3, D1.

40. Furuya, N., Stevens, M. J., Bird, A., Oddou, G., & Mendenhall, M. (2009). Managing the learning and transfer of global management competence: Antecedents and outcomes of Japanese repatriation effectiveness. *Journal of International Business Studies*, 40, 200–215.

41. Black, J. S. (1992). Coming home: The relationship of expatriate expectations with repatriation adjustment and job performance. *Human Relations*, 45, 177–192; Black, J. S., Gregersen, H. B., & Mendenhall, M. (1992). *Global Assignments: Successfully Expatriating and Repatriating International Managers*. San Francisco: Jossey-Bass; Furuya, N., Stevens, M. J., Bird, A., Oddou, G., & Mendenhall, M. (2009). Managing the learning and transfer of global management competence: Antecedents and outcomes of Japanese repatriation effectiveness. *Journal of International Business Studies*, 40, 200–215; Shilling, M. (1993). How to win at repatriation. *Personnel Journal*, September, 40–46.

42. Briscoe, D. R., Schuler, R. S., & Claus, L. (2009). *International Human Resource Management* (3rd ed.). New York: Routledge; Furuya, N., Stevens, M. J., Bird, A., Oddou, G., & Mendenhall, M. (2009). Managing the learning and transfer of global management competence: Antecedents and outcomes of Japanese repatriation effectiveness. *Journal of International Business Studies*, 40, 200–215; Solomon, C. M. (1995). Repatriation: Up, down, or out? *Personnel Journal*, January, 28–37. See also www.coherent.com.

43. Alder, N. J., & Gundersen, A. (2008). *International Dimensions of Organizational Behavior* (5th ed.). Mason, OH: Thompson-South-Western; Bird, A., Mendenhall, M., Stevens, M. J., & Oddou, G. (2010). Defining the content domain of intercultural competence for global leaders. *Journal of Managerial Psychology*, 25, 810–828; Fang, Y., Jiang, G. L. F., Makino, S., & Beamish, P. M. (2010). Multinational firm knowledge, use of expatriates, and foreign subsidiary performance. *Journal of Managerial Studies*, 47, 27–54.

44. Alder, N. J., & Gundersen, A. (2008). *International Dimensions of Organizational Behavior* (5th ed.). Mason, OH: Thompson-South-Western.

45. Adler, N. J., & Gundersen, A. (2008). *International Dimensions of Organizational Behavior* (5th ed.). Mason, OH: Thomson-South-Western.

46. Schuler, R. S., Jackson, S. E., & Tarique, I. R. (2011). Framework for global talent management: HR actions for dealing with global talent challenges. In H. Scullion & D. G. Collings (eds.), *Global Talent Management* (17–36). New York: Routledge. See www.colgate.com/app/Colgate/US/Corp/WorkWithUs/Careers/HomePage.cvsp.

47. Clegg, A. (2011). Multinational people managers. *Financial Times*, August 4, 8.

48. Lublin, J. S. (2005). Job hopping overseas can enhance a career, but it takes fortitude. *Wall Street Journal*, June 7, B1. See www.anamericanabroad.com.

49. Green, S. (2011). The would-be pioneer. *Harvard Business Review*, April, 124–126.

Chapter 12

Building Global Commitment through Labor Relations

There has been an intensification of labour unrest in the past weeks that is probably the most significant spike since the summer of 2010.

—Geoffrey Crothall, China Labor Bulletin
(an advocacy group that tracks labor unrest,
referring to action of late 2011)

We were forced to return to the factory. But we just sit there. No one is operating machines.

—Worker at shoe factory in Dongguan,
China, about consequences of employee
demonstrations against overtime cuts and job
losses in November 2011[1]

This final chapter continues the discussion of concerns regarding both managing diversity and how groups operate across cultures. Working with small multicultural teams is tough enough, as shown in earlier chapters. But when larger labor forces are involved, management challenges cut across entire companies, industries, or countries. The field of labor relations deals with these larger employee–firm relationships. These relations are complex to manage, partly because of many differences in laws and agreements across nations, even for those countries so close that they share a border (e.g., France and Spain; the United States and Mexico). They are also tough to manage because the relationship between management and workers has not been altogether smooth. Indeed, in some countries, those relations have been combative, resulting in frequent protests, strikes, and lockouts, as described in the opening quote. Thus, having knowledge about cross-national labor relations can be a valuable asset for international managers.

LABOR RELATIONS IN AND ACROSS CULTURES

To address issues in labor relations, the perspectives of management and workers are outlined, followed by discussion of agreements or structures that have been devised for soliciting employee input or control.

Workers in all countries are concerned with pay, job security, benefits, and working conditions. Some join labor unions to exert some control over these important work outcomes, including having a say in important firm decisions.[2] In other cases, complex laws control firms in ways that effectively serve the function of a union—even when no organized labor groups exist or when those groups are weak and poorly organized. In fact, some have suggested that laws such as these have supplanted the need for strong and large labor unions.

For years, labor groups have lobbied governments for changes in laws that would permit their needs and demands to be met. Indeed, labor has been late to become involved relative to the multinationals for which they work. Nongovernmental organizations spend billions of dollars in the United States alone to lobby the federal government, with labor groups anteing up their fair share. While there are other ways to exert influence, groups of workers ultimately have more direct control over one method of getting their way on key issues: threatening to reduce or stop work output. This threat may be less credible, however, when the employer is a multinational. The many resources available to large firms allow them to insulate themselves from actions by disgruntled employees. A multinational may simply outlast a union strike by absorbing losses at a particular location. Or, if the company is flexible enough, it could increase production temporarily at another facility to offset production declines where there is unrest. A large company may also threaten to move its operations to another country in response to a strike. Multinationals have considerable power—even more than a domestic firm—over employees.[3]

Hyster Corporation operated a forklift-truck plant in Irvine, Scotland, with 500 employees. Via a grant from the British government, Hyster was ready to invest $60 million in the plant, creating another 100 jobs. But the resulting increase in output would create overcapacity in European operations. Consequently, enlarging its Scottish plant meant that Hyster would have to cut production in the Netherlands. To make matters worse, moving Dutch production capacity to Scotland would mean that Scottish workers had to take a 14% cut in pay. Hyster gave the workers 48 hours to accept the deal. As if this wasn't enough, the next day each employee got a letter from the company. The letter stated that, "Hyster is not convinced at this time that Scotland is the best of the many alternatives open to it. It has not made up its mind. The location of the plant to lead Europe is still open." At the bottom of the page, employees voted for or against the Scotland plant and the pay cut that went with it. Facing job loss, only 11 employees voted no. While Hyster's employees were not unionized, many felt it would not have made a difference. In Hyster's defense, it faced incredible challenges from competition, especially the Japanese who had introduced lower-cost, high-efficiency forklifts on the market. Hyster won an antidumping case it filed with the International Trade Commission resulting in 50% import duties on Japanese products.[4] This situation has been repeated many times across countries, sometimes in more flagrant ways, as when companies take subsidies and then move to lower labor rate locations.

To combat this considerable power of multinationals, unions have tried to use legal means to increase their control. For instance, French unions have begun coordinating lawsuits by members. They turned to this approach because, unlike the

United States, some European countries forbid class action lawsuits (where many plaintiffs band together to sue under a single legal umbrella) to seek redress for alleged breaches of contract.[5]

Many countries have also enacted permanent employment laws, in part as a response to union pressure. These laws provide generous protections for workers. In France, 35 hours is the legal weekly work limit for all employees. Other statutes can make it difficult to fire an employee after a relatively short probationary period. Even if the required termination conditions are met, the employee may be due large amounts of severance pay. Some European countries have extensive laws and requirements regarding termination. The average laid-off worker in the United States receives one week's severance pay for every year of service. German workers, however, receive an average of more than four times as much—one month of pay for every year of employment and up. When you add in other benefits such as relocation and retraining available in Germany, termination costs in the United States seem modest. And even letting a worker go in Germany is difficult. As one executive recruiter put it, "U.S. firms that establish themselves here are shocked by the termination rules. The possibility of firing someone quickly without cause is impossible."[6]

This expert observer may be correct, even with the 1990 passage of the Worker Adjustment and Retraining Notification (WARN) Act in the United States. This law requires firms that are considering a closure or mass layoff of 50 or more employees to provide a 60-day notice. During tough economic times, however, some companies are ignoring the law. Mazer Corporation of Dayton, Ohio, sent e-mails to its 300 employees at 5:00 P.M. one day, informing them that it was their last day, and apologizing for the short notice. Some workers did not receive a final paycheck, let alone the notice and 60 days' pay that is required by WARN. Company owners felt bad but explained that they worked until the last minute to obtain financing. When that fell through, the bank seized the company's assets. Employees, such as Scott Bent in Dayton, have sued to obtain back pay, which they say is required by WARN.[7] The 20-year-old law has rarely been enforced and exempts companies that have "unforeseeable circumstances," providing numerous other exemptions. Between December 2007 (the beginning of the Great Recession) and May 2009, the U.S. Department of Labor says that 3.8 million people lost jobs in nearly 37,000 mass layoffs. Yet only about 8% of firms gave the required notice of termination. Some that did not provide notice rightfully invoked the "unforeseeable circumstances" exception clause.[8]

Enforcement of similar laws in other countries is stricter—and so are the laws themselves. Colgate-Palmolive ran into some of these stricter rules after it announced plans to close its factory in Hamburg, Germany, eliminating the 500 jobs. Colgate offered German employees about $40,000 each—a severance plan costing the company over $20 million. Colgate argued that the plan was similar to or better than what other firms in the area had provided. The union, which by law has an opportunity to approve such decisions, felt the offer was too low given that the operation was profitable. The union attracted much attention to their plight, including stories in local papers about how families had worked for Colgate for three generations. The mayor of Hamburg condemned the company for its move, and the union threatened to drag out negotiations. Colgate raised its offer and agreed to a settlement.[9]

As this example illustrates, managing layoffs can be complex even without navigating the political waters of a different country. Likewise, laws themselves are complex, with wide differences across borders, even within one region such as Europe. In France, for example, those with at least one year of employment receive severance pay. The mandated payment is approximately 30 days for each year and can be graduated for those with more than 10 years of service. A 20-year employee making $60,000 per year might be entitled to termination benefits of $100,000 or more.[10] If a large-scale layoff occurs, the law requires higher compensation payments and more company support (e.g., job retraining, mobility assistance).[11] In addition, a firm-level agreement might provide for even higher payments. France is not alone—other countries are equally generous, as Table 12.1 shows.

Because of these mandated benefits, firms operating in Europe have become creative to avoid costly severance rules and drawn-out union negotiations. For instance, when Dutch IT firm Getronics PinkRoccade NV wanted to shed 700 employees, it terminated people in batches of 19—a process that took almost a year. This bypassed Dutch law that requires firms to negotiate with unions to justify and obtain approval for layoffs of more than 20 employees. Other Dutch firms have simply placed unneeded, but perfectly healthy, employees on disability to eliminate them from payroll, shifting the cost to the government.[12] Figure 12.1 presents data on public expenditures for labor market programs (as a percentage of gross domestic product) for a number of Organisation for Economic Co-operation and Development (OECD) countries. Note that the United States had the lowest percentage in 2006, but that figure steadily rose through 2009. In fact, percentage-wise, the United States had the largest increase (more than 200%) from 2006 to 2009 as it tried to prop up a troubled economy. Most of these expenditures across country reflect passive spending to augment unemployment income and support. Overall, however, the United States is still well below the OECD average, while most of Europe already had a strong employment safety net prior to those tough times.[13]

While the Western European social support mechanisms are solidly in place and have grown in some countries, the influence of unions and restrictive labor laws may be waning. This may be partly due to the power of multinationals to quickly shift production east to lower-wage locations. Volkswagen AG was able to persuade union members at one of its plants in Spain to accept a 5% pay cut by threatening to move production (and jobs) to Slovakia, where wages are 50% less. Indeed, as the European Union (EU) expanded eastward, thousands of union jobs have followed. To preserve jobs, unions have been more willing in recent years to give in to multinational demands on pay raises, more flexible work rules, and greater use of

Table 12.1
Legal Protections for Worker Severance in Five European Countries

Country	Legal Protections	Common Additions/ Summary
Belgium	■ Extensive advanced notice ■ Prorated year-end premium ■ Outstanding holiday pay ■ Outplacement counseling ■ Monthly pre-pension payments for employees over 45	Union-negotiated additions (e.g., closure premiums, employment search costs, moral damages) can often double the cost of the total severance package
France	■ 30 days' pay for each year of service ■ Payments increased if more than 10 years of service ■ Compensation rises if layoff is large-scale ■ If firm has more than 1,000 employees, it must offer full pay leave of four to six months	Payments often exceed these minimums. If court decides there was no genuine or serious reason for layoffs, damages might be added to payments—amounting to at least six months' salary. Employees getting increasingly militant at notice of layoff
Germany	■ Notice of up to seven months ■ Two weeks' pay per year of service ■ Employer not entitled to choose employees based on individual performance alone, but must use social criteria (disability, age, etc.)	Payments vary a good deal on specific characteristics of the employee (age, years of service, more)
Netherlands	■ One month's salary for 35- to 45-year-olds; one and a half months for 45- to 55-year-olds; and two months for those over 55 ■ A variety of other social plans provide additional benefits to workers	Employers must select employees by applying the last-in-first-out system (those with less service first). Dutch labor law does not allow unilateral breaking of employment agreement by employer—employers must consult with works councils
Russia	■ Two months' minimum notice for workers ■ One month's pay plus another from layoff until new job ■ Additional month if employee files for unemployment quickly	Large number of filters used to determine who to lay off (e.g., no women employees with children, single mothers)

Sources: Adapted from *Managing Mass Redundancies across Europe* (2nd ed). Brussels, Belgium: Freshfields Bruckhaus Deringer, 2009; Bush, J., et al. (2009). The hidden perils of layoffs. *Business Week*, March 2, 52–53.

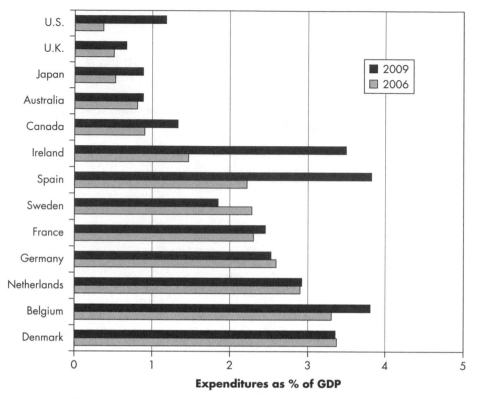

FIGURE 12.1 Public Expenditures on Labor Market Programs as a Percentage of Gross Domestic Product, 2006 and 2009

Source: Adapted from Organisation for Economic Co-operation and Development. (2011). Available at www.oecd.org/document/.

temporary employees, not just in Europe but across the globe. We turn our attention to the status of unions in various countries.[14]

LABOR UNIONS ACROSS COUNTRIES

Unions and multinationals have ways to exert influence over each other, even though it is fair to say that multinationals have the upper hand.[15] This power, however, varies among countries. Nevertheless, there are mechanisms by which employees try to wrest some degree of control from management, the most common being an organized union. Unions in the United States were originally established to bring about reform in the workplace before laws existed to protect worker interests. Now, U.S. unions have a relatively high profile, and that profile is not always positive. In fact, national surveys indicate a relatively negative view of unions by Americans. Perhaps this attitude can partly explain why union membership in the United States has been steadily declining in recent years. In 2011, union members made up 11.9% of the total U.S. workforce, down a half point from the previous year and well down from the 20.1% figure for 1983.[16]

Other highly developed countries have also seen a general decline in union membership. Table 12.2 presents data on union density rates in a large set of OECD countries. As you can see, the percentage of workers who are unionized

Table 12.2
Union Density Rates and Changes over Time

Country	Density (%) in 2008	Change (%) since 1998
Australia	18.6	–33.1
Belgium	51.9	–4.9
Canada	27.1	–5.6
Denmark	67.6	–10.5
Finland	67.5	–13.5
France	7.7	–7.2
Germany	19.1	–26.3
Ireland	32.3	–20.4
Italy	33.4	–6.4
Japan	18.2	–19.1
Korea	10.3	–9.7
Netherlands	18.9	–22.9
Norway	53.0	–2.2
Spain	14.3	–12.3
Sweden	68.3	–16.0
Switzerland	18.3	–15.3
United Kingdom	28.1	–8.2
United States	11.9	–14.2
OCED Countries	17.8	–16.8

Source: Adapted from Organisation for Economic Co-operation and Development. Union density rates in OECD countries. Available at www.oecd.org/document/34/0,3343, en_2649_33927_40917154_1_1_1_1,00.html#union.

Note: Density reflects estimates of the percentage of wage and salary workers who are union members in 2008 and 1998.

varies greatly across countries, ranging from a high of about 68% in Sweden to a low of about 8% in France. The oldest and most well-developed union systems occur in the EU countries. Even among these countries, however, there are differences in the percentage of workers covered by unions. While France has relatively few unionized workers, about 52% of Belgium's workforce is unionized. These national differences have been tied to a number of factors, including the political leanings of the government, how wages are determined, and the size of the public employment sector.[17]

These union density rates should not be taken completely at face value. For one thing, the percentage of union members is only an indirect proxy of union influence. In practice, bargaining agreements reached by unions and management end up covering many nonunion employees.[18] Likewise, a high union density does not necessarily mean that unions are more effective. In reality, a relatively low density rate may belie the true degree of union influence, as is the case in France. In addition, sometimes labor is represented by a political party, which can also increase its influence. Clearly, however, not all unions across borders are structured the same and not all are equally influential. We will discuss the nature and impact of unions in countries around the globe. More emphasis is given to Western countries—ones that have been industrialized longer and, as a result, have had greater opportunity for unions to develop.

Unions in EU Countries

Because union influence is defined in several ways, there is some debate about which unions are influential and why. Nevertheless, union membership has declined over the last two decades in the European Union. Every EU country presented in Table 12.2 saw a drop in membership, many with double-digit drops over a decade. This decline has been more precipitous in some Eastern European states, such as Poland, where union participation has plummeted since the end of the Soviet era more than two decades ago. Then, nearly all workplaces were covered by unions, whereas union participation was only about 14% in 2010. Most EU nations have less than half of the working population involved with unions, with the four most populated countries ranging from a high of 33% (Italy) to a low of 8% (France). Only about one-quarter of those employed in the EU are union members. Membership and strike activity has continued to decline. Nevertheless, unions are still are a force to be reckoned with.[19]

Unions in France

French unions have been dominated by a handful of national unions. Like some other countries (e.g., Japan), most large employers also have a company union, and these groups are among the most political in the world. In fact, the chief difference among French unions is not the industry or occupations they cover, but their political and social leanings.[20]

Membership in these unions is not large by the standards of other countries. The largest, the French Democratic Confederation of Labor, is an industry/public service union affiliated with the Socialist Party and has only 800,000 members. With a figure at around 8%, France has among the lowest national level of union density of all industrialized countries. This statistic partly reflects the fact that there is little need for unions to recruit new members. Likewise, workers do not feel a strong need to seek out unions, in part because, since the mid-1970s, the government has embraced the idea of protecting, if not enhancing, employee rights. There has been a long tradition of extending collective agreements to companies and industries that were not party to the accord. Consequently, workers benefit from the union's influence without having to be a union member. It is fair to say, therefore, that union influence is effectively much greater than the 8% density figure would suggest.

But French unions, like their German counterparts, have been under pressure in recent years to cooperate in government efforts to reform onerous labor regulations.[21] When President Sarkozy took office in 2007, he had public support for pension reform among public workers. During a very disruptive multiweek strike among transport employees, Sarkozy remained defiant: "We will not give in, we will not back down."[22] The union was also reluctant to back down because it was a last chance before a new law requiring a minimal level of service on public transport was to take effect in January 2008. Nevertheless, after nine days, the union voted to begin work again and initiate negotiations. In early 2009, up to 1 million strikers marched through French cities, including 300,000 in Paris, to demand pay raises and job protection, again challenging President Sarkozy. While the one-day strike failed to engage private-sector workers, it was the first time the unions had joined forces since Sarkozy had taken office.[23] Sarkozy's effort to push the retirement age up to 62 was met with large protests. In October 2010, roughly 3.5 million protestors took to the streets, and petrol pumps across the country went dry as unions and oil workers led weeks of strikes. Weeks after the new law was passed, the issue did not even rank among the country's top 10 issues of importance.[24] Perhaps this was because economic tough times have weakened unions and shaken the public's view of French competitiveness.[25]

Unions in Germany

Unlike the United States, where union contracts are negotiated on a company-by-company basis, Germany relies on a centralized system in which some 60,000 contracts are set using industry-wide bargaining. Unions will typically bargain with a group or federation of employers in an industry. There is only one union in most major industries, and membership is entirely voluntary. The German Federation of Trade Unions is actually about 16 unions with a total of 6.6 million members, even though it is dominated by a few larger trades. Contracts usually cover most major work issues, including pay, benefits, and working conditions. As such, the main goals of the union are economic, as opposed to some of the more politically motivated union activity found in other countries. As of 2009, about 19% of the workforce in Germany was involved in trade unions.

Relations between unions and management has been cooperative over the last 20 years or so, with just a handful of days lost to strikes every year. One reason is that workers have input into how the business is run, including representation on the board of directors. Firms with more than 2,000 employees are required to give 50% of board seats to workers. This situation, unique to Germany, is called codetermination. This policy, set up by the Allies after World War II, was designed to prevent industry from being in step completely with a threatening government. In the steel and coal industry, for example, unions select five board members, shareholders select another five members, and this total body then selects an eleventh member. In other industries, union membership on boards varies by industry and company size.[26]

In recent years, German unions have been willing to make concessions on working conditions and pay to increase job security. In some areas, important German unions, such as the giant IG Metall union (Industrial Union of Metal Workers), have been flexible on issues such as the length of work weeks and time off. Nevertheless, the accompanying *Culture Clash* elaborates on the German concern with free time—which remains a top priority for workers. Attitudes toward labor unions have hardened; some blame unions for higher unemployment, rigid labor laws, and a shaky level of German competitiveness. Union participation rates continue to drift downward (see Table 12.2).[27]

CULTURE CLASH

Germans Think Americans Work Too Hard

Angie Clark and Andreas Drauschke have similar managerial jobs and earn similar pay in department stores in Washington, D.C., and Berlin, respectively. The comparison, however, ends there. Drauschke's job as manager of the auto and bicycle division of the store is contractually set at a 37-hour work week with six weeks of annual paid leave. His store closes at 2:00 P.M. on Saturday, is never open on Sunday, and (until recently) stays open only one night each week. He "can't understand that people go shopping at night in America . . . logically speaking, why should someone need to buy a bicycle at 8:30 P.M.?" German law partially explains this incredulous feeling, since, until recently, laws strictly regulated the hours of stores. Stores were first allowed to extend hours at night past 5:00 P.M. to 8:30 P.M., and then to extend hours to a half day on Saturdays. Most recently, Saturday shopping was extended to 8:00 P.M. Control over shopping days and opening hours was handed over to the 16 German states in 2006, none of which has passed laws yet to allow stores to be open on Sunday.

Clark, on the other hand, works at least 44 hours per week, including evening shifts and weekend hours. She often brings work home and has never taken off more than one week at a time. While most Americans admire the stereotypical German industriousness, Clark—a frequent visitor to Germany—has a different view. U.S. workers average roughly 20% more working hours per week than Germans. Estimates of the average hours worked in different countries vary, making this a less-than-precise science.[28] Nevertheless, numbers of hours worked annually provided by the OECD suggest that Americans work about 1,800 hours, more than all but one other OECD country (South Korea) compared to about 1,430 hours for Germans. This means that Americans put in about nine and a quarter weeks more of work per year than Germans. Most Germans receive six weeks off each year, in addition to 11 to 13 single-day, paid holidays. The disparity in hours worked has increased in recent years. "Germans put leisure first and work second," said Clark. Many colleagues at her store hold second jobs and work up to 60 hours or more per week. Drauschke, however, has no interest in working beyond the mandated 37 hours per week, even for more money. "Free time can't be paid for," said the German. He finds the U.S. penchant for holding multiple jobs simply unthinkable.[29]

It is easy for an American to be critical of the German work schedule. But it is worth pondering Germany's history. Germany is a country the size of Montana, with a population of 85 million people. It suffered great physical and economic devastation throughout World War I and World War II, as well as continued political and economic strife in the years following, yet is now the world's fourth-largest economy. These events suggest that, current work hours aside, work ethic and productivity must be high. Plus, the long and irregular work hours and the lack of separation of work from home and family come at a price for many Americans. Turnover at Drauschke's German store is nearly zero, while it pushes 40% per year at Clark's U.S. store. There are clear pluses and downsides to each viewpoint.[30]

Unions in the United Kingdom

The union movement in the United Kingdom has a long history, having been legalized in 1871. British unions are powerful, although their membership and influence has waned (8% drop) over the last decade. Unions have political roots, but not as strong as those of France. In fact, the desire for unions to push political agendas led to the formation of the Labour Party in Britain in 1883. To this day, trade unions play a significant role in the party and provide financial support.

Union density in the United Kingdom is about two and a half times that of the United States. Union participation, however, has seen a big dip recently. At the height of its influence in 1979, membership was around 57%; in comparison, the density rate now is around 28%. A major reason for the drop is that legislation was passed that reduced union power. Additionally, the economy fared reasonably well over the last decade, further reducing the appeal of membership.[31] Nevertheless, unions still wield considerable power and influence. Since a large firm may negotiate with several unions, the process is complex. Cross-union dealings can be fractionated, and this situation has played into the hands of companies that have successfully pushed collective bargaining down from a national to a business level.[32]

Unions in Other EU Nations

Because Europe was the first continent to industrialize, there is great variety of union representation beyond the sample just described. In the Netherlands, for example, trade unions were initially developed by religious and political groups. One example is the largest union in Holland, the FNV, which was a merger between a socialist and a Catholic union. The FNV is not overtly ideological and has participated with the government in many social support initiatives. Experts say that unions are more impactful than their 19% membership rate might indicate.[33] Dutch employees can exert control over the workplace via other unique outlets, as discussed later in the chapter.

Unions in Sweden began as a socialist movement among manual workers. And because of a friendly government, they flourished in a mutually cooperative environment. This can explain why Sweden has such a high density rate. Indeed, despite recent hostility between unions and the government, union membership rates remain relatively high (68%).[34] In fact, Swedish unions have embraced management initiatives to improve productivity, such as technological advances.[35] Belgium, too, has a relatively high union density rate (52%). It might be even higher, however, if there were not as many laws protecting labor. The Belgian workplace is one of the most highly controlled in the world, covering topics such as compensation, severance pay, and other human resource concerns. While the most important unions are organized around religious or political bases, there is a "culture of compromise" in their interactions.[36] Spain is at the other end of the regulated spectrum. Spain has the highest unemployment rate in Europe as of this book's publication, and concern with jobs is high. Expectations of 16% employment in 2010 were exceeded and by the second quarter of 2011 rose to 21%. The population of foreign immigrants (about 5 million) has increased by a factor of about 10 over the last decade, and public spending is at its limit. More trouble looms for Spain.[37]

In general, the long history of union organizing has left many full-time, permanent European workers covered by an extensive set of regulations and protections, especially relative to those of the United States. Many multinationals have long complained about this state of affairs, and there are signs that European countries will slowly roll back these expensive protections. In the meantime, however, firms are coping by reliance on contract, temporary, and part-time workers—in short, workers with few legal protections.[38] In the Netherlands, part-time and short-term workers occupy about one-third of all jobs, compared to less than 15% in the United States. With general economic troubles continuing and these groups likely to be made redundant first, further strains on public spending are likely in the short term.[39] Yet take a look at the accompanying *Global Innovations* box to see how government and private businesses are cooperating in the Netherlands to save jobs in these tough times.

GLOBAL INNOVATIONS

A New Twist on "Dutch Treat": Government and Private Support Combines to Save Jobs in the Netherlands

Governments around the world are looking for ways to improve the job outlook in their economies and to reduce joblessness. While many solutions involve a time-honored formula of direct government bailouts, the Netherlands is trying something new—a twist on the usual formula.

When unemployment rates jumped between 2008 and 2009, in some cases dramatically, governments reacted. Canada, Japan, the United Kingdom, Ireland, Spain, and the United States all saw increases in unemployment numbers. In the United States, for example, the unemployment rate rose from 6.2% to 10.2%. Many businesses cut back personnel and sought loans and bailouts from the federal government. Other countries, such as Germany and the Netherlands, relied heavily on what are called "short-work programs" to keep people employed. These are a collection of actions that either reduce employee work hours or involve hiring of temporary workers. These countries were able to keep unemployment down, with the Dutch leading the pack. Unlike the drastic increase in the United States, France, and Ireland, unemployment rose from 2.7% to only 3.6% during the same time in the Netherlands.

Short-work programs represent a big change in the general European mind-set. Take Theo Witkamp, a nearly 60-year-old machine operator at DAF Trucks in Eindhoven, as an example. Although his work hours have been cut, he is still earning about 85% of what his regular wages would have been from his job, through a combination of company and state contributions. Notably, this is also more than he would earn without the job, a reality that might have happened had the firm not undertaken this joint approach to tackling joblessness. As Witkamp said, "it beats being unemployed."

The Netherlands spent nearly $3 billion on this job-saving program in 2010, a pittance relative to the billions provided to financial and other firms in the United States. The money does seem to be well spent, although some experts give credit to other measures taken during the height of the worldwide crisis. It is true that the Netherlands has of late trimmed back unemployment and other government-provided benefits in an effort to cut costs and keep people working. With such cuts inevitable in an unpredictable global economy, there is all the more reason to work to save jobs. After the global crisis hit, the government, unions, and firms worked to reach an agreement on wage subsidies. Some said this was a harkening back to the Middle Ages for the Dutch, when rival cities and classes grouped to save the dikes when massive floods came. Interestingly, short-work laws were passed in the 1940s, originally during Nazi occupation, but have been rarely used until now. Regardless, they did not apply them haphazardly. Qualifications for subsidies were set up (firms had to show a 30% drop in revenues over three months), and the subsidies were limited to a six-month period. Firms were responsible for paying a substantial percentage of employees' salaries. Plus, the government set up a network of advisors to work with firms. Nearly 1,500 firms participated in the plan, some even paying a higher portion of their employees' salaries than required by the law.

By many accounts, the program was successful, including the low unemployment figures noted above. There were, of course, critics, including some economists who slammed the efforts, saying that is was "a form of creeping communism" and that it was "sharing poverty, pure and simple." Perhaps so, said Dutch finance minister Wouter Bos, adding that it makes it tough for markets to assess firm performance. But, even Bos changed his opinion, saying "you put in some extra money at an early stage, but then you save some money later because people do not have to go for unemployment." Either way, the cost was relatively small compared to some other major bailouts of world economies, including in the United States. And perhaps Bos's traditional Dutch optimism will play out with more firms getting back on their feet in the short and long run. It certainly did for DAF trucks, which saved Theo Witkamp's job. DAF was one of the firms that decided to provide more pay than was required by the state. Better yet, because the firm's orders picked up during the second part of the year, it did not seek further government support.[40]

Unions in Asia

Unions also exert influence in Asia, although—as it does in other parts of the world—this influence varies from country to country.

Unions in Japan

Japan has thousands of enterprise unions.[41] This refers to the fact that many different workers in a company, regardless of their profession or vocation, are represented by one omnibus union. There are some large national unions in the public and private sectors (e.g., municipal workers, teachers), but nearly 95% of all unions have followed the tradition of "one company, one union." In other words, these in-house unions represent only the employees of their respective companies. Membership in these unions is limited to permanent employees; they do not cover an increasing population of part-time and temporary employees. Toyota, for example, has tripled the number of short-term contract workers since 2001. Likewise, Canon relies on outside, temporary help, increasing the percentage of these workers by 19% since 2006, while permanent staff rose only 4% during that time. In firms with more than 1,000 employees, the overall Japanese union density rate (18%) nearly doubles, while among small firms (fewer than 100 employees), only 1% are unionized.[42]

As might be expected from our discussions of Japanese culture throughout the book, the relationship between union and management is largely harmonious. This was not always the case. In fact, after World War II, many Japanese unions were both militant and violent. After many long and backbreaking strikes, Japanese employers basically struck a deal with their unions to obtain job security and good benefits in exchange for no labor strife. Both groups have largely kept the bargain, as there is little friction in Japan. Junior-level managers often occupy union leadership roles. The training received in such union positions is viewed favorably by management and is taken into account for future promotions.[43] Data show that over 15% of directors of large enterprises were former union officials.[44]

Observers often criticize this relationship as being too cozy. Even when Japanese unions go on strike, they do so for very short periods of time—often a half day or less. One union leader at the Japanese subsidiary of Royal Dutch/Shell claimed that the union was getting "tough" with management over wages: "We went on strike the day before yesterday. We stayed out for 45 minutes. Yesterday we struck again for 15 minutes." At lunchtime the next day, workers went on strike briefly again (for higher wages) so that the demonstrators would not have to miss any work. This attitude characterizes most Japanese unions. The average Japanese employee strikes for about 4 minutes per year, compared to 9 minutes in the United States, and 23 minutes in Spain.[45] As the head of the Nissan union said, "Union members want to protect their jobs and preserve their livelihood. The best way to do that is to cooperate with the company." There is some cross-union cooperation in Japan. For instance, several enterprise unions coordinate their bargaining activities during a traditional *shunto*, or spring wage offensive, to establish a national pattern of increases. The individual enterprise unions then use this rate as a standard for their own bargaining.[46] This system remained in place for nearly four decades, delivering wage increases for most union members and for the general population as a whole. In 2002, Japanese unions agreed to the elimination of shunto as hard times settled in. This has led to company-specific agreements and, some think, a reduction in union membership since 2002. With the global economic recession of the late 2000s, the elimination of shunto has also led to more pressure on the government to secure help for the poor. The poverty rate in the world's third-largest economy is among the highest in leading nations (Japan is fourth, behind Mexico, Turkey, and the United States).[47] Through all of Japan's economic troubles of the last two decades, consultation among management and employees about company decisions still occurs.

Unions in China

One of the traditional hallmarks of China's labor relations approach has been full employment. This approach has been referred to as the "iron rice bowl." In other words, China has a cradle-to-grave employment system with a (relatively) egalitarian wage system. In the past, employees could expect that their jobs were secure and permanent. An employee could not be fired, and pay and housing were guaranteed. With dramatic reforms and World Trade Organization and International Labour Organization (ILO) membership, things have changed dramatically and continue to change yearly, with China becoming the second-largest economy in the world in late 2010.

Some pieces of the old system persist, but, for some time now, workers can be laid off and other Western-type managerial prerogatives have been available. But popular sentiment is that this has gone too far and that foreign multinationals have too much control over workers. This was partially the impetus for a new law in 2008 designed to provide greater job security. Passage of the law has raised concern among some multinationals that have been accustomed to a malleable workforce in China. The law provides for treatment of laid-off workers and also provides a system for arbitrating any disputes that might occur.[48] Employers, for example, must give 30 days' notice or at least one month's wages to affected workers.[49] It was less than a decade ago that small, sporadic workers' protests were easily broken up by authorities. Then, a few leaders were arrested, some concessions provided to other strikers, and efforts made to stop unrest from spreading and to prevent workers from connecting and joining forces. But a number of factors have come together to change that. This law, benefited by efforts of state-run media to publicize it, is one factor. Now workers know what they are owed—whether overtime pay or a safer workplace. As one expert puts it, "Every worker is a labor lawyer...they know their rights better than an HR office." Plus, this new labor movement has grown via the ability of far-flung groups to connect. Angry migrant workers use the Internet and the over 800 million mobile phones in China to connect. As the president of the South China Chamber of Commerce states, "There are Internet cafes everywhere...[workers] get information and are asking for more. The days of cheap labor are gone."[50]

Labor unrest is growing. Overall, the number of employees involved in labor disputes handled by arbitration committees is large—nearly 700,000 in 2006 alone, up from 250,000 in 2000.[51] Strikes and work stoppages at several Honda and Toyota factories have received much attention, as has labor unrest at Foxconn Technology, a Taiwanese supplier of iPhones.[52] Foxconn (also known as Hon Hai) received extensive scrutiny because of a series of suicides committed by workers at the world's largest contract manufacturer, which sustains over 850,000 employees in China. Demands by workers for an investigation, intensified by customers such as Apple, Nokia, and Hewlett-Packard, have elevated issues of working conditions at Hon Hai plants to wide audiences.[53]

Chinese and foreign firms are adjusting to this growing voice of labor in several ways. Many are providing both higher pay and a variety of benefits. Hon Hai in particular has announced plans to raise minimum wages and make other safety improvements. Mercedes Benz has begun to offer bonuses to factory workers at assembly plants, and Wal-Mart is making safety changes as well. Others are moving operations from the expensive coast to more inland cities such as Chongqing. This western Chinese city of 32 million people has labor costs that are 20% to 40% lower than those of coastal cities. Some have observed that foreign firms have been especially targeted by labor actions. As one expert said, "It's always easier for workers at foreign-owned plants to gain government support,"[54] especially if there are nationalistic undertones to workplace dissatisfaction. This has strengthened the only union allowed by law—the All-China Federation of Trade Unions (ACFTU). This is the world's largest national trade union, with over 140 million members, at least on paper. The ACFTU recently has been more impactful in pushing for new legislation on worker issues (e.g., protection of women's rights). Recent agreements with Wal-Mart, McDonald's, and Yum Brands help meet ACFTU's goals of signing up 80% of the largest foreign companies by the end of 2011.[55]

Unions in Other Asian Nations

Countries such as India, Indonesia, the Philippines, Thailand, and Vietnam are examples of economies—and labor relations—in a state of transition. Hong Kong has relatively low unemployment and a relatively moderate level of union density (about 21% as of 2008). Despite Hong Kong's Confucian tradition, many have characterized the attitude of Hong Kong workers as "everyone for himself"—an attitude not likely to foster union participation and not one that workers can depend on for advocacy.[56]

The other so-called Asian Tigers—Singapore, South Korea, and Taiwan—have become major influences in the world economy. Although a good deal of government and multinational influence is exerted on workplaces in these countries, there are big differences in the state of their labor relations.[57] Labor issues in Singapore and, to a lesser extent, Taiwan have been relatively calm, with emphasis on social partnership and political stability.[58] In contrast, labor relations in South Korea have been more confrontational. Well-publicized strikes against Hyundai and a proposed GM takeover several years ago illustrate this high level of union activity. This confrontational style has continued through the 2000s, with a large number of strikes and loss of working days, including the country's longest banking strike in 2011.[59]

Unions in Mexico and South America

Since the passage in 1994 of the North American Free Trade Agreement, much attention has been focused on Mexico. A variety of federal laws govern labor relations in Mexico, many of which favor labor—including wage and benefits guarantees. As a result, Mexico is a country with a relatively high degree of union participation. Only 20 employees are needed to form a union in Mexico. This means that Mexican firms are used to negotiating with many different unions within one factory. If the official union declares a strike, all personnel—including management—must vacate the premises. Flags are stationed at each locked entrance, signifying a strike. Union members receive pay during the time that they are out on a (legal) strike.[60] Unions have won many worker rights, mostly through federal legislation rather than direct union activity. On the other hand, the Labor Secretariat has considerable discretionary power to allow strikes. And in the *maquiladoras*, the thousands of factories positioned near the U.S. border, companies are often able to choose submissive, government-affiliated unions.[61] Other major South American economies (Brazil, Argentina) have varying levels of government control and input into labor relations activity.

Unions in Africa

Overall, union activity in Africa is relatively underdeveloped. Nevertheless, there are differences across countries, ranging from the relatively compliant approach in Kenya to the more activist unions in South Africa.[62]

South African labor relations are especially interesting. In the 1970s, when the system of racial segregation called apartheid was at its height, white groups were permitted to form unions and allowed to engage in collective bargaining. In 1980, black groups gained limited union rights, and the number of union members nearly tripled in five years. Even with apartheid still operating, the power of the black unions grew quickly. Strike activity increased greatly in the 1980s, some of it violent. The effect of this organizing was dramatic. One study showed that the increased wage effects for black workers due to union membership approached the (percentage) gains realized by U.S. workers, and these percentages were greater than for European workers.[63] The main gains were among poorer, low-skill workers, whose minimum wages increased much more than those of any other category of employees. So, while future South African president Nelson Mandela was imprisoned for his anti-apartheid work, black union workers were winning concessions of dramatic size.

Once released from prison and elected president in South Africa's first democratic election, Mandela's challenge was to balance the increasingly strident demands made by both unions and businesses—especially foreign ones. The country's big national union federation, COSATU, staged a one-day nationwide strike against a proposal allowing companies to lock out striking workers. Mandela appeared with workers wearing COSATU colors, and the provision was deleted. Many businesses and foreign investors felt that the incident underscored their concern that South African unions had too much influence over government policies. They argued that if South Africa were to be more competitive, it needed more flexible labor rules. Unions protested, claiming that many of apartheid's inequities still needed to be addressed. Mandela's successors, Presidents Mbeki and Motlanthe, continued efforts to balance these competing demands, but challenges remain for current president Jacob Zuma. Just three months after Zuma was elected in 2009, he faced a huge challenge from the municipal workers union that had helped him come to power. Police fired rubber bullets at protesters in a township outside Johannesburg, but the strike continued, with workers seeking 15% wage increases.[64] Even though Zuma is seen as a worker's president, he has hardly been given a pass and is unlikely to get one in the near future.

International Employee Unions

Unions around the world have had varying degrees of membership rates and success in recent years. Perhaps the largest challenge to domestic unions, however, is the multinational firm itself, which can move some or all of its operations to another country.[65] The most noteworthy response to this challenge has been the development of international unions. In fact, as far back as 1919, the League of Nations, as part of the peace agreement ending World War I, created the International Labour Organization. The ILO is composed of representatives from employees, employers, and governments, with each group having a say in policies.[66] Now with more than 170 member countries, the ILO has mainly been responsible for developing guidelines and standards for labor conditions and treatment. These guidelines have the same legal status as an international treaty; they must be ratified and agreed to by each nation. Many countries fail to embrace all of the guidelines, perhaps because of the controversial issues taken on by the ILO (e.g., equal pay). Even if a country ratifies a guideline, ensuring that it complies with the organization's stipulations is tough.[67] In many ways, the ILO operates like its larger parent organization, the United Nations. Other important international organizations have similar goals, including arms of the European Union and the Organisation for Economic Co-operation and Development.

There is also a group of unions with international membership. One of the most important of these is the International Confederation of Free Trade Unions (ICFTU). Its goal is to help national unions in their dealings with multinationals.

The membership of the ICFTU is concentrated in North America and Europe and is a force to be reckoned with by firms. Closely associated with these groups are International Trade Secretariats, which often cover major industry types such as the International Metal Workers Federation. While there are differences among groups, a general goal is to emulate the organization of a multinational and, in so doing, to develop a transnational bargaining system.

That said, most observers suggest that international unions have been largely ineffective.[68] The reasons for this are complex, including the unique laws of various countries and multinational opposition. One of the most insidious reasons, however, has been the ability of multinationals to effectively play one country and its unions against another. There are only a few examples of cross-border coordination among unions, such as the financial backing provided by German union IG Metall to striking workers at British Aerospace.[69] Also, the United Electrical Workers union in the United States supported a Mexican union's efforts to organize a GE plant in Mexico not long ago.

These events, however, are unusual. Many powerful unions within countries are, in effect, political groups and, as a result, are more concerned with national issues than international ones. It is more common for a union in one country to gain jobs by dealing with a multinational that is having labor trouble in another country. This competitive attitude is summed up by a Canadian union member, who stated that "[a]n American union is not going to fight to protect Canadian jobs at the expense of American jobs."[70] For example, some years ago Hoover Appliances (then owned by Maytag Corporation) announced plans to close a 600-employee factory in Dijon, France, and move its operations to Glasgow, Scotland. Hoover's Scottish workers had traded changes in work conditions for job security and the 400 new jobs that would result. The French were outraged and took to the streets to protest. They also crossed the English Channel to take part in a televised debate, during which they accused their Scottish colleagues of taking their jobs. British union leaders were quiet about the incident, except to say that "we have nothing to be ashamed of." It's clear that most workers probably see their foreign counterparts as competitors rather than as allies in the same struggle. This is a large obstacle that international unions will have to overcome to be successful.[71]

OTHER FORMS OF EMPLOYEE INPUT AND CONTROL

Unions are not the only means by which employees can obtain desired outcomes. Employees can be heard and have an impact via a variety of methods. These methods are known by different terms but most commonly as *worker participation*. Participation can include many different forms of input, ranging from having no say at all to having the right to veto management action. Three types of participation are discussed: joint consultation committees, works councils, and board membership.[72]

Joint Consultation Committees

Joint consultation committees (JCC) are common in many Western countries. These are groups of workers who sit on a committee that deals with topics of mutual interest to employees and management. Their charge can range from concerns about product quality to working conditions and even the quality of work life. Typically, JCC members make suggestions that may be adopted by management. In turn, management is often expected to keep workers informed about developments via the committee. The effectiveness of these committees depends on the goodwill and intentions of a firm, with success more likely in paternalistic companies with relatively good employee relations.[73]

Works Councils

Works councils are a form of employee participation that is common in Western Europe (e.g., France, Germany, the Netherlands). While similar to JCCs, works councils often have significant power to block management decisions and actions and to forward solutions to employee concerns. They emerged as a result of societal obligations to seek employee input rather than as a way to necessarily improve competitiveness or the bottom line.[74]

Eventually, national laws were created that mandate their operation. In the Netherlands, for example, law requires that any firm with 35 or more employees must create a works council. They are composed of members elected by employees. Councils must be consulted in important firm decisions, although in practice the issues often relate to personnel policy (e.g., safety programs, pay and benefits, relocation of work). If a firm has 100 or more employees, this consultation could include major financial decisions, such as business acquisitions. Theoretically, the works council should represent the interest of employees. Members of the council, however, may be managers or production employees. In practice, councils can be co-opted by management.[75]

In powerful works councils, such as some in Germany, employees may effectively hold their regular job and one as council representative. Therefore, it is not uncommon to have a second office and perhaps even two staffs right on company grounds. The council representative is thus similar to a shop steward in the United States. The difference is that the works council member has more real input into company decisions.[76] Research on the impact of works councils on productivity is mixed, with some studies showing a positive impact and others showing a weak relation.[77]

Board Membership

Board membership is a third, less common, mechanism by which workers have input—in this case, extensive input. In seven European countries (among them Denmark, France, and Germany), law dictates that workers must have representation on the board of directors. In most cases, these boards are supervisory—the group responsible for selecting a management board that will run day-to-day operations. Typically, workers have only a minority membership on the board. Employee representatives, however, control half of the board seats among companies with more than 2,000 employees. Even though this might seem like a radical idea, research shows that board memberships for workers generally has relatively little effect on the business one way or another. Typically, boards meet very infrequently (often for just a few hours per year), and when talk does turn to substantive issues, workers may be at a disadvantage. At the minimum, boards appear to perform a symbolic function for workers, with some viewing them as a valuable source of information rather than as a lever for wielding power.

PUTTING AGREEMENTS INTO PRACTICE

There are many ways that disagreements can emerge, and they sometimes result in open conflict between labor and management.

Relations between Management and Labor

The general state of relations between management and employees is often evaluated by firms before they choose to invest in a foreign subsidiary. These relations show great variability. One study asked over 10,000 top business executives in 134 countries to rate how cooperative labor–management relations were across these countries. Denmark and Japan ranked very highly, showing that there is a good deal of cooperation between management and labor—a ranking that both nations have received for decades now. On the contrary, Venezuela and France rank at the bottom on this dimension—labor–management relations are contentious. The United States comes in at 16th place out of the 134 countries ranked in this study—a relatively high showing and a marked improvement since the 1990s.[78]

Deterioration of Relations

Sometimes labor–management relations can deteriorate to the point that work slows down, sabotage occurs, and even violence erupts. But events such as slowdowns are difficult to track, and violence against management or security officers (thankfully) is not common. Strikes occur more frequently, however, and are easier to document because of their observable features (e.g., frequency, size, and length).[79] Using strike data, several conclusions can be reached. First, strikes in general have been declining since the 1970s.[80] The number of days lost to strikes has fallen in recent years, and especially so in the EU—outcomes that were accelerated by the recession of the late 2000s.[81] Consider the United Kingdom, where roughly 750,000 working days were lost to strikes in 2008. While this number is large and had a negative impact on the British economy, it pales in comparison to the 30 million days lost in 1979. This drop is probably due to several causes, including the fact that strikes decline during economic downturns and increase in times of prosperity.[82] Data also show that there has been a shift in the *reason* for strikes. Strikes are more likely to involve public services (e.g., transportation systems), and work process issues (e.g., job security, worker participation) rather than workplace outcomes per se (e.g., higher pay). Consider the United Kingdom again, where, in 2008, 94% of all strikes were by public-sector employees, many concerned with job security.

Table 12.3 presents a ranking of a variety of countries on two measures: the number of strikes/lockouts and the number of work days lost from these actions. Note that some countries that are thriving economically have a relatively high number of strikes. Year in and year out, Denmark, France, and Italy rank high among all countries in number of strikes. The total number of lost work days can be in the millions as a result of these work stoppages. And these statistics do not always count the shorter, less-than-one-full-day strikes that seem to be occurring more often. This can be affected by cultural and legal structures in place across countries—a topic that is addressed next, with a discussion of strike activity in a few specific countries.

Table 12.3
Strike Activity and Effects in a Variety of Countries

Country	Number of Strikes and Lockouts	Working Days Lost (per 1,000 Employees)
Spain	811	62
France	699	n.d.
Italy	621	56
Denmark	335	21
Canada	187	280

(Continued)

Table 12.3   (Continued)

Country	Number of Strikes and Lockouts	Working Days Lost (per 1,000 Employees)
Australia	177	28
Portugal	174	7
United Kingdom	144	6
Finland	92	322
Netherlands	21	6
Japan	18	n.d.
United States	16	10
Belgium*	10	n.d.
Switzerland	2	1
Sweden	5	2

Source: Adapted from International Labour Organization Statistical Tables. (2008). Available at http://laborsta.ilo.org/STP/guest.

Note: Number of strikes/lockouts excludes work stoppage involving fewer than 500 workers and lasting less than one full day or shift. Working days lost refers to the number of eight-hour days lost due to strikes/lockouts (per 1,000 employees). Most data are for 2008; data marked with * are from 2006, and # indicates that no data are available. Working days lost per 100 workers = 2006; n.d. = no data available.

Strike Activity in Germany

Despite a long and powerful tradition of union influence, strike activity in Germany is not as common as it is in other Western European nations (about 130,000 work days lost in 2008). For example, days lost per 1,000 employees were about 10 times higher in France than in Germany. This is due partly to the many control mechanisms that workers have in German enterprises, including works councils and the co-determination process. In addition, however, laws constrain German labor relations, making more extreme steps like strikes and lockouts less necessary. For example, laws prohibit either strikes or lockouts when a contract is in effect. Consequently, strikes usually occur when contracts have expired and negotiations are ongoing.

Strike Activity in Japan

Union–management relations in Japan are quite good, as explained earlier in the chapter. Table 12.3 shows that there were only 18 strikes in 2008, which produced relatively few lost work days (only about 2,000). Most disagreements are settled amicably. It is rare for relations to get caustic enough to result in a strike. Even when they do, the strike is brief and not bitter—often it is undertaken either to embarrass management or to bring to their attention a matter of importance. Lockouts by management are very rare. Emotional behavior of union members is tolerated, but management is expected to always be courteous in their language and behavior.[83]

Strike Activity in China

Earlier in the chapter, the increased activity shown by Chinese workers, including a well-publicized strike at Honda in 2010, was discussed. This resulted in a 24% increase in pay (before overtime and benefits) for those Chinese workers. Put in perspective, however, the $3.00 per hour average for Chinese auto workers pales in comparison to hourly pay for German ($58.50), French ($47.81), Japanese ($38.63), U.S. ($33.00), and Spanish ($31.60) workers. National-level data on strike-related activity like that discussed just above are not available.[84]

Strike Activity in the United States

Table 12.3 shows that the United States had 16 official strikes in 2008—this figure has hovered around 20 for the previous five years. But these strikes resulted in over 1 million lost work days for the United States' large labor force. Labor contracts typically prohibit strikes during the period of the agreement. So once a contract is in place, a strike (called a "wildcat strike") is rare and usually not authorized by the union. As in Germany, once a contract expires and a new one is not yet approved, a strike becomes a viable option—and an option that is exercised with some frequency. Employees sometimes choose to continue to work during the negotiation period while threatening a strike. Lockouts by management do occur on occasion, but they are also relatively rare.

Overall Impact of Unions

Many managers find dealings with unions, regardless of where they are, to be challenging. Nevertheless, there are some benefits from a unionized workforce, including a structured bargaining system and clear contractual obligations that must be fulfilled. Perhaps a more subtle benefit of union membership, however, is that it may quell more extreme and militant worker action. In one study of 12 EU countries, militancy was defined as a combination of variables, including labor strife and unrest. The researchers found a negative relationship between the two variables—with higher union membership (density) generally associated with a lower incidence of violence. So despite all the management resistance to unions, there may be a silver lining. Organized employee input—perhaps in many forms—may actually make management–worker relations smoother than would otherwise be the case.[85]

CHAPTER SUMMARY

This chapter looked closely at labor relations and related issues around the globe, focusing mostly on interactions between two important groups—management and employees. There are many differences across countries in both the presence and influence of unions. Nevertheless, employee interests are most commonly represented to management via a union. The percentage of workers who are union members varies across countries and is on the decline worldwide.

One reason for both the variance and the decline is that worker interests can be served by a variety of mechanisms besides unions (e.g., legal mechanisms or political forms of worker input). Indeed, a variety of forms of worker input exist, ranging from weaker methods—such as having some say about or input into work procedures—to having a de facto veto over important firm decisions. Of course, despite the presence of unions and a variety of communication and input methods, sometimes management and employees simply cannot agree. Labor strikes are one response to a lack of agreement. Once again, the nature and prevalence of strike activity or other forms of employee response to labor–management discord can vary across countries.

DISCUSSION QUESTIONS

1. Why might multinationals have the upper hand in dealing with workers, even if those workers are unionized and spread across a variety of countries?

2. What are some of the differences between how North American, European, and Asian unions operate? Why might those differences exist?

3. What is the relationship between the presence of unions and the level of worker militancy? Explain why this is the case.

Developing Your International Career

DEVELOPING EXPERTISE IN INTERNATIONAL LABOR TRENDS

Purpose and Instructions

The purpose of this exercise is to familiarize you with features about labor conditions and trends worldwide. This can be valuable knowledge to have, or to know how to get, for an aspiring expatriate. After all, it is prudent for a firm to vet features about the labor market when considering an investment in a certain country. Likewise, it might be personally valuable to help gauge the difficulty of your job or career path in the international arena.

For this exercise, you will examine characteristics about the labor force in four countries, including features about the *quality* (education, attitudes, skill sets) and *quantity* (workforce size overall and in various sectors; number of available employees; age; growth rate; quantity of trained workers, etc.). Your instructor may assign the countries or provide you with options to choose from, although at least one should be a developing country and at least one other from a developed country. Then use the resources below (or additional ones you may find in your research) to summarize the state of labor relations in each country. There are a number of ways to evaluate each country, and some ideas about this are presented below. Regardless of how you conduct your examination, you should be prepared to present your findings to class in a 10-minute report (or in a paper if directed by your professor).

For each country, present a set of labor quantity and quality variables that convey an accurate picture of the situation in your chosen countries. In your report, comment on the data and, importantly, their implications. For example, if you note that more than 40% of the world's 15- to 20-year-olds live in two developing countries you investigated (China and India), be sure to discuss *why* this might be important.

We also recommend that you assess features about labor conditions in your target countries that may present either opportunities or challenges to firms doing business there. Among other questions to raise about the conditions are the following: (a) Has the labor force been shifting from rural to urban? (b) What is the status of immigrant labor in your target countries and related topics (e.g., brain drain; guest workers)? (c) What about the serious issues of child/forced labor? (d) What is the nature of laws pertaining to various labor groups (e.g., gender, race, etc.)? (e) What are the key employment laws that can impact business functions in your countries (e.g., severance pay, labor force reductions, labor organizing)?

You may wish to create a matrix chart that includes your countries as columns and variable comparisons as rows. Include a final row that is your rating on a scale from 1 (tough labor market) to 10 (favorable market) for the multinational you might work for. In your (brief) report, rely on this chart to talk through your rating as well as the key comparison variables that determined your overall rating.

Resources

A number of useful resources are available on the Internet and in your library to help with this assignment. Here are some especially relevant sources to kick-start your research on this project:

- U.S. Department of Labor, Bureau Labor Statistics (www.bls.gov/fls/chartbook.htm). While this department focuses mainly on the United States, it also includes a set of international labor comparisons.
- Michigan State University, Global Edge (http://globaledge.msu.edu/resourcedesk/statistical-data-sources/). This international business supersite has many resources

and links to those sources that can be of help with this project and that you should bookmark.

■ International Labour Organization (www.ilo.org/global/lang—en/index.htm). The ILO has a complete set of data on labor features of many countries and will be very useful for this assignment.

■ Organisation for Economic Co-operation and Development (www.oecd.org). This website provides a wealth of information and comparable statistics on the 34 OECD member states and can be searched easily.

Making the Case for International Understanding

LABOR RELATIONS ON THE BRINK IN BELGIUM: A CAUTIONARY TALE FOR FIRMS DOING BUSINESS IN TODAY'S EUROPE

Brink's, Incorporated, currently based in Richmond, Virginia, was founded in 1859 in Chicago, Illinois, and is famous for its armored car delivery business. Now one of the largest providers of logistics solutions and secure transport services, it employs 60,000 people in over 150 countries. About three-quarters of Brink's total revenue comes from business outside North America. In fact, about 17% of its 2010 revenue came from France and 40% total from Europe. In principle, the EU is one coordinated economic bloc with free movement of goods and services. For businesses on the ground, especially foreign firms such as Brink's, features such as taxes, labor costs, and business-related laws vary.

This variance can create challenges and hurdles, as it did for Brink's in 2010 in its Belgium business. Since the mid-1970s, Brink's has had two subsidiaries there: a money-making Brink's Diamond delivery business (mostly in the Antwerp diamond district); and Brink's Belgium, a cash delivery unit that provides services to banks. The latter has been losing money (up to $10 million a year), which the firm has attributed to high labor costs. Belgium does have the highest labor costs in the EU. The percentage of employer-paid social security is 31%, nearly twice that of the United Kingdom (17%). Table 12.2 shows that 52% of workers are unionized in Belgium (the fifth-highest percentage in Europe). Law also provides for generous and lengthy paid sick leave, severance for a lost job, and full benefits.

Willem Candel, a senior director at Brink's, characterized the problem: "Sixty-five percent of our costs were labor costs. We were no longer competitive." In the first half of 2010, the firm had losses of $7 million on $32 million in sales, making it clear to management that something had to be done. Their analysis told them that one thing was driving a significant portion of the problems: the nearly 500 staff members who drove the armored cars and serviced the ATMs were classified as white collar (professional) instead of blue collar (hourly/manual labor). This distinction was the result of a late 1800s law that was very favorable to employers and that made Belgium a low-labor-cost country. It was "the China of Europe" at the time. Blue-collar workers were to be paid by the hour, less for overtime, and could be laid off more freely than white-collar employees. Brink's claimed that its large number of white-collar employees cost the company $4.5 million more per year than if the workers were correctly classified as blue collar. Brink's claimed that this mistake prevented the company from winning contracts.

While unions continue their efforts to eliminate the job distinctions, Brink's developed a strategy. In late 2010, it announced a plan to lay off about 60 workers and to reclassify staff from white collar to blue collar. The unions were stunned and announced a strike. Fearing a prolonged union conflict and more losses, Brink's declared bankruptcy as a way to escape financial problems. Employees of the cash delivery business were laid off, and management moved to the Netherlands. The lucrative diamond delivery business was spun off ahead of bankruptcy proceedings.

The union quickly filed suit, contending that changing employees' job status and not providing severance pay was illegal. The union's representative stated that "Brink's acted as if we wouldn't be vigilant, but we have lawyers too." Expert observers say the company probably erred in not providing severance, but Brink's defended itself, arguing that "we never refused a dialog with the unions...they refused to work." Those same experts point out that U.S. firms cannot act the same way about a bankruptcy in Europe, with one suggesting that "U.S. law treats employees as unsecured creditors...it's very different in Europe."

There is one postscript and a big challenge for Brink's—a Brussels court recently rejected the firm's bankruptcy filing. It held that Brink's had no grounds to turn its more profitable diamond transport business into a new firm ahead of the bankruptcy plea. The court suspended Brink's license to operate this business. Court-appointed administrators filed a nearly $29 million claim against Brink's. Brink's has offered $10 million to employees to drop the suit.

ASSIGNMENT QUESTIONS

1. What is your view of how the company handled this problem? Did it handle things correctly? Why or why not?
2. What did it do wrong? What were the key problems in its approach to this situation?
3. What is your view of how the employees and unions handled the situation? What could they have done to provide a satisfactory solution to the impasse?
4. What are the policy implications for U.S. firms and those of other countries doing business in Europe, and in Belgium in particular? What specific factors should be considered as they enter and operate in Europe?[86]

NOTES

1. Both chapter opening quotes from http://edition.cnn.com/2011/11/23/business/china-labor-unrest/index.html.

2. Tan, H. H., & Aryee, S. (2002). Antecedents and outcomes of union loyalty: A constructive replication and extension. *Journal of Applied Psychology*, 87, 715–722.

3. Collings, D. G. (2008). Multinational corporations and industrial relations research: A road less travelled. *International Journal of Management Reviews*, 10, 173–193.

4. Newman, B. (1993). Border dispute: Single-country unions of Europe try to cope with multinationals. *Wall Street Journal*, November 30, A1, A22; Zachary, G. P. (1993). Like factory workers, professionals face loss of jobs to foreigners. *Wall Street Journal*, March 17, A1, A9.

5. Fleming, C. (2004). Europe learns litigious ways. *Wall Street Journal*, February 24, A16, A17.

6. McCann, D. (2005). *Working Time Laws: A Global Perspective. Findings from the ILO's Conditions of Work and Employment Database.* Geneva, Switzerland: International Labour Organization.

7. Bush, J., Scott, M., Rowley, I., Lakshman N., Matlack, C., Ewing, J., & Zhe, H. (2009). The hidden perils of layoffs. *Business Week*, March 2, 52–53.

8. Dugan, I. J. (2009). Companies, workers tangle over law to curb layoffs. *Wall Street Journal*, July 6, A1; *The Worker Adjustment and Retaining Notification Act: Fact Sheet.* (2009). Available at www.doleta.gov/programs/factsht/warn.htm.

9. Steinmetz, G. (1996). Americans, too, run afoul of rigorous German rules. *Wall Street Journal*, February 2, A6.

10. Employee dismissals can prove costly for companies in Europe. *HR Focus*, August 1992, 18.

11. *Managing Mass Redundancies across Europe* (2nd ed.). Brussels, Belgium: Freshfields Bruckhaus Deringer, 2009.

12. Bilefsky, D. (2003). The Dutch way of firing. *Wall Street Journal*, July 8, A14.

13. Walker, M., & Thurow, R. (2009). U.S., Europe are ocean apart on human toll of joblessness. *Wall Street Journal*, May 7, A1, A14.

14. Bourdette, N. E. (2004). As jobs head to Eastern Europe, unions in the West start to bend. *Wall Street Journal*, March 11, A1, A6.

15. Briscoe, D. R., Schuler, R. S., & Claus, L. (2009). *International Human Resource Management* (3rd ed.). New York: Routledge.

16. Union member summary. Bureau of Labor Statistics, Department of Labor, 2010. Available at www.bls.gov/news.release/union2.nr0.htm.

17. Rampell, C. (2009). Trade unions' decline around the work. *New York Times*, November 5. Available at http://economix.blogs.nytimes.com/2009/11/05/trade-unions-around-the-world/; Hollinshead, G., & Leaf, M. (1995). *Human Resource Management: An International and Comparative Perspective.* London: Pitman; Koretz, G. (1990). Why unions thrive abroad, but wither in the U.S. *Business Week*, September 10, 26; Gunnigle, P., Brewster, C., & Morley, M. (1994). European industrial relations: Change and continuity. In C. Brewster & A. Hegewisch (eds.), *Policy and Practice in European Human Resource Management: The Price-Waterhouse Cranfield Survey* (139–153). London: Routledge.

18. Ferner, A., & Hyman, R. (1992). *Industrial Relations in the New Europe.* Oxford, England: Blackwell.

19. Gunnigle, P., Brewster, C., & Morley, M. (1994). European industrial relations: Change and continuity. In C. Brewster & A. Hegewisch (eds.), *Policy and Practice in European Human Resource Management: The Price-Waterhouse Cranfield Survey* (139–153). London: Routledge.

20. Hollinshead, G., & Leaf, M. (1995). *Human Resource Management: An International and Comparative Perspective*. London: Pitman; Brunstein, I. (1995). *Human Resource Management in Western Europe*. Berlin: Walter de Gruyter.

21. Brunstein, I. (1995). *Human Resource Management in Western Europe*. Berlin: Walter de Gruyter; Matlack, C. (2003). France: Labor disarray is giving reform a chance. *Business Week*, June 16, 48.

22. The street fights back: Strikes in France. *The Economist*, November 24, 2007, 55.

23. The street fights back: Strikes in France. *The Economist*, November 24, 2007, 55.

24. Reforming gloomy France. *The Economist*, April 23, 2011, 27–29; Villars-Gauthier, D., & Colchester, M. (2010). French strikers protest higher retirement age. *Wall Street Journal*, October 13, A13; Where the streets have no shame. France's protests. *The Economist*, October 23, 2010, 61–62.

25. A time of troubles and protest: As European economies sink, fears of social unrest arise. *The Economist*, January 24, 2009, 55–56; Tomlinson, R. (2004). Troubled waters at Perrier: Nestle, which owns the brand, and the French workers who bottle it are locked in a nasty fight. *Fortune*, November 29, 173–176. See also Fauthier-Villars, D., & Abboud, L. (2009). In France, boss can become a hostage. *Wall Street Journal*, April 3, B1, B5; Carreyrou, J. (2005). At French utility, union wages war to guard its perks. *Wall Street Journal*, May 10, A1, A10; Wrighton, J., & Sapsford, J. (2005). For Nissan's rescuer, Ghosen, new road rules await at Renault: Will also run French firm taking on powerful unions. *Wall Street Journal*, April 26, A1, A8.

26. German industrial relations: Slowly losing their chains. *The Economist*, February 21, 2004, 49; Wachter, H. (1997). German co-determination—Quo vadis? A study of the implementation of new management concepts in a German steel company. *Employee Relations*, 19, 27–37.

27. How to pep up Germany's economy. *The Economist*, May 8, 2004, 65–67; Rhoads, C. (2003). In deep crisis, Germany starts to revamp vast welfare state. *Wall Street Journal*, July 10, A1, A5; Rohwedder, C. (1999). Once the big muscle of German industry, unions see it all sag. *Wall Street Journal*, November 29, A1; Sims, G. T., & Rhoads, C. (2003). New era for German labor movement? *Wall Street Journal*, July 1, A9; Edmondson, G. (2004). Showdown in the Ruhr Valley. *Business Week*, November 1, 54–55.

28. Fleck, S. (2009). International comparisons of hours worked: An assessment of the statistics. *Monthly Labor Review*, 132, 3–31.

29. Geoghegan, T. (2010). It's even worse than you think. *New York Times*, November 18. Available at www.nytimes.com/roomfordebate/2010/8/4; Prescott, E. C. (2004). Why do Americans work more than Europeans? *Wall Street Journal*, October 21, 1–3.

30. Fleck, S. (2009). International comparisons of hours worked: An assessment of the statistics. *Monthly Labor Review*, 132, 3–31; Biehl, J. K. (2009). German love of leisure worries government. *SFGate.com*, July 3. Available at www.sfgate.com/cgi-bin/articles; Working hours. *The Economist*, August 23, 2003, 80; Germany: Rebirth of a salesman. *The Economist*, July 8, 2000, 22–24; Benjamin, D. (1993). Germany is troubled by how little work its workers are doing. *Wall Street Journal*, May 6, A1, A7; Benjamin, D., & Horwitz, T. (1994). German view: You Americans work too hard—and for what? *Wall Street Journal*, July 14, B5, B6; Koretz, G. (2001). Why Americans work so hard. *Business Week*, June 11, 34.

31. Hollinshead, G., & Leaf, M. (1995). *Human Resource Management: An International and Comparative Perspective.* London: Pitman.

32. Hollinshead, G., & Leaf, M. (1995). *Human Resource Management: An International and Comparative Perspective.* London: Pitman.

33. Brewster, C., & Hegewisch, A. (1994). *Policy and Practice in European Human Resource Management: The Price-Waterhouse Cranfield Survey.* London: Routledge.

34. Visser, J. (2006). Union membership statistics in 24 countries. *Monthly Labor Review,* 129, 1, 38–49; Reed, S. (1997). Will Stockholm give away the store? *Business Week,* February 10, 54.

35. Taylor, R. (1993). Union membership in Sweden still growing. *Financial Times,* December 21, 14.

36. Hees, M. (1995). Belgium. In I. Brunstein (ed.), *Human Resource Management in Western Europe.* Berlin: Walter de Gruyter.

37. Spain's new unemployed—And worse to come: The worrying social fallout from sharply rising unemployment. *The Economist,* January 24, 2009, 56; Spain cuts a Gordian labor knot. *The Economist,* March 10, 2001, 51.

38. Bush, J. (2007). Russian labor raises its voice: A walkout at a Ford plant near St. Petersburg may herald a new era of union activism. *Business Week,* December 10, 34–35.

39. A time of troubles and protest: As European economies sink, fears of social unrest arise. *The Economist,* January 24, 2009, 55–56; Part-time workers. *The Economist,* November 23, 2003, 100; Templeman, J., Trinephi, M., & Toy, S. (1996). A continent swarming with temps. *Business Week,* April 8, 54.

40. Cohen, A. (2010). A Dutch formula holds down joblessness. *Wall Street Journal,* December 28, A10.

41. Benson, J. (2008). Trade unions in Japan: Collective justice or managerial compliance? In J. Benson & Y. Zhu (eds.), *Trade Unions in Asia: An Economic and Sociological Analysis* (24–42). London: Routledge; Clenfield, J. (2010). A tear in Japan's safety net. *Bloomberg Businessweek,* April, 12, 60–61; Tabuchi, H. (2009). In Japan, secure jobs have a cost. *New York Times,* May 20. Available at www.nytimes.com/2009; Inohara, H. (1990). *Human Resource Development in Japanese Companies.* Tokyo: Asian Productivity Organization.

42. Rowley, I., & Hall, K. (2007). Japan's lost generation: Japan Inc. is back, but millions of young workers have been left behind. *Business Week,* May 28, 40–41.

43. Inohara, H. (1990). *Human Resource Development in Japanese Companies.* Tokyo: Asian Productivity Organization.

44. Benson, J. (2008). Trade unions in Japan: Collective justice or managerial compliance? In J. Benson & Y. Zhu (eds.), *Trade Unions in Asia: An Economic and Sociological Analysis* (24–42). London: Routledge.

45. Time lost to strikes: Minutes of lost work per employed person from strikes and lockouts in 2006. *Business Week,* December 3, 2007, 11.

46. Browning, E. S. (1986). Japan's firms have a friend: The unions. *Wall Street Journal,* April 28, sec. 2, 28.

47. Murphy, J. (2009). Joblessness spurs shift in Japan's views on poverty. *Wall Street Journal,* May 2–3, A5.

48. Nyaw, M. (1995). Human resource management in the People's Republic of China. In L. F. Moore & P. D. Jennings (eds.), *Human Resource Management in the Pacific Rim* (187–196). Berlin: Walter de Gruyter.

49. Thornton, E. (2009). The hidden perils of layoffs: Ex-workers are hauling their former companies into court over alleged violations of severance laws. *Business Week,* March 2,

52–53; Roberts, D. (2007). Rumbles over labor reform: Beijing's proposed worker protections are giving multinationals the jitters. *Business Week*, March 12, 57.

50. Roberts, D. (2010). A new labor movement in born in China. *Bloomberg Businessweek*, June 14–20, 7–8; Bradsher, K. (2010). A labor movement stirs in China. *New York Times*, June 10.

51. China's new labour law. The party throws a sop to the workers. *The Economist*, December 8, 2007, 49–50; Brady, R. (2004). China: A workers' state helping the workers? *Business Week*, December 13, 61; Lee, G. O. M., & Warner, M. (2007). *Unemployment in China: Economy, Human Resources, and Labour Markets*. London: Routledge.

52. Shirouzu, N. (2010). Workers challenge Beijing's authority. *Wall Street Journal*, June 14, A7.

53. Bussy, J. (2011). Measuring the human cost of an iPad made in China. *Wall Street Journal*, June 3, B1; Wong, S., Liu, J., & Culpan, T. (2010). Life and death at the iPad factory. *Bloomberg Businessweek*, June 7–13, 35–36; Culpan, T., Lifei, Z., & Einhorn, B. (2011). How to beat the high cost of happy workers. *Bloomberg Businessweek*, May 9–15, 39–40; Ye, J., & Wu, N. (2010). Suicides spark inquiries. *Wall Street Journal*, May 27, B1, B7; Poon, A., Chao, L., & Kane, Y. I. (2011). Factory blast roils tech supply chain: China's Hon Hai closes product polishing plant. *Wall Street Journal*, May 24, B1, B2.

54. Shirouzu, N., Chao, L., & Dean, J. (2010). Foreign firms act on labor in China. *Wall Street Journal*, June 15, B1, B2.

55. Shirouzu, N., Chao, L., & Dean, J. (2010). Foreign firms act on labor in China. *Wall Street Journal*, June 15, B1, B2; Trade unions in China: Membership required; global firms operating in China are being pressured to sign up with a union now, or pay more later. *The Economist*, July 31, 2008, 23–24; Chu, K., & Yun, M. (2010). Wages, conditions improve as workers in China form unions. *USA Today*, November, 19. Available at www.usatoday.com/money/world/2010–11–19-Chinalabor_cv_N.htm; The next China. *The Economist*, July 31, 2010, 48–50; Warner, M. (2008). Trade unions in China: In search of a new role in the "harmonious society." In J. Benson & Y. Zhu (eds.), *Trade Unions in Asia: An Economic and Sociological Analysis* (24–42). London: Routledge; Canaves, S., & Areddy, J. T. (2009). China killing bares anger over reform. *Wall Street Journal*, July 31, A1, A14; Canaves, S. (2009). Chinese stall workers fight privatization effort: Rights group documents overturned police cars and killing of executive in rally against takeover of government company. *Wall Street Journal*, July 27, A10.

56. Chan, A. W. (2008). Trade unions in Hong Kong: Worker representation or political agent? In J. Benson & Y. Zhu (eds.), *Trade Unions in Asia: An Economic and Sociological Analysis* (81–101). London: Routledge; Poon, W. K. (1995). Human resource management in Hong Kong. In L. F. Moore & P. D. Jennings, *Human Resource Management on the Pacific Rim* (214–236). Berlin: Walter de Gruyter.

57. Getting organized, with Western help. *The Economist*, December 1, 2001, 57–58.

58. Leggett, C. (2008). Trade unions in Singapore: Corporatist paternalism. In J. Benson & Y. Zhu (eds.), *Trade Unions in Asia: An Economic and Sociological Analysis* (102–120). London: Routledge.

59. Koch, M., Nam, S. H., & Steers, R. M. (1995). Human resource management in South Korea. In L. F. Moore & P. D. Jennings (eds.), *Human Resource Management on the Pacific Rim* (106–126). Berlin: Walter de Gruyter; Solomon, J., & Choi, H. W. (2001). For Korea's Daewoo Motor, a hard sale. *Wall Street Journal*, May 23, A21; South Korea's longest banking strike: Rebels without a cause. *The Economist*, July 30, 2011. Available at www.economist.com/node/21524882; Rowley, C., & Yoo, K. S. (2008). Trade unions in South Korea: Transition toward neocorporatism? In J. Benson & Y. Zhu (eds.), *Trade Unions in Asia: An Economic*

and Sociological Analysis (43–62). London: Routledge; Brull, S. V., & Lee, C. K. (1997). Why Seoul is seething. *Business Week*, January 27, 44–48; South Korea: Culture clash. *The Economist*, January 11, 1997, 35–36.

60. Briscoe, D. R., Schuler, R. S., & Claus, L. (2009). *International Human Resource Management* (3rd ed.). New York: Routledge.

61. Smith, G. (2000). Mexican workers deserve better than this. *Business Week*, September 11, 127.

62. Stewart, R. M. (2011). Wal-Mart checks out a new continent. *Wall Street Journal*, October 27, B1, B2; Schillinger, H. R. (2005). Trade unions in Africa: Weak but feared. *Occasional Papers: International Development Cooperation*, 1–7. Frankfurt, Germany: Global Trade Union Program; Chege, M. (1988). The state and labor: Industrial relations in independent Kenya. In P. Coughlin & G. Ikiara (eds.), *Industrialization in Kenya: In Search of a Strategy*. Nairobi: Heinemann Kenya.

63. Wonacott, P. (2010). Strike hampers South African Growth: Public service walkout threatens to spread. *Wall Street Journal*, August 28–29, A14; Moll, P. G. (1993). Black South African unions: Relative wage effects in international perspective. *Industrial and Labor Relations Review*, 46, 245–261.

64. Bischof, J. (2011). South Africa's labor pain. *Wall Street Journal*, May 17, A12; Wonacott, P. (2010). Strike exposes unease in South African pact. *Wall Street Journal*, September 3, A13; Childress, S. (2009). South Africa's Zuma faces wide unrest. *Wall Street Journal*, July 29, A7; Matthews, R. (1996). Another burden to carry. *Financial Times*, May 21, 15.

65. Newman, B. (1983). Border dispute: Single-country unions of Europe try to cope with multinationals. *Wall Street Journal*, November 30, 1, 22.

66. Simpson, W. R. (1994). The ILO and tripartism: Some reflections. *Monthly Labor Review*, September, 40–45.

67. Hollinshead, G., & Leaf, M. (1995). *Human Resource Management: An International and Comparative Perspective*. London: Pitman.

68. Dowling, P. J., & Schuler, R. S. (1990). *International Dimensions of Human Resource Management*. Boston: PWS-Kent.

69. Parry, J., & O'Meara, G. (1990). The struggle for European unions. *International Management*, December, 70–75.

70. Martin, D. (1984). A Canadian split on unions. *New York Times*, March 12, D12.

71. Forman, C. (1993). France is preparing to battle Britain over flight of jobs across the channel. *Wall Street Journal*, February 3, A11; Borrus, A. (2000). Workers of the world: Welcome. *Business Week*, November 20, 129–133; Unions: In from the cold? *The Economist*, March 14, 2009, 65–66; Burkins, G. (2000). Labor reaches out to global economy. *Wall Street Journal*, April 11, A2; Cavusgil, S. T., Knight, G., & Riesenberger, J. R. (2008). *International Business*. Upper Saddle River, NJ: Pearson Prentice Hall.

72. Strauss, G. (1982). Worker participation in management: An international perspective. *Research in Organizational Behavior*, 4, 173–265.

73. But please see de Macedo-Soares, T. D. L., & Lucas, D. C. (1996). Key quality management practices of leading firms in Brazil: Findings of a pilot-study. *TQM Magazine*, 8, 55–70.

74. Ramsay, H. (1997). Fool's gold? European works councils and workplace democracy. *Industrial Relations Journal*, December, 119–128; Addison, J., Schabel, C., & Wagner, J. (1997). On the determinants of mandatory works councils in Germany. *Industrial Relations*, 43, 392–420; McFarlin, D., Sweeney, P. D., & Cotton, J. L. (1992). Attitudes toward employee

participation in decision-making: A comparison of European and American managers in a US multinational company. *Human Resource Management*, 31, 363–383.

75. McFarlin, D., Sweeney, P. D., & Cotton, J. L. (1992). Attitudes toward employee participation in decision-making: A comparison of European and American managers in a US multinational company. *Human Resource Management*, 31, 363–383.

76. Stolz, M. (2009). *Works Councils and Labor Relations in Germany*. Chicago: American Bar Association.

77. Wagner, J. (2005). *German Works Councils and Productivity: First Evidence from a Nonparametric Test*. Working paper series in economics. Lüneberg, Germany: University of Lüneburg.

78. Rankings of the degree of cooperative relations between labor and employers. *Global Competitiveness Report, 2008 2009*. Geneva, Switzerland: World Economic Forum, 2008.

79. But while these variables seem relatively objective, directly comparing strikes across countries isn't that easy. There are many nation-specific definitions of what constitutes a strike or other type of work stoppage. Danish statistics, for example, exclude any disputes that result in fewer than 100 days being lost. Despite this, Denmark regularly ranks among the highest in the world on work days lost because of strikes. Groups such as the ILO and the OECD have worked to clarify definitions and make strike data more comparable. For the most part, strike data are usually based on the number of strikes and the number of work days lost because of the strike. See the following for information on this topic: Sparrow, P., & Hiltrop, J. M. (1994). *European Human Resource Management in Transition*. New York: Prentice Hall; Labor disputes. *The Economist*, April 22, 2000, 96.

80. You ain't seen nothing yet. *The Economist*, April 2010, 24; Labor disputes. *The Economist*, May 12, 2001, 108.

81. Taylor, A. (2009). Europe's strikers more scare in the recession. *Time.com*, August 10. Available at www.time.com/time/business.

82. Sparrow, P., & Hiltrop, J. M. (1994). *European Human Resource Management in Transition*. New York: Prentice Hall.

83. Inohara, H. (1990). *Human Resource Development in Japanese Companies*. Tokyo: Asian Productivity Organization.

84. The gulf in auto wages. *Bloomberg Businessweek*, July 12–18, 2010, 15.

85. Sparrow, P., & Hilltrop, J. M. (1994). *European Human Resource Management in Transition*. New York: Prentice Hall.

86. Miller, J. W. (2010). Brink's retreat in Belgium backfires. *Wall Street Journal*, December 21, B8; Krawitz, A. (2010). Belgium diamond shipments halted as Brink's loses its license: Diamonds worth $200 million being blocked at Zaventem airport. Available at www.diamonds.net/news/NewsItem.aspx?ArticleID = 33529.

Index